本书得到北京第二外国语学院
"科技创新服务能力建设-高精尖学科建设-外国语言

中丹对话
文化遗产研究

— 主 编 —

张喜华　　[丹] 因戈尔夫·蒂森 (Ingolf Thuesen)　　郑承军

上海社会科学院出版社
SHANGHAI ACADEMY OF SOCIAL SCIENCES PRESS

图书在版编目(CIP)数据

中丹对话：文化遗产研究 / 张喜华，(丹)因戈尔夫·蒂森，郑承军主编．— 上海：上海社会科学院出版社，2021
 ISBN 978 - 7 - 5520 - 3667 - 1

Ⅰ.①中… Ⅱ.①张…②因…③郑… Ⅲ.①文化遗产—保护—中国—文集 Ⅳ.①K203 - 53

中国版本图书馆 CIP 数据核字(2021)第 169466 号

中丹对话：文化遗产研究

主　　编	张喜华　[丹]因戈尔夫·蒂森　郑承军
责任编辑	章斯睿
封面设计	周清华
出版发行	上海社会科学院出版社
	上海顺昌路 622 号　邮编 200025
	电话总机 021 - 63315947　销售热线 021 - 53063735
	http://www.sassp.cn　E-mail：sassp@sassp.cn
照　　排	南京前锦排版服务有限公司
印　　刷	上海信老印刷厂
开　　本	710 毫米×1010 毫米　1/16
印　　张	29
字　　数	632 千
版　　次	2021 年 11 月第 1 版　2021 年 11 月第 1 次印刷

ISBN 978 - 7 - 5520 - 3667 - 1/K·627　　　定价：98.00 元

版权所有　翻印必究

前　　言

　　文化遗产是人类众多普遍价值中的一种,其重要意义不可小觑。通过铭记历史,缅怀先祖,探访过往,人类才有了解释现世生活的基础,为迎接未来挑战做好准备。因此,遗产是人类财富,反映并塑造了人类的共同价值观,为个人生存及社会发展做出贡献。

　　遗产的存在有赖于社会各阶层的共同价值观,涉及国家民族身份或共通的价值观的家庭及社区成员。联合国教科文组织世界遗产中心的设立便反映了遗产的共通价值。遗产无处不在,具有共享性。与此同时,我们也应意识到遗产是被建构的这一事实。我们总是在不同程度地探讨并界定什么才能称之为遗产。因而,遗产的确立是构建社会及人类共同价值观的重要一环。

　　我们不断对遗产进行探索和思考,很重要的一个原因就是希望可以为未来留存记忆、历史和纪念。遗产的确立意义重大,对社会经济具有一定影响,保护文物古迹可能代价高昂,易碎物品尤为如此。

　　基于这些对遗产以及遗产管理的认识和思考,当今世界拥有专门确立、保护和推动遗产发展的大型机构,其中联合国下属国际组织——联合国教科文组织最负盛名,它致力于处理文化财产有关事宜。文化财产也是一种遗产,它是我们与遗产进行联结的方式。因此,这两个术语很难完全剥离开来。文化财产一词突出了法律属性,而遗产一词更像是一个具有现代特征的口头表达,源于盎格鲁-撒克逊人,并被联合国教科文组织用来定义"世界遗产"。遗产没有反义词,我们在多元文化背景下使用该词时发现,当翻译成某种区域语言时,它的含义不尽相同。丹麦的"kulturarv"一词的确意味着从过去的文化中继承下来的东西,但具体而言,它与丹麦的立法有关,并且丹麦人对遗产一词的理解更多地强调其"实践性"。中国也是一样,当"heritage"一词翻译为中文"遗产"时,其内涵同样映射了中国人对遗产的思考和理解方式。

　　这就表明,当我们在多元文化及多语种的背景下讨论"遗产"这一概念时,我们会下意识认为我们对英文单词"heritage"的理解完全相同,但事实并非如此。

Preface

Cultural heritage is one, however important value, among many universal values of humankind. We all use our perception of the past, our ancestors and our history and memories to explain our present life. And even to prepare for the future. Heritage as such is therefore a fundamental capacity of humans and contributes to survival strategies for individuals and societies as heritage describes and identifies shared values.

Heritage exists as shared values on several levels in the society. Heritage may involve from a few members of a family or of a community through national state identities or universal global values. The latter is reflected in the UNESCO World Heritage Center. Heritage is everywhere, it is shared and it is also constructed. On different levels we are negotiating what is heritage and therefor the making of heritage is an important part of policy making concerning the identification of shared values in societies or for humankind.

An important aspect of heritage thinking is the wish to keep a memory, a history, a tradition or a monument for the future. The making of heritage is therefore an important decision also with economic implications for a society. Protection of heritage monuments can be a very costly enterprise in particular when it comes to fragile objects.

Due to these many aspects of heritage thinking and heritage management the world today houses large institutions with the purpose of identifying, protecting and promoting heritage. Most important is the international organization under the UN, UNESCO, which approaches cultural property. Cultural property is heritage. It is how we associate with heritage. The two terms are therefor difficult to separate. While the cultural property term has a legal character, the heritage term is more a colloquial word of a rather modern character. It was introduced by the Anglo-Saxon world and accepted by UNESCO in defining World Heritage.

However, the term heritage has no antonym and what we discovered when using the term, in a multi-cultural context was, that when translated into a regional language it had a tendency to change meaning. The Danish word "kulturarv" indeed means something inherited from past cultures, but it related specific to the legislation and understanding of heritage as practiced in Denmark. And the same can be said for China where the translation of herit-

因此，我们通过案例来说明英语单词"heritage"在丹麦及中国语境下的具体含义，以期改善并促进人类在遗产这一重要领域的相互理解与合作。读者也可将此书视为一本词典，通过案例介绍的方式，我们将"heritage"一词在中国和丹麦进行文化翻译，"遗产"一词能开启中丹两种不同文化传统之间的重要对话。

1950年5月11日，中国与丹麦正式建立外交关系，到2020年，两国关系已历时70年；2018年中国和丹麦建立全面战略合作伙伴关系10周年；2017年为"中国—丹麦旅游年"（以下简称"中丹旅游年"）。丹麦是北欧国家里第一个同中国建立全面战略伙伴关系的国家，奉行一个中国的政策。两国友谊深厚，合作领域广泛，学者们的学术外交和文化外交更是极大地增进了两国的理解和互信。在中国和丹麦多边合作交流过程中，"文化"和"文化遗产"成了丹麦研究中心学者进行文化交流和学术交流的关键词。文化交流极大地促进了两国人民的民心相通和相知共进。

2017年在"中丹旅游年"背景下，北京第二外国语学院、丹麦哥本哈根大学和上海社会科学院联合举办了"文化遗产·旅游·文化传播"丹麦研究中心年会。来自中国和丹麦的学者以及相关文化交流机构负责人参加了会议。丹麦王国驻上海总领事普励志（Nicolai Prytz）先生回顾了中国与丹麦之间互相学习与交流的历程，高度肯定了北京第二外国语学院丹麦研究中心作为国内首家专事丹麦研究的中心在密切中丹合作研究、促进中丹友好交流与人才培养方面发挥的重要作用，对付出不懈努力的中、丹学者表达诚挚的感谢。与会的中、丹教授和博物馆专家围绕文化遗产进行了多角度阐释。遗产和旅游在构筑未来跨文化友好关系中的作用、文物在文化交流与合作中的作用、"教育旅行"在深化中丹文化交流和提高人才培养国际化方面的举措和意义、文化遗产的意义及其与教育的关系、文化遗产与文化国际传播的关系、数字化时代文化遗产的传播内容与传播策略等都是中丹学者高度关注的内容。

2017年丹麦学者和文化遗产研究专家到广西对万年桂陶开展了为期六天的系统走访与考察。中国陶艺悠久历史、文化传承以及当代生产给专家一行带去深深地震撼。为此丹麦专家特地撰文记录和推广中国陶艺文化遗产及其当代意义。联合国世界文化遗产保护丹麦专家认为，万年桂陶起源及发展脉络清晰，传承完整有序，世界罕见，既具有世界文化遗产的OUV共性，又具有独特性和唯一性，是世界文化遗产的重要部分。2018年丹麦研究中心丹麦专家访问景德镇，就景德镇宋代进坑制瓷遗址陶瓷文化遗产保护开展对话和交流，北欧遇到北宋，文化遗产成为了穿越时空对话的纽带和桥梁。

age becomes .... Which again reflects the Chinese way of thinking and understanding heritage.

This situation means that when we discuss heritage in a multi-cultural and in multi-lingual contexts we immediately think that when we use the English words heritage we all understand the same. But that is not the case. The idea is therefore by examples to illustrate the translation of the English word heritage into its Danish and Chinese meaning in order to improve and facilitate mutual understanding and collaboration in this important aspect of human life. We therefor also see this book as an example of a one-word dictionary: heritage translated into Chinese and Danish through cases. The introduction to an important dialogue between two different cultural traditions.

On May 11,1950, China and Denmark established diplomatic relations. 2020 witnesses the 70th anniversary of the formal establishment of diplomatic relations between China and Denmark; 2018 sees the tenth anniversary of the establishment of a comprehensive strategic partnership between China and Denmark; 2017 is the "China-Denmark Tourism Year". Denmark is the first Nordic country to establish a comprehensive strategic partnership with China and sticks to the One-China policy. The two countries enjoy deep friendship and extensive cooperation in various fields. The academic and cultural exchanges of scholars have greatly enhanced the understanding and mutual trust between the two countries. In the process of multilateral cooperation and exchanges between China and Denmark, "culture" and "cultural heritage" have become keywords for the scholars in Center for Denmark Studies to conduct cultural and academic exchanges, which has greatly promoted the mutual understanding and mutual advancement of the friendship of the people from the two countries.

2017 is the China-Denmark Tourism Year, Beijing International Studies University, the University of Copenhagen, Denmark, and the Shanghai Academy of Social Sciences jointly organized the annual meeting for Center of Denmark Studies with the theme of "Cultural Heritage, Tourism, and Cultural Communication". Scholars from China and Denmark and researchers of relevant cultural exchange institutions attended the meeting. The Danish Consul General in Shanghai, Mr. Nicolai Prytz, reviewed the process of mutual learning and exchanges between China and Denmark, and highly affirmed that Center for Denmark Studies of Beijing International Studies University, as the first Chinese center dedicated to Denmark studies, has strengthened Sino-Danish cooperation in research and exchange. He expressed sincere gratitude to the Chinese and Danish scholars who have made unremitting efforts. The Chinese and Danish professors and museum experts who participated in the meeting gave a multi-angle interpretation of cultural heritage. The topics, such as the role of heritage and tourism in building future cross-cultural friendly relations, the role of cultural relics in cultural exchanges and cooperation, the measures and significance of "educational travel" in deepening Sino-Denmark cultural exchanges and enhancing the internationalization of talent training, and the significance of cultural heritage and

前　言

　　2018年正值中丹建立全面战略伙伴关系10周年,中丹两国政府举行了很多双边庆祝活动,丹麦研究中心的"文化遗产"专题会议正是双边学者们对10周年的献礼。2018年6月18—20日丹麦中心在丹麦哥本哈根大学亚洲动态研究中心召开了主题为"Cultural Heritage, Kulturarv or 文化遗产"的学术会议。汉学家何莫邪(Christoph Harbsmeier)从教育、教养、教化、修养、修身、文、文化、文化遗产等方面阐释了"文"在中国文化和社会中的深厚影响和意义。张喜华教授作了题为"中国文化复兴和文化国际传播中的文化遗产"的主题发言,认为丰富的中国文化遗产在文化身份建构、文化传播和跨文化交流中具有重要作用。中国、丹麦、挪威、英国和德国的其他学者分别对"文化遗产"在不同语言、文化和社会语境中的不同意义进行了阐释,"文化"和"文化遗产"成了意义纷呈的热词,展示着各自语境中的独特魅力。会议进一步促进了中丹学者的跨文化交流,促进了文化互识和互信。中丹两国学者找到了共同的学术兴趣,汇聚一堂,对话交流,学界无边,文化恒常,友谊长青。

　　2020年丹麦研究中心举办中丹建交70周年高端论坛。与会专家学者一致强调中丹关系中"友好"、"合作"是交往的主题。中丹友好关系历史悠久、社会基础广泛、官民并举,具有良好的根基。学者们应继承并弘扬中丹友好交流精神,从国别和区域研究、学科发展、绿色发展、语言文学研究、科技合作、民间交流、经贸合作等方面扎扎实实做事,诚心诚意沟通,建设中丹友好交流平台,不断开拓创新,深化中丹合作和友谊。

　　为了巩固多年在文化和文化遗产领域的合作研究成果,聚焦对话,本书基于中丹学者的研究和实践,汇集了中国学者和青年学子、丹麦专家和汉学家的相关研究成果,以中英文双语形式结集出版,以更好地促进文化对话和文化传播。本书的准备和撰写过程是中丹文化交流对话的宝贵机遇和实践。本书的逐渐成型基于文化交流对话实践,践行平等对话交流的初衷,服务于民心相通的最高目标。哥本哈根大学玛利亚·罗斯格德(Marie Højlund Roesgaard)教授和丹尼斯·金普尔(Denise Gimpel)教授为本书的构思、撰稿、征稿和审稿做了大量工作。郑承军教授从国别与区域研究的学科层面为本书的编辑和出版身体力行,从宏观指导、会议组织到亲自供稿,付出了大量的心血。上海社会科学院马驰研究员发挥学术专长和学术资源优势,为中丹文化交流、研究和实践提供了大量的帮助,撰文向丹麦介绍中国文化。中丹两国学者在文化对话中交流互鉴,践行着"美美与共"的跨文化理想。跨文化研究的青年学子除了撰文,还参与了翻译和校对工作。马亚楠、徐志杰、刘静贤、伍文全、卢嘉欣、余沁、谷健、于春华、孙宁、张家川等参与了部分论文的翻译和校对。本书的出版得到了北京第二外国语学

its relationship with education, the relationship between cultural heritage and cultural international dissemination, the content and communication strategies of cultural heritage in the digital age, attracted Chinese and Danish scholars' close attention.

In 2017, Danish scholars and cultural heritage research experts went to Guangxi to conduct a six-day systematic visit and inspection of Gui Pottery. The Danish experts expressed their shock at the long history of pottery and its contemporary production. To this end, Danish experts wrote articles to record and promote the cultural heritage of Chinese ancient pottery and its contemporary significance. Danish experts on the protection of world cultural heritage of the United Nations, believe that Gui pottery has a clear origin and development context, complete and orderly inheritance, and it is rare in the world. It not only has the OUV commonality of the world cultural heritage, but also has its own uniqueness. In 2018, Danish experts from Center for Denmark Studies visited Jingdezhen to explore the protection of the ceramic cultural heritage of Jingdezhen's Song Dynasty porcelain-making relics. Nordic encounters the Northern Song Dynasty, and cultural heritage has become a link and bridge for dialogue across time and space.

2018 marks the 10th anniversary of the establishment of a comprehensive strategic partnership between China and Denmark. The Chinese and Danish governments have held many bilateral celebrations. The "Cultural Heritage" conference of Center for Denmark Studies and ADC is the gift of bilateral scholars to the 10th anniversary. On June 18-20,2018, the academic conference on "Cultural Heritage, Kulturarv or Cultural Heritage" was held at the Asian Dynamics Center of the University of Copenhagen, Denmark. Sinologist Christoph Harbsmeier explained the profound influence and significance of "wen 文" in Chinese culture and society from the aspects of education, upbringing, cultivation, self-cultivation, culture and cultural heritage. Professor Zhang Xihua gave a keynote speech entitled "Chinese Cultural Renaissance and Cultural Heritage in International Cultural Dissemination", and held that rich Chinese cultural heritage plays an important role in the construction of cultural identity, cultural dissemination and cross-cultural communication. Other scholars from China, Denmark, Norway, UK and Germany have explained the different meanings of "cultural heritage" in different languages, cultures and social contexts. "Culture" and "cultural heritage" have become hot words with various meanings with its unique charm in different contexts. The conference has further promoted cross-cultural exchanges between Chinese and Danish scholars, and promoted mutual understanding. Chinese and Danish scholars have found common academic interests, gathered together for dialogues and exchanges. The academic world is boundless, culture is omnipresent, and Sino-Danish friendship is everlasting.

In 2020, Center for Denmark Studies chaired a forum on the 70th anniversary of the establishment of diplomatic relations between China and Denmark. Experts and scholars attending the conference unanimously empha-

院"科技创新服务能力建设—高精尖学科建设—外国语言文学学科"项目资助。"相知无远近,万里尤为邻",中丹学者和学子携手努力,才有了本书的出版和中丹同步发行。在此一并表示深深的感谢。

张喜华、因戈尔夫·蒂森(Ingolf Thuesen)
北京第二外国语学院丹麦研究中心
2021年3月22日于北京

sized that "friendship" and "cooperation" in Sino-Denmark relations are the themes of exchanges. There is a long history of friendly China-Denmark relation, a broad social foundation for exchanges. Scholars should inherit and carry forward Sino-Denmark friendly exchanges on area studies, green development, language and literature research, scientific and technological cooperation, economic and trade cooperation, etc.

In order to consolidate the results of many years' cooperative research in the field of culture and cultural heritage and focus on dialogue of the two countries, this book is based on the research and practice of Chinese and Danish scholars, and brings together the relevant research results of Chinese scholars and young students, Danish experts and sinologists. It is bilingual in Chinese and English to better promote cultural dialogue and understanding. The preparation and writing process of this book is a valuable opportunity and practice for Sino-Danish cultural exchanges and dialogues. The gradual formation of this book is based on mutual efforts of scholars practicing the original intention of equal dialogue and exchange, and serving the highest goal of people-to-people communication. Professor Marie Højlund Roesgaard and Professor Denise Gimpel from the University of Copenhagen have done a lot of work for the conception, writing, solicitation and review of this book. Professor Zheng Chengjun has contributed to the editing and publication of this book from the disciplinary level of regional studies, outlining, conference organization to paper writing. Prof. Ma Chi from Shanghai Academy of Social Sciences leveraged its academic expertise and academic resources to provide a lot of help for Sino-Danish cultural exchanges, research and practice, and wrote an article to introduce Chinese culture to Denmark. Scholars both from China and Denmark have exchanged and learned from each other in the cultural dialogue, practicing the cross-cultural ideal of sharing with each other and respect each other. In addition to writing articles, students of cross-cultural studies also participated partly in translation and proofreading. Ma Yanan, Xu Zhijie, Liu Jingxian, Wu Wenquan, Lu Jiaxin, Yu Qin, Gu Jian, Yu Chunhua, Sun Ning, Zhang Jiachuan, etc. participated in some translation and proofreading. The publication of this book was funded by Beijing International Studies University.

No matter how far away it is between China and Denmark, we can work and exchange just like friendly neighbors. Chinese and Danish scholars and students have been working hand in hand for the publication of this book to get it circulated both in China and Denmark. No words can express our deep gratitude for the mutual efforts and friendship. The best repay is to work more for our friendship.

Zhang Xihua, Ingolf Thuesen
Center for Denmark Studies
Beijing International Studies University
March 22, 2021

目 录

前言 ··· 001

我国文化复兴与传播中的文化遗产 ················· 张喜华 001

老陶工与他的制陶作坊
——正在中国与丹麦濒临绝迹的史前遗产？
················· 因戈尔夫·蒂森(Ingolf Thuesen)/著 余 沁/译 011

中国和全球历史视野下的文化遗产
················· 何莫邪(Christoph Harbsmeier)/著 徐志杰/译 024

"遗产(Heritage)"和"文化遗产(Kulturarv)"
················· 苏纳·沃肯(Sune Auken)/著 于春华/译 030

如何保护非物质文化遗产的核心价值
——以海宁硖石灯彩为例 ································· 马 驰 037

从用户角度看联合国教科文组织世界遗产
················· 莫滕·沃姆德(Morten Warmind)/著 刘静贤/译 041

考古遗产和当地身份
················· 埃斯本·阿尔斯莱夫(Esben Aarsleff)/著 张家川/译 048

论"Kulturerbe" ········ 莫里茨·金泽尔(Moritz Kinzel)/著 马亚楠/译 055

清代传统技艺和泥塑
················· 约瑟菲娜·巴克(Josefine Baark)/著 卢嘉欣/译 062

丹麦建筑遗产 ·················· 克里斯托弗·施密特（Kristoffer Schmidt）/著　武彦如/译　070

中国古代志怪小说中的人文光辉
　　——以《聊斋志异·陆判》中的异想与妙构为例 ········ 宋紫珍　郑承军　082

少林功夫在世界舞台的传播分析 ······················ 曹洪瑞　089

孔子故里曲阜"三孔"的文化意义建构与海外传播反思 ······ 于春华　096

黄海电影海报设计作品的东方美学意蕴 ················ 武彦如　103

龙泉青瓷在宋士大夫休闲生活中的意境构成
　　——以南宋龙泉窑鬲炉为例 ···················· 余　沁　110

京剧的海外传播问题与对策探析 ······················ 孙　宁　121

关于中国瓷器与中国文化国际传播的思考
　　——以景德镇瓷器为例 ························ 郭戎荣　130

天津美食中的幸福文化身份建构与可持续发展对策 ········ 张家川　137

中国京剧文化的对外传播 ···························· 刘　琦　144

从龙门石窟看文化自信与文化交流 ···················· 沈安童　151

灵魂何处是归路
　　——论长沙马王堆汉墓T形帛画的转生成仙示意功能 ··· 王艳华　157

长白山剪纸艺术在日韩的传播研究 ···················· 于洪鉴　163

向世界递上"中国名片"
　　——以泰山挑山工为例 ························ 郑天娇　170

Contents

Preface ·· 002

Cultural Heritage in China's Cultural Rejuvenation and
    International Communication ················· Zhang Xihua   176
The Old Potter and the Cave
    — Disappearing Prehistoric Heritage in China and
    Denmark? ···································· Ingolf Thuesen   193
Cultural Heritage in Chinese and Global Historical
    Perspective ···················· Christoph Harbsmeier(何莫邪)   208
"Heritage" and "Kulturarv" ······························ Sune Auken   218
How to Preserve the Core Value of Intangible Cultural Heritage
    — Xiashi Lantern as an Example ···················· Ma Chi   226
A UNESCO World Heritage Site from a User's
    Point of View ································ Morten Warmind   233
Archaeological Heritage and Local Identity ········ Esben Aarsleff   243
Kulturerbe (kʊlˈtuːɐ|ɛrbə) ······························ Moritz Kinzel   252
Traditional Practice and Clay Portraiture in Qing
    China ·· Josefine Baark   261
Danish Built Heritage ······················· Kristoffer Schmidt   276
Humanistic Effulgence in the Ancient Chinese Fantasy Novels
    — Take the Wonderful Whimsies and Ingenious Conceptions in
    Strange Tales from the Liaozhai Studio · Judge Lu
    as an Example ············ Song Zizhen, Zheng Chengjun   291

An Analysis of International Communication of Shaolin
　　Kungfu .... Cao Hongrui　305
The Cultural Significance of Construction and International
　　Communication Reflection of *San Kong* in Qufu, Confucius'
　　Hometown .... Yu Chunhua　316
The Eastern Aesthetic Meanings of Film Posters Designed
　　by HUANG Hai .... Wu Yanru　329
The Artistic Conception of the Literati's Leisure Life Reflected
　　on Longquan Celadon in the Song Dynasty
　　— Take the Tripod Censer (*lilu*) from Longquan Kiln in Southern
　　　Song Dynasty as an Example .... Yu Qin　339
Problems and Countermeasures in the Overseas Transmission of
　　Peking Opera .... Sun Ning　358
Jingdezhen Porcelain in China's Cultural Rejuvenation and
　　International Communication .... Guo Rongrong　374
The Construction of Happy Cultural Identity and Sustainable Development
　　Countermeasures in Tianjin Cuisine .... Zhang Jiachuan　385
The External Communication of Chinese Beijing Opera .... Liu Qi　396
Research on Cultural Confidence and Cultural Communication from
　　the Perspective of the Longmen Grottoes .... Shen Antong　407
Gone in the Soul: Study on the Directory Function for Reincarnation
　　and Being Immortal of Mawangdui Han Tomb T Shape Silk
　　Painting .... Wang Yanhua　419
Research on the Dissemination of Paper-cutting in Japan and South
　　Korea .... Yu Hongjian　429
Hand a Name Card of China to the World: Taking Mountain Tai
　　Porters as an Example .... Zheng Tianjiao　441

我国文化复兴与传播中的文化遗产

张喜华

文化遗产,概念上分为"有形文化遗产"和"无形文化遗产"。包括物质文化遗产和非物质文化遗产。物质文化遗产是具有历史、艺术和科学价值的文物;非物质文化遗产是指各种以非物质形态存在的与群众生活密切相关、世代相承的传统文化表现形式。在大多数人的眼中,文化遗产可能仅仅只是某个区域特定的地域象征和世代相传的技艺、风俗等。但是文化遗产所包含的内容远不止这些,它是一个国家和民族历史文化成就的重要标志,对于展现世界文化的多样性具有独特作用。在日趋全球化的今天,文化认同和民族文化身份的构建对于一个国家和民族来说尤为重要,是增强其国际竞争力的有力支撑,是其对外传播文化的重要基础。而文化认同和民族文化身份最有效的载体就是文化遗产。因此,文化遗产在文化复兴以及对外文化传播当中有着不可替代的作用。而在当今文化自信力缺乏的社会环境下,我国在这方面的发展和教育有待进一步深化。

一、我国优秀传统文化复兴已成为国家战略

党的十八大以来,我国文化事业和文化产业不断蓬勃发展,取得了骄人的成绩。现代化公共文化服务体系建设步入发展快车道,文化市场体系进一步健全,"走出去"战略的步伐加快,等等。这些都体现了文化在我国经济社会发展中的重要性。我们现在所处的时代是一个大发展、大变革的时代,全球化的趋势越发明显,树立并保持我国特有的民族文化身份已经成为提高我国在国际社会上的话语权的重要基础。因此,认同、继承和发展我国优秀传统文化,培养高度的文化自信,对中华民族伟大复兴有着十分重要的意义。

作为中华民族伟大复兴的最为基础、最为广泛的一环,我国优秀传统文化内

容包含核心思想理念、传统美德、人文精神三个方面。这其中分别包括五千年来勤劳智慧的中华民族在修齐治平、尊时守位、知常达变、开物成务、建功立业过程中形成的基本思想,比如革故鼎新、实事求是、脚踏实地等;还有丰富的道德理念和行为规范,如天下兴亡、匹夫有责的担当意识,精忠报国、振兴中华的爱国情怀,崇德向善、见贤思齐的社会风尚,孝悌忠信、礼义廉耻的荣辱观念,这些都潜移默化地影响着国人思维和行为方式。中华优秀传统文化积淀了多样、珍贵的精神财富,如求同存异、和而不同的处世方法,文以载道、以文化人的教化思想,形神兼备、情景交融的美学追求,俭约自守、中和方正的生活理念等,是我国人民思想观念、风俗习惯、生活方式、情感样式的集中表达,滋养了独特丰富的文学、艺术、科技、学术,至今仍然具有深刻影响。

　　党的十九大提出"坚定文化自信,推动社会主义文化繁荣兴盛",目的就是要逐渐转变国人逐渐西化的文化思维,提高对自身文化的认同感,提高文化自信,从而推动我国社会主义文化的健康发展。2017年,国务院颁布《关于实施中华优秀传统文化继承发展工程的意见》中强调:到2025年,中华优秀传统文化传承发展体系基本形成,研究阐发、教育普及、保护传承、创新发展、传播交流等方面协同推进并取得重要成果,具有我国特色、我国风格、我国气派的文化产品更加丰富,文化自觉和文化自信显著增强,国家文化软实力的根基更为坚实,中华文化的国际影响力明显提升。同时,国务院还将文化遗产保护工程纳入经济社会发展总体规划,纳入考核评价体系;加大中央和地方的各级财政支持力度,支持中华优秀传统文化发展重点项目。同年,国家又对《文物保护法》加以修订,对我国文化遗产的保护加大了保护力度。这一系列的宏观政策指导,都表明了继承和发扬我国优秀传统文化的紧迫性和必要性。因此,如何继承和发扬我国优秀传统文化成为新时代面临的重大课题。习近平总书记在孔子诞辰2565周年纪念国际学术研讨会暨国际儒学联合会第五届会员大会开幕会上提出,"'创造性转化、创新性发展',是指导传承发展中华优秀传统文化的重要方针"[①]。我们首先就是要尊重传统,文化传统是国家和民族的精神标识、文化血脉和价值系统。只有从传统文化中汲取营养,才能惠及当代、滋养后代。没有这个精神命脉,文化大繁荣就无从谈起,国家和民族的复兴就更没有希望;其次就是要善于古为今用,古代圣贤编撰的大量典籍,老祖宗传下来的文化遗产,这些都是宝贵的精神财富和经验财富,我们要让这些珍贵的财富活起来,学以致用,将这些方

---

① 李军:《坚持"创造性转化、创新性发展"方针弘扬我国传统文化》,《光明日报》2014年10月10日, http://www.71.cn/2014/1010/783444.shtml, 2014 - 10 - 10 09:05。

法与现代观念有机结合,解决当下的问题,发挥好其教化育人的功能,让它们积极有效地为国家为社会服务;最后就是在以上两点的基础上推陈出新,面对诸多种类的传统文化,我们也不能照抄照搬,具体问题也要具体分析,不能作茧自缚。文化的生命力在于创新,每一个时代都要有一种与之相适应的文化来满足社会发展的需要,解决新的问题。习近平总书记指出,"不忘本才能开辟未来,善于继承才能更好创新",我们必须在"两创"方针的指引下,在继承中发展,在发展中继承,秉持扬弃的原则,进行新的文化创造,让中华文明革故鼎新,再创辉煌,完成好我们这一代人应当承担的历史责任。

2018年6月9日是文化和自然遗产日,为贯彻落实党的十九大精神,进一步提高人民群众保护传承非物质文化遗产意识,弘扬中华优秀传统文化,树立文化自信,全国各地都展开了丰富多彩的文化遗产宣传活动。2018年的遗产日主题为"文化遗产的传播与传承"。为贯彻落实习近平总书记关于"让文化活起来"的指示精神,让更多的民众全方位、多角度体会传统文化的魅力,第五届"芳草非遗嘉年华"活动在北京民俗博物馆成功举办。前来的游客纷纷表示这一为期两天的活动,形式新颖,精彩纷呈,突出了本次活动的主旨。本次活动既表明了国家对文化遗产传承和传播文化作用的重视,又切实地让文化遗产的魅力融入了人民群众的生活当中,对增进国民的文化自信起到了极大的推动作用。

另外,在继承和发展优秀传统文化、提高文化自信的同时,有效地加大文化的对外传播也是新时代我们面临的一项重要任务。近十多年以来,国家一直在强调我国文化"走出去",2000年我国第一次明确地提出了"走出去"战略,在文化领域,就是"要以更加开放的姿态融入国际社会,进一步扩大对外文化交流,实施'走出去'战略"[①]。2011年颁布的《关于深化文化体制改革推动社会主义文化大发展大繁荣若干重大问题的决定》强调要推动中华文化走向世界。开展多渠道、多形式、多层次的对外文化交流,广泛参与世界文明对话,促进文化相互借鉴,增强中华文化在世界上的感召力和影响力。2014年习近平总书记提出要讲好中国故事、传播好中国声音、阐发中国精神、展现中国风貌,要向世界宣传推介中国优秀的文化艺术,让国外民众在审美过程中感受魅力,加深对中华文化的认识和理解。2013年提出的"一带一路"倡议中的"五通"里就有一项为民心相通,目的就是加强同沿线各国的文化交流,实现文化传播。

文化复兴迫在眉睫,我们年轻一代要意识到文化自觉与文化自信的紧迫性,

---

① 杨利英:新时期我国文化"走出去"战略的意义,人民论坛,http://history.rmlt.com.cn/2014/0926/323534.shtml,2014-09-26 16:27。

积极主动地去了解、继承并发展我国优秀传统文化,为我国的文化事业不断注入新鲜血液,文化复兴才会早日实现。

二、文化遗产——中华文化复兴和传播中的中流砥柱

作为中国文化基础的载体,文化遗产可以说在中华文化复兴当中的地位可见一斑。中国历史悠久,文化遗产众多,目前已有52项世界自然遗产和文化遗产,其中世界文化遗产或双遗产占40项,位居世界第二。从文化载体的角度上来讲,"我国的实物遗存其实并非最为重要,无论是石质的还是木质的,重要的是借其表达另一种崇高的形态——永恒性"[①],文化遗产凝结了五千年来中华民族的智慧、汗水和中华民族的伟大文明。古往今来,无论是上层建筑的交替更迭,还是民间的繁衍生息,文化都承载着崇高庄严的功能或永恒的精神依托,伴随而生的优秀文明也就自然而然地永恒地蕴含其中。因此,在新时代下强调的文化复兴也就离不开文化遗产。

第一,文化遗产构建了民族文化身份。以故宫为例,故宫是第一批进入《世界遗产名录》的人类文化遗产,拥有世界现存面积最大的古建筑群,代表了中国古代宫廷建筑的最高水准,在世界建筑史中独树一帜。故宫严格地按《周礼·考工记》中"前朝后市,左祖右社"的帝都营建原则建造。整个故宫,在建筑布置上,用形体变化、高低起伏的手法,组合成一个整体。在功能上符合封建社会的等级制度,同时达到左右均衡和形体变化的艺术效果。我国建筑的屋顶形式是丰富多彩的,在故宫建筑中,屋顶的形式就有10种以上。以三大殿为例,屋顶各不相同。故宫建筑屋顶满铺各色琉璃瓦件。主要殿座以黄色为主,绿色用于皇子居住区的建筑,其他蓝、紫、黑、翠以及孔雀绿、宝石蓝等五彩缤纷的琉璃,多用在花园或琉璃壁上。太和殿屋顶当中正脊的两端各有琉璃吻兽,稳重有力地吞住大脊。吻兽造型优美,是构件也是装饰物。这些严谨而又独特的建筑方法,向世界展现了中华民族的伟大建筑智慧和建筑文化。同样,作为世界文化遗产的长城,是我国也是世界上修建时间最长、工程量最大的一项古代军事防御工程。自西周时期开始,长城延续不断修筑了2000多年,分布于我国北部和中部的广大土地上,总计长度达五万多千米。早在汉朝时期,长城就在中西文化的交流起到了很重要的促进作用。汉武帝派遣张骞出使西域诸国,就以长城要塞为根据地,开

---

① 彭兆荣:《"祖宗在上":我国传统文化遗续中的"崇高性"——兼与巫鸿的"纪念碑性"商讨》,《思想战线》2014年第1期第40卷,第6页。

辟和维护着长安至大秦两万余里的交通干道，也就是著名的"丝绸之路"。几千年来，在这条古道上，中外文化融合、交流。至今这条古道仍在发挥着巨大作用。许多外国人了解我国都是从知道长城开始的，长城是世界上其他国家人民了解我国历史、我国文化、中华民族的一个很好的切入点。这一凝结着中华民族几千年的智慧和力量的宏伟建筑，是中华民族贡献给全人类的宝贵遗产。所以，这些伟大的文化遗产已经成为我国文化登上国际舞台的重要名片，在很大程度上构建了我国的民族文化身份，也让中华文化在激烈的全球化竞争面前赫然屹立于世界民族之林，独树一帜。

第二，文化遗产有利于促进文化自觉和文化自信。近年来，随着中国经济的快速发展，文化也受到了世界的广泛关注，越来越多的人想要了解中国。但是，改革开放的40年来，中国基本上只是充当了"世界加工厂"的角色，属于制造大国，自主创新能力与较发达国家相比还有较大差距。虽然我国正在逐步发掘自身的文化创造力，实现从输出产品到输出思想、创意、文化的转变，但是由于我们长期以来对自己的历史文化不够重视，导致当下中国许多年轻人在这一方面知识奇缺，文化素质普遍不高，很大一部分甚至连本民族文化都讲不清楚，文化自觉就无从谈起，更不要说实现文化自信了。所以首先就是要引导他们充分了解并认同本民族的文化，然后再在这个基础上提高文化自信。而文化遗产作为我国优秀传统文化的集中载体，本身就有着文化认同的功能，"在世界遗产运动的影响下，我国的'非遗'运动也风起云涌。非遗界的研究者初步发掘了文化遗产与文化认同的关系，肯定了文化遗产的文化认同功能，对于上至国家、下到个人的文化认同而言，文化遗产的功能也不容忽视"[①]。文化遗产是认识和了解中华民族优秀传统文化的最重要的渠道之一，学者可以通过自己"真听、真看、真感受"，身临其境地去体验个中所蕴含的历史和文化，去了解这些文化瑰宝的背景，领会中华文化的趣味和博大的胸襟，同时还可以选择身体力行地去做诸多非物质文化遗产的保护者和继承者，在行动的过程中感受中华民族文化的魅力，逐渐地去了解并认同我国优秀传统文化，提高文化自信。最近中央电视台综合频道热播的大型文化节目《经典咏流传》积极响应落实十九大报告中"推动中华优秀传统文化创造性转化、创造性发展"的精神，采用"和诗以歌"的形式将非物质文化遗产——诗词与现代流行音乐相融合，在注重节目时代化的同时，也深度挖掘诗词背后的内涵，讲述文化知识、阐述人文价值、解读思想观念，为现代文明追根

[①] 邱硕：《文化遗产与文化认同的新关联——"文化遗产与文化认同"国际研讨会综述》，《文化遗产研究》第三辑，第264页。

溯源,从而树立文化自信。"它带给观众的不仅是复苏文化记忆的历史呈现,更是民族文化发展的时代强音。"①该节目一经播出,就深受广大人民群众赞许,好评如潮,让包括许多年轻一代在内的广大群众在充分了解并肯定我国优秀传统文化的同时,很大程度上实现了文化自觉,促进了文化自信。

第三,文化遗产是文化对外传播的重要载体。这也是文化遗产最重要的作用之一,当今全球化的趋势不断加强,国际旅游市场逐步扩大,在旅游产业发展的过程中,吸引国际游客的内容主要有两大类:独特的自然景观和深厚的历史和文化。而我国作为四大文明古国之一,有着五千多年的悠久历史,文化遗产众多,自然就成了世界旅游大国。而国际游客来到我国参观我国的文化遗产本身就是一种文化的感受过程,是一种文化吸纳和内化的过程,因而本质上是一种文化国际传播过程。从国际游客来到我国,接触我国的文化遗产,到了解部分我国文化的整个过程当中,文化遗产这一环是最重要的,正是因为文化遗产所承载的历史文化信息,才使得他们能够将这些我国文化的内容吸收进来,从而才实现了文化的传播。由此,我国文化遗产可以说是连接我国与世界的一大窗口,许多外国人了解我国也是从听闻我国的某些文化遗产开始的,例如长城、故宫、功夫、唐诗宋词等。近年来,随着互联网科技的发展,许多文化遗产场所都应用了最新的科技元素,采用数字化的交互方式,给文化传播方式带来了革命。北京的故宫博物院充分利用数字技术和互联网技术,建立了故宫数字体验馆,以新媒体形式呈现出一个数字化的历史文化遗产,为古老的故宫注入了现代科技的血液。2016年,故宫博物院与腾讯公司建立长期合作伙伴关系,借助互联网平台把"互联网+传统文化"由理念转变成实践。现在,"视听馆"、"全景故宫"、"V故宫"、故宫App、故宫游戏等文化遗产传播的新形式都有效地传播了故宫文化,其中的"数字故宫"短片将极为复杂的故宫建筑文化和建筑结构生动、形象、立体地呈献给游客,而且有外文版,令海外游客对故宫的文化内涵叹为观止。《韩熙载夜宴图》App以"融汇学术、艺术、科技,贯通视觉、听觉、触觉,动态重现华美夜宴"获得Ipad类最佳奖。《雍正行乐图》动态图片通过微信走红,累计转发超过80万次。

总的来说,所有以不同形式呈现出来的内容都是以文化遗产本身为载体,没有文化遗产这个中流砥柱作为载体,文化的对外传播就很难实现。

---

① 郝静静:《让古典诗词乘着歌声的翅膀飞翔——大型文化节目〈经典咏流传〉评析》,《光明日报》2018年2月27日,http://www.chinawriter.com.cn/n1/2018/0227/c404004-29835848.html, 2018-02-27 06:22。

三、我国文化遗产存在的问题和对策

我国在文化遗产的对待和管理的问题上,制定了许多的相关政策,做出了许多合理妥善的举措,也取得了良好的效果。比如,在非物质文化遗产的保护方面,2005年3月26日,国务院办公厅印发了《关于加强我国非物质文化遗产保护工作的意见》,着力强调了我国非物质文化遗产保护工作的重要性和紧迫性;确立了非物质文化遗产保护工作的目标和方针,建立名录体系,逐步形成有我国特色的非物质文化遗产保护制度;加强领导,落实责任,建立协调有效的工作机制。同年11月,"蒙古族长调民歌"就入选联合国教科文组织第三批"人类口头和非物质遗产代表作"名录。至2009年,全国非遗资源总量近87万项。"到2017年,国务院批准公布了四批共1 372项国家级代表性项目,各地批准公布了13 807项省级代表性项目。文化部命名了四批1 986名国家级代表性传承人,各地命名了14 928名省级代表性传承人。"[①]此外,在对我国文化遗产的保护和国土空间高效利用上,国家建立了国家公园体制,为现有的文化遗产管理制度改革提供了新思路。种种方法都表明了我国正朝着文化遗产保护的程序化、规范化、制度化的方向迈进,未来在这一方面一定会取得令人满意的成绩。

虽然我国在这一方面做出了一些令人满意的成绩,但是总体上还存在着一些问题和不足,还未发挥文化遗产足够的作用,有待改进。

第一,认识不够。我国很多地方对文化遗产的价值认识不够深刻,许多地方对文化遗产场所的利用过度商业化,以此来牟取大量旅游收入,却忽略了对人文的关怀。例如,在2008年汶川地震过后,北川县和汶川县的羌族文化便匆忙登记为国家级和国际级非物质文化遗产,重建羌族村被改为遗产旅游目的地,却忽略了对受伤人员人文情感上的关怀。[②] 我们在对文化遗产价值要有一个清楚的认识,我们的目的是为了保护、继承和传播文化,最后的落脚点是人,不能以牺牲其中的人文内涵为代价,来换取所谓的短期的经济增长。

第二,文化遗产的保护力度不够。在维护和修缮上,有部分城市在城市化进程中,忽略了文化遗产的重要性,对许多可能的文化遗产的损毁态度消极或置之不理,甚至大肆拆建。这些都是极其错误的。"文化遗产是历史发展轨迹的生动

---

① 王学思:《党的十八大以来我国非遗保护工作综述》,新华社,http://www.xinhuanet.com/culture/2017-10/16/c_1121808007.htm,2017-10-16 09:50。
② Katiana Le Mentec, Qiaoyun Zhang, Heritagization of disaster ruins and ethnic culture in China: Recovery plans after the 2008 Wenchuan earthquake, *China Information*, 2017, Vol. 31(3)349.

写照,保存了无法估量的历史记忆和有用信息,具有影响深远的历史价值、科学价值和艺术价值,能够被人保存、传承和发展。城市文化建设要想具有底蕴和文脉,只能以文化遗产作为核心和灵魂,将其作为城市文化集成系统的总指引。"① 在主动记录和传承方面上,我们年轻一代做得还不够,有不少可以作为非物质文化遗产的技艺鲜为人知,如果不被发掘并且继承的话,很有可能这些古老技艺的传承就会出现断代,文化发生不可逆的消逝。

第三,文化遗产的教育功能发挥得不够。文化遗产本是加强文化自觉和文化自信最有力的活教材,但对于我国中小学生和青少年来说并不是很便捷,他们想去通过感受我国的文化遗产来培养自己的文化素养和文化自信就会显得相对乏力。比如,各大文物古迹场馆需要高额门票,也未专门面向中小学生设立单独的体验时段,游客较多,观感体验较差,缺乏欣赏氛围,等等。因此,文化遗产的教育作用还应该得到更大的发挥,从而有利于培养青年一代的民族自信、文化自信和爱国主义精神。

第四,文化遗产在海外传播效度不够。中国虽然地大物博,文化遗产基数大,但是在海外传播出去的大部分是碎片化信息,外国人对中国文化也只是一知半解,认知程度仅停留在提起某些文化遗产就有印象是中国的,对其中蕴含的文化了解不深入。国家也在文化"走出去"上下足了功夫,也取得了一定的成绩。但要想进一步提高我国文化遗产在海外的传播效度,还需要狠修内功,在自身上多下功夫。

对于以上几点存在的问题,最重要的就是要充分发挥文化遗产的教育作用和加大文化遗产海外传播效度。而对于认识不够的问题,国家和政府要出台更多、更全面的保护政策以及经费拨付或限制,有关部门要做好宣传教育工作,鼓励更多的年轻人来参与到文化遗产的保护和传承当中来。对于对文化遗产保护力度的问题,国家可以成立专门的机构或者小组,对不明确的遗址进行评估,针对评估结果来决定是否保留或保护。早在 2012 年 4 月,国家四部局就成立了由建筑学、民俗学、艺术学、规划学、遗产学、人类学等专家组成的专家委员会,评审《我国传统村落名录》,进入名录的传统村落成为国家保护的重点。这样就能有效地保护各个地方的传统村落,而它们所蕴含的非物质文化遗产就能够得到传承。

然而,对于文化遗产的教育功能发挥得不够的问题,有关部门一定要引起重视,这是事关文化自信和文化复兴的关键。青年一代是我国实现文化复兴的希

---

① 宋暖:《城市化进程中的文化遗产保护与文化认同》,《理论学刊》2015 年 9 月第 9 期,第 127 页。

望,承担着民族伟大复兴的重要使命,但我国青年一代在这方面的意识十分薄弱,而且我国对青年一代的文化遗产教育存在严重不足,因而文化遗产教育刻不容缓。在这一点上,可以借鉴意大利在这方面的经验,"意大利充分发挥自身的遗产优势,通过教育来提高居民的遗产保护意识。为了营造'人人了解遗产、人人爱护遗产'的环境和氛围,意大利政府采取多种措施,使遗产景区门票一直保持在相对较低的价位。而且在意大利,经常可以看到有组织的一群大、中、小学生在参观古建筑、古文物,并认真地做着笔记。教师会为他们认真地讲解,学生们参观完后还要参加考试。通过参观学习,学生们对历史知识有了系统地了解,文化遗产保护意识也得以提高。在这种潜移默化的熏陶下,遗产保护意识深入人心"。[1] 让全民感受文化遗产所具有的文化魅力,提高全民的文化自信。经常开展一些丰富多彩的文化遗产教育活动,对青年一代起到一种潜移默化的熏陶作用,让它们自然而然地接受并继承和发扬我国优秀传统文化,提升文化自信。这样一来,我国的文化复兴的动力将会越来越足,民族复兴指日可待。

其次就是对于文化遗产在海外传播效度不够的问题,这一点也是至关重要。我国十几年来一直强调"文化走出去",但效果并不是十分显著,传递出去的"碎片"信息很容易让外国人无法理解或者由于文化差异甚至对我国文化产生误解和偏见,这就是因为这些信息的传递很少结合每个文化遗产的特定语境。因此,我国文化遗产传播工作就应该在自身上大做文章,结合特定时代下的语境,只有做到与特定的语境相结合,传递出来的文化信息才能是完整、客观、真实的。游客才能对文化产生完整的理解,而非"碎片"的,这也就是完成文化传播的一个重要的基础。

最后就是完善好相关的服务设施,尤其是注意外语翻译的准确性和差异性。每个国家和民族文化和语言思维各不相同,所以针对每一个国家都要有一套精准的翻译系统,旅游翻译"是一种跨语言、跨社会、跨时空、跨文化、跨心理的交际活动"[2],是外国旅游者了解我国的必要媒介,文化遗产解说内容的翻译质量对于宣传我国、树立我国的对外形象、进行国际文化交流有着很重要的意义。因此,只有内容、语境、语言思维、基础设施服务等要素得到充分完善后,外国游客就会主动地接近我国,对中华文化产生更大的兴趣,我国优秀文化在海外的传播效度就可能会大大提高。

---

[1] 张晨:《意大利公众如何参与文化遗产保护》,《我国社会科学在线》,http://www.yuanlin.com/gujian/Html/Detail/2013-4/19907.html,2013-04-24 22:50。

[2] 曾文雄:《旅游文化对外传播与旅游经济发展》,《商场现代化》2006年3月(上旬刊)。http://www.docin.com/p-1013790638.html。

总之,文化遗产凝聚和浓缩了我国文化,是我国文化最典型且有效的载体。在全球化进程不断推进的时代背景下,我们要通过充分发挥我们自身的文化遗产优势,时刻保持自身文化身份的独立性,提高我们自身的文化自信。努力做足做好文化遗产教育工作的同时,还要切实做到"结合语境,做好翻译",将中华文化积极有效地传播到世界的每个角落。如果做到以上这些,就一定能早日实现中华民族的伟大复兴。

(作者单位:北京第二外国语学院)

老陶工与他的制陶作坊

——正在中国与丹麦濒临绝迹的史前遗产？

因戈尔夫·蒂森（Ingolf Thuesen）/著　余　沁/译

遗产是时间的增函数。它既能以文物、历史遗址等人造物的形式流传后世，也能以过去历史记忆的形式传存。用理想的话语来说，遗产将时间定格了，所以当下社会明确基于一定原因保护每件文物或历史遗址。而宣布某物为遗产主要是因为我们发现它给我们的生活增添了价值。这是我们就遗产达成的普遍共识，并制定联合国教科文组织公约，为世界各国所遵循。遗产拥有物质与非物质维度，联合国科教文组织分别称之为有形或者无形的文化遗产。下文中来自中国的案例便是兼具有形与无形遗产的例证，它使我们直面一个问题：我们应该保护这一遗产吗？如果应该保护它的话，要怎么保护？此案例还涉及丹麦的陶瓷制作传统，同时分享这一传统可能将相互启发制定遗产保护策略。

在2017年访问中国广西壮族自治区期间，我们考察了一个临近中越边境的村庄。当地博物馆人员介绍我们认识了一名老陶工。我们得知这位陶工已有70多岁高龄，是现今唯一不用窑炉烧制优质陶器的手艺人。要知道，制陶在中国历经数千年的发展，技术已趋于完善。我们被带到一个山洞中，这个山洞就是他从泥塑成型到烧制陶器成品的制陶作坊。接下来我将以图文并茂的方式呈现发生在山洞中的整个制陶流程。这位陶工的技艺娴熟精湛，代表了中国数千年来的陶瓷技术。中国在世界陶瓷发展中占有重要地位，瓷器的发明让中国的手工技艺处于登峰造极的境地。在中国，任何细小的陶瓷传统工艺和技艺都应被记录作为历史档案。在这偏远山村中保留下来的古代制陶技艺正是增进我们对陶瓷技术历史理解的一个重要窗口。

黏土到人造石器的转变

纵观历史，人类的主要创举之一是发现动植物可以被驯养和种植，即所谓新石器时代革命(蔡尔德,1951)。这使得人类对自然界的态度发生了翻天覆地的变化,人类从单纯被动依赖自然的狩猎采集经济,发展为掌控部分自然资源,种植如小麦和大米等谷物,驯养狗、绵羊和山羊等动物的自然农业社会。由此人类一跃到达大自然食物链的顶端。

但与此同时,人类社会产生了另一项引人注目的创举。它不仅与食物采集有关,而且与材料、工具和技术有关。这一创举就是发现了某些泥土经过烧制质地会变得如石头般,因此学会了利用这种方法制作陶器。这确实是石器时代人类的一次革命。数千年来,人类用于制作工具最重要的材料就是石头,它能根据工具所需的功能要求打造成适宜的形状,如锋利的刀刃、箭头、用于研磨的圆形糙面等。所有石制工具的共同点是使用减缩物料手段制成需要的用具。燧石被削成薄片,其他石头则被打磨成不同形状。这种减缩物料制作工具的方法充满挑战性,需要工匠兼具技能和经验。器具制作过程中出现任何差错都无法纠正,否则最终得到的就是功能缺失的工具或者直接成为废品。

一万多年前在中国,人类发现黏土被火烧过后——也许是偶然接近了火堆——改变了它的特性。它变得更加坚硬,犹如一块石头。这一发现引发了一场技术革命,即用火技术(pyro technology)的发明,也就是通过用火加热改变材料性能。用火加热黏土最终可产生一种坚硬的石材——陶。来自中国江西仙人洞遗址的考古证据表明,此处早在两万年前就有了用作炊具的陶器(吴小红等,2012)。这些早期人类生活用具考古考证现已在中国和日本以及其他地区得到证实,这意味着制陶技术这一创举可能是人类在驯养动物、种植植物之前就已经掌握了的更有效进行贮藏和烹饪食物的生存技能。因此,这一能够更好贮藏食物和水等液体以及烹饪食物的技术创举使人类产生了农耕生活。来自约旦沙漠的最新考古发现表明,烤制面包技艺也早于农业耕作。这证实了所谓新石器时代革命取决于技术创新和对用火技术的掌握的观点(阿兰兹·奥泰格等,2018)。

通过考察人类利用诸如燧石等传统石材制作工具,制作陶器比加工石头具有更多优势。打造石器是用减缩物料技术创制一种工具的形状,制陶则变成了通过制模和接加部件让材料做成一定形状的成形技艺。这为制作生活容器提供了新路径。制陶的风险主要是能否成功烧制已成型的坯胎,将柔软的黏土制成如石头般坚硬的器具。掌握了这项技术,人类便能制作人造石器了。石器时代是人类首选天然石料制作工具的时期,同时也是人类发明技术制造人造石器的时代。

最早的陶器是用自然界具有一定韧度的黏土作为原材料,做成一定的器形,采用坑烧或堆烧的方法烧制而成。我们在广西山洞中见识了这种制陶方式。对于长期研究数千年来不同陶瓷文化的考古学家来说,看到这一原始制陶方式时感觉时间突然静止了。这不是在遥远的过去,而是当下亲自看见人类古老技术至今尚存的震撼。它是一份关于如何生产陶瓷的精美的活档案。我们需要这样的档案。下面本文将总结描述我们在洞中陶坊考察到的制陶过程,因为我们都认为在它背后是数千年来几乎未改变的传统制作工艺。

(一)泥料制备

制作陶器的山洞在群峦叠嶂的山谷中。山谷中满是黏土与农田肥沃的田地。农耕是当下生活在小村庄的农民的主要活动。四周青山环绕,山谷中肥沃的土地为这片区域增添了美丽与宁静(图1)。

图1 陶工所在山洞周边风景如画

老陶工带着预先准备的陶坯来到山洞(图2)。这些生坯可能是在村里制作成型的,但他在等待这些陶罐烧成的同时,也在山洞中为我们演示了整个制坯过程。

图2 陶工带着打算烧制的陶罐前往山洞

老陶工使用的泥料是一种褐色细颗粒软泥团,非常适合塑形成各种器物。这种泥料取自当地,经过练泥工序后保持适宜的湿度备用。在山洞中,他用一种白色矿物和这种黏土进行调配。调配这种有韧度的矿物使得器物通常在烧制过程中不变形。这种白色矿物是先用直径约 10 厘米的圆石砸碎成小白石子(图3),然后放入石舂臼,即岩石的凹槽处,舂成细粉末。之后再用木杵进行细舂提高它的韧性,最后将之掺入制陶泥料中。(图 4 和图 5)。

图 3　用石块作为工作台,手握石头砸碎白色矿石

图 4　用天然岩石和木杵做舂臼,将白色矿石舂成粉末

图 5　陶罐成型前用提高烧制韧度的矿粉配制泥料

拉坯成型

在洞中,陶工向我们展示了如何用陶车塑型一个容器。这个陶车是将直径约 40 厘米的圆盘装在一个敦实的圆石柱上。这个转盘就是拉坯成型的工作台。它被放在木轴心顶部,而这根木头可能是用混凝土将其固定在地面上(图 6、图 7)。这个组合装置可以让陶工拉出陶罐这种圆器。圆盘下面的石柱支点可以稳定并平衡转动陶车,手动旋转转盘,拉坯时能保持一定的旋转速度。

图 6　陶工陶车 　　　　图 7　陶车转盘轴心

紧挨着陶车边的是陶工的石凳,另一块石头是他的制陶工作台。这里放着陶工做陶壶用的原材料——泥料、白色矿粉,以及工具——一块布、一壶水、一把 10 厘米长的刮片和一根细绳(图 8)。

图 8　陶工的作坊:陶车、石凳,以及放在石头上的制陶工具和泥料

在开始做陶壶前,陶工会先在转盘中心撒一层薄薄的白色矿粉,然后放上用于做壶底的泥块(图9)。壶底做好后,给壶身下半部添加更多的泥料以塑造壶身的侧面(图10和图11)。这部分工作大约需要4分钟。

图9 制作陶壶第一步:先往陶车转盘上撒白色矿粉

图10 用泥块做壶底

图11 给壶身下半部塑形

壶底和壶身下半部做好后,用手转动转盘。陶工用湿布将壶身从侧面拉起,最后用刮片修饰其形状和表面(图12和图13)。用细绳将壶身与转盘切割分离,将做好的壶身移到旁边的木板上晾干(图14)。然后陶工做壶身大约需要10分钟。总体来说,从将泥料放到陶车上到把做好的壶身放到木板上晾干,整个过程大约需要15分钟。

图12 用湿布辅助拉坯成型

图13　用刮片刮平修饰壶身的形状　　　　图14　晾干陶坯

烧制

　　一般来说，烧制是整个陶瓷生产过程中最关键的阶段。精确控制温度和窑火中的氧气流量是生产高品质陶瓷器物的决定性条件。细微的温度变化都可能导致烧制中的器物变形。例如，烧制完成后的壶盖与壶身之间不再相互吻合匹配。最糟糕的是烧制完全失败，导致不得不丢弃所有的容器，所以陶瓷窑炉边常堆放着成堆的破碎变形的容器。但是这些陶瓷废弃物恰好帮助考古学家找到古代窑址。除非是大自然的馈赠，否则在不用窑炉烧制或者没有烧成温度控制装置的情况下，能亲眼看到一次由陶坯烧成陶器的完整过程是相当令人着迷的事。

　　陶工将烧制所需的必备材料都带到了山洞。燃料是成捆的晒干的玉米叶和玉米梗以及另一捆没晒干的芒萁（别名"铁狼萁"）（图15、图16）。摆放好几块石头，在上面用长约1.5米至2米、直径约5厘米的树枝搭建出一个长方形架子，整个架子离地面约20厘米高（图17）。将干透了的壶坯按照其形状成排放置，一排带壶流和把手的壶身，错落有致放在两排壶身中间的壶盖。总体来说，木架上能放置16个壶身、6个壶盖。先前烧制后留下的废弃品和较大的陶壶碎片则放在边角处，以及待烧的壶身周围和顶部，用于保护壶身并控制它们周围的热量（图18）。

图 15 烧制所需的燃料一：晒干的玉米叶和玉米梗

图 16 烧制所需燃料二：没晒干的芒萁

图 17 正在搭建的堆烧木架

图 18 堆满陶器和废弃品的木架

烧制主要有两个阶段。第一个阶段需要一个半到两个小时。陶工先往木架下面添加玉米细杆，从下方给陶壶进行加热。这个过程进行到一半时，把陶壶翻转，让另一面也得到加热（图19、图20）。第一个阶段主要是为了去除壶坯中残留的水份，为接下来的高温烧制做准备。

图19　烧制的第一个阶段：从下面添柴，加热陶器

图20　将陶器翻个面，重复这一步骤

第二个阶段是高温硬化坯体。此时需要用到芒萁。将芒萁放置在木架下面和壶的顶部，形成一个密闭空间。一开始，绿色的叶子燃烧会产生大量浓烟，这很好解释了为什么要在远离村庄的山洞内烧制陶器（图21、图22）。定期添加燃料，在这不到25分钟的烧制过程中，陶工需要高度集中关注火候（图23）。

用一层芒萁包裹在壶坯四周，在木柴架烧塌前，空气和氧气都会从柴架下面流入助燃（图24）。从许多方面来看，这整个结构和技术都类似于我们所知道的美索不达米亚文明的传统史前窑：泥砖砌成的圆窑分出两个空间，一个是处

图 21 烧制的第二个阶段：将芒萁放在陶器的下面和顶部

图 22 芒萁燃烧后产生了大量浓烟

图 23 烧制的第二个阶段，陶工必须全程持续关注火候

图 24 燃料燃烧碳化成一个圆顶结构，类似于史前建造的窑

于底部的火膛，另一个是放置陶坯的窑室(贾西姆，1985)。美索不达米亚的窑用泥砖砌成，中国南部的这个窑则由有机物、树枝和半干的芒萁构成。从生产出的陶瓷硬度来看，几乎都能在轻叩下听到金属声音。这一烧成工艺产生的温度约为1000摄氏度。

陶工用木棍拨开碳化的枝条层，然后便能看到烧得发红的陶壶，再将它们挑出来慢慢冷却(图25)。这次烧制很成功，没有废品。能把控住烧制火候技艺精湛的陶工可让烧出来的壶盖很好地契合壶身。这种特别烧成工艺制作的陶壶，壶盖和壶身匹配得天衣无缝。

图 25 从火中挑出来烧得发红的陶壶

结语

在当今中国发现一种仅靠天然物质就可完成的陶瓷制作是非常了不起的。如果这个制陶工艺不是代代相传历经千年不断，将早已不复存在。山洞作坊中老陶工的原始手工制陶工艺是最重要的遗产，可帮助我们了解史前陶器的制作过程。将它作为有形和无形的遗产完整记录下来，可以佐证石器时代用火技术是人类利用自然力量改变生活方式的一项重要创举。

这让人们不禁要问：在中国已经进入最发达文明阶段并生产出陶瓷最高端形态——瓷器时，为何依然还保留着这么简单的原始制陶方法？这其中或许有许多答案。当然，高档瓷器并不适合所有人。但每个人都需要用来烹饪和存储的陶制壶罐是一种廉价产品，可满足普通人的需求。

现在让我们来看看在丹麦发生的类似情况。从中世纪开始，到了夏天农夫就雇佣穿梭在村落间的女陶工制作家用陶器。无须建窑搭坊，她们仅靠着祖传的技能，就能就地成型烧成陶器。她们就地取材，用一种简单的方式把泥做的壶罐挖坑埋烧。由于坑烧柴熏，结果产生了一种表面又黑又亮的特别陶器。这就是今天人们熟知的黑陶。它们在日德兰半岛的许多省博物馆都有展出（Lina，2019）。当然，在制作农夫用的黑陶器同时，丹麦各地的作坊或者工厂也生产了高品质的陶瓷。大约1775年，皇家哥本哈根陶瓷厂建成，学习了中国制瓷技术的精英们也生产出了优质瓷器。

最后，不用建造窑炉烧制陶器的工艺已成为一份人类值得保存的重要遗产。珍视这份遗产不仅能让我们了解人类经历的技术创新与发展进步，而且能了解社会发展过程中各种纷繁复杂的变迁。中国和丹麦都面临保护珍贵遗产的困境（图26、图27）。

图26　日用陶瓷。丹麦日德兰半岛坑烧黑陶罐　　图27　中国广西堆烧陶罐

（作者单位：哥本哈根大学）

参考文献：

1. Arranz-Otaegui, Amaia et al. 2018. Archaeobotanical evidence reveals the origins of bread 14,400 years ago in northeastern Jordan. *Proc Natl Acad Sci* USA July 31, 2018 115(31)7925-7930.

2. Childe, V. G. 1951. Man Makes Himself (London: C. A. Watts & Co. Ltd.).
3. Jasim, Sabah A. 1985. The Ubaid Period in Iraq. Recent Excavations in the Hamrin Region. BAR International Series 267.
4. Linaa, J. 2019. Pots for the impoverished: Black pots from Jutland — A Danish contribution to the European Ceramic Market 1600-1850. In *Keramik in Norddeutschland: Beiträge des 48. Internationalen Symposiums für Keramikforschung vom 14. bis 16. September 2015 in Mölln*. Hans-Georg Stephan Ed. (Verlag Beier & Beran) 108-113.
5. Wu, Xiahong et al. 2012. Early Pottery at 20,000 Years Ago in Xianrendong Cave, China. *Science* 29 Jun 2012: Vol. 336, Issue 6089, pp. 1696-1700.

中国和全球历史视野下的文化遗产

何莫邪（Christoph Harbsmeier）/著　徐志杰/译

有些人认为，中华民族源远流长的历史和大英帝国悠久的历史（虽然短但很多）都依赖于精英人士其精神文化遗产的持久性。

中国传统官僚往往接受过，或至少假装接受过深厚的精英文化教育，就像英国殖民主义者和军官往往假装接受过英语以及拉丁语、希腊语这些欧洲经典文化教育一样。此外，中国的考试制度已有两千多年的历史，文学水平很高。中国官员的任命通常依赖于严格的语言和文学考试。

基于以下两个原因，中华民族的历史得以延续数千年：

1. 精英文化遗产，源于公元前9世纪以来的古代经典。
2. 文字体系，源于公元前13世纪中国的甲骨文。

因此，在中国，经典著作和文字体系的研究都备受关注，民族凝聚力和民族认同也因此得以界定。

在中国历史的记载中"文"，一直都是核心文化价值观，既代表着一种严肃的文化规范（文雅），也是一种基本的审美价值和礼仪价值，任何"像样的"、端庄的中国人都必须致力于"文"。但是，"文"根本不涉及教条或教义主义。相反，"文"是一种行事方式，是一种被视为神圣不可侵犯的古老先例。

在中国，"文"也可视为"文字书写"被称为书法。早在公元前10世纪，这种叫法就在官方版本中得到充分肯定，自公元3世纪以来，人们就一直在赞扬个人的书法艺术。书法通过个人的文化素养来表达身份及其种族身份。即使在今天，许多学生仍然选择学习书法，这是对文化遗产的一种积极的审美式沉思。很少有中国家庭能完全脱离书法。在中国，书法艺术遍布城市的各个角落，主宰着街道风光，就像书法遍布日本城市的所有地方一样。书法是自我修养的美学支柱。字写不好的"文明人"常常是矛盾的，甚至是自相矛盾的。

中国典型的文化遗产是指文学、经典和书法,这体现了有教养的人的深厚人格,而这种人格是通过修身养成的。

就物质生产力而言,中国在众多文物古迹的修复方面,也许是最具生产力的超级大国。

从政治角度来看,在基于历史的中国政治认同的建构中,考古学具有核心作用。

同时,"cultural identity"这一概念源于19世纪的西方,哈佛大学的杜维明称,"认同"这一中文术语出现在20世纪80年代。直到20世纪结束,全世界的人们似乎才需要一个像身份认同这样的术语,由此,身份认同不言而喻。

然而,早在19世纪,"民族本质"就已经成为中国话语很重要的一部分,这种本质关系到民族尊严和文化自尊。

在我们这个时代,身份认同已成为全世界的文化流行词。成千上万的人因为无法找到自己的个人身份而自杀。无论城市还是乡村,都不惜花费重金来建立自己的"文化认同"。每个国家堆金积玉般增强民族认同感,在没有文化认同的危险之地更是如此。越来越多的城市和乡村开始效仿。说某种语言或方言被认为是在建立文化身份,表达文化尊严。慢慢地,现代人开始为自己建构一堆各种各样、各种级别的身份。在不同场合,用不同"身份"。当一个人身在中国时,他的欧洲"身份"似乎也变得非常重要。因为共同的文化将身份联系在了一起。

如今,在中国,"文化"(culture)原本一直是单数,没有复数形式。在古汉语中,"文化"就是指中国文化。复数形式的文化是日语中的汉语借词。在日本的影响下,中国人才开始思考"different cultures",即不同的文化。

需要注意的是,在汉语中,没有西塞罗的阿尼米文化("精神农业>精神教育学"),目前也没有与"文化"对立的"自然"这样经典的对立词。天("天堂>自然")与人("人类")的对立代替了"文化"与"自然"的对立。

在欧洲,众所周知,普芬多夫提出了受国际法保护的"cultures"这一复数形式。

"文明"这一概念的提出与之类似。目前,汉语中的"文明"由"civilisation"翻译而来,传统上指的是唯一的、真正的文明,即儒家十三经,这在二十四史中已有记载。

"文明"(civilisation)没有复数,因为没有与中国文明相平等的文明。而且"中国"也不是一个有界限的帝国,当然也不是众多州中的一个。在古代中国,回国(to return to one's state)是指回到其家乡。皇帝所统治并不是老州,也不是其他任何国家中的某个州,而是"天下"(All under Heaven)。中华文明曾被视为天下文明。中国的文化遗产在本质上被认为是阳光下唯一文明的遗产。

汉语中的"遗产"最初是指"inheritance"。受日语对西方语言翻译的启发，"inheritance"又被用来指代"heritage"。起先，这种遗产是指物质资产，但是随着时间的流逝，"遗产"一词也开始指像习俗、宗教、传统，甚至是文学作品之类的无形资产。

教化是对文化遗产中雅这一部分规律性的文化适应。这里，与希腊比得里亚的对比具有启发性："首先，青年接受了民主教育。由于富人的儿子可以接受民主教育，因此穷人的儿子与富人的儿子一起长大可以让穷人的儿子有可能像富人的儿子一样接受教育。"（亚里士多德《政治学》）

通过语法学校和大学，对这种历史悠久的文化习俗的传播进行国家控制，是伟大的语言学家威廉·冯·洪堡的计划，该计划已塑造了世界大范围内的高等教育。洪堡有关传承文化遗产以及教化的概念与那些对拉丁和希腊经典的研究紧密相关，这些经典赋予了欧洲共同的文化遗产和身份认同。目前，丹麦正在抹除这一以语言为基础的古典教化计划的最后痕迹，这也正是整个西欧正在做的事情，目的是为了与美国的主流做法保持一致。在美国，以语言为基础的希腊—罗马文化的传承只留给了一些学术专业人士，因此早已被边缘化。

在英语中，并没有与"Bildung"相对应的令人信服的说法，而在中国，"教化"（Bildung），"修养"（literate cultivation），与较为单调的"教育"（education）一词的流行状态完全不同。因此，尽管《牛津英国文学史》选择用"Bildungsroman"这一英语单词来翻译德国的"Bildungsroman"，但对这一译法进行重新思考也是具有启发性的。丹麦文和中文都不需要借用德语单词来"翻译"它。

中国的古典教育虽然陷入了困境，但国家仍旧大力支持。在一个非常美国化的现代中国，中国儿童发现传统国学没有用时会非常绝望。国家资助的有关黄金时期的孔子和老子的研究比比皆是。小学生要用心学习数百首用古汉语（相当于中华文明的"拉丁文"）写成的诗词。中国古典学术的生产力是巨大的：在英语中，我们没有一本古希腊同义词字典，而我自己就有许多本这样的中文著作。出版商的热情来自国家对中国古汉语研究的巨额资助，与此同时，在哥本哈根大学正在认真讨论废除古希腊语这一学科。

在中国，继承古汉语的遗产是有客观原因的，尽管这种方式与我们西方人与拉丁语之间的关系完全不同。有一本厚厚的书记录了温家宝总理使用的中国古典录，几千年来，这些语录一直被当作经典使用。可以肯定的是，中国领导人在竭尽全力延续中国古典遗产。

公共电视节目尽其所能：大量关于中国功夫的、传统题材的电影以及中国戏曲中都充斥着文言文式的对话。在中央电视台第 10 频道,学者易中天在黄金时段用数百个小时阐述了古典知识,介绍了诸如孔子、老子等哲学家及中国古典文学。他的讲演因其学术内容而风靡一时。此外,他的讲演中充斥着文言文的解释。在数百小时的黄金时段中,易中天用语言学的方式从二十六史中的第一史开始,详细介绍了这一古典历史遗产。二十六史是用古汉语写成的,涵盖了公元前 200 年至公元 200 年间的历史。他的讲演获得了极大的成功,因此他又被邀请就三国这段历史进行类似的讲演,随后他又将这段讲演出版成书,这都是因为它们备受欢迎。我曾现场看过易中天的讲演,必须承认,他那超凡的魅力与他的成功密不可分,而他对传统文化熟练掌握也令人震惊。易中天可以让中国古汉语遗产鲜活起来,当人们将他与国际上颇为成功的人物,如于丹教授相提并论时,他的这种特点就更加突出。于丹教授将他视为古典主义不良品味和传统主义媚俗的典范,但易中天的确做了许多来表达中国大众对传承中国古汉语的郑重承诺。

对古汉语痴迷的人并非只有官方媒体和政治领导。

可以发现,一个受过良好教育的,说普通话的人会说成千上万条谚语,而这些谚语就是中国古典遗产的宝藏。不仅如此,北京话音频词典(http://tekstlab.uio.no/maid/)在线词典也对此进行了证明。在北京话音频词典中,以北京话为母语的人最初是北京的满族人,这表明他们流利地掌握着数千条古代经典谚语,比如当前使用的书面语或口语,也可以具体到社会语境中,在社会语境中使用古典遗产中的一些用法也是有可能的。

此外,必须说明的是,一些中小学生和大学生越来越不认同将文言文列为必修课程。他们认为,如今没有必要再研究中国传统文化,这些研究只会占用他们学习科学和英语的宝贵时间(学习英语是因为要想出国学习就得通过托福考试)。作为香港一所大学的教学质量评估员,我最近看到了许许多多令人惊讶的现象,在说普通话的幼儿园上学的贫困儿童,他们不仅要被迫学习当地的广东方言,还要用普通话来与说广东话的孩子交谈;尤其是要让那些对文言文不感兴趣或负担过重的孩子们了解文言文的基础知识。我很清楚,在某些方面,通过政治命令来保护文化语言遗产具有一定的局限性。

考虑到个人生活和公共媒体中古典语言遗产的未来充满不确定性,转向西方大学中的汉学研究课程的发展史会很有趣。

1812 年,亚伯-勒穆萨被任命为巴黎索邦大学的教授,随后汉学研究开始成为一门学术学科。对他而言,认真对待口语化的汉语,即白话文,是一种革命性行为。这种对中国的认真研究使文言文占据了主导地位。没有文言文的扎实基础,就没有人会想要深入研究中国文化。就像没有拉丁语和希腊语的扎实基础时,没有人想过应该认真研究欧洲文化一样。没有对文化语言遗产坚定的承诺,人们就可能会取消欧洲计划;没有坚定的承诺,人们就会认为这将危害中国的文化认同和精神连续性。

1966年,我在牛津大学学习中文时,汉学研究仍然主要是对中国文化传统以及文言文的研究。这种精神很像伟大的瑞典学者高本汉(Bernhard Karlgren),他有一个习惯,即询问想要跟随他学习普通话的学生:"我看起来像是那种你可以从我这里学到很多普通话的人吗?"他会指着地板继续说:"在那儿,你会发现数以百万的人,跟着他们,你可以学得更快,学得更好!"高本汉非常了解普通话。但是他的主要兴趣在于中国文化和语言遗产。他知道没有人比中国人更有历史意识。如果没有人对这种语言传承给予充分重视,没有人会和他一起学习汉语。

到目前为止,绝大多数(实际上是整个西方世界)汉学研究教授对其文言文的专业能力都非常满意。通常认为,人们对历史语言学的兴趣源于汉学。人们认为它倾向于旧式的语言学。作为语言学的"罪魁祸首",我们开玩笑说:"他们称我为语言学家,我也侮辱了他们。"这就是世界各地或多或少出现的语言学繁荣后的衰落:辉煌的世界已落幕。

社会经济、宗教、历史、文学或哲学的观点已逐渐取代文化历史的观点。一切都那么自然而然。但这里存在一个问题:汉学研究中,社会经济或文学作品的主要来源是文本。我们对中国社会经济、历史、文学、宗教和哲学作品的理解永远比我们对语言和相关原文中概念世界的理解要微妙得多。这种概念性文化遗产的细节完全依赖于历史文献学的坚固基础。柏拉图在他的学院门口写了一个粗暴的标语:"禁止非数学家入内"。人们对此有众多争论,但是不争的一点是:"没有扎实的汉语语言文化遗产学和语言学基础,没有仔细阅读汉语资料这一必备的技能,任何人都不应开展汉学研究。"汉学研究非常看重中国人对事物的看法,因此对于任何要深入研究汉学的人来说,这都是必要的前提。

但是,有时看起来这些似乎都可能发生深刻变化。通常,中国孩子都不喜欢学习文言文。许多中国人可能会从自己的文化和语言传统的深厚根基中"解放"自己。无论在哪里,我们都能看到这些的现象:中国进入了全球可口可乐的精神殖民地,快餐化的文化视角使得中国人越来越以好莱坞的风格看待自己和自己的文化。

中国有时会给人留下这样的印象。但是在某种程度上,我怀疑中国真的会变成那样。在我看来,在中国特色的社会主义的意识形态中,文化遗产和文化认同会发挥其民族主义的功能。《人民日报》上有大量的文言文短语。丰富的中国文化底蕴仍然是中国意识形态的核心部分。爱国主义是中国的核心价值观,而爱国主义和民族主义实质上都是对文化遗产的尊重。

(作者单位:哥本哈根大学)

"遗产(Heritage)"和"文化遗产(Kulturarv)"

苏纳·沃肯(Sune Auken)/著　于春华/译

我们对过去的看法不可避免的是意识形态上的认识。我们对当前的理解发生变化时,我们对过去的理解也会改变。我们所看到的过去,绝不仅仅是过去,而是我们以为的过去。无论过去是好是坏,我们从来都不是中立的观察者。我们总是有一个认知过程,总是有价值审视、兴趣判断。我们所做的和所说的一切都无法改变这一点。

对于像我这样从事流派研究的专业人员而言,隐含意识形态的问题总是近在咫尺。我们的意识形态可以通过我们成长过程中所学的流派,通过教育系统(Devitt, 2009),通过我们成长过程中所体现的价值观,以及通过我们的语言,自然而然地融入我们的生活。所有这些都是习惯性的,它们"只是我们在这里做事的方式"(Schryer, 2002),由此可能会产生一种"常态的幻想"(Paré, 2002),甚至可能导致所谓的"无知的文化复制"(Segal, 2007)。正如基德(Kidd, 2013)所说:"意识形态就像令人悦目的体味……你自己很难注意"(另见Paré, 2002)。

但是,不可避免并非一成不变。我们并非别无他法,也并非注定要成为这一进程的受害者。作为具有反思能力的个体,我们可以选择自我教育并批判性地思考我们的隐含价值。我们并非完全独立,也不是完全孤立。我们只能通过其他流派来批判流派,我们需要语言来批判语言,这都是可以做到的。我们可能很难闻到自己的体味,但是我们总有可能闻到,之后大多数人可以选择洗个澡。

在人文学科领域中,语言几乎是任何跨学科讨论中存在的一个重要问题。英语被确立为世界通用语言,在英语世界之外的两种其他文化之间的交流中,英语甚至也有可能作为交流的语言。对于任何一方而言,英语可能都不是第一语言,但它往往是共同的第二语言。但是,语言中存在意识形态,有时你最需要的词汇可能不可用,或者话到嘴边却含义歪曲,他们要么无法传达你想说的话,要么给你的交流添加了不必要的意思。因此,作为一名丹麦教育者,我尽量使用英语工作。在丹麦教育辩论中,我缺少的不只是一个词,而是缺少两个关键词:"dannelse"和"faglighed"。这两个词在英文中都没有对应词,然而"dannelse"在教育中又是一个非常必要的单词,有时会通过使用德语单词"Bildung"将其翻译成英文。然而,这个单词在交流中又会显得突兀。

与这个问题有关的还有更深层次的意识形态问题。将英语自然化为特定的交流手段也意味着"事物英语(things Anglophone)"成为常态;以英语为条件的世界观将成为一种隐性的、间或显性的规范。这种盎格鲁式的规范性使我们"禁锢在英语中"(Wierzbicka, 2013;另见 Caines, 2015),或者束缚在英语"全球化的狭隘主义"(Wolters, 2013)中。在这些情况下,为了了解我们在切换语言时可能会接受的东西,检查我们使用的语言就显得格外重要。

在我们对待过去的过程中,一个关键问题是我们如何思考和谈论过去留下的痕迹,无论是广义的文化层面、意识形态还是自然层面。与此,最匹配流行的英语单词是"遗产(heritage)",而丹麦语中最正式的单词是"文化遗产(kulturarv)",这个词使用很少。两者有时会可以互为翻译,因此联合国教科文组织的"世界遗产"清单,用丹麦语翻译为"Verdenskulturarv"。

但是,如果我们稍微仔细地看一下"遗产(heritage)"和"文化遗产(kulturarv)"这两个词,它们实际上是大不相同的。参考简单的字典条目[①],韦氏词典里这样定义了"遗产(heritage)"——

1. 属于继承人的财产。
2a. 由前人送出或从前人获得的东西——遗产,继承:
- 对她的中国遗产感到骄傲;
- 丰富的民俗遗产;
- 战场是我们遗产的一部分,应予以保留。
2b. 传统:

[①] 当然,在遗产问题上,有许多不同领域的研究。事实上,遗产研究本身就是一个有组织的研究领域;因此,《国际遗产研究杂志》将"遗产研究、博物馆研究、历史、旅游研究、社会学、人类学、记忆研究、文化地理学、法律、文化研究、解释与设计"等领域的研究结合起来。(https://www.tandfonline.com/action/journalInformation? show = aimsScope&journalCode = rjhs20 见 2018 年 11 月 13 日)。然而,就本文而言,我坚持使用更简单的定义,因为目前的问题与广泛的文化理解有关,而不是与特定的研究知识有关。不出所料,遗产的意识形态性质问题与遗产研究无关(Kryder Reid, 1017; Kryder Reid, Foutz& Zimmerman, 2017;两者都有大量的相关参考文献)。

政党的世俗主义传统。

3. 由于某人的自然状况或出生而拥有的东西：生来就具有的东西——
- 自然自由的遗产早就被抛弃了。①

正式度稍微欠缺的互联网字典Dictionary.com给出了这样的定义——

1. 从过去传下来的东西，作为传统：荣誉、骄傲和勇气的民族遗产；

2. 由于出生而属于或属于某人的东西；继承的批次或部分：贫穷和苦难的遗产；

3. 为某人保留的东西：公义的遗产。

两种定义都与过去的东西在现代生活中的存在和运作方式有关。这两种定义都有共同的释义，即遗产是一个丰富的概念，蕴含着许多意义。此外，遗产是财产的问题，在一定程度上是排他性的。这种东西能使得一群人与其他人不同。同时这也是一个悲观的概念，与戏剧性的感觉，深厚的联系，战场和痛苦，荣誉、骄傲和勇气联系在一起。它与传统、遗产、继承、出生权、其他沉重的词语聚集在一起再合适不过。从历史上讲，这是一个古老的词，通过历史追溯其含义和用法本身就是一个有意思的研究。

"文化遗产(kulturarv)"一词的历史并不长。实际上，这个词在卷帙浩繁的《丹麦语言词典》(*Ordbog Over Det Danske Sprog*)中无迹可循，尽管这本字典详尽地涵盖了1700年至1950年之间的丹麦语。"文化遗产(kulturarv)"的字典含义取自当代丹麦语的主要词典——《丹麦语词典》(*Den Danske Ordbog*)，这本词典如下定义了该词(为清晰起见，此处不再对其进行翻译)——

一大群人或一众人的生活观、生活方式、行为礼仪和艺术表达中传承的部分：

- 的确，如果问我们的文化遗产是什么，那就是语言；
- 通过在与外国文化的会谈中对北欧和欧洲文化遗产的考虑，生活质量得到了改善②。

以其"文化遗产(cultural inheritance)"的字面意思而言，该词本身很近似我们在"遗产(heritage)"中发现的同样深层含义，但是显然从定义中可以看出，在实际使用中，该词要精简得多，或者作为更严格的技术术语。如果我们在 *Den Danske Ordbog* 的定义中看到与它搭配的词，这些特点也很明显。这个词与人

---

① https://www.merriam-webster.com/dictionary/heritage. 见2018年10月12日。

② https://ordnet.dk/ddo/ordbog?query=Kulturarv&tab=for. 见2018年10月12日。该条作了一些编辑，以适应本文件的当地情况。

工制品、文化和文化生活的各种词语相关联,但是这些词热度都不高。

这两个词的词义重合部分与"文化遗产(kulturarv)"的定义相同。也就是说,该词定义涵盖的所有内容都在"遗产(heritage)"一词中。从某种意义上说,"遗产(heritage)"不仅涵盖了"文化遗产(kulturarv)"的整体,还有了别的含义。

但是,从另一种意义上说,我们在不更改含义的情况下无法添加含义。缺失恰恰是一种精干的、技术性的意义,它指示了一种现在对过去的持续生活的兴趣,而不是汲取丰富而悲惨的意义。丹麦语这个词可能是个新词,有点无聊,但它更像是个头脑冷静的代名词。这个词与传统相比,其蕴含的排他性更少,所有权更少,沙文主义更不受欢迎。"遗产(heritage)"一词所指的最著名的机构是一个右翼智囊团,即遗产基金会;而在几年前,以"文化遗产(kulturarv)"的名义命名的最著名的机构是一个行政政府单位——文化遗产局(Kulturarvsstyrelsen),其成立于2002年,在2012年与其他两个目录合并为一个新的大型机构。

为什么这很重要?因为我们将世界概念化的方式永远不可能是完全中立的。在这种情况下,有两个后果,第一个是实践的和学术上的,第二个是思想上的。两者相互联系。

首先是实际的原因:如果我们将历史视为遗产,那么我们很有可能犯下怀特海德(Whitehead)所说的"放错了具体性的谬论"(Whitehead,1997),这意味着我们没有适当地首先考虑它是一个抽象,就将知识抽象强加于现实。有许多解决方法可用,但是该概念本身引起了广泛的高层抽象,也就是说,提出数据应该放在哪里的想法。对于历史学的学生来说,无论哪种形式,材料很少会升到"遗产(heritage)"的层面。在这么漫长的历史中,最无趣的一点,很可能是战场、出生权或骄傲、勇气和荣誉。过去比迷宫更像是一个迷宫,甚至迷宫也不过是隐喻而已。而且,在极端情况下追溯过去的实际因果链并不简单,而且实现从过去到现在的追踪也很困难。

就以眼前的问题为例。如上所述,我选择的研究领域是流派。当你研究历史流派时,你遇到的并不是一套清晰明确的规范文本,每种文本都以有序的方式向着现在发展,并且每种都在深厚的、共享性的遗产中增加了自身的含义。相反,你会被大量具体的文本、话语和其他文化艺术品所淹没,它们与具体的流派有关(尽管流派总是抽象的),被具体的人使用,在具体的情况下达到具体的目的(Miller,1984),并导致具体的吸收(Freadman,1994,2002)和结果。要理解流派的每种用法,你需要将其视为在其特定流派上下文中执行的动作(Devitt,2004)。总是有一个演员,而且总是至少有一种流派。随着历史的变化,流派的背景也发生了变化,很难理解一种流派的含义以及人们过去所做的事情,因为在每种流派使用中理所当然的事情早已跟不上时代潮流。因此,即使你接触伟大的文本——那些已经成为经典的历史文本——你会发现它们的独特性和普适性交织在一起,并且它们的特殊性、动机、作用和影响只能在显然更为平凡的流派用法的背景下才能理解。

从中吸取的教训(可以由多个研究人员从其他角度证实这一点)是,对过去的研究处理的数据是复杂的,并且不可避免地陷入了许多从未遇到过,甚至无法预期的复杂性中。此外,这可能比乍看之下更为重要,历史是非常有趣的,非常人性化(无论好坏),而且常常充满乐趣。可能不仅仅是我发现,在我的研究中给我带来最大乐趣的一些因素是对历史的大发展几乎没有或没有明显重要性的局部细节。最后,我们可能会看到它影响到现在,而无法完全理解这种影响是如何变化的。流派研究的一个基本见解是,任何给定流派中的隐含假设通常对其用户来说自然而然,以至于难以察觉。它们是习惯性的、根深蒂固的,以至于我们认为它们是理所当然的。因此,真正影响我们的是什么,我们认为我们的遗产可能是截然不同的事物,可以使用一个总括的术语,使这种关系在某种程度上脱离了"遗产(heritage)"的热度和讲究性,并将其更多地构架为一个实际的问题,例如"文化遗产(kulturarv)",是一个很大的优势。精简术语很适合进行更丰富的分析。

从上面的这个问题转到意识形态问题。如前所述,意识形态的棘手之处在于,看到自己的意识形态比看到人类同伴的意识形态更难。但是,这是一个公平的问题,当我们使用单词时,我们采用什么假设,以及何时需要质疑这些假设。对于像"遗产(heritage)"这样一个极富传统的术语来说,隐含的假设同样是多种多样的,我们应该谨慎地接受它们。

意识形态永远存在。我们永远不会摆脱它。的确,从诠释学的角度来看,它是我们思维的主要推动力,因为它建立了一个基线理解,从中可以理解所有其他东西(Gadamer,1990)。但是,如果我们要成为选择者而不是意识形态的盲目仆人,我们需要对假设进行反复审查;包括但不限于对塑造我们的意识形态的流派和语言的考察,通过反复审视,我们塑造他人和我们自己的意识形态。

因此,就其价值而言,我们需要将过去及其与之的联系更多地看作是"文化遗产(kulturarv)"问题,而更少地看作是"遗产"问题。语言是它们的本来面目,想要取缔,或者至少抛弃一个像"遗产(heritage)"这样的术语,这是一个愚蠢的差事。此外,考虑到"遗产(heritage)"一词含义丰富,因而绝不可随意禁用或替换;作为历史和语言的学生,我们不想让语言变得贫乏。然而,特别是当英语在世界上获得其独特地位时,(无论好坏)我们确实需要审视该语言中的假设,我们确实需要知道其他的选择。这篇文章只是向这一目标贡献的一份绵薄之力。

(作者单位：哥本哈根大学)

参考文献：

1. Auken, S. (2018). Understanding genre. Journal of Zhejiang International Studies University, 3(2), 14 – 27.
2. Caines, A. (2015). White spaces. Times Literary Supplement(July), 23.
3. Devitt, A. (2004). Writing Genres. Carbondale: Southern Illinois UP.
4. Devitt, A. (2009). Teaching Critical Genre Awareness. In C. Bazerman, A. Bonini, & D. Figueiredo (Eds.), Genre in a Changing World (pp. 337 – 351). Fort Collins, Colorado: Parlor Press.
5. Freadman, A. (1994). Anyone for Tennis? In A. Freedman & P. Medway (Eds.), Genre and the New Rhetoric (pp. 43 – 66). London: Taylor & Francis.
6. Freadman, A. (2002). Uptake. In R. Coe, L. Lingard, & T. Teslenko (Eds.), The Rhetoric and Ideology of Genre (pp. 39 – 53). Cresskill Hampton Press Inc.
7. Gadamer, H. -G. (1990). Wahrheit und Methode (Vol. 2). Tübingen: J. C. B. Mohr.
8. Kidd, B. (2013). Sports and masculinity. Sport in Society, 16(4), 553 – 564. doi: 10.1080/17430437.2013.785757
9. Kryder-Reid, E. (2017). Introduction: tools for a critical heritage. International Journal of Heritage Studies, 24(7), 691 – 693. doi: 10.1080/13527258.2017.1413680.
10. Kryder-Reid, E., Foutz, J. W., Wood, E., & Zimmerman, L. J. (2017). "'I just don't ever use that word': investigating stakeholders' understanding of heritage". International Journal of Heritage Studies, 24(7), 743 – 763. doi: 10.1080/13527258.2017.1339110.
11. Miller, C. (1984). Genre as Social Action. Quarterly Journal of Speech, 70(2), 151 – 167.
12. Paré, A. (2002). Genre and Identity: Individuals, Institutions, and Ideology. In R. Coe, L. Lingard, & T. Teslenko (Eds.), The Rhetoric and Ideology of Genre (pp. 57 – 71). Cresskill: Hampton Press Inc.
13. Schryer, C. F. (2002). Genre and Power. A Chronotopic Analysis. In R. Coe, L. Lingard, & T. Teslenko (Eds.), The Rhetoric and Ideology of Genre (pp. 73 – 102). Cresskill, New Jersey: Hampton Press, Inc.
14. Segal, J. Z. (2007). Breast cancer narratives as public rhetoric: genre itself and the maintenance of ignorance. Linguistics and the Human Sciences, 3(1), 3 – 23.

15. Whitehead, A. N. (1997). Science and the Modern World. New York: Simon and Schuster.
16. Wierzbicka, A. (2013). Imprisoned in English. The hazards of English as a default language. Oxford: Oxford University Press.
17. Wolters, G. (2013). European Humanism in Times of Globalized Parochialism. Bolletino della Societá Filosofica Italiana, 208, 3 - 18.

如何保护非物质文化遗产的核心价值

——以海宁硖石灯彩为例

马 驰

硖石灯彩主要流传于浙江省海宁市硖石街道，是中国浙江著名的传统民间工艺美术，又是海宁三大文化（灯文化、潮文化、名人文化）之一。以针刺工艺独树一帜，堪称"江南一绝"，誉满海内外。硖石灯彩相传源于秦，始于汉，盛于南宋，绵延至今已有两千多年历史。

南宋时，金兵已入寇中原，宋高宗赵构迁都临安（今杭州），偏安于半壁江山，为了粉饰太平，元宵放灯发展到了新的高峰，扎灯、赛灯、赏灯蔚然成风，据《武林旧事》[1]和《乾淳岁时记》等记载，当时，进京朝贡的灯品，有福州白玉灯、新安（安徽）琉璃灯、南京夹纱灯、常州料丝灯、苏州罗锦灯、杭州羊皮灯和硖石万眼罗灯等，各具特色，争奇斗妍。灯品中尤以针工细密的"万眼罗"最奇，南宋诗人范成大《灯市行》中有"叠玉千丝似鬼工，剪罗万眼人力穷"一句，点出了它比用轻罗、织锦剪裁结扎的罗锦灯更加精细、美观，当年硖石灯彩进京朝贡，被选为"灯彩精品"而悬挂在临安（杭州）东华门外凤楼前，故许葆翰（1866—1942）《硖川灯市》诗有"东华门外凤楼前，博得虚名非一年"句。[2]

在唐僖宗乾符年间（874—879），硖石灯彩即已誉满江南，南宋时被列为朝廷贡品。清代乾隆年间，硖石形成了演灯、顺灯、斗灯等相关民俗，下东街的"塔灯"、横港桥的"凌云阁"、横头的"梅亭"等灯会层出不穷。19世纪末至20世纪初，硖石民间制灯、迎灯盛行，灯彩的制作工艺和造型形态亦有较大突破，出现了"龙舟""采莲船"等品种，这种盛况一直延续到民国。新中国成立后，硖石灯彩得到长足发展，技艺不断创新，经过文革的短期沉寂，到20世纪80年代有了新的

---

[1] 周密：《武林旧事》（卷二），中华书局2006年版，第64—65页。
[2] 张镇西：《海宁灯文化》，《文史天地》2009年第9期。

发展。① 2006年5月20日，硖石灯彩经国务院批准列入第一批国家级非物质文化遗产名录。

硖石灯彩有"拗""扎""结""裱""刻""画""针""糊"的八字技法。"拗"，包括拗架和拗彩，将原材料拗出骨架，这便有了灯彩的型。千年传承的手艺，艺精而架稳，一副有型的骨架是决定灯彩好坏的基础。拗彩，则是将金属拗成各式形状的装饰物，包括灯的连接处、顶部装饰等。据灯彩师告知，这样的"拗"容不得半点偏差，没有测量标准，全靠灯彩师多年经验掌控，稍有变形就难以装配和连接。"扎"，乃拼接工艺，现在很多都已采用焊接工艺，现代技术的更新实现了更高难度的灯彩造型，增加了灯彩的稳定性。"结"，灯彩边缘结边，吊流苏，要求细致耐心，一盏灯的品质在于细节的呈现。"裱"，将刻好的灯纸背面裱上一层宣纸，再进行染色、衬色（彩色布料）及"针"等步骤。"刻"，是灯彩的精髓所在，极其考究手法与耐心。灯彩师在画稿基础上，一刀刀将纸刻画成形。磨刀、熟练的刻画刀法已是经历了十多年沉淀，灯彩师不在意每天出多少量，而是精益求精每一个步骤。"画"，一个好的灯彩师，必定是一名优秀的画者。灯彩惯用国画工笔重彩花鸟、人物、山水等，但较之工笔画难度更大，一般两次无法成形，此作便只能作废。"针"，此技艺也是令人叹为观止，利用针在纸上打孔作画，包括排针、勾针、花针、乱针、破花针、补针等不同的针法微刻精雕。针刺密度达到平均每平方厘米18至32孔。一件好的针孔作品需要数百万个针孔，在灯光的映射下可以达到不可思议的效果。"糊"，作为最后的工序，不仅考验灯彩师的技术，更是考验耐心，不可让刻纸在糊的过程中断裂、起皱，才能够达到上乘品质。了解了灯彩师的制灯过程，方知何为匠人、匠心。方知非物质文化遗产及其传人绝非浪得虚名。硖石灯彩的任何一道工艺拿出来都是一门绝学。灯彩师介绍道，他们会的可不止单单其中一个步骤，而是从拗型、刻画到成品都能游刃有余；灯彩师还必须会画画、书法，才能够赋予一盏灯彩艺术的灵魂。②

硖石的灯彩虽然工艺精湛，有很高的审美价值，但价格也不便宜。早些年硖石灯彩基本用于灯会展览，2000年左右开始走向旅游市场。一盏小小的宫灯有六个面，完成需要二十多天，价格在三四千元左右，制作精良的灯彩售价十多万也不足为奇。由此可知，非物质文化遗产已经很难走进寻常百姓家，要保护和传承这份千年技艺更是不容易。

根据有关部门调查，现在海宁会做灯彩的人总共也就七八十人，不过真正

---

① 张镇西：《硖石灯市》，《文史天地》2017年第4期。
② 周郁斌：《探访海宁硖石灯彩》，《浙江日报》2013年4月11日。

在做的只有不到三十人,年轻人愿意学的就更少了。因为纯手工制作,一个灯彩师一天最多可以做两个灯架。如今改用半机械化生产,一天大概可以做成百上千个灯架。不过最后一道裱糊必须手工完成,无法使用机器。为了让灯彩走出博物馆,走进寻常百姓家,海宁利用灯彩开发旅游纪念品方面做了很多尝试,缩小造型。但是,灯彩的形状一小,对技艺的要求更高,售价不降反升。后来,海宁还研制了半机械化的茶壶灯、花瓶灯,只是机器做出来的针刺元素远没有手工刺的那般精致。现在的硖石灯彩有座灯、提灯、壁灯、挂灯和礼品灯五大品种,观赏和收藏价值都有待提升。[1]

非物质文化遗产是一个民族最古老、最鲜活的集体记忆,凝聚着民族的创造与光芒。它向人们展示历史长河中生命的细节,让人们可以感受到古老文化,并由此抵达千百年文明源头的深处。较之有形遗产而言,它又是如此的脆弱,犹如指间之沙,稍有不慎,则将流失于指缝,因而每项非物质文化遗产,几乎都成了它们所属领域的"千古绝响",海宁市的非物质文化遗产"硖石灯彩"也不例外。

硖石灯彩这门民间独特的制作技艺是一种古老的艺术,尽管像一杯陈酿,历久弥香,但在历史上,多以家族传承为主要延续方式,且传男不传女。过于狭窄的传承方式,极容易造成技艺的断层甚至流失。现在拥有不等于永久留存,现在"活着"不等于"长生不老",因此传承才是保护非遗文化的最好方式。传承的首要任务就是保护好传承人,而非遗传承从个体传承转向群众传承,更是避免非遗灭绝的最有力保障。让非遗走进课堂,走进民间,培植起更为广泛、更为肥沃的非遗生存与发展的土壤,是保护与传承非物质文化遗产最直接、最有效的办法。

为了让"绝响"不绝,保护和传承好对文化自信具有重要作用的非物质文化遗产,海宁做了很多有益的尝试。例如,海宁市职业高级中学通过创建并充分利用非物质文化遗产传承人工作室推行非遗进课堂,使非遗传承由个体向群体转变和跨区融合实现。非遗活态传承,令融针刺、绘画、刀刻技艺于一身的世界独有的"硖石灯彩"非遗技艺得到保护、传承乃至发扬光大。

保护与传承硖石灯彩,成了摆在海宁市尤其是作为传播与继承传统文化为己任的学校面前的一个重大课题。要想保护与传承好非遗文化,首先必须要有一块阵地、一个平台,让非遗文化走进校园,让师生们更好地认识和了解硖石灯彩非遗文化。海宁市职业高级中学在成功创建了"浙江省首批非物质文化遗产传承教学基地"的基础上,2017年又创建了浙江省"胡金龙技能大师

---

[1] 朱宁嘉、金海明:《硖石灯彩衍生态研究与设计实践》,《设计》2019年第19期。

工作室"①,并在校园里打造了"非遗会客厅"。"会客厅"里有个可容纳几十人的"灯彩研习工作坊",硖石灯彩技能大师胡金龙会经常来到这间"工作坊",向师生们讲授硖石灯彩文化并亲自传授硖石灯彩制作技艺。平日里,学校还充分利用这间"工作坊",通过知识问答、图片品味、实物鉴赏、动手实践等丰富多彩的形式,提高师生对硖石灯彩非遗文化的感性认识,令师生感受硖石灯彩非遗文化的独特魅力,在学生们心中播下一颗"非遗"种子,点亮他们心中那盏"非遗"的心灯。尤其是通过这块阵地和技能大师的"传帮带",专业教师得到了锻炼,教育教学水平迅速得到提升,先后涌现了省特级教师、省优秀教师、市级名师等名优教师,教师有多篇论文发表在全国及省级核心刊物上。

为了把硖石灯彩制作技艺打造成学校的特色专业,海宁市职业高级中学将非遗文化兴趣班的招生范围,从原先的工艺美术专业扩展到全校,只要是对硖石灯彩感兴趣的学生,都可以在选择性课程体系下,选择这门课程。同时在教学模式上,学校采用了现代学徒制。通过与国家级、省级非遗代表性传承人及省市工艺美术大师密切合作,学校将企业的能工巧匠请进课堂,对学生进行引导和点拨,并组成"大师+非遗传承人+行业能手+老师+学生"的教学团队。采用"大师傅"带"小师傅"、"小师傅"带新生的方式,实行"一对一"或"一对多"的活态传承教学模式,让学生在学习灯彩技艺的同时,领略大师制作技艺的风采和制作精品的风韵,以增强学生对硖石灯彩非遗文化的兴趣和对硖石灯彩绝妙技艺追求的动力。

千百年来,硖石灯彩在传统技艺的基础上,不断得到改进和创新。灯彩制成后以灯映画,能显现出形象逼真、惟妙惟肖的立体画面。由于种种原因,在硖石灯彩列入首批国家非遗之时,多数灯彩学生都已弃艺而去。因此,政府加大了传承人保护力度,以确保独特精湛的制灯工艺不至于濒临失传。

为扩大硖石灯彩在年轻一代学生中的影响、培养灯彩新人,海宁市政府在海宁市博物馆设立"硖石灯彩展览馆",全面展示和弘扬硖石灯彩艺术的历史成果和灯的文化魅力;以节庆活动为依托,每年举办灯会、灯展、灯彩一条街等活动,营造节日观灯氛围;组织参与国内外灯彩大赛,通过参加希腊、新西兰、新加坡等国家和港、澳、台地区的元宵灯会,促进了对外文化交流,提升了硖石灯彩知名度。

(作者单位:上海社会科学院思想文化研究中心)

---

① 胡金龙,国务院认定的硖石灯彩非遗文化传承人,从艺多年来对硖石灯彩传统制作技艺有很深的造诣,其精湛的作品在国内灯彩界有很大的知名度和影响力。

从用户角度看联合国教科文组织世界遗产

莫滕·沃姆德(Morten Warmind)/著 刘静贤/译

如今的耶灵是丹麦中日德兰半岛地区的一个小镇,现共有3 431人住在镇上,但是一些古老的遗迹表明,在过去,这个小镇十分重要。[Et kort over Danmark med Jelling her?]

最明显的遗迹是在一个教堂两侧的两个一模一样的坟墓,坟头青草茵茵。坟墓的直径70米,高11米,两墓之间的距离也为70米。教堂入口外是两块石碑,上面刻有维京时代字母的铭文,称为"符文"。根据这些铭文以及其他资料,可以总结出以下耶灵的历史——

约公元950年,国王哥尔姆为纪念亡妻赛拉在耶灵立碑,称亡妻为"丹麦的装饰品"并刻于石碑之上。此石碑就是现今对碑中之一。大约公元965年,他的儿子,也就是我们所知的哈拉尔德·布鲁吐斯[1],对纪念碑进行了重大修改,将其去世的父亲加了上去,并在较大的一个装饰精美的三面石碑上宣布其(哈拉尔德)"征服了整个丹麦与挪威,并令丹麦人皈依基督教"。仅仅根据较小石头上的铭文并不能知道哥尔姆的纪念碑是什么样的,因此也就不知道哈拉尔德是如何修改了纪念碑。

公元1200年,一位叫萨克索·格拉玛提库斯(Saxo Grammaticus)的丹麦历史学家回忆耶灵的哈拉尔德石碑时暗示(没有任何事实依据)建造纪念碑正是哈拉尔德下台的原因,他的军队因承担了纪念碑的建造工作而心生不满(Saxo 10,8,1-3; edition in English: Friis-Jensen, 2015)。

随着时代变迁,巨大的坟墓和石碑变得老旧过时,无足轻重,最后无人问津,

---

[1] 哈拉尔德的绰号说明他一定有一颗突出的变色牙齿。他因一个以他的昵称命名的通信协议而闻名。蓝牙符号是"H"的符文和"B"的符文的组合。

变得破败不堪。体积较小的哥尔姆纪念亡妻的石碑成了公元1050年建立的石教堂外的长凳。人们住在坟墓附近，随着时间的流逝也可能对它们造成了一定程度的破坏。1820年至1821年，在耶灵进行了第一次考古勘察。1861年，丹麦国王腓特烈七世在位时，对耶灵又进行了一次大型发掘。虽然腓特烈七世对考古学非常感兴趣，但是他的发掘方法并不完善。直到1941年至1948年，戴格才根据现代标准，对耶灵进行考古发掘（Dyggve，1948）。

我们应当注意，耶灵在丹麦历史上的两个关键时刻都曾是人们关注的焦点——第一次是在与德国联邦的两次战争期间，第二次是在德国占领期间。耶灵作为丹麦民族和王室的发源地，具有重要的民族主义意义。

因此，从丹麦的角度来看，1994年耶灵成为联合国教科文组织的世界遗产是相当合理的，但作为一个重要的历史时代——晚期维京时代的证据，该遗址无疑具有更加广泛的意义。2006年，人们决定对耶灵遗址进行一次勘探，尽管人们认为该遗址已被充分发掘，不会再有新的发现，但令人惊讶的是新的发现引起一片哗然。其中最令人振奋的发现是整个遗址由一个看似相当高且难以穿透的栅栏所包围，只留有很窄的入口（Jensen，2015）。这导致了历史学家对这个历史遗迹全面重新评估，并重新制定了如何向公众展示和解释遗迹的计划。自然，联合国教科文组织世界遗产面对的"公众"也还是人类。作为新计划的一部分，为了更好地展示历史遗迹，2012年，耶灵市中心约10%的房屋被拆除，而这可能只是开始。这些计划是在距离耶灵市中心14公里远的市镇瓦埃勒（人口11.1万）制定的，自然给耶灵的社区居民造成了许多困扰，也受到了来自居民的阻力。那里的居民并不会首先认为自己是这个威严的国家历史遗迹的使用者和看守人，他们更认为自己只是普普通通的百姓，只希望能够安安稳稳的生活（Baun Christensen，2016）。而这引发了我去考虑用户一方的观点。

遗址的使用

如果您是游客，则使用该遗址基本上就是在参观包括坟墓、石碑、教堂和曾经由栅栏围着坟墓的较大的区域。虽然栅栏已经看不到了，但在地面标记了以前可能的地方。也可以参观位于坟墓西侧的博物馆，或者更确切地说是"体验中心"。从博物馆的屋顶几乎可以看到整个遗址。

坟墓是景观/城镇景观的特征，因此始终处于"开放"状态，也就是说大家随时可以爬到想去的任一坟墓的顶部。根据丹麦的习俗，位于教堂周围的墓地也是随时可以进入的，因此两块刻有铭文的石碑也随时可以观看。此外还有专门的灯光照明,即使到了晚上碑上铭文和装饰依旧清晰可见。

石碑曾经露天放置,日夜无人看守。游客可能会爬上它们,将自行车靠在上面,这些行为都造成石碑的磨损。几个世纪以来,霜冻也使岩石发生严重的自然腐蚀。更糟糕的是由污染和其他近期因素(上个世纪丹麦的特征)引起的酸雨也造成岩石腐蚀。将所有这些因素综合考虑,人们希望以某种方式覆盖石碑并已经开始着手计划此事。如果操作不正确,将石碑围起来如同露天放置一样危险。此外,重要的是要保证石碑的可参观性。最终,每块石碑都被围在了玻璃罩子里。说来也古怪,2011年2月,在石碑即将入罩之前,一名精神病患者用一瓶绿色油漆涂抹了较大的那块石碑[1]。万幸的是,涂漆能够被去除。尽管这些石碑已经露天放置了几个世纪,而且最近二十年,涂鸦"标记"在丹麦已经非常流行了,但它们在此次事件之前并没有被喷过漆,这很有意思。石碑不是这种破坏行为的常规对象,这可能表明,对于丹麦人而言,它们是所有人都关心的东西。

该教堂从早上八点至晚上八点对公众开放,开放时间比大多数其他丹麦教堂都要长。如果举行仪式,例如婚礼、葬礼,则不对游客开放。教堂的一部分建筑大概能追溯到1050年左右,教堂所在地曾被认为是哈拉尔德建造的丹麦最早的教堂之一。人们在教堂下方发现了木制建筑的痕迹,以及一个单人坟墓,许多人认为这是丹麦第一位国王哈拉尔德的父亲哥尔姆的遗骸。据推测,哈拉尔德从异教徒的坟墓里转移了父亲的遗体,并将其重新埋葬在基督教教堂中,这是一种死后基督教化的行为。只要有机会,大多数参观纪念碑的人也会参观教堂。

"国王的耶灵"

此地有一博物馆始建于1999年,并于2000年开放。从严格意义上讲它并不是博物馆,更像是一座"体验中心",在这里可以了解维京文化、基督教化,还可以对历史遗迹增加了解。中心由国家博物馆管理,从早上十点至下午五点开放,全年免费,可以将其视为遗址的组成部分。

展品利用最新的互动技术,将"维京时代"生动地呈现在游客面前。用网络上的话来说:

> 体验中心提供有关维京人生活和遗产的独特而超现代的感官体验。维

---

[1] 丹麦《政治报》2012年8月13日,https://politiken.dk/indland/art5400828/16-årig-bag-graffiti-på-Jellingesten-skal-i-behandling。

京人生活的方方面面,从养蜂到养龙,不断展现在人们面前,人类的全部感官也随之被吸引。这将是一段奇妙的旅程:从聆听壁炉的光辉中讲述的故事,到观看作为维京人和战士的生活,再到了解维京人通向瓦尔哈拉的道路以及向基督教的过渡。①

博物馆还设有展览,讲述丹麦王室发展的一些重要历史时刻,突出了王室发展连续性中的中断和连结,从而巧妙地向参观者传递了哥尔姆和哈拉尔德以及如今的女王玛格丽特二世和她的家人之间的家族关系。因此,博物馆不仅展示了维京时代国王统治下的耶灵,也展示了当今王室统治下的耶灵。

谁是用户?

世界遗产的用户可以根据几种不同的方式进行分类。在下文中,我选择了两种方法。首先,我将他们简单地按照每个组与遗址的相关性/亲近程度进行分组,然后根据每个组内部对遗址的兴趣高低,又将每个组划分为多个子小组。这种方法存在一定程度地任意性——我以这种方式创建的组也可以有不同的组成——但我认为这样分组在分析上会产生一些区别。

我围绕耶灵历史遗迹划分了三个主要的圈子。最大的圈子是全体人类。下一个圈子是丹麦人,最后一个圈子是那些居住在耶灵的当地人。

对于那些利益相关的用户,也可以称之为"既得利益者",我特别把自己所在的研究过去的学者的组别放在首位。毫无疑问我们是这些古迹的使用者。国家和地方的政客、整个旅游业和当地商家也是使用者,尽管每个团体都有特定的利益。我认为,尽管严格说来联合国教科文组织并不完全符合,但它也必须包括在内。

讨论每个小组分别从遗址中获得什么似乎是公平合理的。但应该记住的是,当我们从一般群体转向更具体的群体时,所有适用于一般群体的自然都适用于其他具体群体。

当然,最大的、定义最不明确的用户组就是整个人类。无论是现在还是这个历史遗迹建造之时,它最直接和最重要的意义就是其独特的设计和令人赞叹的规模,我们所知的其他维京时代遗址几乎难以与之相匹。

除了其庞大的规模令人印象深刻,它还直观地展示了这样一个历史遗迹是

---

① https://en.natmus.dk/museums-and-palaces/kongernes-jelling-home-of-the-viking-kings/experience-center/.

如何建构和维护王权的。现在，对资源的展示令人印象深刻，在维京时代，它一定看起来非同寻常。较大的那块表明哈拉尔德使丹麦人皈依了基督教。哈拉尔德可能就是通过该遗址所展示的原始力量使丹麦的基督教化成为可能，因此该遗址也可以看作是丹麦融入欧洲基督教君主制的纪念碑。由于斯堪的纳维亚半岛是最后一个进行基督教化的地区，因此这也可以看作是欧洲全面基督教化的开始。所有这些都以最简短的形式反映在联合国教科文组织世界遗产网站首页上关于耶灵的描述中：

> 耶灵墓穴和其中一块北欧古石是异教北欧文化的典型，而另一块北欧古石和教堂则表明了10世纪中叶之前丹麦人的基督教化。[①]

有一点需要补充，说起来有点矛盾，但其实仍然相关，尽管耶灵历史遗迹规模庞大，又令人赞叹，但与地中海地区和世界其他地区中较大的当代历史遗迹相比时，它也证明了维京时代生活的荒凉和可用资源的有限性。

耶灵历史遗迹向所有人展示了这些内涵，无论他们来自何方。

下一个圆圈包括整体的丹麦人。对他们来说，耶灵历史遗迹提供了更多的东西，它是对国家起源和王室路线的有形提醒。王室路线在千年统治国家的曲折和王朝斗争中一直在延续。

此外，符文石以一种古老的丹麦语写成，丹麦人可以通过比对碑文和在斯堪的纳维亚地区广泛使用字母表的特征，追溯他们语言的根源；也因此，符文石同时也成为一种与其他斯堪的纳维亚国家联系的可能。

耶灵所在地日德兰也引起了丹麦人的一些兴趣，他们意识到丹麦各地的重要性在不断变化。现在，日德兰并不是那么重要或那么"中心"了，几个世纪以来，人们的注意力都集中在最东端的西兰岛的东侧的首都所在地。对丹麦人来说，耶灵遗址提醒人们，它在遥远的过去是与众不同的。

当然，由居住在耶灵的居民组成的最里面的圈子对这一切都有体验，但可能对这一著名地点的感情稍逊一些。一车车的旅客在城镇里短暂停留，看一个景点，然后继续前行，这并不一定令人愉快。也许一些耶灵居民会因为他们的城镇更加得到重视而倍感骄傲，但事实恰恰相反，这个城镇对耶灵而言无关紧要。在一定程度上，外界认为这个城镇阻碍了历史遗迹的开发和保护。因此，近几年来，在墓地附近的多数房屋遭拆除，这使当地人很难能高兴起来。

---

① https://whc.unesco.org/en/list/697.

另一个问题是,当地的教堂和公墓就坐落在历史遗迹的正中间,显然游客有时会让当地人很难进入这些地方,破坏前来吊唁和缅怀死去亲人的气氛。再者,有人指出,异乎寻常的大量访客意味着教堂必须每天打扫一次,而不是像其他教堂一样每周打扫两次。而这将产生一笔额外的费用,且须由会众支付。[1]

利益相关者

当然,研究维京时代的学者从这个历史遗迹获得同其他所有人一样的益处,除此之外,还有一些其他的方面。联合国教科文组织将这里入列历史遗迹名录意味着该遗址比以前有更好的资金支持和更好的保护。这也使得公众对我们的工作产生了更大的兴趣,这就可能会为我们通过书籍和公开演讲方式获得资金,创造更多机会。但另一方面,也存在不利之处,因为考古工作可能会造成历史遗迹的部分破坏,所以考古工作会变少。

国家政客对这样的历史遗迹很感兴趣,因为他们通过世界遗产获得了一定的荣誉。尽管很难精确地描述这种荣誉,但是至少在历史遗迹正式被认证时,他们促成了一件具有国家和国际双重重要性的完全积极的事件。而在这事件中,甚至他们的政治对手也会认为他们很好,很爱国。

当然,当地政治家也可能会获得荣誉,而且因为可能会名留青史,所以他们获得的荣誉可能更长远。因为世界遗产往往会带动旅游业发展,贸易交往,进而促进经济增长。所以对当地政治家而言更立竿见影的效果是,他们可以树立关注当地利益和发展的形象。

旅游业也期望这样的遗址可以带来更多的旅游商机。该遗址的清晰、有趣的介绍可以反复印刷在宣传手册中,也可连接到联合国教科文组织站点等进行国际广告宣传。随着曝光率提高,该遗址对丹麦的所有旅游业而言都具有重要意义。

城镇中大量的游客使得当地商家的收入有所增长,但是与此同时也使得当地的地区法律变得愈加严格,根本不可能在景点附近再建造新的商店。而且,为了让墓地有更好的景观,要拆除市中心,这也意味着一些商店或客栈就被拆除了(Baun Christensen, 2015)。因此,在这种情况下,耶灵遗址入选世界遗产这等好事对当地商家而言是喜忧参半的。短途游客在购买商品时也很有选择性,因

---

[1] 文章选自当地报纸 *Vejle Amts Folkeblad*,2016 年 10 月 4 日,https://vafo.dk/jelling/Menigheds-raad-er-bekymret-over-slid-paa-hoejomraadet/artikel/445434。

此有些商人比其他人获利更多。

在我的利益相关方名单上,最后一个是教科文组织本身。显然,该组织通过这个遗址在世界交流的地图上又添加了一个小标志,彰显了该组织在保护攸关人类普遍利益的重要遗址和造福人类方面所做的工作。与此同时,这也印证了一种观点,即该组织做着重要的工作,也因此它有存在的价值。

结论

几乎在整个20世纪,耶灵的历史遗迹都是丹麦人的专属建筑。针对这个历史遗迹的挖掘和城镇规划不时发生争论,耶灵发生了巨大的变化。然而,直到此历史遗迹于1994年成为世界遗产之后,才在2006年计划并执行了对该地区的新的广泛勘探,经过勘探,最终历史遗迹改变了它的特征,并且必须拆除市中心的大部分建筑来安置它。

这也许是一个极端的例子来说明当历史遗迹成为人类遗产的一部分时,历史遗迹本身会发生什么,但我认为,845项世界文化遗产中的任何一项都经历了类似的变化,可能变化得更微妙,从一个国家或地方遗址变成一个历史遗迹。

(作者单位:哥本哈根大学)

参考文献:

1. Baun Christensen, L. & Lokalhistorisk Forening for Jelling, Kollerup, Vindelev og Hvejsel Sogne, 2016. Jelling-byen der forsvandt, Jelling: i samarbejde med Forlaget Jelling.
2. Dyggve, E., The Royal Barrows at Jelling, Antiquity no. 88 December 1948 pp. 190 – 197.
3. Friis-Jensen, K. & Fisher, Peter, 2015. Saxo Grammaticus, Gesta Danorum, the history of the Danes, Oxford: Clarendon Press.
4. Jensen, K., 2015. Monumentområdet i Jelling, The monument area in Jelling 1. udgave (1. edition), 1. oplag., Aarhus: Arkitekt Kristine Jensens Tegnestue.

考古遗产和当地身份

埃斯本·阿尔斯莱夫(Esben Aarsleff)/著　张家川/译

从陶器这样的小文物，到金字塔和兵马俑这样的国际奇观，考古遗产都是一种复杂的现象。国际奇观的价值是显而易见的，地方发掘出来小文物的价值同样不可低估，因为它们是我们了解当地历史的关键。进而，我们才能够描绘出一幅与当地现代社会紧密相连的历史画卷。因此人们公认，扎根于地方社区的考古成果是支持，甚至是创造地方特色的宝贵资源。

考古遗产

考古遗产的重点是地方对考古遗产的认识，这种认识主要来源于由建筑工程（例如新房、道路、工业等）引起的发掘工作。

丹麦的所有发掘活动均受《博物馆法》约束。该法规定，所有建筑工程必须承担在其土地上发现的任何考古遗址的发掘成本。在北西兰岛，考古遗址主要包括带有文化层、房屋、壁炉、生产坑和垃圾坑的定居点遗迹。这些遗迹的形成时间可追溯到公元前4000年至公元1000年，涵盖了包括石器时代晚期、青铜和铁器时代的丹麦史前时期。由于某些未知的原因，我们很少发掘出坟墓。上一次发掘出坟墓，也已经是10多年前的事了。

在过去的十年中，我们已经意识到湿地的巨大潜力，这些湿地曾经是北西兰岛的特色。在这些湿地中，我们找到了泥炭切割和原始信仰活动的痕迹，这两种痕迹都为国际所关注。与旱地上的痕迹相似，湿地同时具有神圣性和世俗性，这与以前我们对湿地的认识完全相反。

通常，在我们的挖掘工作中，陶土和其他类型的废品之类的人工制品最为常见，但是也有一定数量的工具和装饰物。尽管时尚发生了变化，工具也得到了改

进，但大多数发掘品还是都由日常垃圾和更精细的人工制品或者人造工具组成。

在挖掘工作中，史前时期的木制建筑和石制建筑很少见。由于现代建筑的兴起，史前建筑几乎都被拆除了。仅有少数幸运的建筑可以被保存下来，并向公众开放。仿佛是一个不成文的规定，只有大大小小的文物才能留下来。

因此，考古遗产的主要部分由保存在博物馆文物库中的文物组成。文物的价值从三方面衡量，分别是稀有性、科学价值和历史价值（即文物讲述的史前人类与社会的故事）。后者通常是将文物和普通发掘物品区别开来的最重要依据。从最小的陶器到最漂亮的珠子，每个文物都有其独特的故事。

图1

为了展示我们考古文物的特征并解释考古成果，我们花了几小时的时间，向公众开放了大部分大型挖掘工具，得到了地方社区对文物遗产的真实性赞赏。

这类"弹出式"博物馆通常会吸引业余地方考古学家，和其他对地方史前史感兴趣的人前来参观。但是在少数情况下，考古遗产在创建，或支持地方特色方面更加重要，具体如以下示例所示。

洛德森·明德（Lodsens Minde）

2010年，我们在呼斯提德镇内进行了一次小规模的挖掘工作，发掘了一些早期石器时代、青铜器时代和中世纪后时代的遗迹（Pantmann，2017）。这些遗迹由石器时代的火石和其他时期的壁炉组成，而壁炉正是我们常常能发掘出来的遗迹类型。

挖掘工作就在当地杂货店的旁边，所以当地人对挖掘工作很感兴趣，许多人都密切关注着每日挖掘工作的进展。一开始，挖掘工作的目的是寻找石器时代的文物，但因为壁炉与当地人的生活息息相关，当地人对壁炉遗迹更加感兴趣。开挖结束后，当地人发起了为期一年的工程，该工程于2016年完工。当时，人们在当地最大的壁炉的原址附近开设了一个小广场，这个广场有两个重建的壁炉，和两个真人大小的钢铁塑像，分别代表石器时代或青铜时代的渔民。我们在广场旁边的发掘中发现了关于这三个时代的一些文字记载。

图 2

但是，为什么这些看似无趣的壁炉突然对当地社区产生了如此大的吸引力？

要理解这个问题，我们必须回顾一下呼斯提德镇的历史。呼斯提德镇最初是一个以捕鱼为生小镇，诞生于 19 世纪中叶（Hansen，1998）。在丹麦人眼中，这是一个年轻的小镇，历史很短。古老的壁炉证明了这座小镇具有史前历史，想在这里生存，前提条件就是学会捕鱼，学会在海边生活，这种情况一直持续到现在。因此，人们可以通过考古遗产理解过去与现在之间的联系，这大大增强了当地渔民的身份认同感。

这个例子表明，即使是日常发现文物中体现的共同特征，也可以上升为当地人民身份认同感的重要基石。

许灵厄山之石

许灵厄山之石重达 8.5 吨，最初矗立在北部的霍尔斯纳斯海滩附近高高的悬崖上，四周视野辽阔。在公元前 1000 年，大约是青铜时代的中期，人们在巨石上刻了几艘船和数百个杯子的标记，代表了青铜时代的宗教象征和信仰（Pantmann，2017）。1983 年，由于海洋对悬崖的自然侵蚀，这座巨石离开了自己原来的位置，落入了海滩。到了 20 世纪 90 年代，巨石被迁往弗雷德里克斯伐克的艺术大厅。后来人们对巨石的兴趣消退了，巨石也最终进入了博物馆的储藏室。

2007 年到 2010 年间，霍尔斯纳斯市的人们开始想念许灵厄山之石，一个当地组织运作了一个耗时很久的项目——将巨石"请回"霍尔斯纳斯市。他们筹集了用于展示的资金,制作了海报,并将石头运回弗雷德里克斯伐克,现在巨石被陈设在当地图书馆的大厅中。

呼斯提德镇是渔民创立的,而在18世纪中叶,来自哥本哈根的企业家创立了弗雷德里克斯伐克(Jacobsen et al,2006)。该镇最初是一座兵工厂,周围有员工专用的房屋。这座小城本身与18世纪中期以前的青铜时代或其他史前时期没有任何联系,但许灵厄山之石是全市的代表。这块巨石周围的地区历史,却可追溯到石器时代之后。因此,考古遗产创造出了一种令当地人拥护的身份认同感,甚至比城区的历史还要久远。

萨尔珀特摩斯

考古遗产的另一个实例是位于希勒勒德郊区——萨尔珀特摩斯的一次发掘,这次发掘为期5年。该发掘历时较长,出土文物种类繁多。最重要的发现之一可能是公元前3600年左右的人类干尸(bog body;Jørgensen & Hagedorn, 2015)。不幸的是,人们可以从图片中一眼就看得出,这具尸体的骨架在发掘过程中被一台21吨重的挖掘机弄得粉碎。

图3　　　　　　　　　　　图4

这位可怜人生前被人用骨制锐器击中,后脑有一处石斧造成的致命伤。死后,他被埋葬在当时村落附近的湖中。我们的猜测是当地人将其杀死,作为祭品,这一传统在当时各地都比较盛行。

这次发掘的另一个重要发现是一片酋长农场的遗迹,该遗迹的历史可追溯到公元250—400年。遗迹中包括房屋、圣物,很多充满文化气息的人工制品和有泥炭切割痕迹的湿地(Pantmann,2014)。

在矿坑中,有各种各样的祭祀动物痕迹,大部分是牛、绵羊、山羊和猪,还有木制的人工制品,陶器和大量发白的石头。这种石头很特殊,可以从新石器时代,一直到追溯到青铜时代和铁器时代。

图 5

虽然开发商属于公共机构,意识不到本地身份的重要性,但是开发商同意必须在推土机和挖掘机进入该地区之前,保存考古遗产。接下来的故事众所周知,当地社区对这些发现非常感兴趣,过去几年一直在进行大规模发掘。博物馆在给群众的解释方面做了很多工作,馆方表示这件事在很多层面上来讲对了解史前史都特别重要。

在这个例子中,当地社区接受了发掘工作的存在,而考古遗产就算没有创造一种身份认同感,也创造了过去与现在之间的纽带。

唯听和渤健——关于两家私人公司例子

渤健是一家美国私营医疗公司,于 2002 年至 2005 年间在希勒勒市建起了一家工厂。2001 年,博物馆在其土地上进行了大规模的农舍发掘,此时期是丹麦的铁器时代(公元 200—400 年;Nielsen & Kramer, 2002)。此处出土了很多文物,大部分是陶器碎片这种生活垃圾。该公司发现当地居民在这片区域生活了 1600 年至 1800 年之久,公司看到了巨大的投资潜力。因此,他们投资在新工厂的大厅设立了一个展览区,与当地历史联系起来,也为促进了当地的分公司员工一定程度上的地方身份认同。

渤健公司发掘工作的第二个成就,是他们将通往总部的道路命名为"铁器时代之路"。只有一种方式来解释这种行为,那就是他们对自己的遗产有极大的兴趣,并感到非常自豪。

唯听也是一家私营公司,于2008年在阿勒德附近建立了新总部。发掘过程中他们发现了定居点和墓地,均可追溯到铁器时代初期,大约是公元前500年至公元元年(Aarsleff, 2009)。该遗址文物稀少,他们最终只找到了一个陶罐,将其展示在了展厅。奇怪的是,这个陶罐竟是在总部的中心地带发现的,它以某种方式成为该公司发掘历史的起点。

图 6

在这两个例子中,考古遗产都成为公司建立与当地联系的积极因素,而不是为了建立身份,因为公司已经具有了世界范围的身份。更重要的是,他们希望通过在大厅安排展览,让当地社区和国际伙伴了解到他们尊重历史,并把历史因素放入了他们的新建筑。对于较大的私营公司来说,考古的保管工作或保管工作的费用渐渐成了其企业社会责任投资的一部分。

考古遗产——地方遗产作为国家遗产的补充

这些例子表明,在像北西兰岛这样的小地区,考古遗产的使用方式也千差万别。在位于霍尔斯纳斯市的呼斯提德和弗雷德里克斯伐克中,壁炉和许灵厄山之石对于当地身份的建立至关重要。

萨尔珀特摩斯的例子中显示,公共机构本不需要本地身份,但是当地人接受了本地身份,并将其视为与当地历史的联系。

两个私人公司的例子表明，考古遗产可以建立与历史的联系，无论是本地身份还是企业社会责任方面，公司都可以加以利用，这两者对大公司都具有一定的价值。

总而言之，考古遗产揭示了地方的微观历史。在考古学家的帮助下，文物和文物结构可以给人们讲述古代日常的生活故事，并使人们意识到，史前史与他们个人或公司、地区或社区的身份，都有千丝万缕的关系。

现代社会难以追根溯源，这使得历史和远古时代与许多丹麦人越来越息息相关。作为考古学家，我们只能包容和寻找更多的历史活动和历史事件，这些活动和事件既代表了地方的考古遗产，又具有与国家遗产的联系。

（作者单位：北西兰岛博物馆）

参考文献：

1. Hansen, E. 1998. *Hundested i gamle Dage. Erindringer fra et kvart Aarhundrede*. Hundested Lokalhistoriske Forening.
2. Jøacobsen et al. 2006. *Friderichs Wærk — Kilder til industribyens fødsel*. Hundested Lokalhistoriske Forening. Frederiksværks Lokalhistoriske Forening og Industrimuseet Frederiks Værk.
3. Jørgensen, T. & L. Hagedorn 2015. Salpetermoseliget. *Alle tiders Nordsjælland. Museum Nordsjællands Årbog 2015*, s. 118-122.
4. Nielsen, L. E. & F. Kramer 2002. Udgravningerne ved Biogen. *NoMus 2/2002*, s. 3-6.
5. Pantmann, P. 2014. Hund og hund imellem. *NoMus 3/2014*, s. 3-11.
6. Pantmann, P. 2017. Ild og vand — kult i bronzealderens Lillerød. *Alle tiders Nordsjælland. Museum Nordsjællands Årbog 2017*, s. 149-156.
7. Pantmann, P. 2017. *Lodsens Minde*. Unpublished Report of the excavation.
8. Aarsleff, E. 2009. Flere kældre fra førromersk jernalder — og lidt grave. *NoMus 1/2009*, s. 24-29.

论"Kulturerbe"

莫里茨·金泽尔(Moritz Kinzel)/著 马亚楠/译

如今,"Kulturerbe"一词在德国引起的争论无处不在,主要就历史遗迹、传统或手工艺品的保护及其管理进行讨论。但是,1986年以来的德国著名的词典Dude以及2004年出版的德语词典Wörterbuch der Deutschen Sprache尚未收录"Kulturerbe"一词。那么,"Kulturerbe"这一术语实际上代表什么呢?它何时首次出现在德语中?在何种背景下出现?它是否真的包含了与"Erinnerungskultur"和"Denkmalwert"相关却又迥然不同的全部含义?本文将就以上部分问题进行讨论。

德国术语"Kulturerbe"

如今,"Kulturerbe"一词得到广泛应用,并且似乎具有一种命令式的严肃性,就像"old"一词一样。但是,1986年的旧版德语词典Duden以及2004年出版的 *Wörterbuchder Deutschen Sprache* 都未包含"Kulturerbe"。这意味着在过去十五年中,德语"Kulturerbe"一词相当于英语中的"heritage"已经得到了认可。杜登德语词典在其最新的在线版本中将"Kulturerbe"定义为"überliefertesKulturgut einer Gemeinschaft, eines Volkes",可译为"传承社会或人民的文化遗产"。[①] 从构词法的角度来说,"Kulturerbe"是由"Kulturelles"和"Erbe"两个单词构成的。尽管"Kulturerbe"和"Kulturelles Erbe"看起来相同,意思也相近,但后者更多的是在强调"Erbe",也就是遗产,而不是我们需要悉心保护的、有价值的文化。2001年,在联合国教科文组织的"非物质遗产"活动中,"Kulturerbe"在德语版中首次

---

① http://www.duden.de/rechtschreibung/Kulturerbe [07.11.2015].

出现。随着2006年备忘录的正式批准,这个术语被正式收录,从此以后被广泛使用。与此同时,如果我们使用"Kulturerbe"作为关键词去搜索,我们可以找到非常多的相关书籍。大量的研究试图去定义这个词,但都不得而终,因为关于这个词的讨论相当复杂,难以获得清晰的定义。"Kulturerbe"本身并不存在,它是导致令人信服的叙事的多种因素的总和,这一叙事为特定的群体或社会定义了可能在某个时间点丢失的"价值"。只有当足够的拥护者参与到拟议的叙事,并且认为围绕某一物体、历史遗迹、特定活动、建筑物或其他人物所编的故事与自己有关联的时候,这种"价值"的重要性才得以凸显。然后,拥护者团体将"消息"(message)传播到全世界,让更多人支持他们所编版本的故事及阐释。但在大多数情况下,只有当历史遗迹的相关叙事中包含"失的威胁"时,其价值才能得到认可(Kinzel,2018)。

然而,"Kulturerbe"不仅仅是一个概念:在德国,关于"历史遗迹"和传统的争论较少基于"继承"某种东西,它更多的是建立在保存和维护概念基础上的,这一概念被称为"Denkmalschutz und Denkmalpflege"(Kiesow,2000)。它的含义和概念与英语中"heritage"一词大不相同,"heritage"被定义为"传给继承人的财产""从前任处继承或获得的东西""遗产、继承物""由于自然条件或出生而拥有的东西""与生俱来的权利"。[①]"Kulturerbe"首先要理解为所继承的东西的相关知识。重要性和历史意义可能导致价值创造和知识转让;只要有关某个地方的故事仍在被讲述,实际地方究竟位于何处就不会失传,可以指出的是文化遗产(Kulturerbe)也就不会丢失——因为它始终为人们所铭记。

价值的概念——文化财产

原则上,"文化遗产/文化财产"概念背后的价值体现在三个方面:

1. **审美价值**:在一个物体、一个地方、一座建筑物或一项活动中发现美丽、平衡和秩序;

2. **历史价值**:满含热情地将过去与历史视为知识的来源:"文化遗产是古老的!";

3. **社会价值或公共价值**:保护的实际行动,即"Denkmalpflege"(文物保

[①] https://www.merriam-webster.com/dictionary/heritage [accessed 03.09.2018]. For a more detailed discussion on the English term "heritage" see S. Auken's contribution ("Heritage" and "kulturarv") in this volume.

护),就是通过实践来保护文化遗产。

"Kulturerbe"一词涉及一系列广泛的可解释价值的概念,这些价值可能赞成或反对什么可被视为文化遗产(参见 Bogner et al,2018;Meier et al,2013):

"Alterswert"(老化和铜锈):李格尔(Alois Riegl,1903—1995)将"Alterswert"定义为老化的痕迹以及与观察者情感直接相关的铜锈。但"Alterswert"还包括持续的老化过程。文化遗产的价值随着持续老化的进程而增长,而不是随着保存下来的识别阶段而增长。

"Bildwert"(审美价值):历史遗迹因其外形美观别致而广受赞赏;包括城市景观、剪影轮廓或以绘画和照片形式呈现的仿制品。

"Erinnerungswert"(记忆):尽管"Erinnerung"一词与历史和"Gedächtnis"(意为记忆)紧密相关,尽管纪念碑和纪念馆实际上是事件、人物和"事物"应被记住的实体见证,但在德国目前的遗产争论中却很少使用"Erinnerung"一词。纪念物、回忆或引起回忆的事物可能会让人回忆起"Erinnerungswert"的某些方面。文化记忆(kulturelles Gedächtnis)具有很强的选择性,其转移、遗忘和掩盖的方面在定义叙事和最终的群体身份方面发挥了重要作用(Assmann,2006;Assmann,2013)。破坏能够中断记忆的发展,但是破坏行为会使得人们能够更深刻地记住一个强有力的标志物(Onu,2018)。

"Erzieherischer Wert"(教学和教育价值):在"Kulturerbe"的背景下"Erziehung"必须被视为具有双重性的事物:一方面通过历史遗迹给人们施加特定的事物加以记忆,以此来教育人们;另一方面,通过为"Bildung"提供机会(一种整体方法),通过对历史及我们从中学到的东西进行更广泛的讨论,以此来教育民众。

"Identität"(身份):身份建立在与众不同的经历及对"他者"明确划分的基础之上。没有对立的"他者",就没有身份。但这并不排除一个人具有其他身份,属于不同群体的一部分。随着"他者"的消失,分界线可能会随着时间的流逝变得模糊。但是,这可能会产生新的叙事,从而导致群体身份的改变。

"Kultwert"(崇拜价值):"Kultwert"的概念是基于对手工艺品的感知以及通过展示或呈现手工艺品而创造的价值,尤其是在宗教和祭奠背景下。"Kultwert"最初旨在描述诸如法令或遗迹的价值,这些通常都在一年一度的游行展览。如今,它更多地用来说明真实地点的价值——其价值要小于真正的纪念碑或物体。

"Kunstwert"(艺术价值):"Kunstwert"一词意为历史遗迹的艺术性。在这一标准下,艺术品的修复和完工才得到支持,因为通常而言,经过修复抛光的外观比其破碎风化的状态更具吸引力,更受赞赏。

"Nachhaltigkeit"(可持续发展)：在"Kulturerbe"背景下，可持续发展不仅要解决历史遗迹本身长期保护的问题，而且还引发了合理利用的概念，即尊重文化财产的完整性，并对这一概念进行了重新阐释。

"Streitwert"(冲突与争论)：历史遗迹或文化遗产的价值及其处理方法可能证明是其实际价值。冲突和讨论的交流使得争论中的 Kulturerbe 具有价值，例如关于重建和新建的"历史"建筑以及真实性问题的讨论。

"Symbolwert"(象征价值)：针对国家、朝代或社会的关键价值在于象征价值，它们构成了纪念物和历史遗迹概念的基本框架。象征价值代表着对某人有价值的古迹或其他文化财产的建造和破坏。象征支持强烈的身份认同感，并设想其与"其他身份"的区别。

"Transkulturalität"(跨文化性)：跨文化性价值是对属于一个或多个国家或地区的遗产的认可，例如由于边界线移动或人口流动产生的文化遗产。在某些情况下，这种"Kulturerbe"容易引发争议、不受欢迎且使人不适，因为它与"其他身份"有关，可能会被视为对"自身"身份的威胁。但是，从全球角度来看，跨文化性也可视为文化以多种方式相互影响，将各种传统和文化融合在一起，创造出新的传统、身份和友谊。

"Urkundenwert"(法律文献)：历史遗迹本身是真实的文献，是其所在时代的见证，可以作为参考。

"Zeugniswert"(见证)：文化遗产是历史事件、经验或技术的证据和见证；与"Urkundenwert"(合法文献)密切相关，也与"Erinnerungswert"(记忆)相关。

上文已简要解释的各个方面和概念，都必须理解为"Kulturerbe"一词的一部分。正如所解释的，该术语源自更合法的术语"Kulturgut"(文化财产)及"Kulturgüterschutz"(文化财产的保护)。最初认为"Kulturerbe"一词仅涵盖历史遗迹和历史建筑。

使人不适、引发争议及不受欢迎的遗产

试图解释德语中"Kultur"一词的复杂性不在本文讨论范围，同样地，对于极其复杂的"Erbe"一词及其管辖范围内的解释同样不属于本文讨论范围。但是，"Erbe"不仅仅涵盖令人舒适的方面。一个人可以继承深度和财产抵押以及"糟糕"的记忆或联想。这意味着"Erbe"一词也总是包含记忆和历史中使人不适、引发争议及不受欢迎的部分(Huse, 1997)。由于德国历史以及建筑物和其他文化财产的所有损失，不仅仅是过去 150 年的损失，"Erbe"一词都是文化遗产争论的

重要组成部分,可能与下列术语存在巨大差异,包括法语中的"patrimoine"、英语中的"heritage"、意大利语中的"patrimonio"(Brandi,1977)、阿拉伯语中的"turath",甚至包括丹麦语中的"Kulturarv"。

在2018年7月于巴林举行的联合国教科文组织世界遗产委员会会议上,关于是否应将"充满负面意义的"(negative-loaded)遗产列入世界遗产名录引起了颇具争议的讨论(ICOMOS,2018)。这一争论在很大程度上表明了"遗产"(heritage)一词的不同含义以及对该术语的不同理解。仅仅将"遗产"视为值得纪念的正面事件是错误的。恐怖暴力事件和相关地点(在各个方面和感官上都使人不适),可能不会仅仅因为它们不是最佳的旅游地点而遭到压制。但这并不意味着真正充满负面意义的遗产,可能会转变为一些积极的、与历史遗产照看的交流共享相关的传统,例如法国—比利时关于"西线"沿线的第一次世界大战公墓和纪念馆的提议究竟代表着什么。由于历史的书写是一个政治过程,历史叙事肩负着创造身份和民族——即定义群体的责任,而文化遗产显然是定义叙事的主要部分。联合国教科文组织的文化世界遗产概念由此变成了一种普遍适用的体系——能够灵活适应物质文化及相关活动和传统的所有不同内涵(UNESCO,1972)。尽管上文已作出了解释,联合国教科文组织仍倾向于回避令人不适和引发争议的文化遗产,因为它的目标之一是通过促进旅游业,通过使遗址成为全球共享遗产的主要积极方面而闻名于世,以此来保护遗产。

结论

这篇短短的文献只是试图开始一个进一步理解的过程。如上文所示,德语"Kulturerbe"一词包含了一个长期争论不休的话题,即我们如何才能最好地定义价值,并以此为依据将传统、建筑物、古迹和其他过去的见证宣称为"活着的"遗产。我们对"Kulturerbe"的理解与我们的文化背景和民族历史息息相关,因此无法一对一转让或翻译。这一困境很难克服,但是了解并意识到差异可能有助于加深理解并进行富有成果的对话。当我们谈论"遗产"时,我们到底在谈论什么,实际上是在谈论"Kulturerbe"一词包含的所有复杂性。

(作者单位:哥本哈根大学)

参考文献:

1. Assmann, A. 2006. Erinnerungsräume. Formen und Wandlungen des kulturellen Gedächtnisses.

3. Auflage. München: Beck.
2. Assmann, J. 2013. Das kulturelle Gedächtnis. Schrift, Erinnerung und politische Identität in frühen Hochkulturen. 7. Auflage. München: Beck.
3. Bogner, S., Franz, B., Meier, H. -R., and Steiner, M. (eds.). 2018. Denkmal — Erbe — Heritage: Begriffshorizonte am Beispiel der Industriekultur, Heidelberg: arthistoricum. net, (Veröffentlichungen des Arbeitskreises Theorie und Lehre der Denkmalpflege e. V., Band 27). DOI: 10.11588/arthistoricum.374.531; https://books.ub.uni-heidelberg.de/arthistoricum/catalog/book/374 [accessed: 04.01.2019].
4. Brandi C. 1977 Teoria del restauro. Torino: Einaudi.
5. Huse N. 1997. Unbequeme Baudenkmale. Entsorgen? Schützen? Pflegen? München: Beck.
6. ICOMOS 2018. 2018 Evaluations of Nominations of Cultural and Mixed Properties. ICOMOS report for the World Heritage Committee; 42nd ordinary session, Manama, 24 June — 4 July 2018 — WHC-18/42. COM/INF.8B1. https://whc.unesco.org/archive/2018/whc18-42com-inf8B1-en.pdf [accessed: 09.01.2019].
7. Kiesow G. 2000; Denkmalpflege in Deutschland — Eine Einführung. Stuttgart: Theiss.
8. Kinzel M. 2016. Von der Zerstörung von Kulturerbe: der Versuch einer Annäherung. In: AIV Forum, Vol. 2016, No. 1, pp. 6 – 15.
9. Kinzel M. 2018. "Once Upon A Time …" Constructing Narratives to Destruct Heritage. In: Moritz Kinzel; Mette Thuesen; Ingolf Thuesen (eds.): Conflict and Culture: Understanding threats to heritage. Copenhagen: Forlaget Orbis, 2018, pp. 14 – 19.
10. Meier H. R., Scheurmann I., and Sonne W. (eds.) 2013. Werte. Begründungen der Denkmalpflege in Geschichte und Gegenwart. Berlin: Jovis.
11. Onu, M. 2018. Spurious Infinity and axiological remembrance. Philosophical approaches on threats to cultural heritage. In: Kinzel — Thuesen — Thuesen (eds.): Conflict and Culture. Copenhagen: forlaget orbis. 2018: 56 – 61.
12. Riegl A. 1903. Der moderne Denkmalkultus. Sein Wesen und seine Entstehung. Wien/Leipzig.
13. Riegl A. 1995. Kunstwerk oder Denkmal? Alois Riegls Schriften zur Denkmalpflege. Bacher E. (ed.). Studien zu Denkmalschutz und Denkmalpflege Bd. 15. Wien/Köln/Weimar.
14. Schmidt L. 2008. Einführung in die Denkmalpflege. Stuttgart: Theiss.
15. Tauschek M. 2013. Kulturerbe. Eine Einführung. Berlin: Reimer.
16. UNESCO 1972. Convention Concerning the Protection of the World Cultural and Natural Heritage. Adopted by the General Conference at its seventeenth Session Paris, 16 November 1972 http://whc.unesco.org/archive/convention-en.pdf [accessed 03.10.2018].

图 1　理解遗产的关键词（HeAT-Project/University of Copenhagen）

图 2　文化遗产价值和术语的英语及德语词云

清代传统技艺和泥塑

约瑟菲娜·巴克(Josefine Baark)/著　卢嘉欣/译

在清初广州生产的众多珍贵文物中,有一批泥塑人像,数量上百,其中大部分由西方收藏家收藏。这些泥塑多是中国和欧洲的商人在广州时委托"捏脸匠"为其制作的肖像。制作肖像的工匠们利用"陵墓雕塑"这一传统技艺制作新型肖像,更易在欧洲世界进行展示。这里的"传统技艺"指的是为了满足当地需求而长期开发的技能,是一种"非物质文化遗产"(Smith and Akagawa, eds., 2008)。如下文所述,这些源于广州的技艺虽然是在传统和"文化遗产"基础上发展起来的,但制作和展示泥塑绝不是对传统技艺的静态重复。如果将文化接触点理解为不断变化的目标,而不是固定的出发点,我们就可以利用这一案例来分析手工艺品是如何适应、融合和反叛传统技艺,并最终产生一种全新的、可共享,甚至"全球化的"文化遗产。

本文简要介绍了清朝中期的广州贸易,中国丧葬仪式中泥塑肖像的使用以及中国机器人的仿真性,以便对两个塑像进行详细研究。广州的贸易环境极大地促进了文化的繁荣,当地旧传统和手工技艺能迎合新的社会需求很快地做出改变。例如,1720—1760年间,一些制作于中国的肖像画采用了"再现相貌"的欧洲做法,但也有一些仍坚持突出衣服、等级和装饰,以表示特定人物。

通过研究作为一个国家"文化遗产"基础的手工传统如何被当地工匠改造以适应新的消费者(即欧洲人),本文从两个方面揭示了18世纪70年代在广州兴起的"全球"文化范畴下,肖像画对社会地位的塑造表现。首先,文化范畴不仅由中国和欧洲商人组成的全球"精英"塑造,工匠们的制作材料与技艺使奢侈品跨越欧洲和中国文化习俗之间的鸿沟,如此技艺同样塑造了多元文化社区;其次,欧洲和中国的精英人士常用衣服来显示社会地位。尽管泥塑人像源于数百年的传统实践,但它也根据广州当地的全球化需求进行了特别调整。到18世纪末,肖像画已成为的"全球化"和"高贵"的象征。随后,相关跨文化背景下描绘社会关系的问题成功揭示了"遗产"适应"文化"的灵活性。

18世纪30年代,英国、法国、丹麦和瑞典的东印度公司到达广州后的几十年里,欧洲对购买、代理、赠送和转售中国艺术品的兴趣日益增强。随着国际贸易的扩大,广州欧洲区周围的小巷遍布商店,售有各种商品:瓷器、丝绸、漆器、草药、微型模型和泥塑肖像。本文重点讲述1730—1760年间藏于丹麦皇室的泥塑。此外还将涉及陈列于瑞典城堡卓宁霍姆宫夏季凉亭中的类似塑像,这一城堡也是斯堪的纳维亚半岛保存18世纪原始陈列品的唯一地方。

斯堪的纳维亚半岛与广州的贸易

丹麦与中国之间的第一次航行始于1730年,而与瑞典之间首航始于1732年。基于贸易、防御、谈判和惯例等多重传统关系,丹麦人在广州的贸易体系得以建立(Perdue, 2015)。1757年后,外国商人禁止与行商以外的居民互动。行商联合会包括近12个商会,他们决定着西方可购买的商品。1757年正式实施"一口通商"(即清朝规定西洋商人只可以在广东通商的政策)之前,欧洲人还可以在广州城西郊逛一逛。他们可以去瓷器街、丝绸店街、漆器街,以及位于欧洲码头的行商会的主要仓库看一看。

随着贸易的迅速发展,大多数广东工匠继续按照中式审美制作装饰物。随后,欧洲商人特别委员会的成立与知识精英之间不断上升的西方主义,共同促进了跨文化审美手工艺品的流行。大量印有欧洲盔甲纹章的瓷器的出现有力地印证了当时欧洲文化对广州市场的影响力。亚洲艺术品在欧洲室内装饰中逐渐流行起来,欧洲人开始陈设具有想象力的中式风格的艺术品(即"中国风")。

在第一次航行中,丹麦亚洲公司(以下简称DAC)雇用的押运员委托了广州工匠用制作微型泥塑。这些泥塑最初在商人家中展出,随后在丹麦皇家艺术馆展出。在丹麦皇室的直接资助下,中丹贸易盈利十分可观。1732—1771年,发往广州的丹麦货物净值近2 000万里格斯德勒(rigsdaler,当时丹麦使用的货币名称),回程货物的总价为3 800万里格斯德勒(Struwe, 1967)。出境货物主要是现金,回程货物则包括茶、作为压舱物的陶瓷以及允许押运员使用的"私人"货物后备箱(Willerslev, 1944)。

尽管中国文人和商人模样的泥塑最为常见,但学界将更多的研究集中在这些泥塑与欧洲商人的相似性上(Broomhall, 2016; Clarke, 2011)。西方学者将相貌相似性作为肖像制作的关键要素。例如,通过与欧洲彩绘肖像进行比较,可

图1 《纪尧姆·德布劳维尔上尉肖像》，18世纪30年代，彩绘黏土，个人收藏品，比利时

图2 布鲁日一位匿名大师作品，《纪尧姆·德布劳维尔及其家人肖像》，1745—1755，布面油画，132.5厘米×170厘米，格罗宁格博物馆

以识别出像纪尧姆·德布劳维尔上尉这样的雕塑（图1；Parmentier，1989）。

虽然迄今还未能在中国人的绘画肖像和雕刻肖像之间找到类似的联系，但这并不意味着不存在这样的联系。对中国肖像画的研究大部分都集中于早期的纪念肖像画和墓葬肖像画（Stuart and Rawski，2001；Hornby，2000）。同时，清朝的肖像画研究多集中于研究对西方绘画技术的引进（Musillo，2008；Kleutghen，2013；Cahill，2010）。这两条研究思路为证明泥塑联系两种文化传统奠定了重要基础。

错置的头部

记载广州生活的欧洲文献提供了有限的街道手工艺生意照片。1732年，丹麦货船——克朗普林斯·克里斯坦号（Kronprins Christian）上的四位押运员带回了自己的泥塑肖像。他们还带回了两座中国精英人士的泥塑——一个是身穿明朝服装的女人，另一个身着清朝服饰的男官（图2）。

库存记录对男性泥塑的描述比女性泥塑更为具体。1737年，货船抵达丹麦的五年后，丹麦皇家艺术节的存货记录中对这两塑像如是描述：

广东省军官。两小像均高13.5英寸，身型和服装为广州风格。中国军官

图3　中国官员肖像。雍正时期(1723—1735),长37厘米,丹麦国家博物馆,哥本哈根

身着穿黑色服饰,妻子穿白色外套,都由黏土制成(Gundestrup,1991)。①

根据此描述,我们可以推测,虽然泥塑没有具体姓名,但是对于欧洲消费者来说,男人的等级和出身极为重要,而衣服则是人物身份的延伸。

男性泥塑有两个鲜明的特征。他身型苗条,两只脚微妙地摆着姿势,其中一只脚非常自然地稍稍向前以保持平衡。他身着官员服饰,黑色吉服上绣有一个大方补。通过他的身型可以推测出与其配对的女性塑像的大小。进一步观察此塑像,可推断补子图案上或是一品鹤,或为六品鹭鸶②。丹麦库存记录将其记录为武官,但武官补子上所绣为兽,而文官绣鸟。因此,丹麦人可能是通过顶戴识别人物,而非身上的补子图案。官员品级还可以通过帽饰的颜色、结构和顶珠来确定,不巧该塑像的顶珠已缺失。虽如此,仍能明显看出这顶帽子是用红色丝线编织而成。安东尼·斯皮罗指出,着装是理解肖像作为中国的特殊象征性工具的关键点。当无法通过铭文区分身份时,官员品级可作为参照指标(Antony Spiro,1990)。

商船抵达丹麦后,丹麦艺术馆收藏了这两个泥塑,该艺术馆有选择地向公众开放。泥塑像皇家收藏后,并无任何对其进行维修的记录。因此,头部更换很可能由广州工匠完成。头部和人物的识别与此处论述并不十分相关,因而留待以

---

① 1737 820/201-202 Een Mandaring over Militair Standen udi Provincesen Canton, ere begge to smaa Figurer 13 1/5 Tommer høi efter deres Lægerns Skikelse og Klædedragt i Canton. Mandarin er i sort og Konen i en hvid Jake, samme ere ligesom forige piorte af Leer. '

② 笔者于2017年11月16日获丹麦国家博物馆允许,亲自研究此塑像。

后研究。关键是，头部似乎是对某一特定相貌的描绘。此外，从修复该人物的广州工匠使用的"文化遗产"或技艺传统的背景考虑，着装的特殊性表明此雕像是某一人物的"肖像"，而不仅仅是"模型"。

欧洲文献对"捏脸匠"作坊以及工匠的技法进行了详细描述。1753年，瑞典水手奥洛夫·托林（Olof Toreen，1718—1753）在前往苏拉特（Suratte）的航行中描述了"泥塑全身像和半身像"（Osbeck, Toren, Ekeberg, and Newton, 1765; Clarke, 2011）。1769年，英国东印度公司员工威廉·希基（William Hickey）说道：

> 有一个中国人擅长用黏土塑像，后期还会上色，成品很是不错。波特和我去了这个人店里……诺丁汉号船的外科医生卡内基（Carnegie）先生，坐在自己的塑像旁，抱怨工匠制造的是该死的丑陋的恶魔。几番埋怨后，工匠放下工具，仔细端详卡耐基，说："嘿，你英俊的脸庞上没有什么可塑造的了。"……卡内基觉得自己被冒犯了……说自己既不会付钱给工匠，也不会将这塑像带走。他确实这样做了，我们再次来到店里时，看到卡内基先生的塑像和其他塑像一起被挂在了梁上，脖子上还挂了绳子。询问这个的含义时，工匠极为恼火地回答："这些都是给那些海盗或是盗贼刻像后留下的，他们不付钱也不带走自己的塑像，净想着要英俊的脸庞，给我带来很多麻烦，我必须把他们吊起来"（Hickey, 1913; Clarke, 2011）。

尽管对中国官员泥塑的记载与希基讲述卡内基先生的塑像被悬挂起来的故事相隔了近一个世纪，但它的确表明，委托工匠制作泥塑很是常见——毕竟这一被挂在"其他几个塑像"中的作品——深受其雕刻者的重视。

中国肖像传统

泥塑有三大特征：强调服饰、尺寸较小、头部可移动。注重描绘服饰是中国肖像画的一个常见特征（Hung, 1997; Kesner, 2007; Stuart and Rawski, 2001; Seckel, 1993）。甚至有早期中国学者也指出了这一点。王绎（1333—1368），在《写像秘诀》中批判了早期绘画中常出现的僵硬姿势，称其为"必欲其正襟危坐如泥塑人"（Wang Yi cited in Stuart and Rawski, 2001）。尽管此类参考文献对泥塑大多持批评态度，但这也的确证明了泥塑与绘画之间的关联性。此外，泥塑虽不如绘画的地位高，却是为皇帝而作。罗友枝（Evelyn Rawski）就提到了一个放置在寿康宫中的雍正皇帝的泥塑（Rawski, 1988）。

虽未曾明确此泥塑的大小，但是泥塑的尺寸对于了解其在清朝广州的文化意义至关重要。从西方的角度来看，小尺寸泥塑很容易带回欧洲。但是，即使泥塑尺寸始终小于真人体形，它们的高度也常常超过一米。因此，这种解释不太合适。相反，小尺寸的特点揭示了泥塑在清朝广州大量出现的两个核心特征：首先，泥塑的尺寸与古老墓葬雕塑有关（Hung，2015；Kesner，1995；Ebrey，1997；Dien，1987；Hay，2010；Spiro，1990）。其次，若不被带去西方大陆，这种联系本身赋予泥塑的是神奇的通灵力量。

在中国，微型化的最早实例是墓葬文物，它们是精神世界的通道（Hung，2015）。这类墓葬雕塑被称为"明器"或"灵器"，"它们是真人的替代品"（Kesner，1995）。另一种彩绘泥塑人物是神庙里的神像，但它们并非肖像，通常是可辨别的"模型"（Howard，Hung，Song，and Hong，2006）。另外，巫鸿（Hung Wu）认为"在坟墓中建造地下室或微观环境时，它不仅为灵魂提供了象征性的住处，而且由于其小巧体积也使灵魂无形中有了微型概念"（Hung，2015）。吕智荣（1992）、王仁波（1987）指出，微型雕塑最初是作为陪葬品出现的，以代替活人献祭。凯斯纳（Kesner）将其称为"替代品"。这并不是说所有微型雕塑都具有无形的灵魂。但一般而言，微型化，尤其是建筑微型化所具有的象征性价值，确实使这些模型变得不再仅仅是玩具。此外，它将微型化概念与旅行的思想联系在了一起。

正如希基对卡尼基先生塑像被"悬挂"的描述所暗示的那样，清朝初期，泥塑人物可能仍被认为具有一定的神秘力量。但是，大卫·弗里德伯格（David Freedberg，1989）也指出，一个例子不能完全说明这些塑像是否与还愿用的四肢或蜡像归属同一种类。斯美茵（Jan Stuart）和罗友枝认为，"外国人制作的一些雕塑也许会受到中国南方一些'船民'中流行的习俗的影响，'船民们'将祖先的小型木雕放在家族祭坛上"（2001，173）。但是，他们并没有将西方人的肖像与那些能显示中国商人遍布欧洲宫廷的塑像联系起来。中国塑像的特征——栩栩如生的点头模样，也许是阻碍这种联系的决定性特征。

如上所述，清代人物塑像的第三个特征是其头部可活动，有些塑像的手也能活动。泥塑并不是严格意义上的自动装置，只是躯干内部具有一个配重系统，用户操作后可其使塑像头部移动。这种仿真性与中文文献中有关机器人或自动装置的早期叙述紧密相关（Schafer，1990；Eichenhorn，1952；Needham，1960）①。《列

---

① 例如，赵国君石虎在位期间（335—345），解飞、魏猛变发明之物："十多名身高超过 2 英尺的木制人物，身披袈裟，以佛陀为中心绕圈行走。每当有人来到佛陀面前时，木人便会鞠躬敬拜佛陀，并将手里握着的一小撮香扔进火盆，与真人没什么不同。"

子》中记载了工匠偃师为周穆王发明的机器人：

> 穆王惊视之，趋步俯仰，信人也。……穆王始悦而叹曰："人之巧乃可与造化者同功乎？"

早期中文文献所记载的仿真机器有一个共同点：反复"低头"或"点头"。当然，奇迹不会止步于此，有些机器人甚至拥有更多能力，例如跳舞、唱歌、调戏宫女，或是大步走出微型门[①]。长此以往，可移动的头部将人物形象置于生活领域，在未被固定的情况下，还将引起其与人类自治的最终联系。

早期机器人展现出了一贯的表演性技能。表演木偶和戏剧是整个东亚表演艺术存在已久的一个组成部分（Law，2015；Liu，2016；Orr，1974）。约瑟夫·尼德姆（Joseph Needham）将传统歌剧和皮影戏联系在一起，有些研究者则认为，中国的整个戏剧传统源于对汉墓中的陪葬者"模型"（黏土和木头）的仿造（Needham，1960）。尽管广东的工匠们会用真人的头发来装饰一些中国泥塑人的辫子或胡须，但似乎不太可能将原本下葬的塑像送交欧洲商人。相反，我认为送去欧洲的是那些在中国从事贸易的商人的塑像（尽管不全部都是）。我还以为，这种交流方式能使泥塑人物在欧洲宫廷的彩绘肖像一样，得到重视，并向公众展示。因此，中国官员泥塑不像欧洲室内装饰用的瓷器艺术品那样，只有装饰的作用。

结论

这些泥塑人物有时只用来展示中国服饰。但通常它们被集成到大型的中国风室内装饰中，例如皇后岛宫的中国宫。

在中国宫里，瑞典王室成员摆脱了严格的宫廷生活，把玩着这些微型塑像。如果我们仔细观察这些塑像，不难看出由于被频繁触摸（让它们点头），头上和手上的颜色都暗了。如此频繁的把玩也说明，虽然从中国进口的瓷器像艺术品一样摆放在这些泥塑旁边，但泥塑却被视为不同的艺术品。根植于中国文化传统的泥塑技艺要求把玩者必须与其进行身体接触。

[①] 东晋一位发明家甚有巧思，造竹木室，作一妇人居其中："人扣其户，妇人开户而出，当户再拜，还入户内，闭户。"（人们敲木娃娃的门，小妇人开门而出；站于门前，她反复鞠躬；回到屋内，便又关上了门）。《中国科学技术典籍通汇》，综合卷 4（郑州：河南教育出版社，1996）：第 752 章。

图4 红屋,中国宫;卓宁霍姆堡,瑞典

　　本文重点强调中国工匠如何发展一种"文化遗产",或者说是一系列容易适应新环境的传统技艺。此外,欧洲精英消费者展示泥塑的同时,也是在长期外交环境下展示肖像的实践。如果我们将"文化遗产"作为一种开放技艺,而不是一套定性规则,那么它可以使人们对全球文化如何在国际领域发展有更加细微的了解。

（作者单位：哥本哈根大学）

丹麦建筑遗产

克里斯托弗·施密特(Kristoffer Schmidt)/著　武彦如/译

2018年是丹麦首部建筑保护法颁布一百周年，为庆祝这一百年事件，丹麦召开了一次社会高度关注的会议，并出版了两部由建筑遗产领域的最重要的学者们撰写的著作(Tønnesen, etc., 2018; Bendsen & Morgen, 2018)。这两本书揭示了虽然保护法保护了一些具有重要文化意义的建筑，但保护当局也为保护同样重要的建筑免遭拆除或大修做了一些徒然的努力。但在其他案例中，同一当局则选择无视对建筑物的保护请求，因为它们没达到保护建筑的标准。后一种情况对于本文的主题非常重要，因为它们显示了关于建筑遗产价值的不同意见，特别是在学者之间的意见差异。本文通过一系列的历史实例及对当代丹麦建筑遗产价值评估的首选方法——SAVE评估法的分析，展示这些关于建筑遗产的不同观点。

"1918保护法"的先声

1918年建筑保护法立法有多方面的原因，包括大量老建筑被拆除，以及一系列不当修复项目对重要历史建筑造成了严重损害。曾有一个源于失火的离奇案例。1859年12月，一场大火摧毁了位于希勒勒市(Hillerød)曾属于克里斯蒂安四世(Christian Ⅳ)的弗雷德里克斯堡城堡(Fredericksburg Castle)主体部分。由于天气严寒及消防装备不足，大火烧毁了城堡的主体。浓烟滚滚的城堡废墟被所有丹麦人视为一场悲剧，关于是否复建弗雷德里克斯堡城堡的讨论很快引起了丹麦全国的关注。一些知名的历史学家反对重建，但他们的声音湮没了。通过公众捐资以及来自腓特烈七世国王(King Frederick Ⅶ)与丹麦政府的两份占比相当多的捐款，城堡被重新建了起来。其外观与文艺复兴时期的典型城堡样式相似,但它的内部很难重现,因为没有人确切地知晓室内细节。此外,负责的建筑师费迪南德·梅尔达尔(Ferdinand Mehldahl)并没有兴趣重建一个在他看来是常见的文艺复兴建筑的完全复制品。最后重建成的城堡可以说是仿文艺复兴与复古主义的混合体(Bligaard,2008;Smidt,2018a)。还有一个更严重的案例是维堡大教堂(Viborg Cathedral)在1864年到1876年间的重建。为监督教堂的保护和修复,丹麦于1861年成立了一个专门的教堂委员会。遗憾的是,建筑学的、文化历史的理想追求并不总是与实际价值相吻合。对于维堡大教堂而言,严重的恶化是从委员会决定整修这座大教堂开始的。负责的建筑师尼尔斯·西格弗雷德·内贝隆(Niels Sigfred Nebelong)、朱利叶斯·索勒(Julius Tholle)、赫尔曼·巴格·斯托克(Hermann Baagøe Storck)以及教堂委员会没有保留这座矗立的建筑,而是选择了一个更激进的方案。除了唱诗班席位下面的地下室外,其他的都被拆除了。建筑师们在原址上建造了一座新的教堂,外观类似于假想中的原汁原味的中世纪罗马式教堂(Smidt,2018a)。维堡大教堂是19世纪

图1 新老维堡教堂

图片来源:丹麦国家图书馆。

和 20 世纪早期许多被误导的建筑整修项目之一，这些整修严重损害了纪念性建筑的遗产价值。

对经济增长的追求，导致了以"De seks Søstre"（六姐妹）为代表的一些历史建筑的整体或局部破坏。尽管名字叫作"六姐妹"，"De seks Søstre"实际上是由三座荷兰文艺复兴风格的连体建筑组成的，建于 17 世纪中叶，矗立在克里斯蒂安四世的证券交易所 Børsen 的右侧。1899 年，大银行 Privatbanken 收购了 De seks Søstre，目的是在这里建一个新总部。尽管遭到抗议，银行还是拆除了这些建筑，并用一座大型的但在历史重要性上不及 De seks Søstre 的建筑取而代之。De seks Søstre 的拆除成了制定建筑保护法的主要论据。更令人费解的是，始建于 1650 年的丹麦皇家艺术馆（The Royal Danish Kunstkammer）（同时也作为皇家图书馆[The Royal Library]）遭到破坏。20 世纪初，丹麦国家档案馆（Danish National Archives）馆长维赫尔姆·阿道夫·塞切尔（Vilhelm Adolf Secher）将丹麦皇家艺术馆视为建设现代档案馆的理想选址。因此，他提议对这处建筑进行大修，而大修会严重损害建筑的遗产价值。通过政治关系，塞切尔成功执行了他的计划（Bendsen & Morgen 2018；Mogensen，2001；Smidt，2018a）。丹麦皇家艺术馆的例子说明，即使是在保护文化遗产的行业中，也存在着对内嵌在建筑物中的文化遗产的漠视。

图 2　1899 年六姐妹

图片来源：Johannes Hauerslev，丹麦国家图书馆。

列入遗产名录的建筑

庆幸的是，上述及其他类似案例激起了群众对忽视建筑遗产的反对，最终促成了"1918 保护法"的诞生。在此之前，丹麦皇家艺术学院（The Royal Danish Academy of Fine Arts）曾以比利时和法国的相关法律为参考，于 1905 年提出了丹麦的第一个建筑保护法案。尽管这一提案对建筑的私人所有权有所限制，但学院认为，遗产之于全社会的艺术、历史和民族价值远在这些担忧之上。与此相反，丹麦国家博物馆（National Museum of Denmark）于 1907 年提出过另一项法案，在该提案中，保护是通过所有者和当局的互谅互让进行的。这两项法案最终都没有被提上丹麦议会，但后者成了"1918 保护法"制定的准绳（Smidt，2018a）。

1918 年 3 月 12 日，丹麦议会通过了"1918 保护法"。该法律明确规定要建立遗产名录，列出全国的在建筑学和文化意义上最重要的建筑。进一步指派了专门的委员会，评估了哪些建筑值得被列入这份名单。到 1920 年，已有 1 145 处建筑进入了遗产名录。这是一个相当可观的数字，但还应提到的是，丹麦国家博物馆和丹麦皇家艺术学院在 1918 年之前就已经为此做了大量准备工作（Smidt，2018b；Tønnesen，2018a；Bendsen & Morgen，2018）。

遗产名录分为两个独立的等级——

一、历史意义或建筑学品质十分优秀的建筑，对其进行拆除、不尊重历史的修改或忽略将造成丹麦国家文化财富的重大损失。

二、历史意义或建筑品质学较为一般，但对其保护仍具有重要意义的建筑（Smidt，2018b）。

对一类和二类建筑的限制政策是完全不同的。未经委员会批准，一类建筑的所有者不得对建筑作任何更改。二类建筑只受到不被拆除的保护，其遗产价值的幸存主要仰赖业主的善念。一名单主要是保护文艺复兴时期和巴洛克早期建筑，而二名单主要是由较新的建筑构成。为防止建筑被拆除，委员会决定在将建筑列入遗产名录前不告知其私人业主（Smidt，2018b；Tønnesen，2018a）。

尽管起初的遗产名录中大部分建筑的收录都是合情合理的，但仍有一些建筑的上榜或缺席以及有一些建筑被评为二类的情况令人不解。例如，委员会将位于霍尔特（Holte）的 18 世纪的乡村庄园（Gammel Holtegård）列入了一类名单，而位于卡拉姆堡（Klampenborg）的更具原真性的 Christiansholm 只获评二类。可能出于某种原因，委员会忽略了 Gammel Holtegård 曾在 1901 年进行过一次扭曲了建筑原貌的大翻修。还有一些复制品也登上了初始名录,如位于赫索姆(Hørsholm)的一座纪念当地农业改革的方尖碑。该纪念碑高5米,由法国建筑师尼古拉斯·亨利·贾尔丁(Nicolas Henri Jardin)设计,原建于1766年。委员会忽略了它的现存实物是1894年按原样建造的复制品。委员会似乎也忽略了某些特定的建筑类型,例如具有重要文化意义的木结构建筑和农舍,特别是富南岛(Funen)的此类建筑,它们直到20世纪80年代末才得到保护。当时,官方意识到这些类型的建筑已遭大面积破坏,因此进行了专门的调查,以便将仍存留的木结构建筑和农舍列入遗产名录。此项调查的清单对诸如车站、学校和乳制品场等其他被忽视的建筑遗产有至关重要的作用,但由于保护成本高昂,它们还是被放弃了。在另一些案例中,建筑能否进入名单则显得更为偶然,往往取决于某些个人或当地团体的认知和努力。例如艺术史学家哈拉尔德·兰伯格(Harald Langberg),他在1940年到1949年间作为主要推动者使895处建筑列入了遗产名录。另一个例子是在1954年到1959年之间共有47家磨坊被列入名录,这主要是专门研究磨坊的专家安德斯·杰斯珀森(Anders Jespersen)努力的成果,他当时是特别建筑委员会的雇员。此外还有一些案例是勤勉的地方历史协会或市政当局游说委员会的结果,一些特定区域的建筑也由此被列入了遗产名录。(Kjær,2010;Smidt,2018b;Tønnesen,2018b;Jensen,2018)随着时间的推移,一些团体开始对委员会和遗产名录提出质疑。尤其是现代主义建筑师们认为遗产名录只看到过去,指责特别建筑委员会是困扰现代城市发展的障碍。另一方面,文化史学家也提出了对委员会忽视的某些建筑类型(如农舍)和地理区域的担忧(Bendsen & Morgen,2018)。

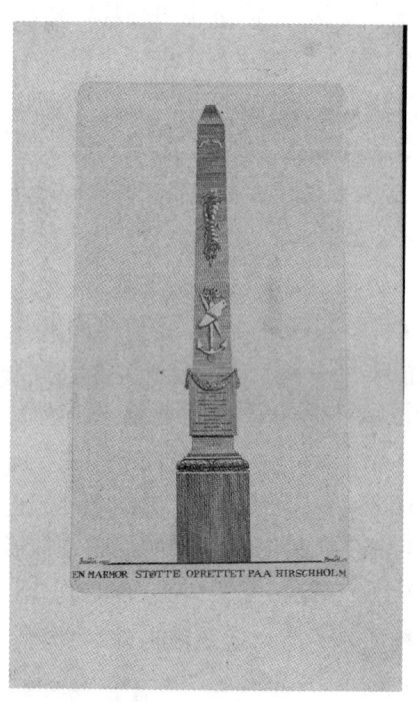

图3 位于霍索姆,刻画了尼古拉斯·亨利·贾丁的方尖碑

图片来源:丹麦国家图书馆。

时隔48年后,对二类建筑的保护需求开始显现。因此,对保护法的第一次立法修改之一,就是二类建筑的外部变更需要获得委员会的批准,然而这项修改并没有生效。此后这两份名单于1979年废止,取而代之的是一份包含着此前的

一类、二类建筑的新名单(Bendsen & Morgen 2018：178-9,211-4)。这一废止意味着之前 B 名单上的建筑将有相当一部分因达不到遗产评估标准而被清出名单。此次除名是由于丹麦对所有列入遗产名录的建筑的建筑学和文化价值，进行了大规模的审查(2010—2016)。到目前为止，遗产名录中包含的约 9000 处建筑中有 7% 被除名，其中大部分是二类建筑。

SAVE 鉴定和 SAVE 评估法

虽然保护法保护了丹麦建筑遗存中很重要的一部分，但还有一些未被列入遗产名录却具有重要文化意义的建筑仍未受到保护，其中许多是关于丹麦最大的一部分人口(即农村人口和贫困城镇人口)的历史的重要史料。相比之下，遗产名录主要收录的是精英阶层使用的建筑，即城堡和庄园。从 20 世纪 40 年代开始，城市更新拆除了一些原属于社会底层的建筑，造成了全国范围的建筑遗产的重大损失。一些市政府注意到了这个问题，对辖区内的此类建筑实施了保护，然而其他市政当局却认为保护这些建筑会妨碍新项目的建设。显然，一种能够评估这些建筑的保护价值的方法已成为现实需要，SAVE 鉴定应运而生，它根据五个方面的价值对建筑进行评估。

理想情况中的 SAVE 鉴定包括三个阶段。第一阶段是初步调查，由一家建筑顾问公司收集该市的地形、历史和建筑信息。为全面了解一个城市的建筑遗产，顾问公司将先进行初步登记。收集的信息以初步报告的形式发布，并附有展示该市现有全部建筑物的地图，经由当地的利益团体审阅后方能获得批准。这个利益团体通常由顾问公司代表、市政当局的项目经理、当地政界人士以及当地博物馆、档案馆、房主协会和遗产协会的代表组成。如果获批，报告将作为后续 SAVE 鉴定的工具(Tønnesen, 2000；Høi & Stenak, 2011)。鉴于初步报告质量的重要性，当地利益团体成员(特别是博物馆或档案馆)的任何建议都应当被纳入考虑。然而不幸的是，情况并非总是如此。要么是因为资金上周转不开，要么是因为人们普遍对文化机构的建议不感兴趣，这使得对报告的任何修改都困难重重。弗雷登斯堡市(Fredensborg)建筑的重新登记就是这样，顾问公司提供的初步报告不能令人满意，因此被当地博物馆否决了。然而，既没有时间也没有资金对报告进行修订，因此随后的 SAVE 登记就是以这份曾被博物馆否决的材料为基础的。[①]

[①] 据 2018 年 10 月 23 日对赫索姆地方档案馆馆员汉斯(Hans Jørgen Winther Jensen)的访谈。

在第二阶段,顾问公司对每处建筑进行实际的 SAVE 登记。为防止鉴定范围过大或花费过高,市政当局将范围限制在某一特定年份(如 1940 年)前建造的建筑(Tønnesen,2000;Høi & Stenak,2011)。市政当局也可以以地理分布或主题(如农舍)进行限定。

在第三阶段,实际结果以地图集的形式发布,其中包括对该市的地形描述、对其历史发展的叙述以及对当地建筑及其特征的评述。这些地图集还包含建筑物的制图说明,并附有描述其具有保护价值的文化品质的文本。另有地图以三种颜色标示已登记的建筑,分别代表较高保护价值、中等价值及较低价值(Tønnesen,2000;Høi & Stenak,2011)。

现行的评估建筑保护价值的 SAVE 评估法,由建筑学价值、文化历史价值、环境价值、原真性和保存状况共五个中间价值组成。一座拥有较高建筑学价值的建筑首先对外在品质有要求,诸如良好的比例、各部分之间的协调以及建筑学上的形式、材料与功能间的相互作用。建筑还将被与该地区的同类建筑作比较,以甄别其在当地背景中属特定建筑类型或地方建筑风格的优良、一般或较差个案。文化历史价值由多方面评判标准决定,例如建筑是否代表一种地方建筑风格或一个特殊时期的风格,以及它是否展现了某种特殊的建造技艺。设计和材料方面的技术创新也要被评估。最终,一个有点流于表面的审查决定了该建筑是否具有某种历史价值,这种历史价值必须在建筑自身中得以体现。只有在极少数情形中,重要历史人物与建筑的关联才会影响到文化历史价值的评估。环境价值与建筑在特定文化区域的意义相关,如果建筑的存在提高了邻近建筑物、建筑群或景观的整体文化价值,则认为该建筑的环境价值较高。建筑的原真性与外观的原始度相关,如果重建破坏了原始外观,那就有必要测定能否进行复原。在某些情况下,后期修改实际上能够维护原始外观的价值。某些修改甚至具有其自身的建筑学和文化历史价值。建筑的技术状况与得当的维护相关。一般来说,建筑的保存状况对整体价值的影响不大,因为恰当的修复可以保护建筑的建筑学、文化历史和环境价值。不过在拆除被认为值得保护的建筑时,技术状况仍是一个决定性因素。在过去几年里,就有一些值得保护的建筑由于技术状况不佳而被拆除。

每项价值由 1—9 的分数决定,1—3 分为较高价值,4—6 分为中等价值,7—9 分为低价值。评分在 1—4 分的建筑被视为值得保护。当地的博物馆和档案馆通常扮演顾问和监督的角色。然而,如果市政当局决定拆除具有高 SAVE 值的建筑,博物馆除了指责也无可奈何。整体价值不是五个中间价值的平均值。诸多案例表明,是某些中间价值决定了整体价值。根据最新的

SAVE 评估法操作指南，建筑学价值、文化历史价值和环境价值比原真性和技术状况重要。奇怪的是，在旧版的介绍和描述中，建筑学价值是整体价值的决定性因素。

从 20 世纪 80 年代末开始，许多市决定采用 SAVE 评估法来获取具有保护价值的建筑名单。迄今约有 12.5 万处建筑被登记为有保护价值的建筑。SAVE 值只是作为一种参考，不同于被列入遗产名录的建筑，并没有法律去保护具有高 SAVE 值的建筑。尽管如此，SAVE 评估法和登记册仍是市政当局借以了解在建筑学和文化意义上具有重要性的建筑的必要工具，在某些情况下，它能够保护建筑，使其不被拆除、破坏结构或损毁外观。

SAVE 登记册中的遗产名录建筑

尽管丹麦建筑遗产事实上有很大一部分是通过 SAVE 评估法确定的，但关于该方法有效性的研究却很少（如 Bech-Nielsen，1998；Vadstrup，2017）。评价 SAVE 评估法的一种路径是评估列入遗产名录的建筑的 SAVE 评分。遗产名录建筑的外部（及内部）代表着最高的建筑和文化标准（Bendsen & Morgen，2018），因此我们推测这些建筑理应也获得较高的 SAVE 评分。然而，情况并非总是如此，在使用 SAVE 评估法评估时，许多列入遗产名录的建筑只获得了 3 分或 4 分的总分。例如位于希勒勒市的一座 1775 年的新古典主义建筑，第一任主人 F.C. 布拉默（F. C. Brammer）将其命名为安纳堡（Annaborg），是一座四合院庄园的主翼。它既是布拉默家族的住所，同时也是布拉默作为郡总管（Amtmann；the senior retainer of an Amt）的办公室。根据遗产报告记述的建筑外部细节，包括纪念碑式的花岗岩基座、细檐口和大型花岗岩楼梯入口等，显示该建筑是一位高级官员的家。安纳堡的重要的建筑学和文化价值还包括它独立式的、简洁的结构和灰泥墙，同时它也是一座典型的新古典主义建筑。因此安纳堡 4 分的 SAVE 总评分就有点令人诧异。[①] 与安纳堡位于同一条街的还有另一座 18 世纪的建筑。这座建于 1721 年的橘红色粉刷建筑，是负责皇家马匹繁育和改良的官员的家和办公场所。该建筑是由皇家建筑师约翰·科尼利厄斯·克里格（Johan Cornelius Krieger）主持建造，这成为保护它的一个重要理由。克

[①] 遗产报告见：https://www.kulturarv.dk/fbb/downloaddokument.htm?dokument=123776567. （2018 年 10 月 8 日获取）；SAVE 评分见：https://www.kulturarv.dk/fbb/bygningvis.pub?bygning=6199762. (2018 年 10 月 8 日获取)。

里格的才华比不上 18 世纪的丹麦建筑大师劳力兹·德·图拉（Laurids de Thurah's）、尼古拉·艾格特维德（Nicolai Eigtved）和尼古拉·亨利·贾尔丁（Nicolas Henri Jardin），但他的建筑成就仍令人赞叹，并且他的建筑作品只有少量存世，于是位于希勒勒的这一座就成了能够代表其技艺的罕见之作。此外，这座建筑是巴洛克晚期建筑中的一个有趣的案例，一些原始的细节和建筑元素，如门、窗等，也被保留了下来。这一次，SAVE 评估法又给出了一个意外的结果，该建筑的总评分只有 3 分。①

有人可能会说这两个例子是少数失误，不代表 SAVE 登记册的一般倾向。为了进一步校验，我们对北西兰岛（Northern Zealand）诸市以及格莱萨克瑟（Gladsaxe）、巴勒鲁普（Ballerup）、海莱乌（Herlev）和根措夫特（Gentofte）等地的所有遗产名录建筑进行了鉴定，获得了它们的 SAVE 评分，累计 474 处。其中，115 处获得 1 分，124 处获得 2 分，190 处获得 3 分，40 处获得 4 分，有 2 处获得 5 分，还有 3 处只获得 6 分。②

分析还显示某些特定类型建筑的评分总体高于其他类型的建筑。城堡、庄园和年久的乡村田园等纪念性建筑通常能达到 1 分或 2 分，20 世纪丹麦著名建筑师如莫根·拉森（Mogens Lassen）、约恩·奥伯格·乌特松（Jørn Oberg Utzon）和阿恩·雅各布森（Arne Jacobsen）等人的建筑正是如此。相比之下，遗产名录中列出的联排房屋，如埃尔西诺（Elsinore）老城中心的那些联排房屋，通常总分为 3 分或 4 分，很少能得到 2 分，没有 1 分。很难确定造成这种差异的确切原因。仅从审美角度来看，联排房屋可能不能代表丹麦最好的建筑，埃尔西诺的情况似乎就是如此。在这里，被列入遗产名录的城镇房屋的建筑学价值都没得到 1 分，它们更有可能拿到 5 分而不是 2 分。审美外观并不是评估的正式要素（Høi & Stenak, 2011），然而人们不禁这样怀疑，尤其是在我们考虑到一个顾问必须在 20 分钟内完成对一处建筑的 SAVE 评估时。另一个看似可信的解释是，埃尔西诺的 SAVE 鉴定在授予建筑较高 SAVE 值时明显趋于保守。埃尔西诺是此次调查中拥有遗产名录建筑最多的城市。尽管如此，顾问们只对 6 处建筑给出了最高 SAVE 值。其中两处是教堂，即圣·奥拉夫教堂（Saint Olaf's Church）和圣·玛丽教堂（Saint Mary's Church）（教堂未被列入遗产名录）；后四处是列入遗产名录的建筑，包括卡梅利特修道院（Carmelite Priory）的两座建

---

① 遗产报告见：https://www.kulturarv.dk/fbb/downloaddokument.htm?dokument=123776636.（2018 年 10 月 8 日获取）；SAVE 评分见：https://www.kulturarv.dk/fbb/bygningvis.pub?bygning=6207840.（2018 年 10 月 8 日获取）。
② SAVE 登记册网站未更新，一些列入遗产名录的建筑可能还没有被纳入。

筑、玛丽恩利斯特城堡(Marienlyst Castle)的主体建筑和克伦堡城堡(Kronborg Castle)的主体建筑。

保守的评估并不局限于埃尔西诺。2008 年,弗雷登斯堡市决定重新启动 SAVE 评估。官方称始于 2007 年的一项改革扩大了城市的地理边界,因此旧有的 SAVE 评估不再能覆盖整个城市。[①] 市政委员会决定在全市范围进行新的 SAVE 鉴定,而不是沿用先前评估的 SAVE 值。一个主要原因就是第一次 SAVE 鉴定中有一些评估是保守的,因此不符合弗雷登斯堡市房屋的实际遗产价值。[②]

我们还可以识别出少量但存在问题的遗产名录建筑,它们的中间价值 SAVE 评分与总评分出现偏差。例如,埃尔西诺的一处城镇房屋得到了 4 分、4 分、3 分、5 分、5 分的中间价值评分,其总分为 3 分。鲁泽斯代市(Rudersdal)有一处原属于腓特烈七世(Frederik Ⅶ)的情人的乡村庄园,其中间价值评分为 3 分、2 分、4 分、3 分和 5 分,总分为 1 分。根措夫特的一家 1939 年的加油站的总分也是 1 分,尽管它的中间分为 2 分、2 分、3 分、5 分和 2 分。

图 4　鲁德斯达尔市伯爵夫人路易丝·丹纳(弗雷德里克七世的第三任妻子)乡村庄园

图片来源:Ramblersen,维基共享资源。

[①] 奇怪的是,同样的改革也要求市政当局负责监督被认为值得保护的建筑,使它们和城堡与文化委员会一道成了丹麦建筑遗产的主要管理者。
[②] 据 2018 年 10 月 23 日对赫索姆地方档案馆馆员杰森(Hans Jørgen Winther Jensen)的访谈。

结论

毫无疑问，遗产名录和 SAVE 登记册对保护众多具有重要文化意义的建筑发挥了重要作用。然而正如本文所揭示的，SAVE 评估法也有其自身缺陷。在被调查的市镇中，一些 SAVE 评分与遗产名录建筑的实际遗产价值不符。在 474 处列入遗产名录的建筑中，245 处获得了 3 分或更低的 SAVE 评分。尽管 SAVE 评分 3 分（190 处）也算较高的遗产价值，但人们会预期那些遗产名录中的建筑将自然获得最高分数（1 分或 2 分），而不应该是 4 分（40 处）、5 分（2 处）或 6 分（3 处）。导致这些不合规则和甚至有些错误的评估出现在 SAVE 登记册中的原因可能是多方面的。当地政治利益或对建筑遗产的不关心会影响实际的评估。顾问公司可能准备不充分或没有资格进行调查——或许是因为严格的预算。如果我们考虑到对一处建筑的 SAVE 评估可能最多只需要 20 分钟，而且在许多情况下审美偏好决定了实际评分，那这就特别成问题了。换言之，建筑遗产也许是可以被衡量的，但人们不应忽略，政治利益、经济利益、准备不足或不同的学术偏好都可能会影响任何建筑遗产评估的结果。

（作者单位：北西兰岛博物馆）

参考文献：

1. Gert Bech-Nielsen 1998, *SAVE-Survey of Architectural Values in the Environment. En kritisk analyse*, Copenhagen.
2. Jannie Rosenberg Bendsen & Mogens A. Morgen 2018, *Fredet — Bygningsfredning i Danmark 1918 - 2018*, Copenhagen.
3. Mette Bligaard 2008, *Frederiksborgs genrejsning. Historicisme i teori og praksis*, Copenhagen.
4. Arne Høi and Morten Stenak 2011, *SAVE Kortlægning og registrering af bymiljøers og bygningers bevaringsværdi*, Copenhagen.
5. Torben Lindegaard Jensen, 2018, "De fredede bygninger i landdistrikterne" in Allan Tønnesen et al (ed.), *Hele Samfundets eje. Bygningsfredning i 100 år*, Odense, pp. 119 - 129.
6. Ulla Kjær 2010, *Nicolas-Henri Jardin — en ideologisk nyklassicist*, Copenhagen.
7. Margit Mogensen 2001, *Rigsarkivet. Husene på Slotsholmen*, Copenhagen.
8. Claus M. Smidt 2018a, "Fredning og bevaring før bygningsfredningsloven" in Allan

Tønnesen et al (ed.), *Hele Samfundets eje. Bygningsfredning i 100 år*, Odense, pp. 13 – 45.

9. Claus M. Smidt 2018b, "De første fredninger" in Allan Tønnesen et al (ed.), *Hele Samfundets eje. Bygningsfredning i 100 år*, Odense, pp. 61 – 74.
10. Allan Tønnesen 2000, *InterSAVE International Survey of Architectural Values in the Environment*, Copenhagen.
11. Allan Tønnesen et al (ed.), *Hele Samfundets eje. Bygningsfredning i 100 år*, Odense.
12. Allan Tønnesen 2018a, "Det særlige bygningssyn" in Allan Tønnesen et al (ed.), *Hele Samfundets eje. Bygningsfredning i 100 år*, Odense, pp. 47 – 59.
13. Allan Tønnesen 2018b, "De senere fredninger" in Allan Tønnesen et al (ed.), *Hele Samfundets eje. Bygningsfredning i 100 år*, Odense, pp. 75 – 100.
14. Søren Vadstrup 2017, *ny-SAVE-metoden til udpegning af bevaringsværdige bygninger*, Copenhagen.

中国古代志怪小说中的人文光辉

——以《聊斋志异·陆判》中的异想与妙构为例

宋紫珍　郑承军

　　《聊斋志异》是清代蒲松龄写就的文言志怪小说,奠定了蒲松龄"中国文言短篇小说之王"的地位。《聊斋志异》"一书而兼二体",既有对六朝志怪小说的继承、将奇闻异事进行简单记述的篇章,也有对唐代传奇进行汲取、用生动的描写和曲折的故事情节进行构建的篇章,具备了小说的要素[1]。后者在创作题材上融古出新,在叙述艺术上引人入胜。这些篇章的题材取材于民间传说或前人志怪书籍,也有的来源于蒲松龄的个人创作[2]。在内容上,蒲松龄对人物、环境、事物的描写紧紧围绕着"异"字铺陈,而在故事情节的展开上,蒲松龄多用悬念、转折,使得不同的故事片段完美衔接,写成妙事。

　　想要读懂《聊斋志异》,必须先了解《聊斋志异》所描绘的世界。这个世界中,万物有灵,不仅有人、鬼、神,还有动植物化作的精怪。在《聊斋志异》里,人、鬼、神、精怪可以自由地交往,形态和身份上也存在相互转换的可能性,并不存在不可逾越的鸿沟[2]。故事发生的地点是人世间,人是这个世界的主角,但鬼神精怪的不时介入使得《聊斋志异》中的世界在与真实世界重合的基础上可以随时变为一个奇幻的世界。这是因为鬼神精怪在蒲松龄笔下的世界里,往往比人更神通广大,这种神通广大体现在智谋上,也体现在行为能力上。但是《聊斋志异》里的世界仍然是人的主场,神鬼精怪都在一定的规则内或某些程度上对人产生影响。神可能是天上的飞仙,也可能是地下的阎罗,他们往往掌管人的命数轮回,是人祭拜敬畏的对象。人死为鬼,这里的鬼经常残存着为人时的记忆与理智,分善恶,甚至有的可以在一定时间内与人混居交往。《聊斋志异》中的精怪有在原本

---

[1] 袁世硕:《蒲松龄与〈聊斋志异〉》,山东文艺出版社2004年版,第67页。
[2] 冯伟民:《蒲松龄和〈聊斋志异〉》,中华出局1984年版,第24、58页。

的动植物形态和人之间变换的能力,其智商与情商并不亚于人,可以以其超自然的能力帮助或破坏人的活动。而《聊斋志异》中的人往往有着蒲松龄所处时代存在的各种社会角色,其中,书生是一个经典形象。在《聊斋志异》中,书生、美女、狐仙、鬼神往往会在同一时空交错出现,进行交往,产生爱恨纠葛,甚至出现身份转换,从而演绎出曲折离奇的故事。本文以《聊斋志异》中的《陆判》为例,试图探析蒲松龄蕴藏于其中的奇思异想与精构巧设。

一奇引多奇:《陆判》中的异神、异人、异行、异事

在《陆判》的故事里,神是奇异之神,"人是奇异之人,行是奇异之行,事是奇异之事"。①

故事的主人公朱尔旦,是一名书生,"性豪放。然素钝,学虽笃,尚未知名"。② 朱尔旦"学艺"不高,但人胆大,对于众人的戏言,他信以为真,只身夜赴十王殿,把殿内左廊"绿面赤须,貌尤狰恶"的判官神像背到了众人面前。朱尔旦不仅独自"径去""人者,毛皆森竖"的十王殿,还把背来的陆判"置几上",敬酒邀请判官至其家"觅饮"。第二天,判官真身如约而至,朱尔旦与其"易盏交酬",获悉了判官的"陆"姓。蒲松龄除了正面描写朱尔旦的大胆,还通过侧面描写其他人见到陆判神像或者真身的反应来烘托朱尔旦的大胆。最开始怂恿朱尔旦的诸人见到判官像后"瑟缩不安于座,仍请负去",在得知朱尔旦通过结交陆判得中秋闱之后,又请求朱尔旦为他们引见陆判,但见到"赤髯生动,目炯炯如电"的陆判真身之后,又"茫乎无色,齿欲相击,渐引去"。此外,朱尔旦妻子得知陆判至其家时,也"大骇,戒勿出",但朱尔旦并未听取。就算是出于功利的目的,除朱尔旦外的众人都无法克服对陆判的畏惧,可见朱尔旦的大胆已经不是一般意义上的大胆,可以跨越对鬼神的畏惧之心。因此,朱尔旦的际遇不是其他人能随意拥有的,只有朱尔旦这样与众不同的异人,才有机会结交陆判那样的异神。陆判令人畏惧的外表算是鬼神的标准配置,并不是他的奇异之处。陆判的奇异之处在于他通晓人间学问,并愿意与人交游。朱尔旦初见陆判至其家,以为是自己前一日冒犯陆判,"殆将死矣",不料陆判并未感到冒犯,到访反而是"蒙高义相订",趁着"夜偶暇,敬践达人之约"。更奇的是,朱尔旦与陆判谈论古籍,陆判都能"应答如

---

① 王少华:《一篇换心革面的惊世故事——略论〈聊斋·陆判〉对奇异的叙述》,《档案》2017 年第 4 期,第 31—32 页。
② 本文关于《陆判》故事的引文出自蒲松龄:《聊斋志异》(会校会注会评本),张友鹤辑校,上海古籍出版社 1986 年版,第 1—4、139—146 页。

响",还通晓制举应试的八股文,会时常用朱笔批改朱尔旦习作的文稿,并直率地给予"不佳"的评价。陆判作为冥界的神,常与鬼神打交道,却熟知人世的风俗典章,乐于结交士人,这种人情味正是陆判之异。

朱尔旦与陆判人神结交的异行,来自他们奇想与陆判奇术的完美契合。陆判"三两日辄一来"朱尔旦居所,饮酒论文章,与朱尔旦"情益洽",对于朱尔旦不佳的文思,陆判想出一个办法,即为朱尔旦"破腔出肠胃,条条整理""为君易慧心"。对于蒲松龄那个时代的人来说,人的文思是与心相关的,并没有大脑的概念,因此陆判为朱尔旦换一颗慧心,就是为朱尔旦提升了智力才情,朱尔旦自此"文思大进,过眼不忘",在当年的秋闱中夺得魁首。陆判作为神,有着凡人想不到的奇思,能想到为朱尔旦易心,已经使故事够奇异了,而朱尔旦在易心得益之后,竟然也发出奇想,认为"心肠可易,面目想亦可更",提出了让陆判帮妻子换一颗美人头的想法,陆判应允了朱尔旦,几日后在朱尔旦的协助下成功为朱尔旦妻子换了头。蒲松龄笔下陆判的易心与换头奇术,都是建立在陆判的职务之便与异能基础上的,这两方面的细节使得朱尔旦与陆判的异行更有细节可循。陆判的判官身份使得他可以"在冥间,于千万心中,拣得佳者一枚",才得以为朱尔旦换心理肠,但还需要把朱尔旦"毛窍塞耳"之心带回冥界,"以补阙数"。答应了朱尔旦为其妻换头之后,陆判"徐图之","向艰物色",直至"得一美人首,敬报君命"。蒲松龄对于陆判易心和换头的过程并没有一笔带过,而是通过细节描写凸显陆判的技术之精。朱尔旦换心后,"视榻上亦无血迹","天明解视,则创缝已合,有线而赤者存焉"。陆判为朱尔旦的妻子换头时动作一气呵成,"朱妻醒,觉颈间微麻,面颊甲错;搓之,得血片"。这里朱妻的一些不适和遗留的一些血迹反而让故事更有了一些真实感。朱妻洗漱之后,"举首则面目全非",如画中美人。换头痕迹蒲松龄也写明了:"解领验之,有红线一周,上下肉色,判然而异。"这些易心与换头细节合情合理,符合发展规律,写幻如真。让陆判与朱尔旦的异行更栩栩如生地呈现在读者眼前。

朱尔旦和陆判一个异人,一个异神,在交往中共有异行,演绎出几番异事,既包括朱尔旦易心后际遇的奇妙变化,也包括陆判为朱妻换头后引发的官司和侦破的奇案。朱尔旦换心后,当年就从"尚未知名"转而秋试夺魁,在三十年后即将身死的前五日,有陆判提前告知,得以从容准备身后事。神奇的是,朱尔旦死后,受陆判推荐,在阴间授有官爵,作为鬼,十年间时常能回家照顾妻子、教导儿子。十年后,朱尔旦要赴任成为华山山神,才与妻子儿子永诀。从人到鬼再到山神,朱尔旦每种身份下的奇遇和每次身份的转换都令人称奇。蒲松龄除了在朱尔旦的整体际遇上笔触出奇,还不忘在细节情节上进行奇遇补充。陆判为朱尔旦所易的心来自阴间,也有换下来的朱心补缺数,所以不会引发后续故事。但陆判为朱妻所换的美人头蒲松龄一开始并未说明来处,为后面引发的官司和奇案做了铺垫。美人头的原主是死于非命的吴侍御之女,在停尸期间首级失踪。吴家久寻不得之际,"渐有以朱家换头之异闻吴公者",在核查无误后,便将朱尔旦诉至公堂。此时,陆判出面,以奇术让吴侍御之女托梦父母,指明真凶,并通过"陆判官取儿头与之易之,是儿身死而头生也。愿勿相仇"之言,不仅使得杀人案件水落石出,还使得朱尔旦从此成了吴家的翁婿。换头这一异行引出了无头奇案,朱尔旦从被告变为原告翁婿,这一情节即使是作为朱尔旦奇异人生的插曲,也精彩不减。

《陆判》中,异人遇异神,两者出异行,异行引异事,一波未平,一波又起,"由一奇而引出多奇,层层推进,波澜迭起"①。

文学渊源与思想意蕴:《陆判》中蒲松龄的妙思巧构

《陆判》的故事奇异纷涌,但环环相扣,构思巧妙。构思巧妙之处,一是其情节的文学渊源,二是故事中寄托的思想意蕴。

文学渊源这里涉及《陆判》中情节的本事考证。根据刘勇强先生的定义,本事指"为小说家直接依据的、具有一定情节、人物的文本性素材"②。之所以进行《陆判》情节的本事探寻,是因为本事研究对理解小说的思想内涵和艺术价值有重要意义。叶德均认为《聊斋志异》中因袭晋唐志异、传奇,元明戏曲的本事的地方很多,还提到了王晫的《今世说》和徐芳的《换心记》可以作为《聊斋志异的本事》。③ 而朱一玄也直接指出,刘义庆的《幽明录·贾弼之》、皇甫氏的《原化记·刘氏子妻》、徐芳的《换心记》、王晫的《今世说·赏誉》、钮琇的《觚剩》,皆是《陆判》的本事。④

《陆判》中朱尔旦与判官结交的本事则可见于《觚剩》。《觚剩》里的张生"屡就童子试不遇",在寺庙与判官结交后,在判官的帮助下做了官。《陆判》中的换头洗肠的本事可见于刘义庆的《幽明录·贾弼之》和王晫的《今世说·赏誉》。

---

① 王少华:《一篇换心革面的惊世故事——略论〈聊斋·陆判〉对奇异的叙述》,《档案》2017年第4期,第31—32页。
② 刘勇强:《古代小说创作中的"本事"及其研究》,《北京大学学报(哲学社会科学版)》2015年第4期,第71页。
③ 叶德钧:《戏曲小说丛考》下册,中华书局1979年版,第591页。
④ 朱一玄:《〈聊斋志异〉资料汇编》,南开大学出版社1984年版,第50—55页。

《幽明录·贾弼之》中,贾弼之被梦中"面查丑甚"之人换去了自己的头。《今世说》里,周立五面相不好,"颧未高,两颐逼而秃,面有槁色",参加科考也不顺利,梦到被人换上了"须髯如戟"的头,醒来后"颧渐高,两颐骨渐丰,须髯髵然日益长",过了几年,又梦到一个老者"涤其脏腑",后来"文学日进,历试两闱皆获售"。而易心的本事可见于徐芳的《换心记》,该故事中的进士公在夜半被金甲神换心之后,从连"寻常书卷,不能辨句读",变为"胸次开朗""所授书,辄能记诵"。蒲松龄在《聊斋自志》中曾写明自己"才非干宝,雅爱搜神;情类黄州,喜人谈鬼:闻则命笔,遂以成编……集腋为裘,妄续幽冥之录"[①],从蒲松龄的自述中可以看到蒲松龄对南北朝以来各种志怪者和志怪作品的关注,因此,上述对《陆判》本事的考证有其合理性。刘勇强认为,本事研究最值得关注的内容包括情节的再生、文体的转换、叙述的调整,其中叙述的调整包含叙述结构的裁剪与重组、叙述角度与方式的改动、叙述者身份的变化等。[②]蒲松龄汲取了前人志怪小说中与判官交友、易心、换头、洗肠的情节,对于判官交友进行情节和细节填充,对易心、换头的效果进行重新包装,将已有故事通过整合重塑糅合在了一起,使它们环环相扣,达到了融古焕新的效果。

在巧妙构思串联奇异情节的同时,蒲松龄也将他的道德观念和政治理想镶嵌到了各个情节中,就如蒲松龄在《聊斋自志》中所提到的:"浮白载笔,仅成孤愤之书。"

朱尔旦与陆判的交往故事体现出了蒲松龄对于文思举业的期望,也有对命运天定的不甘与无奈。朱尔旦在陆判帮其易心后,文思畅达,得中秋闱,但陆判也提前告诫过:"君福薄,不能大显贵,乡、科而已",果然,朱尔旦参加后来的会试时,三次都因为违反场规失败,自此"灰心仕进。积三十年"。这里易心的效果是有限的,还不能完全改变朱尔旦的命数。包括陆判告知朱尔旦其即将身死时,也提出了"惟天所命,人何能私?且自达人观之,生死一耳,何必生之为乐,死之为悲"的开解。而朱尔旦从人变成鬼后,也一直陪伴着家人,操心儿子的读书事宜直至儿子长大,在临行赴任华山山神之际,朱尔旦还叮嘱儿子不要荒废学业,把自己在人世间未竟的科考理想寄托在了儿子身上。不管是科举还是生死,这里都有对命数的不甘,但最后只能妥协。蒲松龄自19岁得中秀才之后,便再没有在科举上有所成,他在《陆判》篇末的"异史氏曰"中感叹道,"陆公者,可谓

---

① 蒲松龄:《聊斋志异》(会校会注会评本),张友鹤辑校,第1—4、139—146页。
② 刘勇强:《古代小说创作中的"本事"及其研究》,《北京大学学报(哲学社会科学版)》2015年第4期,第71页。

媸皮裹妍骨矣。明治至今,为岁不远,陵阳陆公犹存乎?尚有灵焉否也?为之执鞭,所忻慕焉"。蒲松龄感叹陆判貌丑心善,能在朱尔旦的举业上援手相助,自己如今的年龄,如果能得见陆判,就是为他赶车也愿意。表现出了蒲松龄对于自己举业现状的不满,对陆判的向往其实也是一种对现实的无可奈何。

朱尔旦身死后终于在阴间满足了自己对仕途的期盼,受陆判推荐,在阴司"授有官爵",但也没有马上割舍在阳世间的妻子与儿子,仍然常回阳世间陪伴妻与子。朱尔旦对儿子跨越生死的舐犊情深,蒲松龄做了充分的描摹。"子玮,方五岁,来辄捉抱;至七八岁,则灯下教读。子亦慧,九岁能文,十五入邑庠,竟不知无父也";儿子长大成人行将永别时,朱尔旦叮嘱儿子不要荒废学业,与儿子约定十年后再相见。十年后再见时,朱尔旦已是华山山神,儿子也已为官。朱尔旦只肯定了儿子官声好,自己可以瞑目,便离去了,但"去数步,回望,解佩刀遣人持赠",以让儿子"佩之当贵"。配刀上刻有寄语:"胆欲大而心欲小,智欲圆而行欲方"。这句话出自《旧唐书》,告诫儿子要有壮志,也要细心筹谋,行事要灵活圆滑,但也一定要正大光明。后来朱尔旦还托梦让儿子在孙子中挑选继承配刀的继承人,保佑孙子也仕途通达。这种跨越时空、人鬼、人神的舐犊牵挂,与中华传统的"父母之爱子"的亲情相符合,充满温情。

当然,朱尔旦从寂寂无名的考生到让同社生"相视而惊"的秀才,再到身死后得以在阴司里做官,都离不开陆判的相助。陆判与朱尔旦跨越人神的友情也是《陆判》想要传达的能量。凡人朱尔旦不因陆判是面貌骇人的鬼神而像其他人一样对陆判避而不见,而是待之以礼,诚心与之畅饮交谈,"时抵足卧"。通晓世俗典籍的陆判也不因为朱尔旦文思不佳而嫌弃这个凡人,反而利用自己的异能帮助朱尔旦在举业上更进一步。对于朱尔旦对美貌配偶的追求,陆判也予以满足,并在朱尔旦陷入无头公案时帮助朱尔旦脱困。在朱尔旦即将身死前提醒其早做准备,在其身死后推荐他在阴间做官,这才使朱尔旦有了仍然能够在阳世间照顾妻与子、日后升为华山山神的机会。朱尔旦这个异人和陆判这一异神各异其异,但又刚好意气相投。陆判方对朱尔旦的帮助与投入明显更多,但是,朱尔旦对陆判的陪伴之功也不能小觑。两人的友谊是《陆判》各色奇异情节发生的基础,也是《陆判》中的一抹人情暖色。

结语

《陆判》是《聊斋志异》中内容丰富多彩、情节曲折多变、构思绝妙精巧、意蕴耐人寻味的范例。蒲松龄以一奇引多奇,由异人朱尔旦引出异神陆判,而后才有一系列因两者生出的异行与异事。而《陆判》中的经典奇异情节,很多都有本事可寻,是对志怪小说题材的继承与发展,对这些情节的巧妙改编与串联,也体现了蒲松龄高超的创作艺术。而贯穿于全文的思想意蕴,也体现了蒲松龄乃至他所处时代的道德观念和政治理想。《陆判》对中国古代志怪小说和中国古代文化人文光辉的体现,一方面在于志怪小说创作者创作主观能动性的充分发挥,并且这种发挥是基于所处时代大众所广泛接受的文化氛围和幻想逻辑,进而经营出一个便于创作者展开故事推演的奇异世界的;另一方面在于志怪小说的创作里既有对前人创作的继承与推进,也有借言虚幻世界才可能之异事,阐发真实世界确存在之义理的文化匠心。通过对《聊斋志异》中《陆判》篇异想与妙构的解读,既可以展示中国古代文言志怪小说的创作思路,也可以展示蒲松龄所在时代的人所追求的道德情感及政治理想,这对于了解中国古代文言志怪小说和中国古代文化的人文光辉,是一个很好的助力。

(作者单位:北京语言大学、北京第二外国语学院)

少林功夫在世界舞台的传播分析

曹洪瑞

"一部单车,一碗粥,一个沙发,是一种生活,也是一种哲学。"这就是"Hygge"。"Hygge"可谓是丹麦的金字招牌,这个仅有五个字母的单词向人们揭示了丹麦成为全球幸福指数排行前三的国家的秘密。"Hygge"是一种心态,也是一种哲学,让人们选择使自己安逸舒适的方式,从忙碌的生活中、从种种繁琐事情中脱离出来。这让我联想到中国的禅文化。禅宗文化使人修身养性,通过静心调息的方法忘却现实中的一切烦恼,收获健康,愉悦身心。禅宗思想又同武道精神相融合,其中少林功夫尤为突出。

少林功夫(又称"少林武术")是指在嵩山少林寺这一特定佛教文化环境中历史的形成,以佛教神力信仰为基础,充分体现佛教禅宗智慧,并以少林寺僧人修习的武术为主要表现形式的传统文化体系[①]。2006 年被录入国家级非物质文化遗产名录之中。据史料记载,虽然尚未有详细的少林功夫出现的确切时间,但有"拳始北魏稠功著"的记载,少林寺最早的武僧稠禅师便是少林功夫的创始者。地处中原腹地,交通便利,连接天南海北,又处五岳之一的嵩山,自然是兵家必争之地。为保护寺院不受攻击,为在战乱的年代幸存下来,加上长时间的打坐静卧,身体素质下降,少林众僧在他的倡导下,逐渐习拳,这便是少林武术的雏形。少林功夫只为自卫,不为攻击,所以少林功夫以防为先,攻击为后[②]。少林功夫技术体系庞大,但主要可以归为两大类别:如七星拳这样的徒手搏斗和少林棍这样的持械搏斗。除此之外,另有七十二绝技以及点穴、气功等独特的功法。练习少林功夫可以健身养生,其还能展示"静若处子,动若脱兔"的人体动作美感。

---

① 释永信:《禅武一体的少林功夫》,《少林与太极》2015 年第 1 期,第 4 页。
② 吕宏军、滕磊:《少林功夫》,浙江人民出版社 2005 年版,第 8 页。

少林功夫是中华文化瑰宝。少林功夫是经过上千年的不断发展,通过少林寺师父的言传身教和少林子弟的刻苦训练而一代代传承下来。它在演变发展的过程中,以开放的心胸不断吸收文学、哲学等方面的理论。其灵活的的武术套路与中国古典文学有着密切的联系。如少林棍中的"悟空藏棍"的出处正是中国四大名著之一的《西游记》;中国古典哲学认为"气"是构成世界的基本要素,这种"气"的哲学思想在少林功夫中体现得淋漓尽致,如少林硬气功讲究把人体体内的"气"运作起来,以抵挡武器或外来其他攻击。少林功夫丰富的文化内涵使其成为东方武术文化的代表。

少林功夫起源河南嵩山少林寺,这座"天下第一名刹"有着 1500 年的历史。"少林者,少室之林也。"寺居少室山阴的丛林之间,定名"少林"①。少林寺历史悠久,1963 年被河南省人民政府公布为第一批省级重点文物保护单位;2007 年被国家旅游局正式批准为第一批国家 5A 级旅游景区;2010 年包括少林寺常住院、初祖庵、塔林在内的天地之中历史建筑群被联合国教科文组织列为世界文化遗产。公元 495 年,北魏孝文帝为天竺高僧修建少林寺,少林寺便成为传播佛学的宗教场所。这座千年古刹经历过风吹日晒的自然损坏,也经历过历朝历代的人为破坏,仍屹立至今,成为具有较多历史、文学、科学价值的名胜古迹。今之少林寺常住院,为住持僧及众执事僧主持佛寺活动和起居活动的场所,为寺院中心院落,现通称少林寺②。寺内有七进院落,四周西有塔林、北有达摩洞、南有二祖庵、东有广慧庵。少林建筑不只是诵经的地方,也是寺内僧人的训练场。比如,千佛殿以殿内"十三棍僧救唐王"等壁画而闻名遐迩,是少林寺现存最大的殿宇。殿内有四十八个脚踏陷坑与几根斜柱,据说,这些脚坑是上百年的功夫训练所形成,武僧练武时贯通的气运行到脚,再用脚蹬地,强大的撞击力在地上留下了这些印记。这些斜柱是武僧练武时用肘臂撞击,强大的撞击力使柱子偏离基座。"罗马不是一日建成的",少林功夫也不是一日就能练成的,这些都是武僧苦练功夫的见证。

少林功夫与少林寺不可分开而论,少林寺是少林功夫的摇篮,对推广创新少林功夫起着重要的作用,少林功夫让全中国乃至全世界知晓这座古刹,使众功夫爱好者慕名而来。少林功夫在世界范围的传播,为少林寺吸引不少粉丝,不仅拉动了少林寺旅游业的发展,还使少林功夫成了少林寺与世界沟通的媒介,与来自五湖四海的功夫爱好者探讨少林武术的奥秘。

---

①② 吕宏军:《嵩山少林寺》,河南人民出版社 2002 年版,第 2 页。

少林功夫在国际上的传播形式与现状

古话有"谈武侠,必言少林",可从其中看出少林功夫在中国享有极高的地位及影响力。中国自改革开放以来,打开国门,走向世界,传播中国文化,少林寺主持释永信大师也抓住改革开放的机遇,自1987年主持少林寺以来,搭上开放的顺风车,使少林寺走在中华文化世界传播的前列,让少林功夫成为世界文化中的一颗耀眼的星星。少林功夫在国际上主要有三种传播方式。

一是少林功夫与影视艺术结合走上世界舞台。有"天下第一门派"美誉的少林功夫基本上是中华武术题材电影创作与改编的首选。1982年,电影《少林寺》在全球范围内上映,好评如潮,这不但吸引世界的功夫爱好者前往少林寺,拜师学"术",也掀起了少林功夫的热潮,在影视圈里刮起一阵"少林风"。之后,出现了更多少林题材的影视作品,如《少林小子》《新少林五组》《新少林寺》等。电影为追求影视效果,可能会虚构一些故事使之出彩,而纪录片则不同,纪录片是以真实生活为素材,以真人真事为对象、以完整记录真实的一种影视方式,少林题材的纪录片意在为世人展现真正的少林。由中央电视台与河南电视台联合制作的纪录片《功夫少林》向全球观众展示了21世纪的今天,代代功夫人如何通过少林功夫领悟生存之道以及对生命的理解[①]。

功夫与舞台艺术的融合是传统武术在现代发展的新方式。一部少林功夫与现代舞蹈结合的跨界舞剧《空间》,在伦敦著名剧场——沙德勒之井剧院(Sadler's Wells Theatre)首次公演后,在欧美等国进行巡回演出。《空间》通过音乐、舞蹈、武术等方式使中华传统文化与现代艺术的发生碰撞[②],这完美的融合与创新不仅让观众通过崭新的方式了解少林禅宗精神,领略少林功夫之美,也给中国传统文化的传播与发展路径开辟了新的道路,使文化传播更上一层楼。

二是少林功夫与武术表演结合走上世界舞台。少林功夫始于中原,但并未局限于中原。释永信大师担任少林寺住持以来,少林众僧参加的国际性会议与对外交流日益增多,少林访问团应邀前往多个国家的多所城市,进行少林武术表演。少林武术表演活动逐渐成为少林文化国际传播的主要方式之一。少林寺武僧团在释永信的带领下已在世界60多个国家与地区进行了少林功夫表演,民间

---

① 《少林功夫今何在?》,央视网,http://jishi.cctv.com/2016/04/26/ARTIW67JOmLD9UJOnEezrhYf160426. shtml? spm = C86503. P4DfMPxErwxg. EMvoNGpSUemF. 2,2016 - 04 - 26。
② 母雨潼、胡平:《跨界舞剧〈sutra〉视角下少林文化的创意研究》,《艺术科技》2020年第33卷第20期,第137页。

还有许多其他团体为少林功夫走向国际做出了巨大的贡献，其中少林塔沟武术学校尤为突出。

少林武术塔沟学校（以下简称"塔沟武校"）是以少林武术为主要特色的学校，自其成立学校以来，共参加国内外重大武术比赛近千场次，2003年至2020年计有十七次参加中央电视台春节联欢晚会并五次获奖，学员先后参加了雅典奥运会、上海特奥会、北京奥运会和残奥会、广州亚运会、南京青奥会、G20峰会、国庆70周年群众游行等重要活动的相关演出，既得到了国家领导人的赞扬，也获得了国内著名导演的高度评价[①]。2008年北京奥运开幕式，塔沟武校2008名学员为世界观众准备了视觉饕餮盛宴——《自然——太极拳》(图1)，该节目以太极阴阳理论为基础，将少林拳的刚猛之劲之与太极拳的阴柔之美完美地结合。塔沟武校通过这样的大舞台用精湛的武术表演、极高的默契度以及团结一致的精神，惊艳四座，将少林元素乃至中华武术元素完美地呈现出来，将中国传统文化与武术瑰宝的魅力充分地展现给全世界。

图1　塔沟武校学员参加北京奥运会开幕式演出《自然》

三是少林功夫与武术比赛结合走上世界舞台。随着少林寺及少林功夫在世界范围内享有盛誉，到少林寺参观、学习少林功夫的人日益增多，为此郑州市政府为了弘扬少林禅宗文化，于1991年举办首届"郑州国际少林武术节"。迄今为止，已经成功举办了十二届少林国际武术节。（前四届为一年一届，之后为扩大规模，改为两年一届。）尽管前七届参赛的国家和地区较少，但成功举办了七届后，少林功夫的知名度得到了提高，广大功夫爱好者也更积极地练习少林功夫。

---

① "集团介绍"，少林塔沟教育集团官方网站，http://www.shaolintagou.com/jituanjieshao，2020 - 11 - 05。

大赛设置不同的比赛项目,同时分设了男女组别,扩大了参赛者的范围,调动了全球范围内功夫人的积极性,为全球功夫人提供练习与切磋少林功夫的国际舞台。2018年10月,第十二届郑州国际少林武术节在登封开幕,来自65个国家与地区的武林高手聚集于此,以武相会,参赛选手年龄最小的2岁,最大的79岁[1]。在武术节期间,郑州市还举办武术表演、嵩山文化展示、非遗项目展示等一系列活动,进一步扩大少林功夫的影响力[2]。

少林功夫在国际传播中存在的问题与对策

少林功夫尽管作为中华文化走向国际的领头羊,但在走向世界舞台的过程中,还是存在很多问题的。

首先,重"艺"轻"禅"。在全球化商业化的大背景下,少林功夫为了能加快走出去的步伐,这个过程中,少林功夫更侧重于武术艺术而不是禅宗文化。在许多国际影视里都出现了少林功夫的身影,然而,为了能达到影视需要的艺术效果,许多影视中把焦点聚焦在少林武术之艺术上,更多绝伦的武打场面的出现使得观众认为少林武功盖世,少林拳法迅猛,少林功夫天下第一,从而产生这样一种错觉,即少林功夫仅仅只是一种艺术表现形式,这完完全全忽略了少林功夫背后的禅宗文化内涵。

少林功夫与禅是不可分割的。针对现在重"艺"轻"禅"的现象,应该加强少林功夫禅、武文化的宣传。功夫,本意远不只是"武术",它在佛教中最初是指打坐的功夫[3]。因此无论是搏击修炼还是打坐静心,皆为功夫。禅修的"静"与武术的"动"的相互之作用才有了今日之少林功夫。如果不对此现象做出相应的措施,无论是国内年轻一代还是国际友人,都丢失少林功夫之禅、武文化这块拼图,就无法拼出一副完整的少林文化拼图。这也凸显了在传播少林功夫的过程中,要做到"禅""武"并重。

其次,从"武"到"舞"。自20世纪以来,传统中国武术受到西方体育竞赛模

---

[1] 银新玉:《第十二届中国郑州国际少林武术节在登封开幕》,《河南日报》,https://www.henan.gov.cn/2018/10-21/712311.html,2018-10-21。

[2] 陈冠男:《第十二届中国郑州国际少林武术节明天在登封举办》,《河南日报》,http://newpaper.dahe.cn/hnrb/html/2018-10/19/content_288740.htm,2018-10-19。

[3] 释永信:《佛教实践中的功夫与禅——在美国加州伯克利学院的主题演讲》,少林寺官方网站,http://www.shaolin.org.cn/templates/T_newS_list/index.aspx?nodeid=26&page=ContentPage&contentid=42435,2020-12-09。

式的影响,以及各种新型形式的舞台艺术,少林功夫的表现形态发生了变化。一方面,1990年,少林功夫被纳入体育竞赛项目,少林功夫中朴实无华小幅度的讲求内劲和攻防的传统风格,被类似杂技和舞蹈的高空旋转、大幅度冲踢等比赛规定动作所取代[①]。这样虽然提升了少林功夫的观赏感,但却使少林功夫变了质,把它变成了类似体操的体育项目。另一方面,固然少林功夫与舞台剧的惊艳搭配能吸引不少观众前去观看,一探传统文化与舞台剧能擦出怎样的火花,但是,舞台剧的内容单一,团队对武术一知半解,导致舞台剧更偏向艺术方面而削弱武术部分,这不利于少林功夫在世界范围的传播。

不忘初心,回归少林的"武"。无论是少林功夫成为体育竞技项目还是与舞台剧的融合,这样做的重要原因之一是有利于少林功夫走出去。一方面要发挥少林功夫的特色,与体操等其他项目区别开来。专门建立武僧团,不仅在体育赛事上,在国际事务方面,调动积极性,更加有力的保护和弘扬少林的"武"。另一方面要与专业人员打造一部既有艺术观感又富有武术文化的精品舞台剧。

最后,"传"而不"宣"。少林功夫对外传播的前提是在国内为大众所知并引以为傲。然而,在国内,无论是国内举行的国际武术比赛还是巡演的武术舞台剧,宣传力度是不够的,官方的宣传不到位,媒体介入太少,所以导致人们在日常生活中很少接触到少林功夫,更别提了解和学习少林功夫及文化了。这无疑是少林功夫走出去道路上的一块绊脚石。

政府采取相关措施,媒体加大宣传力度。政府可以出台相关法律法规保护少林文化,让少林文化走进校园,比如推广少林广播体操,举行少林拳比赛评比等活动。邀请媒体介入,运用现在主流媒体及新媒体方式,加大宣传力度,如发布相关微信公众号消息,拍摄抖音视频,邀请"网红"发布相关微博文案运用流量等方式让更多的人参与相关活动,了解少林功夫。这样的做法可以使国人自己更了解少林功夫,中国现在是个国际化的国家,许多国人走出国门,无论是求学还是旅游,每一个了解少林功夫的中国人,都是少林功夫在国际舞台的实实在在的传播者。

当今的世界是相互包容、相互联系、多姿多彩的。世界文化在这样的大环境下可以相互交流、学习。自中国改革开放以来,中国与世界其他文化的交流往来越来越频繁,中国"一带一路"倡议,也为世界多元化的发展提供了温床,借助多元、包容、自由的文化环境,使少林功夫走向世界,成为世界文化之林的一部分,丰富世界文化,增加世界文化多样性。但世界许多国家或地区因对中国及中华

---

① 吕宏军、滕磊:《少林功夫》,浙江人民出版社2005年版,第186页。

文化缺乏了解,产生了对中国不符事实的刻板印象。少林功夫是"讲述中国故事"的世界语言[①],是中华武术的品牌,是中华文化的典型载体,国际友人可以通过少林功夫进而了解其背后的少林文化乃至中华文化,这也有助于打破刻板印象。"禅""武"并重的少林功夫架起中华文化与世界文化沟通的桥梁,对中华文化及世界其他文化的世界传播起着重要的借鉴意义。

(作者单位:北京第二外国语学院英语学院)

[①] 方国清、王润、骆红斌:《武术传播:讲述"中国故事"的"世界语言"——一项关于国家形象的理论建构》,《浙江体育科学》2011年第1期,第93页。

孔子故里曲阜"三孔"的文化意义建构与海外传播反思

于春华

20世纪初,《安徒生童话》传入中国,为几代中国孩子编织了美好的"童话梦"。丹麦成为当之无愧的"童话王国"。时至今日,安徒生俨然成为丹麦王国的文化符号。如果说于历史长河中,选一人代表中国文化,非孔子莫属。孔子开创的儒家学说是中国传统文化的基本内核。近年来,"孔子热"在全球范围内持续升温,相比之下,作为中国儒学的发祥地、孔子故里曲阜却遭到冷落。在丹麦,安徒生故里菲英岛欧登塞市,几乎成为国内外游客游览丹麦的必经之地。在丹麦旅游局中文官网上,安徒生文化节被推至首页,安徒生博物馆是菲英岛必游景点的第一位。然而,曲阜"三孔"景区却没有如此热度。

世界文化遗产:曲阜"三孔"景区

20世纪,世界范围内大战爆发,现代化进程迅猛推进,给自然景观和历史遗迹带来巨大破坏。联合国教科文组织意识到自然文化遗产正面临着演变和消失的威胁。1972年,教科文组织制定《保护世界文化和自然遗产公约》,以期保护世界上无法替代的文化和自然财产。该公约明确了文化遗产的三类:文物、建筑群和考古遗址。1994年,曲阜"三孔"景区被列入世界文化遗产名录,兼具物质遗产的性质,包括孔庙、孔府、孔林的古建筑和馆藏文物。

曲阜孔庙最初是孔子生前居所。至汉朝,孔子的思想在中国广受推崇。常言道,"千年礼乐归东鲁,万古衣冠拜素王"。汉高祖刘邦曾来曲阜孔庙祭祀孔子。东汉桓帝在位期间,鲁相韩敕主持整修孔庙,曲阜孔庙初具官设庙堂的性质。唐太宗时期,中央下令全国上下兴建孔庙,曲阜孔庙得到进一步修缮,规格提升,规模扩大。"孔庙表率""祭祀孔子"沿袭成为中国社会传统。祭祀乃国之大事,孔庙内十三碑亭里的石碑上记载了历代皇帝曲阜祭孔的经历。历代皇帝为孔子追封谥号,古宅不断扩建,形成如今的规模。曲阜孔庙的主建筑大成殿,仿皇宫而建,十根石柱将大成殿分为九间,进深五间,代表中国传统文化里的"九五至尊"。大成殿檐上由黄色琉璃瓦装饰,在当时只能用于皇室建筑,"四周围以红墙,四角配以角楼"①,大气恢弘,是中国传统建筑的最高规格,足以看出孔子在中国历史上的"至圣"的地位,是中国文化的"皇帝"。曲阜孔庙与北京故宫、承德避暑山庄并称为中国三大古建筑群。"孔庙实际象征着孔子和儒家思想在中国古代社会中所占的崇高地位。可以这样说,一部孔庙的从祀史,就是一部官方意识形态的发展史,就是正统思想文化学说的演变史,同时也是中国传统文化的缩影和象征。"②

孔府,又称衍圣公府,是孔子嫡系子孙——世袭衍圣公居住的府第。孔子一生仕途失意,思想未得到重视。直至汉朝,汉高祖行至曲阜孔庙祭祀孔子,封孔子第八世孙孔腾为"奉祀君",爵位世袭。自此,尽管朝代更迭,孔氏家族与皇族并荣,成为历史上最尊贵的家族。北宋至和二年(1055),宋仁宗赵祯改封孔子46代孙孔宗愿为"衍圣公",并赐新第,衍圣公府(孔府)由此而来。孔子一生推行"周礼",其中宗法制影响至深,直至近代,中国都是典型的宗法社会。"孔氏家族是这一社会中最具典型意义的历史标本。自孔子至其77代嫡孙孔德成,2400多年之间,世次清晰,支脉完整,有明确的家训族规,有严密的管理系统,形成了一个特殊的社会历史景观。"③历代衍圣公居住于此,守护孔子遗物,珍藏御赐祭祀礼器。现孔府占地约7.4公顷,有古建筑480间,分前后九进院落,中、东、西三路布局。从建筑规模和建筑布局来看,现在的孔府"是一座典型的中国贵族门户之家,有号称'天下第一人家'的说法"④。孔府馆藏历史文物十万余件,不仅包含历朝历代皇帝御赐青铜礼器,还收藏有金石、陶瓷、玉器、玛瑙、珍珠及历代名人字画。由此,孔府又兼具部分博物馆的功能。孔氏家族是中国传统家族沿袭传承的范本,历代孔氏子孙辈分均可考据,2005年还被列为吉尼斯世界纪录的"世界最长家谱"。孔府不仅承担了儒学文化发扬的重任,更为世界考察中国宗法传承提供了范例。

孔林,又称"至圣林",位于曲阜城北1.5公里处,占地三千余亩,是孔子及其

---

① 《世界文化遗产——孔府、孔庙、孔林》,中华人民共和国中央人民政府,http://www.gov.cn/test/2006-03/28/content_238291.htm,2006-03-28 13:38)。
②③ 杨朝明:《游访孔庙孔府孔林·东方的文化圣地》,上海:上海古籍出版社2004年版,第4页。
④ 《世界文化遗产——孔府、孔庙、孔林》,中华人民共和国中央人民政府,http://www.gov.cn/test/2006-03/28/content_238291.htm,2006-03-28 13:38)。

后裔埋葬的家族墓地,有坟冢10万余座,"已有2500多年历史,也是目前世界上延时最久,面积最大的氏族墓地。它是我国规模最大、持续年代最长、保存最完整的一处氏族墓葬群和人工园林"。① 孔林内有孔子神道与城门相连,孔子墓位于孔林中部,与二世祖孔鲤、三世祖子思的墓排列在一起,"成掎角之势,按旁听导游的说法,是'携儿抱孙'"②。携儿抱孙是中国古代家族坟墓的布局。孔林地上文物丰富,对于研究中国墓葬制度的沿革和古代政治、经济、文化、风俗、书法、艺术等都具有很高的价值。时至今日,仍有孔子后人葬于此地。家族绵延,代代不息。

孔府、孔庙、孔林,并称"三孔","是中国历代纪念孔子,推崇儒学的表征,以丰厚的文化积淀、悠久的历史、宏大的规模、丰富的文物珍藏,以及极高的科学艺术价值而著称"。③ 作为先圣孔子故里,曲阜被奉为"东方圣城",其文化意义值得从多方面考察,曲阜"三孔"景区作为孔子思想和孔氏家族发展的物质载体,值得国内外学者、游客深入了解。

曲阜"三孔"文化意义

"作为儒家文化之发源地,曲阜旅游景区的主体文化为儒学,其主要思想特色为'圣',以孔子为核心人物,汇集中国两千余年的文化里程碑。"④泱泱华夏,万古江河,上下五千年,作为四大文明古国中,文明唯一没有中断的古国,一脉相承的中华文明是中华儿女的骄傲。有学者评曰,"孔子集前两千五百年之大成,开后两千五百年之新统"。孔子开创的儒学,光照千秋,彪炳日月。孔子一生倡导"仁"的实践,我国著名社会学家费孝通先生在随笔《孔林片思》中曾言,"这次到了孔庙我才更深刻地认识到中国文化中对人的研究早已有很悠久的历史。孔子讲'仁'就是讲处理人与人之间的关系,讲人与人之间如何相处。孔子的家族现在已经到了七十六代了,这说明中国文化具有多么长的延续性!为什么老百姓要保护它?说明它代表着一个东西,代表着中国人最宝贵的东西,这就是中国人关心人与人如何共处的问题"。⑤ 费老的一段话表达了曲阜"三孔"存在两个

---

① 《世界文化遗产——孔府、孔庙、孔林》,中华人民共和国中央人民政府,http://www.gov.cn/test/2006-03/28/content_238291.htm, 2006 - 03 - 28 13:38。
② 干春松:《我们为什么要去曲阜》,《粤海风》2014年第4期。
③ 《世界文化遗产——曲阜三孔景区》,《中国旅游报》2015年3月16日。
④ 孙江虹:《曲阜三孔旅游景区与儒家文化的结合方案》,《兰台世界》2014年第7期。
⑤ 费孝通:《孔林片思》,《读书》1992年第9期。

维度的历史文化意义。一是"三孔"的存在,"在某种意义上是中国文化持续恒久发展的一个重要证据,虽然历史上的每座城池都基本会遭到异族的侵略和来自内部的破坏,但是,对于曲阜的争议却很少"①;二是"三孔"作为孔子思想的物质载体,实质上承载了中国思想体系的独特之处。费老强调了孔子思想中"人与人相处"的精神内核,点出了儒学与其他信仰的根本不同,即"儒家素来'借天道明人事',核心是关心人与人、人与社会的事,而不太关心死后的世界。所以梁漱溟先生说中国文化早熟,很快就走出了信仰,进入了理性主义的时期"。② 由此,中国历史进程中没有演化出西方社会中教会式的宗教。

孔子作为中华文化的代表,他身上有太多思想奥秘值得我们探究。当今,我们处在一个"万物皆媒"的时代,曲阜"三孔"当之无愧成为解码孔子思想产生、传承和接受的媒介符号。孔庙葆圣贤遗韵,道洽大同;孔府秉诗礼垂家,垂范百世;孔林存礼制典范,慎终追远。以孔庙为例,李纪祥教授曾在世界儒学大会上讨论了"孔庙"空间坐落与意义探源问题,从狭义与广义两个维度探讨了孔庙的现世意义。他提出,孔庙首先是血缘性的家庙,又是非血缘性的宗庙世界——血缘性的孔氏后人祭祀祖先;另一方面,孔庙又是"非血缘性的以孔子为主、为之祖的祭祀及其儒家之域世界"。③ 孔庙作为祭祀孔子的场所,其血缘后裔是第一类祭祀者;作为教育者的孔子,孔门弟子祭祀先师,形成了另一种特殊的文化礼仪。孔子修"六书",述《论语》,上至治国安邦,下至待人接物,思想经天纬地,泽被后世。从广义上说,包括全部中国人在内的许多人都受教于孔子,皆为孔子"后学"。祭祀孔子、敬仰孔子已然跨越了血缘限制。"孔庙"作为文化据地突破了血缘、国界限制,为儒家奉行的"天人合一"思想作了最完美的注解。

孔府和孔林也是考察儒家文化的现实标本。孔氏后人衍圣公恪守先祖圣训,孔府至今有一处红漆长凳称之为"冷板凳",又称"阁老凳"。相传明朝权臣严嵩被朝廷弹劾,严嵩为自保,前往曲阜请姻亲衍圣公孔尚贤为其向嘉靖帝求情,衍圣公不为所动,严嵩坐在门外长凳一天无果,最后只得悻悻离开。一处文物,一段历史。诸如此类典故,孔府还有许多,历代衍圣公无疑成为孔子思想优秀的实践者,对学习和感受儒家思想提供了鲜活的案例。孔林亦然。松柏参天,虬枝盘曲,但孔林绝不只是一处自然景观,儒学思想中的家族观念、师生情谊体现得淋漓尽致。

---

①② 干春松:《我们为什么要去曲阜》,《粤海风》2014年第4期。
③ 李纪祥:《"孔庙"的空间坐落与意义探源——文化空间、祭祀空间、政教空间》,《第三届世界儒学大会学术论文集》,2010年。

曲阜"三孔"海外传播反思

1956年,联合国教科文组织公布"世界十大文化名人",孔子位于名单之首。曲阜"三孔"不仅代表了中华文化渊远流长,也为世界文明提供了现实可考的物质载体。孔子不仅是中国的孔子,更是世界的孔子。

近年来,我国采取了相关举措,为曲阜"三孔"走向国际助力:

第一,举办曲阜国际孔子艺术节。"中国(曲阜)国际孔子文化节是为了纪念伟大的思想家、教育家、儒家学派的创始人孔子,进一步弘扬中华优秀传统文化,加强国际间的文化交流与合作而举办的大型国际性节庆活动。迄今为止,已成功举办了36届,在海内外产生了广泛的影响。"[1]孔子文化节每年固定在曲阜举办,为国内外学者、游客通过走进"三孔"了解儒家文化起到了宣传和媒介的作用。除此之外,孔子文化节一直也在努力一步步主动走向国际视野。"1990年,孔子文化节与联合国教科文组织携手办节,孔子文化节的国际性质初现端倪。2004年,孔子文化节组委会组成代表团赴韩国和日本等国家开展推介会,主动出击将孔子文化节推向全世界。2005年与2006年,孔子文化节先后举行了'全球联合祭孔'和'海峡两岸同祭孔'活动。2010年,孔子文化节首次走出国门办节,与联合国教科文组织在巴黎举办'孔子文化周'活动。至此,孔子文化节已经走出国门,走向世界。"[2]由此,曲阜"三孔"更加成为世界了解儒家文化的一个重要窗口。

第二,飞机高铁助力曲阜旅游。2008年,曲阜机场建成并投入使用,方便境外游客飞行直达。京沪高铁于2008年正式开工,2011年,京沪高铁通车,北京—上海段高铁经停曲阜东站。自此,北京至曲阜高铁仅需2小时,上海到曲阜也仅需3小时。实践证明,曲阜机场的落成和高速铁路的贯通为曲阜"三孔"引入了更多的游客。

第三,打造与5A级景区匹配的导游队伍。"2011年8月,曲阜市被确立为山东省三个全国导游管理体制综合改革试点城市之一。曲阜先后推出了'三孔'5A级景区讲解员资格认证制度、县级市单独导游年审试点、成立股份制导游公司、实施导游等级评定制度、全程监管过错退出制度等措施,取得了初步成效,社

---

[1]《世界文化遗产——孔府、孔庙、孔林》,中华人民共和国中央人民政府,http://www.gov.cn/test/2006-03/28/content_238291.htm,2006-03-28 13:38。

[2] 丰诚诚:《基于节事活动的曲阜城市形象传播研究——以曲阜国际孔子文化节为例》,《新闻研究导刊》2018年第1期。

会反响良好。"①建立系统的曲阜"三孔"导游培训体系,有助于提升游客的游访体验,为游客提供准确到位的历史文化讲解,促进儒学思想的传播。

尽管曲阜"三孔"的传播取得了一定发展,但曲阜"三孔"的热度仍无法与世界范围内的"孔子热"相匹配。其海外传播还尚有巨大提升空间。

第一,国际孔子文化节宣传力度不够。"孔子文化节每年的举办时间都在 9 月下旬,与国庆'十一黄金周'的时间重合,在各旅游地都在施展拳脚吸引游客的时候,孔子文化节每年的前期宣传都显得相对不足。"②浏览相关报道,可以发现,孔子文化节缺乏前期宣传,没有形成良好的舆论氛围,更难以对国外游客实现有效传达,结果是孔子文化节只是持续性地影响山东甚至曲阜境内。因此,相关部门可以深度发掘孔子思想内涵,将孔子思想与当代课题集合,制造孔子文化节话题,以解决问题的实用性为导向,吸引中外学者、游客来此探讨。

第二,充分利用当地便捷的交通优势,达成与周边文化名城的深度合作。国外游客游览中国,他们最基本的期待就是能感受"异域风情"的中国文化。孔子作为中国的文化符号,作为世界文明的里程碑式人物,足够具有吸引力。曲阜"三孔"可以以此为出发点,达成与北京故宫、济南趵突泉、东岳泰山等历史文化名胜的合作,形成诸如"中国文化寻踪"等主题游览活动,以此借其他名胜的热度为曲阜"三孔"引流,促进曲阜"三孔"的对外传播。

第三,积极促成与境外孔子学院的合作。一方面,孔子学院作为国外学子了解中国文化的平台,他们的学习不该只囿于书本和传统课堂,游访孔庙、孔府、孔庙能为他们认识中国文化提供更直观、更形象的方式,让他们实地体会儒学思想的绵延流长;另一方面,随着曲阜"三孔"的国际化性质不断加强,"对于外语人才的需求以及高端旅游从业人才的需求很迫切。下一步,曲阜将完善人才的培养和引进机制,为曲阜旅游发展提供智力支持"。③

第四,推动孔子和曲阜"三孔"题材的影视化。在高度信息化的今天,影视成为大众传播行之有效的媒介。宫廷剧的海外传播,促使一批海外游客来中国故宫参观皇帝妃嫔的生活场所。相比故宫,关于孔子或涉及曲阜"三孔"题材的影视作品明显不足。曲阜"三孔"的对外传播可以搭上影视传播这趟顺风车:一是"运用电视纪实节目直接介绍",二是"通过剧情产品直接或间接展现"。④将文

---

① 张令伟:《打造与 5A 级景区匹配的导游队伍》,《中国旅游报》2013 年 1 月 7 日。
② 丰诚诚:《基于节事活动的曲阜城市形象传播研究——以曲阜国际孔子文化节为例》,《新闻研究导刊》2018 年第 1 期。
③ 张令伟:《打造与 5A 级景区匹配的导游队伍》,《中国旅游报》2013 年 1 月 7 日。
④ 吕乐平:《影视跨文化传播导论》,中国广播电视出版社 2016 年版,第 68—69 页。

化遗产与影视媒介结合,为海外观众提供了对文化遗产的多感官认识,有助于促使更多人亲临曲阜"三孔",探寻圣人足迹。

1988年,诺贝尔物理学奖获得者汉内斯·阿尔文曾说:"如果人类要在21世纪生存下去,必须回到2500多年前,去汲取孔子的智慧。"曲阜"三孔"为了解孔子思想开放了直接有效的窗口,对于21世纪人类开创兼收并蓄、文化多元的文明新局面具有重要现实意义。曲阜"三孔"海外传播效力尚且不足,需要顺应现代化和信息化的大背景,优化传播路径,推动自身走向国际。

(作者单位:北京第二外国语学院英语学院)

黄海电影海报设计作品的东方美学意蕴*

武彦如

自为2014年许鞍华执导的电影《黄金时代》设计的系列海报引起广泛的关注和好评以来，黄海在电影海报设计界的知名度和个人品牌效应迅速提升，其作品将对电影海报的审美带入了大众对电影艺术的品评视野内，以具有感召力的视觉设计为电影的宣传和推广带来了实际的效益。除了为《我在故宫修文物》《道士下山》《大鱼海棠》《影》《江湖儿女》等不同类型的热门华语电影设计海报，黄海的设计也受到了海外影业公司的青睐，先后为《哆啦A梦伴我同行》《龙猫》《小偷家族》《超能查派》和《生化危机：终章》等日本、欧美影片设计了中国版海报。综观黄海的电影海报设计作品，无论是为何种类型、什么题材和哪一地区的影片所作，均映衬着挥之不去的中国传统文化底色，蕴含着或浓或淡的东方美学趣味。

"德有所长而形有所忘"——精神之美

庄子在《德充符》中讲述了申徒嘉、叔山无趾、哀骀它等贤人虽外貌丑陋甚至残缺，然因其德行之美更加受人尊敬、爱戴和追随的故事，以至于卫灵公、齐桓公再看那些形体健全的人，反而觉得他们不美了。所谓"德有所长而形有所忘"，世人"非爱其形也，爱使其形者也"，"使其形者"就是他们的精神。庄子透过这些寓言表明了"形骸之外"之美高于"形骸之内"之美的思想和审美观念，赞颂了超越于形体的精神人格美。中国传统美学在不忽略形体美的同时，更加重视和追求精神的美。

将电影视作一个整体的审美对象，大腕云集的演员阵容、光鲜靓丽的明星形

---

* 本文是山西省艺术科学规划课题（编号：2016G16）的阶段性研究成果。

象属于电影的外在的"形",是作为整体的外在形体中最表层也最容易吸引到观众的部分。因此,以往的电影海报常根据角色的重要性和演员的票房号召力,将人物形象依主次排列于画面中,作为首要视觉元素占据着画面最核心的空间。黄海则不将明星形象作为海报的主要表达内容,这正是他设计的电影海报区别于其他电影海报设计的一个明显特征。

在外在"形"之内,故事情节和精神内涵就是电影的"使其形者",这是决定一部电影优秀与否的最核心的内容,黄海设计的电影海报直指向这个核心,始终秉持着为这个核心服务的理念。如为2009年上映的电影《花木兰》设计的海报(图1),画面中的主要视觉元素只有代表战士的符号头盔和代表女性的符号红唇,花木兰巾帼英雄的形象即跃然纸上。人物面部的其他部分完全被省略,因此有效地避免了演员的容貌对观众的视觉及心理的干扰,帮助观众将注意力完全集中于影片故事的核心。同时面部的省略也营造了神秘感,留给了观众丰富的主动思考的空间,包括对演员形象、服装道具和角色的命运的想象等。这样含蓄、克制的设计不仅极易引起中国观众的共鸣,也可以让不同文化背景的人都能够通过此海报准确理解影片的主题。这幅海报成了各个版本的海报中最令人印象深刻、回味无穷的一幅,这正是崇尚精神之美的海报设计所具有的模糊了时空界限的魅力。

图1

"孰知天下之正色哉"——相对之美

"毛嫱、丽姬,人之所美也,鱼见之深入,鸟见之高飞,麋鹿见之决骤,四者孰知天下之正色哉?"(《庄子·齐物论》)面对同一个审美对象,人与鸟兽的截然不同的反应,是由于主体的审美经验不同,"其好恶故异"(《庄子·至乐》),"人之所美也"的"毛嫱、丽姬",却不能引起鸟兽之共情,庄子通过这个小寓言明示了美是相对的、有条件的。黄海设计的电影海报,特别注意结合不同地区特定的文化背景,尊重观众的审美习惯,以此为前提和支点传达电影的主旨,针对同一影片在不同国家和地区的宣传,以差异化的视觉表现来帮助观众理解和接受影片。其设计在不失去中国传统美学底蕴的前提下,将他者文化纳入到自己的设计体系中来,是对传统的积极创新,推动了电影向全球市场的推广。

影片《黄金时代》系列海报就是尊重和体现美的相对性规律的一个经典案例。如美国版和法国版的海报同样以表达电影主人公萧红的作家身份为创意点,但根据两国观众不同的视觉经验和审美偏好,以风格迥异的视觉设计实现了精准的传达:美国版海报(图2)的主图形是一只金色钢笔笔尖,笔尖中,主人公小小的身影孑然独立,孤对寒梅,准确地传达了电影的意象——在苦难中磨砺出的金色灵魂,画面明暗对比极强烈,图形边缘清晰明确,体现出美国式的现代视觉艺术风格特征;法国版海报(图3)则以法国观众熟悉的现代小说家玛格丽特·杜拉斯为创作灵感,画面的中心是女主人公的局部侧影,将命运的飘零和文人的倔强借左手的香烟和右手的钢笔表达出来,透过这一对简洁、有力同时富于矛盾性和想象空间的符号,映射了出影片的主旨,整体调性浪漫而柔和,拉近了影片与观众之间的心理距离。韩国版海报(图4)则以人物含泪的面部特写为主要图形,借助了演员汤唯在影片《晚秋》中给韩国观众留下的深刻印象,同时也抓住了韩国文化中的"恨"的美学特征——悲而不哀,因悲而更振奋、更坚韧的情感,与影片主人公的性格、命运不谋而合。

图2　　　　　　　　图3　　　　　　　　图4

"以实为虚,化景物为情思"——虚实之美

虚和实的关系问题,是中国传统哲学宇宙观的一个典型问题,这种宇宙观念表现在审美追求上,体现为中国艺术特别讲求虚实结合,以此反映出生命的活跃和无穷。在艺术作品中,"艺术家创造的形象是'实',引起我们想象的是'虚',由

形象产生的意象境界就是虚实的结合"。①"以实为虚,化景物为情思。"(〔宋〕范晞文《对床夜语》)"虚实相生,无画处皆成妙境。"(〔清〕笪重光《画荃》)黄海的电影海报作品也特别注重以虚实结合的视觉造型元素营造意境悠远的画面空间,具体体现在以下两个层次:

第一层次,画面中的虚与实。中国书画讲究"计黑当白",向来注重对虚空间的营造和运用,对空白的重视也贯穿在黄海的海报作品中,如图1《花木兰》海报的角色面部留白,图2《黄金时代》海报笔尖处的空白人物剪影,图3大幅的黑空间以及图4面向左侧的人物侧面剪影,均有效地利用了画面的空白处,丰富了画面的内容,增加了画面的空间层次,体现了对视觉元素运用的节制、冷静和内敛、含蓄的东方审美旨趣。如果说西方的卢宾反转图形(正负形)是一种精心设计的视觉游戏,而黄海的传承了中国美学虚实相生理念的作品,则以对虚空间的把握和运用,将电影海报从视觉美的层次推向了更高的精神美的境界。

第二层次,画面与精神的虚实。面对黄海设计的电影海报,观众的目光或聚焦、或游移于这些海报画面的空白处,虚实结合的形象触发了观众的想象和思索,画面未曾直接表现出来的情感于观众的心中、思想中萌生、建构和完成,留白化为可产生万千种的意象的生生不息的母体,使空白非但不空,还更加内涵丰富、意味深长。海报画面形象为实,引发的神游为虚,达成了"以实为虚,化景物为情思"。这种虚虽不是视觉可见之实,但却触及了海报所传达的电影精神核心的真实,画面的空白象征着隐藏和无限的可能,具有无穷的生命力,正如老子所说:"有无相生","虚而不屈,动而愈出"。

"刚柔相推而生变化"——运动之美

《周易》认为世界是在阴阳两种一柔一刚的根本力量的相互作用下生成、运动、变化的,"刚柔者,立本者也","刚柔相推而生变化"(《周易·系辞上》)。老子认识到了自然和社会中普遍存在的对立面之间的相互依赖和转化的动态过程,从运动中寻找不变的"道";庄子认为整个世界都处在变化之中,"芴漠无形,变化无常,死与生与,天地并与,神明往与!"(《庄子·天下》)在此哲学观念影响下,中国美学特别追求体现气势、韵律、力量的运动之美。在各种造型元素中,中国传统视觉艺术最注重以线条表现形体。这样的美学思想体现在黄海的电影海报设计中,表现为通过各种视觉元素间的力量的交织、对比、律动,达到了动中有静、

---

① 宗白华:《美学散步》,上海人民出版社1981年版,第39页。

静中有动、动静结合、气象万千的艺术境界。

以《黄金时代》的法国版海报和韩国版海报对线条的应用为例,法国版海报(图3)右上方的几缕缥缈的青烟是整幅画面中唯一轻盈的部分,形似翩翩起舞的女性形象,线条灵动、优美,好比是主人公坚毅的精神世界中的一段柔美而浪漫的旋律,突破了暗色调的沉闷,增加了画面的节奏感和层次感,营造了冷清空寂、余韵悠长的东方美感。而在韩国版海报(图4)中,面向左侧的人物剪影是整幅画面中唯一边缘整齐而肯定的线条,与其余视觉元素形成了力度上的对比,通过这种对比体现了在个人选择与时代命运交织的洪流中,主人公内心深处的始终如一的坚定,增强了画面张力,增加了海报所表现的内容的广度和深度。这两幅海报对线条的运用恰好是相反的,动与静、虚与实、柔与刚,但无论是以轻盈灵动的线条点缀还是以边缘清晰的线条肯定,都富含有由刚柔对比而的生成内在的生生不息的力量,在静态的平面空间中引发动态的联想,引导观众进入到主人公故事背景、人物命运和视觉意象的世界中去。在视觉力量的互相作用中,黄海设计的电影海报也达到了中国传统艺术的指导原则"气韵生动"与"骨法运笔"(谢赫《古画品录》)的要求,呈现出由"刚柔相推"所带来的变化运动之美。

"天地与我并生,万物与我为一"——无限之美

"枕上见千里,窗中窥万室。"(王维《和使君五郎西楼望远思归》),中国人于有限中见出了无限,于视觉艺术,追求在有限的画面空间内表达无穷的境界。"夫道,覆载万物也,洋洋乎大哉,"(《庄子·天地》)庄子及其后学一再指出,美具有无限性,最高的美是囊括整个宇宙,无比广大的。[1] 在无限的面前,任何的有限和相对的事物都是有缺陷的。庄子在《秋水》中赞美东海"不为顷久推移,不以多少进退者"的"大乐",即永恒的无限的大美。黄海的海报设计作品中体现着对无限之美的追求,传达给观众东方式的审美心灵体验,将电影海报设计从视觉可表现的有限美推向了精神方可及的无限美的境界。

中国人对无限之美的追求,扩大了到整个宇宙,达到"天地与我并生,万物与我为一"(《庄子·齐物论》)的境界。《道士下山》的海报(图5)画面采用郭熙三远说的"平远"的视角,脚下是大山巍巍,头上是乌云压境,小道士的身影在其中渺小若天地间的一粒沙,片景孤境自成一个丰满的宇宙,"我"之小与天地之"大"

---

[1] 李泽厚、刘纲纪:《中国美学史》(第一卷),中国社会科学出版社1984年版,第252页。

形成了鲜明的对比,将小道士初次下山的复杂心绪精妙地传达了出来,引发了观者对电影的观察、理解和对生命的思考。① 为宫崎骏的动画电影《龙猫》设计的中国版海报(图6),以"俯察"的视角描绘在龙猫肚皮上嬉戏的小梅和小月,宛若奔跑在风轻轻抚过的无边麦田里,由视觉引发了触感联想,将温情传导至观者的心中。这个俯察的视角,是一种使观者抽离世事、以仁爱之心看待生命的视角,同时也在这种独特的视角中观照到自身,感受到信仰、救赎和宁静。该海报引得日本网友评论"是因为中国国土面积广阔吗?中国人视角下的大自然,仿佛藏着一种对秘境的憧憬"。这藏着的秘境,正是对无限之美的追求所打开的超越于物我之分的纯粹审美境界。

图 5　　　　图 6

结语

电影海报的首要目的和任务是表达电影本身,黄海设计的电影海报始终从电影的精神核心出发,以多变的设计风格和独具匠心的设计创意表达电影的故事内容和精神内涵。根植于中国文化的土壤,黄海的设计在采用现代设计手法和设计语言的同时,始终带有一抹中国文化与东方美学的印记。在视觉元素符号的选择上体现出对精神之美的崇尚,在针对不同受众的不同版本设计中体现对相对之美的尊重,通过留白手法营造出虚实之美,在动静变化、刚柔对比中表

---

① 胡佳音:《点景:黄海电影海报设计的重要形式语言》,《电影评介》2017 年第 21 期,第 107—109 页。

现运动之美,最终达到无限之美的大美境界。极具东方美学意蕴的视觉表达,使黄海的作品总能触动到观众微妙的内心世界,达到了民族性、艺术性和现代性的完美平衡与融合。

(作者单位:上海大学上海电影学院)

龙泉青瓷在宋士大夫休闲生活中的意境构成

——以南宋龙泉窑鬲炉为例

余 沁

图 1 南宋龙泉窑鬲炉

高 6.2 厘米,口径 8.8 厘米,德清县博物馆藏。

资料来源:李辉柄主编:《中国陶瓷全集》第 8 卷"宋(下)",上海人民美术出版社 1999 年版,第 121、264 页。

龙泉窑作为中国陶瓷史上最后形成的青瓷窑业系统,自晚唐时期开始瓷器生产,北宋中期生产初具规模,最终于南宋中期走向成熟并形成自己的独特风格——以釉色和造型取胜,较少纹饰。

在上述整个发展演进过程中,龙泉青瓷的使用阶层从普通民众拓展到达官贵人,甚至最后进入宫廷成为御用瓷器之一。本文以现藏于德清县博物馆的南宋龙泉窑鬲炉(图 1)为例,通过分析其进入以宋代士大夫为代表的上层阶级的视野并融入他们生活的路径,为龙泉青瓷在宋代士大夫休闲生活的意境构成中所起作用提供线索。

一、理学背景下宋士大夫观念的生成

赵宋王朝以武力平定天下,并通过"杯酒释兵权"的谋略在制度上消除了其内部隐患。在文化策略上,尽管恢复并重建了礼制、建立了权威的国家系统,但仍需要文化与教育的支持系统。因此,自宋初开始,皇家一直重文轻武,因为只有由知识阶层表述的知识、思想与信仰系统,才能有效地建构着政治与伦理秩序[①]。在

---

① 葛兆光:《中国思想史》第二卷,复旦大学出版社 2019 年版,第 154 页。

这一重建思想世界的过程中,因"治统"与"道统"之间的权力重心拉锯,形成了皇帝与士大夫"共治天下"的基本政治格局。理学正是在此背景下兴起。

鉴于五代十国的更迭动荡使得旧的思想秩序失去了原有的约束力,宋代士大夫为确立思想秩序的同一性和合理性,对知识、思想和信仰的有效性进行了重新思考,并逐渐重新确立起来关于"道"、"理"与"心"、"性"的一整套观念系统。[①] 到了南宋朱熹时,则集前人研究成果(特别是程颐系统)之大成,形成了新儒学体系——理学,并兼容了佛、道等思想。

天地万物皆有理。所谓"理",是一种超越个体、权利、地域的普遍性真理,具有普遍化、普世化的特点。在"理"字的思路中,首先要"理一分殊",明确宇宙万象总有一个根本处,也就是终极处有一个实在的"理"。在理学家话语中,这个"理"便是天道,应以"诚"的态度去对待。所谓"诚者,真实无妄之谓,天理之本然也"。[②] 然后,体验与把握"理"的途径则是"格物穷理"。"格,至也。物,犹事也。穷至事物之理,欲其极处无不到也。"[③]也就是说,对各种事物进行观察、揣摩、分析与涵咏,用自己的知性与理性彻底领悟变化万端中的终极"道理"。事实上,这种获取知识与思想的路径丰富多样,而"正心诚意"不仅是"格物"前的心理预设,也是"格物"之后所得。[④] "诚之者,未能真实无妄,而欲其真实无妄之谓,人事之当然也。"[⑤]如此,天道与人道在"诚"上便实现了贯通统一。当通过"格物穷理"体验与把握"理"之后,则进入"理"字思路的最后一步——"穷理尽性"。因为"天地间只有一个道理。性便是理"。[⑥] 性作为道之形体,需由心收拾并发用出来。因此,诠释中的所谓"穷理尽性"的涵意,便似乎成了体验与探究万事万物之"理",以凸显人的自我本真的"性",而格物穷理的终极目标,也就成了对内在心性的探寻。[⑦] 这最终将聚焦于内在的道德伦理。

综上,在如此理学背景之下,宋代士大夫将宇宙终极道理与心性本原融通,从"天"转向"人",并将得到的"理"用于指导生活,确立秩序。以"诚"的态度在原

---

① 葛兆光:《中国思想史》第二卷,复旦大学出版社 2019 年版,第 186 页。
② 〔宋〕朱熹:《四书章句集注》,中华书局 1983 年版,第 31 页。
③ 同上书,第 4 页。
④ 《大学章句》云:古之欲明明德于天下者,先治其国;欲治其国者,先齐其家;欲齐其家者,先修其身;欲修其身者,先正其心;欲正其心者,先诚其意;欲诚其意者,先致其知;致知在格物。物格而后知至,知至而后意诚,意诚而后心正,心正而后身修,身修而后家齐,家齐而后国治,国治而后天下平。详见〔宋〕朱熹撰:《四书章句集注》,中华书局 1983 年版,第 3—4 页。
⑤ 〔宋〕朱熹:《四书章句集注》,中华书局 1983 年版,第 31 页。
⑥ 〔宋〕黄士毅编:《朱子语类汇校》(全十册)第一册,徐时仪、杨艳汇校,上海古籍出版社 2016 年版,第 82 页。
⑦ 葛兆光:《中国思想史》第二卷,复旦大学出版社 2019 年版,第 183 页。

儒家传统思想基础上生成了内在超越的观念取向，即通过对人更内在的"性"进行体认，于内省自身、涵养心性中凸显道德本原并完成个体生命的意义。

二、理学影响下龙泉青瓷的艺术风格建构

鲍桑葵(Bernard Bosanquet)认为，艺术超越自然状态是以美的形态明确表现的观念①。而最高的美，无论是自然美还是艺术美，并不是按照普通人的感觉本身的一致性来进行判断的，而是按照与教育和经验发展程度相应的人类情感的一致趋向来判断的。②作为宋代的知识阶层，士大夫在遵循"理"字的思路治学修身时普遍秉持着"正心诚意以治国平天下，最终确立自身生命价值"的观念。因而从一般意义上讲，他们的审美价值更倾向于"重道尚雅"，这也由此奠定了他们所处整个时代的审美意识和美的标准。一方面，以伦理道德为本位的"道"重视对本体性理的探寻。作为宋代文化精神的核心要义，其外在表征为秩序和稳定之美。另一方面，"雅"即正也，且有"高雅""高尚""美德"之意③。此外，以求理为要义的文化本身意味着一种纯粹的高雅生活④。因此士大夫对于"雅"的追求表现为对平淡含蓄之美的喜爱。

鉴于宋代各类教育事业的普及化、平民化，理学所确立的原则以及理学背景下士大夫生成的审美价值取向由上到下深入到社会。换句话说，民众不仅潜移默化中受到理学中"格物穷理"思想的影响，在处事、造物时自觉遵从这一法度，而且在发达的城市经济推动下所造之物均不自觉迎合了士大夫"重道尚雅"审美价值下的美的形态。同理可推，龙泉青瓷在发展过程中一直致力于观察并吸收其他名窑的优点以改善自己的产品，形成以本文案例中的鬲炉为代表的"端巧优雅、简洁清淡、纤细挺拔"的艺术风格。这正是受此影响的具体例证。

纵观龙泉青瓷两宋时期的制瓷情况可知，北宋中期生产初具规模的龙泉窑主要受越窑、瓯窑、婺州窑等周边窑场的影响，但尚未形成自己的艺术风格。除了淡青釉色与其他窑场有差异之外，器形、装饰手法以及装烧工艺均具有同时期越窑，甚至瓯窑等其他诸窑的风格。⑤两宋之际或南宋早期，全国政治经济文化

---

① [英]鲍桑葵:《美学史》，李步楼译，商务印书馆2019年版，第19页。
② 同上书，第14页。
③ 郭学信:《宋代士大夫群体意识研究》，中国社会科学出版社2017年版，第168页。
④ 赵玉强:《优游之道：宋代士大夫休闲文化及其意蕴》，上海古籍出版社2017年版，第70—71页。
⑤ 沈岳明:《北宋时期的龙泉窑业》，沈岳明、郑建明主编《北宋龙泉窑纵论》，文物出版社2018年版，第2—7页。

中心南移，北方汝窑、定窑等名窑技术随着人口南迁传入南方。龙泉窑再次吸收汝窑、官窑的烧制技艺，改进了胎土配方，即在瓷土中掺入适量的紫金土，提高了其抗弯度，使得器物在高温下不易变形。① 这为之后龙泉青瓷形成自己独特的艺术风格并由此走进士大夫的视野奠定了重要基础。

本文案例中的鬲炉从器形、釉色、装饰三个方面展现了胎质改变后带来的造型设计、上釉方法以及装饰艺术等方面的重大改变和提高。

首先，因龙泉青瓷无需再担心器形在高温下轻易变形，在对其足部、腹部等部位修整时可做到恰到好处地厚薄均匀，使得其整体造型成功克服"笨重粗厚"，在塑造上也更易适应不同受众群体的审美需求。赵宋王朝为了证明自己政权的合法性，表明自己精于古代礼乐，占有并保存古代的青铜器成了其有力象征。② 因此当时宋代社会从上至下复古之风盛行，但凡有条件的士大夫大都喜欢收藏金石、书画等物，其中宋徽宗更敕令王黼编撰《宣和博古图录》。文中鬲炉正是以《宣和博古图录》中收录的周帛女鬲（图2）的标准样式进行烧造，以供宫廷和士大夫使用。但这并不是简单的样式仿制。在宋代，鬲不仅是祭祀用具，其形制更被模仿制成士大夫的文房雅玩——鬲炉。所以在器形设计上不仅要考虑到祭祀时的庄重大方，还要统摄士大夫的审美旨趣。丹纳（Hippolyte Adolphe Taine）认为，物质文明与精神文明的性质面貌都取决于种族、环境、时代三大因素③。因此，了解士大夫审美旨趣的最直接方式便是观察、揣摩、分析同时期的其他艺术门类，如宋代绘画和书法。作为士大夫生活中息息相关的一部分，它们是"重道尚雅"审美价值下最高之美的最直接呈现。其中，宋代山水、花鸟等题材的画作的创作趋向于追求平淡恬静的意境，而人物画和书法中的艺术表现则趋向于纤细雅淡之风。综上，此鬲炉于器形设计上主要做了两

图2 周帛女鬲

资料来源：王黼编：《宣和博古图录》卷十九，泊如斋重修，明万历1603年本。

---

① 沈岳明：《龙泉窑厚釉技术和粉青釉瓷器的烧造》，《故宫博物院院刊》2020年第5期，第16—17页。
② [美]艾朗诺：《美的焦虑：北宋士大夫的审美思想与追求》，杜斐然等译，上海古籍出版社2013年版，第9页。
③ [法]丹纳：《艺术哲学》，傅雷译，生活·读书·新知三联书店2016年版，第3页。

处改良：其一，更加修长的束颈使得鬲炉在整体视觉上拥有了挺拔之感；其二，三角形乳足的应用使得其较之周帛女鬲三足的敦厚风格增添了一分线条上的曲直变化。由此便建构了稳定形制秩序中端巧优雅、纤细挺拔却明快圆润的艺术风格。

其次，此鬲炉的粉青釉光泽柔和，属于龙泉青瓷中典型的厚质青釉，标志着青瓷釉色之美的极致。这种釉层丰厚的瓷器，一般需要经过多次素烧、多次施釉方可生成[1]，若没有二元胎土配方奠定适宜的胎体薄厚和烧成状态基础，仅釉料改良则无法达到青釉厚而不流的效果。当然从审美的角度来说，龙泉青瓷一直致力于改革和突出"青"的呈色，这是对自然之美不懈追求的表现。自古以来，中国人崇尚自然。到了宋代，"理"字思路下于"理一分殊"和"格物穷理"中完成了天道与人道之"诚"的贯通统一，也就是天人合一的境界，并以此态度去对待追寻的终极"道理"。鉴于教育普及平民化下龙泉窑的工匠文化素质和综合技能的整体提高，其造物受到这一法度潜移默化的影响。因而他们细致入微地观察自然界中各种晶莹青绿之美的特点，并探寻其背后永恒之美的本质，不断试烧最终成功的过程正是"重道"的另一种表现。

最后，此鬲炉表面光洁，仅在器形转折处有"出筋"装饰，是龙泉窑工匠技艺和智慧的体现。因为基于成熟期龙泉青瓷厚釉薄胎的特点，早前薄釉厚胎时使用的刻画装饰变得不再适合，易被隐藏在厚釉之下无法凸显。因此，南宋成熟期的龙泉青瓷几乎没有装饰，但这又会产生臃肿的视觉效果。工匠在揣摩其烧制技艺特点之后，最终采取了在浑圆的鬲式炉肩部及三乳足正面处贴加三角泥条装饰的"出筋"手法，使鬲式炉浑圆的形体产生棱角转折的视觉感。与此同时，因为采用了"出筋"装饰手法，鬲式炉表面上的厚釉与出筋处的露白产生了色差变化[2]，使得鬲炉的艺术风格简约而不简单。

总体而言，本文案例中的南宋龙泉窑鬲炉于器形、釉色、装饰达到了和谐完美的统一。它作为成熟期龙泉青瓷的典型作品，不管是工艺还是设计上都受到了以"格物穷理"为代表的理学思想的影响。与此同时，因士大夫"重道尚雅"的审美价值引导以及同时代其他艺术门类的艺术风格作为参照系，最终它被塑造成为符合宋代士大夫审美的艺术作品，"端巧优雅、简洁清淡、纤细挺拔"，进入士大夫的视野。

---

[1]《龙泉青瓷简史》，载朱伯谦《揽翠集：朱伯谦陶瓷考古文集》，科学出版社2009年版，第157页。
[2] 雷国强、李震：《南宋龙泉青瓷香炉鉴赏与研究》（中），《东方收藏》2015年第2期，第58页。

三、理学语境下龙泉青瓷的道德理念象征

朱熹在《与陆子静书》中有云:"凡有形有象者,即器也;所以为是器之理者,则道也。"[1]也就是说,器是形而下的具体现象与事物的世界,超越形下之器后则是形而上之道,即理学家话语中的"理"之根本。而在"理"字思路最后一步"穷理尽性"中,实质上是对内在心性的探寻,以凸显人的自我本真的"性"。因为"道即性,性即道,固只有一物"。[2] 性作为实理,更具有以仁义礼智为代表的道德理念。

因此,以本文案例中的鬲炉为代表的龙泉青瓷自进入宋代士大夫视野的那刻起,便自觉处于预设的理学语境之下。作为形而下之器的构成,龙泉青瓷有赖于气,气凝聚处便有理,从而也就有了性。士大夫通过在把玩和鉴赏中运用他们的想象力、情感体验和价值观等建构属于龙泉青瓷的意象,从而在材质、工艺与意象之间形成一种张力,由此体味龙泉青瓷艺术风格特点背后象征的道德理念。

第一,龙泉青瓷光泽柔和的"青"色象征了"和谐仁爱"的道德理念。《鸡肋编》云:"处州龙泉县多佳树,地名豫章,以木而著也。……又出青瓷器,谓之'秘色'。"[3]正是龙泉窑址坐落在崇山峻岭之中,被群树环绕,使得龙泉青瓷天然具有一种自然韵味,这是人与自然和谐相处的表现。当它走进士大夫生活时,一方面它将自然之色带入士大夫的书斋雅室,与室内的其他文房雅玩共同营造了"天人合一"的自然之景,另一方面也通过人与自然这个意象将自然之乐与道德之乐贯通,进一步隐喻实际生活中人与人之间的和谐相处,通向"仁"这个道德本原。

第二,龙泉青瓷莹润如玉的釉色象征了"尚玉比德"的道德理念。在传统儒家文化中,玉是礼的代表。《礼记·聘义》中孔子与子贡论玉说:"夫昔者君子比德于玉焉:温润而泽,仁也;缜密以栗,知也;廉而不刿,义也;垂之如队,礼也;叩之,其声清越以长,其终诎然,乐也;瑕不掩瑜、瑜不掩瑕,忠也;孚尹旁达,信也;气如白虹,天也;精神见于山川,地也;珪、璋特达,德也;天下莫不贵者,道也。《诗》云:'言念君子,温其如玉。'故君子贵之也。"[4]由此可知,礼学不仅是传统儒

---

[1] 《与陆子静书》,《文集》卷三十六,"四部丛刊"本,第14页。转引自冯友兰《中国哲学史》(下),生活·读书·新知三联书店2009年版,第371页。
[2] 〔宋〕黄士毅编:《朱子语类汇校》(全十册)第一册,徐时仪、杨艳汇校,上海古籍出版社2016年版,第94页。
[3] 〔宋〕庄绰撰:《鸡肋编》,萧鲁阳点校,上海书店出版社1983年版,第5页。
[4] 胡平生:《礼记》(下),张萌译注,中华书局2017年版,第1225页。

家最重要的组成部分之一,重视"礼"被认为是极为重要的品格,而且"尚玉"之风也正是源于以玉比君子之德。这在青瓷体系中表现得尤为突出。自唐代越窑瓷第一次靠近玉的失透感,陆羽在《茶经·茶之器》中便赞道:"若邢瓷类银,则越瓷类玉,邢不如越一也。"① 也就是说,类玉的龙泉青瓷在士大夫心中是其首选,因为它激发了他们心中对于追求君子之德的道德情感,从而成为日常生活中可视的道德理念的表征。

第三,龙泉青瓷器形、釉色、装饰的和谐统一象征了"道器并重"的道德理念。在理学语境下,"一物两体,气也"。也就是说,一气之中有阴阳二性。其中气聚则物成,气散则物毁。② 万事万物是在二元对立中得以生成。与此同时,"事事物物皆有个极,是道理之极至"。③ 换句话说,每个事物都有其最完全的形式,即其最高的标准,那么这便穷尽这一事物之理。以造型和釉色取胜,极少纹饰的龙泉青瓷便是这一最完全形式的典型。完整的龙泉青瓷无论是线条、比例还是色彩搭配都完全符合了人体视觉的舒适度,是其艺术风韵之美的根本,是形而下之器与形而上之道结合的完美阐释者。若器形线条出现微小变化,抑或釉色与纹饰之间搭配不当,都将影响龙泉青瓷试图营造的规整稳定、平淡含蓄之感。

综上所述,鉴于"格物穷理"的终极目标是对内在心性的探寻,而"天下之物,至微至细者,亦皆有心,只是有无知觉处尔"。④ 由此,作为物的龙泉青瓷因以高超技艺下最完全的呈现激发了士大夫的洞察力,从而使得他们"寓心"于此。当物之心与人之心合二为一时,则意味着他们通向了终极之"道",即不再执着于龙泉青瓷之物的外在美的形态,而是在理学语境下反思体味其艺术风格特点背后象征的"和谐仁爱、尚玉比德、道器并重"的道德理念,从而调节因喜爱引发的"情"。也就是说,士大夫在喜爱之"情"与道德之"性"间自我调整,最终在内省自身、心性涵养的过程中达到了"道""理"与"心""性"之"和"的境界。

四、龙泉青瓷在宋士大夫休闲生活中的意境构成

休闲作为一种美好的生活状态与人生境界,体现着时间与空间的统一,人(主体、主观)与物(客体、客观)的统一,身(身体感受)与心(心理感受)的统一,休

---

① 〔唐〕陆羽:《茶经》,晋云彤主编,黑龙江美术出版社2017年版,第134页。
② 冯友兰:《中国哲学史》(下),生活·读书·新知三联书店2009年版,第331—332页。
③ 〔宋〕黄士毅:《朱子语类汇校》(全十册)第六册,徐时仪、杨艳汇校,上海古籍出版社2016年版,第2377页。
④ 同上书,第72页。

闲本身具有内在的正向价值,尤其重视道德涵养与休闲的一致性,氤氲着审美、艺术与诗性的气质,蕴藏有丰富的哲学文化意义。[1] 对于以理为基础的宋代士大夫来说,情理兼摄是他们休闲思想的主要特征,实现生命之真是他们休闲生活中的核心价值追求。也就是说,士大夫在性情圆融的意境中完成个体生命的意义。其中,以龙泉窑鬲炉为代表的品香炉又在整个意境的实现中发挥着重要作用。

首先,将本文案例中的龙泉窑鬲炉与香结合,还原至宋代士大夫休闲生活这一"原境",从其口径尺寸(8.8厘米)可知,它属于品香炉。根据宋《都城纪胜》记载,"烧香点茶,挂画插花"这四种事是宋代士大夫生活中不可或缺的乐趣。[2] 其中烧香也叫焚香,位列四事之首。在香事中,香炉是其重要主体,它与香一起成为士大夫休闲生活中不可或缺的一部分。宋代陆游于《假中闭户终日偶得绝句》中有云:"官身常欠读书债,禄米不供沽酒资。剩喜今朝寂无事,焚香闲看玉溪诗。"可见一炉香烟已经超越了物质带来的束缚,是士大夫享受并体悟人生过程中的重要媒介。

纵观中国香学文化的历史,它起源于殷商以至更遥远的新石器时代晚期,初步成形于两汉,在宋代达到高峰。[3] 鉴于香的美好气味可以改善人的心情,使人安宁愉悦,因此无论是皇室、权贵还是大众,用香逐渐发展为他们生活中的常事。当然,对于士大夫来说,当他们在一炉香烟的环绕下安静下来,增添一丝雅趣之余更是进入其精神家园观照内心的开始。在细节上,用香注重思想感受的传递、韵味和含义,以及意会感悟。所以,中国香学文化本质仍是"香以载道",是士大夫实现性情圆融意境的重要外在条件。在此"澄怀虑性"的氛围之下,士大夫的休闲生活无时无刻不透露出"重道尚雅"的审美价值以及对自我道德心性涵养之道的追寻。

比如,书斋研修。研修广义上包含观书诵读、伏案书写、静坐冥想等,这往往发生在士大夫的书斋雅室。如图3所示,士大夫坐于江畔松下的书斋中,案上放置了书籍与小香炉,这正是书斋中焚香研习的惬意景象。士大夫精神在此刻的独处中必须保持专一凝定,而香的气味通过"鼻观",可静心虑性、远离是非杂念。最终与室外的自然之景一起,为士大夫营造了一个"慎独"的空间,即在安宁和愉悦中智慧思索、探寻本体性理,进一步完成内在道德的修养实践,最终达到提升精神境界的目的。

---

[1] 赵玉强:《优游之道:宋代士大夫休闲文化及其意蕴》,上海古籍出版社2017年版,第16页。
[2] 吴清、韩回之主编:《澄怀观道:传统之文人香事文物》,上海科学技术出版社2014年版,第14页。
[3] 贾天明:《中国香学》,中华书局2018年版,第19页。

图 3　宋刘松年《秋窗读易图》(局部)

绢本设色,纵 25.7 厘米　横 26.0 厘米,辽宁省博物馆藏。

资料来源:浙江大学中国古代书画研究中心编:《宋画全集》第三卷 2,浙江大学出版社 2009 年版,第 201—202 页。

图 4　宋刘松年《松荫鸣琴图》(局部)

绢本设色,纵 24.0 厘米　横 24.9 厘米,克利夫兰艺术博物馆藏,Leonard C. Hanna, Jr. 基金会。

资料来源:浙江大学中国古代书画研究中心编:《宋画全集》第六卷 2. 浙江大学出版社 2008 年版,第 47—48 页。

当然,抚琴也是士大夫之间一项非常流行的休闲活动(图 4)。由于琴乐追求"和雅清淡、弦外之音"的意境,因此在抚琴过程中,琴声背后人的胸襟气度的展示更为重要。它是士大夫寻求极致体验并展现其人格形象与精神风范的重要方式。[1] 以琴会友,要达到这样的意境,无论是弹琴人还是听琴人,都需将外在环境与自己的内在心境合二为一。此时,空灵美妙的香韵不仅能够帮助去噪入静,营造一个清幽静雅的环境,而且也展示了一种"正心诚意"的端敬态度,有助于在琴乐中进入更广阔的物我合一乃至天人合一的内心境界。

其次,从材质的角度,本文案例中的龙泉窑鬲炉属于瓷质炉。宋代的出香方法承袭唐中晚期的隔火熏香法。这是一种高端用香方式,比之直接将香料放入火中烧,其香气更加醇和宜人,而且能增添许多情趣,深得文人雅士的青睐。[2] 对于香炉的材质,本不限于银、铜、铁等材质,全随人的喜好去做。但宋代烧瓷技术在理学思想的影响下于借鉴中不断提高,使得瓷质香炉在造型上可以随意模仿前代其他材质的香炉或者另有创新。此外,瓷质香炉不同于金属材质香炉,不易过度精雕细琢,反而呈现出古朴雅致、简洁清淡的风格。加之制作成

---

[1] 赵玉强:《优游之道:宋代士大夫休闲文化及其意蕴》,上海古籍出版社 2017 年版,第 159 页。
[2] 〔宋〕陈敬著,严小青编著:《新纂香谱》,中华书局 2012 年版,第 163—164 页。

本相对较低,这为需视自身情况挑选适宜香炉的士大夫提供了更加自由的选择。

与此同时,宋人品香,除了将品香炉置于矮桌"鼻观"外,更有握炉品闻的需要。因此品香炉的束颈较高,以便一手把握。此时,若香炉为金属材质,不免传热过快,而且手执炉后也会留有相应的金属残味,影响品香过程中的雅趣。简而言之,瓷质炉因本身的艺术风格特征和材质特性最终成为士大夫雅室的首选。其中生产瓷质炉的窑口,又以龙泉窑等为巨。宋代杨万里有《烧香七言》诗云:"琢瓷作鼎碧于水,削银为叶轻如纸。"说的便是以本文案例龙泉窑鬲炉为代表的符合宋代士大夫喜好的龙泉青瓷品香炉。

最后,本文案例中的鬲炉属于龙泉青瓷,而龙泉青瓷本身在理学语境下所指特定的道德理念。受理学影响的士大夫在观念上注重体认天理,内观以涵养自己的道德。这种完成个体生命意义的方式能够将人心涵养得丰厚博大,随之而来的是在现实生活中真正实现心的休闲。一炉香烟首先营造的澄怀静寂的意境便是使人居静,然后人的内心逐渐变得空闲、虚明。当然,"理"字的思路也明确指出,道不离物。也就是说,士大夫是要在闲淡、虚静的心境下于日用之中随事观省体认[①],于"物"与"我"间自由切换。因此,龙泉青瓷便自然融入到士大夫"自得"之乐的休闲时空中,起到寄托其道德价值期许的作用。这也反向证明了宋代瓷质香炉多产自龙泉窑。

总而言之,士大夫休闲生活实质上追求的是性情圆融的意境。以本文案例中鬲炉为代表的龙泉青瓷从品香炉的实用层面和其艺术风格特征层面,因符合士大夫的真实情感所需,呈现出"玩物适情"的状态。但此"情"背后又紧密联系着道德目标。也就是说,从龙泉青瓷所指的道德理念层面,在士大夫居静的状态下对"道"、"理"体悟之后,通过物我之心合一,使得情欲引发的杂乱慢慢在道德理念的表征引导下趋向心性的纯然,完成"人心"到"道心"的转换,恢复到情之未发时的合乎"理"的"性",由此便完成了士大夫所追求的自由自在的生命之真的价值意义。

结论

处于理学背景的宋代士大夫一直致力于体认人内在的"性",并于内观中凸显道德本原并完成个体生命的意义。受此观念影响,宋代的主流审美意识和美的标准为"重道尚雅"。以南宋龙泉窑鬲炉为代表的龙泉青瓷在工艺和设计上正

---

① 赵玉强:《优游之道:宋代士大夫休闲文化及其意蕴》,上海古籍出版社 2017 年版,第 353 页。

是受此影响,形成了符合宋代士大夫审美的"端巧优雅、简洁清淡、纤细挺拔"的艺术风格,并成功走进他们的视野。在融入士大夫生活的过程中,它所具有的光泽柔和的"青"色、温润如玉的釉色以及来自完整器形的和谐统一在理学语境下被转化为"和谐仁爱、尚玉比德、道器并重"的道德理念象征,使得它在引发士大夫"情"的同时,又调节了士大夫自我本真的"性",从而在心性涵养的培养过程中达到了"道"、"理"与"心"、"性"之"和"的境界。当然,它一方面作为品香炉这一类别器物,与香一起参与到士大夫的休闲生活中,从中国香学文化层面辅助为士大夫营造了一个静心虑性、澄怀雅致的外在环境。另一方面作为龙泉青瓷本身,从人物相交实践的层面,通过对物之"道"、"理"的体悟,"人心"转"道心",完成了士大夫休闲生活追求的物与我、身与心、道德与休闲之间的统一,体悟道德本原的同时实现了生命之真的价值意义。由此可知,龙泉青瓷在宋代士大夫休闲生活的性情圆融意境构成中是重要的媒介之一。

(作者单位:上海大学上海电影学院)

京剧的海外传播问题与对策探析

孙 宁

2018年8月1日晚,京剧版《哈姆雷特》——《王子复仇记》于丹麦克隆堡(莎士比亚名作《哈姆雷特》故事发生地)上演,以此拉开了2018年丹麦莎士比亚艺术节的序幕。演出引起了观众的广泛赞誉。《王子复仇记》最早于2005年首演于丹麦,以京剧的做、念、唱、打艺术程式为《哈姆雷特》经典剧目注入了新鲜血液,体现了东方与西方的友好对话与艺术融合。来自中国的艺术家们用最纯粹的中国传统戏剧艺术形式为丹麦观众重新诠释了莎士比亚的这部经典剧作的精神,展示了中西文化交融所迸发出的巨大力量。同年8月11日,黑龙江省京剧院在丹麦趣伏里主题公园上演了《贵妃醉酒》与《天女散花》两出京剧剧目。2000余名丹麦民众和游客们共同沉浸在京剧的独特魅力中。京剧,作为一种浓缩着中国文化的艺术符号,通过这样的演出,流入了丹麦人的心中,促进了丹麦对中国的了解,加深了中国与丹麦的情谊,其文化价值不可估量。正如哥本哈根中国文化中心主任张力所言:"文化交流对增进不同国家之间的民心相通起着独特和不可替代的作用,丹麦民众能有机会领略到中国国粹艺术的魅力,可以帮助他们更好地了解中国文化,促进中丹人民的交流,有利于两国关系的进一步加深。"①

京剧具有深厚的中国文化底蕴。中华文化是世界上最为古老的文化之一,凝聚着几千年来人类智慧的结晶,滋养了一代又一代的中国人。而京剧是中华文化中的精华所在,即为"国粹"。京剧之所以能够同中国画、中国医学并称为三大中国的"国粹",与其虚实结合的表现手法;唱、念、做、打的表演艺术;气势恢宏

---

① 《中国京剧在丹麦古老乐园上演》,新华网 http://www.xinhuanet.com/world/2018-08/13/c_129931905.htm,2018-08-13。

的表演风格以及京剧中所蕴含的民族精神密不可分。首先,京剧是"虚实相生"的艺术,能够通过道具的变换、演员的表演等为观众呈现出时间以及空间的变化,带给观众一种"浸入式"戏剧欣赏体验。其次,京剧是一种程式化的、成熟的艺术,一场京剧剧目可涉及文学、武打、念白、唱腔、服饰、脸谱等多种艺术形式,这些元素共同谱写出华丽的京剧舞台效果。最后,京剧的形成距今已有 200 余年的历史,京剧所包含的中国文化元素以及民族精神更是孕育于中华 2000 年的文明进程中,每一段剧目都是中国传统文化的载体,因而是世界了解中国的一个窗口,是中西方文化艺术交流的使者。

2010 年 11 月,京剧被列入"人类非物质文化遗产代表作名录"。"京剧以其深刻的思想内容,程式化的舞台表演,旋律优美的音乐构成,色彩鲜明的服饰、脸谱,共同构成富有民族特色的戏剧文化。"[1]京剧是中国传统文化的载体,也是人类共同的文化遗产和艺术瑰宝。然而,京剧的海外传播受到一定的阻碍。国外民众对京剧的感知力、认识力与兴趣度与京剧本身的文化价值不匹配。京剧浓缩的文化符号,独特的文化韵律,丰富的表演形式未能尽然展现在世界人民的面前。因而如何延续京剧这一表演艺术在海外的横向生命力值得我们探讨。

自梅兰芳先生访美后,京剧在当时的美国红极一时,打开了在海外立足的空间。但后来,京剧这种表演艺术再也没有达到过当时的文化盛况。整体而言,目前京剧在海外的发展还面临着较大的困境。作为一种与西方戏剧风格迥异的东方戏剧形式,京剧在异质文化中容易被误读,京剧的接受也收到较大的阻碍。鉴于此,有必要用科学的模式对京剧的海外传播进行策略分析。美国传播学奠基人拉斯韦尔提出的 5W 传播模式,对人类社会的传播活动进行了模式分析,主要包括谁(Who)、说什么(Says What)、通过什么渠道(In Which Channel)、对谁说(To whom)、效果如何(With What Effects)五个要素。[2] 笔者借助拉斯韦尔的 5W 模式,从传播主体、传播内容、传播渠道、传播客体四个方面对京剧的海外传播的困境及对策进行分析,以期增强京剧的对外传播效果。

一、传播主体

京剧的对外传播涉及两个方面的主体力量,一是以中国政府相关机构及组

---

[1] 刘席珍:《论京剧的审美特质——从休闲性与娱乐性说开去》,《吉首大学学报(社会科学版)》2006 年第 2 期,第 46—50 页。
[2] 哈罗德·拉斯韦尔:《社会传播的结构与功能》,中国传媒大学出版社 2013 年版。

织的官方传播和与戏曲相关的个人、组织、企业等民间主体。① 二是京剧的译者。这两个主体力量在京剧的对外传播中缺一不可。然而,京剧的传播主体面临着不聚焦、不广泛,以及专业译者短缺的问题。

中国高度重视中外之间的文化交流,积极主动地去引导中国戏剧文化对外传播,在京剧的对外传播中起着主导的作用。但与京剧相关的个人、组织、企业等民间主体在传播过程中仍然是较为"零星"的状态。这里的"零星"有两方面含义,一是传播主体缺乏代表性。我国京剧在海外演出大多都是"组织""剧团"的形式,导致传播主体身份模糊,没有代表性。而"相较概念化的官方机构或组织,独具人格魅力的戏曲演员'个人'更能打动观众"。讲好中国故事要以小见大,唱好中国京剧同样要落点到京剧演员本身。1930年梅兰芳访美前,曾专门印发关于梅兰芳本人的英文介绍手册,包括梅先生在中国京剧界的地位、影响力等,同时也在多家报社进行刊登介绍,其结果就是,海外民众对中国京剧有了具体的感知力,能够聚焦到具体的人物魅力中。正如中国对丹麦"童话王国"印象的建立是通过"美人鱼""丑小鸭""拇指姑娘"这一个个具象的人物。京剧的传播也一定要聚焦于代表性的人物。"零星"的第二层含义是京剧传播主体仍然较为局限。传播学者施拉姆指出:"人类传播是人做的某种事。"② 人是京剧艺术传播的载体,是京剧能够可持续发展,不间断传承的动力来源,对京剧艺术的生命力起着决定性作用。京剧需要进一步拓宽其传播主体,将更多的社会力量吸纳进传播主体团队中,而不仅仅局限于地方剧院、京剧协会等。来华留学生群体在中外文化交流中起着至关重要的作用,2017年以来,来华留学生人数已经在世界留学生人数中位列第三,在亚洲位列第一。留学生们可以亲身体验中国文化,拥有着年轻的、鲜活的思想,是国与国之间交流的桥梁。除了来华留学生,海外侨胞同样是京剧发展的重要社会力量。"客居异国的华人华侨既是海内外信息的接受者,也是中华传统文化的承载者和传播者,他们会通过多种途径在海外推广祖国的戏剧艺术。"海外侨胞与来华留学生都是中外文化交流的重要使者,在京剧的对外传播中国起到了重要的作用,是京剧拓展传播主体的重要方向。

译者也是京剧对外传播的重要主体,在京剧的对外传播中起到了决定性的作用。京剧的翻译不仅是语言的翻译,还涉及了文化符号的翻译。这就使得对京剧的翻译不同于普通翻译。它要求翻译人才具备京剧的专业知识,深厚的外语素养以及跨文化交流视野。艺术是相通的,没有国界,但表达艺术的语言却各

---

① 张安华:《当代中国戏曲对外传播的策略探析》,《戏剧文学》2017年第5期,第122—130页。
② 威尔伯·施拉姆:《传播学概论》,陈亮等译,新华出版社1984年版。

有不同。京剧平仄交错的音律、目不暇接的招式、色彩鲜明的服饰以及丰富奇特的脸谱，深深吸引着世界各地的人们。然而没有字幕的京剧却使他们困惑，看不懂其中的韵味，进而产生了跨文化交流的鸿沟。然而我国的京剧翻译人才出现断层，以京剧翻译为主要翻译方向的人才少之又少。我国应完善京剧翻译人才的培养机制，充分利用好高校的人才培育能力，进一步细化翻译专业的划分，引导学生接触、认识并熟练操作京剧翻译。培养既有扎实的外语应用能力，又具备开阔的国际视野以及戏曲知识的复合型翻译人才。同时也应加强中外译者的合作交流，通过海外研修、国际主题研讨会以及人员互派等形式，稳步扩充专业化京剧翻译队伍。

二、传播内容

京剧的对外传播内容即为京剧本身。京剧这种独特的表演艺术使其对外传播的历程并不是一帆风顺。

第一，京剧是中华传统文化的载体精华所在，而中西方文化属于异质文化，因而京剧在传播过程中面对着中西方文化差异带来的阻碍。"中国传统文化以儒家文化为主，主张'人治''中庸''均贫富'，强调人与人的和谐相处。是直觉感性认识的曲线思维模式。中国是典型的农耕文化，而西方文化属于外倾性商业海洋文化，重视个人权利和自我价值的实现，依赖理性表述，是一种直线型的逻辑思维模式。"[1]这样的文化差异性在中西方戏剧中也有所体现。西方戏剧重在"写实"，强调对现实生活的"摹仿性"；而京剧重在"表意"，舞台设置往往强调"空"的意境，摆一张小桌子即可。演员拿一个马鞭就可日行千里，是高度虚拟化的表意艺术。这样的"写意"使得京剧具有极强的艺术性，但同时也有可能造成海外观众的"误读"或者"不知所云"，针对这种情况，演出前的讲解是极为重要的。

第二，京剧的情节推动缓慢，和西方文化的快节奏文化有所冲突。从内容上讲，京剧剧情简单明了，注重通过演员精湛的技艺、舞台配置、念白等方式来描写人物丰富而又细腻的内心世界，整体情节推动较为缓慢。这可以使观众可以闲适地欣赏，即使错过其中一段，也无须惶恐，返回来依旧能读懂大意。如《贵妃醉酒》中，描述的就是杨贵妃身赴百花亭，而久侯不见唐玄宗，进而借酒消愁，抑郁

---

[1] 李孝敏：《构建和谐社会视阈下的中西文化研究》，《西安社会科学》2010年第28卷1期，第142—144页。

悲伤的心情。剧目情节简单,然而在各种道具、人物、声音的配合下,贵妃的内心世界被刻画得出神入化。而对于生活节奏较快的西方人来讲,可能会造成观剧过程中产生"急切"的心情,影响观剧体验。

第三,京剧对观众的文化背景知识有一定的要求。京剧是高度程式化、浓缩化的艺术。这种程式化表现为,"它载歌载舞,节奏鲜明,念白有调,动作有式,锣鼓有经,歌唱有曲牌和板式,武打有套路和档子"。因而京剧具有其独特的内容与形式。京剧中"唱""念""做""打"的艺术形式融为一体。其中"唱"为唱词,"念"为念白,"做"为京剧的表演动作,而"打"指的是格斗和武打场面。这几种艺术形式融为一体,塑造出独特的京剧文化。除此之外,京剧角色还有生、旦、净、末、丑(伶俐风趣或阴险狡黠的角色)五大行当之分。脸谱的样式、颜色也极为讲究,代表着某种人物性格。因此,想要真正看懂京剧,确实需要一定程度的文化知识。否则,文化差异会给观众带来认知负荷,从而使观众无法尽心地欣赏京剧。

鉴于中西文化差异以及京剧自身的程式性,京剧的对外传播一定要做好充分的准备工作。在梅兰芳先生访美前,前后共用了8年的时间来完成准备工作。出发前,梅兰芳的团队刻制了有关京剧的英文的宣传册,提前刊登在演出所在地的报刊上,并且在每场演出前都会发放给观众加以阅读。齐如山等人还精心绘制了200幅图画,涵盖了剧场、行头、古装衣、冠巾、胡须、扮相、脸谱、舞谱、乐器、钟、宫谱、角色等15类,都配以中英文的双语说明[1],更加形象直观地展现了中国京剧之美。考虑到海外观众的语言文化障碍,梅兰芳有意减少了京剧中"唱"和"念"的部分,增加了"做"和"打"的部分。顾及美国观众快节奏的生活习惯,梅兰芳将演出缩短至每晚一场,共四段,总计不超过两小时。反过来,梅兰芳这长达8年的准备工作也得到了美国观众的极大认可。根据当地文化做好相应的准备工作,可以大大减少海外观众在京剧接受中的认知负荷,为观众营造中轻松愉悦的艺术体验。

面对京剧异质文化中的受众群体,除了大量的准备工作,还应当对京剧的形式及内容进行"对话式"创新,从京剧内部进行发力。所谓的"对话式"创新,就是在最大限度保留京剧的原汁原味的基础上,着重于中外之间可"对话"的共通部分。京剧之所为成为"国粹",能够作为中国文化的表征,建构了中国人民的文化身份,在于其京剧独特的板式,在于其浓缩了的中国文化符号与中华文明价值

---

[1] 沈静、景义新:《跨越文化鸿沟——梅兰芳赴美演出成功原因探析》,《新闻世界》2009年第3期,第55—56页。

观。切不可为了迎合大众审美将京剧"平庸化",不可对京剧进行全切式删减、全否式创新,这样的京剧便不再是京剧。然而,京剧在其对外传播过程中确实也遵循"变则新,不变则湮"的艺术发展规律,如果不在形式和内容上进行创新,势必也会沦落至曲高和寡的田地。山东省京剧院院长郑少华表示"中国戏曲中蕴含的忠孝节义仁义礼智信,包含着基本的人性教化,这是全人类共通的东西"。人类艺术是相通的,他以著名的爱情剧《拾玉镯》为例,爱情是人类共同的追求,而京剧所表现出的又是另一种文化中的爱情。[①] 在京剧艺术传播的过程中,我们可以关注并发扬京剧中有人性深度和历史内涵的普适性价值以及民族特质,尽量减少因文化差异而造成的艺术接受困难。"对话式"创新的另一种方式就是用中国京剧的"四功五法"来演绎西方经典戏剧,如京剧版《哈姆雷特》和京剧版《浮士德》,这些戏剧的大获好评就是中西方文化"对话""交融"的果实。文化间的友好对话是人类社会繁荣发展的必要条件,正如著名哲学家哈贝马斯所言:"不同文化类型应当超越各自传统和生活形式的基本价值的局限,作为平等的对话伙伴相互尊重,并在一种和谐友好的气氛中消除误解,摒弃成见,以便共同探讨对于人类和世纪的未来有关的重大问题,寻找解决问题的途径。这应当作为国际交往的伦理原则得到普遍遵守。"[②]

三、传播渠道

传播渠道是传播中重要的一环,影响着传播内容的散落范围。许多海外民众并不是对京剧不"感冒",而是根本没有接触过京剧这种艺术形式。京剧要主动地走向世界,或许将来的某一天就会在某位观众的心中生根开花。京剧"走出去"必须依托有效的传播渠道。京剧,作为一种表演艺术,其过去主要的传播渠道是通过各个剧院进行实体的表演。在这样的传播形式下,京剧演员与观众得以面对面直接接触,这就大大增加了戏剧演出的感染力。但这种实地剧场的传播形式同时也大幅度限制了京剧的受众面积。20 世纪 90 年代以来,随着互联网的发展,京剧得以通过网络的方式传播,京剧被"送"入到海外民众的视野中,然而却没能够"走"进人们的心里。这是因为宏阔的京剧元素都被压缩至一小方屏幕前,大大减弱了京剧现场的艺术性与震撼性。京剧应紧随现代科技的脚步,

---

[①] 《550 名留学生体验"带讲解的京剧"想拜师学"真功夫"》,中国新闻网,http://www.chinanews.com/cul/2016/11-30/8078509.shtml,2016 - 11 - 30。
[②] 哈贝马斯:《从感性印象到象征表现》,李黎译,中国社会科学出版社 1999 年版,第 57 页。

发挥其独特的魅力,虚拟现实技术就是一个很好的选择。中山大学非遗中心段晓卿博士在《虚拟现实在戏曲类非遗保护中的应用模式的研究》提出:"常见的数字化保护手段难以全面、深入地介入戏曲传承与保护,虚拟现实作为'融媒介'典型代表,能够实现对现实空间的高度还原,通过多通道感官信息的自然交互产生强烈的临场感,为戏曲艺术的数字化传承与保护提供新的可能。"①将京剧以现代化的形式构造出一个虚拟化的空间,使得观众在这个虚拟世界中与京剧进行交互,不失为一种好的传播方法。只有善于向新兴的媒体技术借势,京剧的传播才有可能实现其最大效度。

其次,京剧的传播也要借助好市场的力量。国家和市场的互动是动态的、交互的。国家在京剧的传播中要起到把控全局的引导作用,同时要发挥文化企业的市场主体作用。京剧只有大胆走出"博物馆",融入市场,并进行适度的产业化转化,才有可能实现其可持续发展。可通过加强京剧文化IP化管理,提高京剧与受众之间的互动频率。"随着人们对知识产权的认识逐渐加深,当前娱乐文化产业IP化管理进一步成熟,IP化管理理念也成为跨产业、跨领域行业管理的重要参考。"②要努力打造属于京剧的文化IP,催生出相关的文创产品、产业。

最后,京剧的海外传播也可依托孔子学院的力量打造京剧传播的平台。孔子学院是世界了解中国、学习中国文化的重要窗口,是中华文明走出去的重要窗口。③ 京剧是中华文化的名片,因而依托孔子学院传播京剧文化与孔子学院自身的"中外文化交流"使命相契合。截至2018年,我国已在154个国家和地区建立了548所孔子学院和1 193个中小学孔子课堂,学员总数达187万人④,这部分庞大的人群是中国与世界友好交往的重要力量。孔子学院应充分发挥文化交流平台作用,采取各式各样的形式激发学员对京剧的兴趣,如举办京剧知识竞赛、脸谱DIY、京剧研讨会、京剧艺术节等,促进京剧文化在更多中外文化使者的心中生根。

四、传播客体

"受众是信息传播的'目的地',是信息传播链的一个重要的环节。受众又是

---

① 倪彩霞:《非物质文化遗产学的研究现状、热点及趋势——中国非物质文化遗产与民族民间艺术学科建设研讨会综述》,《文化遗产》2019年第2期,第139—144页。
② 卢强:《非遗视角下的山东农村土陶历史与文化创新》,《核农学报》2021年第2期,第516页。
③ 白紫薇:《孔子学院转型发展研究》,《中国人民大学教育学刊》2020年第4期,第63—72页。
④ 《世界各地已有548所孔子学院》,新华网,http://www.xinhuanet.com/world/2018-12/05/c_1210009045.htm,2018-12-05。

传播效果的'显示器'。"因此,中国戏曲对外传播效果实现的根本途径是海外受众的艺术接受。"京剧的海外传播的客体是与异质文化中的国外民众,有着语言和文化的差异。京剧与其传播客体间的语言差异使得京剧在对外传播的历程中面临着极大的困难,因而如何用异质文化中的人听得懂的语言去展现出京剧的真实面貌极为重要。正如中国人民大学国剧研究中心执行主任孙萍所言:"传播重点是京剧的翻译问题,从过去到现在,你都会发现,国内京剧院团赴国外演出时,因为翻译不当导致观众无法理解剧情,从而无法深入了解京剧。"①剧场翻译所涉及的不光是字对字的转换,而是两种文化的协商。"剧场翻译是一种流动性很强的实践,在这种实践中,没有固定的翻译程式,因为在戏剧翻译中,不仅有着语言和文化的差异,还涉及不同的戏剧体系,包括表演惯例和观众期望。"②这就使得剧场翻译被误读的可能性大幅度增加,艺术接受也变得困难起来。

"中国传统戏曲的翻译与传播不仅能保护我国非物质文化遗产的民族性,而且能促进各民族之间的交流,提升我国非物质文化遗产的世界性。"③京剧是极具独特性与民族性的艺术,其中所产生的巨大文化鸿沟的弥补必须由资深的译者以及成熟的翻译方法来弥补。京剧的翻译人才需要同时具备一定的京剧知识以及高深的翻译技能,京剧的翻译也不能是译者的单打独斗,而必须由一定的团队合作完成。正如苏姗·巴斯内特(Susan Bassnett)所言:"和其他类型的翻译不同,戏剧的翻译很明显是一种合作活动。"④这个合作团队中除了译者外,还应包括具备一定英语能力的本国京剧专家和英语为母语且对京剧感兴趣的外国专家。译后还需要采取科学的、实践的方式对翻译效果进行检验。美国夏威夷大学亚洲戏剧与表演系教授就是合作翻译的实践者,并以此取得了很好的效果。她的翻译实践是:"以中文为母语且懂英文的译者和以英语为母语且懂中文的译者合作,合作双方都必须精通京剧,最好达到能表演的程度,这样对京剧表演就有一种直觉,才能产生好的译文。而后通过京剧艺术家的评判以及剧院观众的反应对翻译的效果进行检验。"⑤客体的反馈是检验传播效果的重要途径之一。梅兰芳剧团在出国之前,"只要遇到欧美人士便问他们梅兰芳演戏哪些地方最

---

① 杨雪、孙萍:《京剧的传播任重道远》,《人民政协报》2016年8月15日,第009版。
② Johnston, D. *Metaphor and Metonymy: the Translator-Practitioner's Visibility. In Staging and Performing Translation* (pp. 11–30). London: Palgrave Macmillan, 2011.
③ 于强福:《非遗戏曲"走出去"译介研究述评》,《戏剧之家》2020年第35期,第15—16页。
④ Bassnett, Susan. *Translation*. London/New York: Routledge, 2013.
⑤ 黄庆欢:《京剧剧本翻译实践与思考——夏威夷大学魏莉莎教授访谈录》,《中国翻译》2019年第4期,第99—103页。

好,这就侦察了外国人的心理,好做出国演戏的准备。差不多有六七年的时间,问过的外宾就有一千多人"。通过这样的合作翻译,可以确保京剧的翻译同时具有可读性与可演性,保障了客体的艺术接受效果。

　　爱因斯坦曾说过:"物理给我知识,艺术给我想象力,知识是有限的,而艺术所开拓的想象力是无限。"优秀的文化、艺术值得世界上每一位人感受和欣赏。京剧艺术来源于一代又一代人中国人的智慧结晶,塑造了中华民族的身份认同。京剧海外传播需直面现状,保持包容开放的心态,以主动的姿态与世界文明进行平等对话。面对京剧当前对外传播的困境,首先应进一步拓展并塑造有代表性的京剧传播主体,完善京剧翻译人才的培养机制。其次要根据受众文化,积极对京剧进行"对话式"创新。再次,京剧应主动拥抱新的媒介手段和技术以拓宽传播渠道。最后,京剧的翻译需采取合作翻译的形式,用异质文化中的人听得懂的语言去展现出京剧的真实面貌,提升传播效果,全方位推动形成京剧海外传播新格局。

　　　　　　　　　　　　　　(作者单位:北京第二外国语学院英语学院)

关于中国瓷器与中国文化国际传播的思考

——以景德镇瓷器为例

郭戎荣

艺术是共通的,它可以通过人类情感的共鸣,跨越时间与种族的界限,直击人的心灵;艺术是流动的,优秀的艺术文化一旦被发觉就会自觉向外扩散,影响其他的民族。在漫长的历史岁月中,中国与世界的交流可以追溯到 2000 年前的丝绸贸易上。据公元前 5 世纪希腊历史学家希罗多德的著作《历史》记载,希腊人早就将以产绢而著名的东方大国称之为"绢国"。丝绸传到西方被看作是极其稀有之物,价格高昂,一度成为罗马帝国境内最名贵的奢侈品。不仅是丝绸,西方对中国外销瓷器的热爱可以从现存的早期绘画作品、文学描述中找出蛛丝马迹。17 世纪末 18 世纪初,中国瓷制餐具风靡欧洲,中国器物成为上流社会彰显品位的代表,让人们对神秘的东方大国充满了好奇与向往。瓷器上所装饰的亭台楼阁、花鸟鱼虫、名山大川、神仙吉兽、高士美人、民俗宗教、戏曲故事,成了西方想象认知中国的重要媒介,让西方人足不出户就得以窥探华夏之美。[1] 由此可见,中国瓷器通过艺术与商业途径在文化国际传播中的重要作用。

在千百年来的贸易往来和文化交流中,中国瓷器吸纳了其他国家的文化元素生产出了融合异域风情的彩瓷,例如销往欧洲的"珐琅彩瓷""粉彩瓷""耶稣会瓷""菲茨休瓷"等。同时,欧洲也自中国瓷器传入当地就开始了对其的仿制和研发,丹麦的"皇家瓷"是其中之一。1775 年建立的哥本哈根窑厂从模仿中国瓷器起家,到后来生产出具有自身特色的瓷器。[2] 作为丹麦最好的瓷器工厂,皇家哥本哈根窑厂的每件瓷器都由陶瓷艺术家手工绘制,工序精致繁杂,图案融合了丹

---

[1] Reed, Marcia. Paola, Dematte, ed. *China on Paper*: *European and Chinese Works from the Late Sixteen to the Early Nineteen Century*. Getty Research institute, 2011. p. 1.

[2] 陈进海:《世界陶瓷美术史》,黑龙江美术出版社 1995 年版,第 506 页。

麦特色,设计别出心裁。1790年,丹麦国王曾下令制作一套精美又具有代表性的"丹麦之花"瓷器赠送给俄国女王凯瑟琳二世作为礼物,所有瓷器的图案都是以丹麦植物园图鉴为蓝本绘制的。以瓷器作为国礼相赠,足见"丹麦皇家瓷"在丹麦国内的重要地位。由中国传统工艺品的商业贸易流传至欧洲,再到欧洲各国对中国商品的接受与内化吸收,都体现了古老中国强大的文化软实力,以传统工艺品为载体,作为艺术品、商品在海外贸易与文化传播发挥作用。因此,瓷是中华文化的海外传播的重要部分。

景德镇瓷器的历史与文化意义

"中国瓷都"景德镇是窑火千年不断的中国产瓷胜地。据《南窑笔记》记载:"新平之景德镇,在昌江之南,其冶陶始于季汉",江西景德镇陶瓷手工制陶业早在千百年前从农业中分离出来,是世界上唯一的以单一行业发展起来的城市。景德镇地处赣、皖、浙三省交界地带,是黄山、怀玉山余脉与鄱阳湖的过渡地带,地势平缓,境内以低山和丘陵为主,周边山区蕴含着大量优质瓷土资源。优越的地理条件为景德镇瓷器制造与区域贸易提供了天然条件。自唐朝起,景德镇就开始了瓷业烧造。在宋代,景德镇窑业异军突起,"天下咸称景德镇瓷器"。[1] 宋真宗景德元年(1004)因镇产青白瓷质地优良,遂以皇帝年号置景德镇,并沿用至今。元朝时期,是景德镇瓷器发展的重要时期,政府设置"浮梁瓷局",并更以景德镇税课监为提领,由此全国制瓷业逐渐向景德镇集中。到了明清时期,集瓷器生产优越条件于一身的景德镇,其制瓷业达到了鼎盛时期,形成了以市场为主导的精细化瓷业生产模式。不同瓷器制作工序由专门的瓷业生产者分工进行,既能保证了瓷器质量,又能满足外界瓷器需求。在传统手工生产背景下,景德镇制瓷业分工模式的优势,保证其在一段时间内,领先于全世界瓷业的发展。因此,在中国瓷器发展的历史长河中,历代瓷业工人的智慧和劳动造就了景德镇瓷器名扬海外,对中国乃至世界陶瓷文化发展有重大贡献。

景德镇瓷器自身拥有独特的审美价值。美国学者艾布拉姆斯曾提出构成艺术系统的四大要素为,艺术品、艺术家、宇宙(艺术品的主题)以及观赏者。景德镇瓷器作为艺术品,满足了人对美的追求,为人们提供了"赏心悦目"的视觉享受,阐释并外化人们心中的情感诉求,引发人们精神上的共鸣。马克思曾说过:"一个歌唱家为我提供的服务满足了我的审美的享受。"艺术品与观赏者彼此成

---

[1] 朱顺龙:《陶瓷与中国文化》,汉语大词典出版社2003年版,第248页。

就,古今名瓷,作为珍贵的工艺品,传播到世界各地,不仅是一种工艺品为其实现自身精神价值的追求,同样也满足了国外观赏者的艺术审美追求与艺术体验。

景德镇瓷器承载了千百年来中国社会的历史文化。从文化内涵角度来看,各民族的独特文化都需要依靠艺术手段来表达,中国传统瓷工艺品也是中华民族发出自我之声的载体与手段。景德镇承载了中华几千年的民俗、伦理、道德、哲学、宗教内核,从造型到图纹花样折射出中国社会的千姿百态。此外,中国瓷业工人在历史变革年代对瓷器的传承和改良,映射出中国社会历史的转折点。自清末至民国,景德镇的瓷业工人,以己之长奋力与外瓷抗争,使景德镇的传统技艺得以保留。仿古瓷、美术瓷均有很高成就,许多雕塑能手,例如"珠山八友"彩绘画家等优秀艺人脱颖而出。因此,景德镇陶瓷承载中华文化,反映民族历史,它的背后是一代又一代的中国瓷业工人对中国传统技艺的守护与传承,为弘扬中国的陶瓷文化做出了贡献。

景德镇瓷器拥有多样的人文内涵。对于瓷的人文记载不胜枚举:唐代柳宗元的《代人进瓷器状》,宋代蒋祁的《陶记》,明代王宗沐的《江西省大志·陶书》和宋应星的《天工开物·陶埏》,清《南窑笔记》(佚名)、唐英的《陶冶图编次》、朱琰的《陶说》、蓝浦和郑廷桂的《景德镇陶录》,民国时期有郭葆昌《瓷器概说》、江思清《景德镇瓷业史》、黎浩亭编撰的《景德镇陶瓷概况》、向焯编撰的《景德镇陶业纪事》等。1949年以来,又有江西轻工业厅景德镇陶瓷研究所编著的《中国的瓷器》(1963)、中国硅酸盐协会编的《中国陶瓷史》(1982),其中景德镇瓷器均占一定的篇幅。被国家授予有突出贡献中"青年专家"称号的刘新园所著瓷器考古文章已被国外报刊登载,其本人也曾多次赴国外讲学。

景德镇制瓷业也是一种科学技术。景德镇的科技事业在古时就有人对制瓷的科技成果进行总结,有《陶记》、《陶录》、《历法大论》、《痘疹订讹》、《东木堂医方集钞》等专业书籍。中华人民共和国成立后,对陶瓷发展史、古陶瓷、古建筑研究以及其他社会科学研究的人员逐渐增多,成果不断出现,有的专著已影响到国外。

当代景德镇瓷器海外传播的现状

中国,在西方语境下以"瓷国"著称,景德镇瓷器(以下简称"景瓷")是中国传统工艺最典型的代表。近些年来,社会的生产力得到了极大地提高,科学技术发展迅速,国际间的交通越来越便捷,网络媒体等传播媒介遍及各地,促进了跨国文化交流更加频繁。中国瓷器也在今天有了更多元化的传播途径,包括商业路径、展览路径、收藏路径、旅游路径、教育路径、媒介路径。

第一,景瓷作为商品的其商业路径。自古以来,经济利益可以显著有效地促进中国传统商品的商业传播。作为中国的"瓷都",江西景德镇自改革开放以来研发瓷器品种多达20类、2 000多款器型、7 000多种图案纹饰,形成了仿古瓷、旅游瓷、日用瓷等多种门类的陶瓷产品体系,远销130多个国家和地区。[①] 中国瓷器在国外有多个销售模式与途径,一是作为日用品在超市商场等零售,二是作为艺术品在艺术市场或艺术博览会交易、拍卖。为满足不同的客户需求,瓷器制造商满足不同质地、形态、图纹的定制,现代化批量生产使得景德镇瓷业再次蓬勃发展。

第二,景瓷作为物质文化遗产的展览路径。作为中国传统特色工艺品,近年来中国瓷器在各大展览会场作为中国传统工艺的代表出席,作为历史文物瓷器的独立外展、中国受邀参与的海外大型艺术展、博物馆间的合作展览、纪念特殊节庆的艺术品特展、国际选拔性艺术展览等。瓷器跨国展览多为公益性机构组织举办,常伴有媒体宣传推广、学术研讨会专题讲座、新闻发布会、宣传册和衍生品的售赠等途径吸引大众关注,但不以营利为目的,重在文化传播。同时,景德镇瓷器作为传统工艺品的对外传播,实现瓷器作为艺术载体的审美价值,推动中外艺术的交流和发展,因此跨国展览常作为中国文化国际传播的重要途径。

第三,景瓷作为艺术品的收藏路径。艺术收藏融合了以上两种传播路径的特点:其一,瓷器收藏是一种经济积累、保值和增值的投资手段,作为艺术品的不可再生性和稀缺性为其带来了巨额的利润,民间古董商和私人藏家视艺术收藏为一种商业投资;其二,艺术收藏也是一种文化传播活动,经由不同的收藏者延续收藏、私人展出的瓷器藏品等都对文化传播有一定推动作用。

第四,景瓷作为地方特产的旅游路径。旅游作为一种向异域游客展示当地文化的有效途径,是当今世界促进文化交流、国际合作的重要手段。景德镇是国家首批公布历史文化名城之一,陶瓷文化是其主体。在众多的古文化遗存中,已列入国家级重点保护单位的有湖田古窑遗址,列入省级重点保护单位的有浮梁镇北宋红塔和湖田、塘下、杨梅亭3处古窑址,市级文物保护点44处。现有陶瓷馆、陶瓷历史博物馆、古窑瓷厂、文物商店以及其他有关文博单位,为收藏、保存、考古、宣传做了大量的工作,吸引了大批专家学者和游客。商业旅游方面,游客可以在博物馆参观、参与陶瓷手工坊的瓷器制作、购买纪念品的过程中感受东方传统工艺品的魅力,且瓷器既富含艺术性又具有实用性,对于国内外游客来说有

---

① 李胜利:《建立景德镇"十大瓷厂"陶瓷纪念馆之思索》,《景德镇陶瓷》2009年2月号,第21页。

着较强的文化吸引力和艺术感染力。

第五，景瓷作为精湛技艺的教育路径。景德镇陶瓷教育已初步形成多层次、多规格、多形式的教育体系。直属轻工业部的景德镇陶瓷学院，还有省陶瓷工业公司主管的景德镇陶瓷职工大学，省轻工业厅所属景德镇陶瓷学校，一批陶瓷职业高中等，都是培养陶瓷技艺人才的基地。近些年来，随着中国经济发展日益向好，中华优秀传统文化得到了国内外的重视与关注。在海外的教育平台上，中国高校的国学教育课程被广泛注册学习，国外高校近年来也开设了中国艺术史、汉学研究相关科系，中国瓷器是其中的重要课题。中国在世界各地开设孔子学院、中国文化中心等机构开设艺术类课程，瓷器作为中国传统工艺品的优秀代表也取得了海外广泛认可和关注。

第六，景瓷作为一种传统文化符号的媒介传播路径。随着新媒体时代的发展，大众传媒的发展为瓷器的海外传播起到了重要作用。景德镇公开发行的刊物有《景德镇陶瓷》《陶瓷研究》。以陶瓷为题材创作的电影剧本有《瓷娃娃》《滴水观音》，分别由上海美术电影制片厂和上海电影制片厂摄制，填补了市场上电影创作的空白。还有一批文艺、戏剧、音乐舞蹈、美术、书法、摄影作品，发表、展出或演出，反映瓷城特色，体现了景德镇瓷器独有的文化魅力。景德镇瓷器作为一种文化符号，在各大媒体运营平台都可见其身影，其典雅独特的文化气质感染了众多对瓷器文化感兴趣的人。

综上所述，景德镇瓷器在海外传播中包含多种路径，从寻常家用餐具到正式外交场合相赠的特色国礼，从阳春白雪到下里巴人，瓷器对中国文化的对外推广渠道多样，范围广泛，同时在科技飞速发展的今天其仍然存在较大的发展空间。

景德镇瓷器在文化海外传播中的问题与对策

第一，过度追求利益导致的日用瓷器品质降低。国内价格战导致的市场竞争严重影响了日用瓷器的品质，市场上假货和残次品的出现导致了"劣币驱逐良币"的现象，日用瓷器生产商不断降低瓷器质量，原有中等质量瓷器在购买量降低的情况下提高了价格。因此出现了消费者对国货质量的不信任心理，使得日本瓷器和西方进口瓷器在国内更受消费者青睐。这进一步强化了中国民众的"崇洋媚外"心理。不只是景德镇瓷器，对于多数中国传统工艺品都面临着"对内价格战，对外质量战"的矛盾情况，使得部分商品价格低但质量差，质量稍好却价格虚高。文化自信的前提离不开商业经济的蓬勃发展，但不良的市场经济问题会间接影响人们的心理，观察中国现今对外传播成功的商业案例，例如家电、科技产品等,可以发现只有在国内得到中国消费者认可的商品,才有可能走出国门冲击海外市场,传扬中国思想与文化,被海外消费者广泛接受。因此,只有保护传统工艺,制定瓷器等级监查标准,提升市场品质才有利于中国传统工艺品传承发展、对外传播。

第二,制瓷艺术家逐年减少,景德镇瓷器艺术品数量少。尽管景德镇政府加大了瓷业教育的投入,但大机器生产时代的发展导致更多流水线工人的增加,而制瓷艺术家基数仍然较小,瓷器作为艺术品的审美内涵被大部分制造商忽略。缺少文化内涵的特色商品在海外贸易流通中艺术感染力降低,难以承载传扬中国优秀传统文化的重任。因此,要从内部对艺术教育的重视和为物质文化遗产传承艺术家的保护应得到重视,才能实现对外的传播和影响。

第三,景德镇瓷器存在与现代流行文化的融合度低的问题。近年来,汉服在青年群体中受到追捧与喜爱,在地铁、商场等公共场合出现了年轻一代身着汉服长袍披肩的现象,彰显了文化身份与传统内涵,青年人作为具有创造力、想象力的活跃群体对传统文化的兴趣有效的帮助了中国文化的继承与发展。但传统中国瓷器、漆器、雕刻等中国传统工艺品仍然常被认为"陈旧古板""不符合当代审美"。因此,改善这一问题还需要艺术审美教育得到重视,加强景德镇瓷器的国内外宣传,提高年轻一代对中国传统人文知识的兴趣与素养,为传统工艺品的现代发展注入活力。

总之,景德镇瓷器的传承与发展的内部发力不足是当今中国文化对外传播中面临的主要问题。其次,在对外交流融合过程中需要扩展传播路径和受众范围。在对外传播过程中,将官方与民间相结合,艺术与商业相结合,以官方渠道为主导,例如在官方场合作为外交国礼、珍贵遗产藏品的国际合作活动、教育系统中重视传统文化的学习与研究等;以民间渠道为核心力量,充分发挥群众的力量,人民群众对传统工艺品的接受程度决定了其对外传播的深度与广度。

结语

中国瓷器是中国物质文化的主要载体之一,瓷器、丝绸、雕塑等"丝绸之路"中的贸易商品是最早被海外接受的中国工艺,中国传统的审美情趣、思想内涵、价值观念在传统工艺品的海外流通中得到传播与融合。景德镇瓷器就是其中最典型的代表。如今,瓷器的市场被现当代西方主导的流行文化所冲击,"传统"二字似乎与当代追求"时髦"的年轻群体格格不入,曾经风靡西方上流社会的景德镇瓷器被"北欧冷淡风""日式简约风""美式复古风"等产品所取代,时尚的标准被西方重新定义。随着中国经济的快速发展，近年来文化自信概念，例如"文化软实力""文化竞争力""文化影响力"等被不断强调，中国文化"走出去"相关政策也成为中国文化建设的重点，景德镇瓷器作为兼具艺术性、文化性、商业性的产品有助于以民族艺术特色打开国际市场，通过艺术语言塑造中国形象，传扬优秀中华传统文化，进一步在文化层面实现中华民族实现文化复兴。

（作者单位：北京第二外国语学院英语学院）

参考文献：

1. 陈敬海：《世界陶瓷：人类不同文明和多元文化在交融中延异的土与火的艺术》（第五卷），沈阳画报出版社 2006 年版。
2. 陈进海：《世界陶瓷美术史》，黑龙江美术出版社 1995 年版。
3. 郭丹英：《中国古代外销陶瓷茶具研究》，浙江大学 2007 年版。
4. 李智：《文化外交——一种传播学的解读》，北京大学出版社 2005 年版。
5. 李胜利：《建立景德镇"十大瓷厂"陶瓷纪念馆之思索》，《景德镇陶瓷》2009 年 2 月号。
6. 王一川：《艺术学原理》，北京师范大学出版社 2011 年版。
7. 袁胜根，钟学军：《论清代广彩瓷与中西文化交流的关系》，《中国陶瓷》2004 年 6 月。
8. 张文婧：《中西文化交流视域下洋彩瓷的传承与发展》，《中华文化论坛》2016 年 4 月。
9. 朱顺龙：《陶瓷与中国文化》，汉语大词典出版社 2003 年版。
10. M. H. 艾布拉姆斯：《批评理论的趋向》，罗务恒译，《文艺理论研究》1986 年 6 月刊。
Reed, Marcia. Paola, Dematte, ed. *China on Paper：European and Chinese Works from the Late Sixteen to the Early Nineteen Century*. Getty Research institute，2011.

天津美食中的幸福文化身份建构与可持续发展对策

张家川

中国美食文化博大精深,由"鲁、川、粤、苏、浙、闽、湘、徽"构成的八大菜系基本涵盖了中国人自古至今大多的美味佳肴,同时也在世界美食中占有不可替代的地位。天津作为九河下梢的港口城市,是我国的四大直辖市之一,最早以"直沽寨"的名字出现在《金史》。清朝初期进一步发展出商业密集区,道光年间逐渐涌现出一批富商巨贾。商业的繁荣与商人的活跃,自然对消费行业产生巨大的推动力量。作为人们主要消费内容的饮食行业的发展表现得更为明显[1]。公元1662年,天津八大成之首"聚庆成"开张,这标志津菜体系的正式产生[2]。经过多年演变,天津菜已经成为天津文化的重要组成部分,也是天津人认识自己身份的重要参考。天津人开朗热情、乐观幽默,根据各个年度"十大幸福城市"的评比,在大城市中,天津的"上榜率"极高,在直辖市中,也经常力压北京、上海,挤进榜单之中[3]。天津作为中国面积比较小的城市,和同样小面积的欧洲国家丹麦一样,以小博大,在"幸福"这一文化软实力方面引人注目。

丹麦的幸福文化广为人知,最新的《2020年全球幸福指数报告》[4]显示,丹麦是世界上幸福指数排名第二的国家,仅在芬兰之后。事实上,丹麦几乎每年都保持在前两名的位置,在2012年、2013年和2016年都被评选为世界上最幸福的国家。丹麦文化中的"Hygge"更是作为幸福模式传遍世界。在食物方面,丹麦人的饮食追求善待自己,宠爱自己,纵容自己,给自己一个逃离健康生活需求的

---

[1] 由国庆:《天津卫美食》,天津人民出版社2011年版,第1页。
[2] 来新夏:《天津历史与文化》,天津人民出版社2008年版,第218—219页。
[3] 赵青:《城市居民幸福感的地域性分析——以天津为例》,《商业文化》2012年第11期(下半月)。
[4] 《2020年全球幸福指数报告》,https://happiness-report.s3.amazonaws.com/2020/WHR20.pdf,2020 - 12 - 20。

时刻[1],这与天津人乐观的精神不谋而合。天津人的饮食也以取悦自己为主,海鲜、肉食、甜食居多,但多盐多油也同样是天津菜的特点。在饮食中藏有文化的密码,天津文化作为中国文化的组成部分,需要根据自身的特点建构属于自己的文化身份。中国文化要批判的继承和发展,文化身份也要取其精华去其糟粕。丹麦人饮食上的幸福密码可以为天津美食提供解决方案。建构起天津文化身份的天津美食,也有很多改进的空间。食物作为文化软实力的展现,也可以构建更加有特色的中国文化身份。

天津饮食文化的历史和声誉

天津美食种类众多,历史悠久并广为传播,享有不俗的名誉。

从金代的"直沽寨",到明朝永乐二年被正式名为天津,这里地处九河下梢,拥有"七十二沽"的广阔水域。俗话说:吃鱼吃虾,天津为家。早在乾隆年间,就有了"十里鱼盐新泽国,二分烟月小扬州"的美誉[2]。古代天津盛产河豚,元末明初诗人成始终途经天津时,留下了"杨柳人家翻海燕,桃花春水上河豚"的诗句。乾隆十七年进士董元度曾到过天津,他对天津人吃河豚"顾嘴不顾命"的情形也大为惊叹。天津的小黄花鱼早在明清就已经是很金贵的朝中美味,《清稗类钞》有记载,黄花鱼在皇上品尝后就变成了酒楼里奇货可居的珍馐。罾蹦鲤鱼虽是八国联军侵华时期才诞生的美食之一,也被天津名士陆辛农在《食事杂诗集》中赞誉道"明川第一白洋鲤,烹做津沽罾蹦鱼"。天津爱吃刀鱼,分河刀鱼、海刀鱼两种,清道光年间的诗人周楚良记载说:"刀鱼如船上纤板,以入河口淡水网获得……无海腥味,最为鲜美。"除了鱼类,各种各样的虾也是天津人爱不释口的美味。清末的《津门竹枝词》说"争似春来新味好,晃虾食过又青虾"。陆辛农在《食事杂诗集》中同样说:"数来佳节说新正,百里鱼群海上争。夺命小舟轻似叶,青梭白晃供调烹。"每到春暖四五月间,渤海梭子蟹黄满顶盖肥,哪家正赶上囊中羞涩,借钱也要吃,就好像天津老话说的一样:"借钱吃海货,不算不会过。"现如今,海鲜海货依旧是津门的一大特色。

除了海鲜海货,天津的老店美食也远近驰名。随着政治经济文化的发展,天津的餐饮业已经在明末清初初具规模,到了清代中叶以后达到鼎盛,几百家小饭店遍布街巷。为庆贺康熙皇帝登基,在1662年热烈的鞭炮声中聚庆成饭庄在繁

---

[1] [丹麦]迈克·维金:《丹麦人为什么幸福》,中信出版社2017年版,第71页。
[2] 由国庆:《天津卫美食》,天津人民出版社2011年版,第4—180页。

华的估衣街宝宴楼胡同开业。《津门竹枝词》中记载："估衣街捏赵洪远,一饭寻常费万钱。"20世纪40年代津菜大繁荣,高档饭店的名厨大多掌握"五鬼闹判"的技能——同时掌控两个主火,一个次火,一个汤火。素菜、素席是天津饮食文化的重要组成部分,光绪三十二年,在天津文化名士林墨清的倡议下,真素楼选址大胡同中间坐西朝东的门面开业。"真素"二字援引《世说新语》中"亦缘其性真素"之句。狗不理包子是天津美食三绝之一。20世纪20年代末,冯问田在《丙寅天津竹枝词》中说:"包子调和小亦香,狗都不理反名扬。末夸今日林风月,南阁张官久擅长。"除此之外,经典的八大碗与烧肉,隆冬四珍——银鱼、紫蟹、铁雀、韭黄、四大扒,都能在不同程度上代表天津美食的各个历史阶段。

除了正餐,天津人还对早餐非常重视,甚至是茶余饭后的小吃和甜点,在天津的饮食中都从来不会被忽略,反倒成为别具特色的风景线。馃子从宋代就传入了天津地区,人们痛恨秦桧,让他变成"油炸鬼"。大致是清朝的时候,渐渐改名为"棒槌馃子"。煎饼果子是最具特色的风味小吃,也是最受老百姓喜爱的早餐。锅巴菜在天津方言中常念作"嘎巴菜",清康熙年间蒲松龄的《煎饼赋》中的"汤合盐豉,末锉兰椒,鼎中水沸,零落金缕"形象的比喻了锅巴菜的情状。"天津甘栗"也是驰名四海,甚至出口创汇的名品特产。清光绪年《津门纪略》记载道天津东门牌坊下的郑三糖炒栗子远近闻名,口碑极佳。其他的如大梨糕、熟梨糕、豆根糖,也都是充满天津特色的小吃。

想要了解天津美食,百闻不如一见,实地考察品尝更能体验先贤笔下描绘的美味。

天津的幸福饮食中的文化身份

文化身份这一话题自本世纪初以来饱受争论。中国在改革开放之后经济快速发展,社会的快速发展与全球化的影响交织在一起,中国自身的文化身份也不再一成不变,而是动态的,发展的。全球化刺激了不同国家、不同文化的民族自我意识,并强化了对于自身文化认同的需要。① 在中国,大城市的城市化进程快速推进,大城市人民对自身文化身份的认识也不再局限于本国、本民族,而是一种可以被感知的文化融合过程。在这种碰撞之中,一方面要警惕强势话语的文化霸权,避免在认识自我和发展自我文化认同时,被强大的"东方主义"话语所吞没,也就是避免一种"东方主义"话语的内在化。另一方面,在建构文化身份

---

① 苏勇:《文化身份认同与建构中的文化主体性》,《贵州师范大学学报(社会科学版)》2009年第1期。

时,又要避免极端民族主义的傲慢与偏狭①。中国要建设成为富强民主文明和谐的现代主义国家,和谐、幸福感高的文化身份值得推崇。

北京是首都,上海被称为"魔都",天津却被称作"哏都"。"哏"在天津方言中的意思是有趣、幽默的意思,天津人的幽默和开朗重点体现在天津的"吃文化"和"玩文化"上。赞赏某人见多识广、阅历丰富,天津人用"吃过见过"形容,这显然比"读万卷书行万里路"来的直观和实在,在更深的思维层次中,读书、行路是受罪的,吃是享福的。中国各菜系饭庄遍布全城,虽没有创造出本地的品牌菜系,但以"狗不理"包子、"十八街"麻花为代表的速食快餐还是闻名全国的。爱吃会吃、爱玩会玩在天津是被认为是享福的生活②。

天津人可以从饮食中感到幸福,在食品的制作和命名中可见一斑。"狗不理包子"的创始人高贵友出生在直隶武清县下朱庄(今天津市武清区)。中国有句古话,歪名好养活,高友贵的父亲中年得子,便将这个孩子取个小名叫作"狗子"。高贵友从小心灵手巧,跟师傅学得手艺后,开了一家专营包子的小吃部——"德聚号"。由于高贵友手艺精湛,料精馅足,做出来的包子口感柔软,鲜香不腻,形似菊花,煞是可人,因此生意十分火爆,以至于他忙得根本无暇跟进店的顾客打招呼,于是老食客们都戏称高贵友"狗子卖包子——不理人"。这样口口相传,喊顺了嘴,"狗不理"包子由此诞生,而"德聚号"这几个字却戏剧性地被人们淡忘了③。现如今,狗不理包子作为天津美食三绝之首,成了游客到天津必吃的一道美食。甚至国外友人也对这种有着奇怪名字的包子深感兴趣,狗不理包子作为人们想到天津必然联想到的美食标志,同样从侧面建构了天津文化。天津人对狗不理包子这个稍显"粗俗"的名字并不抗拒,反而自豪地邀请各地友人前来品尝。天津人的幽默导致平时交流中开玩笑的自由度很高,根据霍尔的文化维度理论来看,天津人的权力距离似乎并不远,每个人对自己的面子并无特别看重,快乐在文化中的占比更大。

甜食同样也是天津美食文化的重要组成部分,春天吃油蜡纸包裹着的大梨糕,夏天吃透心凉的二斗刨冰,秋天吃蘸糖的切糕,冬天吃推着呜呜响小车的老爷爷卖的熟梨糕。一年四季天津人对甜食的喜爱都不会间断。天津是海洋性气候,冬天不会非常寒冷,夏天也没有炎热到不可忍受,这就导致了天津人很喜欢在晚饭后或者周末的闲暇时间出去遛弯。对于有小孩的家庭来说,晚上孩子出

---

① 苏勇:《文化身份认同与建构中的文化主体性》,《贵州师范大学学报(社会科学版)》2009 年第 1 期。
② 赵青:《城市居民幸福感的地域性分析——以天津为例》,《商业文化》2012 年第 11 期(下半月)。
③ 钱国宏:《"津门三绝":天津人的地标美食》,《时代邮刊》2018 年第 7 期。

去玩耍,自己和邻居聊一聊家长里短,是再舒服不过的日常生活。通常街边都会出现各式各样的小贩推车叫卖,家长遍会经不住孩子的央求,买些甜食让孩子和小伙伴们分食。天津的甜食更多存在于街头巷尾,而不是正式的聚会和宴会,甜食也作为茶余饭后的调和剂,增进了邻里之间的关系。虽然过于多的甜食摄入不利于健康,但是天津人的一个主要性格特点是信奉"知足常乐"。小富即安,安就是幸福,对那些生活富足仍奋力打拼的人,天津人常常表现出不解:有吃有喝,干嘛这么拼命?"不知足"是天津人对生活现状不满意的人的一种温和的批评。比上不足,比下有余是大部分天津人可以接受并乐于保持的状态。就算有一天的不愉快,几口甜到心眼里的熟梨糕,就能化解大部分烦恼。

北京有炸酱面,河南有烩面,天津人的特色是"捞面"。天津捞面和其他面种不同,并没有固定的配料和菜码。一般来说,天津的捞面一家一个样,甚至每位大厨,面对不同的群体,做出来的捞面都有所不同。捞面自然也以面为底,但面只能盛到碗的三分之一处,剩下三分之二全部堆满了不同的菜码。要说可以加的菜可太多了,以土豆、西红柿、木耳、鸡蛋、虾仁为底的卤子,豆芽菜或者菠菜,紫甘蓝或者洋白菜,土豆丝炒胡萝卜丝或者豆角炒肉,只有你想不到,没有天津人加不到。传统的做法中还有用花椒、香菜、热油和酱油调制而成的花椒油,在拌好捞面之后撒在上面,最后撒上一把黄瓜丝和黄豆,吃的时候配上宝坻大蒜,真是神仙一般的感受!天津人好客而包容,每当家里来客人,捞面是必不可少的标准招待套餐。不仅如此,捞面由于菜码过多,制作的过程也非常繁琐,耗时比较大,所以很多时候天津人也把捞面当成家中团圆的大餐。一家人和和美美,一起准备具有家庭特色的捞面,天津人的幸福就是如此的简单。

天津美食文化身份可持续发展对策

在生活节奏日益加快,竞争越发激烈的 21 世纪,简单的幸福渐渐变成一种奢侈品。符合国家核心价值观的天津美食文化应该担负起发扬中国文化的责任,做助力中国文化传播的助推器。饮食是人们日常生活的刚需,非常适合作为文化传播的抓手,做好可持续发展的对策尤为重要。

首先,天津的美食文化应该进行内部改良。文化是发展的,不是一成不变的,不能因为害怕失去自己的特点而故步自封,停滞不前。资料显示,天津人的肥胖率在全国排名中遥遥领先,这很有可能源自天津人饮食中的高糖分摄入。虽然随着科技的进步,医疗设施的普及和医疗服务的完善,疾病的治愈率得到显著提升,但没有科学的饮食习惯,重盐重糖,逞一时口舌之快,仍会对身体造成伤害,导致心血管疾病,严重的会危害生命安全。幸福的饮食文化不该以健康为代价,而是应该认识到健康饮食的重要性,给幸福加上一层保障,让幸福更加长远与持久。对于天津美食文化,要取其精华去其糟粕。天津人比较重视饮食的可持续发展和减少浪费,比如天津人在购买煎饼馃子的时候总是习惯带去自己家里的鸡蛋,而不是使用店里的鸡蛋,经济又实惠。

其次,天津美食文化应该强化文化身份意识,增强文化自信,发挥文化凝聚作用。天津美食由于历史原因,发展较早,很多美食属于传统美食,不太适合现今社会的快节奏,当代年轻人熟悉的美食越来越少,传统美食的意义也渐渐忘却。各个民间组织和单位可以通过组织阅读会、交流会,与传统大厨面对面,带领本地人加强对传统天津美食的认识,增强对自己文化身份的自信。本地政府也应该在改良的基础上加强对美食文化的扶植力度,挽救濒临灭绝的小吃和传统菜肴,让物质力量和精神力量相结合,在满足社会需要的基础上加强文化的传播。比如聚集了天津各种小吃的南开区南市食品街,由于多年未变,室内半开放导致供暖问题无法解决,宣传力度不够,虽然距离南开大悦城很近,仍是无法吸引人流。本地政府可以加强相应的保障措施,让天津美食文化"活起来""动起来",反过来加强天津人的身份认同和文化凝聚作用,促进文化的传播。

最后,借着时代的东风,天津美食文化可以结合其他天津优秀文化,适应社会需要,利用新媒体短视频的快速传播来满足大众的期待。天津菜不在中国的八大菜系之中,但是提到相声,中国人会首先想到天津这个城市。天津经典相声之中的《报菜名》,"蒸羊羔,蒸熊掌,蒸鹿尾儿,烧花鸭,烧雏鸡儿,烧子鹅,卤煮咸鸭,酱鸡,腊肉,松花,小肚儿……"几乎全国各地的每个人都能来一段。这种传播较广的,已经成为天津特色的艺术方式,可以同天津美食的传播结合起来,既满足了观众对于娱乐的需求,又通过天津的美食传播了天津文化,促进了文化身份的可持续发展。近年来短视频平台兴起,很多传统艺术都采用这种新媒体的方式进行传播,关于天津美食的传播目前还只是通过个别天津人自己的个人号进行平时的探店与美食制作方法的分享。官方媒体可以借时代东风,用官方短视频账号的方式传播天津美食文化。在快乐稀缺的现在,传播幸福的文化和价值观,一定程度上也满足了大众的期待。

天津美食作为中国美食不可分割的一部分,由于其中蕴含的"幸福"元素而在新时代焕发出新的生命力。不论是饱受赞誉的海鲜传统老店,还是小食早餐,天津人的幸福基因在天津美食中充分展现,并参与建构了天津人的文化身份。但是文化需要进步,文化的传播也需要在改善的基础上加强,天津的美食文化应该在内部改良的基础上强化本地人心中的文化意识和文化自信,并利用短视频等新媒体的方式,强化自身文化身份的可持续发展,为传播中华文化尽一份力,增强中国的文化软实力。

(作者单位:北京第二外国语学院英语学院)

中国京剧文化的对外传播

刘 琦

了解京剧

2010年11月6日,联合国教科文组织政府间保护非物质文化遗产委员会第五次会议在肯尼亚首都内罗毕举行,这次会议对于中国有着特殊意义,24个成员国共同审议并通过了中国京剧的申报材料,中国京剧成功入选"人类非物质文化遗产代表作名录"。中国京剧在世界的文化领域有了一席之地,在中华民族优秀传统文化宝库中占有独特地位的京剧艺术,进一步得到了世界性的公认和肯定。

京剧是我国流行范围最广、影响力最大、最能代表中国戏曲文化的剧种,不仅在国内广为流传,在国外也成了中国戏曲的代表。京剧被称为"中国国粹",亦有"国剧"之称。京剧因形成于北京而得名。京剧表演继承和发扬了中国载歌载舞的戏剧传统,经过多年在舞台上的实践和改进,逐渐有了自己的一套体系。京剧是综合性表演艺术,集唱(歌唱)、念(念白)、做(表演)、打(武打)、舞(舞蹈)为一体,通过程式化的表演手段叙演故事,刻画人物,表达喜、怒、哀、乐、惊、恐、悲的思想感情。[1] 唱、念、做、打具有严格程式,不同角色、行当也有着不同的规范和路数。京剧表演要求各角色之间配合密切,演员与乐队彼此互相照应、默契合作,使得表演节奏紧张而有条不紊,战斗场面激烈并具有美感。京剧的角色行当现在主要分为生、旦、净、末、丑五大类。这五大行当的表演程式都各有特点,所表现出该行当人物的性格特点也各不相同,人物有忠奸、美丑、善恶之分,各个栩

---

[1] 周育德:《中国戏曲文化》,中国戏剧出版社1995年版。

栩如生,形象鲜明。从京剧的行头能看出中国几千年主流的服装文化形态,经过改进其有利于京剧演员进行唱、念、做、打表演技巧的表现。不同角色行当的服饰装扮有着严格的规定和精细的分类。从服装我们能分辨出角色所处的朝代和在社会中的地位,戏装的样式是表现角色社会地位的重要标志。脸谱也是京剧装扮中重要的一项,在京剧发展的过程中,京剧脸谱经过多个剧种的脸谱融合改造形成了独特的京剧脸谱。脸谱色彩明艳,用色大胆,用具有高对比度的颜色大笔勾勒出人脸的五官。其造型夸张独特,不同的五官造型显示出不同的人物性格,脸谱是辨认善、恶、忠、奸的象征。不同角色行当脸上的颜色象征了这个人的性格、品质和命运,是理解剧情的关键,也是京剧艺术的一大特色。

中国戏曲文化的对外传播已有几百年的历史,京剧作为世界古老的戏剧文化之一,具有其独特的艺术风格,东方美学价值和综合艺术的表现手法。京剧作为中国传统文化的重要标志,在东西文化交流过程中起到传播、介绍中国文化的作用。从13世纪开始,中国戏曲先后在欧洲、美洲及东南亚等海外地区进行了传播,与当地的戏剧艺术等文化交流融合。自15世纪起,世界文化交流越发频繁,使得中国戏曲对外有了更深一步的交流。中国戏曲和演员登上了欧洲舞台,西方人也开始领略到中国戏曲艺术的独特魅力。17世纪起,有关中国的著作在欧洲大量出现,东方文化带给西方不一样的文化体验,为西方戏剧的艺术创作提供了新鲜的素材。20世纪前半叶,尤其是20世纪二三十年代,以梅兰芳的访美演出为代表的京剧文化交流传播活动成了中国戏曲跨文化传播的高潮。1915年,梅兰芳应中华民国政府外交部要求接待了一个美国教士团,演出《嫦娥奔月》,这可能是中国京剧演员最早在中国土地上向外国人正式介绍京剧。此后,他在北京无量大人胡同的寓所成了"外交公寓",接待了包括大文豪泰戈尔、英国哲学家伯特兰·罗素在内的各国文艺界、政界、实业界、教育界等各界人士六七千人。[1] 梅兰芳的演出改变了当时西方对中国戏曲甚至对中国人的偏见,推广了中国戏曲以及中国文化,也为出国访问做了铺垫。1930年,梅兰芳率访问团抵达美国。这次访美活动在文化交流层面取得了极大的成功,美国主流媒体争相报道和评论,梅兰芳和团队得到了艺术界人士的热情款待。随后,梅兰芳又出访苏联,在苏联同样掀起了一阵欣赏评议中国戏曲的热潮。此外,1932—1933年间,另一位京剧名角程砚秋也前往苏联和欧洲多国进行游学,在游学的过程中进行京剧表演的同时也参加了各种形式的文化交流活动,他使欧洲国家进一步了解了中国京剧,进行京剧研究,并改进西方戏剧。

---

[1] 刘珺:《中国戏曲对外传播的跨文化障碍》,《戏曲艺术》2010年第31期。

虽然京剧几百年来一直坚持对外传播并取得了一些不错的进展,但是传播的过程并不是一帆风顺的,在历史的每个阶段都遇到了不同的困难。在全球化背景下,中国京剧的跨文化传播又一次面对挑战,只有认识到中国京剧在传播中所遭遇的文化认同上的冲突和困难,才能在当今历史条件下迈向新征程、再上新台阶,进行更好的跨文化交流。

京剧对外传播面临的困境

1. 翻译难,理解更难

语言是传播的工具,京剧院团赴国外演出时,如果没有适当的翻译会导致观众无法理解剧情,从而无法真正了解京剧所传达的内容。一直以来,戏曲的翻译一直是对外传播过程中的一个难题。戏曲唱词并不是白话文,理解起来有一定难度,在翻译中既不能字字直译,又不能完全抛开字面意思进行意译。既要照顾国外观众的理解习惯,还要力争保持戏曲唱词的音韵。京剧词汇的翻译的确很难,很多词语是现在白话文中不常使用的表达,也是中国人特有的表达,很难在外文中找到相对应的词语。光是京剧名称的翻译就有很大的难度,有很多剧名是以地名作为剧名,比如《武家坡》《三岔口》等,如果以拼音直译,国外观众很可能不知所云。

表演在一定程度上能跨越语言障碍,观众可以通过情景设置和人物表演猜测人物的性格和故事的发展脉络,但这种猜测对于剧情的理解是模糊的,也可能是错误的,无法深入,因此合适的翻译在对外传播的过程中必不可少。梅兰芳在美国表演时,会提前请翻译向观众讲述故事梗概,并简要介绍京剧的表演形式,这样让观众在观看演出前有一定的准备,不至于一头雾水。目前,除极少数的经常对外演出的剧目外,很多剧目都缺乏合适的翻译。英语翻译很多,但精通戏曲的翻译人才缺口很大。大多数译者对专业戏曲知识了解甚少,甚至看不懂台词,翻译的准确性难以保障,更不要说表现出传统戏曲特有的意境和韵味了。戏曲唱词对的翻译的要求极高,译者需具备扎实的语言基础、高超的翻译技巧、对不同文化的了解和对戏曲文化的熟悉。如何提高戏曲的翻译水平,从而打破语言壁垒让外国观众有更好的观赏体验,是中国戏曲深层次跨文化交流迫切需要解决的问题之一。

2. 文化差异大,欣赏门槛高

中国戏曲的自身固有虚拟性、程式化的风格特点和独特的审美取向。对于不了解京剧的人来说有比较高的欣赏门槛,观众对信息的理解难度较高。

西方戏剧表演是写实派的，日常生活什么样，戏剧就怎么演，而中国的戏曲表演较为抽象，有独特的程式化符号，比如经常出现在京剧中的开门洒扫、上马赶路等特定情节都是由一系列固定的规范动作来表达的。而这些符号和规范都是约定俗成的，脸谱的不同颜色、画法代表了什么人，已经具有了程式化规范。观众仅通过脸谱就能很大程度上识别出人物的形象，也能通过脸谱蕴含的象征意义进一步猜测接下来剧情的发展。对于熟悉戏曲的观众来说，这些程式没有理解上的困难，不会造成观看表演中的阻碍，但对于之前没有戏曲艺术知识储备的观众来说，理解所有的程式符号是非常困难的。西方观众缺乏中国文化背景知识，解读京剧时会产生额外的认知负荷，这也降低了京剧的亲和力、感染力和吸引力。

除此之外，中国戏曲的音乐与西方的音乐样式差异很大，无论是乐器还是音律，这种中国传统的音乐形式不同于其他任何一个国家的音乐，很难取得共鸣。对于敲锣打鼓、丝竹齐奏的场面，许多国外观众最初是难以接受的。中国古典音乐有着长期的历史渊源，国外观众对此缺乏了解和审美认同。因此，仅靠一两场戏曲演出，是很难让国外观众充分体会到中国戏曲的韵味，也很难了解中国几千年文化的精髓和内涵。

虽然中西方文化中有很多不同之处，但这不是我们对传播中困难妥协的理由。文化正是因为不同才异彩纷呈，我们应该更加勇于表达，积极传播自己独特的文化。京剧工作者应有文化自信，善于挖掘带有中国特色的文化亮点，表达出中国文化传神、写意、内敛和抒情的深刻内涵。

3. 兴趣不足，缺乏市场

对于文化交流的欲望应该是相互的，而不是"一厢情愿"的。文化传播面临着一个很残酷的现实，那就是无论传播的人多么卖力，如果目标观众缺乏了解的兴趣，那么所有的努力都是徒劳。只有真正引起国外观众的兴趣，吸引他们主动了解京剧，才能算得上是对外传播的成功。中国戏曲在国外的演出重交流而轻市场。梅兰芳的对外访问虽然掀起了一波中国京剧热潮，这股热潮来的快散的也快，没能开辟出中国戏曲的长期海外市场。传播戏曲文化，是希望来自其他民族、其他文化的观众通过认识和理解中国戏曲，能够更好的了解中华传统文化的内涵、价值观和审美观。如果缺少海外演出的固定观众，这一目的将无法实现。京剧的中国市场吸引了很多外国游客，他们会观看一两出京剧演出体验中国的传统文化。这类观众有极大的不稳定性和流动性，戏曲表演对于他们来说只是旅游项目中的一项活动，对京剧缺乏进一步了解的兴趣，很难成为中国戏曲的固定消费者和欣赏者。

上述三个方面指出了一些京剧传播中一直存在的问题,这些问题并不全面。在新的历史时期,我国以京剧为主的戏曲对外传播交流工作中还有一些其他的困难。纵观历史,这些问题究其根本都是由文化差异所引起的。在全球化的今天,国家与国家、文化与文化之间的距离被不断的拉近,科学技术的发展使得交流有了更多便捷的工具,这是机遇也是挑战。只有以积极的心态解决文化传播中的困难,在文化交流的过程中求同存异,才有可能解决当前戏曲对外传播的问题,让戏曲文化真正在世界舞台上传递中国声音、讲好中国故事。

从《霸王别姬》看京剧的影视化交流

电影是一门现代综合性艺术,融合音乐、美术、舞蹈、文学等多种形式为一体,相对京剧艺术来说,是一门较新的艺术形态。目前电影只有百余年历史,却在世界上形成了空前的文化影响力。随着时代的发展,电影越来越受到人民群众的喜爱。看电影成了现代人日常生活中不可缺少的一部分,也成了现代人了解不同文化的主要形式。1895年卢米埃尔兄弟拍摄了世界上第一部电影,1905年中国人终于开拍了属于自己的电影——由著名京剧大师谭鑫培主演的名段《定军山》。在这个具有重大里程碑意义的作品中,任景丰选择的题材便是国粹——京剧[①],京剧与电影的结合既能让中国人迅速地接受电影这一新鲜的艺术形式,又能把京剧这一传统中国艺术搬到大银幕上,走出国门,走向世界。

1993年,电影《霸王别姬》上映,导演陈凯歌通过影片向观众展示了一对戏子的爱恨情仇、时代的浮沉变迁,京剧艺术贯穿始终,推动了故事情节的发展。《霸王别姬》曾获得第46届戛纳电影节金棕榈奖,金球奖最佳外语片奖等多个国际大奖,同时,还入选了美国《时代周刊》评出的"全球史上百部最佳电影"名单。《霸王别姬》在多个国家上映并获得了不错的票房,在韩国、日本等国多次重映。可见,艺术是不分国界的,各国观众对于中国的传统艺术充满兴趣。不少看过《霸王别姬》的国外影迷,都对我国的京剧艺术产生了很大的兴趣,这是一次传统文化的传承,也是一次传统文化的传播,《霸王别姬》完成了一次有力的文化输出,在电影史上留下了一笔浓墨重彩的京剧色彩。

《霸王别姬》这部影片以时间顺序发展,横跨几个时代,讲述了一个动人的故事。主人公的命运和京剧艺术的命运连结在一起,在社会政局极为动荡的历史

---

① 陈旋:《论中国传统戏曲在电影中的魅力与价值——以〈霸王别姬〉和〈活着〉为例》,《戏剧之家》2018年第32期。

背景下经历了几起几落。影片用京剧作为线索推动叙述,在经过清末、民国、抗战、解放、"文革"等几个时期的变换更迭下,主人公程蝶衣和段小楼从风光至极的名角落魄到穷困潦倒的路人。虽然外国观众可能对于中国的历史,或者京剧文化不太了解,但是观众通过电影讲述的故事了解主人公的爱恨情仇,通过感受主人公的命运,了解到他们和京剧深深的羁绊,和主人公一起走过了与京剧相伴的一生。以戏曲融于影片并以其为主要叙事线索,具有强烈的形式美和造型美,成就了电影独一无二的中国特色的具有戏曲元素的视听美学风格。影片尽心设计的画面以及背景音乐,都让观众置身其中,近距离的沉浸在一个推崇京剧艺术的环境之中。戏曲的造型艺术在视听上呈现别样的形式美感。电影《霸王别姬》中最先夺人眼球的便是京剧的造型艺术,电影开头便是程蝶衣与段小楼扮上虞姬和霸王的角色去馆里走台,程蝶衣身着锦衣霞帔,头戴虞姬凤冠,手里拿着红绸宝剑,段小楼则是黑白脸谱,身着霸王战袍,头顶将冠,黑色长髯,奠定了电影的戏曲服装的整体风格,使之呈现出强有力的视觉冲击,展现戏服之精美,京剧之精妙。《霸王别姬》这首电影中的同名曲是由著名作曲家赵季平先生作曲的,紧扣京剧中的曲调,结合了多种中国传统乐器,乐音悦耳、凄哀,衬着宏大悲壮的乐队声,把剧中的人物命运和情感波动营造得跌宕起伏,具有历史的厚重感。

纵观《霸王别姬》全片,传统文化国粹京剧从纵向时空上贯穿始终,而影视艺术则在横向上与其相辅相成,我们可以从中看到一部京剧的发展史话。电影镜头追随着历史的脉络,不停地带领观众以各种视角徜徉、穿梭、沉浸其中。影视艺术为观众赋予了一种特殊视角,可以随时切近,仿佛亲身经历影片中的故事。《霸王别姬》的杰出之处不只在于中华传统文化与电影艺术表现形式的深度融合,而更在于这部影片表达出来的那种对于传统文化的深沉的感情,而这份深沉的感情可以引发全球观众的共鸣。通过电影的美学表达和情感共鸣,京剧的魅力得到了放大,越来越多的观众对京剧产生了主动的兴趣,兴趣是打破文化差异最好的动力。

新时代中国京剧的对外传播

京剧艺术博大精深,剧本、表演、音乐、服饰、舞台美术,不管从哪个单独的角度深入研究,都足以编写成一部巨著。面对这样深邃的艺术,需要我们在"专而精"与"博而全"之间寻找平衡,这也是京剧对外传播必须要努力贴近的标准。

影视化传播是我国传统艺术走出国门的一种有效途径,我们还需要结合时代特征寻找更多京剧艺术对外传播的新型途径、科学模式,为中国优秀传统文化更好地走出去探索出一条行之有效的道路。让海外的观众通过电影、电视、互联网等多个平台,接触、学习戏曲知识,了解中国的经典艺术作品,熟悉中国的传统文化,理解中国人的情感、价值观,从而对中国有更全面深刻的认识。

因此,想要弘扬我国传统文化,让京剧文化真正的"走出去",我们应该大力拓宽市场,学习使用新的媒体平台,大胆创新京剧表演形式。我们可以用京剧的形式演绎西方人所熟知的故事,用开放的姿态拥抱西方文明,实现中西文明的碰撞,在拓宽国际市场的同时,还要了解国外观众的兴趣取向,引起更多情感上的共鸣,吸引外国观众主动了解中国,让他们领略到中国传统文化的无穷魅力。

从龙门石窟看文化自信与文化交流

沈安童

中国文化遗产作为中华优秀传统文化的一部分,是文化自信的重要源泉,它见证了中华文明的发展,彰显了中华文化的活力,承载了中华民族的灵魂。中华文化源远流长,自然有着丰富的文化遗产,到目前为止,中国先后申报并批准列入《世界遗产名录》的遗产有55项,其中有37项文化遗产、4项自然与文化双遗产。这些文化遗产丰富了中国文化的内涵,在展现文化自信上发挥了重要作用。龙门石窟坐落在中国河南省洛阳市,于2000年被列为世界文化遗产,是世界上营造时间最长、造像最多的石窟之一,体现了中国独特的人文景观和深厚的历史文化底蕴。龙门石窟作为文化遗产,参与构成了优秀的国家文化,激发了民族自豪感,是文化自信的坚实基础。丹麦的小美人鱼铜像虽然不是石刻艺术,但与中国的龙门石窟有共通之处。作为丹麦的文化遗产,小美人鱼铜像蕴含着丹麦人的精神追求,塑造出"童话王国"的国家形象,展现了优秀的童话文学,成了丹麦的国家象征。因此,应该重视文化遗产的作用,把文化遗产看作文化自信的根与魂,通过文化遗产进行文化交流,实现文化走出去,这样才能发挥文化遗产的作用,提高国家文化软实力。

龙门石窟,作为文化自信的底气

龙门石窟是中国四大石窟之一,毗邻伊河,近靠香山,依山傍水,自然风景优美,开凿于北魏,营造时间长达400余年,现存洞窟像龛2000余个,造像10万余尊,文化景观丰富。联合国世界遗产委员会将其列入《世界遗产名录》时给予其高度评价:"龙门地区的石窟和佛龛展现了中国北魏晚期至唐代(493—907)期间,最具规模和最为优秀的造型艺术。这些翔实描述佛教中宗教题材的艺术作品,代表了中国石刻艺术的最高峰。"①除此之外,龙门石窟还是中国的全国重点文物保护单位和国家 5A 级旅游景区。它是古代中国发展的缩影,体现了不同时期的政治、经济、宗教、文化、艺术、科技的发展情况,具有丰富的文化价值和文化生命力。龙门石窟蕴藏了高深的石刻技艺、书法艺术、佛教文化、历史底蕴,是文化自信的底气。

第一,高超的石刻技艺。科学技术的水平受到历史条件的限制,数千年前的中国乃至世界都无法拥有现在的各项发达科技,但是都留下了诸多令人惊叹的文化遗产。埃及金字塔由石头搭建而成,没有使用任何黏合剂,却屹立至今,被称为世界奇迹;中国长城工程浩大,长达万里,是古代中国劳动人民的伟大创造。龙门石窟与两者相比稍显逊色,但其高超的石刻技艺是不可否认的,在没有任何机器的帮助下凿山刻石,一刀一斧,完成了规模巨大、数量众多的造像工程,突破了当时的历史条件,值得惊叹。而且,龙门石窟造像大则高 17 米,小则 2 厘米,大小造像皆雕刻精湛,栩栩如生,造像的五官面相、身材比例、服饰衣纹展示出古代能工巧匠的石刻技艺,他们的雕刻手法是无法比拟的。

第二,独特的书法艺术。汉字形态多变,从甲骨文、金文到大篆、小篆、隶书,再到草书、行书、楷书,经历了多次演变,在文化交流与继承中发挥着重要作用。在汉字演变的过程中形成了中国独特的书法艺术,有着极高的艺术价值,同时不同书体也体现了不同的时代精神和价值追求。龙门石窟的书法艺术由碑刻保存,是古代书法艺术的再现,碑刻题记 2800 余块,体现了不同时期的书体风格和民族性格。其中最有名的分别是《龙门十二品》和《伊阙佛龛之碑》,分别代表了魏碑和唐楷书法艺术,兼具考古价值和艺术价值。以《龙门十二品》为例,它的书法艺术体现了北魏时期的社会特征和书法家的文化素养及审美观念,反映出南朝细腻典雅和北朝雄健质朴的融合②。因此,龙门石窟的书法艺术价值超越了文字层面,它承载了丰富的历史文化背景,保存了众多经典文献书籍。

第三,盛行的宗教文化。中原地区是中华文明的发源地,也是古代中国的统治中心,因此佛教最先传入中原,在河南洛阳落地生根,使其成为佛教文化氛围最浓郁的地方,白马寺和玄奘西游皆是见证。因统治者的推崇和僧尼的大力宣传,佛教逐渐在中国发展壮大,龙门石窟就是佛教传入中原之后发展下的产物,是佛教文化的艺术表现,有着丰富的佛教文化内涵。龙门石窟的佛像造像题材

---

① 《龙门石窟》,河南省人民政府门户网站,http://www.henan.gov.cn/ztzl/system/2009/06/12/010140064.shtml, 2009 - 06 - 12。
② 张婷:《从北魏龙门石窟书法看南北文化交融》,《文物鉴定与鉴赏》2019 年第 23 期,第 50 页。

多样,有释迦牟尼、弥勒佛、无量佛、地藏菩萨和观世音菩萨等,造像风格多变,佛像的五官服饰等变化都折射出佛教文化在中国的演变。龙门石窟成了佛教文化在中国的见证者,是研究佛教发展的可靠资料。

第四,深厚的历史底蕴。龙门石窟不是某一特定历史阶段的产物,它经历了数个朝代、上百年的打造,所以龙门石窟除了体现不同时期的石刻技艺、书法艺术、佛教文化之外,从历时的角度看,还反映了古代中国的发展进程,将400多年的历史再次呈现在人们眼前。造像活动的兴衰、造像形态的变化等反映了政治形势、意识形态、文化艺术和经济水平的变化和发展,展示了中国历史的辉煌与灿烂。

龙门石窟展示了古代中国优秀的石刻技艺、书法艺术,见证了宗教文化在中国的发展,体现了中国深厚的历史底蕴,是中华文化的沃土,它所体现出的中华优秀传统文化使其成了文化自信的底气。

龙门石窟,作为文化交流的产物

龙门石窟不是在某一时间由某一文化创造的结果,它历经数朝,受到多种因素的影响,在不同文明和文化的交融中得以孕育。汉族和少数民族、外来宗教和本地教派、异国文化和中华文化在此碰撞,最终形成了如今的龙门石窟,可以说,没有文化间的互相交流,就没有龙门石窟的产生。

第一,汉族和少数民族的交流。北魏孝文帝为了稳固统治,迁都洛阳,推行汉化政策,学习和效仿汉族文化,使北方鲜卑族文化与中原汉族文化开始交融。魏晋南北朝时期的其他少数民族政权,继续沿袭汉化政策,不断吸收和借鉴汉族文化,实现了文化交流与民族融合。龙门石窟是汉族和少数民族文化融合的产物,北魏时期的造像保留了鲜卑族强壮挺拔的身材体格,但佛像相貌贴近中原人,且佛像服饰具有汉族特色,有着明显的中原艺术风格。这种中原艺术风格"是北魏迁都洛阳之际在民族及文化大融合的历史条件下的产物,是北方鲜卑族文化与中原汉族文化为主的文化的融合"[①]。自北魏之后,龙门石窟的汉族文化元素日益增多。历经魏晋南北朝的混乱,诸多民族文化互相影响、互相渗透、互相吸收养分,在民族文化交流和融合中形成了龙门石窟这件伟大的艺术品。

第二,佛教和儒学、道教的交流。自北魏时期,"儒、释、道三教合流成为宗教发展的趋势。佛教为民众提供精神寄托与心理抚慰,儒家学说维护着传统社会

[①] 周斌:《试论龙门石窟的造像艺术》,《文物世界》2013年第5期,第34页。

的秩序与稳定,而依托神仙方术发展起来的道教也受到民间欢迎"①。佛教作为外来文化,与本土儒家、道家文化的融合使其更容易被人们接受,因此龙门石窟造像保留了诸如袈裟、璎珞之类的佛教元素,同时融入道家服饰特征和飞天形象,延续了儒学精华,"其含蓄适中的审美、宽厚仁慈的表达、兼容不同文化的态度等将'仁义''中庸'内涵体现备至"。②

第三,异国文化和中华文化的交流。始于汉朝的丝绸之路是中国进行对外文化交流的桥梁,丝绸之路使中国接触到了异国文化。比如,它引入了印度文化,使佛教传入中国,从此印度僧侣来中国传教,中国僧侣去西天取经,开始了频繁的文化交流活动。中原地区作为当时的文化中心,是文化交流传播的主要地点,佛教在此传播迅速,龙门石窟建造的初衷便是佛教信仰,因此它不可避免地带有印度文化元素,有印度佛教造像的特点。"这种中印文化交流使古代中国第一次开始了对'西方'的探询与认识,从认识古代印度而最终认识到真正'西方'的欧洲,也使得中国对于西方世界的探索,除了一般意义上的地理探索之外,更增添了文化传播与沟通的意义。"③除了与印度的文化交流,龙门石窟还展现了古代中国与韩国、希腊、波斯等亚欧国家进行文化交流的痕迹,石窟造像带有西洋乐器、欧洲花纹、希腊石柱等异国文化元素,证明了龙门石窟是不同文明交融的结果,具有高度的国际化。另外,龙门石窟还有莲花等植物纹样和龙等神兽造型,说明石窟造像有着丰富的中国传统文化元素。由此可以看出,龙门石窟深受不同国家文化的影响,吸收不同的文化特征,博采众长,是异国文化和中华文化融合的结果,也正因为此,龙门石窟具有普世的艺术价值,更具吸引力。

龙门石窟作为中华优秀传统文化遗产,是文化自信的重要组成部分,但是文化自信不同于狭隘的民族中心主义,在对自身文化的生命力和创造力充满信心的同时,敢于审视自我,接纳外来优秀文化。龙门石窟体现了佛教艺术的民族化、世俗化、中国化,是不同民族、不同信仰、不同国家的文化长期交流融会的结果,吸收了世界优秀文明的发展成果,展现了中华民族开放包容的文化自信。一个国家的文化发展需要广泛开展对外文化交流,主动学习世界上的优秀文化,实现优秀文化、文化自信、文化交流的循环,所以要利用文化遗产,提高文化自信,在文化自信的基础上坚持对外文化交流,在交流中发展更优秀的中国文化。

---

① 徐婷:《从龙门石窟造像题记探析北魏女性佛教信仰特征》,《宗教学研究》2020年第3期,第130页。
② 黄智高:《"巨变"与"不变":龙门石窟造像服饰世俗载映之揆度》,《美术大观》2020年第8期,第70页。
③ 金勇强:《"一带一路"视野下河南佛教文化旅游转型升级研究》,《郑州轻工业学院学报(社会科学版)》2017年第18卷第5期,第42页。

利用文化遗产,坚持文化自信,深化文化交流

龙门石窟不仅是中华优秀传统文化的代表和中华民族文化自信的源泉,也是优秀文化交流借鉴的结果,文化交流的重要性不言而喻。因此,在利用文化遗产提高文化自信的同时,需要深化文化交流,促进自身文化的发展,推动自身文化走向世界。发挥文化遗产最大作用的前提是文化遗产的保存和维护,这样才能延续优秀文化,维持文化自信的资本;提高文化遗产的吸引力和影响力要从两方面着手,从内对文化遗产进行创造性发展,与现代文化有机统一;对外进行文化遗产的传播,用不同手段进行文化输出,使自身文化走向世界,最终利用文化遗产开展双向文化交流,不同文明进行平等对话以达到互利共赢的目的,使世界文明更加丰富多彩。

1. 文化遗产的保护

物质文化遗产具有特殊性,因其不可再生、不可替代性需要加强保护力度,始终把保护放在第一位。中国丹霞地貌同为世界文化遗产,曾发生过游客翻越护栏踩踏景区和在景点刻字等事件,对丹霞景区造成了难以弥补的破坏,因为破坏痕迹无法人工修复,自然修复需要 600 余年的时间。龙门石窟因为早期监管和保护不力,石窟偷盗现象十分严重,被盗雕像难以追回造成了巨大的文物损失,另外游客触摸佛像也使现存雕像受损。丹麦的小美人鱼铜像也有类似的经历,铜像曾被锯断、被盗走,被人泼上油漆。因此文化遗产保护首先要加强景区监管力度,阻止人为破坏,严厉打击文物犯罪,同时进行文物修复,使人类的优秀文化得以传承,维持世界文化的多样性。

2. 文化遗产的发展

文化遗产不能止步于过去,停留在历史中,它需要冲破时间,与现代社会相适应,进行创造性发展,从而激发文化活力,取得进步。文化遗产可以结合自身特点衍生出众多创意文化产品,比如,河南博物馆推出了考古盲盒,使用河南各个历史文化名城的土质,将出土文物的仿制品放置其中,附送洛阳铲和小刷子,让普通人体验考古过程,感受发掘乐趣。这一文创产品利用了人们的好奇心理,将近年流行的盲盒文化和文物考古活动结合起来,吸引了众多目光。文化遗产还可以利用现代科技,将互联网技术与文化发展相结合,许多文化遗产景区采取线上购票、游园、管理、宣传的模式,实现了传统历史文化景区的转型升级,所以要"充分利用互联网工具,激活文化遗产,丰富旅游形态,将'互联网+'作为活化

历史文化的有效手段"①。

3. 文化遗产的传播

纪录片等视频形式是文化传播的最佳媒介之一。《我在故宫修文物》记录了故宫文物修复的故事,"展现了中华优秀传统文化的独特样貌,突出了民族文化独树一帜的风格,展现了古人精湛的技艺和无穷的智慧"②,掀起了一阵"文博热",向世界讲述中国文化遗产的故事。英国广播公司(BBC)在 2020 年推出了《杜甫:中国最伟大的诗人》这部纪录片,向世界讲述了中国诗词之美,让中国诗人散发出跨文化的魅力,让人们知道,这世上不只有但丁,有莎士比亚,有安徒生,还有杜甫。因此,文化遗产需要拓宽对外传播路径,除了文旅融合,利用旅游吸引注意力,还可以利用视频等记录形式,制作高质量的纪录片、电视剧、综艺节目等等,推动自身文化走向世界。

4. 文化遗产的交流

文明在互相交流借鉴中进步,文化遗产的双向平等对话有利于文化发展。进行文化遗产交流的重要途径之一就是开展论坛以进行文明对话,中国和荷兰曾经举办过"中国—荷兰文化传媒论坛",以论坛为文化交流的平台,让中荷两国文化遗产专家就保护和利用文化遗产、实现其当代价值交流经验与心得。第二届"中国—中东欧国家文化遗产论坛"曾在洛阳开幕,国家文物局局长在论坛上表示"中国和中东欧国家文化遗产交流合作呈现稳中有进的良好态势,文物展览更加活跃、人员交往更加密切、机制建设实现突破"③。文化遗产论坛和文化遗产展览可以作为文化遗产交流的重要手段,促进不同文化的交流和对话,在互相学习中提高文化竞争力和吸引力。

文化遗产是一个民族文化发展的宝贵财富,是民族自信心的重要来源,在利用文化遗产提高文化自信的同时,需要加强对外文化交流,正如习近平主席在《在敦煌研究院座谈时的讲话》中说的那样,"只有充满自信的文明,才会在保持自己民族特色的同时包容、借鉴、吸收各种不同文明"④,在文化交流互鉴中吸收人类优秀文明成果,促进文化强国建设,提高文化软实力,让世界文明更加丰富多彩。

(作者单位:北京第二外国语学院英语学院)

---

① 满奇伟、陶建超、杨鸿雁等:《洛阳"互联网+智慧景区"龙门模式的实践与思考》,《河南日报》2015 年 8 月 6 日。
② 敬菲菲:《中华优秀传统文化纪录片的价值与传播》,《当代电视》2019 年第 9 期,第 70 页。
③ 《第二届中国—中东欧国家文化遗产论坛在洛阳开幕》,《遗产与保护研究》2019 年第 4 期,第 12 页。
④ 习近平:《在敦煌研究院座谈时的讲话》,《求是》2020 年第 3 期。

灵魂何处是归路

——论长沙马王堆汉墓 T 形帛画的转生成仙示意功能

王艳华

从 20 世纪 70 年代发掘开始至今,国内外对马王堆汉墓的相关研究已经持续了近 50 年。相关资料显示,马王堆汉墓是汉初的首任轪侯、长沙国丞相利苍的家族墓地。此汉墓共由三座墓组成,即一号利苍夫人辛追墓、二号利苍的封土墓和三号利苍之子的墓地。在持续了三年的发掘工作中,马王堆共出土了 3 000 多件文物。历经 2000 年却保存完好的辛追遗体震惊全国,同时也吸引了全世界的目光。时任国务院总理周恩来对汉墓的发掘工作给予了高度重视,来自不同国家和地区的约 160 家报社也对其争相进行了报道[1]。马王堆汉墓的发掘是中国考古学上多学科研究相结合、多单位大协作的范例,它开创了中国考古的新格局[2]。

在诸多出土文物中,T 形帛画以其精美的构图和玄妙的功能成了湖南省博物馆马王堆汉墓成列中的镇馆之宝。实际上,马王堆一号墓和三号墓都出土了 T 形帛画,两幅帛画出土时都覆盖于内棺之上,都由单层细绢制成。帛画呈 T 形,一号墓的帛画 T 形横部长 92 厘米、宽 67 厘米,T 形下部长 47.7 厘米,宽 138 厘米。帛画总长 205 厘米。T 形帛画上端横部的图案为日、月、上升的龙及蛇身神人等,下方则绘有蛟龙及墓主人等的图像。帛画顶部设有一根竹竿,用于张举悬挂,一条棕色丝带缠绕其上。帛画中部和下部的两个下角,缀有青色细麻线织成的筒状绦带,长度均为 20 多厘米[3]。学界通过研究墓葬的葬制、葬仪及陪葬品特点,基本确定了马王堆汉墓是一个受黄老道家思想及楚文化共同影响

---

[1] 山西博物院、湖南省博物馆编著:《马王堆汉墓文物精华》,山西人民出版社 2011 年版。
[2] 喻燕姣:《马王堆汉墓的历史文化价值》,《文物天地》2017 年第 12 期,第 23—30 页。
[3] 湖南省博物馆:《长沙马王堆一号汉墓发掘简报》,文物出版社 1972 年版,第 39 页。

的汉代墓葬。因而有人提出,马王堆一号汉墓出土的 T 形帛画在一定程度上反映了道家的神仙思想①。本文试图以一号墓的 T 形帛画的功能为窗口,来探讨道家思想中"转生成仙"的观念。并基于跨文化的视角,来讨论源于道家的生死观与古埃及文明的异同之处,由此呼应一个经典的哲学命题,即我们将要去哪里?

汉代丧葬仪式中的"招魂"之礼

杨树达先生在《汉代婚丧礼俗考》中阐述道,汉代的丧葬礼仪大致可分为三个阶段:一为葬前之礼,这一阶段包括招魂、沐浴饭含、大小殓、哭丧停尸等内容;第二阶段是葬礼,包括告别祭典、送葬、下棺三个环节;第三是葬后的服丧②。"亡魂知返"是中国古代生死观中一个固有的概念(时至今日中国民间也还盛行着清明节与重阳节),招魂之礼因而贯穿于葬前与葬礼阶段。亲人不舍亡者的离去,担心其沦为孤魂野鬼,往往设飨招魂,保佑其免遭厄运,促使魂归复生。

古人的招魂过程一般分为两种,即初亡招魂与入圹招魂③,前者发生于葬前阶段,后者发生于葬礼举办期间,入圹招魂还可再分为地面仪式与地下仪式。具体的招魂步骤为:"复者"身穿朝服,左手持死者衣服,登上屋顶朝北大喊"某某某,回来吧",以此重复三次。三次召唤后,招魂者会将招魂所用的衣服扔给堂前接应的人"司服"。"司服"用小筐接住衣服,从"阼阶"下到安放死者之处,再将招魂衣覆于尸体上,以此等待死者的魂回归到肉体中来④。但由于古人讲究"用生施死",因此招魂的"复衣"一般都不会入殓,也就是说它不可能覆于内棺上一同下葬。因此,马王堆一号墓的帛画并非此阶段中复者所用的招魂之具。

初亡招魂失败后,死者彻底结束了在阳间的生命历程,于是从阳转阴,在阴间开始了新的生命历程。经沐浴穿衣、牺牲祭奠和捆扎,亡者的尸体最终安放于棺中⑤。但此时死者的形貌已经不能再为人们所见,于是"铭旌"作为死者的替代品而登场。人们借铭旌来承载对死者的爱与思念。在此后的送葬过程中,铭

---

① 邓辉、陈华丽:《魂归何处:马王堆一号汉墓 T 形帛画中的阴阳、神仙思想》,《吉首大学学报(社会科学版)》2020 年第 1 期,第 94—101 页。
② 徐杰舜主编:《汉族风俗史·第二卷·秦汉、魏晋南北朝汉族风俗》,学林出版社 2004 年版。
③ 王晓玲:《非衣与招魂——马王堆、敦煌、吐鲁番及丝路沿线墓葬文化关系研究》,《南京艺术学院学报(美术与设计)》2017 年第 3 期,第 46—53 页。
④⑤ 冯娜:《浅析马王堆一号汉墓 T 形帛画的功能》,《科技信息》2009 年第 27 期,第 491—492 页。

旌继续发挥着作用。它被高举在枢车的前部,作为表明死者身份的符号,来引导枢车前行。同时,它还指引着死者的游魂,魂跟随躯体,最终走向安息的场所①。时至下葬,铭旌便覆在灵柩上、放入棺木中,一同葬于地下,这象征着现实世界中溢出躯体的魂被引领到了生命的最后安息地②。回到对马王堆一号墓的讨论,尽管T形帛画是覆于棺上的,但此棺为内棺,且帛画的画面没有朝上,因此可以判断它并没有发挥宣示死者身份和生前权威与富贵的作用③。T形帛画画面朝下其实是在昭示,随棺入圹后的帛画之观者不再是吊唁者或亡者亲属,而是亡魂自身。而且如果为了发挥标识死者身份和招魂的功能,帛画上只需有墓主人画像,而无需画得如此繁复精美且构思严整。可见,T形帛画图像在很大程度上的服务对象会是墓主亡魂而非其他人④。

基于上述丧葬仪式的流程,我们可以得出如下结论:T形帛画没有参与葬前的招魂仪式。在葬礼阶段,它可能参与了地上入圹招魂之礼,发挥着标识死者身份与引魂入棺的功能,相当于"铭旌"。但到了墓室空间里,帛画则成了墓主人"转生成仙"的程序示意图⑤。

"非衣"上的成仙之径

从丧葬仪式可以看出,T形帛画至少具备两项功能。其一类似于"铭旌",起着标识死者身份、引导灵车前行的作用;其二为"魂幡",起着"招魂"的作用。然而马王堆汉墓的遣策既未将其命名为"铭旌",也非"魂幡"。T形帛画有自己专属的名称,"非衣"。此名称或许是绘制这幅帛画的人起的,或许是根据墓主家族而命名的,只在长沙国利仓家族中使用⑥。那么,作为"非衣"的T形帛画在招魂之后还发挥着什么作用? 亡者的魂魄又去了哪里?

我们首先可以以帛画的形状、构图与图案为切入点。在中国传统文化中,T形有着"空间"上的意义。研究T形帛画的学者曾提出,T形旨在突出"天"的高高在上,T字横部所描绘的天上日月与神话传说彰显了天神能量的恢弘伟大⑦。但其实重点并非只在于顶端的横部,整张帛画都是对汉初信仰中的死后世界图

---

①② 冯娜:《浅析马王堆一号汉墓T形帛画的功能》,《科技信息》2009年第27期,第491—492页。
③④⑤ 王晓玲:《非衣与招魂——马王堆、敦煌、吐鲁番及丝路沿线墓葬文化关系研究》,《南京艺术学院学报(美术与设计)》2017年第3期,第46—53页。
⑥ 廖俊:《长沙马王堆汉墓T形帛画名称及局部内容探究》,《西部学刊》2018年第8期,第67—69页。
⑦ 邓辉、陈华丽:《魂归何处:马王堆一号汉墓T形帛画中的阴阳、神仙思想》,《吉首大学学报(社会科学版)》2020年第1期,第94—101页。

景的呈现。马王堆汉墓 T 形帛画采用的是典型的"天界""人间""地府"三层构图法(与之相似的还有山东临沂金雀山 4 号、9 号汉墓帛画①):T 形下部的纵向空间描绘了一个理想的太阴世界,它是死后尸解成仙过程中的一个关键要素②;帛画中部描绘的是人间,中心部分绘有一块"引魂灵璧",玉璧两侧绘有长龙。这样的构图意味着灵魂从地府召回之后就沿着灵璧的孔与长龙的躯体进入到 T 形横幅上端的神仙世界③;T 形的顶部横向空间即为灵魂的终点——神仙世界,这一部分展示了成仙后上升九天、变形而仙的情景④。

  其实,汉初已形成了一套从冥界到天界的生命转化成仙的信仰。这一信仰体系综合了山海文化、融会了区域传统,是一种新的宗教形态⑤。"成仙"必须先"得道","得道"载以"厚葬"。这样一套精细的思想体系使世人关注重心不再是墓葬本身抑或是冥界享受,而是墓葬所构成的生命转换功能。这样的思想驱使着古代中国人"竭财以事神,空家以送终"⑥,甚至贫寒子弟愿为此卖身为奴。死后成仙成了先人大兴丧事、大造坟墓的真正动力,而非简单的实现孝道。可以说实现孝道只是厚葬的表象,其实质是人们对死后成仙的追求⑦。辛追夫人和其子均为当时的"道者",他们深信形解销魂之术,坚信生前修炼得道、死后亡魂接受仙官指点并服食玉浆就能形解而成仙⑧。于是,他们将对不死之乡的美好期许化作追求成仙的技术手段,并广泛传播、运用到墓葬结构之中⑨。我们可以感受到,马王堆汉墓在文化结构和物理空间结构上提供了一整套仪式架设,组成了一个中间环节,用来传达生命转换这一过程的话语符号,而 T 形帛画就是其中的一个闪亮的符号。

  但有关学者指出,西汉初期的主导思想"黄老学说"宣扬的是在世成仙升天,并非死后引魂升天⑩,因此 T 形帛画的"引魂升天"功能还有待商榷,取而代之的是"招魂安息"说。后者强调的是帛画把死者的魂从地府召回,不是进入天国,也

---

① 王晓玲:《非衣与招魂——马王堆、敦煌、吐鲁番及丝路沿线墓葬文化关系研究》,《南京艺术学院学报(美术与设计)》2017 年第 3 期,第 46—53 页。
② 姜生:《马王堆帛画与汉初"道者"的信仰》,《中国社会科学》2014 年第 12 期,第 176—199、209 页。
③ 巫鸿:《礼仪中的美术:巫鸿中国古代美术史文编》,郑岩等译,生活·读书·新知三联书店 2016 年版,第 35 页。
④⑤⑥⑦ 姜生:《马王堆帛画与汉初"道者"的信仰》,《中国社会科学》2014 年第 12 期,第 176—199、209 页。
⑧ 王晓玲:《非衣与招魂——马王堆、敦煌、吐鲁番及丝路沿线墓葬文化关系研究》,《南京艺术学院学报(美术与设计)》2017 年第 3 期,第 46—53 页。
⑨ 姜生:《马王堆帛画与汉初"道者"的信仰》,《中国社会科学》2014 年第 12 期,第 176—199、209 页。
⑩ 邓辉、陈华丽:《魂归何处:马王堆一号汉墓 T 形帛画中的阴阳、神仙思想》,《吉首大学学报(社会科学版)》2020 年第 1 期,第 94—101 页。

不局限于小小的墓穴，而是进入永恒的神仙世界①。此后亡者在指引下修炼成仙，与神一样超脱时空约束，同时在这个平行时空里平静地享受着尘世俗乐。

跨越文明边界的"转生"观念

作为四大文明古国的古埃及和古中国，其文明都具备鲜明的丧葬文化特色，古埃及的金字塔、狮身人面像、木乃伊、人形棺，以及古中国的帛画、画像石、画像砖等都是典型的代表。制作于公元前1070—前715年的底比斯神庙彩绘人形棺是一个典型的装置木乃伊的木质棺材，其作用是保障灵魂归来前遗体的完整性。彩绘棺上的图案描绘着死后引魂轮回、获得永生的路径与指南②。从功能上看，人形棺彩绘和T形帛画似乎具备一个共同特点，即指引亡魂。然而，究竟是指引亡魂"重生"还是"安息"，两者存在着差异。但更为重要的是，两者展示了两大文明对死后生活的不同向往以及对亡后身体认知的差异。

首先，人形棺彩绘体现的是对"死后成神"的向往。人形棺彩绘主要以"面"造型来体现神灵、法老王、贵族等重要的神或人的形象。这种长期稳定的古埃及造型方式源于强烈的宗教情感③。而T形帛画强调的是"修仙"。秦汉时期保存尸体是为了让死者遇仙、聚精气，令魂魄回到肉体之中，并且从此成为仙人，跟神仙们在一起④。其次，在古埃及人的身体观念中，生命是由可见的躯体和不可见的灵魂组合而成，灵魂可以不灭。人和宇宙万物一样，都是永恒的。因此，只要尸体保存得当，灵魂就能回归，人就能死而复生。所以他们将遗体制作成木乃伊，并精心绘制存放木乃伊的人形棺⑤。然而，中国的神仙方术之说强调精神肉体的双项永存。因为在道家的观念中，万物构成的质料是气，而万物之源的气只有清浊之分，所以精神和肉体是同质的。在这种一元论思维的影响下，人们认为精神可以不灭，肉体当然也就得以长存⑥，也就对于尸身的保存不是特别重视。最后，中国古人的希冀在于活的永恒而非死而复生，于是人们通过厚葬来满足丧葬和陪葬物品都能够在阴间使用的幻想。

不论是人形棺彩绘还是T形帛画，两者都展现了千年前的人们精湛的造型水平和天马行空的想象力。同时它们还展现了埃及和中国两大文明古国的艺术

---

①④ 邓辉、陈华丽：《魂归何处：马王堆一号汉墓T形帛画中的阴阳、神仙思想》，《吉首大学学报（社会科学版）》2020年第1期，第94—101页。

②③⑤ 邓鸿涛、陈欣缘、刘冠：《底比斯神庙祭司人形棺彩绘与马王堆汉墓T形帛画形象辨析》，《艺术教育》2019年第12期，第280—281页。

⑥ 俞伟超：《马王堆一号汉墓帛画内容考》，《先秦两汉考古论集》，文物出版社1985年版。

魅力,对后世艺术的发展产生了深远的影响。但更重要的是,两者都以丧葬文化为窗口,通过或"重生"或"安息"的生死观呈现了古人对死亡的尊重和对生命的思考,从而引导了人们在世事浮沉中静心去思考生命的意义,去思考我们是谁?我们从哪里来?我们要往哪去[①]?

(作者单位:北京第二外国语学院英语学院)

---

① 王晓玲:《非衣与招魂——马王堆、敦煌、吐鲁番及丝路沿线墓葬文化关系研究》,《南京艺术学院学报(美术与设计)》2017年第3期,第52页。

长白山剪纸艺术在日韩的传播研究

于洪鉴

人们都知道享誉世界的丹麦作家安徒生有着"童话大王"的美誉,而殊不知这位作家闲时最大的兴趣在于剪纸,他灵活运用对称、均衡的技法特色,作品充满了童话色彩。丹麦和东北地区同处于北半球高纬度地区,有着相似的气候特点,更是有着相似的动植物生态,东北地区的稀有动物乌苏里貂在丹麦也有分布,丹麦人民的"Hygge"生活理念和东北人民的"及时行乐,随处幽默"的生活态度高度类似,两地的文化有着很多相似点。丹麦虽然不曾有着东北地区常年冰天雪地的豪迈风景,但是冬季的旅游项目也是经常被人津津乐道的娱乐项目,处在温带海洋性气候的丹麦人民,虽然不曾有得天独厚的自然资源,但是来到丹麦的游客往往总是被这个国家的文化软实力所折服,无论是其高品质的生活情调,还是到处可见的幸福笑脸,都能体现出丹麦文化的深厚功底。

长白山地区的满族人由于生活的独特地理位置,由于气候导致的特色生活使得他们产生了独特的生产、生活习俗,如:"棒打獐子、瓢舀鱼,野鸡飞进饭锅里""关东三大怪:窗户纸糊在外,大姑娘叼个大烟袋,养个孩子吊起来"等俗语。这些俗语都表现了满族人的生活状态,起源于长白山地区的满族,生活的气候特点是冬季漫长寒冷,满族的先人在长白山地区这一四季分明,冬季漫长的严酷自然环境里生息繁衍距今已经有4 000多年的历史。

长白山满族民间剪纸究竟产生于什么年代,史料并无记载,难于查证,但是在剪纸的发展上推断,早在16世纪,满族的先民女真就已经开始用树皮、鱼皮、皮革、麻布等材料,进行剪刻,剪成的图案粗犷,富于民族特性。用纸来剪刻的"纸上剪纸"可以推断是开始于明代以后。据《满族史论丛》载,后金皇太极期,女真人已开始自己造纸。纸张的出现是"纸上剪纸"产生与发展的先决条件。而满族早期的民间艺术家们用其他材料剪刻而成的"非纸剪纸",是在造纸术发明之前就出现了,那是用野兽皮、桦树皮、鱼皮、苞米叶、麻布等材料来完成剪纸艺术的。长白山满族民间剪纸在这种独特的历史环境和自然条件下形成了自己的面貌。在长期的历史发展中,长白山满族民间剪纸艺术成为留存在民间的文化遗产,一直深受民间的喜爱,包括与满族人民共同生活的汉人也受其影响。虽然这些形式的剪纸没有留下更多的实物和文字资料,但在白山黑水间,通过口传心授,不断发展和不断创新下,代代相传。在20世纪20年代后,长白山满族剪纸沉淀在民间,许多作品表现满族所生活的长白山区域自然面貌、自然生活状态、传说、地方特产。长白山满族文化研究人王纯信老先生在1982年就开始田野调查这种民间艺术,并进行了深入的研究和收集,带动了东北满族民间文化的发展。如吉林省九台市的关云德在由"中国民间文艺家协会"组织实施的《中国民间文化遗产抢救工程》重点项目中,被正式确认为"中国民间文化杰出传承人"。2000年年初,满族剪纸被文化部公示为"国家级第二批非物质文化遗产项目",代表性传承人金雅贞,是中国"十大剪纸大师"之一。她的剪纸,流传于大江南北,甚至漂至了大洋彼岸。很多标有满族特征和表现生活自然的剪纸作品又重现在全国乃至世界各地艺术展览和艺术刊物上。剪纸是满族古老民族文化的瑰宝,它是满族人对生活、自然和情感的艺术沉淀,是反映满族习俗的艺术品,极其珍贵。长白山满族剪纸这一充满东北满族乡土气息的民间艺术,充满了强大的生命力和艺术感染力,这朵中国民间艺术的奇葩在我们的保护传承下必然开得更加灿烂。

如今在世界文化不断交融的背景下,国际游客对于非物质文化遗产中的文化底蕴十分感兴趣,也是吸引游客旅游的重要原因之一。据统计,日韩两国在海外游客来长白山的占比达到了近七成,是来到吉林省旅游的首选之地。长白山剪纸艺术在非物质文化遗产传播和保护上有着自己的一套特色模式,将地方民族特色作为主战场,不断增强国际影响力,值得学习与借鉴。本文就长白山剪纸艺术的文化传播意义,结合在日韩传播的现状,提出一些建议。

长白山剪纸艺术的文化传播意义

满族民间剪纸是古朴、粗犷、浑厚稚拙的,是长白山地区文化千百年来积淀的历史产物,全面而集中地体现了我国民间美术的造型观念、哲学观念,满足了大众的审美观念。它不仅具有极强的实用功能,而且在扎根这片黑土地的发展中,它形成了自己独有的艺术特点。以下将从艺术表现形式、剪纸的题材内容出发,并结合近些年剪纸艺术在海外传播中的案例,讨论长白山剪纸艺术海外传播的实际意义。

首先,从艺术表现形式上来看,长白山满族民间剪纸在长期的流传与发展过程中,在满族人民不断的发展与创新过程中,逐步演变形成了多种多样的表现形式。例如单色剪纸、拼色剪纸、折叠剪纸、熏样剪纸、手撕剪纸等。而最常见和最具有代表性的还是单色剪纸和手撕剪纸,主要材料是红色纸。这是由于中国人自古崇尚红色。红色在中华民族的色彩喜好中,象征着太阳、光明、温暖和幸福,2007年,在武汉举行的第二届国际剪纸艺术博览会上,吸引了包括中、美、英、韩在内的十余个国家,共2 400多幅剪纸作品参赛。吉林市民间剪纸艺术家李侠女士的剪纸作品《长白山神》喜获博览会金奖,《长白山神》是一幅运用满族技法制作完成的剪纸作品,具有粗犷豪放、简约大方等独有的满族剪纸特点。该幅作品构图新颖、错落有序,主要由"萨满面谱""东北三大怪""东北三宝""长白山四季""东北大秧歌"五个部分组成。强烈的民族性剪纸艺术虽是静态的纸质作品,但由于其栩栩如生的艺术表现形式,这是在剪纸艺术海外传播中走出去道路的巨大跨越。

其次,在剪纸的题材内容上,以现实生活中最为常见的事情、事物作为题材,凭借着纯朴的感情与直觉对形象进行观察,以此为基础,逐步形成了长白山满族剪纸独特的单纯、浑厚、简洁、明快的特殊艺术风格,以生活习俗和传说故事为主要内容。《人参姑娘》《白山狩猎》《姐妹易容》,每一个作品剪纸背后,都会有一个生产、节令、婚丧习俗及民间传说的故事。2010年,长白山满族剪纸被吉林省官方带到了上海世博会,这让具有浓郁民族和地域特色的满族剪纸艺术被更多人所熟知,各国游客纷纷驻足观看,剪纸展品亦被抢购一空。2018年,在深圳文博会,剪纸艺术家陈维珍的《晒参姑娘》《萨满》等剪纸艺术作品,将满族人民狩猎、娶亲、打场等情景创新运用到剪纸周边产品,受到广泛欢迎,走出了一条剪纸文化与产业相结合的创新之路。

长白山满族剪纸渗透到几乎所有的长白山民俗当中,包括服饰、居住、饮食等,作为一种具有民族特色的艺术形式,所包含的民族传统文化得到了广大民众的认可。特别是其所传递的民间传说和故事,对于萨满文化的史料研究有很大的贡献,能够很好地还原历史原貌,在文化海外传播的过程中更是富有文化底气,透过小小的红色剪纸,就能一窥东北大地上的原始民俗。

长白山剪纸艺术在日韩的传播现状

日本现代剪纸以表现神话、民间故事、传奇人物、自然景色为主要题材。在风光剪纸中,富士山、樱花等是常见的题材。韩国剪纸与长白山剪纸技法相似,都是以讲故事的方式见长,不断在吸收前人的方式下进行研究。日本剪纸的发展深受中国剪纸的影响,"二战"后,日本现代剪纸随日中友好活动日益频繁而逐渐发展壮大,希娜吉拉尼青山是日本女性艺术家,旅居法国,她依靠一把剪刀和灵巧的双手,完成了许多精美的剪纸作品.她的剪纸艺术汲取了很多长白山剪纸艺术的养料,具有典型的东方韵味,令人叹为观止。在韩国的文化交流中,长白山剪纸也发挥了不小的作用。剪纸艺术在舞台上闪闪发光,2019 年,文登区交流团表演的《共筑中国梦》,将中国剪纸文化与音乐元素巧妙结合,充分展现了优秀的传统民间艺术。在电视节目和综艺中,长白山剪纸更是屡见不鲜。2019 年,第二届中韩剪纸文化艺术交流展在韩国首尔举行,大量的剪纸艺术作品,其中就包括了长白山剪纸,在本次中韩国际交流会中起到了巨大的作用。

长白山剪纸在日韩的文化传播中取得了不小的进步,但在传播中依然存在着不小的阻力,这些阻力也或多或少影响了海外文化传播。首先,就社会环境而言,日本和韩国相继在 20 世纪 80 年代成立了剪纸协会,虽然剪纸艺术在日本、韩国的推广和发展取得了长足的进步,但与此同时,近年来长白山剪纸艺术的发展进程较为缓慢,通过访问日本和韩国的剪纸协会网站,在网站的建设中存在着更新不及时,网页导航混乱的情况,通过检索也只有近 10 条左右的新闻报道出现了长白山剪纸的身影,由此也可以看出长白山剪纸艺术在海外的尴尬处境。其次,就商业环境而言,剪纸艺术衍生出各种剪纸产业,如服装上剪纸元素的应用、赛事举办、剪纸产品等取得一定市场化成效。由于市场化的推广力度不足,没有建立清晰的发展路线,致使衍生产业形成的盈利尚不能以资金的形式反馈到剪纸艺术的推广中。甚至一些韩国、日本的民间手艺人,仍然存在着"自负盈亏"的尴尬处境。最后,文化异同共存现象时常发生,三个国家在剪纸艺术的海外传播方式上都采取了"讲故事"的方法,透过剪纸中的故事来进行文化价值输出,这对蕴涵百年文化传承的长白山剪纸的传播来讲,具有文化理念的优势。近年来尤其韩国由于受西方剪纸文化的冲击较大,接受以"静态中传达美学""艺术是用来欣赏"等思想,剪纸艺术越来越曲高和寡,而长白山剪纸大部分作品来源于朴实的农耕生活,对比之下,这种剪纸艺术如果不经过适当包装和恰当传播,恐怕是难入他国"法眼"。

长白山剪纸艺术在日韩传播的对策和建议

第一,政府层面要做好"把关人"角色。在全球化语境下,无论是长白山剪纸艺术的负责方和剪纸人应该具备国际化视野,摒弃单一视角和过重的本土情结,用全球化的视角来关注长白山剪纸艺术的国际传播。近年来,在吉林省大力扶持东北亚经济圈的政策下,长白山地区与日本和韩国的文化交流开展甚多。但对于非物质文化遗产来说,相较于其他的文化旅游资源来说,其自身的经济价值相对较低,政府对其的重视程度明显不高,传承与发展力度较小,许多传承保护工作的开展无法得到保障。个人层面上,对于剪纸艺术而言,研究不够深入,仅仅只是停留在欣赏的层面上,没有继续深入了解下去的态度,在政府重视程度不高的情况下,国内有通化师范学院开展了专门保护传承剪纸艺术的活动中心,另外在选修课上开设剪纸课程,而就吉林省其他高校来说对于剪纸艺术的重视程度不足,学习缺乏延续性。由于其强烈的地域特性,在南方这项技艺已经十分罕见,在海外传播的阻力上可见一斑。同时在教学手段不足的现状下,许多学生学习兴趣不足,没有看到学习此类技艺的前景,不愿意学习此类技艺。除此之外,政府在进行长白山剪纸艺术保护与发展的过程中,出台相应的政策法规实施性不强,在财政支出方面投入有限,很难为非遗发展提供保障,使得其海外传播中存在较大的阻碍。

针对此问题,在长白山剪纸艺术传承与发展过程中,政府必须充分发挥自身的文化职能,为传承和发展提供保障。首先,需要鼓励当地艺人走出去,通过本地人的"活靶子"作用,积极宣传本地文化,吸引更多的人与到长白山剪纸艺术的学习当中,为满族剪纸的传承与发展提供文化基础。其次,政府需要组织专业的分队,对于长白山满族剪纸开展保护工作,重点发掘传统的艺术形式,同时为艺人提供政策和物质两方面的支持与保障。最后,政府通过出台相应政策,在全社会内形成良好的宣传风气,例如,鼓励学校开展非遗文化课程,也鼓励更多年轻人走进这古老神秘的非遗文化,在街边道路上多利用剪纸宣传家乡文化。

第二,内容层面要做好"讲述者"角色。长白山剪纸是一项具有极强的文化底蕴的民间艺术,做好这方面的研究有助于在日韩传播中更好地推广我们的民间艺术,了解背后的历史渊源。前人的研究多集中于收集整理、民俗因素或形象分析等方面。现在距离历史发生的事情已经年代久远,很多文化故事我们不得而知,对于此项"非遗"的文化研究如果不深入的话,其中演变的过程所得出的结果就很难找到根本原因。这些研究多为从宏观角度讨论非遗的研究,范围太广。现在的研究成果论文发表的刊物级别不高。关于长白山人参故事研究的国家级项目较少,高水平论文不多。到目前为止,关于长白山剪纸研究的相关著作及论文数量较少,通过检索论文类仅有10篇左右。同时,研究的深度还有待于挖掘,目前的研究多集中于非遗文化本体研究,而本体研究也只是表面研究,针对非物质文化遗产的具体内涵研究、文化价值研究、地域特色研究不多,跨学科、交叉学科的研究更少。

鉴于上面提出的情况,长白山剪纸文化研究虽然取得了不小的成果,但也依然存在着研究的不足,突出问题主要是研究内容有待进一步丰富,研究质量有待提高,研究数量亟须增加。对于研究学者来说,如果在前期更多的发掘背后的故事,这样在传播的时候就更加易于理解,找到符合自己兴趣所在的因素,从而促进剪纸艺术传播。应当保持与非物质文化遗产传承者更加紧密的联系,通过实地走访调查等,加强学术写作的深度,在研究方法和研究角度上也应当推陈出新,要站在前人的肩膀上,不断发现问题,总结新经验,为长白山人参故事研究,乃至整个非物质文化遗产研究提供新的思路。

第三,受众层面要做好"引导者"角色,在长白山剪纸艺术的日韩传播中,有时在传播中面临"失语"情况,日本和韩国的游客常常不能理解我们剪纸中样式、技法传达的内涵,也不能体会剪纸中的深层文化,在传播中,长白山剪纸艺术将"自我"为中心,没有了解学习剪纸者的诉求。而在受众群体中,长白山剪纸艺术在海外传播中也存在着潜在受众缺失的情况,年轻的一代作为宣传的主力军,从成长环境影响下,对非物质文化遗产的接触不多,也很难对其理解,不容易自觉形成传播意识。观众更关注于与生活黏合度高的节目、民生、娱乐、电影等。在近几年的知名国际艺术展览中,中国参展作品中剪纸作品参展数量较其他类别作品而言数量较少,而且得到国外艺术家青睐的作品也较少。

打铁还需自身硬,传播在国际化语境下的剪纸也应"入乡随俗",从而吸引更多人加入海外传播中,在文化海外传播中,传播的主体不能以自我为中心,应该了解学习者诉求的表达,例如剪纸爱好者对剪纸的学习难度感到难以应对,对长白山剪纸艺术甚至对长白山旅游有愿望,但是由于指导者不足或者深奥难以理解等诸多的需求,在长白山剪纸传播过程中,要关注学习者的自身的需求,之后调整传播策略,合力引导,促使更加深入的了解和学习长白山剪纸艺术。对日韩来讲,潜在的受众人群不在少数,在策略制定上要让潜在受众通过对长白山剪纸的了解来深入了解中国文化,又由中国文化反馈提高其学习此类技艺的兴趣,通过生活环境与文化氛围的潜移默化,促使受众群体在本民族文化的惯性思维之下,自然地接受长白山剪纸,使个人在无意识中对长白山剪纸产生认可。

结语

长白山剪纸艺术是一种地域性的原生态文化,是原汁原味的民间文化,积淀着中华民族的潜在意识和社会心理。随着剪纸艺术的发展和创新，这种艺术形式越来越多的受到国外受众的接受和喜爱。在文化"走出去"这一文化传播背景之下，适当地、有方法有策略地对外传播更容易跟受众的审美需求产生心理共鸣，跟当地文化形成对话沟通。因此，从文化传播的角度来看，剪纸艺术在对外传播中就不能仅仅局限于物态文化本身，而是要让受众在了解剪纸的造型、技巧所呈现出来的物态美感之外，进一步了解这一物态形式所承载的精神内涵。这样才能使受众在认知艺术作品的同时，激发其对中华民族的探究兴趣，从而了解中华民族的文化心理，进一步接受和认同中国文化，这也正是文化传播的最终目的。

（作者单位：北京第二外国语学院英语学院）

参考文献：

1. 宋春梅.延边州非物质文化遗产旅游开发研究[D].吉林：延边大学，2016.
2. 李辉，仲昭曦：《吉林省满族文化旅游营销组合策略初探》，《长春师范大学学报》（自然科学版），2017，36(1)：87—90.
3. 董仁杰，金石柱，刘畅：《我国非物质文化遗产跨文化传播研究动向》，《湖北经济学院学报》（人文社会科学版），2019，16(2)：99—102.
4. 郑媛媛：《一带一路背景下吉林省生态旅游农业发展研究》，《时代农机》，2017，(12)：143—144.
5. 李阳，刘文超，刘明菊等：《基于网络游记分析的度假型综合体旅游体验研究——以长白山国际度假区为例》，《地域研究与开发》，2019，38(1)：116—122.
6. 孙鹏程：《吉林省民族特色乡村生态旅游资源开发存在的问题与对策》，《乡村科技》，2020，(20)：26—27.
7. 马倩雯：《长白山满族剪纸在学前美术教育中的传承与发展》，《艺术科技》，2017(12)：145—146.

向世界递上"中国名片"

——以泰山挑山工为例

郑天娇

随着社会的高速发展,人们总是为了追赶时代的步伐而只顾埋头向前冲,却忘记了为何出发。人心浮躁、物欲横流的社会需要精神支柱来指引人们更好地认识自我、发展自我,从而促进社会的良性运转。每个国家的发展都离不开精神支持,如果说中国有以爱国主义为核心的民族精神和以改革创新为核心的时代精神,丹麦就有著名的工匠精神。虽然"二战"后现代化浪潮强劲,但丹麦的工业化姗姗来迟,即使起步晚,这样一个人口少、国土面积小、资源匮乏的北欧小国却走出来了一大批处于全球领导者地位的著名企业,如"全球最大的集装箱航运公司马士基、全球最大的循环泵生产制造商格兰富、全球最大的玩具制造商乐高、全球催化剂领导品牌托普索等等"[①]。丹麦的工匠精神内涵包括专注与创新,丹麦的企业始终专注于开发产品,精益求精,直至达到世界最高水平;重视培养人才以不断进行创新。丹麦凭借持之以恒的工匠精神开创了自己的一片天地,成为丹麦在世界上的一张名片。

"中国精神"包含了中国传统文化的精华,是中国传统文化长期发展的思想基础,也能显示中国文化软实力。习近平总书记多次强调在当代提高国家文化软实力的重要性,有助于增强民族凝聚力,塑造国家形象。如今,人们在生活各个方面都追求速度:5G、高铁、抖音等,但同时也有越来越多的人渐渐在速度中迷失了方向,失去了前进的动力,这时就需要放慢脚步,反省初心,从而整装上阵,以更好的精神面貌面对未来,泰山挑山工精神可以激励我们不断进步。凡是爬过泰山的人,无不赞叹其雄伟壮观,泰山无疑是中国的形象代表,以"埋头苦

---

① 郭芳:《为什么研究丹麦?——丹麦工匠精神铸造的那些全球领先者》,《中国经济周刊》2016年第42期。

干、勇挑重担、永不懈怠、一往无前"为核心的泰山挑山工精神也应该被中国人和全世界所熟知并铭记。

泰山挑山工为何如此重要？

泰山隶属于山东省泰安市，"泰"意为极大、通畅、安宁，虽然泰山的实际海拔高度在五岳占第三位，但其具有不可比拟的历史政治与文化地位。作为"五岳之首"，其自古便被视为是社稷稳定、政权巩固、国家昌盛、民族团结的象征。无论是帝王将相，还是名人宗师，都对泰山仰慕备至。从先秦七十二君至明清，4000年中，有数以百计的帝王之使臣朝拜祭祀泰山，尤其自秦始皇东巡登临泰山大举封禅活动后，历代帝王更是或亲赴或派使臣纷纷登泰山祭祀封禅。[1] 历代文人名士也纷至沓来，孔子、司马迁、张衡、李白、杜甫，都为之留下了不朽之作。孟子的"登泰山而小天下"传为佳话，杜甫的"会当凌绝顶，一览众山小"热情赞美了泰山高大巍峨的气势和神奇秀丽的景色，成千古绝唱。历代赞颂泰山的诗词、歌赋多达1000余首。泰山在1987年被联合国教科文组织列入首批世界文化与自然双重遗产，是中国也是世界上第一个自然文化双遗产，兼具自然与文化之美，是名副其实享誉中外的"天下第一山"。据泰山风景名胜区管理委员会统计，2014年至2019年，每年平均接待进山进景点游客550万人左右，可以看出泰山正在以自己的魅力吸引着越来越多的人。

泰山挑山工是一个古老的职业，历代皇帝祭祀所用的物品及后来建设所需的材料都是靠挑山工攀登7800多级台阶挑到山上去的。20世纪80年代是挑山工职业的黄金时期，随着泰山开始搞大规模建设，泰山的旅游业逐步繁荣，山上的盘道、庙宇、宾馆、通讯、索道等基本设施建设规模空前，运送物资的需求迫切，很多家庭困难的农民利用农活之余的时间来做挑山工。[2] 渐渐地沿途有了越来越多供登山者消费和休息的场所，小到食品，大到机器设备，挑山工都是运输的主力。好的登山体验有助于吸引更多游客，提高泰山在海内外的知名度，因此挑山工代表了泰山的形象，在向世界宣传泰山的过程中充当了基石的作用。主峰玉皇顶海拔1532.7米，挑山工行走在一级一级石板台阶上，甚至要经过倾角70°至80°的十八盘等险峻陡峭的路段，成为泰山一道不可忽视的风景线。冯骥才的文章《挑山工》先后选入高中及小学语文教材，是泰山题材的著名散文之

---

[1] 李丰：《泰山：唯天为大　五岳独尊》，国际在线（www.crionline.cn），2006年1月18日19:06:26。
[2] 徐从芬：《跨越千年的攀登　泰山挑山工的前世今生》，《联合日报》2019年12月31日。

一,文中刻画了泰山挑山工的形象:"又矮又粗""黑黝黝的肌肉""肩上搭一根光溜溜的扁担,两头垂下几根绳子,挂着沉甸甸的物品"①,速度不快但却一步不停地向山顶攀登。汪国真在诗歌《山高路远》中写道:"没有比脚更长的路,没有比人更高的山"②,泰山挑山工完美地诠释了这句诗的含义。党的十八大以来,习近平总书记多次引用泰山挑山工不敢在"快活三里"久留的故事来激励广大党员干部以永不懈怠的精神状态和一往无前的奋斗姿态,真抓实干,做新时代泰山挑山工。③

泰山挑山工是不可替代的存在,他们参与并支撑着泰山的发展,是历史的见证者,中华民族精神的传承者与弘扬者。泰山挑山工精神是经历时间积淀的精神财富,其内涵应当随着时代发展有新的解释。

泰山挑山工精神的内涵新解

习近平总书记充分肯定和赞扬了泰山挑山工埋头苦干、勇挑重担、永不懈怠、一往无前的精神特质,即挑担不畏难、登山不畏艰,坦途不歇脚、重压不歇肩。④随着现代生活节奏不断加快,人们时刻承受着巨大的竞争压力,很多人会抓住机会使自己不断进步,但不乏有人会慢慢失去奋斗的动力,放松对自己的要求,消极度日,重新审视泰山挑山工精神可以给迷茫中的现代人以启示。

首先是为明确的目标而不懈奋斗。泰山挑山工的目标只有一个,短期来看就是将物品挑到山顶,长期来看就是追求幸福的生活。为了完成每次的挑山任务,当游客们在什么地方饱览壮丽的山色,或者在道边诵读凿在石壁上的古人的题句,或者在喧闹的溪流边洗脸洗脚,挑山工们就会不声不响地从游客身旁走过,悄悄地走到游客的前头去了。⑤不为沿途风景所惑,不为所遇风雨所动,始终坚信会到达山顶,这之前决不会停下攀登的脚步。现代人也应当像泰山挑山工一样,设定清晰可行的目标,步伐可以平稳,但切忌懒惰、彷徨与放弃。很多知名的丹麦企业都致力于达到世界最高水平,也在为这个目标不断努力,尽管会不断出现很多竞争对手,但仍在坚持,可以看出精神确实可以看作前进的动力。

其次是勇敢挑战自己。泰山挑山工一次要挑 100 多斤的担子,走 7 公里多的陡峭山路,勇于挑最重的担子,从不拈轻怕重。如今很多 90 后选择裸辞,其动

---

①⑤ 冯骥才:《挑山工》,1981 年。
② 汪国真:《汪国真经典代表作》,作家出版社 2010 年版。
③④ 崔洪刚:《大力弘扬泰山"挑山工"精神》,人民网 2019 年 4 月 3 日 08:08,http://theory.people.com.cn/n1/2019/0403/c40531-31010547.html。

机之一便是"逃避"[1],出于工作压力和人际关系处理等原因而决然辞职。这种逃避心态可能会带来一时的解脱,但从长远来看,绝非解决问题的有效途径。年轻人在遇到困难时应当不断尝试去解决存在的问题,勇敢挑战自己去适应新的环境。

再次是不安于享乐。"快活三里"位于泰山中天门以北,地势平坦,风景宜人,疲惫不堪的游客可在此处坐下来休息放松,然而负重上山的挑山工却从不随便在这里止步,因为一旦停留,腿脚就懒了,心气就泄了,前方更险峻的"十八盘"就更难攀登。[2] 如今智能手机的不断普及使得"低头族"越来越多,无疑手机等通讯设备是能够让人们产生依赖的"快活三里"。时间不等人,因此应当把时间分配到更有意义的事情上去,而不是一味沉迷在虚拟世界中享受安逸。

最后是专注当下,不沉迷过去,不担忧未来。泰山挑山工们脚踏实地,一步一个脚印向前走,专心走好每一步。丹麦企业不断运用过去的经验进行创新,在专门的领域不断进步,从而变得世界知名。只纠结过去的得失不利于做出下一步的行动,甚至会退步。挑山工专注当下的精神特质可以指引人们拥有良好的心理状态。

以上四点是结合当代社会出现的一些问题而作出的对泰山挑山工精神的重新阐释,理解并实践该精神有利于现代人更好地认识自己,发展自己。然而现实情况是:随着盘山公路的修通,车辆可以从山脚下开到中天门,中天门至南天门有高山索道,2003年从桃花源到北天街货运索道建成,成批的货品已不再依赖挑山工了,挑山工的数量在不断减少。因此不禁要问:泰山挑山工到底该何去何从?

传承泰山挑山工精神,讲好中国故事

随着科学技术的创新,运输方式变得多样,人们创造出很多可以取代人力的机器,这是不可逆转的发展潮流,这样一来就会有很多人失去原来的工作,尤其是依靠力气来谋生的人群,当然泰山挑山工也无法改变这一残忍的现实,目前,泰山挑山工有50多人,固定人员仅30多人,大多数人都选择改行。现在已经很少能见到挑山工了,虽然他们在发展历史上扮演着重要的角色,但了解他们的人也在不断减少,更不用说泰山挑山工精神的传承了。国学大师季羡林说:"泰山

---

[1] 刘红霞、黄颖:《90后白领"裸辞"为哪般——基于对18位90后白领"裸辞"动机的访谈分析》,《中国青年研究》2014年第9期。
[2] 李善禹:《"快活三里"莫流连》,《解放军报》2019年12月16日。

是中国文化的主要象征之一,欲弘扬中华文化,必先弘扬泰山文化。"博大厚重的泰山孕育了泰山挑山工这一独特群体,人们不应该因为看不见而忘记他们身上的挑山工精神,这种精神又可以是代表中国形象的一张"名片"。

习近平总书记在2013年8月19日召开的全国宣传思想工作会议上提出"要精心做好对外宣传工作,创新对外宣传方式,着力打造融通中外的新概念新范畴新表述,讲好中国故事,传播好中国声音"。讲好中国故事的目的是要传播中国声音,再现中国梦想,阐发中国精神,展现中国风貌,传递中国价值。[①] 无论是同一语境的对内传播还是对外的跨文化传播,都要解决两个问题,即讲什么故事和怎样讲。前者是讲好中国故事的基础,后者决定了故事的传播力。

首先是所讲故事的内容,即挑山工精神,阐发这种精神也可以看作讲述挑山工这一群体的故事。中国的发展依靠全体人民辛勤劳动,挑山工也是万千职业中的一种,普通的中国人凭借不懈奋斗创造美好生活的故事可以折射出中国的发展。讲述挑山工的故事时可以包括该职业发展的历史、主要职责、他们身上的精神对泰山及中国的重要意义。

在明确了故事内容后,还要选择恰当的传播方式。为了弘扬挑山工精神,政府有关部门做出了很多努力。2016年,泰山风景名胜区管理委员会开始编纂《中华泰山文库》,文库分为古籍、著述、外文及口述影像四大书系,《挑山工》作为口述影像书系中的一本,历时两年,已经成书。中央美术学院教授张润垲、张得蒂夫妇是中国第一代雕塑艺术家,他们在2019年创作了雕塑作品《泰山挑山工》。2020年12月19日,院线电影《挑山》的开机仪式在泰安举行,导演郑春雨希望以电影、影像等形式,把泰山挑山工群体记录下来,为家乡做好宣传。可以看出,人们也渐渐注意到了挑山工这一群体身上折射出的精神品质的可贵,传播手段虽然多样,但传播力仍不理想。以下是为了有效阐发挑山工精神而提出的两点建议:

第一,精神的世代传承可以把学校看作主场,民族的未来掌握在下一代手中,梁启超也在《少年中国说》中说道:"少年智则国智,少年富则国富,少年强则国强,少年独立则国独立,少年自由则国自由,少年进步则国进步。"因此学校可以将挑山工精神当作教育专题来使不同年龄段的学生都能在了解之后意识到传承该精神的意义,也可以开设相关课程来系统地介绍挑山工精神,有条件的话还可以组织爬山或访谈活动,使学生们在接触挑山工的过程中亲自体会他们身上的精神品质。

---

① 苏仁先:《讲好中国故事的路径选择》,《中国广播电视学刊》2016年第2期。

第二，泰山景区可以设置专门的宣传地点向前来参观的游客们介绍挑山工文化及其历史意义。为了加快跨文化传播，让全世界了解到挑山工精神，相关的文章或影片等艺术创作都应被翻译成多语种，以吸引更多外国游客。互联网开辟了全新的传播方式，利用其传播者多元化、传播行为互动化等优势来拓展弘扬挑山工精神的广度和深度。不必局限在国内的互联网媒体平台（如抖音、微博等），景区可以利用他国的媒体平台（如 Youtube、Twitter、Instagram 等平台）开展多语种的国际传播。

作为泰山建设者的组成部分，挑山工的工作贯穿于泰山的一草一木之中，辛勤的挑山工早已与雄伟壮丽的泰山融为一体。泰山的保护和发展，永远离不开挑山工，泰山挑山工与泰山同在。挑山工身上的精神品质在当代看来也有巨大的意义，可以给现代人很多重要启示。因此，传承和弘扬挑山工精神是必要的，可以指引我们行走在正确的道路上，保证社会的良性运转。中国故事的讲述及中国精神的弘扬需要家庭和学校的共同参与，在孩子的成长道路上投以精神指引，除此之外，挑山工精神的弘扬还应结合时代发展的特点来开展，利用互联网媒体进行多语种跨文化传播。泰山是中国优秀文化的象征，其养育出的泰山挑山工也将精神面貌刻在"中国名片"上向世界展示，再一次向世界述说中国的故事。

（作者单位：北京第二外国语学院英语学院）

Cultural Heritage in China's Cultural Rejuvenation and International Communication

Zhang Xihua

Cultural heritage can be conceptually divided into "tangible cultural heritage" and "intangible cultural heritage". Tangible cultural heritage refers to the cultural relic which is endowed with historical, artistic, and scientific value, while intangible cultural heritage refers to an intangible carrier with a variety of traditional cultural values and is closely related to the lives of the people for generations. In the eyes of most people, cultural heritage may simply be the symbols of a specific region and may refer to the skills, customs, and so forth that have been passed down from generation to generation. However, cultural heritage contains much more than that. It is also a significant symbol of the historical and cultural achievements of a country or a nation, and it plays a unique role in showing the diversity of world culture. In today's increasingly globalized world, cultural awareness and the construction of cultural identity are of significant importance for a country or a nation in that these two elements are powerful supports for enhancing international competitiveness and are fundamental bases for international communication of Chinese culture, whereas the most effective carrier of the two elements is cultural heritage. Therefore, cultural heritage plays an irreplaceable role in cultural rejuvenation and the international communication of Chinese culture. While in today's social environment cultural confidence is still lacking, Chinese education needs to be further deepened in this regard.

The rejuvenation of Chinese excellent traditional culture has become a national strategy.

Since the 18th National Congress of the Communist Party of China, Chinese cultural undertakings and cultural industries have continued to flourish and achieved remarkable results such as the building of a modern public cultural service system and the cultural market system has advanced. On the other hand, the pace of the "going global" strategy has accelerated. All these show the importance of culture in Chinese economic and social development. The era we are in now is an era of great development and transformation, where the trend towards globalization is becoming increasingly pronounced. Establishing and maintaining Chinese unique national cultural identity has become an important basis for China to improve its right of discourse in the international arena. Therefore, the self-consciousness, inheritance and development of excellent Chinesetraditional culture and the cultivation of a high degree of cultural confidence are of great significance to the great rejuvenation of the Chinese nation.

As the most basic and extensive part of the great rejuvenation of the Chinese nation, Chinese excellent traditional culture can be divided into three aspects: the core ideas, Chinese traditional virtues, and Chinese humanistic spirit. Chinese excellent traditional culture includes the core ideas such as being innovative, hard-working, seeking truth from facts and so on which have been formed by the industrious and wise Chinese people for about 5,000 years during the process of improving themselves, running the country, keeping their position in accordance with the laws of time and day, understanding thoroughly the truth of all things on earth and then handling affairs successfully accordingly and making contributions to the world. There are also rich moral concepts and behavioral norms contained in the excellent Chinese traditional culture, such as a sense of responsibility, faithfulness, patriotism, morality, filial piety, self-discipline and collectivism, all of which exert an influence on the Chinese way of thinking and behavior in a subtle manner. Chinese excellent traditional culture has accumulated a variety of precious spiritual treasures, such as the interacting philosophy of seeking common ground while reserving differences and harmony, the educational philosophy of educating the common people with literature and culture in that they bear the function of inheriting Taoism, the aesthetic pursuit of both the external form and the internal spirit with the scenery depicted and the emotions expressed in perfect harmony, and the life philosophy of leading a diligent and integrated life. It is a condensed expression of the Chinese people's ideology, customs, lifestyles, and emotional styles that accelerates the development of a unique literature, science and technology, humanities and academics, and still have a profound impact on modern society.

    The 19th National Congress of the Communist Party of China proposed the strategy of "building stronger cultural confidence and helping socialist culture to flourish". The purpose is to gradually change the increasingly westernized cultural thought pattern of the Chinese people, improve the recognition of their own cultural identity and enhance the cultural confidence of the entire nation to promote the healthy development of the socialist culture in our country. In 2017, the State Council promulgated the *Opinions on the Implementation of the Inheritance and Development Program for Excellent Chinese Traditional Culture* with the aims by 2025: a system of inheritance and development of excellent traditional Chinese culture will basically take shape and significant progress can be achieved through the co-ordinational advance of research and development, education popularization, heritage protection, innovative development, communication and exchange, and other aspects; cultural products with Chinese characteristics and Chinese style will be more abundant; cultural self-consciousness and cultural confidence will be enhanced; the foundation of the country's cultural soft power will become more solid, and a significant increase in the international influence of Chinese culture. At the same time, cultural heritage protection project will be incorporated into the plan for economic and social development and will be included in the assessment system; the central and local levels of financial support will be increased to support Chinese outstanding traditional cultural development. In the same year, the state amended *the Cultural Relics Protection Law* to increase the protection of

Chinese cultural heritage. All this policy guidance from the macro level has demonstrated the urgency and necessity of inheriting and developing Chinese excellent traditional culture. Therefore, how to inherit and develop Chinese excellent traditional culture has become a critical issue in the new era. General Secretary Xi Jinping proposed at the opening meeting of the International Academic Symposium and the Fifth Member Conference of the International Confucian Federation celebrating the 2565th anniversary of the birth of Confucius "'Creative transformation and innovative development' is an important policy to guide the inheritance and development of Chinese outstanding traditional culture"[1]. The priority is to respect traditions. Cultural traditions are the spiritual identity, cultural heritage and value system of a country or a nation. Only by drawing nutrition from traditional culture can we benefit contemporary people and nourish future generations. Without this spiritual lifeline, there is no way to achieve the great prosperity of the country, let alone hold the hope for the rejuvenation of the country and the nation. Tradition and talents go hand in hand. Secondly, it is necessary to revive cultural heritage into modern application. The ancient sages' books, inventions with wisdom and philosophy have made up our cultural heritage for generations. These are valuable spiritual and empirical wealth. Keep them and apply them in modern times so that they can actively and effectively serve modern development and lessen alienation. In the end, an innovative and dialectic attitude to traditional culture is needed. In the face of many types of traditional culture, we cannot copy them without any changes. The vitality of culture lies in innovation. A culture meeting the needs of social development to solve new problems will survive. To inherit and develop traditional culture is to renew and rejuvenate it. General Secretary Xi Jinping also pointed out that "Only by not forgetting one's origin can one open up the future and only by being good at inheriting can one innovate better." Under the guidance of the "two innovations" principle, we

---

[1] Li Jun. To Promote Traditional Chinese Culture with the Principle of "Creative Transformation and Innovative Development". *Guangming Daily*. 2014.10.10(李军:《坚持"创造性转化、创新性发展"方针弘扬中国传统文化》,《光明日报》),http://www.71.cn/2014/1010/783444.shtml,2014-10-10 09:05。

are supposed to make development with the inheritance of our tradition and inherit our tradition in a developing view. We should uphold the principle of "taking the essence and discarding the dregs" and make new cultural innovations, so that the Chinese civilization will be more rejuvenated and make better achievements, and thus we can fulfill the historical responsibility of our generation.

June 9th, 2018 is the Cultural and Natural Heritage Day. In order to put the guiding principles from our 19th National Congress into action, to further improve the people's awareness of protecting and inheriting intangible cultural heritage, to promote the excellent traditional culture of China, and to establish cultural confidence, various cultural heritage promoting activities have been carried out all over the country. The theme of the Cultural and Natural Heritage Day in 2018 is "dissemination of cultural heritage and its inheritance". The 5th Fangcao intangible cultural heritage carnival was successfully held in the Beijing Folk Museum for the sake of implementing the guiding principles from general secretary Xi Jinping's instructions on "Make Culture Come Alive" and making more people obsessed with the opportunity of experiencing the charm of traditional culture from all aspects. The visitors who have experienced the activities all said that they were equipped with both novelty and splendor and could highlight the purpose of the event successfully after the two-day event. It not only demonstrated Chinese emphasis on cultural heritage inheritance and cultural dissemination, but also practically integrated the charm of cultural heritage into the lives of the common people and played a great role in promoting cultural confidence.

In addition, it is also an important task for us to effectively increase the validity of our cultural external communication in the new era while inheriting and developing excellent traditional culture and improving cultural confidence. For more than a decade, China has been emphasizing the "going out" of Chinese culture. In 2000, for the first time, China explicitly put forward the "going out" strategy, which is "to integrate into the international community with a more open attitude and to further expand the cultural exchanges with other countries" in the cultural field.[①] In 2011, *the decision on deepening the reform of the cultural system to promote development and prosperity of socialist culture* was issued, a policy and proposal to promote Chinese culture to the world. It is necessary for us to carry out multi-channel, multi-form and multi-level cultural exchanges with other countries and to participate extensively in the dialogue of world civilizations. Only in this way can we promote the mutual learning between cultures, and enhance the appeal and influence of Chinese culture in the world. In 2014, "Telling Chinese Stories" was proposed by Xi Jinping. He stressed that we should spread Chinese voices, elucidate the Chinese spirit, and show the Chinese appearance, and introduce the country's excellent culture to the world, so that foreign people can feel the charm in an aesthetic way, and thus deepen the understanding of Chinese culture. One of the "Five Links" of the "Belt & Road Initiative" proposed in 2013 is Closer People-to-People Links with the purpose of strengthening cultural exchanges with countries along the B & R.

Cultural rejuvenation is imminent. The younger generation must realize the urgency of cultural self-consciousness and cultural confidence, proactively understand, inherit and develop Chinese excellent traditional culture, and continuously inject "fresh blood" into Chinese cultural undertakings with the aim of bringing about the cultural rejuvenation at an early date.

Cultural Heritage, Mainstay in the Revival and International Communication of Chinese Culture

As the carrier of China's cultural foundation, Chinese cultural heritage can be said to have a significant role in the rejuvenation of Chinese culture. China has a long history and many cultural heritages. At present, there are 52 world natural heritages or cultural heritages in China, of which 40 are World Cultural Heritage or World Nature and Culture Heritage, ranking top

---

① Yang Liying. The Significance of Chinese Culture "Going Global" Strategy in the New Era. *People's Forum*. 2014. 9. 26(杨利英:《新时期中国文化"走出去"战略的意义》,人民论坛) http://history.rmlt.com.cn/2014/0926/323534.shtml, 2014 - 09 - 26 16:27。

2 in the world. From the perspective of the cultural carrier, "the physical relics in China are not the most important, whether made of stone or wood, the value lies in the expression of a kind of noble form — eternity"[①] However, the cultural heritage has condensed the wisdom, civilization and contribution of the Chinese nation for 5000 years. Throughout the ages, cultural heritage has carried noble and solemn functions or an eternal spiritual support even during a turbulent period of history. The excellent civilization that comes along with it is also naturally and eternally contained in it. Therefore, the cultural rejuvenation stressed in the new era cannot be separated from cultural heritage.

First, cultural heritage builds up national cultural identity. Taking the Forbidden City as an example, the Forbidden City is the first batch of human cultural heritage to be incorporated in the World Heritage List. It has the largest ancient building group in the world, representing the highest level of ancient Chinese palace architecture, and is extremely unique in the history of world architecture. The Forbidden City was built in strict accordance with the principles of the construction of the imperial capital: "the court is in front of the royal palace and behind the north palace is the city; the temple is on the left side and the altar on the right side" as recorded in *the Kaogong ji* (考工记), translated as *the Record of Trades*. it is a classic work on science and technology in ancient China and was compiled towards the end of the Spring and Autumn period. The entire Forbidden City has formed an integrated whole in its architectural layout by applying physical changes and up-down fluctuations and it was built functionally in accordance with the hierarchy of feudal society. At the same time, it achieves the artistic and aesthetic effect of left and right balance and physical changes. There are various types of roofs in Chinese architecture. In the Forbidden City, there are more than 10 different types of roofs. Taking the "three big halls" as an example, the roofs are all different. The roof of the Forbidden City is covered with

---

[①] Peng Zhaorong. "Ancestral ancestors above": Nobleness in the continuation of Chinaese Traditional Culture and Discussion with Wu Hong's "Monumentality". *Ideological Front*. 2014, Issue 1, Volume 40, p. 6. (彭兆荣:《"祖宗在上":我国传统文化遗续中的"崇高性"——兼与巫鸿的"纪念碑性"商讨》,《思想战线》2014 年第 1 期第 40 卷,第 6 页)

colored glazed tiles. The dominant color of the major hall is yellow. Green is used in the buildings of the residence of the prince. Other colors like blue, purple, black, emerald, and peacock green, sapphire and other colorful glazed tiles are mostly used in the garden or on the glazed wall. At the two ends of the principal ridge on the roof of the Hall of Supreme Harmony, there are glazed Wenzhou, a spinal animal of ancient Chinese architecture, at both ends, which swallow the big ridge firmly and forcefully. The Wenzhou has a beautiful shape, and it is both a component and a decoration. These rigorous and unique Chinese-style building methods show the world the great architectural wisdom and building culture of the Chinese nation. Similarly, the Great Wall, a world cultural heritage, is a Chinese ancient military defense project with the longest constructional period and the maximum amount of work in the world. It was continuously built for more than 2,000 years since the Western Zhou Dynasty, and is in the vast areas of northern and central China. The total length of the Great Wall is over 50,000 kilometers. As early as the Han Dynasty, the Great Wall played a great role in promoting cultural exchanges between China and the West. When Emperor Wu of the Han Dynasty sent Zhang Qian on a diplomatic mission to the western regions, he took the Great Wall fortress as the base and opened and maintained the trunk road stretching more than 20,000 miles from Chang'an to the Daqin, which was also known as the Silk Road. For thousands of years, Chinese and foreign cultures have merged and exchanged here, on this ancient road, and they still play a huge role today. Many foreigners know about China starting from the Great Wall. The Great Wall is a good entry point for people in other countries in the world to understand Chinese history, Chinese culture, and the Chinese nation. This magnificent building that condensed the wisdom and strength of the Chinese nation for thousands of years is a precious legacy left by the Chinese nation to all mankind. Therefore, Chinese great cultural heritage has become an important business card for Chinese culture to enter the international arena, which has largely built up our national cultural identity and allowed Chinese culture to stand out in the world in the face of fierce global competition.

Second, cultural heritage is conducive to the improvement of cultural self-consciousness and cultural confidence. In recent years, with the rapid development of the Chinese economy, Chinese culture has also received widespread attention from the world, and more and more people want to understand China. However, in the past 40 years since the reform and opening up, China has basically only played the role of a world's processing plant, namely a large manufacturing country. Compared with developed countries, there is still a big gap in the capacity of independent innovation. Although China is gradually enhancing its own cultural creativity for the purpose of changing from exporting products to exporting ideas, creativity, and culture. Seeing that we have not paid enough attention to our history and culture for a long time, many young people in China are lack of knowledge in this aspect, and their cultural quality is generally not high. A large number of them cannot even explain their own national culture clearly, let alone cultural self-consciousness and cultural confidence.

So, first of all it is necessary to guide them to a full understanding and identification with their own culture, and then to increase their cultural confidence. And cultural heritage, as the concentrated carrier of Chinese outstanding traditional culture, has the function of cultural identity per se. "Under the influence of the World Heritage Movement, Chinese 'intangible cultural heritage' movement is also surging. Researchers in the heritage field have preliminarily figured out the relationship between cultural heritage and cultural identity and affirmed the cultural identity-developing function of cultural heritage. The function of cultural heritage should not be ignored in terms of the development of cultural identity whether it is for the country as a whole or the individual person."[1]

Cultural heritage is one of the most important channels for learning and understanding the excellent traditional culture of the Chinese nation. Scholars can experience the history and culture contained in these cultural heritages through their "true listening, real watching, and actual feelings"

---

[1] Qiu Shuo. The New Link between Cultural Heritage and Cultural Identity — A Summary of the International Seminar on Cultural Heritage and Cultural Identity. *Cultural Heritage Research*. Volume 3, p. 264. (邱硕:《文化遗产与文化认同的新关联——"文化遗产与文化认同"国际研讨会综述》,《文化遗产研究》第三辑,第 264 页)

and thus can have a better understanding of the background of these cultural treasures, the pleasure and tolerance of Chinese culture. At the same time, they can choose to be the protector and successor of many intangible cultural heritages to feel the charm of Chinese culture in the process of action, and gradually to understand and identify with Chinese excellent traditional culture, and then improve cultural confidence.

Recently, "Classic Chant Spreads", was a hit large-scale cultural program on CCTV's comprehensive channel. The program actively responds to and implements the spirit of "promoting the innovative transformation and innovative development of excellent traditional Chinese culture" proposed in the report of the 19th CPC national congress. It promotes Chinese intangible cultural heritage with poems and songs in the form of modern pop music, while deepening the connotation behind the poetry, illustrating cultural knowledge, humanistic value, the origin of modern civilization with the aim of building cultural awareness of the young. "It brings to the audience not only the historical presentation of revived cultural memories, but also the strong voice of the times with the development of national culture."[1] Once the program was broadcast, it was highly praised by most of the people and received rave reviews, which meant the audience, including many younger generations, had fully realized and affirmed Chinese excellent traditional culture and, at the same time, promoted cultural self-consciousness and confidence to a large extent.

Third, cultural heritage is an important carrier for the spread of culture, which is also the most important role played by cultural heritage. Nowadays, the trend of globalization is continuously strengthened, and the international tourism market is gradually expanding. With the development of tourism, there are two main categories that attract international tourists: unique natural landscapes and attractions with deep historical and cultural meaning. As one of the four ancient civilizations, China has a long history of more

---

[1] Hao Jingjing. Let Classical Poetry Fly on the Wings of Singing — Comment on the Large-scale Cultural Program "Singing Classic". *Guangming Daily*, 2018. 2. 27. (郝静静:《让古典诗词乘着歌声的翅膀飞翔——大型文化节目〈经典咏流传〉评析》,《光明日报》) http://www.chinawriter.com.cn/n1/2018/0227/c404004-29835848.html, 2018 - 02 - 27 06:22。

than 5,000 years and numerous cultural heritages. Naturally, China has become a world tourism power. And the phenomenon that international tourists coming to China to visit Chinese cultural heritage per se is a process of cultural experience the process of cultural absorption and internalization, and therefore essentially can be defined as a process of cultural international dissemination. In the whole process of international tourists coming to China, learning about Chinese cultural heritage, and understanding part of Chinese culture, the cultural heritage is the most important. It is the historical and cultural information carried by cultural heritage that enables them to absorb the contents of Chinese culture and realize the successful dissemination of culture. Therefore, Chinese cultural heritage can be said to be a bridge connecting China with the world. Many foreigners who learn about China also started by hearing about some of Chinese cultural heritages, such as the Great Wall, the Forbidden City, Kung Fu, Tang poetry, songs, and so on. In recent years, with the development of Internet technology, many cultural heritage sites have applied the latest technology and adopted digital interaction methods, which has revolutionized the modes of cultural communication. The Palace Museum has made full use of digital technology and Internet technology to establish the Digital Experience Museum of the Palace Museum, presenting digital historical and cultural heritage in the form of new media to inject the blood of modern technology into the traditional Palace Museum. In 2016, the Palace Museum and Tencent established a long-term partnership with the Internet platform to transform "Internet + traditional culture" from idea to practice. Now the new methods in the spread of cultural heritage such as the audio-visual hall, the panoramic Forbidden City, the Forbidden City, the Forbidden City APP, and the Forbidden City games have effectively spread the Forbidden City culture. The "Digital Forbidden City" short film presents the extremely complex architectural culture and structure of the Forbidden City to tourists in a vivid three-dimensional way, and has a foreign language version, which makes overseas tourists marvel at the cultural connotation of the Forbidden City. The Han Xizai Night Banquet Map APP won the best prize in the IPAD category for "Integrating Academic, Art, and Technology, providing the visual, auditory and tactile sense altogether, and reproducing the Beautiful Night Banquet in a dynamic manner". The "Yongzheng Xing Le Tu" motion picture became popular through WeChat, and was reposted more than 800,000 times.

In general, all contents presented in distinct forms are based on cultural heritage. Without the mainstay, cultural heritage as the carrier, it is difficult to achieve the external spread of culture.

Suggestions on Chinese Cultural Heritage Protection and Communication

China has formulated many related policies on the treatment and management of cultural heritage, has taken many reasonable and appropriate measures, and also obtained good feedback. For example, on March 26, 2005, the State Council issued *Opinions on Strengthening the Protection of Intangible Cultural Heritage of China* to strengthen management, responsibilities and coordination, which emphasized the importance and urgency of the protection of Chinese intangible cultural heritage; established objectives and guidelines for the protection of intangible cultural heritage, established a list system, and gradually formed an intangible cultural heritage protection system with Chinese characteristics; strengthened leadership, implemented responsibility, and established a coordinated and effective working mechanism. In November of the same year, the "Mongolian Long Tune Folk Songs" were included in the UNESCO representative list of world intangible cultural heritage. By 2009, there were nearly 870,000 intangible cultural heritage resources nationwide. "By 2017, the state council had approved and published 1,372 state-level representative projects in four batches, 13,807 provincial-level representative projects, and the ministry of culture had named 1,986 state-level representative inheritors in four batches, while the provinces, autonomous regions and municipalities had named 14,928 provincial-level representative inheritors."[1] In

---

[1] Wang Xuesi. Overview of Chinese Intangible Cultural Heritage Protection since the 18th National Congress of the CPC, *Xinhua News Agency*. 2017. 10. 16. (王学思:《党的十八大以来我国非遗保护工作综述》,新华社)http://www.xinhuanet.com/culture/2017-10/16/c_1121808007.htm, 2017 - 10 - 16 09:50。

addition, the state has established a national park system for the protection of Chinese cultural heritage and the efficient use of land space, which provides new ideas for the reform of the existing cultural heritage management system.

All these methods indicate that our country is moving towards the direction of procedural standardization and institutionalization of cultural heritage protection, and will certainly achieve satisfactory results in this regard in the future. Although China has made some satisfactory achievements in this regard, there are still some problems and deficiencies in general.

First, it is not enough to realize the value of cultural heritage in many places in China. Many places have over-commercialized the use of sites of cultural heritage to obtain a large amount of tourism revenue without concern for humanity. For example, after the Wenchuan earthquake in 2008, the Qiang culture in Beichuan and Wenchuan counties was hastily registered as national and international intangible cultural heritage, and the aim of reconstructing of the Qiang village was turned into building a heritage tourism destination, whereas the humanistic and emotional care for the injured people was totally neglected. "These initiatives tend to reshape Qiang culture elements into fetishized commodities ... The disaster and Qiang culture heritage tourism not only failed to bring about sustainable economic development to the earthquake-stricken areas, but also ignored to a large extent the initial goal of 'post-disaster cultural recovery' and the virtues of cultural heritage in recovery processes."[1] Therefore, we must have a clear understanding of the value of cultural heritage. Our purpose is to protect, inherit and spread culture and the most significant one is the care for people. We can't sacrifice the cultural connotations for so-called short-term economic growth.

Secondly, the protection of cultural heritage is not enough in terms of maintaining and repairing. In the process of urbanization, some cities ignore

---

[1] Katiana Le Mentec, Qiaoyun Zhang, Heritagization of disaster ruins and ethnic culture in China: Recovery plans after the 2008 Wenchuan earthquake. *China Information*, 2017, Vol. 31(3)349.

the importance of cultural heritage, and take a negative or indifferent attitude to the destruction of many possible cultural heritage sites, or even wantonly demolish and rebuild, which is extremely wrong. "Cultural heritage is a vivid portrayal of historical development trajectory. It preserves immeasurable historical memories and useful information and has far-reaching historical, scientific and artistic value, which can be preserved, inherited and developed. If urban cultural construction wants to excavate local context and culture, it should take cultural heritage as its core and soul, and take it as the general guide for the urban cultural integration system."[1] In terms of active recording and inheritance, our younger generation has not done enough. There are many techniques that can be regarded as intangible cultural heritage that are rarely known. If they are not discovered and inherited, it is likely that these ancient techniques will be lost for generations and the culture will undergo irreversible damage.

Thirdly, the educational function of cultural heritage is not fully implemented. Cultural heritage is the most powerful teaching material to strengthen cultural self-consciousness and confidence, but it is not very convenient for our primary and middle school students and adolescents if they want to cultivate their own cultural literacy and cultural confidence by feeling the cultural heritage of our country. For example, major cultural relics and venues require high-value tickets. The venues do not have separate periods for primary and secondary school students. There are numerous tourists in the venues, poor experience, lack of appreciation atmosphere and so on. Therefore, the educational role of cultural heritage should be given greater play, which is conducive to fostering national self-confidence, cultural self-confidence, and patriotism of the younger generation.

Fourthly, the effectiveness of spreading cultural heritage overseas is insufficient. Although China has a large land area and a rich natural and cultural heritage, most of the information that is transmitted overseas is merely

---

[1] Song Nuan. Cultural Heritage Protection and Cultural Identity in the Process of Urbanization, *Theory Journal*, September 2015, Issue 9, p. 127. (宋暖:《城市化进程中的文化遗产保护与文化认同》,《理论学刊》2015 年 9 月第 9 期,第 127 页)

fragmented information, with which foreigners are only half acquainted. The extent to which they know about China may just stay at the primary level. For example, when certain cultural heritage sites are mentioned, they may get the impression that they are from China while they know little about Chinese culture. The country has also worked hard on cultural international communication and has achieved certain results. However, in order to further improve the effectiveness of the dissemination of Chinese cultural heritage overseas, we still need to work harder to improve ourselves.

Regarding the problems mentioned above, the most important thing is to give full play to the educational role of cultural heritage and increase the effectiveness of cultural heritage overseas dissemination. As for the problem of insufficient understanding, the state and government should introduce more and more comprehensive protection policies, as well as pay attention to the allocation of funds. Relevant departments should conduct related work in publicity and education well to encourage more young people to participate in the protection and inheritance of cultural heritage. To evaluate how much effort should be put into the protection of cultural heritage, the state can set up special institutions or groups to evaluate unclear sites and then decide whether to preserve or protect them based on the assessment results. As early as April 2012, four sections of the State set up a committee of experts for architecture, folklore, art, science, heritage, anthropology to assess "the Chinese traditional village list", and the traditional folk villages became the focus of state protection for their intangible cultural heritage. In this way, the traditional villages in various places can be effectively protected, and the intangible cultural heritage contained in them can be passed on.

However, as for the problem that the educational function of cultural heritage is not fully developed, our country's relevant departments must pay attention to it. This is the key to building cultural confidence and realizing cultural rejuvenation. The younger generation carries our country's hope for cultural rejuvenation, and bears the important mission of great national rejuvenation. However, our younger generation's cultural awareness is very weak, and there is a serious deficiency in the cultural heritage education of the younger generation. Therefore, cultural heritage education is urgent. In this regard, it is possible to learn from Italy's experience in this area. "Italy makes full use of its heritage advantages and raises people's awareness of the heritage protection through education. In order to create an atmosphere where everyone appreciates the heritage and cherishes it, the Italian government has taken various measures to keep the tickets for heritage scenic spots at a relatively low price. Moreover, in Italy, an organized group of students from primary school, middle school and university can often be seen visiting ancient buildings, ancient relics, and taking notes seriously. The teacher gave the students a sound explanation, and stipulated that after the visit, the students would have to pass an examination. Through the visit and study, students will have a systematic understanding of historical knowledge and cultural heritage protection awareness can also be improved. Under this kind of imperceptible edification, the awareness of heritage protection is deeply rooted in students' hearts."[1] It is necessary to make people feel the cultural charm of cultural heritage and raise their cultural confidence accordingly. The frequent conduct of colorful cultural heritage educational activities for the younger generations would have the imperceptible edification effect that they would realize, inherit and carry forward the excellent traditional culture naturally. In this way, the power of our country's cultural rejuvenation will be getting stronger, and national rejuvenation just around the corner.

The second critical issue is the ineffectiveness of the dissemination of cultural heritage overseas. Our country has been emphasizing international cultural communication for more than ten years, but the effect is not obvious. The fragment-like information transmitted to foreigners can easily make them fail to understand it or even misunderstand and generate prejudice to our culture due to cultural differences, which is because the transmission of such information rarely combines with the specific context of each cultural heritage. Therefore, Chinese cultural heritage should make great efforts on

---

[1] Zhang Chen. How the Italian Public Participate in the Protection of Cultural Heritage. *Chinese Social Science Online* http://www.chla.com.cn/htm/2013/0425/166688.html? userid = 293. （张晨：《看意大利公众如何参与文化遗产保护》,《中国社会科学在线》2013 年 4 月 25 日）

its own, combining with the context of a specific era. Only in this way can the cultural information conveyed be complete, objective and true. Tourists can understand the complete culture knowledge instead of fragment-like information, which is an important basis for cultural communication.

The last suggestion is that we are supposed to improve the relevant service facilities, especially pay attention to the accuracy and nuances of foreign language translation. Each country and nation are endowed with different culture and language logic, so there must be a precise translation system for each country. Tourism translation is "a cross-language, cross-social, cross-temporal, cross-cultural, cross-psychological communication activity"[①]. It is a necessary medium for foreign tourists to become acquainted with China. The translation quality and interpretation of cultural heritage plays an important role in promoting Chinese national image and conducting international cultural exchange. Therefore, only when the content, context, language logic, infrastructure services and other elements are fully improved, will foreign tourists proactively approach China. They will have a greater interest in Chinese culture, and the validity of the spread of Chinese excellent culture abroad may be greatly improved.

In short, cultural heritage condenses Chinese culture and is the most typical and effective carrier of Chinese culture. Under the era of globalization, we must make full use of our own cultural heritage advantages while maintaining the independence of our cultural identity, and improve our own cultural confidence. Efforts should be made in the field of cultural heritage education. On the other hand, we also need to "combine the context and generate a pertinent translation" to actively and effectively disseminate Chinese culture to every corner of the world. Only in this way can the great rejuvenation of the Chinese nation be realized at an early date.

(Beijing International Studies University)

---

① Zeng Wenxiong. Tourism Culture International Communication and Tourism Economic Development. *Market Modernization*. March 2006, Early Issue. http://www.docin.com/p-1013790638.html. (曾文雄:《旅游文化对外传播与旅游经济发展》,《商场现代化》2006 年 3 月,上旬刊)

The Old Potter and the Cave

— Disappearing Prehistoric Heritage in China and Denmark?

Ingolf Thuesen

Heritage is a function of time. Heritage is what survives either as a product of humans, artifacts and monuments, or as memories of the past. Ideally speaking heritage stops time and preserves an artifact or a monument for reasons formulated by a contemporary society. A major reason for declaring something as heritage is that we find it adds value to our own life. This is the universal understanding of heritage and is followed by world societies through UNESCO conventions.[①] Heritage has a material and an immaterial dimension labelled by UNESCO as tangible or intangible culture. The following case from China is an example of both tangible and intangible heritage and is presented here as it inevitably confronts us with the question: shall we protect this heritage and if so, how do we protect it? Also the case relates to a ceramic tradition in Denmark which may inspire us to share heritage strategies.

During a visit to Guangxi Province in China in 2017 we visited a village close to the Chinese-Vietnamese border where the local museum authorities introduced us to an old potter. We were told that this man, who was more than 70 years old, was the only person left who could produce a quality ceramic without the kiln technology which otherwise China has developed to perfection through thousands of years. We were guided to a cave in the

---

[①] Conventions concerning culture and heritage can be found on this link: http://portal.unesco.org/en/ev.php-URL_ID=13649&URL_DO=DO_TOPIC&URL_SECTION=-471.html.

mountains which was his workshop for making pottery from the building of the vessel until it had been fired. The following presentation is an attempt to begin to document in writing and in pictures the entire production process taking place in the cave which is remarkable and an expression of thousands of years of ceramic technology in China. Considering the important position of China as a prime developer when it comes to ceramics culminating with the invention of porcelain, *China* — 瓷器, no history or event dealing with ceramic tradition in China is too small to be recorded. What in this case immediately is seen as a simple relic of the past surviving in a distant countryside is actually an important example that improves our understanding of the history of ceramic technology.

Turning clay into stone

One of the major innovations of humankind through history was the discovery that plants and animals could be domesticated, the so-called Neolithic revolution (Childe 1951). It was a tremendous change in the human attitude to nature from the hunter gatherer economy, where humans were dependent on nature to taking control over parts of nature, cereal grains, wheat and rice, and animals, dogs, sheep and goats. Humans had become the ultimate top link of nature's food chain.

However, at the same time another dramatic innovation was made, not connected to food procurement, but to materials, tools and technology. This innovation was the discovery that firing certain types of earth would make the material stone-like, the making of ceramics. This discovery was indeed a revolution to Stone Age man. For thousands of years human's most important material for tool production was stone that could be chipped or polished into an adequate shape determined by its function as a tool. A sharp edge for a knife, rounded rough surfaces for grinding, points for arrows, etc. Common to all stone tools was that they were made using a reducing technique. Flint or chert were chipped, other stones were ground into shape. Such a reducing technique was challenging and required skill and experience of the tool maker. Mistakes could not be corrected and resulted in a less functional tool or waste.

More than ten thousand years ago in China humans discovered that clay that had been heated — perhaps accidentally by being close to a fireplace — changed character. It became harder and similar to a stone. The discovery led to a technological revolution namely the invention of pyro technology, changing materials by heating. Heating clay eventually produced a stonehard material, ceramics. Archaeological evidence from the Xianrendong cave in the Jiangxi province of China shows that at this location ceramics were produced for cooking vessels as early as 20,000 years ago (Wu et al. 2012). Those very early dates have now been confirmed from other sites in China and Japan, meaning that the technological innovation of ceramics made it possible for humans to store and cook food in more efficient ways and preceded the domestication of plants and animals. Therefore farming life may be understood as a result of technological innovation that meant better ways of storing food and liquids and preparing meals by cooking. A recent archaeological find from the Jordanian desert shows that the baking of bread also preceded farming confirming that the so-called Neolithic revolution was determined by technological innovation and understanding of pyro technologies (Arranz-Otaegui et al. 2018).

Looking at the traditional stone materials for tool production, flint and chert, ceramics also offered additional advantages than working in stone. The reduction technique for creating the shape of a tool was changed into a forming technique where material were shaped by modelling and adding. This opened a new world of opportunities for producing vessels and the risk was now primarily associated with the firing of the modelled shapes and turning the soft clay fabric into a stone-like material. Humans became stone makers. The Stone Age was the era when natural stone was a preferred material for tool production, but also the era when humans invented the technology of making stone wares.

The earliest ceramics were produced from raw materials available in nature, clay and temper, and fired in fire pits or a bonfire. That was also how we experienced the making of pottery in Guangxi province in a cave. For an archaeologist who has been studying ceramics from many different cultures produced during thousands of years, time suddenly stopped. This was not the past, but the present and a fine documentation of how ceramic production had taken place from the very discovery of this revolutionary technology. A documentation was needed. In the following a summarizing description of how we experienced the process of making ceramics in a cave is attempted as we all felt it had thousands years of almost unchanged traditions behind it.

Preparing a clay

The landscape around the cave where ceramics wee produced consists of low mountains separated by valleys. The valleys are filled with a sediment of clay and silt forming a fertile soil for agriculture. Farming is a major activity today with the farmers living in small villages. The mountains are covered with a green vegetation and the fertile fields in the valleys add beauty and tranquility to the region (Fig. 1).

Fig. 1　The picturesque landscape around the potter's cave.

The old potter arrived at the cave bringing pre-prepared pots with him (Fig. 2). These were probably produced in the village. But he also demonstrated the entire process of production for us in the cave while waiting for the firing of the pots to be completed.

The clay, a brown fine grained soft paste very suitable for forming vessels, came from the area and had been extracted and kept with the right humidity. In the cave the clay was mixed with a white mineral, a temper that normally stabilizes the shape during the firing. The white mineral came as small white stones which first were crushed with a round stone, ca. 10 cm in

The Old Potter and the Cave

Fig. 2 The potter arriving at the cave with pots ready for firing.

diameter (Fig. 3). Hereafter the material was put into a mortar, a hollow in the rock, and ground into a fine powder. A double-ended wooden tool was used for this final preparation of the temper, before it was mixed with the clay (Fig. 4 and 5).

Fig. 3 Crushing a white mineral temper with a hand stone using the rock as table.

Fig. 4   Turning the white mineral into a powder using the natural rock and a wooden pounder as a mortar.

Fig. 5   Tempering the clay as a final preparation before forming the pot.

Throwing a pot

In the cave the potter showed how to form a vessel by using a rotating wheel. The wheel consisted of a disc, c. 40 cm in diameter, attached to a heavy circular stone. This is the table for throwing pottery. The table is placed on top of a pivot of wood which is fixed to the ground probably with some concrete (Fig. 6 and 7). This construction makes it possible for the potter to throw pots. The heavy stone under the disc adds momentum to the rotation of the table and the well-balanced turning table keeps the right speed as long as it is necessary for throwing the pot.

Next to the turntable is a stone used as a seat for the potter and another stone is used as a table. Here the potter placed the raw materials for the pot, clay and the white powder together with his tools, a piece of cloth, a pot with water, a 10 cm long spatula and a string (Fig. 8).

Before the potter begins to form a new pot some of the white powder is poured in a thin layer to the center of the table where the lump of clay for the

The Old Potter and the Cave

Fig. 6 The potter's wheel.  Fig. 7 The pivot carrying the wheel.

Fig. 8 The potter's workshop, turntable, chair and a stone with tools and raw materials.

base of the pot is placed (Fig. 9). The base of the pot is formed together with the lower part of the body by adding more clay and modelling the sides (Figs. 10 and 11). This part of the work lasts around four minutes.

With the base and the lower part of the pot formed, the wheel is rotated by hand. The potter pulls up the sides using a wet cloth and the final touch is made by the spatula which evens the shape and the surface (Figs. 12 and 13). The pot is now cut loose by a string and moved to some wooden plank nearby for drying (Fig. 14). It took the potter around 10 minutes to turn the pot. In total it took around a quarter of an hour to make this shape from the clay being placed on the table until the finished shape stood on the plank for drying.

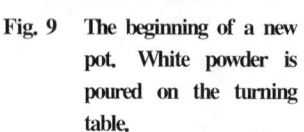

Fig. 9 The beginning of a new pot. White powder is poured on the turning table.

Fig. 10 The base of the pot prepared.

Fig. 11 Modelling the lower part of the body of the pot.

Fig. 12 Throwing the pot using a wet cloth.

Firing

The firing of clay is normally one of the most critical phases in the production of ceramics. A precise control of temperatures and flow of oxygen for the fire is a condition for producing vessels of a high quality. Small variations can mean warping of the vessels. For instance a lid may no longer

Fig. 13 Smoothing the shape with a spatula.

Fig. 14 The finished pot left for drying.

fit on the pot after the firing. In the worst case a firing completely fails and all the vessels have to be discarded. Therefore ceramic kilns are often found surrounded by heaps of broken and deformed vessels. This helps archaeologists in locating ancient kiln sites. It was extremely fascinating to follow how a firing took place without any technical means of kiln constructions or temperature control except for what nature might offer.

The potter brought with him to the cave all the necessary materials for the firing. Fuel was bundles of dried corn stems and leaves and other bundles of undried fern, 芒萁 (*Dicranopteris dichotoma* Fig. 15 and 16). Long straight branches measuring 1.5 - 2.0 meters and ca. 5 cm in diameter were used for building a rectangular grill elevated ca. 20 centimeters above the ground by stones (Fig. 17). The bone-dry unfired pots were placed in rows according to their shapes, one row of spouted jars with a handle and two rows of pots with their lids placed in between. In total 16 vessels and six lids were placed on the wooden grill. Waste from earlier firings, large sherds and fragments of pots, were placed at the corners, around and on top of the pots to be fired probably in order to protect and contain the heat around the pots (Fig. 18).

Fig. 15　Fuel for the fire. Dried corn leaves and stems.

Fig. 16　Undried fern.

Fig. 17　The wooden grill being built.

Fig. 18　Stacked with pottery and wasters.

The firing consists of two main phases. In the first phase, which lasts for 1½-2 hours, the potter heats the pots from below by inserting burning corn twigs under the grill. Half way through the process the pots are turned in order to be heated on the other side as well (Fig. 19 and 20). The first phase removes remaining water in the clay of the pots and prepares them for high temperatures.

Fig. 19　The first phase of the firing. The pottery is heated from beneath.

Fig. 20　Turned and the process repeated.

In the second phase the temperature is increased in order to harden the clay. This is when the ferns are used. The plants are placed under the grill and piled on top of the pots creating a containment. In the beginning the green leaves generates a large amount of dense smoke, a good reason for doing the firing in a cave away from the village (Fig. 21 and 22). Fuel is added regularly and during this firing which lasts for less than 25 minutes the potter gives all his attention to the firing (Fig. 23).

Fig. 21　The second phase of the firing. Ferns are placed beneath and on top of the pottery.

Fig. 22　Generating thick smoke.

Fig. 23　During the second firing phase the potter keeps his attention constantly on the firing.

It seems that the ferns create a crust around the pots and until the wooden grill collapses air and oxygen can feed the fire from beneath (Fig. 24). In many way the entire structure and technique resembles a traditional prehistoric kiln as we know them from Ancient Mesopotamia: a dome built of mud bricks divided into two chambers, a firing chamber at the bottom and the chamber for the vessels to be fired above separated by a clay floor (Jasim 1985). The Mesopotamian kiln was built by bricks of clay; the southern Chinese kiln built by organic materials, branches and semi dried fern. To judge from the hardness of the ceramics produced, it has an almost metallic sound; this technique generates temperatures of around 1000 C.

With a wooden stick the potter now opens the shell of carbonized weed and branches. The red glowing pots become visible and can be removed for cooling (Fig. 25). This firing was successful and no pots were lost. A good indicator of the precision and skill of the potter is how well the lids fit the pots. This particular firing produced pots where the lids fitted perfectly.

Fig. 24 The fuel carbonizes into a domed structure resembling prehistoric kilns.

Fig. 25 A red glowing pot is removed from the fire.

Conclusion

It is remarkable in modern China to find a ceramic production that only requires natural products such as clay for the pots and organic materials for the firing. This would not have happened if the craft of making pottery had not been there for thousands of years and inherited through generations of craftsmen. The old potter's work in the cave is a time pocket of heritage of highest importance in order to understand prehistoric pottery production. It is tangible and intangible heritage that should be fully documented as it explains how pyro technology became one of the most important innovations during the Stone Age.

It is also obvious to ask why such a simple way of making ceramics could survive when China in the meantime developed into one of the most advanced civilizations producing the ultimate ceramic, porcelain. There are many possible answers to the question. Of course the high end products such as porcelain were not for everybody. But everybody needed pots for cooking and storage and therefore an inexpensive product was needed to fulfill the need of ordinary people.

Let us now make an excursion to Denmark where we find a similar situation. Since the medieval period female potters travelled around during the summer in the countryside and were hired by farmers to produce household pottery. They only carried with them their inherited skill, and they also needed no kilns. The pots they made were fired in a pit in a simple way using locally available materials. The results became a special type of pots blackened and burnished on the surface due to the firing technique. They are well known today as black pots and can be seen on display in many provincial museums in Jutland (Linaa 2019). Parallel to the production of black pots for the farmers high quality ceramics were also produced in workshops and factories around Denmark. And around 1775 the Royal Copenhagen porcelain factory was established producing fine porcelain for the elite heavily inspired by China.

Making ceramics without a built kiln is therefore an important heritage to document not only to understand technological innovation and development, but also to understand the social complexity of societies. This situation has been encountered in both China and Denmark (Fig. 26 and 27).

Fig. 26　Ceramics for everyone. Pots produced without kilns in Jutland, Denmark.

Fig. 27　In Guangxi Province, China.

(University of Copenhagen, Denmark)

Bibliography

1. Arranz-Otaegui, Amaia et al. 2018. Archaeobotanical evidence reveals the origins of bread 14,400 years ago in northeastern Jordan. *Proc Natl Acad Sci* USA July 31,2018 115 (31)7925 – 7930.
2. Childe, V. G. 1951. Man Makes Himself (London: C. A. Watts & Co. Ltd.).
3. Jasim, Sabah A. 1985. The Ubaid Period in Iraq. Recent Excavations in the Hamrin Region. BAR International Series 267.
4. Linaa, J. 2019. Pots for the impoverished: Black pots from Jutland — A Danish contribution to the European Ceramic Market 1600 – 1850. In *Keramik in Norddeutschland: Beiträge des 48. Internationalen Symposiums für Keramikforschung vom 14. bis 16. September 2015 in Mölln*. Hans-Georg Stephan Ed. (Verlag Beier & Beran) 108 – 113.
5. Wu, Xiahong et al. 2012. Early Pottery at 20,000 Years Ago in Xianrendong Cave, China. *Science* 29 Jun 2012: Vol.336, Issue 6089, pp.1696 – 1700.

Cultural Heritage in Chinese and Global Historical Perspective

Christoph Harbsmeier(何莫邪)

There are those who believe that the extraordinary persistence of the Chinese Empire and the disproportionate (though much shorter) persistence of the British Empire both depended on the persistence of a spiritual cultural heritage in the elites.

Traditional Chinese bureaucrats tended or at least pretended to be educated in their deep elite cultural heritage just as British colonialists and officers tended at least to pretend to be educated in their English as well as European classical heritage of Latin and Greek. Besides, the highly literary Chinese Examination System is two thousand years old, and official appointment often depended on passing demanding linguistic and literary tests in China.

Two things have held the Chinese Empire together for millennia:

1. the cultural heritage *wen* 文 of an elite inherited from the ancient classics from the 9th century BC onwards.

2. the writing system *wen* 文 inherited from the 13th century BC Chinese oracle bone inscriptions.

Both the study of the classics and the studies of the writing system are therefore quite naturally of great national concern in China to define national cohesion and national identity.

Wen 文 elegant culture has been a core cultural value concept throughout recorded Chinese history, it expresses an elevated cultural norm (*wen* 文雅).

Wen 文 social decency is also an aesthetic and ritual basic value.

Any "proper" dignified Chinese must be committed to *wen* 文.

But *wen* 文 involves absolutely no dogma or catechism.

On the contrary, *wen* 文 is a *Way* of going about things, a *Way* that is thought of as sacrosanct by revered ancient precedent.

Wen 文 writing is celebrated in China as calligraphy *shūfǎ* 书法, which — in an impersonal version, is well attested already from the 10th century BC, artistic personally expressive calligraphy is celebrated since the third century AD. Calligraphy came to express personal identity and ethnic identity through literate cultivation of the cultural heritage. Many students opt for calligraphy lessons even to this day as an aesthetic active kind of meditation on their cultural heritage. Few Chinese homes are completely free from calligraphy. Artistic calligraphy dominates the street scenery anywhere in urban China, as it does anywhere in urban Japan. Calligraphy is the aesthetic backbone to serious self-cultivation. A civilised person with bad calligraphy used to be an oxymoron, or even a *contradictio in adjecto*.

Cultural heritage then, in China, is quintessentially literary, scribal in the appreciation of calligraphy as conveying the deep personality of a civilised person, of someone whose formation is based on *xiū shēn* 修身 "cultivation of the personality. (And, incidentally, if you are curious to find out more about these kinds of terms you may want to look them up in the Thesaurus Linguae Sericae **url: tls. uni-hd. de** which I have spent most of my research time compiling with the help of a large number of colleagues from all over the world during the last 35 years, and which concentrates on Chinese conceptual history in a comparative context. You are warned: comparative philology is my passion. I may be overestimating its importance. ...)

In terms of material productivity, China is perhaps the most productive superpower regarding the continuing recovery of its incredibly rich archeological cultural heritage.

From a political point of view, archeology plays a central role in the historically-based construal of the Chinese political identity (*nt — ng* 认同).

Meanwhile, the concept of cultural identity is an invention of the 19th century in the West, and Tu Weiming of Harvard University claims to have coined and invented the Chinese term *rentong* in the 1980ies. Until the twentieth century people throughout the world did not seem to need a term like identity. Identity went without saying.

However, the national essence was very much part of Chinese discourse already in the 19th century, there being such an essence was a matter of national dignity and cultural self-regard.

In our time identity has become a cultural buzzword throughout the world. Thousands commit suicide for failure to find in themselves any personal identity. Cities and even villages spend large sums establishing their cultural identities. States of all kinds frantically spend billions of whatever their currency is to promote national identities, especially where it is dangerously self-evident that such identities do not exist. Increasingly cities and villages follow suit. Being a speaker of a language or a dialect is taken to establish a cultural identity and thus to convey cultural dignity. Increasingly, modern man construes herself as a bundle of identities of various sorts, at various levels. And on different occasions different identities become relevant. When one finds oneself in China, even a European identity seems to become very relevant. Identity is tied up with perceived common culture.

Now in China *wenhua* 文化 culture is originally always always in the singular. *Wenhua* 文化 has no plural. In traditional Chinese *wenhua* was quintessentially Chinese culture. As a word with a plural, *wenhua* is a Japanese loanword in Chinese. It is only under Japanese influence that the Chinese began to think in terms of different cultures.

Note that in Chinese there is nothing like Cicero's *cultura animi* agriculture of the spirit＞pedagogy of the spirit, and there is no current classical Chinese opposition of *wenhua* culture versus *ziran* 自然 nature. The opposition between *tiān* 天 Heaven＞Nature and 人 human took the place of culture versus nature.

In Europe, Pufendorf (died 1694) famously invented the plural of cultures to be protected by international law.

Similar observations apply to the concept of civilisation. The Chinese term *wenming* 文明 which is the current translation for civilisation refers traditionally to the one and only real civilisation, that of the Thirteen Classics of Confucianism, the one described in the 26 Dynastic Histories.

And I note in passing that Mao Zedong really had installed a complete set of these 26 massive dynastic histories in the train he used to travel in, thus making sure that these sources on the Chinese cultural heritage were at no point of his life beyond his reach.

Wenming 文明 civilisation has no plural because Chinese civilisation has no equal. And China was not a bounded empire, certainly not one *gu* — 国 state among others. In ancient China, *hui guo* — 回国 to return to one's state was to return to that part of China from which one's family originated. What the emperor governed was not any old state, not any one state among others, but *tiānxia* 天下 All under Heaven. Chinese civilisation was experienced as the defining civilisation of All under Heaven. The cultural heritage of China was taken to be essentially the one and only civilised heritage under the sun.

Heritage, in Chinese *yichǎn* 遗产 is primarily inheritance. Inspired by Japanese translations from western languages, inheritance came to be used to refer to heritage. Primarily this heritage was taken to be material, but with time the term *y'chǎn* came to apply to intangibles like customs, religions, traditions, and even literary works.

Educational heritage, *jiaohua* 教化, was disciplined acculturation to the finer (*yǎ* 雅) parts of the cultural inheritance. Here, the contrast with Greek *paideia* is instructive: In the first place the youth receive a democratic education. For the sons of the poor are brought up with the sons of the rich, who are educated in such a manner as to make it possible for the sons of the poor to be educated like them. (Aristotle, *Politics* 1294b20).

The state-controlled institutional transmission of this historically based cultural *paideia* through grammar schools and Universities was the project of the great linguist Wilhelm von Humboldt which has shaped higher education throughout large parts of the world. Humboldt's notion of the cultivation cultural heritage and *Bildung* was closely linked to the study of those Latin and Greek classics which have given Europe its common cultural heritage and identity. Denmark is currently rooting out the last vestiges of this project of language-based classical *Bildung* which is being discontinued throughout Western Europe bringing it in line with dominant practice in the USA where the language-based cultivation of the Graeco-Roman heritage has long been marginalised and left to a few academic professionals.

There is no convincing way of saying Bildung in English, whereas in China the words 教化 *Bildung*, 修养 literate cultivation have a completely different buzzword status from the more humdrum 教育 education. Thus it is instructive to ponder the thought that whereas the Oxford History of English literature chooses to translate the German *Bildungsroman* by the English (sic!) word Bildungsroman. Neither Danish nor Chinese need to take over the German word to translate it.

Classical education is in trouble in China, but the state does what it can to support it. Much to the despair of Chinese children who find no use for a traditional Chinese *Bildung* in a very Americanised modern China. State-sponsored studies of the Chinese golden age of Confucius and Laozi abound everywhere. Primary school children are made to learn by heart literally hundreds of poems written in classical Chinese, the Latin of the Chinese empire. The productivity of classical Chinese scholarship is immense: In English we do not have a single dictionary of classical Greek synonyms, whereas I alone own many dozens of such works on Chinese. Publisher's enthusiasm is funded by very large state subsidies for classical Chinese studies in China while Denmark is seriously discussing the abolition of classical Greek as a subject in the University of Copenhagen.

There is objective reason to cultivate the classical Chinese linguistic heritage in China, though, in a way that is quite alien to our Western relation to Latin. There is a fat book on Prime Minister Wen Jiabao's use of classical Chinese quotations, quotations in a language that has been dead as a spoken medium for several millennia. And we also have a comprehensive account of Xi Jinping's more lame attempts to live up to his pretensions to being a civilised leader, acculturated to the Chinese literary tradition.

The Chinese leadership makes every effort to continue the classical Chinese heritage, that is for sure.

Public television does their bit: a huge wave of Chinese *gongfu* films and films on traditional themes as well as Chinese operas are replete with dialogue in *wenyanwen*. The anthropologist Yi Zhōngtiān 易中天 has been offered many hundreds of hours of prime time in the public TV Channel 10 expounding the philology of the intellectual classical heritage, the classical Chinese texts from the philosophers like Confucius and Laozi and many more. His lectures were almost embarrassingly popular given their academic content and their distinguished academic author. I have been able to buy most of them as CD disks. In addition, in his lectures replete with *Wenyanwen* 文言文 explanations, Yi Zhōngtiān has been given hundreds of hours prime TV time to present in philological detail the classical historical heritage from the first of the 26 Dynastic Histories written completely in classical Chinese covering the period 200 BC to 200 AD. His success was so great that he was invited to do similar lectures on the History of the Three Kingdoms, again in many dozens of lectures which had to be published in book form because they were so unbelievably popular. I have attended Yi Zhōngtiān's lectures, and I must confess that his charismatic charm played as important a role in his success as his unbelievable fluency in traditional Chinese culture. He has a way of making the classical Chinese linguistic heritage sexy that becomes even more evident when one compares him with his internationally quite successful epigones like Professor Yu Dān 于丹, who strike one as paragons of classicist bad taste and traditionalist *kitsch*, but who do all the more to demonstrate the depth of popular commitment to the classical Chinese linguistic heritage in China.

The official media and the political leadership are not alone in demonstrating this infatuation with the distant linguistic tradition. Of the slogans displayed on Tiananmen, and very carefully documented by the Taiwanese authorities, practically none were composed in the current spoken vernacular celebrated by the linguist Chao Yuen Ren 赵元任 as Sayable Chinese. All of these slogans were in classical Chinese *Wenyanwen* 文言文. And the heritage of Chinese popular wisdom is enshrined most importantly in their proverbial idioms known as *chéngyǔ* 成语. Now these proverbial idioms *chéngyǔ* belong most visibly to the classical Chinese linguistic heritage, in that they are in plain classical Chinese *Wenyanwen*, the Latin of the Chinese tradition.

A reasonably educated speaker of modern Mandarin Chinese can be demonstrated to have a repertoire of thousands of proverbs from the treasury of the Chinese classical heritage. Not only can it be demonstrated: it has been demonstrated by the on-line project of a *Mandarin Audio Idiolect Dictionary* (http://tekstlab. uio. no/maid/), where a native speaker of Peking Mandarin Chinese as spoken by the original Manchu population of that great city demonstrates fluent spontaneous command of many thousands of specific such classical sayings, providing examples of their current use in written or in spoken modern Chinese, and specifying in particular the social contexts in which the use of these elements from the classical heritage is expected to occur.

When all this is said and done, I must report that among the schoolchildren and university students today the obligatory curriculum requirement for study of classical Chinese is exacerbatingly unpopular. The study of their classical Chinese heritage is felt to be a manifest irrelevance in the modern world, takes away precious time from the study of science and of English for the TOEFL examinations required for study abroad, and being totally detached from the five modernisations which are to make China great again. As a Quality Assessor of a University in Hong Kong I have recently seen quite varied striking evidence how not only the local Cantonese dialect has to be forced down the throats of the poor little children these days, who grow up in Mandarin-speaking kindergarten and answer back their Cantonese-speaking children in Mandarin: especially the basic knowledge of classical Chinese 文言文 has to be forced down the throats of totally uninterested and overburdened children. It became clear to me that there are limits to the extent a cultural linguistic heritage can be kept truly alive by political decree.

Given the precarious future of the classical linguistic heritage in private life as well as in the public media of all kinds, it is interesting to consider the history of curriculum development in Chinese Studies in Western Universities.

When Chinese Studies began to become an academic discipline with the appointment of Abel-RŽmusat as a Professor in the Sorbonne in Paris in 1812, it was a revolutionary act on his part to take colloquial Chinese, *báihuà* 白话, seriously at all. The serious study of China took seriously the dominant status of *Wenyanwen*, the Latin of China. No one would dream of studying the Chinese culture with any depth, but without a sound background the classical Chinese language. Just as no one should — of course — ever have been dreaming of seriously studying European culture with any depth, but without a sound background in Latin and Greek. Without such deep commitment to cultural linguistic heritage one might as well call off the project Europe, and without such deep commitment it is felt that one would endanger Chinese cultural identity and spiritual continuity.

When I enrolled for Chinese in Oxford in 1966, Chinese Studies were still dominated by the study of the Chinese cultural tradition and of classical Chinese and *Wenyanwen*. The spirit was much like that of the great Swedish linguist Bernhard Karlgren who developed the habit of asking prospective students wanting to study Mandarin Chinese with him asking Do I look as if you could learn a lot of Mandarin Chinese from me? He would point to the floor and go on: Down there you'll find millions of people from whom you'd be able to learn the language much faster, and much better! Karlgren, the dialectologist, knew Mandarin very well. But his main interest was in the Chinese cultural and linguistic heritage. He knew that no people are more historically-minded than the Chinese. No one was going to study Chinese with him without paying due attention to that linguistic heritage.

By now, a solid majority of China Studies professors are blissfully innocent of professional competence in classical Chinese, in fact all over the western world. An interest in historical linguistics is widely regarded as demeritorious in sinology. It is taken to indicative of a leaning towards old-fashioned philology. And as philology-minded culprits we joke among one another: They called me a philologist and I insulted them, too. Such has been the decline of the glory of philology more or less all over the world: *sic transit gloria mundi*.

Socio-economic, purely religious, historical, literary or philosophical perspectives have tended to replace perspectives of cultural history. And all that is natural enough. But here is the snag: The sources for socio-economic or literary affairs in China Studies are predominantly texts. Our understanding of Chinese socio-economic, historical, literary, religious, and philosophical affairs is never going to much more subtle than our understanding of the language and conceptual world of the relevant source texts. The details of this conceptual cultural heritage are totally dependent on a solid grounding in historical philology. Plato had a cruel sign at the entry to his Academy: No Entry to Non-Mathematicians. One can quarrel about this in many ways. But one thing out to be indisputable: No one should be allowed to enter Chinese Studies without a solid grounding in the science of the Chinese linguistic cultural heritage, philology, the indispensable art of the close reading of Chinese sources. This science is a *conditio sine qua non* for any in-depth form of China Studies that values the autochthonous Chinese vision of things.

However this may be, it can sometimes look as if all this may change profoundly. Chinese children typically hate to learn classical Chinese. Many Chinese may come to emancipate themselves from the deep roots of their own cultural and linguistic heritage. Everywhere we see the signs China's entry into a global Coca-colonisation of the spirit, of a MacDonaldisation of cultural perspectives that will increasingly make the Chinese view themselves and their own culture in a Hollywood style.

China may sometimes give such an impression. But I somehow doubt that it will ever **really become** like that. It looks to me as if the new state-capitalist China will develop its own style of absolutist autocratic globalised ideology (with Chinese characteristics) in which cultural heritage and cultural identity play their proper nationalist part. The *People's Daily* in Peking is replete with classical Chinese phrases. In the new China, as in the old, the use of classical Chinese phrases is a mode of linguistic domination. The rich Chinese cultural heritage remains a central part of the new Chinese Socialist and nationalist ideology. Patriotism is a core value in China. And patriotism as well as nationalism essentially feed on respect for cultural heritage.

(University of Copenhagen, Denmark)

Bibliography

1. Abel-Remusat, Jean-Pierre, *Les ŽlŽmens de la grammaire chinoise*, Paris: Gauthier, 1822.
2. Chao, Yuen Ren, *A Grammar of Spoken Chinese*, Berkeley: University of California Press, 1968.

3. Falkenhausen, L. von, The Concept of Wen in the Ancient Chinese Ancestral Cult, in Chinese Literature: Essays, Articles Reviews (Clear), vol. 18, 1996, 1–22.
4. Harbsmeier, C., "The Axial Millennium in China" in Johann P. Arnason, S. N. Eisenstadt and Bjšrn Wittrock, eds., Axial Civilisations and World History, Leiden: Brill, 2005, pp. 468–507.
5. Harbsmeier, C., "Globalisation and Conceptual Biodiversity", Quatre-vingt-uniŽme session annuelle du ComitŽ, Oslo, du 1er au 6 juin 2007, Compte Rendu, SecrŽtariat Addiminstratif de l'Union AcadŽmique Internationale Palais des AcadŽmies, Bruxelles, pp. 23–39.
6. Harbsmeier, C. ÒVergleichende Geschichte der Nachdenklichkeit, NEWSLETTER des MŸnchner Zentrums fŸr Antike Welten und der Graduate School Distant Worlds, 2021, no. 1, p. 2.
7. Jaeger, Werner, *Paideia: The Ideals of Greek Culture Volume I. Archaic Greece: The Mind of Athens*, Second Edition Translated from the German *by Gilbert Highet*, Oxford: OUP, 1986.
8. *Wēnwéněryǎ* 温文尔雅 (Explanation of classical quotations used by Wen Jiabao), Beijing: Zhongguohuabao Chubanshe, 2010, 355 + 14 pages.

"Heritage" and "Kulturarv"

Sune Auken

Our perception of the past is inevitably ideological. We cannot avoid it. When our understanding of the present changes, so does our understanding of the past. The past, as it appears to us, is never just the past, it is always the past *as it appear to us*, and we are, for better or worse, never neutral observers. We always have an agenda, we always have values, and we always have interests. Nothing we do and nothing we say can change that.

For me as researcher whose professional topic is genre, the question of implied ideology is always close at hand. Our ideology may be naturalized to us through the genres we have learned as we grow up and move through the education system (Devitt, 2009), through the values represented in our upbringing, and through our language. All of these things are habitual, they are "just the way we do things around here" (Schryer, 2002,76), and thus may acquire an "illusion of normalcy" (Paré, 2002,61) that might even lead to what has been called a "cultural reproduction of ignorance" (Segal, 2007, 4). As Kidd says: (2013):"Ideology is like B.O. [...] you never smell your own." (553; see also Paré, 2002,60)

However, inevitable is not immutable. We are not without agency; we are fate-bound to be victims of the process. As reflective beings, we have the option to educate ourselves and to think critically about our implied values. We are not fully independent or fully at a distance. We can only criticize genres through other genres, and we need language to criticize language, but it can be done. We may have a hard time smelling our own body odor and it may always return, but the option of a bath is recurrently available to most of us.

A particular problem in a cross-boundary discussion of well-nigh any subject in the humanities is language. English is established as the world's lingua franca, and even in communications between two cultures outside the Anglosphere English is likely to be used as the language of the exchange. It may not be a first language to either party, but it *is* a shared second language. However, with language comes ideology, and sometimes the words you need most are not even available or they twist between your fingers as false friends that either do not communicate what you are trying to say, or even add undesired meanings to your communication. Thus, as a Danish educator trying to work through the English language, I lack not just one, but two keywords in the Danish educational debate: "dannelse" and "faglighed", neither of which have a parallel word in English, albeit "dannelse" is so necessary a word that it is sometimes rendered in English through the use of the German word "Bildung". However, it sticks out like a sore thumb in your discourse.

There are deeper ideological issues connected to this problem. The naturalization of English as the given vehicle of communication also means that "things Anglophone" become the natural state; and a worldview conditioned by the English language is taken as a norm, implicitly and sometimes explicitly. This Anglo-normativity leaves us *Imprisoned in English* (Wierzbicka, 2013; see also Caines, 2015), or under the yoke of an English language, "Globalized Parochialism" (Wolters, 2013). Under those circumstances, it becomes even more crucial to examine the language we use to become aware of what we may adopt as a given thing when we switch languages.

In our approach to the past, a crucial question is how we think and talk about the traces or the remains of the past in the present, be they broadly cultural, ideological, or physical. The prevalent English word for this is "heritage", whereas the most official word in Danish, albeit in much less common use, is "kulturarv". The two are sometimes posited as translations, thus Unesco's list of "World Heritage", translates the expression as

"Verdenskulturarv" in Danish (where "world" = "verden").

If, however, we take a slightly closer look at the two words, "heritage" and "kulturarv", they turn out to be quite different. Sticking to simple dictionary entries,① *Merriam-Webster* defines "heritage" thus:

1. Property that descends to an heir.

2a. Something transmitted by or acquired from a predecessor: LEGACY, INHERITANCE

- Proud of her Chinese *heritage*.
- A rich *heritage* of folklore.
- The battlefields are part of our *heritage* and should be preserved.

2b. TRADITION

- The party's *heritage* of secularism.

3. Something possessed as a result of one's natural situation or birth: BIRTHRIGHT

- The *heritage* of natural freedom was long since cast away.②

A less formalized internet dictionary, *Dictionary.com*, gives this definition.

1. Something that is handed down from the past, as a tradition: *a national heritage of honor, pride, and courage.*

2. Something that comes or belongs to one by reason of birth; an inherited lot or portion: *a heritage of poverty and suffering.*

3. Something reserved for one: *the heritage of the righteous.*

Both definitions have to do with the way something from the past is present and working in contemporary life. There is a joint understanding in both these definitions that heritage is a rich concept that carries a lot of

---

① There is, of course, much research done from many different fields on questions of heritage. In fact, Heritage Studies is in itself an organized research field; thus the International Journal of Heritage Studies, combining research from fields like "Heritage Studies, Museum Studies, History, Tourism Studies, Sociology, Anthropology, Memory Studies, Cultural Geography, Law, Cultural Studies, and Interpretation and Design" (https://www.tandfonline.com/action/journalInformation? show = aimsScope&journalCode = rjhs20 Seen November 13th, 2018). For the purpose of the present essay, however, I stick to the simpler definitions, as the question at hand has to do with broadly shared cultural understandings, not with specified research knowledge. Unsurprisingly, the question of the ideological nature of heritage is not foreign to heritage studies (Kryder-Reid, 1017; Kryder-Reid, Foutz & Zimmerman, 2017; both with numerous further references).

② https://www.merriam-webster.com/dictionary/heritage. Seen October 12th, 2018.

meaning. Moreover, a heritage is a question of property, and it is exclusive to an extent; it is something a group has that sets it apart from others. It is also a concept of high pathos; connected to dramatic feelings, deep connections, battlefields and suffering, honour, pride, and courage. Fittingly, it clusters with other heavy words: tradition, legacy, inheritance, birthright. Historically speaking it is an old word, and tracking its meaning and use through history would make for an interesting study in itself.

The word "kulturarv" on the other hand doesn't have a very long history. In fact, it is completely absent from the otherwise huge dictionary *Ordbog over det danske sprog*, which covers the Danish language between 1700 and 1950 in painstaking detail. The dictionary definition of "kulturarv", taken from the major dictionary of contemporary Danish, *Den danske ordbog* defines the word thus (I leave the word itself untranslated for clarity):

The part of a large group of people or a population's view of life, life style, manners, and artistic expression that has been taken over from previous generations.

- indeed, if anything is our kulturarv, it's language.
- Through the contemplation of Nordic and European kulturarv in the meeting with foreign cultures, quality of life is improved. [1]

Taken in its literal meaning, "cultural inheritance", the word itself could easily have been laden with the same deep layers of meaning we find in "heritage", but as is evident from the definition, in actual use it is a much leaner, or more strictly technical, term. This is evident too if we see the words that it cluster with in the definition on *Den danske ordbog*. It is connected to various words for artifacts, culture, and cultural life, but none of these are very heated either.

The overlap between the two words is identical to the definition of "kulturarv". Everything covered by that definition is present in the word "heritage". In one sense, "heritage" covers "kulturarv" whole and then adds something.

---

[1] https://ordnet.dk/ddo/ordbog?query = Kulturarv&tab = for. Seen October 12th, 2018. The entry has been edited somewhat to fit into the local context of the present paper.

However, in another sense you cannot add meanings without changing the meaning. Missing is precisely the lean, technical meaning that designated an interest in the continued life of the past in the present without drawing in layers and layers of rich, pathos-laden significance. The Danish word may be new and slightly boring, but it is also much more a term for cooler heads; less exclusionary, less proprietary, and much less inviting of chauvinism than heritage. The most prominent institution designated by the term "heritage" is a right-wing think-tank, *The Heritage Foundation*; whereas the most prominent institution with "kulturarv" in its name was, until some years ago, an administrative government unit, *Kulturarvsstyrelsen* (The directorate of kulturarv), established 2002 and merged with two other directories into a new larger institution in 2012.

Why is this important? Because the way we conceptualize the world is never innocent or fully neutral. In this case there are two consequences, the first practical and scholarly, the second ideological. The two may very well prove to be connected.

The practical reason first: if we conceive of history as heritage, we are very much in danger of committing what Whitehead calls "the fallacy of misplaced concreteness" (Whitehead, 1997, 52), meaning that we impose an intellectual abstraction on reality without properly taking into account that it was an abstraction in the first place. There are many work-arounds available, but the concept itself invites a sweeping high-level abstraction, that — so to speak — puts the idea where the data should have been. For a student of history, of whatever kind, the material very rarely rises to the level of "heritage"; so much of history, and not necessarily the least interesting bits, are not battlefields, birthrights, or pride, courage, and honour. The past is much more a maze than a monument, and even the maze is too limited as a metaphor. Moreover, tracking actual chains of cause and effect in the past is difficult in the extreme, and tracing connections from past to present equally hard.

To use the example closest at hand. As stated, my chosen field of study is genre. When you study genres in history, what you meet is not a clear set of well-defined canonical texts, each moving in an orderly fashion towards the present, and each adding its own meaning to a deep, shared heritage. Instead, you are overwhelmed by a cornucopia of concrete texts, utterances and other cultural artefacts, relating to concrete genres (although, genres are always an abstraction), used by concrete people, in concrete situations to achieve concrete purposes (Miller, 1984) and leading to concrete uptakes (Freadman, 1994,2002) and outcomes. To understand each of these uses of genre you need to see them as actions performed within their particular context of genres (Devitt, 2004). There is always an actor, and there is always at least one genre. As history changes, contexts of genre change, and it may be devilishly hard to catch what a genre meant, and what people did with it in the past, as things that were taken for granted in each use of genre, have long gone out of vogue. Thus, even when you approach Great Texts — texts that have gone on to become canonical; heritage texts — you will find that they intertwine the unique and the generic, and that their particular character, their motivation, their role, and their influence, can only be understood on a background of apparently much more mundane genre uses.

The lesson learned from this — and one that can be corroborated by multiple researchers working on historical topics from other angles — is that a study of the past deals with data that is mixed and manifold and that invariably catches you in numerous complexities you had not, and could not, anticipate. Moreover, and this could be more crucial than it seems at first sight, history is highly interesting, very human (for better or worse), and often a lot of fun. I am probably not alone in finding that some of the elements that have given me the most pleasure in my studies are local details of little or no apparent importance to the greater movements of history. Finally, we may well be able to see that this influences the present, without being fully able to understand how this influence moves. One of the fundamental insights of genre research is that the implied assumptions in any given genre are often so naturalized to its users as to be made well-nigh invisible; they are habitual, ingrained, to such an extent that we take them for granted. Thus, what actually influences us, and what we see as our heritage may be wildly different things, and we need access to an overarching term that moves the relationship somewhat out of the heat and high oratory of "heritage" and frames it a little more as a practical question, a term like "kulturarv", is a great advantage. The leaner term lends itself well to a richer form of analysis.

Moving from this to the question of ideology. As noted, the slippery thing about ideology is that it is inherently more difficult to see your own ideology than that of your fellow human being. However, it is a fair to ask what assumptions we adopt when we use a word, and when we need to question such assumptions. In the case of a rich, tradition-laden term like "heritage" the implied assumptions are equally manifold, and we should be wary of accepting them.

Ideology is always there. We are never free from it. Indeed, from the point of view of hermeneutics, it is a central enabler of our thinking as it establishes a baseline understanding from which everything else is understood (Gadamer, 1990). However, we need a recurrent examination of our assumptions if we are to be choosers and not blind servants of our ideology; including, but not limited to, examinations of the genres and language that shapes our ideologies, and through which we shape the ideologies of others and ourselves.

Therefore, for what it is worth, we need to see the past, and our connection to it, more as a question of "kulturarv" and less as a question of "heritage". Languages being what they are, seeking to ban, or at least abandon a term like "heritage", is a fool's errand. Moreover, given the rich, yes, heritage of the word, it wouldn't even be a desirable thing to do; as students of history and language we don't want to impoverish language. However, in particular when English has — for better *and* worse — acquired its unique status in the world, we do need to interrogate the assumptions carried in the language, and we do need to know about the alternatives. This short essay has been one small contribution to such an endeavor.

(University of Copenhagen, Denmark)

Bibliography

1. Auken, S. (2018). Understanding genre. *Journal of Zhejiang International Studies University*,

3(2), 14-27.
2. Caines, A. (2015). White spaces. *Times Literary Supplement* (July), 23.
3. Devitt, A. (2004). *Writing Genres*. Carbondale: Southern Illinois UP.
4. Devitt, A. (2009). Teaching Critical Genre Awareness. In C. Bazerman, A. Bonini, & D. Figueiredo (Eds.), *Genre in a Changing World* (pp. 337-351). Fort Collins, Colorado: Parlor Press.
5. Freadman, A. (1994). Anyone for Tennis? In A. Freedman & P. Medway (Eds.), *Genre and the New Rhetoric* (pp. 43-66). London: Taylor & Francis.
6. Freadman, A. (2002). Uptake. In R. Coe, L. Lingard, & T. Teslenko (Eds.), *The Rhetoric and Ideology of Genre* (pp. 39-53). Cresskill Hampton Press Inc.
7. Gadamer, H.-G. (1990). *Wahrheit und Methode* (Vol. 2). Tübingen: J. C. B. Mohr.
8. Kidd, B. (2013). Sports and masculinity. *Sport in Society*, 16(4), 553-564. doi: 10.1080/17430437.2013.785757.
9. Kryder-Reid, E. (2017). Introduction: tools for a critical heritage. *International Journal of Heritage Studies*, 24(7), 691-693. doi: 10.1080/13527258.2017.1413680.
10. Kryder-Reid, E., Foutz, J. W., Wood, E., & Zimmerman, L. J. (2017). "'I just don't ever use that word': investigating stakeholders' understanding of heritage". *International Journal of Heritage Studies*, 24(7), 743-763. doi: 10.1080/13527258.2017.1339110.
11. Miller, C. (1984). Genre as Social Action. *Quarterly Journal of Speech*, 70(2), 151-167.
12. Paré, A. (2002). Genre and Identity: Individuals, Institutions, and Ideology. In R. Coe, L. Lingard, & T. Teslenko (Eds.), *The Rhetoric and Ideology of Genre* (pp. 57-71). Cresskill: Hampton Press Inc.
13. Schryer, C. F. (2002). Genre and Power. A Chronotopic Analysis. In R. Coe, L. Lingard, & T. Teslenko (Eds.), *The Rhetoric and Ideology of Genre* (pp. 73-102). Cresskill, New Jersey: Hampton Press, Inc.
14. Segal, J. Z. (2007). Breast cancer narratives as public rhetoric: genre itself and the maintenance of ignorance. *Linguistics and the Human Sciences*, 3(1), 3-23.
15. Whitehead, A. N. (1997). *Science and the Modern World*. New York: Simon and Schuster.
16. Wierzbicka, A. (2013). *Imprisoned in English. The hazards of English as a default language*. Oxford: Oxford University Press.
17. Wolters, G. (2013). European Humanism in Times of Globalized Parochialism. *Bolletino della Societá Filosofica Italiana*, 208, 3-18.

How to Preserve the Core Value of Intangible Cultural Heritage
— Xiashi Lantern as an Example

Ma Chi

Xiashi lanterns, a well-known kind of traditional Chinese folk art in Xiashi, a county-level city in Haining, Zhejiang Province, is one of three major cultural forms in Haining along with tide culture and celebrity culture. The distinctive needling of Xiashi lantern has received a commendation at home and abroad. It is said that the Xiashi lanterns boasts of a history of more than 2 000 years, originating from the Qin and Han dynasties and prospering in the Southern Song Dynasty.

In the Southern Song Dynasty, minority forces from Northeastern China invaded the Central Plains. Therefore, Emperor Zhao Gou moved the capital to Lin'an, which is Hangzhou today. The Emperor reconciled himself to the political situation. The custom of flying lanterns on the Lantern Festival developed to a new peak, which is actually window dressing. Making, racing and admiring lanterns became common practice at that time. According to the historical literature by Zhou[①], a man of letters in Song Dynasty, different kinds of lanterns were shipped to the capital as tributes including jade lanterns in Fuzhou, glass-colored lanterns in Xi'an, yarn-weaved lanterns in Nanjing, silk-made lanterns in Changzhou, brocade lanterns in Suzhou, sheepskin lanterns in Hangzhou and silk fabric lanterns in Xiashi. These lanterns with their own characteristics competed with each other.

---

① Zhou Mi, *Wulin Jiu Shi*, Beijing, Zhonghua Book Company, 2006, Volume 2, pp. 64 - 65. (周密:《武林旧事》(卷二),北京,中华书局 2006 年版,第 64—65 页)

Regarded as the most marvelous lanterns, Xiashi lanterns are called "lanterns with thousands of eyes" because of their fine needling. Fan Chengda (1126 – 1193), a poet in the Southern Song Dynasty, wrote in his poem A Visit to Lantern Fair, "The lantern is so delicate that it does not look like an earthly work of art. The thousands of holes exhaust manpower". His writing shows Xiashi lanterns were more delicate than other lanterns. At that time, a Xiashi lantern was displayed as a tribute to the emperor and hung in front of the city gate. Xu Baohan (1866 – 1942) also pointed out in his poem Xiashi Lantern Fair that the lantern was worthy of the fame.①

From 874AD to 879AD, in the Tang Dynasty, Xiashi Lanterns became renowned in the South of the Yangtze River. In the Southern Song Dynasty, Xiashi Lanterns were on the list of tributes. During the reign of Emperor Qianlong in the Qing Dynasty, various lantern shows, such as lantern acting and racing, emerged in many districts of Xiashi. At the turn of the 20th century, with making and decorating lanterns becoming popular among the locals, a breakthrough was achieved in craftsmanship and shaping, and many kinds of lanterns in the form of dragon boats and lotus gathering boats appeared. Xiashi lanterns kept popular in the Republic of China (1912 – 1949) and enjoyed rapid development and technical innovation after the founding of new China. After a period of stagnation during the Cultural Revolution, Xiashis gained new opportunities for development. ②On May 20th, 2006, approval was gained from the State Council and Xiashi lanterns were the first to be inscribed on the List of National Intangible Cultural Heritages.

The process of making Xiashi Lanterns mainly includes eight steps: bending, tying, knitting, mounting, engraving, painting, needling and pasting. Bending focuses on the lantern's skeleton and decoration. Materials are bent to make a skeleton, which decides the quality of a lantern. The workmanship passed down from the past, ensures the stability of the

---

① Zhang Zhenxi, "Haining Lantern Culture", *Literature and History World* by Haining CPPCC, 2009 [9]. (张镇西:《海宁灯文化》,海宁市政协《文史天地》2009 年第 9 期)
② Zhang Zhenxi, "Xiashi Lantern Market", *Literature and History World* by Haining CPPCC, 2017 [9]. (张镇西:《硖石灯市》,载海宁市政协《文史天地》2017 年第 4 期)

skeleton. Decoration refers to transforming medals into ornaments of different shapes including joints and top decoration of a lantern. Lantern masters allow no deviation which may lead to deformation. Masters' work depends on their experience rather than measurement standards. Tying depends on a modern technique of welding, which renders it possible to make difficult shapes and ensures the stability of a lantern. Knitting requires patience to hang fringes on the lantern edges, which shows the importance of details. Xuan paper, a kind of special paper for calligraphy produced in Anhui Province, then needs to be mounted upon the backside of the lantern paper and dyed and needled. Engraving is the quintessence of a lantern. It takes the skill and patience of a lantern master to make shapes based on their painting drafts. Decades of hard work contributes to the artistry of wielding the graver. The quality of detail-seeking outweighs quantity. A lantern masters must be an outstanding painter. The master paints flower and birds, characters, landscapes with the Chinese tradition of fine brushwork. This painting process is very difficult because it would be useless if the painting went wrong. The skill of needling is also breathtaking. Various traditional Chinese needling methods such as row needling, crochet needling and messing needling, are used to form a painting on lantern paper. The needling density of a lantern is 18 to 32 holes per square centimetre. An excellent piece of needling work usually has millions of holes, which looks remarkable in the light. Pasting as the last process of lantern making requires not only the skills but also the patience of a lantern master. The superior quality allows no split or fold. The ingenuity of a craftsman is demonstrated through the lantern-making process, and the title of intangible cultural heritage and its inheritors is well-earned. A lantern master is a designer of extraordinary versatility, thus endowing each lantern with a soul of art.[1]

The price of Xiashi a Lantern is proportional to its delicate artistry and great aesthetic value. The lanterns were displayed at lantern exhibitions in early years and have now begun to appear on tourism market. It takes more

---

[1] Zhou Yubin, "Exploring Haining Xiashi Lantern" *Zhejiang Daily*, April 11,2013. (周郁斌:《探访海宁硖石灯彩》,《浙江日报》2013 年 4 月 11 日)

than twenty days to complete making a small palace lantern with six facets. Its average price is about 3000 to 4000 RMB. And it would be no surprise to charge more than 100,000 RMB for an extremely delicate lantern. Therefore, Xiashi lanterns are beyond reach of ordinary people, and it is not easy to preserve this ancient artistry.

According to official data, there are about eighty people who can make Xiashi Lanterns today, among whom less than thirty people are working on them. Fewer and fewer young people are willing to acquire this traditional craft. A lantern master could make only two lantern skeletons in one day by hand. However, hundreds of lantern skeletons are produced in the way of semi-mechanization production. The last process of pasting must be completed by hand instead of machine. In order to make lanterns accessible to ordinary people rather than confined to museums, many attempts have been made in developing mini-sized lantern souvenirs which requires more skills and thus a higher price. Pot and vase-shaped lanterns are made by semi-mechanization production, but their needling is far less delicate than those made by hand. There are five kinds of Xiashi lanterns now including floor lamps, hand lanterns, wall lamps, pedant lamps and gift lanterns, all of which need more room to increase their aesthetic and collection value.[1]

The intangible cultural heritage of mankind epitomizes the most ancient and living collective memory of a nation and its invaluable wisdom and innovation. It manages to demonstrate life details in the course of history, help people to perceive ancient culture and touch the deepest part of a millennium of civilization. In contrast to tangible heritage, intangible cultural heritage is so fragile that it may be easily lost between the fingers much like sand in the hand. Thus, intangible cultural heritage seems to have met its doom in every domain, and Xiashi lanterns are no exception.

The ancient art of the Xiashi lantern is like old wine which gets more fragrant with age. It is worth attention that the artistry of Xiashi lanterns is passed down to family members, and only to male members, which narrows

---

[1] Zhu Ningjia Jin Haiming, "Derivative Ecological Research and Design Practice of Xiashi Lantern", *Design*, 2019[19]. （朱宁嘉、金海明：《硖石灯彩衍生生态研究与设计实践》,《设计》2019 年第 19 期）

its channels of inheritance and results in the loss of artistry. There is no elixir for life, what we have today may fail to exist permanently. Priority should be given to the protection of inheritors. Keeping intangible cultural heritage from extinction depends not so much on individual inheritance as mass inheritance. The most direct and valid way to preserve intangible cultural heritage is to introduce it to classroom and civil society, thus developing a better environment for its growth.

Many important attempts to preserve and inherit intangible cultural heritage, which helps build cultural confidence, have been made in the city of Haining. For example, Haining Vocational High School introduces intangible cultural heritage to classes by establishing inheritor studios, and promotes the transformation from individual inheritors to mass inheritors, thus preserving, inheriting and promoting the unique artistry of the Xiashi lantern with a mixture of needling, painting and engraving.

Schools in Haining, especially those whose duty is to preserve and promote traditional Chinese culture, have met difficulties in preserving and inheriting intangible cultural heritage. A platform through which teachers and students can have more access to the Xiashi lantern is needed to preserve and inherit intangible cultural heritage. Haining Vocational High School is one of the schools in Zhejiang Province which succeed in establishing first teaching bases for intangible cultural heritage in Zhejiang. In 2017, the school established a studio for Master Hu Jinlong, who is recognized by the State Council as an inheritor of the Xiashi Lantern. With years of experience, Master Hu is a man of great achievements in making Xiashi lanterns and his works are well-known at home and abroad. The school opens a salon of intangible cultural heritage in which there is a workshop for Xiashi lanterns for dozens of people. Master Hu frequently gives a lecture about Xiashi lanterns in the workshop and teaches in person the techniques of making Xiashi lanterns. The workshop has been fully used to hold many activities such as question & answer, picture appreciation, lantern display and practice, thus enhancing teachers' and students' perception of Xiashi lanterns and providing opportunities for them to feel its unique charm. Gradually, a seed of intangible cultural heritage has been sowed in student's hearts, thus lighting up their lanterns of hope. Thanks to the master-and-apprentice ties and relevant platforms, many teachers have made progress in teaching, won many honorary titles at different levels, and published numerous articles about intangible cultural heritage in national and provincial core journals.

In order to build a featured major on Xiashi lantern artistry, Haining Vocational High school has expanded enrollment. Any student interested in Xiashi lanterns can enroll in the course of Xiashi lantern artistry. In the meantime, the school has adopted modern apprenticeships which focus on the cooperation between the representative inheritors of national and provincial intangible cultural heritage and art masters, thus introducing skilled craftsmen to class to instruct students. The teaching group of "master + inheritors + skilled craftsmen + teachers + students" and the dynamic teaching pattern of "one-to-one" or "one-to-more" makes it possible for students to learn lantern artistry and perceive the charm of masters and the beauty of artistic works, thus enhancing students' interest in Xiashi lanterns and promoting their pursuit of lantern artistry.

For hundreds of years, the Xiashi lantern has based its improvement and innovation on its traditional artistry, developing five kinds of lantern including floor lamps, hand lanterns, wall lamps, pendant lamps and gift lanterns with more aesthetic and collection value. The picture cast by the light on the lantern is as vivid as life. When the Xiashi lantern was included in the List of National Intangible Cultural Heritage, many students ceased their pursuit of lantern artistry for various reasons. Therefore, the Haining government strengthened its efforts to protect inheritors and ensure the inheritance of the unique artistry.

In order to expand the impact of Xiashi Lanterns among young people and cultivate new inheritors, Haining government has established the Xiashi Lantern Exhibition Hall in Haining Museum to demonstrate and promote the historical achievements and charm of Xiashi lanterns. The government also holds many festive activities, such as lantern fairs and lantern streets at festivals, to create a festive atmosphere of admiring lanterns. Moreover, Haining government organizes many lantern competitions at home and abroad, taking an active part in lantern competitions in countries, such as Greece, New Zealand, Singapore and Regions of Hong Kong, Macao and Taiwan, to promote cultural exchanges and the popularity of the Xiashi lantern.

(Center for Thought and Culture, Shanghai Academy of Social Sciences)

A UNESCO World Heritage Site from a User's Point of View

Morten Warmind

Today Jelling is a small town with 3431 inhabitants in the Danish region Central Jutland, but there are ancient remains which show that it once was far more important. [Et kort over Danmark med Jelling her?]

The most salient remains are two identical mounds made of grass-turf on either side of a church. The mounds are 70 meters in diameter and 11 meters in height, and the distance between them is also 70 meters. Outside the entrance to the church are two stones with inscriptions in the Viking Age alphabet called "runes". These inscriptions, as well as other sources, make it possible to summarize the history of Jelling as follows:

In about 950 of our era a king called Gorm created a memorial in Jelling for his dead wife Thyrvi, whom he called "the ornament of Denmark" on an inscribed stone, which now forms one of a pair. In around 965, his son, whom we know as Harald Bluetooth[1], made major changes to the memorial so that it included his dead father and he further declared on a large three-sided stone with elaborate decorations that he, Harald, "won for himself all of Denmark and Norway and made the Danes Christian". Apart from the inscription on the smaller stone, it is unknown what Gorm's monument looked like, and therefore also how Harald changed it.

---

[1] Harald's nickname shows us that he must have had a prominent miscolored tooth. He has become famous through the communication protocol named after this nickname. The Bluetooth symbol is a combination of the rune for "H" and the rune for "B".

In 1200 a Danish historian called Saxo Grammaticus hinted at a memory Harald's memorial in Jelling — declaring (without any basis in factual evidence) that it was the cause of Harald's downfall, because his army was dissatisfied with being forced to work on its construction (Saxo 10,8,1 – 3; edition in English: Friis-Jensen, 2015).

The monumental mounds and the stones somehow became obsolete and unimportant in the course of a couple of generations, and they were then left to themselves pretty much, and subsequently decayed. The smaller stone of Gorm was used as a bench outside the stone church which was constructed in 1050, for instance. People lived right next to the mounds, and probably also damaged them somewhat over time. In 1820 – 1821 the first archaeological examinations were carried out in Jelling, and in 1861 the Danish King Frederik VII arranged a major excavation in Jelling. The king was extremely interested in archaeology, but his excavation was not methodologically satisfactory. Only in 1941 – 1948 were excavations according to modern standards carried out by E. Dyggve (Dyggve, 1948).

It should be noticed that Jelling was the focus of interest at two critical points in Danish history — the first time in the period between the two wars with the German Confederation, the next during the German occupation. Jelling has a strong nationalist significance as the birthplace of both the Danish nation and the Royal House.

It was therefore quite reasonable from a Danish point of view that in 1994 Jelling became a UNESCO World Heritage site, but the site certainly is of a general interest as evidence of a significant historical era — the late Viking Age. In 2006 it was decided to make a survey of the Jelling site, and surprisingly, for the site was thought to be quite fully explored, new finds were made of a sensational nature; among these the most exciting was the discovery that the whole site had been enclosed behind a seemingly rather high and impenetrable palisade, with only a very narrow entrance (Jensen 2015). This led to a complete re-evaluation of the monument, and to renewed plans for how to display and explain it to the public. The "public" of a UNESCO World Heritage site is, naturally, humankind, no less. As part of the new plans, in 2012 10% of the houses in central Jelling were torn down to display the monument, and probably more houses will have to go. These plans were made in the chief town of the municipality, Vejle (111,000 inhabitants), which is 14 kilometers distant, and the plans naturally caused a lot of distress and some resistance in the very small community in Jelling, where the population did not see themselves primarily as users and custodians of an impressive national monument, but rather as ordinary people wishing to be left in peace (Baun Christensen 2016,163ff). This is the starting point for my considerations about the user's point of view.

Using the site

If you are a visitor, using the site consists basically of simply looking at it, taking in the mound, the inscribed stones, the church and the larger palisaded area, which once surrounded the mounds. The latter is not directly visible, but has been marked on the ground, where it is possible. It is also possible to visit a museum, or rather an "experience center", which lies directly to the west of the mounds. From the roof of the museum, almost the whole site is visible.

The mounds are a feature of the landscape/townscape and they are therefore always "open", meaning that you can climb to the top of either one at any time you might wish to do so. The graveyard, which is situated around the church according to Danish custom, is also always accessible and thus the two large, inscribed stones are always visible. At night they are illuminated, so that the inscription and the decorations are especially easy to see and take in.

The stones used to stand in the open air, unguarded day and night. Visitors might climb on them, lean their bicycles against them or wear them down in other ways. The natural decay of rocks through frost must also have taken a toll through the centuries. Worse, probably, is the acidic rain caused by pollution and other recent factors, which have been a feature in Denmark throughout the previous century. All of this combined made it desirable that the stones should be covered in some way, and a plan to do this was set into motion. Enclosing the stones could be as dangerous as leaving them in the air if was not done correctly. Further, it was important that they should not lose any of their accessibility. Eventually each stone was encased in a box with glass sides. Curiously, in February 2011, right before the stones were to be encased, a mentally ill young man defaced the larger stone with graffiti from a spray can of green paint[①]. Fortunately it was possible to remove the paint, and it is interesting to note that the stones had not been spraypainted before, even though they had been completely exposed for centuries, and even though graffiti- "tagging" has been popular in Denmark at over least the last twenty years. That the stones were not regular objects of this kind of vandalism may demonstrate that for Danes, they were regarded as something everyone cared about.

The church is open to the public from 8 in the morning to 8 in the evening, which is more than most other Danish churches. If a ritual takes place, such as a Sunday service, a wedding or a funeral, there is no admission for tourists. Parts of the church are most likely from around 1050 and the building is thought to have been placed at the spot where Harald built one of the first churches in Denmark. Traces of wooden buildings were found under the church, together with the grave of a man, and many think that these are the remains of the first king of Denmark, Harald's father Gorm. It is supposed that Harald removed his body from the Pagan mound and reburied it in the Christian church as an act of posthumous Christianization. Most people who visit the monument also enter the church if it is possible.

"Jelling of the Kings"

The museum, which was begun in 1999 and opened in 2000, is not a museum in the strict sense of the word. It is rather an "Experience Center" where it is possible to learn about the culture of the Vikings, Christianization and what is known about the monuments. The Center is run by the National Museum. It is open from 10 to 5 all year, and the admission is free, so it can be regarded as an integral part of the site.

---

① Article in the Danish newspaper Politiken Aug. 13,2012: https://politiken.dk/indland/art5400828/16-årig-bag-graffiti-på-Jellingesten-skal-i-behandling.

The exhibits make use of the newest interactive technology to make the Viking Age come alive for the visitors, both adults and children. In the words of the web-site:

"The Experience Center offers a unique and super modern sensory experience regarding the life and legacy of the Vikings. The whole range of the human senses will be tantalized as the life of the Vikings unfolds with everything from bee-keeping to dragons. It will be a voyage from the stories that were told in the glow of the fireplace, to the life as a Viking and a warrior, the path to Valhalla as well as the transition to Christianity."[1]

The museum also contains a display, which tells some highlights of the history of the royal line of Denmark, emphasizing the various breaks and bridges in the continuity of the line and thus subtly carrying the message of the familial relations between Gorm and Harald and the present queen Margrethe II and her family. Thus the museum presents not only Jelling of the Viking Era kings, but also of the royalty today.

Who are the users?

Users of a World Heritage site may be classified in several different ways. In the following I have chosen two approaches. First, I group them simply with regard to how relevant/close the site is for each group and secondly I have formed a number of groups, based on the interest each group would have in the site. This method is somewhat arbitrary — the groups I have created in this way could also have been made up differently — but I think it creates some useful analytical distinctions.

I see three main circles, as it were, around the monument. The largest circle comprises humankind in general; the next circle is made up of the Danish population in general, and finally in the inner circle is the local population living in Jelling.

As for groups of people, who are users based on a vested interest, and

---

[1] https://en.natmus.dk/museums-and-palaces/kongernes-jelling-home-of-the-viking-kings/experience-center/.

who could be termed "stakeholders", I have, idiosyncratically, put my own at the top: Scholars who study the past. We are certainly users of the monuments. So are the national and the local politicians, the tourist industry at large and the local businesses, albeit each group has specific interests. UNESCO must, I believe, also be included in this list, though not strictly speaking as a group.

It seems fair and reasonable to discuss what each of these groups gets out of the site respectively. It should be kept in mind, that when we move from the general to the more specific groups, everything that goes for the most general group naturally goes for all the rest.

The largest and least well-defined group of users is of course Mankind as such. The most immediate and general importance of the monument, now as when it was constructed, is its unique plan, and its impressive size, given that no other Viking Age site that we know of comes even close.

Given its size and impressiveness, it also provides a first-hand impression of how such a monument works to construct and uphold royal power. The demonstration of the command of resources is impressive now, and in the Viking Age it must have seemed very extraordinary. The larger stone declares that Harald made the Danes Christian. Possibly the raw power demonstrated by the site was part of what made Harald's command of the conversion-process possible, and the site can therefore also be seen as a monument to Denmark's integration into the "civilized" European community of Christian monarchies. As Scandinavia was the last area to be Christianized, this can also be seen as the beginning of the complete Christianization of Europe. All this is reflected in the briefest possible form in the description of Jelling on the UNESCO World Heritage Site home-page:

"The Jelling burial mounds and one of the runic stones are striking examples of pagan Nordic culture, while the other runic stone and the church illustrate the Christianization of the Danish people towards the middle of the 10th century."[1]

Somewhat contradictory, but nevertheless relevant, it should be added

---

[1] https://whc.unesco.org/en/list/697.

that the Jelling monument, for all its size and impressiveness, also demonstrates the starkness of Viking Age life and the limited resources available, when compared to much larger contemporary monuments in the Mediterranean area and other parts of the world.

The monument affords these insights to anyone, no matter their origin.

The next circle comprises the Danes in general. To them it has more to offer, being a tangible reminder of the origins of the nation and of the royal line, which has continued through the twists and turns and dynastic battles over a millennium.

Further, the rune-stones are in an old form of Danish, and Danes can relate to the roots of their language through the inscriptions and the characteristic alphabet, which was in use all over the Scandinavian area; it therefore at the same time provides a possible tie to the other Scandinavian countries.

The setting of Jelling in Jutland is also of some interest to Danes, who are aware of the shifting importance of the various parts of Denmark. Central Jutland is not as important or "central" now, where attention for centuries has centered on the capital on the east side of the easternmost island of Zealand. To Danes, the Jelling site is a reminder that it was different in the distant past.

The innermost circle, comprising the population living in Jelling may, of course, experience all of this, but possibly with somewhat less affection for the famous site. It is not necessarily pleasant to have busloads of outsiders stopping briefly in your town to look at an attraction and then move on. Maybe the heightened awareness of their town is a source of pride to some of the Jelling-dwellers, but the town was never the most important thing about Jelling — quite the opposite. The town has to some degree been perceived by outsiders to lie in the way of the monument, so a large number of houses in the proximity of the mounds have been torn down over the years, hardly to the delight of the local population.

Another problem is, that the local church and the local cemetery is placed right in the middle of the monument, and obviously tourists make the access for the local people to these places difficult at times, creating an atmosphere which is not good for those who come to mourn and remember their dead relatives. It has further been claimed that the unusually large number of visitors means that the church must be cleaned once a day, instead of twice a week like other churches. This is an extra expense which must be paid for by the congregation. [1]

Stakeholders

Scholars who study the Viking Age of course derive the same benefits from the monument as everyone else, but there is something added. The conferral on the monuments of UNESCO-status means that the site is better funded and better protected than before this was the case. Then we also experience a greater interest from the public in our work, which may even result in more opportunities to earn money from books and public lectures etc. On the other hand, it may be a downside that archaeological work becomes less possible since it entails partial destruction of the monument.

National politicians have an interest in such a monument, because they gain a certain amount of honour from a World Heritage site. This honour may be difficult to pinpoint precisely, but at the very least, when inaugurating the site, they will gain a completely positive event of both national and international importance, where they can look good and appear to be patriotic even in the eyes of their political opponents.

Local politicians also gain honour, of course, and possibly of a more long-lasting kind, as they may become a part of the local history. They can also more immediately be seen to have an interest in the locality, as a World Heritage site always brings with it a promise of increased tourism, trade and consequently of economic growth.

The tourist industry itself also expects that such a site will bring in more tourism. The site gets a coherent and interesting narrative, which can be repeated in brochures and put in international advertising with links to the

---

[1] Article in the local newspaper "Vejle Amts Folkeblad" Oct 4, 2016, https://vafo.dk/jelling/Menigheds-raad-er-bekymret-over-slid-paa-hoejomraadet/artikel/445434.

UNESCO site etc. This makes such a site important for all tourism to Denmark through the heightened exposure.

Local businesses have seen a growth in income through a greater number of tourists in the town, but on the other hand local zoning laws have become stricter, making it impossible to build new shops near the attractions. Further the demolition of the town center to make the mounds more visible has also meant that some businessmen have seen their shops or inns demolished (Baun Christensen 2015,154ff). So the blessing is mixed in this case. Tourists on a short visit are also highly selective in what they buy, so some tradespeople profit more than others.

Last on my list of stakeholders is UNESCO itself. Obviously, the organization gets to add another little flag to its interactive map of the world through such a heritage site. This is a demonstration of the work of the organization to preserve important sites that are of general interest and provide benefits to all of mankind. At the same time this of course strengthens the argument that the organization is doing work that is necessary, and hence that its existence is worthwhile.

Conclusion

The monument at Jelling was a matter exclusively for the Danes through most of the twentieth century. Excavations and town-planning were debated and discussed from time to time and great modifications took place. It was not, however, until the monument became a World Heritage Site in 1994 that new extensive examinations of the area were planned and executed in 2006, with the result that the monument changed its character and that much of the town center would have to be demolished to accommodate it.

This is maybe an extreme example of what happens to a monument when it becomes part of the heritage of Mankind, but I think that many of the 845 cultural World Heritage sites have undergone a similar change, possibly more subtly from a national or local site into what is much more a monument.

(University of Copenhagen, Denmark)

Bibliography

1. Baun Christensen, L. & Lokalhistorisk Forening for Jelling, Kollerup, Vindelev og Hvejsel Sogne, 2016. Jelling — byen der forsvandt, Jelling: i samarbejde med Forlaget Jelling.
2. Dyggve, E., 1948, The Royal Barrows at Jelling, Antiquity no. 88 December pp. 190 - 197.
3. Friis-Jensen, K. & Fisher, Peter, 2015. Saxo Grammaticus, Gesta Danorum, the History of the Danes, Oxford: Clarendon Press.
4. Jensen, K., 2015. Monumentområdet i Jelling, The monument area in Jelling 1. udgave (1. edition), 1. oplag., Aarhus: Arkitekt Kristine Jensens Tegnestue.

Archaeological Heritage and Local Identity

Esben Aarsleff

Archaeological heritage is a complex phenomenon, from the smallest local finds like potsherds, to the international wonders like the pyramids and the Terracotta Army. The value of the latter is evident, but the microscale local finds must not be underestimated, as they are our key to understanding the past on a local level, thereby enabling us to draw a picture of the ancient times that the local modern community can relate to. Thus, the archaeological finds are rooted in the local community and are accepted as a valuable resource that either creates or, at the least, supports the local identity.

Archaeological heritage

The focal point is the local perception of the archaeological heritage, mainly derived from excavations that are carried out because of construction work, for instance new houses, roads, industry and so on.

All excavations in Denmark are regulated by the Museums Act. The act states that all construction work must bear the cost of the excavation of any archaeological sites that may be found on their land. In Northern Zealand the archaeological sites mainly consist of remains of settlements with culture layers, houses, fireplaces, production pits and refuse pits from the period between 4000 BC and 1000 AD, which covers the prehistoric times from the late Stone Age, Bronze and Iron Age in Denmark. For some unknown reason graves are only found on rare occasions; the last time we excavated a burial ground was over 10 years ago.

During the past ten years we have become aware of the massive potential of the wetlands which used to characterize the landscape of Northern Zealand. In these wetlands we have been able to find traces of peat cutting and sacred actions, both of which are of international interest. The wetlands display both sacred and profane uses similar to the traces on drylands and this contradicts the former perception of wetlands as exclusively sacred places.

In general, artefacts such as potsherds and other types of waste are most common on our excavations, but there is also a certain amount of tools and decorative items, and although the fashion changes and the tools are improved over the centuries, the combination of every day rubbish and finer artefacts/tools is seen on most excavations. (Fig. 1)

Fig. 1

Constructions of wood and stone from the prehistoric periods are rarely seen in the excavations, and due to modern construction work, they will almost always be demolished; the ancient constructions are only preserved and opened to the public in a few fortunate examples. As a rule, only the artefacts, both large and small, are preserved for the future.

Thereby the main part of the archaeological heritage consists of artefacts that are kept on the museum's storage facilities. The value of the artefacts is measured based on a combination of their rarity, their scientific value and the story that they tell about prehistoric man and society. The latter is often the most import argument for keeping all artefacts from any excavation — every find has a unique story, from the smallest potsherd to the most beautiful beads.

Examples

We open most of the larger excavations to the public for some hours to show our archaeological artefacts and features and explain the results. The authenticity of the heritage that an excavation offers is appreciated by the local community.

This kind of "pop-up" museum on site normally attracts the locally based amateur archaeologists and others who are interested in the local prehistory. But on rarer occasions the archaeological heritage has a greater importance in the creation of the local identity, or at the least as a support to local identity, as the following examples will show.

Lodsens Minde

In 2010 we excavated a small area within the town of Hundested. We found traces from the early Stone Age, Bronze Age and post-medieval times (Pantmann 2017). The traces consisted of artefacts made of flint from the Stone Age and fire places from the other periods, the latter is a common feature on our excavations.

The excavation found great local interest and many followed the daily progress, as the excavation was situated next to the local grocery shop. (Fig. 2)

Fig. 2

The Stone Age finds were the reason why the excavation was carried out in the first place, but the locals found a lot more interest in the fire places, as they were something they could relate to. After the excavation was finished a local group instigated a yearlong process that ended in 2016, when a small square was set up near the original site of the biggest fireplaces on the site. The square consisted of two recreated fireplaces, together with two life-size steel figures that represent fishers from the Stone or Bronze Age. Next to the square there were some texts about the three periods that we uncovered during the excavation.

But why did some seemingly uninteresting fireplaces suddenly constitute such a great appeal for the local community?

To understand this question, we must look at the history of the town of Hundested. It was originally a small fishing community, founded in the middle of the 19th century (Hansen 1998). In Danish perspective it is a young town, with only a marginal history. The ancient fireplaces indicated that the area had a prehistory, where fishing and living by the sea were a living condition, just as it was almost up until present day. The archaeological heritage thereby provided an understandable link between past and present, and enhanced the local identity as fishermen.

This example shows that even common features can rise from everyday finds to important cornerstones in the local identity.

The Hyllingebjerg stone

This boulder weighing 8,5 tons was originally placed on a high cliff with a wide view near the northern beach of Halsnæs. In the middle of the Bronze Age, around 1000 BC., it was engraved with several ships and hundreds of cup marks, representing the religious symbolism and beliefes of the Bronze Age (Pantmann 2017). In 1983 is was discovered on the beach, no longer in its original place, due to the natural erosion of the cliffs caused by the sea. In the 1990's is was displayed in a hall/local arts house in Frederiksværk, but interest faded, and the stone ended up in the museum's storage.

In the years between 2007 - 2010 the people in the municipality of

Halsnæs began to miss the Hyllingebjerg stone, and a local group began the time-consuming work of "repatriating" the stone to Halsnæs. They raised the money for a showcase, posters and the moving of the stone back to Frederiksværk, where is now stands in the lobby of the local library.

Where Hundested was founded by fishers, Frederiksværk was founded by an entrepreneur from Copenhagen in the middle of the 18th century (Jacobsen et al. 2006). The town was originally a cannon and gunpowder factory, with surrounding houses for the employees. The town itself has no links to the Bronze Age or other prehistory before the middle of the 18th century. Instead the Hyllingebjerg stone represents the wider picture of a municipality, where the areas surrounding Frederiksværk contain a prehistory that dates to the Stone Age and onwards. The archaeological heritage thereby creates an identity that, of course, predates the main town and which the locals embraced.

Salpetermosen

Another example of archaeological heritage is the excavation in the Salpetermose, on the outskirts of Hillerød, which has been carried out over the past five years. The site and finds cover a wide range of periods and types. One of the most important finds is perhaps a bog body from the period around 3600 BC (Jørgensen & Hagedorn 2015). Unfortunately, he was discovered using a 21-ton excavator, which means the skeleton was shattered, as one can see in the picture. (Fig. 3 and Fig. 4)

The poor man had been shot with a bonepoint and had had a fatal blow to the back of his head from a stone axe. Afterwards he was placed in a lake, near a contemporary settlement. We presume that the people at this settlement were the ones who killed him as a sacrifice, a tradition of which there are some examples from all over the country.

Another important find that we excavated was the remains of a chieftain's farm, which dates to the period around 250 – 400 AD with remains of houses, sacred deposits, culture layers with lots of artefacts and wetlands with traces of peat cutting in the form of pits (Pantmann 2014).

Fig. 3   Fig. 4

In the pits there were different kinds of sacred depoists of animals, mostly cattle, sheep, goats and pigs, but also wooden artefacts, pottery and an abundance of whitish stones. The latter are a peculiar type of offering that we can trace back to the Neolithic and all the way up through the Bronze and Iron Age. (Fig. 5)

Fig. 5

The developer is a public authority, who does not see the need for a local identity, but who does accept that the archaeological heritage must be salvaged, before the bull-dozers and excavators enter the area. The local community has, on the other hand, taken a great interest in the finds, and everybody knows that there have been large scale excavations going on for the past years. The museum has undertaken a great deal of work in explaining that this site is of a particular importance regarding the understanding of the prehistory at so many levels.

In this example the local community embraces the excavations and the finds, and the archaeological heritage creates, if not an identity, then at least a bond between the past and the present.

Widex and Biogen — two examples of private companies

Biogen is a private American-based medic company that constructed a factory in Hillerød in 2002 – 2005. In 2001 the museum carried out large scale excavations of farmstead from the period around 2 – 400 AD on their land, which is the Iron Age in Denmark (Nielsen & Kramer 2002). The excavation yielded lots of artefacts, mostly in the form of potsherds from the household waste. The company saw a great potential in the fact that people had been living on their area 16 – 1800 years ago, and they invested in an exhibition in the lobby of their new factory, thus creating a link to the past, and thereby some sort of local identity for the local branch of the company.

A secondary remark on the Biogen excavation was that they named the road to the headquarter: "Iron Age road." This can only be interpreted in one way, that they took great interest and pride in the heritage.

Widex is another private company that built a new headquarter near Allerød in 2008. Excavations uncovered both a settlement and a burial site dating to the early Iron Age, the period around 500 BC – 0 (Aarsleff 2009). (Fig. 6) The artefacts were scarce, and we ended up with just one pot that they could exhibit in their lobby. Oddly enough, the pot was found in what was to be the center of the new concentric headquarter, and it, somehow, became the company's anchor to the past.

In both cases the archaeological heritage became an active component in the companies wishes for a local connection, not identity, as they already have a worldwide identity. More importantly they wanted to let the local community, as well as their international connections, know that they

Fig. 6

respected the past and invited it into their new buildings by arranging exhibits in their lobbies. For the larger private companies, the caretaking of the archaeological past, or paying for the caretaking, becomes part of their CSR (Corporate Social Responsibility) investment.

Archaeological Heritage — The local heritage as a supplement to the national heritage.

These examples show a great variety in the use of the archaeological heritage in a small area such as Northern Zealand. In the municipality of Halsnæs, where both Hundested and Frederiksværk are situated, the fireplaces and the Hyllingebjerg stone have become important for the local identity.

In the example of the Salpetermose the public authority did not need the local identity, but the locals embraced the finds and saw them as a link to the past.

The two examples of private companies show that the archaeological heritage can create a link to the past, which the companies can exploit both in terms of local identity and CSR — both elements represent a certain value to the larger companies.

To conclude one might say that the heritage, on a local level, uncovers the microhistory. With the archaeologist as a mediator the artefacts and structures can tell the stories of daily lives in ancient times and hopefully make people realize that the prehistory is relevant to them, both personally and in terms of identity either of companies, areas or communities.

In the modern rootless community, history and ancient times have become more and more relevant for many Danes, something that we, as archaeologists, can only embrace and meet with more activities and events that present the archaeological heritage locally but preferably with links to the national heritage.

(Museum of Northern Zealand, Denmark)

Bibliography

1. Aarsleff, E. 2009. Flere kældre fra førromersk jernalder — og lidt grave. *NoMus 1/ 2009*, s. 24 - 29.
2. Hansen, E. 1998: *Hundested i gamle Dage. Erindringer fra et kvart Aarhundrede.* Hundested Lokalhistoriske Forening.
3. Jacobsen et al. 2006. *Friderichs Wærk — Kilder til industribyens fødsel.* Hundested Lokalhistoriske Forening. Frederiksværks Lokalhistoriske Forening og Industrimuseet Frederiks Værk.
4. Jørgensen, T. & L. Hagedorn 2015. Salpetermoseliget. *Alle tiders Nordsjælland. Museum Nordsjællands Årbog 2015*, s. 118 - 122.
5. Nielsen, L. E. & F. Kramer 2002. Udgravningerne ved Biogen. *NoMus 2/2002*, s. 3 - 6.
6. Pantmann, P. 2014. Hund og hund imellem. *NoMus 3/2014*, s. 3 - 11.
7. Pantmann, P. 2017. Ild og vand — kult i bronzealderens Lillerød. *Alle tiders Nordsjælland. Museum Nordsjællands Årbog 2017*, s. 149 - 156.
8. Pantmann, P. 2017. *Lodsens Minde.* Unpublished Report of the excavation.

Kulturerbe (kʊlˈtuːɐ|ɛrbə)

Moritz Kinzel

The term "Kulturerbe" is nowadays omnipresent in German debates dealing with the preservation of monuments, traditions or artefacts and the management of those. However the Duden — the well-known German dictionary — e.g. from 1986 as well as the "Wörterbuch der Deutschen Sprache" of 2004(!) do not knew the term "Kulturerbe" yet. So what does the term "Kulturerbe" actually stand for? When did it first appear in the German Language and in what context? Does it actually incorporate all the much differentiated meanings related to "Erinnerungskultur" and "Denkmalwert"? The contribution will discuss some of these aspects.

The German term "Kulturerbe"

Nowadays the term "Kulturerbe" is widely used and seems to have authoritarian gravity — as of "old". However, my old German dictionary — "Duden" from 1986 — as well as the later "Wörterbuch der Deutschen Sprache" published in 2004, do not contain the term "Kulturerbe". This means that the term "Kulturerbe" has established itself in the last fifteen years as the German equivalent for the English term "heritage". In its recent online version the Duden defines "***Kulturerbe***" currently as "***überliefertes Kulturgut einer Gemeinschaft, eines Volkes***" which would translate as:

"handed down cultural property of a community, a people".[①]

The word "Kulturerbe" stems from the term 'kulturelles Erbe'. Although it may resemble the same words and imply the "same" meaning, the focus for the latter is clearly on "Erbe" — *Inheritance* rather than on "culture" and on something valuable to take care for. The word construct "Kulturerbe" was introduced to the German language in the framework of the UNESCO programme for "intangible cultural heritage" in 2001. With the ratification of the memorandum in 2006 the term was officially introduced and has spread widely since then. Meanwhile one could fill entire libraries with books with the term "Kulturerbe" in their titles (c. f. Schmidt 2008; Meier et al. 2013; Tauschek 2013). Numerous contributions try to get hold of the "term" and to define it, but most of them fail as the point of discussion is too complex and ambivalent to be clearly defined. "Kulturerbe" does not exist per se. It is the sum of a number of factors which lead to a convincing narrative which defines a "value" that might be lost at one point in time for a specific group or community. This "value" gains importance only when enough supporters are engaging with the proposed narrative and identify themselves with the story built around an object, a monument, a certain action, a building or other people. The group of supporters will then carry the "message" into the world to gain more supporters for their version of the story and their interpretation. However in most cases the value is only recognised when a threat of loss is incorporated into the narrative (Kinzel 2018).

However, "Kulturerbe" incorporates so much more than only one concept. In Germany the debate about "monuments" and tradition was less based on "inheriting" something; it is rather built upon the concept of preservation and maintenance known as "Denkmalschutz und Denkmalpflege" (Huse 1984; Kiesow 2000). These differ in their meaning and conception substantially from the English term "heritage" which is defined as "property that descends to an heir", "something transmitted by or acquired from a predecessor: legacy [or] inheritance [...]; [or] something possessed as a result of one's

---

[①] http://www.duden.de/rechtschreibung/Kulturerbe [07. 11. 2015].

natural situation or birth: birthright"①. "Kulturerbe" must be understood primarily as knowledge about something inherited. Materiality and historical significance may lead to value creation and knowledge transfer; as long as stories about a place are still told and the knowledge where the actual place was is not lost and can be pointed out cultural heritage ("Kulturerbe") is not lost; as it is remembered.

The concept of value — cultural property

In principle there are three driving values behind the idea of cultural heritage/cultural property:

1) **Aesthetical Values**: seeing in an object, a place, a building or an activity **beauty, balance and order**.

2) **Historical Values**: seeing the past as a sources of knowledge with the excitement: **"it is old!"**.

3) **Social Values or Communal Values**: the actual act of care taking: "**Denkmalpflege**", the maintenance of cultural heritage by practicing traditions.

The term "Kulturerbe" involves a wide range of concepts defining values that may argue for or against what could be seen as cultural heritage (e. g. Bogner et al. 2018; Meier et al 2013; Cnattingius and Cnattinigus 2007):

Alterswert — *Ageing and patina*: Alois Riegl (1903; 1995) defines "Alterswert" as the traces of ageing and the patina that links emotionally directly to the observer. Yet it also includes the ongoing ageing process. Value grows with the ongoing ageing process and not with a preserved stage of identification.

Bildwert — *Aesthetic values*: A monument is appreciated because of its very specific aesthetic and picturesque appearance; including cityscapes, silhouettes, or their reproduction in the form of paintings and photographs.

Erinnerungswert — *Memory*: Although the term "Erinnerung" is closely

---

① https://www.merriam-webster.com/dictionary/heritage [accessed 03.09.2018]. For a more detailed discussion on the English term 'heritage' see S. Auken's contribution ("Heritage" and "kulturarv") in this volume.

linked to history and "Gedächtnis" it is rarely used in the current heritage debate in Germany; although monuments and memorials are actually physical testimonies that events, persons and "things" should be remembered. Remembrance, recollection or reminder may recollect some of the aspects of "Erinnerungswert". Cultural memory ("kulturelles Gedächtnis") is very selective and the aspect of displacing, forgetting, and concealing also play a major part in defining remembered narratives and group identities (Assmann 2006; Assmann 2013). Destructions can interrupt the development of memory, but through the act of destruction a powerful marker may be implemented for even stronger remembrance (Onu 2018).

Erzieherischer Wert — *pedagogical and educational value*: "Erziehung" has to be seen in the context of "Kulturerbe" as a duality: on the one hand to actually educate the people by imposing specific things to remember by monuments to them; and on the other hand by offering the chance for "Bildung" — as a holistic approach — by having a wider discourse on history and what can we learn from it.

Identität — *Identity*: Identity is based on the experience of being different and a clear demarcation towards the "other". Without an opposing "other" there is no identity; but it does not exclude someone from being part of various groups with a different identity. Demarcation lines may blur over time as the "other" dissolves. However this may create new narratives which can lead to the modification of group identities.

Kultwert — *cult values*: The concept of "Kultwert" is based on the perception of artefacts and the value created by exhibiting or presenting them, especially in religious and sacred contexts. Initially meant to describe the value of e. g. a statute or relic exhibited in an annual processions or shrine, it is used nowadays more to explain the value of an authentic location — less the actual monument or object.

Kunstwert — *artistic values*: The artistic quality of a monument defines the "Kunstwert". With this criteria often the restoration and completion of an artwork is argued for as a renewed, polished appearance may be generally more attractive and is much more appreciated than a fragmented and weathered state.

Nachhaltigkeit — *sustainability*: Sustainability in the context of "Kulturerbe" not only deals with the long-term preservation of the monument itself, it also evokes sensible use-concepts that respect the integrity of the cultural property and opens up for re-interpretations.

Streitwert — *conflict and debate*: Debating about the values of a monument or cultural heritage and their treatment may prove to be the actual value of it. The conflict and the arguments exchanged give value to the debated "Kulturerbe"; e. g. in the case of reconstructed and newly built "historical" buildings and the question of authenticity.

Symbolwert — *symbolic values*: The key values for nations, dynasties or communities are symbolic values. They form the basic framework for the concept of memorials and monuments. The symbolic value stands for the construction and destruction of monuments or other cultural property considered to be of value to someone. Symbols very much support the creation of strong identities and the visualisation of the differences from the "others".

Transkulturalität — *Transculturality*: The value of transculturality is the recognition of heritage that belongs to more than one group or nation, e. g. caused by shifting borderlines or migration movements. In several cases this kind of "Kulturerbe" can easily become contested, unwanted or uncomfortable, because it is related to "the others" and may be seen as a threat to one's "own" identity. However, transculturality can also be seen in a global perspective being entangled in many ways and bringing various traditions and cultures together to create new traditions, identities, and friendships.

Urkundenwert — *legal document*: The monument itself is an authentic document and testimony to its time and can stand as a reference, for instance a charter or legal document.

Zeugniswert — *testimony*: cultural heritage is testimony and witness to a historical event, experience or technology. It is closely related to "Urkundenwert", but also to "Erinnerungswert".

All these various aspects and concepts, briefly explained above, have to be understood as a part of the term "Kulturerbe". As explained the term derives from the more legal term 'Kulturgut' (cultural property) and its protection known as "Kulturgüterschutz". This was initially thought to cover only monuments and (historical) buildings.

Uncomfortable, contested and unwanted heritage

It would go beyond the scope of this paper to try to explain the complexity of the term "Kultur" in German. The same is true for the very complex term "Erbe" (heritage) and its interpretation in jurisdiction. However, "Erbe" does not cover only comfortable aspects. One can inherit depths and obligations as well as "bad" memories or associations. This means the word "Erbe" always also includes the uncomfortable, the contested and unwanted parts of memory and history (Huse 1997). As a result of German history and all the loss of buildings and other cultural goods, not only over the last 150 years, this is very much part of the cultural heritage debate and may represent a major difference to the terms "*patrimoine*" in French, "*heritage*" in English the Italian "*patrimonio*" (Brandi 1977) and the Arabic تراث/*turath*, or even the Danish "*Kulturarv*".

At the UNESCO World Heritage Committee meeting at Bahrain in July 2018 it was controversially discussed whether "negative-loaded" heritage sites should be listed on the World heritage list or not (ICOMOS 2018). The debate showed very much the different connotations of the term "heritage" and our different understandings of the term. It would be wrong to see "heritage" only as something positive, something to remember. Horrible, violent events and sites — uncomfortable in every aspect and sense — may not be suppressed only because they do not produce a positively perceived tourism destination. However this does not mean that a genuine negatively loaded heritage may be turned into some positive traditions of communication and shared caretaking of heritage monuments, e. g. the French-Belgian proposal for the World War I cemeteries and memorials along the "West front". As history writing is a political process and narratives are responsible for creating identities and nations — defining groups — cultural heritage is clearly a major part of defining narratives. UNESCO's cultural world heritage concepts turned into a universal applicable system, flexible enough to fit all the different connotations of material cultural and related activities and traditions (UNESCO 1972). Although, as explained above, there is a tendency to avoid uncomfortable and contested heritage since one goal is to protect heritage by promoting tourism and making sites known globally as a primarily positive aspect of a global shared heritage.

Conclusion

This short contribution can only be an attempt to start a process of better understanding. As shown the German term "*Kulturerbe*" incorporated a long and still ongoing debate of how we can best define values to turn traditions, buildings, monuments and other testimonies of the past into a "living" heritage. Our perception of "Kulturerbe" is strongly linked to our cultural backgrounds and national histories and cannot be transferred or translated one to one. It will be hard to overcome this dilemma, but knowing and being aware of the differences may help to come to a better understanding and a fruitful dialogue about what we are actually talking about when we say "heritage" but actually mean "Kulturerbe" with all its complexity.

(University of Copenhagen, Denmark)

Bibliography

1. Assmann, A. 2006. Erinnerungsräume. Formen und Wandlungen des kulturellen Gedächtnisses. 3. Auflage. München: Beck.
2. Assmann, J. 2013. Das kulturelle Gedächtnis. Schrift, Erinnerung und politische Identität in frühen Hochkulturen. 7. Auflage. München: Beck.
3. Bogner, S., Franz, B., Meier, H. -R., and Steiner, M. (eds.). 2018. Denkmal — Erbe — Heritage: Begriffshorizonte am Beispiel der Industriekultur, Heidelberg: arthistoricum. net, (Veröffentlichungen des Arbeitskreises Theorie und Lehre der Denkmalpflege e. V., Band 27). DOI: 10.11588/arthistoricum.374.531; https://books. ub. uni-heidelberg. de/arthistoricum/catalog/book/374 [accessed: 04.01.2019].

4. Brandi C. 1977. Teoria del restauro. Torino: Einaudi.
5. Cnattingius, L and Cnattinigus, N. 2007. Ruiner. Historia, Öden och Vård. Stockholm: Carlssons.
6. Huse N. (ed.) 1984. Denkmalpflege: Deutsche Texte aus drei Jahrhunderten München: Beck.
7. Huse N. 1997. Unbequeme Baudenkmale. Entsorgen? Schützen? Pflegen? München: Beck.
8. ICOMOS 2018. 2018 Evaluations of Nominations of Cultural and Mixed Properties. ICOMOS report for the World Heritage Committee; 42nd ordinary session, Manama, 24 June — 4 July 2018 — WHC-18/42. COM/INF. 8B1. https://whc.unesco.org/archive/2018/whc18-42com-inf8B1-en.pdf [accessed: 09.01.2019].
9. Kiesow G. 2000. Denkmalpflege in Deutschland — Eine Einführung. Stuttgart: Theiss.
10. Kinzel M. 2016. Von der Zerstörung von Kulturerbe: der Versuch einer Annäherung. In: AIV Forum, Vol.2016, No.1, pp.6–15.
11. Kinzel M. 2018. "Once Upon A Time ..." Constructing Narratives to Destruct Heritage. In: Moritz Kinzel.
12. Mette Thuesen; Ingolf Thuesen (eds.): Conflict and Culture: Understanding threats to heritage. Copenhagen: Forlaget Orbis, 2018, pp.14–19.
13. Meier H.R., Scheurmann I., and Sonne W. (eds.) 2013. Werte. Begründungen der Denkmalpflege in Geschichte und Gegenwart. Berlin: Jovis.
14. Onu, M. 2018. Spurious Infinity and axiological remembrance. Philosophical approaches on threats to cultural heritage. In: Kinzel — Thuesen — Thuesen (eds.): Conflict and Culture. Copenhagen: forlaget orbis. 2018: 56–61.
15. Riegl A. 1903. Der moderne Denkmalkultus. Sein Wesen und seine Entstehung. Wien/Leipzig.
16. Riegl A. 1995. Kunstwerk oder Denkmal? Alois Riegls Schriften zur Denkmalpflege. Bacher E. (ed.). Studien zu Denkmalschutz und Denkmalpflege Bd. 15. Wien/Köln/Weimar.
17. Schmidt L. 2008. Einführung in die Denkmalpflege. Stuttgart: Theiss.
18. Tauschek M. 2013. Kulturerbe. Eine Einführung. Berlin: Reimer.
19. UNESCO 1972. Convention Concerning the Protection of the World Cultural and Natural Heritage. Adopted by the General Conference at its seventeenth Session Paris, 16 November 1972 http://whc.unesco.org/archive/convention-en.pdf [accessed 03.10.2018].

Fig. 1　Key aspects for understanding threats to heritage (HeAT-Project/University of Copenhagen).

Fig. 2　Word cloud with cultural heritage values and terms in German and English.

Traditional Practice and Clay Portraiture in Qing China

Josefine Baark

Among the many precious artefacts produced in Canton in the early Qing Dynasty were hundreds of clay portrait figures, the majority of which are now found in Western collections. These sculptures show both Chinese and European merchants, who sat for portraits by "facemakers" in Canton. The artisans making the portraits relied on traditional practices, namely the making of burial sculpture, to produce this new type of portraiture that could easily be adapted to display in a European context. Here, "traditional practices" are taken to mean skills that have been developed over a long period of time to satisfy a local requirement and can be put in the category of "intangible cultural heritage" (Smith and Akagawa, eds., 2008). As will be shown in this article, the practices developed in Canton relied on tradition and "cultural heritage". Nevertheless, the production and display of the clay sculptures was by no means a static repetition of traditional skills. If we conceptualize points of cultural contact as a constantly moving targets, rather than fixed points of departure, we can use this example to trace how artefacts can adapt, blend into and resist traditional practices. Ultimately, this process engenders new, shared and even "global" cultural heritage.

This article presents a brief description of the Canton trade in the mid-Qing dynasty, the use of clay portraits in burial ceremonies in China, and the "lifelike" qualities of Chinese automata in order to look in detail at two portrait figures. The parameters of trade in Canton were particularly conducive to a culture of growth, where old traditions and artisanal practices could be easily adapted to new social requirements. For instance, while certain portraits produced in China from 1720 - 1760 had adapted the European practice of reproducing physiognomic likeness, others maintained the Chinese emphasis on clothes, rank and ornament to signify a particular person.

By tracking how artisanal traditions (in this case Chinese), which are often seen as foundational in defining a nation's "cultural heritage", could be developed by their practitioners to accommodate a new consumer (in this case European), this article uncovers two central aspects of how portraiture fashioned social status within the parameters of the "global" culture that developed in Canton in the 1700s. First, cultural parameters were not shaped only by the global "elite", made up of Chinese and European merchants. Instead, social practices that shaped multi-cultural communities, such as that in Canton, were influenced by the artisans who provided material and skills that enabled luxury objects to straddle the divide between the "European" and "Chinese" cultural practices. Second, the use of clothes to signify social rank was shared by both the European and Chinese elite. Although the practice of clay portrait sculpture derived from centuries old practices, it was uniquely adapted to local Canton society's global needs. By the end of the eighteenth century, portraiture had become the entrenched global and noble signifier. Ultimately, the questions raised about how social relationships are portrayed in a cross-cultural context shed light on the porous nature of how "heritage" adapted itself to "culture".

In the decades following the arrival of the British, French, Danish and Swedish East India Companies in Canton in the 1730s, European enchantment with purchasing, commissioning, gifting and re-selling trade artefacts from China intensified. As international trade expanded, the alleys and side streets surrounding the European Quarter in Canton boomed with shops selling a fantastic array of commodities: porcelain, silk, lacquer, herbal medicine, miniature models and clay portraits. This article focuses on the collection of clay portrait sculptures accumulated by Danish royalty in the period 1730 - 1760. In addition, it references the display of similar portrait sculptures in a summer pavilion at the Swedish Castle of Drottningholm, the only place where the original, eighteenth-century display has been preserved in Scandinavia.

Scandinavian Trade with Canton

The Danes first began to sail directly to China in 1730, while the first Swedish ship set sail in 1732. The Chinese system, within which the Danes at Canton traded, was based on a tradition of multiple relationships of trade, defense, negotiation and ritual (Perdue, 2015). Officially, foreign merchants were barred from interacting with the local population, excepting the *Hong* merchant network in 1757. The *Hong* merchants were an association of approximately 12, who controlled the goods available for the Westerners to purchase. Prior to the formalized implementation of the Canton System in 1757, Europeans had been permitted to roam through the western suburbs of the city. Here, they might have visited the porcelain shop street, the silk shop street or lacquerware street, as well as the *Hong* merchants' main warehouses located on the European quay.

In the midst of burgeoning trade relations, the majority of Guangdong artisans continued to make objects decorated according to Chinese taste. Yet, it was not long before a combination of special commissions by European traders and a rising Occidentalism among the literati elite facilitated the rise of aesthetically cross-cultural artefacts. Opulent porcelain services featuring European armorial crests were perhaps the most recognizable result of European influence on the Canton marketplace. Ultimately, Asian artefacts made their presence in European interiors so indispensable that Europeans began to commission European designs for objects in an imaginative Chinese style, known as "chinoiserie".

On the first voyage, the supercargoes employed by the Danish Asiatic Company (henceforth DAC) commissioned miniature sculpted portraits of themselves from Canton artisans, fashioned in clay. These portraits were initially displayed in the merchants' homes, but they eventually found their way into the royal Danish Kunstkammer, where they joined clay portraits of Chinese people. With direct funding from the Danish royalty, the Sino-Danish trade had proved lucrative. From 1732 – 1771 the net value of Danish cargo sent to Canton was almost 20 million Rdlr, whereas the return cargos sold for altogether 38 million Rdlr (Struwe, 1967, p. 215). The outbound cargo consisted mostly of ready cash, while the return cargo comprised tea, with porcelain for ballast and a 'private' trunk of good allowed to each supercargo (Willerslev, 1944).

Although the clay sculptures that depict Chinese literati and merchants are most numerous, the likenesses of the European merchants have generated the most scholarship (Broomhall, 2016; Clarke, 2011). This bias in Western scholarship continues to prioritize physiognomic likeness as a key element of portrait making. For instance, sculptures like that of Captain Guillaume de Brouwer can be identified by comparison with a European painted portrait (Fig. 1; Parmentier, 1989).

Fig. 1 Portrait of Captain Guillaume de Brouwer, c. 1730s, painted clay, Private Collection, Belgium.

Fig. 2 Anonymous master from Bruges, Portrait of Guillaume de Brouwer and his family, circa 1745 - 1755, oil on canvas, 132.5 cm × 170 cm, Groeninge Museum.

As yet, it has not been possible to identify a similar connection between a painted and a sculpted portrait of a Chinese person. This is not to say that no such connection exists, but merely, that the majority of research into the practice of portraiture in China has focused on commemorative and burial portraiture from earlier periods (Stuart and Rawski, 2001; Hornby, 2000). Meanwhile, Qing dynasty portraiture studies have often focused on the introduction of Western painting techniques (Musillo, 2008; Kleutghen, 2013; Cahill, 2010). These two lines of research have created a vital foundation for demonstrating that clay portrait sculptures connect the two cultural traditions.

A Misplaced Head

European sources describing life in Canton provide a limited picture of the artisanal services available in the streets. In 1732, the four supercargoes on the Danish ship, *Kronprins Christian*, brought back clay portrait figures of themselves. In addition, they brought back two sculptures of people from the Chinese elite. One is a woman, in a Ming dynasty style dress. The second sculpture wears a far more contemporary dress (Fig. 2).

Fig. 3　Portrait of a Chinese Civil Administrator, c. Yongzheng (1723 – 1735), 37 cm, National Museum of Denmark, Copenhagen.

Moreover, the description of him from the inventory records is far more descriptive than that of the female sculpture. The inventory of the Royal Danish Kunstkammer describes them in 1737, five years after their arrival in Denmark:

A Mandarin of Military rank from the province of Canton. Both small figures 13 ½ Inches tall, their bodies and costumes in Canton style. Mandarin is wearing black and the wife is wearing a white jacket. They are both made of clay (cited in Gundestrup, 1991).[i]

From this description, we can surmise that although no specific name is given, the man's rank and origins were important pieces of information for the European consumer. Given the brief allusion to the color of the figures' jackets, clothing was clearly integral to identifying the figures.

The male figure is a composite of two very distinctive figures. The body is slim and delicately posed on two feet, one of which is pushed slightly forward for balance in a very naturalistic way. Dressed in the manner of an official, he sports a large rectangular *pu zi* (rank badge) on his black *ji fu* (long, official coat for men). The size of his body conceivably matches that of the paired female sculpture.

A close analysis of the figure has demonstrated that the rank badge features either a first rank crane or a sixth rank egret.[ii] Although the Danish inventory identifies the man as being of military standing, rank badges of the military type feature quadrupeds, while those of the civil service feature birds. Hence, the Danish identification of the figure may have been based on the knob on the hat worn by the head, rather than the body's rank badge. Rank could also be identified by the hat's colour, structure and knob. Unfortunately, the head has lost its knob. Nevertheless, there are clear indications that the hat was made of red silk threads. Dress was a key feature in understanding portraiture as a specific representational tool in China, as has been raised by Antony Spiro (1990). When identity could not be distinguishes by an inscription, the rank of the official was the remaining symbolic indicator of singularity.

Upon their arrival in Denmark, the two figures were immediately deposited in the Danish Kunstkammer, which was selectively open for the public. Danish records do not show evidence of any repairs commissioned after the figures entered the royal collection. Hence, it is likely that the head replacement was done by craftsmen in Canton. Identification of the head and the figure is not strictly relevant to the argument presented here and shall be left for later research. The point is rather that the head seems to be a physiognomic portrait. Moreover, seen within the parameters of 'cultural heritage' or artistic traditions available to the craftsmen in Canton who repaired the figure, the specificity of dress indicates that the body was a 'portrait' rather than a 'type'.

European sources describe the 'facemaker' workshops and the practices of these craftsmen in some detail. In 1753, a Swedish sailor, Olof Toreen (1718 – 1753), described 'images and busts of clay' in his *Voyage to Suratte* (Osbeck, Toren, Ekeberg, and Newton, 1765; Clarke, 2011, pp. 18 – 19.). Meanwhile in 1769, William Hickey, a British East India Company employee, noted that:

> There was a China man who took excellent likenesses in clay, which he afterward coloured, and they were altogether well executed. To this man's shop, Pott and I went to see [...] Mr. Carnegie, surgeon of the ship Nottingham, sitting for his portrait, and complaining violently what a damned ugly phiz he was making. After repeating this several times, the artist lay down his tools and looking significantly at Carnegie, said, "Hy you handsome face no have got how can make" [...] Carnegie was offended [...], declaring he would not pay for or take the model away. He kept his word, and the next time we called at the shop we saw Mr. Carnegie tucked up, hanging by a rope around the neck, to a beam, among several others. Enquiring the meaning of this, the performer with much anger answered, "All these have too much ee grand Ladrones [i. e. pirates or thieves], give me too much trouble, make handsome face, no pay, no take, so must ee hang up" (Hickey, 1913; Clarke, 2011, p. 20).

Although almost a century divides the clay portrait of a Chinese civil official and Hickey's account of Mr. Carnegie's unsettling hanging, it does show that not only was commissioning clay portrait figures a common practice — after all, the portrait hung 'among several others' — it was one that was taken very seriously by its practitioners.

Chinese Portrait Traditions

Three things characterize the clay sculptures: their attention to dress, their diminutive size and their movable heads. The focus on accuracy in dress is a familiar feature of portraiture in Chinese painting (Hung, 1997, pp. 22 – 27; Kesner, 2007, pp. 33 – 56; Stuart and Rawski, 2001, p. 79; Seckel, 1993, p. 22). This similarity was even remarked upon by earlier Chinese scholars. The *Xiexiang mijue* (Secrets of portraiture) written by Wang Yi (ca. 1333 – 1368), critiques the stiff poses often seen in earlier paintings by calling them 'stiffly erect, with garments neatly arranged, like clay statues' (Wang Yi cited in Stuart and Rawski, 2001, p. 79). Although the majority of this type of reference is pejorative toward the art of clay portraiture, it does demonstrate the consistency with which clay portraits have been connected to painted ones. Moreover, clay portraits — though not considered as high a status as a painted portrait — were even made for emperors. Evelyn Rawski mentions a clay statue depicting the Yongzheng emperor, which was placed in the Palace of Longevity and Health (*Shoukang gong*) (Rawski, 1988; Gugong Zhoukan (Palace Museum Journal) 88,1931, p. 47.

No mention is made of how big or small this sculpture was, yet the size of the clay sculptures are of integral significance to understanding their cultural role in Qing Dynasty Canton. Seen from a Western perspective, it would be unproblematic to assume that the small size of the sculptures made it easy to bring back on the long journey back to Europe. However, the sculptures are frequently more than a meter tall, even if they are still consistently smaller than human-sized. Hence, this explanation does not quite fit. Instead, the diminutive size reveals two core features about why these sculptures appeared abundantly in Canton in the Qing Dynasty. First, their size connects them to older, burial sculptures (Hung, 2015; Kesner, 1995; Ebrey, 1997; Dien, 1987; Hay, 2010; Spiro, 1990). Second, this connection in itself connects them to the ability to magically travel to spiritual realms, if not to the Western continents.

The earliest instances of miniaturization in China were burial artefacts that functioned as passageways to the spiritual realm (Hung, 2015). These types of burial sculptures are known as *ming qi* or spirit vessels, "who compensate for the absence of real people" (Kesner, 1995, p. 126). Another type of painted clay figure are the sculptures of deities found on temple alters, although these are often recognizable "types", rather than portraits (Howard, Hung, Song, and Hong, 2006, pp. 405 – 408). Alternatively, Hung Wu has charted the ways in which "when an underground house or a microcosmic environment was constructed in a grave, it did not just provide the soul with a symbolic home — its diminutive size also framed the soul as an invisible subject in miniature" (Hung, 2015, p. 291). Moreover, miniature portraits may initially have been meant to accompany the dead, as a replacement for real human sacrifice as argued by Lu Zhirong (1992) and Wang Renbo (1987). Kesner terms this the "substitute for absence account". This is not to suggest that all miniature sculptures also housed miniature invisible souls. However, the symbolic value attached to miniaturization in general and architectural miniaturization in particular does heighten the sense that these models were more than mere toys. Moreover, it connects the idea of miniaturization to that of travel.

As is suggested by Hickey's account of Mr. Carnigie's "hanging", the clay figures may have still had a certain magical quality in the early Qing dynasty. However, one instance cannot fully determine that these images were in the same category as votive limbs or wax figures, such as those discussed by David Freedberg (1989, pp. 14 – 20, 157). Still, Jan Stuart and Evelyn Rawski suggest that "some of the sculptures the foreigners had made may have been influenced by a tradition popular among some of south China's 'boat people,' who placed small wooden sculptures of their ancestors on family altars" (2001, 173). Yet, they do not connect the portraits of Westerners with the plethora of sculptures showing Chinese merchants that also pervaded European courts. Perhaps one final feature of the Chinese sculptures prevents this connection: their lifelike nodding.

As mentioned previously, the third characteristic of Qing portrait sculptures was their ability to move their heads, and in some cases their hands. The clay sculptures are not strictly speaking automata, but merely have a system of weights inside their torso that allows their heads to continue moving after having been set in motion by a consumer. This seemingly lifelike quality is deeply connected to early accounts of living machines or automata in Chinese texts (Schafer, 1990, p. 149; Eichenhorn, 1952; Needham, 1960, p. 159).[iii] An automaton purportedly invented by Yan-Shi for King Mu of Zhou Dynasty (1023 – 957 BC) was described in the *Liezi*:

> The King looked at it in amazement; it was striding quickly, looking up and down, undoubtedly it was a man [...] The King was at last satisfied and said with a sigh: 'Is it then possible for human skill to achieve as much as the Creator?' (Graham (trans.), 1990, pp. 110 – 111; Chen, 1996; Needham, 1960, p. 53).

Early Chinese texts describing life-like automata have one thing in common: the automata repeatedly "bow" or "nod" their heads. Certainly, the wonder does not stop there and the figures are sometimes capable of much more, such as dancing, singing and making passes at the court ladies or simply striding out of sight through miniature doors.[iv] Persistently, the movable head grounds the figure in the realm of life and introduces, if not cements, its ultimate connection to the human autonomy.

The skills that early automata exhibit are always performative. Performing puppets and puppet plays are a long-standing part of the repertoire of performative arts throughout East Asia (Law, 2015; Liu, 2016; Orr, 1974, pp. 69 – 84). Joseph Needham connects traditional opera and shadow/puppet plays, while others have proposed that the entire theatrical tradition in China originated in attempts to enliven models of human beings (clay and wood *yūng*) that were placed in Han graves as servitors of the dead (Needham, 1960, 157). Although Canton artisans appear to have used real human hair to decorate some of the Chinese clay sculptures' queue or moustache, it seems unlikely that this would be a means of sending a sculpture that had been meant for burial to a European court. Instead, I would like to suggest that some, though not all, of the Chinese clay sculptures that made the journey to Europe were portraits of merchants engaged in the China trade. Moreover, I believe that the way in which the figures were interacted with enabled them tap into European courtly traditions that valued and displayed painted portraits in royal spaces. Thus, the clay sculptures of Chinese officials were able to resist the merely decorative role of *objet d'art* that was given to the trade porcelain displayed in European interiors.

Conclusion

These figures were sometimes isolated in their own right as demonstrations of Chinese dress. However, frequently, they were integrated into large-scale chinoiserie interiors, for instance in the Kina Slott pavilion in Drottningholm.

Fig. 4　The Red Room, Kina Slott, Drottningholm Castle, Sweden

Here, the miniature figures, were set to move by the Swedish royal family, as they used the summer pavilion to escape from the rigid structures of court life. If we look closely at these figures, each has been touched (set to nod) so often that the paint has been rubbed off on their heads and hands. Engaging with the sculptures frequently demonstrates that while the porcelain that was imported from China was put on display alongside these sculptures like art objects, the clay sculptures were not considered art objects in the same way. Instead, their abilities — derived from Chinese cultural traditions — demanded that they be engaged with physically.

The key focus of this simple outline has been to highlight how artisans in China had developed a "cultural heritage" or rather a set of traditional practices, which could be easily adapted to changing circumstances. Moreover, the European elite consumers, who displayed the sculptures did so while engaging with a long-standing practice of displaying portraits in a diplomatic context. If we treat "cultural heritage" as an open practice, rather than a prescriptive set of rules, it allows for a more nuanced understanding of how a "global" culture could develop in international nodes, such as Canton.

Notes:

i "1737 820/201 - 202 Een Mandaring over Militair Standen udi Provincesen Canton, ere begge to smaa Figurer 13 1/5 Tommer høi efter deres Lægerns Skikelse og Klædedragt i Canton. Mandarin er i sort og Konen i en hvid Jake, samme ere ligesom forige piorte af Leer."

ii The author was permitted to examine the figure first hand at the National Museum of Denmark on 16 November 2017.

iii For instance, an invention by Xie Fei and Wei Mengbien, court of Shi Hu (335 - 345 A. D.):"More than ten wooden Men of the Way, over two feet tall, all cloaked in *kasaya*, circumambulated the Buddha. Each time one came in front of the Buddha, it bowed and reverenced the Buddha. Moreover, they took pinches of incense in their hands and cast them into a brazier, in no way different from human being."

iv An inventor in the Chin dynasty was famous for his wooden dolls' house, with figures which opened doors and bowed:"*rén kòu qī hù, fù rén kāi hù ér chū, dàng hù zài bài, húan rù hù nèi bì hù*" (people touch her door, the woman opens the door and comes out; when she is in the door, she bows repeatedly; returning inside the door she closes the door) [own translation]. Zhōngguó kēxué jìshù diǎnjí tōng huì. Zònghé juǎn 4 (Zhengzhou: Hénán jiàoyù chūbǎn shè, 1996): chapter 752.

Bibliography

1. Broomhall, S., 2016. Face-making: Emotional and gendered meanings in Chinese clay portraits of Danish Asiatic Company men. *Scandinavian Journal of History*, 41 (3), pp. 447-474.
2. Cahill, J., 2010. *Pictures for Use and Pleasure: Vernacular Painting in High Qing China* (p. 32). Berkeley: University of California Press.
3. Chen, J. C., 1996. *Early Chinese work in natural science: A re-examination of the physics of motion, acoustics, astronomy and scientific thoughts* (Vol. 1). Hong Kong University Press.
4. Clarke, D., 2011. *Chinese Art and its Encounter with the World* (Vol. 1). Hong Kong University Press.
5. Dien, A. E. 1987. "Chinese Beliefs in the Afterworld," in The Quest for Eternity: Chinese Ceramic Sculptures from the Peoples Republic of China, ed. G. Kuwayama. Los Angeles County Museum of Art, pp. 9-14.
6. Ebrey, P., 1997. Portrait Sculptures in Imperial Ancestral Rites in Song China. *T'oung Pao*, 83 (Fasc. 1/3), pp. 42-92.
7. Eichhorn, W. 1952. "Wang Chia's Shih-i chi," *Zeitschrift der Deutschen Morgenländischen Gesellschaft* (ZDMG CH), I, pp. 130-142.
8. Freedberg, D., 1989. *The power of images: Studies in the history and theory of response*. Chicago: University of Chicago Press.
9. Graham A. C. (trans.), 1990. *The book of Lieh-tzu: a classic of the Tao*, New York: Columbia University Press.
10. Gundestrup, B., 1991. *Det kongelige danske Kunstkammer 1737: The Royal Danish Kunstkammer 1737*. Copenhagen: Nationalmuseet.
11. Hay, J., 2010. Seeing through dead eyes: How early Tang tombs staged the afterlife. *RES: Anthropology and Aesthetics*, 57(1), pp. 16-54.
12. Hickey, W., 1913. *Memoirs of William Hickey* ... (Vol. 4). Hurst & Blackett, Limited.
13. Hornby, J., 2000. Chinese ancestral portraits: some late Ming and Ming style ancestral paintings in Scandinavian museums. *Bulletin*, (70), pp. 173-271.
14. Howard, A. F., Hung, W., Song, L. and Hong, Y., 2006. *Chinese sculpture*. Yale University Press.

15. Hung, W., 1997. "The Origins of Chinese Painting" in Barnhart, R. M., Xin, Y. and Chongzheng, N., *Three thousand years of Chinese painting*. Yale University Press., pp. 22-27.
16. Hung, W., 2015. The Invisible Miniature: Framing the Soul in Chinese Art and Architecture. *Art History*, 38(2), pp. 286-303.
17. Kesner, L., 2007. "Face as artifact in early chinese art". *RES: Anthropology and Aesthetics*, 51(1), pp. 33-56.
18. Kesner, L., 1995. Likeness of No One: (re) presenting the First Emperor's army. *The Art Bulletin*, 77(1), pp. 115-132.
19. Kleutghen, K., 2013. Staging Europe: Theatricality and painting at the Chinese imperial court. *Studies in Eighteenth-Century Culture*, 42(1), pp. 81-102.
20. Law, J. M., 2015. *Puppets of Nostalgia: The Life, Death, and Rebirth of the Japanese "Awaji Ningyō" Tradition*. Princeton University Press.
21. Liu, S. ed., 2016. *Routledge Handbook of Asian Theatre*. Routledge. Inge C. Orr, 'Puppet Theatre in Asia', Asian Folklore Studies, Vol. 33, No. 1 (1974), pp. 69-84.
22. Lv, Z., 1992. "Qin Shi Huang ling bing ma yong peizangzhi zhi yuanyuan tansuo" (The origins of burial pits of soldier and horse figures at the tomb of the First emperor of Qin), *Wenbo*, no. 2, pp. 50-54.
23. Musillo, M., 2008. Reconciling Two Careers: The Jesuit Memoir of Giuseppe Castiglione Lay Brother and Qing Imperial Painter. *Eighteenth-Century Studies*, pp. 45-59.
24. Osbeck, Pehr., Olof. Toren, Carl Gustav. Ekeberg, J. G. Georgi, and Alfred Newton. *Reise Nach Ostindien Und China: Nebst O. Toreens Reise Nach Suratte Und C. G. Ekeberg's Nachricht Von Der Landwirtschaft Der Chineser Translated from the Swedish by J. G. Georgi*. (Rostock: Koppe, 1765).
25. Parmentier, Jan. "Søfolk og supercargoer fra Oostende I Dansk Asiatisk Kompagnis tjeneste 1730-1747." *Handels-og Søfartsmuseets årbog* (1989): 142-173.
26. Perdue, P. C., 2015. The tenacious tributary system. *Journal of Contemporary China*, 24(96), pp. 1002-1014.
27. Rawski, E. S., 2001. "The Imperial Way of Death: Ming and Ch'ing Emperors and Death Ritual." In Stuart, J. and Rawski, E. S., *Worshiping the ancestors: Chinese commemorative portraits*. Stanford University Press.
28. Schafer, E. H., 1990. The "Yeh chung chi". *T'oung Pao*, pp. 147-207.
29. Seckel, D., 1993. The Rise of Portraiture in Chinese Art. *Artibus Asiae*, 53(1/2), pp. 7-26.
30. Smith, L. and Akagawa, N. eds., 2008. *Intangible heritage*. Routledge.

31. Spiro, A. G., 1990. *Contemplating the ancients: Aesthetic and social issues in early Chinese portraiture*. Univ of California Press.
32. Struwe, K., 1967. *Dansk Ostindien 1732 - 1776: Tranquebar under kompagnistyre*.
33. Stuart, J. and Rawski, E. S., 2001. *Worshiping the ancestors: Chinese commemorative portraits*. Stanford University Press.
34. Wang, R., 1987. General comments on Chinese funerary sculpture. *The Quest for Eternity: Chinese Ceramic Sculptures from the People's Republic of China*, pp. 39 - 61.
35. Willerslev, R., 1944. Danmarks første aktieselskab. *Historisk Tidsskrift*, 10, 633 - 636.

Danish Built Heritage

Kristoffer Schmidt

The year 2018 marks the hundred-year anniversary of the first Danish building preservation law. It was celebrated with a highly publicized conference and the publication of two books, written by some of the foremost scholars on the field of built heritage (Tønnesen et al ed. 2018; Bendsen & Morgen 2018). Both books reveal that despite the fact that the preservation law protected several culturally important buildings the preservation authorities also fought several futile battles to save equally important buildings from demolition or overhaul. In other cases, the same authorities opted to ignore requests for protection of buildings because they did not meet the standards worthy of a preservation. The latter cases are important for the subject of this article because they reveal that opinions about the value of built heritage differ especially among scholars. This article attempts to display these varying views regarding built heritage through a series of historical examples as well as an analysis of the SAVE method, which is the preferred method to value built heritage in contemporary Denmark.

Prelude to the law of 1918

There were several reasons for the preservation law of 1918. One was the demolishment of numerous older buildings. Another was a series of misguided restoration projects, which did costly harm to important historical buildings. A curious example of the latter came about because of a conflagration. In

December of 1859, a large fire ravaged the main part of Christian IV's Fredericksburg Castle in Hillerød. Due to freezing weather and an ill-equipped fire brigade, the fire destroyed the main part of the castle. The smoking heap of ruins became a Danish tragedy and a discussion of whether to resurrect Fredericksburg Castle quickly received national attention. Some notable historical experts argued against a reconstruction, but they were ignored. Through public subscription and substantial contributions from King Frederick VII and the Danish state, the exterior of the castle was re-erected. While the exterior resembled the original Renaissance castle, the interior was difficult to recreate, since no one actually knew the exact inertial appearance. Furthermore, the responsible architect Ferdinand Mehldahl had no interest in recreating an exact copy of the, in his opinion, unexceptional Renaissance quarters. The result was a fascinating mix of imitated Renaissance and historicism (Bligaard 2008; Smidt 2018a: 15 - 6). A graver example was the restoration of Viborg Cathedral from 1864 to 1876. In 1861, a church council was established to oversee the protection and restoration of Danish churches. Unfortunately, the architectural and cultural historical ideals did not always coincide with the actual values. In the case of Viborg Cathedral, a severe deterioration meant that the council decided to restore the cathedral. Instead of preserving the standing building, the responsible architects, Niels Sigfred Nebelong, Julius Tholle, Hermann Baagøe Storck as well as the church council opted for a more radical solution. (Fig. 1) All but the crypt beneath the choir was demolished. In its place, the architects build a church resembling the hypothetical appearance of the original medieval Romanesque styled church. (Smidt 2018a: 17 - 19). The case of Viborg Cathedral is one among many 19th and early 20th century misguided restoration projects, which severely damaged the heritage values of otherwise monumental buildings.

Interest regarding economic growth and progress also resulted in the complete or partial destruction of several historical buildings epitomized by the demolishment of "De seks Søstre" (The Six Sisters). Despite the name "De seks Søstre" consisted of three mid-17th century conjoined buildings erected in Dutch Renaissance style on the right side of Christian IV's stock

Fig. 1　Print depicting the old and new Viborg Cathedral
Photo: The National Library of Denmark.

exchange "Børsen". (Fig. 2) In 1899, the large bank "Privatbanken" bought "De seks Søstre" with the purpose of replacing them with a new headquarter. Despite protests, the bank demolished the buildings and replaced them with a monumental but historical less important building. The demolishment of "De seks Søstre" became a leading argument for the creation of a building preservation law. An even more inexplicable case was the partial destruction of The Royal Danish Kunstkammer — also known as The Royal Library building — from 1650. In the beginning of the 20th century, the head of the Danish National Archives, Vilhelm Adolf Secher, saw the Kunstkammer building as an ideal location for a modern archive. He therefore proposed an overhaul of the building, which severely damaged the heritage values. Through political connections, Secher was able to carry out his plan (Bendsen & Morgen 2018: 11 - 12; Mogensen 2001: 39 - 55; Smidt 2018a: 34 - 35). The case of The Royal Danish Kunstkammer illustrates that indifference towards cultural heritage embedded in buildings existed even among persons, whose job it was to protect cultural heritage.

Fig. 2　Photo of "The Six Sisters" from 1899

Photo: Johannes Hauerslev, The National Library of Denmark.

Heritage listed buildings

Fortunately, the above-mentioned as well as other similar cases created an opposition against this negligence of Danish built heritage, which eventually resulted in the preservation law of 1918. In 1905, The Royal Danish Academy of Fine Arts proposed the first preservation law. The proposal was inspired from similar laws in Belgium and France. The proposed law would limit the private ownership, but the academy argued that artistic, historical and national values of the society overruled these concerns. As a counterproposal, the National Museum of Denmark proposed an alternative law in 1907, where preservations were conducted through mutual understanding between owner and authority. Both proposals never reached the Danish parliament, but the latter became a yardstick for the preservation law of 1918 (Smidt 2018a 36 – 37,43).

On the 12th of March 1918, the Danish parliament passed the preservation law of 1918. The law specified the creation of a heritage list containing the architecturally and culturally most important buildings in the country. A specially appointed council assessed, which buildings were worthy to be placed on the list. By the 1920, the council placed 1.145 properties on the heritage list. This was an impressive figure, yet one should mention that The National Museum of Denmark and The Royal Danish Academy of Fine Arts conducted much of the preparatory work before 1918 (Smidt 2018b: 62; Tønnesen 2018a: 47 – 49 Bendsen & Morgen 2018: 54 – 56,60 – 62).

The heritage list was divided into two separate ratings:

A. "Buildings whose [historical or architectural] qualities are so excellent that their demolishment, unhistorical modifications or neglect would result in a significant loss of the [Danish] nation's cultural treasures."

B. "Buildings whose [historical or architectural] qualities are less than excellent but whose preservation still is of significant importance (translated from Danish in Smidt 2018b: 61).

The restrictions were quite different between A and B listed buildings. Owners of A listed buildings could not make any changes without the approval of the council. B listed buildings were only protected from demolishment, while the heritage values of the buildings survived by the mercy of the owners. The A list was primarily reserved for Renaissance and early Baroque buildings, whereas the B list mostly consisted of newer architecture. To prevent demolishment the council decided not to warn the private owners in advance before they placed their buildings on the heritage list (Smidt 2018b: 61 – 62; Tønnesen 2018a: 49).

Although the main part of the buildings on the initial heritage list are understandable, the presence of some buildings as well as the absence or B rating of others seem unintelligible. For example, the council placed the 18th century country estate Gammel Holtegård in Holte on the A list, while the far more original Christiansholm in Klampenborg received a B rating. For some reason the council forgot that Gammel Holtegård received a major overhaul in 1901, which distorted the original architecture. Copies also found their way to the initial list. In Hørsholm the council listed a five meters high obelisk by the French architect Nicolas Henri Jardin and erected in 1766 to commemorate a local agricultural reform. (Fig. 3) The council ignored that the monument was a copy of the original from 1894. The council also seemed to omit certain building types, like the culturally important timber framed buildings and farmhouses, especially on the island of Funen, who remained unprotected up until the late 1980ies. At that time, the authorities realized a widespread destruction of these building types, whereby they conducted thematic surveys in order to place the remaining timber framed buildings and farmhouses on the heritage list. Thematic listings became instrumental in protecting otherwise neglected built heritage such as station buildings, schools and dairies. They were however expensive and as a result abandoned. In other cases, listings were far more fortuitous and depended on certain individuals' or local groups' knowledge and diligence. One example was the art historian Harald Langberg. From 1940 to 1949, he was the main force behind placing 895 properties on the heritage list. Another example was the listing of 47 mills from 1954 to 1959. These were predominantly a result of mill expert Anders Jespersen, who at the time was an employee of the special building council. In other cases, industrious local history associations or municipalities lobbied the council to list several buildings in specific geographical areas (Kjær 2010: II 799 – 801; Smidt 2018b: 61 – 74; Tønnesen 2018b: 75 – 95; Jensen 2018: 119 – 125). Over time, several groups has voiced their criticism against

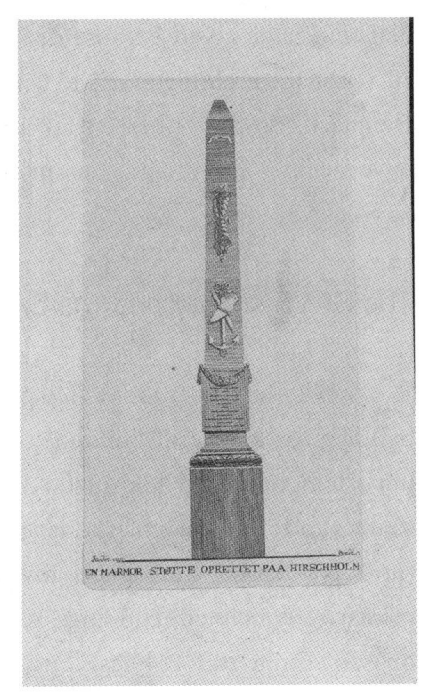

Fig. 3 Copper engraving depicting Nicolas-Henri Jardin's obelisk in Hørsholm

Photo: The National Library of Denmark.

the council and the heritage list. One group in particular, the modernist architects, regarded the heritage list as backward looking and criticised the special building council as a problematic obstacle for urban development. Cultural historians on the other side voiced their concern about the council's neglect of certain building types (farmhouses) and geographical areas (Bendsen & Morgen 2018: 121-123).

After 48 years, it became apparent that B listed buildings needed some sort of safeguard. Therefore, one of the first legislative changes to the preservation law was that external changes on B listed buildings needed approval from the council. The legislative change was however ineffective and from 1979 the two lists were annulled and replaced by one list with all former A and B listed buildings (Bendsen & Morgen 2018: 178-179, 211-214). The annulment meant that a large part of the former B listed buildings risked delisting because they did not meet the heritage standards. This delisting came about because of a large-scale review (conducted from 2010 to 2016) of the architectural and cultural values of all heritage listed buildings in Denmark. So far, 7 percent of approximately 9.000 heritage listed buildings have been delisted and the main bulk of these were originally B listed buildings.

The SAVE survey and the SAVE method

While the preservation law protected an important fraction of the Danish building stock several buildings unworthy of the heritage list but culturally important remained unprotected. Many of these buildings were important sources to the history of the largest part of the Danish population, i.e. the rural population and poor townspeople. In contrast, the heritage list primarily contained buildings used by the elite, i.e. castles and manor houses. From the 1940ies, city redevelopment destroyed several buildings originally belonging to the lower social classes, which resulted in a significant loss of heritage values throughout the country. Some municipalities took notice of the problem and implemented the preservation of such buildings in the zoning. However, other municipalities saw such preservation as an obstacle for new building projects. It soon became apparent that a method was needed in order to assess the preservation value of these buildings. To do this the SAVE survey was created, where each building was assessed on the basis of five values.

Ideally, a SAVE survey consists of three phases. The first phase is a preliminary investigation, where an architectural consultant firm collects topographical, historical and architectural information about the municipality. In order to acquire an overview of the building heritage of a municipality, the consultant firm conducts an initial registration. The gathered information is published in a preliminary report along with maps showing all existing buildings in the municipality. A local interest group reads the report for a final approval. The interest group usually consists of representatives from the consultant firm, a project manager from the municipality, local politicians, as well as representatives from the local museum, local archive, local homeowner's association and local heritage association. If approved, the report serves as a tool for the subsequent SAVE registration (Tønnesen 2000; Høi & Stenak 2011). Given the importance of the quality of the preliminary report any recommendations from members the interest group — especially the local museum or archive — should be taken into account. Unfortunately, this is not always the case. This is either because of a minimal economic leeway or because of general disinterest in suggestions from cultural institutions, which prevents any rewriting of the report. An example of this was a re-registration of buildings in Fredensborg municipality. Here the consultant firm could not deliver a satisfying preliminary report, whereby the local museum rejected it. There was however, neither time nor money for a revision, whereby the subsequent SAVE registration was based on the rejected material. [1]

In the second phase, the consultant firm carries out the actual SAVE registration of each building. To prevent a survey becoming to extensive or expensive the municipality limits the survey to buildings built before a certain

---

[1] Interview with archivist at Hørsholm Lokalarkiv Hans Jørgen Winther Jensen on the 23rd of October 2018.

year (e. g. 1940) (Tønnesen 2000; Høi & Stenak 2011). The municipality may also limit the survey geographically or thematically (e. g. farmhouses).

In the third phase, the actual results are published in an atlas, containing a topographical description of the municipality, a description of its historical development and a review of the local architecture along with its characteristics. The atlases also contain cartographic presentations of structures with explanatory texts describing cultural qualities worth protecting. Another cartographic presentation illustrates the registered buildings with three color codes representing a high preservation value, a medium value and a low value (Tønnesen 2000; Høi & Stenak 2011).

The actual SAVE method for evaluating the preservation values of a building is composed of five intermediary values: architectural value, cultural-historical value, environmental value, originality and condition. In order for a building to achieve a high architectural value, it needs exterior architectural qualities such as good proportions, harmony of composition and the architectural interaction between form, material and function. The building is also compared to similar buildings in the area to determine if it in a local context is a good, average or poor example of a specific type of architecture or local building style. The cultural-historical value is determined by a number of criteria, such as if the building represents a local architectural style or a special style period, and whether it is an expression of special craftsmanship. Technical innovations in design and material are also assessed. Finally, a somewhat superficial examination determines if there is a historical value attributed to the building. This historical value must materialize itself in the building. Only in rare cases does a historically important person's connection with a building influence the cultural-historical assessment. The environmental value relates to the building's significance in a specific cultural area. If the presence of a building improves the overall cultural value of neighboring buildings, a building complex or a landscape the environmental value is high. The originality of a building relates to the originality of the exterior. If a rebuilding has ruined the original exterior, it is necessary to determine if a restoration is possible. In some cases, later alterations actually support the values of the original exterior. Later changes might even have their own architectural and cultural-historical values. The technical state of a building concerns proper maintenance. Typically, the condition of a building has little effect on the overall value because a correct restoration can protect the architectural, cultural-historical and environmental values. The technical state is still a deciding factor in the demolition of buildings deemed worthy of protection. Over the last years, several buildings worthy of protection were demolished due to a poor technical state.

Each value is determined by a score from 1 to 9. A score from 1 to 3 is regarded as a high, 4 to 6 as a mediocre and 7 to 9 as a low value. If a building is valued between 1 and 4, it is deemed worthy of preservation. Local museums and archives usually have the role of advisory parties and watchdogs. However, the local museums can do nothing more than point the finger if a municipality decides to demolish buildings with a high SAVE value. The overall value is not an average of the five intermediary values. From case to case, it is decided, what intermediary values determine the overall value. According to the latest instructions about the SAVE method the architectural value, the cultural-historical value and the environmental value outweighs originality and technical state. Curiously, in older instructions and descriptions of the method the architectural value is the determining parameter of the overall value.

From the end of the 1980s and onwards numerous municipality councils decided to use SAVE method and thus obtained a list of buildings worthy of protection. Today approximately 125,000 buildings have been registered as worthy of protection. The SAVE values merely function as guidelines and unlike heritage listed buildings there is no legislation that protects buildings with a high SAVE value. Still, the SAVE method and registry was and still is a vital tool for municipalities to get an overview of architecturally and culturally important buildings, which in some cases leads to protection from demolition and structural damage or disfigurement.

Heritage listed buildings in the SAVE registry

Despite the fact that a large part of the Danish built heritage is identified by the SAVE method, studies regarding the validity of the method are scarce (e. g. Bech-Nielsen 1998; Vadstrup 2017). A way to evaluate the SAVE method is to assess the SAVE scores of heritage listed buildings. Since the exterior (as well as the interior) of heritage listed buildings represent the highest architectural and cultural standards (Bendsen & Morgen 2018: 17), one would suspect that heritage listed buildings receive high SAVE scores. This is however not always the case. Numerous heritage listed buildings have received and overall score of 3 or 4, when using the SAVE method. An example of this is a neo-classical building from 1775 in the town of Hillerød. Named Annaborg by its first owner F. C. Brammer, the building was the main wing of a quadrangle manor. It served as home for the Brammer family as well as office for Brammer in his role as *Amtmann* (the senior retainer of an *Amt*). According to the heritage report the architectural details in the exterior, such as a monumental granite plinth, a fine cornice and a large granite stair entrance; reveal that the building was home to a high-ranking official. Other important architectural and cultural values of Annaborg's exterior is its freestanding and simple structure with plastered walls as well as it being a fine example of neo-classical architecture. It is therefore somewhat surprising that the overall SAVE score of Annaborg is 4. [1] On the same street as Annaborg lies another 18th century building. This orange red plastered building from 1721 served as the home and office of the official responsible for the breeding and refinement of the royal horses. The fact that the building is attributed to the royal architect Johan Cornelius Krieger is one of the essential arguments for its preservation. Krieger's talents do not measure up to those of 18th century Danish architectural juggernauts like Laurids de Thurah's, Nicolai Eigtved's and Nicolas Henri Jardin's. Still Krieger's architectural accomplishments are impressive, and since only a handful of his buildings exist today, the house in Hillerød represents a rare example of his skills. Furthermore, the building is an interesting example of late Baroque

---

[1] For the heritage report see: https://www. kulturarv. dk/fbb/downloaddokument. htm? dokument = 123776567. Accessed 8. 10. 2018. For the SAVE score see: https://www. kulturarv. dk/fbb/bygningvis. pub? bygning = 6199762. Accessed 8. 10. 2018.

and several original details and building elements, such as doors and windows, are preserved. Once again, the SAVE method tells another story, since the overall score is 3.[①]

One could argue that the two examples are uncommon mistakes, and not a general tendency in the SAVE registry. To examine this further a survey of all heritage listed buildings with a SAVE score in the municipalities of Northern Zealand as well as the municipalities of Gladsaxe, Ballerup, Herlev and Gentofte has been conducted. This amasses to 474 heritage listed buildings. Of these, 115 achieved an overall score of 1, 124 a score of 2, 190 a score of 3, 40 a score of 4, two a score of 5 and three a score of 6.[②]

The analysis also reveals that certain types of buildings achieve a higher score than others. Monumental buildings such as castles, manor houses and older country estates usually achieve an overall score of 1 or 2. As is the case with buildings by famous 20th century Danish architects, e. g. Mogens Lassen, Jørn Oberg Utzon and Arne Jacobsen. In contrast, heritage listed townhouses such as the ones in the old town centre of Elsinore often have an overall score of 3 or 4, rarely 2 and never 1. It is difficult to determine the exact reason for this difference. From a solely aesthetic point, townhouses might not represent the very best Danish architecture. This seems to be the case in Elsinore. Here none of the heritage listed town houses achieve an architectural value of 1 and they are more likely to have a value of 5 than 2. Aesthetical appearance is not officially part of the assessment (Høi & Stenak 2011). Still, one cannot help but suspect this to be the case, especially when we consider that a consultant must conduct a SAVE assessment of a building within twenty minutes. Another plausible explanation is that the SAVE survey in Elsinore is noticeable conservative when awarding buildings high SAVE values. The town of Elsinore has the highest number of heritage listed buildings in the examined municipalities. Nonetheless, only six times did the

---

① For the heritage report see: https://www.kulturarv.dk/fbb/downloaddokument.htm?dokument=123776636. Accessed 8.10.2018. For the SAVE score see: https://www.kulturarv.dk/fbb/bygningvis.pub?bygning=6207840. Accessed 8.10.2018.

② Unfortunately, the website of the SAVE registry is of an older date and some heritage listed building complexes are not probably registered.

consultants award the buildings with the highest SAVE value. Two of these are churches, i.e. Saint Olaf's Church and Saint Mary's Church (churches are not heritage listed), while the last four are heritage listed buildings, i.e. two of the buildings of the Carmelite Priory, the main building of Marienlyst Castle and the main building of Kronborg Castle.

Conservative assessments are not confined to Elsinore. In 2008, Fredensborg municipality decided to redo their original SAVE evaluation. The official reason was that the old SAVE evaluation no longer covered the whole municipality, because a reform from 2007 extended its geographic borders.① Instead of reusing the SAVE values from the previous assessment, the municipality board decided to initiate a SAVE survey of the whole municipality. A primary reason for this was that the first SAVE survey was conservative in several of its estimates, and thus did not correspond with the actual heritage values of the houses in Fredensborg municipality.②

One can also identify a small yet troublesome number of heritage listed buildings with intermediary SAVE values that does not correspond with the overall value. A town house in Elsinore for example received the scores 4,4, 3,5,5, which amounted to an overall score of 3. A country estate in Rudersdal municipality originally belonging to Frederik VII's lover scored 3, 2,4,3, and 5, resulting in an overall score of 1. (Fig. 4) A gas station from 1939 in Gentofte municipality also received and overall score of 1 despite intermediary scores of 2,2,3,5 and 2.

Concluding remarks

There can be no doubt that the heritage list and the SAVE registry has been instrumental in protecting numerous culturally important buildings. Still, as revealed in this article, the SAVE method does have its flaws. In the

---

① Curiously, the same reform also made the municipalities responsible for the oversight of buildings deemed worthy of preservation making them — alongside Slots-og Kulturstyrelsen — the primary caretaker of Danish building heritage.
② Interview with archivist at Hørsholm Lokalarkiv Hans Jørgen Winther Jensen on the 23rd of October 2018.

Fig. 4 Photo of countess Louise Danner's (Frederik VII's third wife) country estate in Rudersdal municipality

Photo: Ramblersen, Wikimedia Commons.

examined municipalities, several SAVE scores do not correspond with the actual heritage values of heritage listed buildings. Out of 484 heritage listed buildings 245 received a SAVE score of 3 or poorer. Although the SAVE score 3 (190 buildings) equals a high heritage value, one would anticipate that heritage listed buildings automatically receive the highest scores (1 or 2) and certainly not a score of 4 (40 buildings), 5 (two buildings) or 6 (three buildings). There may be several reasons, why these irregularities and somewhat erroneous estimates exist in the SAVE registry. Local political interest or disinterest in building heritage can influence the actual estimates. The consultant firm may be unprepared or unqualified to perform the survey — perhaps because of a strict budget. This is particular problematic if we take into account that a SAVE estimate of a building may take twenty minutes at most and the fact that aesthetic preferences in many cases determine the actual scores. In other words, built heritage may be measurable, but one should keep in mind that political interests, economic interests, unpreparedness or differing scholarly preferences might influence the outcome of any built heritage assessment.

Bibliography

1. Gert Bech-Nielsen 1998, *SAVE-Survey of Architectural Values in the Environment. En*

kritisk analyse, Copenhagen.
2. Jannie Rosenberg Bendsen & Mogens A. Morgen 2018, *Fredet — Bygningsfredning i Danmark 1918 -2018*, Copenhagen.
3. Mette Bligaard 2008, *Frederiksborgs genrejsning. Historicisme i teori og praksis*, Copenhagen.
4. Arne Høi and Morten Stenak 2011, *SAVE Kortlægning og registrering af bymiljøers og bygningers bevaringsværdi*, Copenhagen.
5. Torben Lindegaard Jensen, 2018, "De fredede bygninger i landdistrikterne" in Allan Tønnesen et al (ed.), *Hele Samfundets eje. Bygningsfredning i 100 år*, Odense, pp. 119-129.
6. Ulla Kjær 2010, *Nicolas-Henri Jardin — en ideologisk nyklassicist*, Copenhagen.
7. Margit Mogensen 2001, *Rigsarkivet. Husene på Slotsholmen*, Copenhagen.
8. Claus M. Smidt 2018a, "Fredning og bevaring før bygningsfredningsloven" in Allan Tønnesen et al (ed.), *Hele Samfundets eje. Bygningsfredning i 100 år*, Odense, pp. 13-45.
9. Claus M. Smidt 2018b, "De første fredninger" in Allan Tønnesen et al (ed.), *Hele Samfundets eje. Bygningsfredning i 100 år*, Odense, pp. 61-74.
10. Allan Tønnesen 2000, *InterSAVE International Survey of Architectural Values in the Environment*, Copenhagen.
11. Allan Tønnesen et al (ed.), *Hele Samfundets eje. Bygningsfredning i 100 år*, Odense.
12. Allan Tønnesen 2018a, "Det særlige bygningssyn" in Allan Tønnesen et al (ed.), *Hele Samfundets eje. Bygningsfredning i 100 år*, Odense, pp. 47-59.
13. Allan Tønnesen 2018b, "De senere fredninger" in Allan Tønnesen et al (ed.), *Hele Samfundets eje. Bygningsfredning i 100 år*, Odense, pp. 75-100.
14. Søren Vadstrup 2017, *ny-SAVE-metoden til udpegning af bevaringsværdige bygninger*, Copenhagen.

Humanistic Effulgence in the Ancient Chinese Fantasy Novels[①]

— Take the Wonderful Whimsies and Ingenious Conceptions in *Strange Tales from the Liaozhai Studio* · *Judge Lu* as an Example

Song Zizhen, Zheng Chengjun

Written by Pu Songling in the Qing Dynasty, *Strange Tales from the Liaozhai Studio* is a Fantasy Novel in the classical Chinese language. This work established Pu Songling's status as the "king of short stories in classical Chinese language". *Strange Tales from the Liaozhai Studio* is "one novel with two narrative styles". One style is the inheritance of ancient Chinese fantasy novels in Six Dynasties (225 – 589), briefly recording strange events. The other style refers to the vivid description and the tortuous storyline of the Legend in Tang Dynasty (618 – 907), which has the elements of a novel.[②] The latter combines the past with the new in writing subjects, and keeps fascinating in narrative art. The subject matters of these stories are based on folklore or predecessors' fantasy works, as well as come from Pu Songling's creations.[③] In terms of content, Pu Songling's descriptions of characters, environments, and things are laid out closely around whimsies. In

---

[①] Ancient Chinese Fantasy Novels: A type of Chinese classical novel with featured deities, ghosts, and spirits in stories. (志怪小说：古典小说的一种，以神灵鬼怪故事为题材。)

[②] Yuan Shishuo. *Pu SongLing and his "Strange Tales from the Liaozhai Studio"*. Jinan: Shandong Publishing House of Literature and Art. 2004: 67. (袁世硕：《蒲松龄与〈聊斋志异〉》，济南：山东文艺出版社 2004 年版，第 67 页)

[③] Feng Weimin. *Pu SongLing and his "Strange Tales from The Liaozhai Studio"*. Beijing: Zhonghua Book Company. 1984: 24&5.8. (冯伟民：《蒲松龄和〈聊斋志异〉》，北京：中华书局 1984 年版，第 24—58 页)

the development of the storyline, Pu Songling uses suspense and turns to make separate plot segments perfectly coherent, presenting a wonderful story.

To understand *Strange Tales from the Liaozhai Studio*, one must first understand the world depicted in it. In this world, all things have their spirituality. Besides human beings, ghosts (from the underworld), and deities (both from the underworld and heaven), there are also spirits (beings with human shapes) transformed from animals and plants. In *Strange Tales from the Liaozhai Studio*, people, ghosts, deities, and spirits can communicate freely, and there is also the possibility of mutual conversion in their form and identity. That is to say, there is no insurmountable gap among them.[①] Space, where the story takes place is in the human world, and people are the dominant character of this world, but the intervention of deities, ghosts, and spirits from time to time makes the world in *Strange Tales from the Liaozhai Studio* become a fantasy world at any time, overlapping with the real world. This is because, in Pu Songling's writing world, deities, ghosts, and spirits often have far-reaching supernatural abilities that human beings do not possess. Such supernatural abilities are embodied in resourcefulness and superpower. However, the world in *Strange Tales from the Liaozhai Studio* is still the home court of human beings, and the deities, ghosts, and spirits only can influence human beings within certain rules or to some extent. Deities may be flying immortals living in heavy, or the lords of death in the underworld. They often control the fate and reincarnation of human beings and human beings often worship them with awe. After dying, human being's spirits remain and become ghosts. The ghosts here often retain the same memory and reason that they have when they were human beings. There are good and evil ghosts. Some of them can even interact and live with human beings within a certain period of time. The spirits in *Strange Stories from the Liaozhai Studio* have the ability to transform between the original animal or plant forms and the shape of human

---

[①] Feng Weimin. *Pu SongLing and his "Strange Tales from The Liaozhai Studio"*. Beijing: Zhonghua Book Company. 1984: 24&5.8. (冯伟民:《蒲松龄和〈聊斋志异〉》,北京:中华书局 1984 年版,第 24—58 页)

beings. Their IQ and EQ are no less than those of human beings, and they can help or block human activities with their supernatural abilities. The human beings in *Strange Tales from the Liaozhai Studio* often have various social identities that existed in Pu Songling's time, among which, the male intellectual is a classic image. In *Strange Tales from the Liaozhai Studio*, male intellectuals, beauties, fox-spirits, ghosts, and deities may appear at the same time and in the same space. This article takes "Judge Lu", a story in *Strange Tales from the Liaozhai Studio* as an example to try to explore Pu Songling's fanciful whimsies and ingenious designs in this novel.

Serial Whimsies: Unusual Human Beings, Unusual Deities, Unusual Behaviors, and Unusual Things in "Judge Lu"

In the story of "Judge Lu", the deities are unusual, so are human beings, their behaviors and things going on. ①

The protagonist of the story, Zhu Erdan, the intellectual, "was bold and outgoing by nature, though tending to be gullible. He studied industriously but had not yet made a name for himself". ② Zhu had limited academic achievements but had a strong nerve. He took his literary club members' joke seriously and went to "the Hall of the Ten Kings of Hell"③ alone in the middle of the night, and bring back from the left gallery the Underworld Judge④ Statue "with green face and red beard, quite frightful in appearance". Zhu

---

① Wang Shaohua. A Shocking Story of Heart and Head Substitution — A Brief Discussion on Whimsies in *Strange Tales from The Liaozhai Studio · Judge Lu*. Dang An. 2017(04): 31-32. (王少华:《一篇换心革面的惊世故事——略论〈聊斋·陆判〉对奇异的叙述》,《档案》2017年第4期,第31—32页)

② All citations about "Judge Lu" there come from Pu Songling, Edited by Zhang Youhe. Translated by Huang Youyi & Zhang Qingnia & Zhang Ciyun & Yang Yi & Denis C. Mair & Victor H. Mair. *Selections from Strange Tales from the Liaozhai Studio* Ⅰ. Beijing: Foreign Language Press. 2007: 207-225. (蒲松龄:《聊斋志异》(会校会注会评本),张友鹤辑校,上海:上海古籍出版社1986年版,第1—4、139—146页)

③ The Hall of the Ten Kings of Hell: The name of the temple. The Ten Kings is the general name of ten Yamas in charge of the hell in Chinese Buddhism. Taoism also uses this term. (十王殿:庙宇名。十王,中国佛教所传十个主管地狱的阎王之总称,也称"十殿阎君",略称"十王"。后道教也沿用此称。)

④ The underworld judge: Official in charge of documents for Yama in the underworld. (判官:此指迷信传说中为阎王掌簿册的佐吏。)

not only "went straight out" to "the Hall of the Ten Kings of Hell" which made "the hair of those who entered stand chillingly on end", but also came back carrying the Judge and "set him on a table", and inviting the Judge to his home "to come for a drink". The next day, the Judge showed himself to follow Zhu's invitation, and "toasted back and forth" with Zhu, when the Judge's surname, "Lu", was learned of by Zhu. In addition to describing Zhu's boldness directly, Pu Songling also used indirect descriptions of other people's reactions when seeing Judge Lu himself or his statue, to set off, by contrast, Zhu's bold moves. In the beginning, literary club members who put Zhu up to carry back Judge Lu's statue fidgeted "in their seats" and asked Zhu "to carry the image away". After learning that Zhu won an honorable title in the provincial examinations because of his friendship with Judge Lu, Zhu's friends in the literary club asked Zhu to introduce Judge Lu for them, while, on seeing Judge Lu himself, whose "red beard wagging" and "eyes glinting like lighting", "the group members were pale and dazed", and "their teeth were on the point of chattering", at last, "gradually they all withdraw". In addition, Zhu's wife was also "greatly distraught at hearing of their guest" and warned her husband "not to leave the inner rooms", but Zhu did not take her advice. Even for utilitarian purposes, nobody except Zhu could overcome the fear of Judge Lu. It can be seen that Zhu's boldness is not in a general sense and can surmount the fear of deities and ghosts. Therefore, Zhu's chances and fortunes are not something other people can have at will. Only an unusual person like Zhu has the opportunity to make friends with an unusual deity like Judge Lu. Judge Lu's fearsome appearance is not unusual but is regarded as the standard configuration of deities and ghosts. What is unusual about Judge Lu is that he is familiar with the knowledge of the mortal world and is willing to interact with human beings. When he first found Judge Lu come to his home, Zhu thought that he had offended Judge Lu the day before and he supposed he was "about to die". Unexpectedly, Judge Lu was never offended. Instead, the visit was because Judge Lu was honored by Zhu's kind invitation, and he was "glad to accept an invitation from such a liberal-minded man" when he had leisure. What's more unusual is that Judge Lu's "replies came as quickly as echoes" when Zhu "brought up subjects from the classics". Judge Lu was also familiar with the examination essay style and often corrected Zhu's article with a red ink brush, after which Judge Lu always bluntly gave negative comments. As a deity of the underworld, Judge Lu often got along with deities and ghosts, but he was conversant with the customs of the mortal world and willing to make friends with the intellectuals. This kind of human touch is exactly the unusual point of Judge Lu.

Zhu and Judge Lu's unusual behaviors came from the perfect fit of their fanciful ideas and Judge Lu's unusual abilities. Judge Lu "came once every few days" to Zhu's house, drinking and discussing articles. "Their friendship grew even closer". For Zhu's poor composition, Judge Lu came up with an idea of improvement, that is "drawing entrails out of Zhu's rent abdomen and putting the coils in order" and "putting in a brilliant heart in place of" Zhu's. For the people of Pu Songling's time, human literary thought was related to the heart, and there was no concept of the brain. Thus, Judge Lu exchanged Zhu a wise heart, which could improve Zhu's intelligence and literary grace. Since then, Zhu "showed great improvement in his ability to express thought in writing. When he passed his eyes over a page, he never forgot it". Zhu finally took the top honor in that year's provincial exam. As a deity, Judge Lu's fanciful ideas went beyond that of mortals. That is why Judge Lu could come up with the idea of exchanging wise heart for Zhu, which has made the story fanciful enough. While, after having benefited from the exchanged heart, Zhu also had whimsical ideas. In his opinion, "if vitals can be exchanged, I supposed that facial features can be replaced too". Zhu wanted Judge Lu to help his wife exchange a head with a beautiful face. Judge Lu agreed and a few days later, with Zhu's assistance, successfully exchanged the head for Zhu's wife. According to Pu Songling's description, the practice of unusual abilities of heart and head substitution was based on Judge Lu's official post convenience and supernatural magic, which makes Zhu and Judge Lu's unusual behaviors have details to be followed. Judge Lu's work as an underworld judge in the underworld allowed him to pick "out one excellent heart among tens of thousands" in the nether region, so he could exchange wise heart for Zhu, but Judge Lu also needed to bring back Zhu's heart, whose "apertures were blocked", "to make up for the missing one".

After promising to help exchange the head for Zhu's wife, Judge Lu needed more "time to work out the details", because it was "hard to select". Judge Lu had not made it until he "obtained the head of a beautiful woman" as Zhu requested. Pu Songling did not glide over the exchange process of heart and head. Instead, he used detailed descriptions to highlight Judge Lu's technical skills. After Zhu's heart was exchanged, "there were no traces of blood to be seen on the bed". "At dawn, Zhu undid the bandage to have a look: the incision had already closed, leaving only a thin red line". "When the daylight is clear, the wounds are closed, and those who are wired but red will remain.". When Judge Lu exchanged her head for Zhu's wife, the operation was done in one go. "Zhu's wife awoke with a slight tingling in her neck and a crust on her cheeks. Rubbing them she discovered flakes of dried blood". Here, Zhu's wife's discomfort and some bloodstains left behind make the story seem like a true one. After Zhu's wife washed her face, "Looking up, the maid saw a set of features that in no way resembled those of her mistress"[5], and Zhu's wife looked like a beauty in the painting. Pu Songling also pointed out the trace of head substitution:"Zhu loosened her collar for a closer look and found a red line encircling her neck. Then skin above and below her neck was of two distinct colors". These details of heart and head substitution are reasonable and in line with the law of plot development, making fantasy a truth-like story, through which, the unusual behaviors of Judge Lu and Zhu are presented vividly for readers.

Zhu, an unusual man, and Judge Lu, an unusual deity, shared unusual behaviors in their process of getting along and encountered several unusual things, including the unusual fate changes of Zhu after exchanging his heart, and the unusual lawsuit caused by Judge Lu's behavior of exchanging heads for Zhu's wife. After exchanging his heart, Zhu changed from having "not yet made a name for himself" to winning the first prize in that years' provincial examination. Thirty years later, in the first five days of his death, Zhu got informed in advance of his death by Judge Lu and was able to prepare for his funeral at ease. Dramatically, after he had died, Zhu was recommended by Judge Lu to be an official in the underworld. As a ghost, Zhu went back home to take care of his wife and taught his son for ten years.

Ten years later, Zhu had to go to his appointed post as the deity of Huashan Mountain, when he bade farewell to his wife and son. From a human being to a ghost, and from a ghost to a mountain deity, Zhu's adventures under each identity and the conversion of each identity are amazing. In addition to his unusual brushstrokes in the description of Zhu's overall encounter, Pu Songling also did not forget to supplement details to the story plot. The heart that Judge Lu exchanged for Zhu came from the underworld, and Zhu's heart was used to make up for the missing one, so that follow-up undesirable effects will not be triggered easily. But Pu Songling didn't mention where the beauty's head, being exchanged for Zhu's wife, came from at the beginning, paving the way for unusual lawsuits and cases that followed. The daughter of Provincial Censor Wu, who had an unnatural death, is the original owner of the head exchanged for Zhu's wife. The head was missing in the morgue. Wu Family couldn't find the missing head for a long time. "Eventually Master Wu was apprised of the wondrous head substitution in Zhu's house". After verifying that his suspicion was the truth, Master Wu brought changes against Zhu. At this time, Judge Lu showed up and used his supernatural abilities to make Master Wu's daughter appeared in her parents' dream to tell them the real murderer and make a request that, "Judge Lu exchange my head for hers (the head of Zhu's wife). This way my head lives on, even though my body is dead. I hope you will bear no grudge against him (Zhu)". Such a dream not only made the murder case come to light but also made Zhu become the son-in-law of the Wu Family. The head substitution drew forth an unusual case of missing head. Zhu was the defendant at the beginning but became the son-in-law of Master Wu at last. Although this plot was just a little episode of Zhu's unusual life, it was wonderful enough.

In "Judge Lu", an unusual man met an unusual deity. The two conducted unusual behaviors, which drew forth unusual things. These serial whimsies "progress one after the other with continuous dramatic plots".[1]

---

[1] Wang Shaohua. A Shocking Story of Heart and Head Substitution — A Brief Discussion on Whimsies in *Strange Tales from The Liaozhai Studio · Judge Lu*. Dang An. 2017(04): 31-32. (王少华:《一篇换心革面的惊世故事——略论〈聊斋·陆判〉对奇异的叙述》,《档案》2017 年第 4 期,第 31—32 页)

Literary Source and Mental Implication: Pu Songling's Ingenious Conceptions in "Judge Lu"

The story of "Judge Lu" is filled with whimsies, which are serial, as well as with ingenious conceptions. There are two aspects of such ingenious conceptions: one is the literary source of its plot, and the other is the mental implications entrusted in the story.

The literary source here refers to the textual research of the plot's literary origin in "Judge Lu". According to Liu Yongqiang's definition, literary origin refers to "textual materials with certain plots and characters, which novelists are directly in terms of"[1]. The reason for exploring the plot's literary origin in "Judge Lu" is because the research of literary origin is of great significance for understanding the mental connotation and artistic value of the novel. Ye Dejun believes that *Strange Tales from the Liaozhai Studio* follows many literary origins of the Ancient Chinese fantasy novels and legends in Jin (226 – 420) and Tang (618 – 907) Dynasties, and operas in Yuan (1271 – 1386) and Ming (1368 – 1644) Dynasties. He also mentioned that Wang Zhuo's *The way of the Current World* (Jin Shi Shuo) and Xu Fang's *The Story of Heart Substitution* (Huan Xin Ji) can be used as literary origins of *Strange Tales from the Liaozhai Studio*.[2] Zhu Yixuan also directly states that Liu Yiqing's "Jia Bizhi" in his *Hidden and Visible Realms* (You Ming Lu), Huang Fushi's "The Wife of Liu (Liu Shi Zi Qi)" in his *Record of Fanciful Metamorphose* (Yuan Hua Ji), Xu Fang's *The Story of Heart Substitution* (Huan Xin Ji), Wang Zhuo's "The Given Honor (Shang Yu)" in his *The way of the Current World* (Jin Shi Shuo), and Niu Xiu's *The*

---

[1] Liu Yong Qiang. Studies on Literary Origin in Ancient Chinese Novel. *Journal of Peking University* (*Philosophy and Social Sciences*). 2015(04): 71. (刘勇强:《古代小说创作中的"本事"及其研究》,《北京大学学报(哲学社会科学版)》2015 年第 4 期,第 71 页)

[2] Ye Dejun. *Textual Research on Chinese Opera and Novels* (Volume 2). Beijing: Zhonghua Book Company. 1979: 591. (叶德钧:《戏曲小说丛考》下册,北京:中华书局 1979 年版,第 591 页)

Notebook (*Gu Sheng*) are the literary origins of "Judge Lu"[①].

The literary origin of Zhu's friendship with Judge Lu can be found in *The Notebook* (*Gu Sheng*). Zhang, a male intellectual in *The Notebook* (*Gu Sheng*), "always failed the Qualification Exam for Imperial Examination"[②]. After making friends with an Underworld Judge in a temple, Zhang got help from the Underworld Judge and later held office in the government. The literary origins of exchanging heads and neatening entrails in "Judge Lu" are said to be in Liu Yiqing's *Hidden and Visible Realms* (*You Ming Lu*) and Wang Zhuo's *The way of the Current World* (*Jin Shi Shuo*). "Jia Bizhi" is a story in *Hidden and Visible Realms* (*You Ming Lu*), in which, Jia Bizhi's head was exchanged by an ugly person in his dream[③]. In *The way of the Current World* (*Jin Shi Shuo*), Zhou Liwu had poor physiognomy. "His cheekbones were low, having a narrow face, beardless and wizened"[④]. Also, Zhou went not well in the Imperial Examination. He dreamed that he was exchanged a head with a thick beard. Since then, "Zhou's cheekbones have been getting higher, the cheeks getting wider, and the whiskers getting more"[⑤]. After a few years, Zhou dreamed of an old man "cleaning his viscera"[⑥]. Then Zhou's ability to "express thoughts in writing improved day by day, and made it in the Imperial Examination at both the provincial level and the national level"[⑦]. In addition, the literary origin of heart substitution comes from Xu Fang's *The Story of Heart Substitution* (*Huan Xin Ji*). In the story, Jin Shigong "could not have punctuated simple sentences correctly"[⑧], but after a deity in golden armor exchanged heart for Jin Shigong, "he was suddenly enlightened and had a good command of learned knowledge"[⑨]. In "Liao Zhai Zi Zhi", the author's preface in *Strange Tales from the Liaozhai Studio*, Pu Songling claimed that he "is not a talent like Gan Bao, the founder of Ancient Chinese Fantasy Novel, but loves to collect stories about deities", and his hobby is similar to that of Su Shi, a famous litterateur in Earlier Song Dynasty (960 – 1127), appreciating talks about ghosts. Once

---

[①②③④⑤⑥⑦⑧⑨] Zhu Yixuan. *Document Compilation about Strange Tales from the Liaozhai Studio*. Tianjin: Nankai University Press. 1984: 50 – 55. (朱一玄:《聊斋志异》资料汇编,天津:南开大学出版社 1984 年版,第 50—55 页)

hearing of fanciful stories, Pu Songling would record them and these stories gradually came into being a tales collection, attempting to expand *Hidden and Visible Realms* (*You Ming Lu*). In the author's preface, Pu Songling showed his constant attention to various Fantasy Novels and their writers from the Northern and Southern Dynasties (420 - 589) to Pu Songling's time. Therefore, the above-mentioned textual research on the literary origins of "Judge Lu" is reasonable. Liu Yongqiang asserts that the most noteworthy content of the research on literary origin includes plot regeneration, stylistic transformation, and narrative adjustment. The narrative adjustment involves the tailoring and reorganization of narrative structure, the change of narrative angle and manner, and the shift of the narrator's identity.[1] Pu Songling draws on the plots of making friends with judges, heart and head substitution, and entrails washing in the predecessors' Fantasy Novels, enriching the plots and details of making friends with judges, repacking the effects of heart and head substitution. Through integration and remodeling, the existing plots are combined to make them interlocked, rejuvenating the ancients.

While cleverly conceiving the series of unusual plots, Pu Songling also embeds his moral values and political ideals into each plot, just as Pu Songling had mentioned in "Liao Zhai Zi Zhi": "drinking freely while I'm writing to express indignation at the realistic situation".

The story of Zhu's interaction with Judge Lu reflects Pu Songling's expectations for literary talent and official advancement. Of course, there is also his unwillingness and helplessness towards destiny. After Judge Lu exchanged a wise heart for Zhu, Zhu's ability to express thoughts in writing greatly improved, and came out first in the provincial exam. However, Judge Lu also warned in advance: "your blessings are meager", and "you cannot win any great honors", which means "the prefectural and provincial examinations are as far as you'll go". Sure enough, when Zhu participated in the Imperial Examination at the national level, he failed three times for breaking rules of

---

[1] Liu Yong Qiang. Studies on Literary Origin in Ancient Chinese Novel. *Journal of Peking University* (*Philosophy and Social Sciences*). 2015(04): 71. (刘勇强:《古代小说创作中的"本事"及其研究》,《北京大学学报(哲学社会科学版)》2015 年第 4 期,第 71 页)

deportment rules. "At this, the goal of official advancement soured on him. Thirty years passed". The effect of heart substitution here was limited, and it could not completely change Zhu's fate. Besides, when informing Zhu that he was about to die, Judge Lu also tried to straighten Zhu out: "what good are personal wishes in the face of heaven's decree? And any life and death are one in the eyes of a man of broad perspective. Why should you rejoice at life and grieve at death?" After dying and became a ghost, Zhu had still accompanied his family and had taught his son by himself until his son grew up. Before leaving for his newly appointed post of deity in Huashan Mountain, Zhu also urged his son not to neglect his studies. There Zhu put his unfinished ideals of official advancement on his son. Life and death, or the Imperial Examination, there was the unwillingness to fate here, but in the end, there was always a compromise. Pu Songling had no advancement in the Imperial Examinations since he took top honors in the provincial exam when he was 19 years old. He commented at the end of the "Judge Lu" that, "this Master Lu was repulsive on the outside but attractive on the inside. It has not been all that many years from the end of the Ming Dynasty to the present. Is Master Lu of Lingyang still around? Does his supernatural power still work as of old? I would like nothing more than to serve, whip in hand, as his charioteer." Pu Songling signed with emotion that Judge Lu was ugly but kind, and could help Zhu's career of the Imperial Examination. At his age, if Pu Songling could meet Judge Lu, he would be willing to serve as a coachman. These comments show Pu Songling's dissatisfaction with his constant failures of the Imperial Examination at the national level, and his vision of Judge Lu in fact shows his helplessness towards reality.

After his death, Zhu finally realized his dream of an official career in the underworld. He was recommended by Judge Lu to "have an official title" in the underworld, but he did not immediately part with his wife and son in the mortal world. Zhu often returned to the mortal world to accompany his wife and son. Zhu's deep love for his son is beyond life and death, which Pu Songling has made a full description of. Zhu "always hugged his son Wei, who was five years old at the time of his death. When the boy was about seven he taught him to read by lamplight. The boy, too, was brilliant. At nine he could write a composition; at fifteen he entered the local academy, never realizing that he was fatherless". When Zhu's son grew up and Zhu was about to leave forever, Zhu told his son not to neglect his studies and made an appointment with his son to meet again in ten years. When they met again ten years later, Zhu has already been the deity of Huashan Mountain, and his son was also an official in the government. Zhu approved that he was satisfied with his son's good name as an official, and then just left. However, "when he had gone several paces he turned, unfastened a sword from his waist, and had an attendant hand it to his son", blessing that his son will prosper. A line of words was engraved upon the sword: "Be long on courage and short on foolhardiness; be round in wisdom and square in conduct". This sentence comes from the *Old Book of Tang History* (*Jiu Tang Shu*). It was used to caution Wei, Zhu's son, to be ambitious, but to plan carefully; to be tactful, but also to be upright. Later, Zhu also gave a dream to his son to choose an heir among his grandsons to inherit the sword, blessing his grandsons to have a good official career too. This kind of care and love spans time and space, human beings and ghosts, and human beings and deities, which, accords to parents' deep love for their children. It is a traditional Chinese family affection, full of warmth.

Of course, Zhu could not have made it without Judge Lu's help, from being an unnamed examinee to the top in the provincial exam and making his fellow examinees look "at one another in amazement", to being able to serve as an official in the underworld after his death. The friendship between Judge Lu and Zhu that spans human beings and deities is also the positive energy that "Judge Lu" wanted to convey. Zhu, a mortal, did not avoid meeting Judge Lu like others because of Judge Lu's terrifying appearance as an underworld deity, but treated him with courtesy, sincerely drinking and talking with him, and "sometimes they slept together with the soles of their feet touching". Judge Lu, who had a thorough understanding about literary classics in the mortal world, did not mind Zhu's poor writing skills but used his supernatural abilities to help Zhu's advancement in the Imperial Examination. For Zhu's wish of his wife having a fair appearance, Judge Lu helped him, too. Besides, Judge Lu also helped Zhu when Zhu got into trouble, a murder case. Before he was about to die, Zhu was reminded to prepare in advance by Judge Lu. After Zhu's death, Judge Lu recommended him to serve as an official in the underworld, which allowed Zhu to still be able to take care of his wife and son in the mortal world and to have further opportunity to be promoted as the deity of Huashan Mountain in the future. Zhu, an unusual human being, and Judge Lu, an unusual deity, are different in their unusual characteristics, but they coincided perfectly. It is obvious that Judge Lu's devotion to Zhu is greater, but Zhu's role as a companion to Judge Lu can also not be underestimated. The friendship between the two is the basis for the various whimsical plots in "Judge Lu", and it is also a warm touch of human affection in "Judge Lu".

Conclusion

"Judge Lu" is a good example with the fanciful contents, varied plot twists, ingenious ideas, and mental implications in *Strange Tales from the Liaozhai Studio*. Pu Songling made serial whimsies progresses one after the other. Zhu, an unusual human being, drew forth Judge Lu, an unusual deity, and the two together conducted unusual behaviors and dealt with unusual things. Many of the classic whimsical plots in "Judge Lu" have their literary origins, which is the inheritance and development of the subject matters of fantasy novels. The ingenious adaptation and connection of these plots also reflect Pu Songling's high level of literary creation. The mental implications throughout "Judge Lu" also reflect the moral values and political ideals of Pu Songling at his time. Humanistic effulgence in Ancient Chinese Fantasy Novel and ancient Chinese culture can be concluded based on the above-mentioned studies of "Judge Lu". On the one hand, the author of Ancient Chinese Fantasy Novel bring their subjective initiative into full play, and such subjective initiative is on the strength of the cultural atmosphere and fanciful logic which are widely and well accepted by people at that time, so that, an unusual and whimsical world is built to have stories develop smoothly. On the other hand, the creative works of Fantasy Novel not only have inheritance and development to predecessor's creation but also have cultural ingenuity to set forth the existing moral principles in the real world by describing unusual things only happening in the wonderland. Through interpreting the wonderful whimsies and ingenious conceptions in "Judge Lu" of *Strange Tales from the Liaozhai Studio*, the train of thought for Ancient Chinese Fantasy Novel's creation can be presented, as well as the moral values and political ideals of people at Pu Songling's time, which could serve to understand the humanistic effulgence in Ancient Chinese Fantasy Novel and ancient Chinese culture.

(Beijing Language and Culture University, Beijing International Studies University)

An Analysis of International Communication of Shaolin Kungfu

Cao Hongrui

"A bicycle, a bowl of porridge, and a piece of sofa. What these three things stand for is a kind of life as well as a philosophy." This is a saying describing Hygge, a mindset from the Kingdom of Denmark. This five-letter word unveils the secret of why Denmark is on the list of the top three happiest countries in the world. Hygge is a philosophy that allows people to choose a way to make themselves comfortable and detach themselves from their busy lives. This reminds me of Chan Buddhism — a Chinese mindset that allows people to cultivate their bodies and minds, forget all the secular worries through meditation, and reap the benefits of health and happiness. The mindset of Chan is also integrated into the spirit of martial arts, of which Shaolin Kungfu is particularly prominent.

Shaolin Kungfu (also known as "Shaolin Wushu") refers to the traditional cultural system that has developed in the particular Buddhist cultural environment in Shaolin Temple of Songshan Mountain over a long history. It is based on a belief in the supernatural power of Buddhism and fully reflects the wisdom of Chan Buddhism. The martial arts practiced by monks in Shaolin Temple is the major form.[1] It has been on the list of China Intangible Cultural Heritage since 2006. There are no exact historical records

---

[1] Shi Yongxin. "Shaolin Kungfu keeping perfect balance between Chan Buddhism and Martial Arts". *Shaolin and Tai Chi*. 2015, Issue 1, p. 4. (释永信:《禅武一体的少林功夫》,《少林与太极》2015 年第 1 期,第 4 页)

about the time when Shaolin Kungfu appeared, but there does exist a record that "the beginning of Shaolin Kungfu dates back to the Northern Wei Dynasty, related to a Chan master named Chou". This man, the earliest monk of Shaolin Temple, was regarded as the founder of Shaolin Kungfu. Shaolin Temple, located in the Central Plains, enjoyed convenient transportation and connected the south to the north. Its great location attached vital military importance to itself. Besides, long-time meditation and sitting gradually resulted in poor physical fitness. Therefore, with the purpose of protecting the temple from attack and exercising physical abilities, Shaolin monks, under his advocacy, started to play with their fists. This is the embryonic form of Shaolin martial arts, which is only for the sake of self-defense, not attack. That's why this kind of martial art puts great heed to self-defense.[1] It has a huge and well-developed technical system, and it can be basically divided into two main categories: unarmed combat and armed combat, such as Seven Star Fist and Shaolin Staff respectively. In addition, there are seventy-two unique sets of skills and all kinds of special types of Kungfu techniques, such as, Qi Gong, attacking a vital point of the body, etc. Practicing Shaolin Kungfu can keep people fit and healthy, and this form of exercise can also demonstrate the beauty of human body movements. After thousands of years of continuous development, being one of treasures of Chinese culture, it has been passed on from generation to generation through the teaching and oral instructions of the masters as well as the diligent training and practicing of disciples. In the process of evolution and development, Shaolin Kungfu has absorbed literature, philosophy, and other theories with an open mind. There is a close connection between Shaolin martial arts and classical Chinese literature. For example, a classic move in Shaolin Staff called "Wukong hiding the staff" is exactly from *Journey to the West*, one of the Four Great Classical Novels of Chinese literature. Besides, Chinese classical philosophy believes that "qi" is the basic element of the world, and the philosophical thinking of "qi" is vividly

---

[1] Lü Hongjun, Teng Lei. *Shaolin Kungfu*. Zhejiang People's Publishing House. 2005, p. 8. (吕宏军、滕磊:《少林功夫》,浙江人民出版社 2005 年版,第 8 页)

reflected in Shaolin Kungfu. For example, Shaolin Hard Style Qigong emphasizes the operation of the "qi" in the human body against attacks from weapons. The rich cultural connotation of Shaolin Kungfu provides a chance to make itself a representative of Eastern martial arts.

Shaolin Kungfu originates from Shaolin Temple located in Henan Province, having a 1,500-year history and being one of the most famous temples in the world. The temple's name literally means "temple in the thick forests of Shaoshi Mountain". [1] So that is how Shaolin got its name. Because of its long history, it was treated as one of the provincial key cultural relics protection units by the People's Government of Henan Province in 1963; it was officially approved for the first batch of national 5A level tourist attractions by the National Tourism Administration in 2007; Historic Monuments of Dengfeng in "The Centre of Heaven and Earth" (which includes Shaolin Temple) was listed as a world cultural heritage by UNESCO in 2010. Shaolin Temple was built in 495 AD by Emperor Xiaowen of the Northern Wei Dynasty for the Indian monk Batuo. And it became a religious place for promoting Buddhism. This old temple has witnessed changes of dynasties and experienced damage by man-made and natural disasters, but it still stands. Nowadays, it has become a famous monument with historical, literary, and scientific value. Shaolin Monastery mainly refers to the central courtyard of the temple where abbot monks and deacon monks host the Buddhist activities and living activities. [2] It has seven main halls on the axis and seven other halls around, with several yards around the halls. [3] There is Bodhidharma Cave in the north, Second Patriarch Temple in the south, Pagoda Forest in the west and Guanghui temple in the east. Buildings in Shaolin Temple are not just places of prayer and quiet contemplation but training courts. Taking the example of the Old Hall of A Thousand Buddhas,

---

[1] Lü Hongjun. *Shaolin Temple*. Henan People's Publishing House. 2002, p. 2. (吕宏军:《嵩山少林寺》,河南人民出版社 2002 年版,第 2 页)

[2] Lü Hongjun. *Shaolin Temple*. Henan People's Publishing House. 2002, p. 19. (吕宏军:《嵩山少林寺》,河南人民出版社 2002 年版,第 19 页)

[3] Description of Historic Monuments of Dengfeng in "The Centre of Heaven and Earth". Official website of UNESCO. https://whc.unesco.org/en/list/1305/, 2020.12.27.

the largest existing hall in Shaolin Temple, it is famous for murals such as "Thirteen Monks Using Staff Saved Emperor Taizong of Tang". Inside this building, there are 48 small depressions in the floor and several inclined pillars. It is said that these are all formed by hundreds of years of Kungfu training. As the monks channeled the "qi" through their feet, they then struck the ground with incredible force, leaving marks on the ground; as monks practiced martial arts, they hit pillars with their elbows and arms so hard that the strong impact force made the pillars deviate from the base. Like the saying goes, "Rome was not built in a day". Neither was Shaolin Kungfu. The depressions and inclined pillars are evidence of monks' hard practice.

Shaolin Kungfu and Shaolin Temple are inseparable — as the cradle of this martial arts, Shaolin Temple also plays a vital role in promoting it. Moreover, it is Shaolin Kungfu that has made this ancient temple known around the globe and has attracted many Kungfu fans. The international communication of Shaolin Kungfu has attracted many fans to this temple, both boosting the development of its tourism industry and turning this martial art into a vehicle of communication between the world and Shaolin culture. In this way, it allows Kungfu lovers from all over the world to find out the mysteries of Shaolin Kungfu.

Shaolin Kungfu's Communication Forms and Current Status in the World

There is an old saying: "When it comes to martial arts, it is hard not to mention Shaolin Kungfu", from which it is apparent that Shaolin Kungfu enjoys a very high status and influence in China. Since the reform and opening-up policy, China has opened its gate to the world and started to interact with foreign cultures. Abbot Shi Yongxin of Shaolin Temple has also seized this opportunity. Since his being in charge in 1987, he has led Shaolin Temple out of China; under his guidance, this ancient temple has become a successful case of international communication of Chinese culture and an important part of world cultures. The following part will introduce three main communication forms of Shaolin Kungfu around the globe.

Firstly, Shaolin Kungfu combines with film art. With the reputation of "the best school", Shaolin is always the first choice for film creation and adaptation relevant to Chinese martial arts. A film named *Shaolin Temple* was widely reviewed and highly praised in the world in 1982, which not only attracts worldwide kung fu lovers to Shaolin Temple to learn kung fu but also goes on a kung fu binge in the film industry. After that, more movies related to Shaolin theme mushroomed, such as *Kids from Shaolin*, *The New Legend of Shaolin*, *Shaolin*, etc. In pursuit of visual and artistic effects, the film may fictionalize some stories to make it outstanding, while the documentary is different — it is based on real life, recording real lives of certain real persons. A documentary concerning Shaolin attempts to show the world what the real Shaolin is. Coproduced by China Central Television (CCTV) and Henan Television, a documentary named "Kung Fu Shaolin" has been produced to show the public how generations of people practicing Chinese martial arts have learned the way of survival and an understanding of life in the 21st century.[①]

The combination of this art and theatre is a brand new way of developing traditional martial arts in modern times. A dance drama, *Sutra*, has toured Europe, America and other countries since its debut at the prestigious Sadler's Wells Theatre in London. It produces amazing chemistry between Chinese traditional culture and modern arts through music, dance, and martial arts.[②] This perfect combination and innovation not only allows the audience to grasp the spirit of Shaolin Chan Buddhism and the beauty of kung fu in a new way, but also paves the path for the communication and development of Chinese traditional cultures.

Secondly, Shaolin Kungfu combines with martial arts performances.

---

① "Where is Shaolin Kungfu now?" CCTV. 2016.04.26.《少林功夫今何在?》央视网）http://jishi.cctv.com/2016/04/26/ARTIW67JOmLD9UJOnEezrhYf160426. shtml? spm = C86503. P4DfMPxErwxg. EMvoNGpSUemF. 2,2016-04-26.

② Mu Yutong, Hu Ping. "A Study of the Innovation of Shaolin Culture from the View of a Dance Drama, Sutra." *Art Science and Technology*. 2020, Volume 33, Issue 20, p. 137. （母雨潼、胡平：《跨界舞剧 sutra 视角下少林文化的创意研究》，《艺术科技》2020 年第 33 卷第 20 期，第 137 页）

Even though Shaolin Kungfu originated in the Central Plains, it never got stuck in this place. Since Master Shi Yongxin served as the abbot of Shaolin Temple, the number of international conferences and foreign exchanges monks have participated in has been surging. Shaolin has been invited to many cities in many countries to perform Shaolin martial arts. This type of performance has gradually become one of the major ways of international communication of Shaolin culture. Shaolin Kungfu Group has performed in more than 60 countries and regions in the world. What is more, there exist many private organizations that have made great contributions to the spread of Shaolin Kungfu, especially Shaolin Wushu Tagou Group.

Shaolin Wushu Tagou Group is a martial arts school. Since its founding, it has participated in nearly a thousand major domestic and foreign martial arts competitions. From 2003 to 2020, it participated in the CCTV Spring Festival Gala 17 times and won five awards. Its members have taken part in many ceremonies of important events, such as the 2004 and 2008 Summer Olympic Games, the 2007 Special Olympics World Summer Games, the 2008 Summer Paralympics, the 2010 Asian Games, the 2014 Youth Olympic Games, the 2016 G20 Hangzhou Summit, and the mass pageantry of a grand gathering to celebrate the 70th anniversary of the founding of the PRC. Their performance has been highly praised by the public and famous domestic directors.[1] At the opening ceremony of the 2008 Summer Olympic Games, 2008 members from this school prepared a visual feast, "Nature — Tai Chi", for the worldwide audience (Fig. 1). On the basis of Tai Chi's yin-yang theory, the hardness of Kungfu is marvelously mixed with the softness of Tai Chi. On such big stages, this school has amazed the world with its superb performances, excellent teamwork, and the spirit of unity. It perfectly presents the elements of Chinese martial arts, and fully shows the charm of Chinese traditional culture and martial arts to the whole world.

Thirdly, Shaolin Kungfu combines with Wushu competitions. With the growing worldwide popularity of Shaolin Temple and Shaolin Kungfu as well

---

[1] Introduction. Official Website of Shaolin Tagou. 2020. 11. 05. (集团介绍,少林塔沟教育集团官方网站)http://www.shaolintagou.com/jituanjieshao, 2020 - 11 - 05.

Fig. 1 Members from Shaolin Wushu Tagou Group performed "Nature" at the opening ceremony of the 2008 Summer Olympic Games.

as the increasing number of visitors and Kungfu learners, the People's Government of Zhengzhou held the 1st Zhengzhou International Shaolin Martial Arts Festival in 1991 to further promote Shaolin Chan culture. The 12th was successfully held in 2008. (The first four festivals were organized once a year, and later it was changed to once every two years in order to expand the scale.) Although there were participants from fewer countries and regions before the 7th, seven-time successful holdings raised the popularity of Shaolin Kungfu and also motivated the majority of Kungfu fans to practice this kind of martial art. The competition set up different events and divided the participants by gender. That expanded the scope of contestants, motivated Kungfu lovers around the world, and provided a big stage to learn and compete. In October 2018, the 12th Zhengzhou International Shaolin Martial Arts Festival was run in Dengfeng, Zhengzhou, Henan Province. Kungfu masters from 65 countries and regions gathered there to compete with each other. The youngest contestant was only 2 years old and the oldest was 79 years old.[①] During the festival, Zhengzhou also held a series of activities, say, martial arts performances, exhibitions of

---

[①] Yin Xinyu. The 12th Zhengzhou International Shaolin Martial Arts Festival Opens in Dengfeng. *Henan Daily*, 2018.10.21. (银新玉:《第十二届中国郑州国际少林武术节在登封开幕》,《河南日报》) https://www.henan.gov.cn/2018/10-21/712311.html, 2018-10-21.

Songshan culture, and intangible cultural heritage projects to further expand the influence of Shaolin Kungfu.[①]

Problems and Corresponding Measures in the International Communication of Shaolin Kungfu

Although Shaolin Kungfu sets a great example for Chinese cultural exchanges on the world stage, there still exist several problems in the process of international communication.

First of all, the essence of Shaolin Kungfu, Chan Buddhism, has been neglected. In the context of globalization and commercialization, Shaolin Kungfu has appeared in many films for the sake of expanding its global impact. With time passing by, it has put more focus on the performance of martial arts in order to achieve the artistic effect required by the film industry, presenting powerful and fast martial arts scenes. However, that misleads the audience to believe that Shaolin Kungfu is only a form of artistry, which completely ignores the Chan cultural connotation behind it.

Shaolin Kungfu and Chan Buddhism are inseparable. Given the current phenomenon, more heed should be put to the promotion of Chan culture. The actual meaning of Kungfu is more than just "martial arts". It originally referred to the time spent meditating in Buddhism.[②] Therefore, whether it is the practice or meditation, both are called kung fu. It is the interaction between the "stillness" of meditation and the "movement" of martial arts that has made Shaolin Kungfu what it is at present. Assuming that no corresponding measures are taken to tackle this phenomenon, both young

---

[①] Chen Guannan. Dengfeng Will Hold the 12th Zhengzhou International Shaolin Martial Arts Festival Tomorrow. *Henan Daily*, 2018. 10. 19. （陈冠男：《第十二届中国郑州国际少林武术节明天在登封举办》,《河南日报》） http://newpaper.dahe.cn/hnrb/html/2018-10/19/content_288740.htm, 2018-10-19.

[②] Shi Yongxin. Kungfu and Chan Buddhism in the practice of Buddhism — A Speech at the University of California, Berkeley. Official Website of Shaolin Temple, 2020. 12. 09. （释永信：《佛教实践中的功夫与禅——在美国加州伯克利学院的主题演讲》,少林寺官方网站） http://www.shaolin.org.cn/templates/T_newS_list/index.aspx? nodeid = 26&page = ContentPage&contentid = 42435, 2020-12-09.

generations in China and overseas Kungfu lovers would not be able to get to know the whole concept of Shaolin Kungfu, like losing a piece of the puzzle. This is the reason why it is necessary to pay equal attention to martial arts and Chan Buddhism when Shaolin Kungfu interacts with other cultures in the world.

Secondly, Shaolin Kungfu shares fewer differences with gymnastics. Since the 20th century, traditional Chinese martial arts have been influenced by Western sports competition models as well as various kinds of theatre; a great change has happened to the performance of Shaolin Kungfu. For one thing, it became a sports event in 1990. The traditional style of Chinese martial arts, which emphasizes internal strength, attack, and defense, has been replaced by acrobatic skills like somersaulting, kicking, and other compulsory exercises.[①] Although this adds to the appreciation, it has greatly changed Shaolin Kungfu, turning it into a gymnastics-like sport. For another, it is undoubted that the stunning combination of Shaolin martial arts and plays can catch many audiences' eyes to enjoy the chemistry they create. Nevertheless, the content of plays stands alone and the actors have little knowledge of martial arts. Both lead to the result that the play highlights the artistic aspect and weakens the martial arts part, which provides little help to the international promotion of Shaolin Kungfu.

It is vital to maintain the feature of kung fu. Whether we look at Shaolin Kungfu's turning into a sports event or its integration with theatre, one of the crucial reasons for doing so is to expand its global influence to interact with other cultures, which is the original intention that should be kept in mind. To realize this aim, firstly, the characteristics of this kind of martial art should be fully used, and distinguished from other sports, for instance, gymnastics. If necessary, a special team of monks should be formed to both keep the feature of kungfu and motivate it in sports events and international affairs. Secondly, a play, related to Shaolin Kungfu that is rich in artistic enjoyment and martial arts elements, should be produced with professionals.

---

① Lü Hongjun, Teng Lei. *Shaolin Kungfu*. Zhejiang People's Publishing House. 2005, p. 186. (吕宏军、滕磊:《少林功夫》,浙江人民出版社 2005 年版,第 186 页)

Lastly, relevant promotions need to be better organized. The premise of Shaolin Kungfu's global communication is that it should be known by the public and make people of it in China first. However, whether we speak of domestic international Wushu competitions or touring martial arts plays, there is a lack of enough promotion from both authorities and the mass media. As a result, people rarely have the opportunity to experience Shaolin Kungfu in daily life, let alone understand and learn its culture. This is undoubtedly a stumbling block on the path of the international communication of Shaolin Kungfu.

Authorities should take relevant measures and the media should put more efforts on promoting it. The government can introduce relevant laws and regulations to protect Shaolin culture and let Shaolin culture enter the campus, such as promoting Shaolin radio calisthenics and running Shaolin Fist competitions, etc. Inviting the media to spread awareness is also a good choice. Professional mass media runners can make good use of mainstream media and new media methods, such as posting relevant WeChat official account messages, uploading videos on Tiktok, and inviting influencers to post relevant Weibo to reach more people to encourage them to participate in related activities and learn about Shaolin Kungfu. China is now an increasingly international nation. Many Chinese go abroad either for education or traveling. This can also enable Chinese people to understand Shaolin better. Every Chinese who understands Shaolin culture can make great contributions to the international communication of Shaolin Kungfu.

Nowadays, the world is tolerant, interconnected, and colorful, and world cultures can interact and learn from each other. Since China's reform and opening-up policy, the frequency of China's exchanges with other cultures has increased a lot. The advocacy of the Belt and Road Initiative has also provided a breeding ground for the diversified development of the world. With the help of a diverse, inclusive, and free cultural context, as an invaluable part of the world culture, Shaolin Kungfu gradually becomes international, assisting the increase of diversity in world culture. However, due to the lack of understanding of China and Chinese culture, many countries or regions still maintain some stereotypes not corresponding to reality. Shaolin Kungfu plays the role of telling China's stories in an international way.[1] It has been an outstanding representative of Chinese martial arts and a typical vehicle of Chinese culture. Foreign visitors can acquire knowledge of the whole iceberg of Chinese culture from its tiny piece, Shaolin Kungfu, which also helps to shatter stereotypes. Shaolin Kungfu, emphasizing both Chan Buddhism and martial arts performance, builds a bridge between Chinese culture and the world, setting a remarkable example for the international communication of Chinese culture and other cultures in the world.

(Beijing International Studies University)

---

[1] Fang Guoqing, Wang Run, Luo Hongbin. Wushu: To Tell China's Stories in an International Way — A Theoretical Framework on the Country's Image. *Zhejiang Sport Science*. 2011, Issue 1, p. 93. (方国清、王润、骆红斌:《武术传播:讲述"中国故事"的"世界语言"———项关于国家形象的理论建构》,《浙江体育科学》2011 年第 1 期,第 93 页)

The Cultural Significance of Construction and International Communication Reflection of *San Kong* in Qufu, Confucius' Hometown

Yu Chunhua

At the beginning of the 20th century, Andersen's fairy tales were introduced into China, and they built beautiful fairy dreams for several generations of Chinese children. Denmark has become the "kingdom of fairy tales". Today, Andersen is regarded as the cultural symbol of the kingdom of Denmark. If only one person in China were to be chosen to represent Chinese culture in its long history, Confucius would be the best option. The Confucianism initiated by Confucius is the basic core of Chinese traditional culture. In recent years, "Confucius fever" has continued to heat up all over the world. In contrast, Qufu, the birthplace of Chinese Confucianism and the hometown of Confucius, has been neglected to a great extent by the rest of the world. In Denmark, Andersen's hometown, Odense on Funen Island, is a must for domestic and foreign tourists visiting Denmark. On the Chinese official website of the Danish Tourism Administration, the Andersen Cultural Festival is presented on the front page, and the Andersen museum is a must scenic spot on Funen island. However, the attractions in Qufu, especially *San Kong*, cannot receive such widespread coverage.

World Cultural Heritage: *San Kong* in Qufu

In the 20th century, the world wars broke out and modernization advanced rapidly, which brought great damage to the natural landscapes and historical sites. UNESCO was aware that there was a growing tendency for the natural and cultural heritages to deteriorate. In 1972, UNESCO formulated the Convention Concerning the Protection of the World Cultural and Natural Heritage with a view to protecting irreplaceable cultural and natural properties in the world. The convention defines three categories of cultural heritages: cultural relics, buildings and archaeological sites. In 1994, *San Kong* in Qufu were included, which characterize material heritages, consisting of the ancient buildings and cultural relics of the Temple and Cemetery of Confucius and the Kong Family Mansion.

The Temple of Confucius in Qufu was originally the residence of Confucius. In the Han Dynasty, Confucius' thought was highly respected in China. As the saying goes in China, "China's rites and music for thousands of years belong to Qufu, and the uncrowned king (refers to Confucius) is worshipped for thousands of generations." Liu Bang, the first emperor of the Han Dynasty, came to the Temple in Qufu to offer sacrifices to Confucius. During the reign of emperor Huan in the Eastern Han Dynasty, Han Chi, the Prime Minister of Lu (in the southwest of Shandong province now), presided over the renovation of the Temple, so that it became an official temple. During the period of Emperor Taizong of the Tang, the central government ordered to the building of Confucius temples throughout the country, and the Confucius temple in Qufu was further repaired, upgraded and expanded. "Confucius temples as national examples" and "offering sacrifices to Confucius" have become Chinese social traditions. Sacrifice is a national event. The stone tablets among the Thirteen Stele Pavilion in the Temple of Confucius in Qufu record the experience of offering sacrifices to Confucius. The successive emperors granted Confucius posthumous titles, and continued to rebuild and expand the former houses, forming today's scale. Dacheng hall, the main building of the Temple in Qufu, is modeled after the imperial palace, and signifies that Confucius is the emperor in Chinese traditional culture. The eaves of Dacheng Hall are decorated with yellow glazed tiles, which could only be used for royal buildings at that time. The main building of the Temple is "built by red walls and with turrets at the four corners", [1] typifying the highest standard of Chinese traditional architecture. Accordingly, Confucius has a "holy" status in China. The Temple of Confucius in Qufu, the Forbidden City in Beijing and Chengde Mountain Resort (Imperial Summer Villa) are known as the most famous ancient architectural complexes in China. "The Temple of Confucius actually symbolizes the lofty position of Confucius and Confucianism in ancient Chinese society. It can be said that the history of worship in the Temple of Confucius is a history of official ideology, the evolution of orthodox ideological and cultural theories, and the epitome and symbol of Chinese traditional culture."[2]

The Kong Family Mansion was the historical residence of the direct descendants of Confucius. Confucius was frustrated in his official career all his life, and his thoughts were not valued when he was alive. In the Han Dynasty, Emperor Gaozu of the Han went to the Confucius Temple in Qufu to offer sacrifices to Confucius, and granted Kong Teng, the 8th generation of the descendant of Confucius, the title of "Lord Fengsi" (also called "Ceremonial Officer"). Since then, despite the change of dynasties, the Kong family and the royal family have become the most respected families in Chinese history. In 1055, Zhao Zhen, the emperor Renzong of the Song, bestowed on Kong Zongyuan, the offspring of Confucius in the 46th generation, the title of "Duke Yansheng". A new mansion was awarded to Duke Yansheng, which was the original version of the Kong Family Mansion in existence now. Confucius carried out "*Zhou Li*" (the Rites of Zhou) all his life, in which the patriarchal system had a profound and everlasting influence in China up to modern times when China remained a typical patriarchal society; "the Kong family is the most typical historical specimen.

---

[1] World Cultural Heritage: the Temple and Cemetery of Confucius and the Kong Family Mansion, the Central People's Government of the people's Republic of China, 《世界文化遗产——孔府、孔庙、孔林》,中华人民共和国中央人民政府)http://www.gov.cn/test/2006-03/28/content_238291.htm, 2006-03-28 13:38.

[2] Yang Chaoming, *Visiting the Temple and Cemetery of Confucius and the Kong Family Mansion: the holy land of Oriental culture*, Shanghai: Shanghai Ancient Books Publishing House, 2004 edition, p. 4. (杨朝明:《游访孔庙孔府孔林·东方的文化圣地》,上海:上海古籍出版社 2004 年版,第 4 页)

From Confucius to his 77th generation, Kong Decheng, over 2,400 years, a special social and historical landscape has been formed with complete branches, clear family precepts and strict management system". [1] Duke Yansheng lived here to protect Confucius' relics and collect royal sacrificial vessels. Now the Kong Family Mansion covers an area of about 7.4 hectares, with 480 ancient buildings, nine courtyards in front and back, and three roads in the middle, east and west. From the perspective of architectural scale and layout, the present Kong Family Mansion is "a typical Chinese aristocratic mansion, which is regarded as 'the most honorable family in China'". [2] There are more than 100,000 pieces of historical relics in the collection, including not only bronze ritual vessels bestowed by the emperors of all dynasties, but also gold and stone, ceramics, jade, agate, pearls and calligraphy and paintings of celebrities of all dynasties. As a result, the Kong Family Mansion plays a role as a museum of Chinese cultural relics. The Kong family is a model for the inheritance of traditional Chinese families. The descendants of the Kong family can be supported by historical records. In 2005, the Kong family was listed as "the world's longest genealogy" in the Guinness Book of Records. The Kong Family Mansion is not only of great use in promoting Confucian culture, but also sets an example for the world to study the inheritance of the Chinese patriarchal clan system.

The Cemetery of Confucius is located 1.5 kilometers north of downtown Qufu, covering an area of more than 3.6 square kilometers. It is the family cemetery where Confucius, his disciples and his descendants were buried, with more than 100,000 tombs. "It has a history of more than 2500 years, and it is also the oldest and largest clan cemetery in the world. It is the largest, longest lasting and best preserved clan tomb group and artificial

---

[1] Yang Chaoming, *Visiting the Temple and Cemetery of Confucius and the Kong Family Mansion: the holy land of Oriental culture*, Shanghai: Shanghai Ancient Books Publishing House, 2004 edition, p. 4. (杨朝明:《游访孔庙孔府孔林·东方的文化圣地》,上海:上海古籍出版社 2004 年版,第 4 页)

[2] World Cultural Heritage: the Temple and Cemetery of Confucius and the Kong Family Mansion, the Central People's Government of the People's Republic of China, (《世界文化遗产——孔府、孔庙、孔林》,中华人民共和国中央人民政府) http://www.gov.cn/test/2006-03/28/content_238291.htm, 2006 - 03 - 28 13:38。

garden in China."① There is the Confucius Shinto in the Cemetery of Confucius, which is connected with the city gate. Confucius tomb is located in the middle of the Cemetery of Confucius, and is lined up with the tombs there, of his son Kong Li, and his grandson Zisi. "The momentum of horns, according to the guide, is 'son and grandson as companion'."② This is the layout of family tombs in ancient China. The Cemetery of Confucius is rich in cultural relics on the ground, which is of great value to the study of the Chinese burial system and ancient politics, economy, culture, customs, calligraphy and art. Today, there are still descendants of Confucius buried there. The family has lasted for generations.

The Temple and Cemetery of Confucius and the Kong Family Mansion are usually known as *San Kong* or "the Three Confucian Sites". "They are the symbol of commemorating Confucius and advocating Confucianism in Chinese history. They are famous for their rich cultural accumulation, long history, grand scale, rich cultural relics collection and high scientific and artistic value."③ As the hometown of Confucius, Qufu is regarded as the "holy city of the East", and its cultural significance is worth investigating from many respects. As the material carrier of Confucian thought and the development of the Kong family, the Three Confucian Sites in Qufu worthy of in-depth understanding by scholars and tourists at home and abroad.

The Cultural Significance of *San Kong* in Qufu

"Qufu is the birthplace of Confucian culture, and the scenic spots in Qufu characterize the culture of Confucianism, the main ideology of the 'sage', with Confucius as the core figure, presenting more than 2,000 years

---

① World Cultural Heritage: the Temple and Cemetery of Confucius and the Kong Family Mansion, the Central People's Government of the People's Republic of China,(《世界文化遗产——孔府、孔庙、孔林》,中华人民共和国中央人民政府)http://www.gov.cn/test/2006-03/28/content_238291.htm, 2006 - 03 - 28 13:38。

② Gan Chunsong, Why Do We Go to Qufu? *Guangdong Haifeng*, 2014, Issue 4, p. 91.（干春松:《我们为什么要去曲阜》,《粤海风》2014 年第 4 期,第 91 页）

③ World Cultural Heritage — *San Kong* Scenic Spot in Qufu, *China Tourism News*, March 16,2015.（《世界文化遗产——曲阜三孔景区》,《中国旅游报》2015 年 3 月 16 日）

of culture in China."[1] China is a vast country with five thousand years of history. As the only ancient country whose civilization didn't get interrupted among the four ancient civilizations, China takes the pride in its lasting civilization. Chinese scholars comment that "Confucius sorted out the great achievements of 2500 years before him and opened a new unification of 2500 years after him". Confucianism initiated by Confucius has been shining for thousands of years. Confucius advocated the practice of "Ren" (Benevolence) all his life. Mr. Fei Xiaotong, a famous sociologist in China, once said in his essay "Notes on Thinking in the Cemetery of Confucius", "this time I came to the Confucius Temple, I realized that the study of human beings in Chinese culture and has a long history. Confucius said 'Ren' is the way to deal with the relationship between people and how to get along with each other. The Kong family has been passed to the 76th generation, which shows how long the continuity of Chinese culture is! Why do people want to protect it? Because it represents the most precious thing for the Chinese people, that is, how the Chinese people care about the coexistence of people".[2] Professor Fei's writing expresses the historical and cultural significance of Qufu's *San Kong* in two dimensions. First, the existence of *San Kong* is "important evidence of the sustainable development of Chinese culture in a certain sense. Although historically several cities were invaded by foreign nations and destroyed from the inside, there have been few disputes about Qufu".[3] Second, *San Kong*, as the material carrier of Confucius thought, essentially show the unique features of China's ideological system: Fei emphasizes the spiritual core of "people's getting along with each other" in Confucius thought, and points out the fundamental difference between Confucianism and other beliefs, that is, "Confucianism has always

---

[1] Sun Jianghong, The Combination of Three Confucius Scenic Spots in Qufu and Confucian Culture, *Lantai World*, 2014, No. 7, p. 141. (孙江虹：《曲阜三孔旅游景区与儒家文化的结合方案》,《兰台世界》2014 年第 7 期,第 141 页)

[2] Fei Xiaotong, Notes on Thinking in the Cemetery of Confucius, *Reading*, 1992, No. 9, p. 4. (费孝通：《孔林片思》,《读书》1992 年第 9 期,第 4 页)

[3] Gan Chunsong, Why Do We Go to Qufu? *Guangdong Haifeng*, 2014, No. 4, p. 90. (干春松：《我们为什么要去曲阜》,《粤海风》2014 年第 4 期,第 90 页)

'enlightened people through heavenly principles', and its core is to care about people, the society people live in, but not much about the world after death. Therefore, Mr. Liang Shuming has said that Chinese culture was precocious and soon went out of belief and entered the period of rationalism."[1] That's the reason why in China's history there are no church religions like those in western society.

Confucius, the representative of Chinese culture, still remains a mystery that needs to be explored. Today, we are in an era of "all things are media". *San Kong* in Qufu has become a media symbol to decode the inheritance and acceptance of Confucius' thought. The Confucius Temple maintains the legacy of sages, and the truth of world harmony; the Kong Family Mansion adheres to poetry and rites, and sets a good example for all generations; The Cemetery of Confucius keeps a good example of rites, and honors the late sages for their virtues. Taking the Confucius Temple as an example, Professor Li Jixiang once discussed the location of the Confucius Temple and the origin of its meaning at the world Confucian Congress where he also discussed the earthly significance of the Confucius Temple from two aspects. He points out that the Confucius Temple is a family temple of consanguinity because the descendants of Confucius sacrifice to their ancestors, but also represents "an ancestral temple world of non-consanguinity because of Confucius as the master and ancestor and the domain of Confucianism".[2] The descendants of Confucius are the first kind of worshipers, offering sacrifices to Confucius in the Confucius temples; also Confucius is an educator, so Confucius' disciples offer sacrifices to their ancestors, which form another special cultural etiquette. Confucius compiled "six books" and narrated *the Analects of Confucius*, ranging from governing the country, stabilizing the country and dealing with people. Confucianism is well-

---

[1] Gan Chunsong, Why Do We Go to Qufu? *Guangdong Haifeng*, 2014, No. 4, p. 90. （干春松：《我们为什么要去曲阜》,《粤海风》2014 年第 4 期,第 90 页）

[2] Li Jixiang, Space Location and Significance of "the Temple of Confucius" — Cultural Space, Sacrificial Space, Political and Religious Space, *Proceedings of the Third World Congress of Confucianism*, 2010, p. 459. （李纪祥:《"孔庙"的空间坐落与意义探源——文化空间、祭祀空间、政教空间》,《第三届世界儒学大会学术论文集》2010 年,第 459 页）

established and respected by later generations. In a broad sense, many people, including all Chinese people, are taught by Confucius, and they are all the students of Confucius. Offering sacrifices to Confucius and worshiping Confucius is not limited by the blood connection. As a cultural base, the Confucius Temple breaks through the limitation of blood relationship and national boundaries, and makes the most perfect annotation for the Confucian idea of "unity between man and nature".

The Cemetery of Confucius and the Kong Family Mansion are also realistic specimens for the investigation of the Confucian culture. Duke Yan Sheng, the descendant of the Kong family, abides by the precepts of their ancestors. Up to now, there is a red painted bench in the Kong Family Mansion, which is called "cold bench", also known as "Gelao bench". It is said that Yan Song, a powerful official of the Ming Dynasty, was impeached by the imperial court. In order to protect himself, Yan Song went to Qufu to ask his daughter's father-in-law, Kong Shangxian, who was Duke Yansheng at that time, to intercede with emperor Jiajing for him. Duke Yansheng was not moved. Yan Song sat on the bench outside the door for a day and had to leave bitterly. Accordingly, a cultural relic can be invested with a period of history. There are many such allusions in the Kong Family Mansion. Duke Yansheng has undoubtedly become an excellent practitioner of Confucius' thought, which provides a fresh case for studying Confucianism. So does the Cemetery of Confucius. The pines and cypresses towering overhead, the Cemetery of Confucius is not only a natural landscape, but also the overview of the family concept and the friendship between teachers and students in Confucianism.

Reflection on International Communication of *San Kong* in Qufu

In 1956, UNESCO identified the world's top ten cultural celebrities, with Confucius at the top of the list. *San Kong* in Qufu represent the long history of Chinese culture, and provides a realistic material carrier for world civilization. Therefore, Confucius has not only had a great influence in China, but also been beneficial to the world.

In recent years, China has taken relevant measures to make *San Kong* in Qufu known in the world:

First, the International Confucius Cultural Festival is held in Qufu every year. "The International Confucius Cultural Festival in China (Qufu) is a large-scale international festival to commemorate Confucius, the great thinker, educator and founder of the Confucian school. To some extent, the festival provides the rest of the world with exposure to the excellent traditional Chinese culture, international cooperation and global understanding in culture. So far, it has been successfully held 36 times, which has exerted extensive influence at home and abroad."[1] The International Confucius Cultural Festival is held in Qufu every year, which provides opportunities for foreign scholars and tourists to understand Confucian culture by visiting *San Kong*. In addition, the International Confucius Cultural Festival has been making efforts to become cosmopolitan. "In 1990, the Confucius Cultural Festival and UNESCO jointly set the activities, attracting more attention in the globe. In 2004, the Organizing Committee of the festival sent a delegation to South Korea, Japan and other countries to carry out cultural communication seminars, to increase know the ledge of festival. In 2005 and 2006, the Confucius Cultural Festival held activities both in the mainland of China, Taiwan, and the other areas to globally jointly sacrifice to Confucius. In 2010, the Confucius Culture Festival officially went abroad, when 'the Confucius Week' was held with UNESCO in Paris. So far, the Confucius Cultural Festival has aroused more international attention."[2] Thus, "the Three Confucian Sites" in Qufu have become an important window for the world to better understand Confucian culture.

---

[1] World Cultural Heritage: The Temple and Cemetery of Confucius and the Kong Family Mansion, the Central People's Government of the People's Republic of China, (《世界文化遗产——孔府、孔庙、孔林》,中华人民共和国中央人民政府)http://www.gov.cn/test/2006-03/28/content_238291.htm, 2006 - 03 - 28 13:38.

[2] Feng Chengcheng, Based on the Festival Activities of Qufu City Image Communication Research — Take Qufu International Confucius Culture Festival as an Example, *Journal of News Research*, 2018, No. 1, p. 51. (丰诚诚:《基于节事活动的曲阜城市形象传播研究——以曲阜国际孔子文化节为例》,《新闻研究导刊》2018 年第 1 期,第 51 页)

Second, growing air and high-speed traffic is of great help to tourism in Qufu. In 2008, Qufu airport was built and was fully operational, which is convenient for foreign tourists for visiting Qufu directly by air. The Beijing-Shanghai high-speed railway was officially started in 2008. In 2011, the Beijing-Shanghai high-speed railway was put into operation and passed by Qufu east station. Since then, the journey from Beijing to Qufu only takes two hours by the high-speed railway, and that from Shanghai to Qufu only takes three hours. It turns out that the completion of Qufu airport and the Beijing-Shanghai high-speed railway have brought more tourists to *San Kong* in Qufu.

Third, a tour guide team has been improved to much like in 5A scenic spots. "In August 2011, Qufu was established as one of the three pilot cities of comprehensive reform of the national tour guide management system in Shandong province. Qufu has successively launched such measures like establishing a qualification certification system of 5A level scenic spot announcer for *San Kong*, setting up an annual independent guide trial pilot in Qufu, founding a joint-stock guide company, implementing the guide rating system, the whole process of supervising the fault exit system, etc. These practices have proved effective and won good social response."[1] The establishment of a systematic guide training system for *San Kong* in Qufu benefits the tourist experience, provides tourists with an accurate explanation of history and culture, and promotes the global understanding of Confucianism.

Although the international communication of *San Kong* in Qufu has had results, the popularity of *San Kong* in Qufu still can not match the worldwide "Confucius fever". Its overseas communication remains to be improved.

First, publicity of the International Confucius Cultural Festival needs to be generated. "The Confucius Cultural Festival is held every year in late September, which coincides with National Day Golden Week. When all tourist destinations are competing to attract tourists, the publicity of the

---

[1] Zhang Lingwei, Building a Tour Guide Team Matching with 5A Scenic Spots, *China Tourism News*, January 7, 2013. (张令伟:《打造与5A级景区匹配的导游队伍》,《中国旅游报》2013年1月7日)

Confucius Cultural Festival is relatively insufficient every year."[①] Browsing the relevant reports, we can find that the International Confucius Cultural Festival lacks early publicity, which makes the fact that it is more difficult to convey effectively to foreign tourists. As a result, the Confucius cultural festival only continuously affects people in Shandong or those in Qufu. Accordingly, the relevant departments can deeply explore the connotation of Confucius thought, integrate Confucius thought with contemporary topics, generate topics for the Confucius Culture Festival, and therefore attract Chinese and foreign scholars and tourists to Qufu for discussion with the practicality of solving problems.

Second, full use should be made of the local convenient transportation to achieve in-depth cooperation with the surrounding cultural cities. When foreign tourists visit China, their basic wish is to experience the Chinese culture, which is distinct from their native culture. Confucius, as a symbol of Chinese culture and a landmark figure of world civilization, is attractive for them. *San Kong* in Qufu can make the best of cultural aspects to build up cooperation with the Forbidden City in Beijing, Baotou Spring in Jinan, Mount Tai in Taian and other historical and cultural attractions, carrying out theme tourism activities such as "Chinese culture tracing", so as to take advantage of the popularity of other attractions to promote international communication of *San Kong* in Qufu.

Third, to actively advance cooperation with overseas Confucius Institutes. On the one hand, Confucius Institutes are a platform for foreign students to understand Chinese culture, where their study should not be limited to books and traditional classrooms. Visiting the Temple and Cemetery of Confucius and the Kong Family Mansion is a great opportunity and a vivid lesson for them to understand Chinese culture, so that they can experience the continuous development of Confucianism on the spot. On the

---

① Feng Chengcheng, Based on the Festival Activities of Qufu City Image Communication Research — Take Qufu International Confucius Culture Festival as an Example, *Journal of News Research*, 2018, No. 1, p. 51. (丰诚诚:《基于节事活动的曲阜城市形象传播研究——以曲阜国际孔子文化节为例》,《新闻研究导刊》2018 年第 1 期,第 51 页)

other hand, with the internationalization of *San Kong* in Qufu constantly strengthened, "the demand for foreign language talents and high-end tourism talents is very urgent. Furthermore, Qufu will improve the talent training and introduction mechanism to provide intellectual support for Qufu's tourism development". [1]

Fourth, making films and TV programs about Confucius and *San Kong*. Against the backdrop of high informationization, film and television has become an effective medium for mass communication. The overseas spread of palace drama has prompted a group of overseas tourists to visit the living places of emperor and concubines in the Forbidden City. Compared with the programs about the Forbidden City, the number of films and TV programs about Confucius or *San Kong* in Qufu are obviously insufficient. The international communication of *San Kong* in Qufu can be done along film and TV communication: on the one hand, we can "directly introduce *San Kong* through TV documentary programs", On the other hand, we can "directly or indirectly offer plot products". [2] The combination of cultural heritage and TV media provides overseas audiences with a multi-sensory understanding of cultural heritage, which helps to attract more people to visit *San Kong* in Qufu and explore the footprints of sages.

Conclusion

In 1988, the winner of the Nobel Prize in physics, Hannes Alvin, once said, "if mankind is to survive it must go back 25 centuries in time to tap the wisdom of Confucius." *San Kong* in Qufu opens a direct and effective window to understand Confucius' thought, which is of great practical significance for mankind to create a new situation of inclusive and multicultural civilization in the 21st century. The overseas communication effectiveness of *San Kong* in

---

[1] Zhang Lingwei, Building a Tour Guide Team Matching with 5A Scenic Spots, *China Tourism News*, January 7, 2013. (张令伟:《打造与 5A 级景区匹配的导游队伍》,《中国旅游报》2013 年 1 月 7 日)

[2] Lu Leping, An Introduction to Film and Television Intercultural Communication, Beijing: China Radio Film and TV Press, 2016 edition, pp. 68 – 69. (吕乐平:《影视跨文化传播导论》,北京:中国广播电视出版社 2016 年版,第 68—69 页)

Qufu still has a long way to go. It needs to adapt to modernization, optimize communication and promote itself to be internationally.

(Beijing International Studies University)

The Eastern Aesthetic Meanings of Film Posters Designed by HUANG Hai

Wu Yanru

The series of posters designed for the 2014 film *The Golden Era* directed by XU Anhua has attracted widespread interest and good reviews. From then on, HUANG Hai's popularity and personal branding in the field of film poster design is rapidly increasing. His work brings the aesthetic criticism of film posters within the audience's evaluation of the film. These posters bring a real gain to the promotion of the film with their inspiring visual design. In addition to designing posters for popular Chinese films of different genres such as *Masters in Forbidden City*, *Monk Comes Down the Mountain*, *Big Fish & Begonia*, *Shadow* and *Ash Is Purest White*, HUANG Hai's designs have also been favored by overseas film companies. He has designed Chinese versions for Japanese, European and American films such as *Stand by Me Doraemon*, *Tonari no My Neighbor Totoro*, *Shoplifters*, *Chappie* and *Resident Evil: The Final Chapter* posters. HUANG Hai's film posters, no matter what genre, theme or region they are made for, all reflect traditional Chinese culture to a greater or lesser extent, and contain an oriental aesthetic interest.

"Good morals make people forget the defects of appearance." — the beauty of the spirit

Chuang-Tzu tells the story of Shan-thu Kia, Shu-shan the Toeless and Ai-thai Tho, who, despite their ugly appearances and even disabilities, were respected, loved and followed because of their virtues. They were so virtuous that the Duke of Wei-Ling and the Duke of Qi-Huan looked at those who were able-bodied, but found them unattractive. As the saying goes, "Good morals make people forget the defects of appearance", and people "do not love their appearances, but love the thing what makes their appearances", the good morals.[①] Through these parables, Chuang-Tzu demonstrates the aesthetic concept that beauty beyond appearances is higher than the form itself. He celebrates the beauty of the spiritual personality that transcends the appearances. While traditional Chinese aesthetics does not ignore the beauty of appearances, it attaches greater importance to and pursues spiritual beauty.

As an aesthetic object, the cast of actors and actresses and the image of the stars are appearances of films. These are the most superficial and appealing parts of the external form. Therefore, film poster designers often arrange the characters in the frame in order of importance and the popularity of the actors. The image of the actor is the primary visual element of these posters, occupying the central spaces of the posters. HUANG Hai, however, does not use the stars as the main expression of the poster, which is a distinctive feature that sets his film posters apart from other film poster designs.

Fig. 1

Within the external "appearance", the storyline and spiritual connotation are "the things what make their forms" of the films. These are the things determine whether a film is good or not. HUANG Hai points directly to this core, and always uphold the concept of serving this core. For example, in the poster designed for *Mulan*, which was released in 2009 (Fig. 1), the only main visual elements in the picture are the symbolic helmet representing a warrior and the symbolic red lips representing a woman. These sketch the female heroic image of Mulan. The

---

① Chuang-Tzu, *Teh Khung Fu*. (庄子:《德充符》)

rest of the character's face is completely omitted, thus effectively avoiding the visual and psychological distraction of the actor's appearance and helping the audience to focus entirely on the narrative of the film. The omission of the face also creates a sense of mystery, leaving the audience with plenty of space for reflection, including imagining the actress' appearance, the costumes, the props, and the fate of the character. This subtle and restrained design not only resonates with Chinese audiences, but also allows people from different cultural contexts to understand the film's themes accurately through this poster. The poster one of the most impressive and evocative of the various versions of the poster. Poster design that celebrates the beauty of the spirit has an appeal that blurs the boundaries of time and space.

"Who knows true beauty?" — the beauty of the relativity

"All the people regarded Mao Qiang and Li Ji as beauties, but if fish encountered one of them, they would dive deep; if birds met one of them, they would fly away; if deer met one of them, they would scatter. Among these four, who knows true beauty?"[1] The very different responses of humans and animals when confronted with the same aesthetic object are due to the different aesthetic experiences of the subjects. "Their likes and dislikes are therefore different."[2] What people consider beautiful does not evoke the empathy of animals. Through this little story, Chuang Tsu makes it clear that beauty is relative and conditional. The film posters designed by HUANG Hai pay special attention to the specific cultural context of different regions and respect the aesthetic habits of the audience. For the promotion of the same film in different countries and regions, he uses differentiated visual design to help audiences understand and accept the theme of the film. His designs incorporate the culture of the Other into his own design system while retaining the traditional Chinese aesthetic. This is a positive innovation to the tradition and promotes films to the global market.

---

[1] Chuang-Tzu, *Khi Wu Lun*. (庄子:《齐物论》)
[2] Chuang-Tzu, *Kih Lo*. (庄子:《至乐》)

The posters for the film *The Golden Era* respect and reflect the law of relativity of beauty. For example, the posters for both the American and French versions use the identity of the film's heroine XIAO Hong as a writer as a creative point. However, he has designed two posters in very different styles, based on the different visual experiences and aesthetic preferences of audiences in the two countries. The main image on the US poster (Fig. 2) is a golden pen nib, in which the small figure of the heroine stands alone against a blossoming wintersweet. This accurately conveying the film's imagery — a golden soul sharpened by hardship. The contrast between light and dark is very strong and the edges of the graphics are well defined, reflecting the American style of modern graphic art. The French version of the poster (Fig. 3) is inspired by Marguerite Duras, a modern novelist familiar to French audiences. The center of the picture is a partial profile of the heroine. The drifting fate and the tenacity of the literati are expressed by the cigarette in the left hand and the pen in the right. With this pair of simple, powerful, contradictory and imaginative symbols, the main idea of the film is mapped out. The overall tone is romantic and soft, bringing the film closer to the audience on a psychological level. Drawing on the deep impression that actress TANG Wei made on Korean audiences in the film *Late Autumn*, the Korean version of the poster (Fig. 4) features a close-up of the heroine's tearful face as the main graphic. At the same time, it also captures the aesthetic characteristic of "hate" in Korean culture — the emotion of sorrow without sadness. Emotions are more uplifting and tougher because of sorrow. The character and fate of the film's heroine coincide with this.

"Expressing nihility with reality, Transforming scenery into emotions." — the beauty of the nihility and reality

The relationship between nihility and reality is a classic issue of traditional Chinese cosmology. When this cosmic concept is mapped onto aesthetic pursuits, Chinese art pays special attention to the combination of nihility and reality as a way to reflect the vitality and infinity of life. In a work of art, the image created by the artist is the "reality", what causes our

Fig. 2 　　　　　　　　　　　Fig. 3 　　　　　　　　　　　Fig. 4

imagination is the "nihility", and the imaginary realm generated by the image is the combination of the nihility and reality.① "Expressing nihility with reality, Transforming scenery into emotions."② "Nihility and reality support each other, and spaces without painting become wonderful places."③ In order to create a meaningful and long-lasting picture space, HUANG Hai's design also pays special attention to the combination of nihility and reality. This is manifested in the following two levels.

The first level is the nihility and reality in pictures. Chinese painting emphasizes "black as white" and has always focused on the creation and use of blank space. HUANG Hai's design also attaches importance to the handling of blank space. For example, in Figure 1 Mulan's face is blank. In Figure 2, the blank space in the nib outlines the figure's shape. The large black space in Figure 3 and the silhouette of the figure in Figure 4 both make effective use of the blank space in the pictures. The blank space enriches the content of the picture and increases the depth of space. HUANG Hai's restraint in the use of visual elements shows the restrained and subtle oriental aesthetic interest. If Rubin's vase is an elaborate visual game, HUANG Hai's

---

① ZONG Baihua, *Strolling in Aesthetics*, Shanghai: Shanghai People's Publishing House, 1981, p. 39. （宗白华：《美学散步》. 上海：上海人民出版社 1981 年版, 第 39 页）
② FAN Xiwen, *Night talk*. （范曦文：《对床夜语》）
③ DA Chongguang, *Painting the Quan*. （笪重光：《画筌》）

work, which inherits the concept of Chinese aesthetics of nihility and reality, pushes the film poster from the level of visual beauty to a higher level of spiritual beauty with the use of blank space.

The second level is the nihility and reality of the picture and the spirit. Facing the film posters designed by HUANG Hai, the audience's eyes either focus or wander to the blank space of these posters, the combination of nihility and reality triggers the audience's imagination and thoughts. The emotions that are not directly expressed in the picture are sprung up, constructed and completed in the viewer's heart and mind. The blank space is transformed into a living matrix that can generate thousands of images, making it more informative and meaningful. The image of the poster is the reality, and the spiritual travel triggered by it is the nihility, this is what happens, "expressing nihility with reality, transforming scenery into emotions." This nihility though not visible, but touches the core of the spirit of the film conveyed by the poster, this is true. The blankness of the picture symbolizes the hidden and infinite possibilities, with endless vitality. As Lao-Tzu said, "Being and Not-being grow out of one another" and "It is empty, but gives a supply that never fails".[①]

"Change occurs when *gang* and *rou* interact." — the beauty of the movement

In *Book of Changes*, the world is created, moves and changes under the interaction of two fundamental forces, *yin* and *yang*. *Yin* is *rou*, it is soft and flexible. *Yang* is *gang*, it is hard and firm. "*Gang* and *rou* are the basics," "Change occurs when *gang* and *rou* interact"[②]. Lao-Tzu recognized the dynamic process of interdependence and transformation between the prevailing opposites in nature and society, and searched for the unchanging "Tao" from the movement. Chuang Tsu believed that the whole world was in a state of change, "that the shadowy and still is without bodily form; that

---

① Lao-Tsz, *Tao Te Ching*. (老子:《道德经》)
② *Book of Changes*. (《周易》)

change and transformation are ever proceeding, but incapable of being determined."[①] Under this philosophical concept, Chinese aesthetics particularly pursues the beauty of movement that embodies momentum, rhythm, and power. Among the various styling elements, traditional Chinese visual art is characterized by the use of lines. Such aesthetic thought is reflected in HUANG Hai's film poster design. Through the interweaving, contrast and rhythm of the power between various visual elements, the picture achieves the artistic realm of stillness in motion, stillness in movement, combination of motion and stillness, a realm of infinite variation.

Lines are applied to both the French and Korean posters of *The Golden Era*. The misty blue smoke on the upper right of the French poster (Fig. 3) is the only lightsome part of the whole picture, resembling the image of a dancing woman. The lines are flexible and elegant, like a soft and romantic melody in the heroine's strong spiritual world. They broke through the dullness of dark tones, increased the rhythm and layering of the picture, and created a cold, empty and silent oriental aesthetic with long after-effects. In the Korean version of the poster (Fig. 4), the silhouette of the character is the only neat, sure line in the whole picture, contrasting in strength with the other visual elements. This contrast shows the heroine's consistent determination in the torrent of the times. It enhances the tension of the picture and increases the breadth and depth of the content. The use of lines in these two posters is exactly the opposite, dynamic and static, blurry and clear, soft and rigid. However, whether it is embellished with flexible lines or affirmed by lines with clear edges, it is rich in the inherent infinite power generated by the interaction between *gang* and *rou*. Dynamic imagination is produced in a static two-dimensional space, guiding the audience into the world of the heroine's background, destiny and visual imagery. In the interaction of the power of visual elements, the poster also meets the requirements of the guiding principles of traditional Chinese art: "rhythmic vitality" and "anatomical structure".[②] It shows the beauty of change and

---

[①] Chuang-Tzu, *Thien Hsia*. (庄子:《天下》)
[②] XIE He, *Hua Pin*. (谢赫:《古画品录》)

movement brought about by interaction between *gang* and *rou*.

"Heaven, earth, and I were produced together, and all things and I are one." — the beauty of the infinity

"A dream on the pillow can reach a thousand miles away, and from the window you can peer into a thousand homes."[1] The Chinese see the infinite in the finite, and in the visual art, they seek to express the infinite realm in the limited picture space. "It is the Tao that overspreads and sustains all things. How great It is in Its overflowing influence!"[2] Chuang-Tzu and his followers repeatedly pointed out that beauty is infinite, and the highest beauty encompasses the entire universe and is extremely vast.[3] In the face of infinity, any finite and relative things are flawed. Chuang-Tzu praises the East Sea, "it is that no change is produced in its waters by any cause operating for a short time or a long, and that they do not advance nor recede for any addition or subtraction, whether great or small".[4] This is the eternal and infinite beauty. HUANG Hai's poster design works embody the pursuit of infinite beauty and convey the oriental aesthetic spiritual experience to the audience. His designs push the limited beauty that can be expressed visually to the infinite beauty that can be reached spiritually.

The Chinese pursuit of infinite beauty extends to the entire universe. "Heaven, Earth, and I were produced together, and all things and I are one."[5] The poster of *Monk Comes Down the Mountain* (Fig. 5) features a *Ping-Yuan*[6] perspective, one perspective of GUO Xi's "three distances"[7] theory. At the feet of the young monk is a large mountain, above him is the

---

[1] WANG Wei, *Looking Far Away and Thinking of Home on the West Tower*. (王维:《和使君五郎西楼望远思归》)

[2] Chuang-Tzu, *Thien Ti*. (庄子:《天地》)

[3] LI Zehou & LIU Gangji, *History of Chinese Aesthetics*, vol. 1, Beijing: China Social Sciences Press, 1984, p. 252. (李泽厚、刘纲纪:《中国美学史》(第一卷),北京:中国社会科学出版社 1984 年,第 252 页)

[4] Chuang-Tzu, *Khiu Shui*. (庄子:《秋水》)

[5] Chuang-Tzu, *Khi Wu Lun*. (庄子:《齐物论》)

[6] Like a one-point perspective, but from very far away.

[7] GUO Xi, *The Elegance of The Bamboo and Spring*. (郭熙:《林泉高致》)

dark clouds, in which he is as small as a grain of sand between heaven and earth, the lonely realm of the scenery forms a rich universe of its own. The contrast between the small character and the vast world is sharp, so the complex feelings of the young monk on his first trip down the mountain are conveyed. It triggered the audience to observe, understand and think about life.① The Chinese version of the poster for Hayao Miyazaki's animated film *My Neighbor Totoro* (Fig. 6) uses a top view. The children are playing on Totoro's belly, like running in the boundless wheat field blown by the breeze. The visual triggers a tactile association that transmits warmth to the audience's heart. This observing perspective is a perspective that draws the audience away from mundane things and treats life with love. The audience also observes themselves from this unique perspective, feeling faith, salvation and tranquility. Japanese netizens commented on this poster, "Is it because China is vast? The nature from the Chinese perspective seems to hide a longing for a secret realm." This secret realm is just the pure aesthetic realm that transcends the distinction between things and self-opened by the pursuit of infinite beauty.

Fig. 5   Fig. 6

---

① HU Jiayin, *Dian Jing*: *The Important Formal Language of Huanghai's Film Poster Design*. In: *Movie Review*, 2017(21), pp. 107-109. (胡佳音:《点景:黄海电影海报设计的重要形式语言》,《电影评介》2017 年第 21 期,第 107—109 页)

Conclusion

The primary purpose and task of film posters is to express the film. HUANG Hai always start from the spiritual core of the film, and express the story content and spiritual connotation of the film with changeable design styles and original design creativity. Rooted in the soil of Chinese culture, HUANG Hai's design has always been imprinted with Chinese culture and oriental aesthetics while adopting modern design techniques and design language. The choice of visual element symbols reflects the admiration of spiritual beauty. He expresses respect for relative beauty in different versions designed for different audiences. In the blank space, the beauty of virtual and reality is created, and the beauty of movement is expressed in the contrast of dynamic and static changes, gang and rou, and finally reaches the realm of infinite beauty. The visual expression with great oriental aesthetics makes HUANG Hai's works always touch the delicate inner world of the audience, and achieve the perfect balance and integration of nationality, artistry and modernity.

(Shanghai University)

The Artistic Conception of the Literati's Leisure Life Reflected on Longquan Celadon in the Song Dynasty
— Take the Tripod Censer (*lilu*) from Longquan Kiln in Southern Song Dynasty as an Example

Yu Qin

Longquan began to produce porcelain in the late Tang Dynasty, developed its producing scale in the mid-Northern Song Dynasty, and matured its industry in the mid-Southern Song Dynasty and finally established its last celadon production system in the history of Chinese ceramics. It earned its unique style of its outstanding glaze color, shape and little decoration.

In the above-mentioned evolution, consumers of Longquan celadon expanded from ordinary people to officials and nobles. Finally, the celadon became one of the imperial wares. This article takes the tripod censer (*lilu*) from Longquan kiln in the Southern Song Dynasty (Fig. 1), which is currently in the Deqing Museum, as an example. By analyzing its path to be appreciated by the upper class represented by the literati of the Song Dynasty and integrate into their life, it provides clues for exploring the roles of Longquan celadon in the artistic conception of the leisure life of the literati in

Fig. 1　Longquan *lilu*, Southern Song Dynasty

Height 6.2 cm, Caliber 8.8 cm
Deqing Museum
Li Huibing ed.. *The Complete Works of Chinese Ceramics (Volume VIII) Song (Part II)*. Shanghai: Shanghai People's Fine Arts Publishing House, 1999, p. 121 and 264. ［李辉柄主编:《中国陶瓷全集》第 8 卷,宋(下),上海:上海人民美术出版社 1999 年版,第 121、264 页］

the Song Dynasty.

The Founding of the Concept of the Literati of Song Dynasty Under Neo-Confucianism

The Song Dynasty was established by force. It eliminated its internal hidden dangers with the strategy of deprivation of military power (*Bei Jiu Shi Bing Quan*). Besides reconstructing the ritual system and establishing an authoritative national system, it still required a support system of culture and education. Therefore, the emperors kept valuing civility over military because only the system of knowledge, ideology and belief expressed by the intellectual class could effectively construct the political and ethical order[1]. In this process of rebuilding the ideological world, a basic political structure that the emperor and the literati "governed the country together" was formed due to the power struggles between "governor" and "scholar". Then Neo-Confucianism arose.

Without the binding from the old ideological order with the changes and turbulences during the Five Dynasties and Ten Kingdoms, the literati in the Song Dynasty reflected the validity of knowledge, ideology and belief in order to establish the identity and rationality of the ideological order. And they gradually re-established a whole set of conceptual system about "*Dao*", "*Li*" (exploring the law of nature) and "*Xin*" (self-reflection), "*Xing*" (the internal temperament of human being).[2] By the time of Zhu Xi in the Southern Song Dynasty, Neo-Confucianism was formed after inheriting the achievements of predecessors (especially the Cheng Yi system). It also was compatible with Buddhism and Taoism.

Everything is reasonable. The so-called "*Li*" or principle is a universal truth that transcends individuals, power, and regions, and has the characteristics of universalization. As far as "*Li*" is concerned, firstly, there

---

[1] Ge Zhaoguang. *The History of Chinese Thoughts* (*Volume II*). Shanghai: Fudan University Press, 2019, p. 154. [葛兆光:《中国思想史》(三卷本)第二卷,上海:复旦大学出版社 2019 年版,第 154 页]
[2] Ge Zhaoguang. *The History of Chinese Thoughts* (*Volume II*). Shanghai: Fudan University Press, 2019, p. 186. [葛兆光:《中国思想史》(三卷本)第二卷,上海:复旦大学出版社 2019 年版,第 186 页]

is one *Li* (universal principle), which exists in diverse forms (*Li Yi Fen Shu*). It means to make it clear that there is a fundamental in the universe. For Neo-Confucianists, the "*Li*" is the rules of the universe and should be treated with a "sincere" attitude. The so-called sincerity is true and innocent and it is the nature of the rules of the universe.[①] For second, study the truth (*Ge Wu Qiong Li*) which is the way to experience and grasp the "*Li*". *Ge*, the most, that is to be able to understand matters anytime and anywhere. What objectively exists is what we are required to understand its law. Explore the truth and be fully understood.[②] That is to say, by observing, speculating, analyzing and contemplating the world, human may comprehend the truth of the changes with his intellectuality and rationality. In fact, there are various ways of acquiring knowledge and ideas. And self-reflection to rectify one's mind and keep sincerity (*Zheng Xin Cheng Yi*) is the psychological presupposition of respectfully following the law and the result of understanding and studying what one experienced.[③] Only the one learns the principles of nature, follows the laws of nature, then he may be called sincere.[④] In this way, the universe and humanity have achieved the unity of "sincerity". The final stage is to thoroughly explore the truth and completely understand human nature (*Qiong Li Jin Xing*), for the goodness of human nature comes from following the law. For only one truth in the universe, that

---

[①] Zhu Xi. *Collected Notes on Aphorisms of Four Confucian Classics*. Beijng: Zhonghua Book Company, 1983, p. 31. 〔〔宋〕朱熹撰:《四书章句集注》,北京:中华书局 1983 年版,第 31 页〕

[②] Zhu Xi. *Collected Notes on Aphorisms of Four Confucian Classics*. Beijng: Zhonghua Book Company, 1983, p. 4. 〔〔宋〕朱熹撰:《四书章句集注》,北京:中华书局 1983 年版,第 4 页〕

[③] *Da Xue Zhang Ju* (The Aphorisms of *the Great Learning*) said: "The ancients, who wished to promote illustrious virtue under heaven, first had to rule their own states well. Wishing to govern their states well, they first had to manage their family well. Wishing to manage their family well, they first had to cultivate themselves. Wishing to cultivate themselves, they first had to rectify their mind. Wishing to rectify their mind, they first had to make their thoughts sincere. Wishing to make their thoughts sincere, they first had to acquire knowledge. And the way to acquire knowledge is to understand and study what they experienced." See Zhu Xi. *Collected Notes on Aphorisms of Four Confucian Classics*. Beijng: Zhonghua Book Company, 1983, pp. 3 - 4. 〔〔宋〕朱熹撰:《四书章句集注》,北京:中华书局 1983 年版,第 3—4 页〕

[④] Zhu Xi. *Collected Notes on Aphorisms of Four Confucian Classics*. Beijng: Zhonghua Book Company, 1983, p. 31. 〔〔宋〕朱熹撰:《四书章句集注》,北京:中华书局 1983 年版,第 31 页〕

is the internal temperament of human being.① As the form of *Dao*, temperament depends on the mind of self-reflection. Therefore, the meaning of the so-called "*Qiong Li Jin Xing*" seems to experience and explore the "truth" of the nature, so as to highlight the true "temperament" of human beings. And the ultimate goal of "*Ge Wu Qiong Li*" becomes the search for inner nature.② The above result is to focus on the inherent moral ethics.

In summary, under such a background of Neo-Confucianism, the literati in Song Dynasty blended the ultimate truth of the universe with the nature of the mind, which was from "the universe" to "humanity", and used the obtained "truth" to guide their lives and establish the order. With an attitude of "sincerity", an idea of internal transcendence was generated on the basis of the Confucian traditional thoughts. Through the recognition of the more internal "temperament" of human beings, the moral origin was highlighted in introspection and self-cultivation. In the end, the meaning of individual life was completed.

The Construction of the Artistic Style of Longquan Celadon under the Influence of Neo-Confucianism

Bernard Bosanquet considers that art is more than nature. The definite presentation of ideas is in beautiful shape.③ The highest beauty, whether of nature or of art, is judged by the consensus, not of average feeling as such, but rather of the tendency of human feeling in proportion as it is developed by education and experience.④ As the intellectual class in the Song Dynasty, the literati generally adhered to the concept of "administering the country with all sincerity, and establishing the value of their own lives" when they

---

① Huang Shiyi ed., Xu Shiyi and Yang Yan conflate. *The Conflation on Conversations of Master Zhu Xi* (*Volume I*). Shanghai: Shanghai Guji Press, 2016, p. 82. ［〔宋〕黄士毅编,徐时仪、杨艳汇校:《朱子语类汇校》(全十册)第一册,上海:上海古籍出版社 2016 年版,第 82 页］

② Ge Zhaoguang. *The History of Chinese Thoughts* (*Volume II*). Shanghai: Fudan University Press, 2019, p. 183. ［葛兆光:《中国思想史》(三卷本)第二卷,上海:复旦大学出版社 2019 年版,第 183 页］

③ Bernard Bosanquet, M. A.. *A History of Aesthetic*. London: George Allen & Unwin Ltd. 1917, p. 11.

④ Bernard Bosanquet, M. A.. *A History of Aesthetic*. London: George Allen & Unwin Ltd. 1917, p. 7.

followed the thought of "*Li*" (exploring the law of nature) in pursuing their academic studies. Therefore, in a general sense, they were inclined to "valuing the truth and advocating elegance" (*Zhong Dao Shang Ya*), which became the aesthetic consciousness and standard of beauty throughout the entire era they lived. On the one hand, "*Dao*", which is based on ethics and morality, attaches great importance to the exploration of ontological temperament. As the core of the cultural spirit of the Song Dynasty, its external representation was the beauty of order and stability. On the other hand, "*Ya*" is righteousness, which means "elegance", "noble" and "virtue"[1]. In addition, the culture based on seeking truth means a purely elegant life[2]. Therefore, the scholar-officials' pursuit of "*Ya*" was manifested in their love for plain and subtle beauty.

With the popularization of various educational undertakings in Song Dynasty, the principles established by Neo-Confucianism and the aesthetic value of the literati in the context of Neo-Confucianism penetrated into the entire society. In other words, the masses were imperceptibly influenced by the idea of "*Ge Wu Qiong Li*" of Neo-Confucianism, so that they consciously abided in their behaviors and production. Under the impetus of the developed urban economy, the articles they made unconsciously catered to the forms of beauty under the aesthetic value of "valuing the truth and advocating elegance". The same as Longquan celadon, it had been observing and absorbing the advantages of other famous kilns to improve its products in its development process, and initiated the artistic style of "elegance, simplicity, and slenderness". The "*lilu*" (tripod censer) case in this article serves as its concrete example.

Reviewing the porcelain-making of Longquan celadon during the two Song dynasties (the Northern Song and the Southern Song), it is evident that

---

[1] Guo Xuexin. *A Study on Scholar-Bureaucrats' Group Consciousness in Song Dynasty*. Beijing: China Social Sciences Press, 2017, p. 168. (郭学信:《宋代士大夫群体意识研究》,北京:中国社会科学出版社 2017 年版,第 168 页)

[2] Zhao Yuqiang. *Leisure Philosophy: The Leisure Culture of Scholar-Bureaucrats in Song Dynasty and Its Implication*. Shanghai: Shanghai Guji Press, 2017, pp. 70 – 71. (赵玉强:《优游之道:宋代士大夫休闲文化及其意蕴》,上海:上海古籍出版社 2017 年版,第 70—71 页)

the Longquan kiln began to launch its production scale in the mid-Northern Song Dynasty, influenced by the surrounding kilns such as *Yue* kiln, *Ou* kiln, and *Wuzhou* kiln. But it had not yet formed its own artistic style. Excluding the light greenish glaze, its shape, decoration and firing techniques were similar to those of *Yue* kiln and even *Ou* kiln etc. in the same period. [1] During the transitional period of the two Song dynasties or the early Southern Song Dynasty, the national political, economic and cultural center moved to the south. The technologies of famous kilns such as *Ru* kiln and *Ding* kiln in the north were introduced to the south with the migration of population. Meanwhile Longquan kiln once again absorbed the firing techniques of *Ru* kiln and *Guan* kiln, and improved the formula of the clay by adding a proper amount of *Zi Jin* clay in the porcelain clay. It increased the bending resistance of the body, and the utensils were not easily deformed at high temperature. [2] This laid an important foundation for the formation of Longquan celadon's unique artistic style, and aroused the literati's interest.

The case of "*lilu*" in this article shows the major changes and improvements in the shape design, glazing method, and decorative art after changing of the quality of porcelain body.

Firstly, since the deformation of vessels at high temperature became rare, the feet, abdomen and other parts of Longquan celadon could be trimmed symmetrically. Then their overall shape successfully overcame the bulky and thick characteristic, and adapted to the aesthetic needs of different groups in terms of shaping. The court had a special interest in being able to claim expertise in ancient rituals and music, since such knowledge had a powerful legitimizing effect and aura. The possession and preservation of ancient bronze vessels was a key means by which such knowledge was

---

[1] Shen Yueming. Longquan Ceramics in the Northern Song Dynasty//Shen Yueming and Zheng Jianming ed.. *Longquan Kiln in the Northern Song Dynasty*. Beijing: Cultural Relics Press, 2018, pp. 2–7. (沈岳明:《北宋时期的龙泉窑业》,载沈岳明、郑建明主编《北宋龙泉窑纵论》,北京:文物出版社 2018 年版,第 2—7 页）

[2] Shen Yueming. Thick Glaze Technology of Longquan Kiln and Firing of Celadon Porcelain. *Palace Museum Journal*. 2020, Issue 5, pp. 16–17. (沈岳明:《龙泉窑厚釉技术和粉青釉瓷器的烧造》,《故宫博物院院刊》2020 年第 5 期,第 16—17 页）

acquired.[1] At that time, the retro style was prevalent in the entire society. Most scholar-officials liked to collect bronzes, steles, paintings, calligraphy etc. Especially, Song Huizong ordered Wang Fu to compile *Xuanhe Bo Gu Tu* (A Collection of Ancient Bronze Wares). The *lilu* in the article was fired according to the standard style of the *Zhou Bo Nü Li* (Fig. 2) in *Xuanhe Bo Gu Tu* for the court and scholar-officials. But it was not a simple imitation of the style. In the Song Dynasty, the *li* was not only a sacrificial utensil, also its shape was imitated to make into one of the supplies in the literati's study-*lilu*. Besides the solemnity of the sacrificial ceremony, the aesthetic interest of the literati had to put in consideration for the design of its shape. Hippolyte Adolphe Taine considers that the nature of material civilization and spiritual civilization depends on the three major factors: race, environment, and era.[2] Therefore, the most direct way to understand the aesthetic interest of the literati is to observe, speculate, and analyze other art categories in the same period such as painting and calligraphy. As the essential part of the scholar-officials' lives, painting and calligraphy were the most direct manifestation of the superb beauty under the aesthetic value of "valuing the truth and advocating elegance". Among them, the landscape paintings, flowers and birds in the Song Dynasty tended to pursue a calm and quiet artistic conception. The artistic expression in figure

Fig. 2　Zhou Bo Nü Li

Wang Fu ed., Bo Ruzhai revise. *Xuanhe Bo Gu Tu Lu* (Volume XIX). Ming Wanli 1603.（王黼编：《泊如斋重修》，《宣和博古图录》卷第十九，明万历1603年本）

---

[1] Ronald Egan. *The Problem of Beauty: Aesthetic Thought and Pursuits in Northern Song Dynasty China*. Cambridge (Massachusetts) and London: Harvard University Press. 2006, pp. 13–14.

[2] Hippolyte Adolphe Taine. *The Philosophy of Art*. Fu Lei translate. Beijing: SDX Joint Publishing Company, 2016, p. 3. （[法]丹纳：《艺术哲学》，傅雷译，北京：生活・读书・新知三联书店 2016 年版，第 3 页）

painting and calligraphy tended to be delicate and elegant. In summary, there are two major improvements in the shape design of the *lilu*: For one thing, the more slender neck makes the *lilu* look upright and straight. For another, the application of triangular breast feet makes a bit of curve and straight changes from the rounded style of *Zhou Bo Nü Li*'s feet. As a result, an artistic style in a elegant, slender, stable but round form order was constructed.

Secondly, the greenish glaze of this *lilu* looks soft, which is the typical thick glaze in Longquan celadon. It marks the ultimate beauty of the celadon glaze. This kind of porcelain with a rich glaze layer generally requires multiple sintering at low temperature and multiple glazing.[①] Without the binary clay formula to lay a suitable foundation for the thickness of the body and the firing state, only the improvement of the glaze cannot achieve the effect of thick glaze without fluid. From an aesthetic view, Longquan celadon has been committed to reforming and highlighting the appearance of "green", which is a manifestation of the unremitting pursuit of the beauty of nature. Since the ancient times, the Chinese have admired the nature. In the Song Dynasty, the unity of the "sincerity" between the universe and humanity was fulfilled by "*Li Yi Fen Shu*" and "*Ge Wu Qiong Li*" under the idea of "*Li*", which was the realm of the harmony of nature and man. Then in this way they treated the ultimate "truth" they pursued. With the popularization of education, the overall improvement of the cultural quality and comprehensive skills of the craftsmen in Longquan kiln had made their creation subtly affected by this thought. So they carefully observed the characteristics of various greenish beauty in nature, and explored the essence of their eternal beauty. The process of continuous firing trials reflects "emphasizing truth".

Finally, this *lilu* looks smooth. Only the turning parts are decorated with protruding lines (*chu jin*). This technique embodies the skill and wisdom of craftsmen in Longquan kiln. Because of the characteristics of the thick glaze and thin body of Longquan celadon in the mature period, the

---

① A Brief History of Longquan Celadon//Zhu Boqian. *Lan Cui Ji*: *Zhu Boqian Ceramic Archaeological Collection*. Beijing: Science Press, 2009, p. 157. (《龙泉青瓷简史》,载朱伯谦《揽翠集: 朱伯谦陶瓷考古文集》,北京: 科学出版社 2009 年版,第 157 页)

carving decoration used in the thin glaze and thick body has become no longer suitable: it is easy to be hidden under the thick glaze and cannot be highlighted. Then, there is almost no decoration on Longquan celadon in the mature period of the Southern Song Dynasty, so it looks bloated. After trying its firing technique, the artisans finally adopted the protruding lines decoration to stick out triangular clay on the round shoulders and the front of the three breast feet so that the round shape produced the visual sense of angle. In this way, the thick glaze on the surface of the incense burner and the whiteness on the protruding part make a color change because of the "chu jin" decoration.[1] Such initiates the artistic style of *lilu* clear but not simple.

In general, the shape, glaze color and decoration of Longquan *lilu* of the Southern Song Dynasty in this article have achieved a harmonious and perfect unity. As a typical piece of Longquan celadon in the mature period, it had been influenced by the Neo-Confucianism represented by "*Ge Wu Qiong Li*" in both craftsmanship and design. At the same time, it was portrayed as a work of art in the style of "elegance, simplicity, and slenderness" due to the aesthetic value guidance of scholar-officials' "valuing the truth and advocating elegance" and the artistic style of other art categories in the same period as the frame of reference. So it became the scholar-officials' favourite.

The Symbol of Moral Ideas of Longquan Celadon in the Context of Neo-Confucianism

In *Yu Lu Zijing Shu* (The Collection of Discussions with Lu Zijing), Zhu Xi said: "Everything that has shape and form is an instrument (*Qi*). That constitutes the principle of this instrument is *Dao*."[2] In other words,

---

[1] Lei Guoqiang and Li Zhen. The Appreciation and Research of Longquan censer in Southern Song Dynasty (Volume II). *Oriental Collection*. 2015, Issue 2, p. 58. (雷国强、李震:《南宋龙泉青瓷香炉鉴赏与研究》(中),《东方收藏》2015 年第 2 期,第 58 页)

[2] *The Collection of Discussions with Lu Zijing*, *Collected Works* (Volume XXXVI), *The Four Series Books*, p14. Quoted from Feng Youlan. *The History of Chinese Philosophy* (Volume II). Beijing: SDX Joint Publishing Company, 2009, p. 371. (《与陆子静书》,《文集》卷三十六,"四部丛刊"本,第 14 页,载冯友兰《中国哲学史》(下),北京:生活·读书·新知三联书店 2009 年版,第 371 页)

the instrument is the expression of the concrete phenomena and objects in the physical form. And the metaphysical *Dao* is beyond the physical instrument, which is the root of "*Li*" in the discourse of Neo-Confucianism. The last stage of the "*Li*" thought is exploring the truth and completely understanding nature, so its essence is to explore the inner nature to highlight the true "nature" (*xing*) of human being himself. The reason is that *Dao* is equal to nature.[1] As a real truth, nature has the moral idea represented by benevolence, justice, etiquette and wisdom.

Therefore, Longquan celadon represented by the *lilu* in this article has consciously been in the context of Neo-Confucianism since it entered the field of scholar-officials of the Song Dynasty. As the composition of a physical vessel, Longquan celadon relies on *qi* or spirit. When *qi* condenses, it reflects *Li* and nature. Then, the art conception of Longquan celadon was constructed while the literati appreciated it by employing their imagination, emotional experience, values etc. Meanwhile, a tension was formed among materials, crafts and art conception, reflecting the moral ideas behind the artistic style of Longquan celadon.

Firstly, the soft "green" of Longquan celadon symbolizes the moral idea of "harmony and benevolence". *Ji Lei Bian* (Narrative Anecdotes in the Song Dynasty) records:"there are lots of good trees in Longquan County Chuzhou. In there a place named Yuzhang is well known for its precious wood … There also produced celadon wares, named '*mi se*' (jadish green or icelike green)."[2] Longquan celadon possesses a natural charm for the Longquan kiln site is located in the mountains and surrounded by trees, which is a manifestation of the harmony between man and nature. When it entered the life of scholar-officials, it brought the color of nature into their study, and created a natural scene of "the harmony between man and nature" together

---

[1] Huang Shiyi ed. , Xu Shiyi and Yang Yan conflate. *The Conflation on Conversations of Master Zhu Xi* (*Volume I*). Shanghai: Shanghai Guji Press, 2016, p. 94. [〔宋〕黄士毅编,徐时仪、杨艳汇校:《朱子语类汇校》(全十册)第一册,上海:上海古籍出版社 2016 年版,第 94 页]

[2] Zhuang Chuo. Xiao Luyang revise. *Narrative Anecdotes in Song Dynasty*. Shanghai: Shanghai Bookstore Publishing House, 1983, p. 5. [〔宋〕庄绰撰,萧鲁阳点校:《鸡肋编》,上海:上海书店出版社 1983 年版,第 5 页]

with other objects in the room. Meanwhile, it also implied the harmonious coexistence among people in actual life when the image of man and nature narrated the enjoyment of nature and morality, leading to the moral origin of "benevolence".

Secondly, the glaze color of Longquan celadon like jade symbolizes the moral idea of "advocating jade and virtue". In traditional Confucian culture, jade is the representative of ritual. *Pin Yi in the Book of Rites* (the part of *the Book of Rites*) records Confucius and Zi Gong's discussion on jade: "In the past, the virtues of gentlemen were compared with jade. Jade is warm and moist, resembling benevolence; Being meticulous and organized, it bears semblance to wisdom; It is angular but not hurt, signifying its righteousness. When it is hung, it falls in a line, showing its ritualism. It has clear and melodious sound after knocking, like music. Its flaws and beauty will not be covered up by each other, revealing its faithfulness. There is no concealment in its brilliance and appearance, indicating its credibility. The surface of jade is like a white rainbow in the sky. Its essence appears in the mountains and rivers, attesting its staunchness. Kyu and Zhang can be used separately as gifts for the imperial betrothal, and specially delivered, demonstrating its noble virtue. No one in the world would ignore jade, professing its *Dao*. *The Book of Songs* said that as far as a gentleman was mentioned, he should be gentle and kind, with a character like jade. So gentlemen value jade."[1] It is inferred that the study of rituals is not only one of the most important components of traditional Confucianism, also the emphasis on "etiquette" is considered an extremely important character. Furthermore, the fashion of "advocating jade" is also derived from using jade to compare the virtue of a gentleman. And it is particularly prominent in the celadon system. Since the glaze color of Yue porcelain in the Tang Dynasty was similar to jade's color, Lu Yü praised in *Tea Vessels in Cha Jing* (A Comprehensive Introduction of Tea): "If Xing ware is similar to silver and Yue ware is like jade, Xing ware

---

[1] Hu Pingsheng and Zhang Meng translate. *The Book of Rites* (Volume II). Beijing: Zhonghua Book Company, 2017, p. 1225. [胡平生、张萌译注：《礼记》(下)，北京：中华书局 2017 年版，第 1225 页]

is not as good as Yue one. "[1] In other words, the jade-like Longquan celadon was the first choice for the literati because it had developed their moral sentiment towards the pursuit of the virtue of a gentleman, and had become a representation of the visible moral ideas in their daily life.

Thirdly, the harmonious unity of the shape, glaze color and decoration of Longquan celadon symbolizes the moral idea of "equal importance to *Dao* and instrument". In the context of Neo-Confucianism, one thing is in two fundamental states controlled by *qi* (vital force)[2]. In other words, there are both *yin* and *yang* in *qi*. When *qi* accumulates, things are formed, and when *qi* disperses, things are destroyed.[3] Everything is created in a binary opposition. At the same time, any existence has a pole, which is the ultimate truth.[4] In other words, a matter has its most complete form with its superb standard. Then it is to explore the truth of its existence. With exceptional shape, glaze color and little decoration, Longquan celadon is the typical example of this most complete form. Its complete form is in line with the human visual comfort in terms of lines, proportions, and colors. It is the foundation of the beauty of its artistic charm and the perfect interpreter of the combination of physical instrument and metaphysical *Dao*. If there are slight changes in the shape of the vessel, or the glaze color and the pattern are not properly matched, it will affect the sense of regularity, stability, and plainness of Longquan celadon.

To sum up, the ultimate goal of "*Ge Wu Qiong Li*" is to explore the inner nature. And all the existence in the world including the micro matter

---

[1] Lu Yü. JinYuntong ed. *A Comprehensive Introduction of Tea*. Harbin: Heilongjiang Fine Arts Publishing House, 2017, p. 134. [［唐］陆羽著,晋云彤主编:《茶经》,哈尔滨:黑龙江美术出版社 2017 年版,第 134 页］

[2] It consists of pairs of contradictory states, such as the real and the unreal, motion and stillness, concentration and diffusion, and clarity and opacity. Without interaction between the opposite states, the whole cannot exist.

[3] Feng Youlan. *The History of Chinese Philosophy* (Volume II). Beijing: SDX Joint Publishing Company, 2009, pp. 331-332. [冯友兰:《中国哲学史》(下),北京:生活・读书・新知三联书店 2009 年版,第 331—332 页］

[4] Huang Shiyi ed., Xu Shiyi and Yang Yan conflate. *The Conflation on Conversations of Master Zhu Xi* (*Volume VI*). Shanghai: Shanghai Guji Press, 2016, p. 2377. [［宋］黄士毅编,徐时仪、杨艳汇校:《朱子语类汇校》(全十册)第六册,上海:上海古籍出版社 2016 年版,第 2377 页］

have its heart, but lacking of their perception.① So Longquan celadon inspired the insight of scholar-officials. Its most complete presentation under superb skills made them "indulge their hearts". When the object merged into the mind of human beings, it means that they had achieved the ultimate "*Dao*". Besides appreciating the external beauty of Longquan celadon, they preferred the moral idea of "harmony and benevolence, advocating jade and virtue, and equal importance to *Dao* and instrument" symbolized by the characteristics of its artistic style was reflected in the context of Neo-Confucianism. Thereby, it regulated the "temperament" caused by affection. That is to say, the scholar-officials adjusted themselves between the "temperament" of affection and the "nature" of morality. Finally, they reached the realm of "harmony" of "*Dao*", "*Li*" and "*Xin*", "*Xing*" in the process of self-introspection and self-cultivation.

The Artistic Conception of Longquan Celadon in the Leisure Life of the Literati in the Song Dynasty

Leisure, as a beautiful state of life and realm of life, reflects the unity of time and space, the unity of people (subject, subjective) and things (object, objective), and the unity of body (physical feeling) and heart (psychological feeling). Leisure itself has an inherent positive value, especially emphasizing the consistency of moral cultivation and leisure. It contains aesthetic, artistic and poetic temperament, and contains rich philosophical and cultural significance.② For the scholar-officials of the Song Dynasty who were based on *Li*, the combination of emotion and principles was the main feature of their leisure thoughts. Realizing the truth of life was the core value pursuit in their leisure life. In other words, the scholar-officials completed the meaning

---

① Huang Shiyi ed., Xu Shiyi and Yang Yan conflate. *The Conflation on Conversations of Master Zhu Xi (Volume I)*. Shanghai: Shanghai Guji Press, 2016, p. 72. [〔宋〕黄士毅编,徐时仪、杨艳汇校:《朱子语类汇校》(全十册)第一册,上海:上海古籍出版社 2016 年版,第 72 页]

② Zhao Yuqiang. *Leisure Philosophy: The Leisure Culture of Scholar-Bureaucrats in Song Dynasty and Its Implication*. Shanghai: Shanghai Guji Press, 2017, p. 16. (赵玉强:《优游之道:宋代士大夫休闲文化及其意蕴》,上海:上海古籍出版社 2017 年版,第 16 页)

of individual life in the artistic conception of mellow temperament. The censer represented by the Longquan *lilu* played an important role in the realization of the entire artistic conception.

First of all, the Longquan *lilu* in this article is classified to appreciating incense by restoring to the "context" of the leisure life of Song scholars and measuring its caliber (8.8 cm). According to the record of *Du Cheng Ji Sheng* (An Overview of the Capital Lin'an), "burning incense, making tea, decorating with paintings and arranging flowers" were indispensable pleasures in the literati's life in Song Dynasty.[1] And burning incense ranked first among the four appreciations. In incense activity, the incense burner is the principal subject. It turned into an indispensable part of the literati's leisure life together with incense. In the Song Dynasty, Lu You wrote in *Staying at Home* (*Jiazhong Bihu Zhongri Oude Jueju*):"An Official often owes reading debts, And rice as salary is not worth wine. Happen to be disengagement today, So burn incense to read Yuxi poems." It is proved that incense appreciation surpassed the constraints brought by material. It served as the important medium for scholar-officials to enjoy and understand their lives.

Chinese incense culture originated in the Yinshang Dynasty or even in late Neolithic period, initially formed in the Han Dynasty, and reached its peak in the Song Dynasty.[2] The enjoyable smell of incense can improve people's mood to make them peaceful and pleasant. So, whether for the royal family, the noble or the public, the enjoyment of incense had gradually developed into a common thing in their lives. Of course, for scholar-bureaucrats, when they calmed down surrounded by burning incense, it was the time to put themselves at their spiritual home to contemplate their hearts besides adding a sense of elegance. In detail, the process of appreciating incense enjoyed the transmission, charm, meaning and perception of thoughts and feelings. Therefore, the essence of Chinese incense culture was

---

[1] Wu Qing and Han Huizhi ed.. *Clear the Mind to Comprehend Dao: Traditional Incense Artifacts of the Literati*. Shanghai: Shanghai Scientific & Technical Publishers, 2014, p. 14. (吴清、韩回之主编:《澄怀观道: 传统之文人香事文物》,上海: 上海科学技术出版社 2014 年版,第 14 页)

[2] Jia Tianming. *The Study of Chinese Incense*. Beijing: Zhonghua Book Company, 2018, p. 19. (贾天明:《中国香学》,北京: 中华书局 2018 年版,第 19 页)

still "to comprehend *Dao* by means of incense". It was classified the important external condition for scholar-officials to achieve the artistic conception of perfect temperament. Under this contemplating atmosphere, the leisure life of the literati always revealed the aesthetic value of "valuing the truth and advocating elegance" and the pursuit of self-cultivation and morality.

For example, the literati studied in their study. In a broad sense, study includes reading, writing, meditating, etc. These often happened in their study. As shown in Figure 3, a scholar-official sits in the study room under a tree near a river. In the room, there are books and a small censer on the desk. Such is the pleasant scene of burning incense and studying in the study room. A scholar must devote himself in solitude. At this moment, the smell of incense could help calm his mind and stay away from the distracting thoughts. In the end, a space suitable for solitude was created for the literati by burning incense with the outdoor natural scenery. In such a space, they reflected and explored the ontological principles in the sense of peace and happiness, further completed the cultivation and practice of inner morality, and finally achieved the goal of improving the spiritual realm.

Of course, playing Chinese zither was also a very popular leisure activity among the literati (Fig. 4). Because Chinese zither music pursues the artistic conception of "harmony, elegance, purity, lightness and implied meaning", it is more important to show the player's mind in the process of playing it. It acted as the important way for scholar-officials to seek the ultimate experience and show their personality and spiritual demeanor.[1] In order to achieve the artistic conception of making friends with Chinese zither, a player or a listener is required to combine the external environment with his own inner mood. At this moment, the beautiful fragrance can not only help eliminate noise and create a quiet and elegant environment, but also show a respectful attitude of "righteousness and sincerity". And it helped the literati enter a broader inner state of the oneness between matters and man, even the

---

[1] Zhao Yuqiang. *Leisure Philosophy*: *The Leisure Culture of Scholar-Bureaucrats in Song Dynasty and Its Implication*. Shanghai: Shanghai Guji Press, 2017, p. 159. (赵玉强:《优游之道：宋代士大夫休闲文化及其意蕴》,上海：上海古籍出版社 2017 年版,第 159 页)

Fig. 3 Reading the Book of Change in a Cottage (partially enlarged to 170%)

Liu Songnian, Song Dynasty
Ink and color on silk, 25.7 cm × 26.0 cm
Liaoning Provincial Museum
Research Center of Ancient Chinese Painting and Calligraphy, Zhejiang University ed.. *The Complete Works of Song Painting* (Volume III). Hangzhou: Zhejiang University Press, 2009, pp. 201 - 202. (浙江大学中国古代书画研究中心编:《宋画全集》第三卷 2,杭州: 浙江大学出版社 2009 年版,第 201—202 页)

Fig. 4 Listening to the Qin (Zither) (partially enlarged to 170%)

Liu Songnian, Song Dynasty
Ink and slight color on silk, 24.0 cm × 24.9 cm
The Cleveland Museum of Art
Leonard C. Hanna, Jr. Fund, 1983.85
Research Center of Ancient Chinese Painting and Calligraphy, Zhejiang University ed.. *The Complete Works of Song Painting* (Volume VI). Hangzhou: Zhejiang University Press, 2008, pp. 47 - 48. (浙江大学中国古代书画研究中心编:《宋画全集》第六卷 2,杭州: 浙江大学出版社 2008 年版,第 47—48 页)

unity between the universe and man.

Secondly, the Longquan *lilu* belongs to the porcelain furnace in terms of the material. The method of producing incense in Song Dynasty inherited the method of roasting incense with charcoal in ash during the middle and late Tang Dynasty. Compared with directly firing incense, the aroma in this advanced method was more mellow and pleasant. Moreover, the method won the favor of the literati with more interest.[1] The material of the incense burner was not limited to silver, copper, iron and other materials. It could be chosen according to one's preferences. However, under the influence of Neo-

---

[1] Chen Jing. Yan Xiaoqing ed.. *A Comprehensive Introduction of Incense*. Beijing: Zhonghua Book Company, 2012. pp. 163 - 164. [[宋]陈敬著,严小青编著:《新纂香谱》,北京: 中华书局 2012 年版,第 163—164 页]

Confucianism, the ceramic firing technology had been continuously improved through reference from the others. Moreover, the shape of ceramic censer could imitate the ones of other materials of the previous dynasties or innovate by themselves. In addition, different from the metal ones, the ceramic incense burner was not easy to be overly decorated, which presented a simple, elegant, and simple style. Moreover, it provided more choices for scholar-officials because of its relative low production cost.

At the same time, people in the Song Dynasty also had the need to hold the censer to smell the incense. So its neck was made higher for hold. If it was made of metal, heat transferred faster. Furthermore, there was the residual metal smell after holding it, which affected the taste. In short, the ceramic censer finally became the first choice for the scholars due to its artistic style and material characteristics. And Longquan was one of the largest kilns to produce ceramic censer. In the Song Dynasty, Yang Wanli had a poem entitled *Appreciation of Incense* (*Shao Xiang Qi Yan*): "Ceramic tripod caldron (*ding*) is as green as water. Silver insulation is as light as paper." What the poem described is that the Longquan censer was preferred by the scholar-officials in the Song Dynasty represented by the *lilu* in this article.

Finally, the *lilu* in this article is apart of Longquan celadon implied the specific moral ideas in the context of Neo-Confucianism. The scholar-officials influenced by Neo-Confucianism stressed to understand the principles of the nature in their concepts, and introspected to cultivate their own morals. The way of comprehending the meaning of individual life can nurture the mind richly and broadly to realize the leisure of the heart in real life. The artistic conception of calmness and quietness created by the incense burner is to make people calm down and to make their heart become clear and bright. The thought of "*Li*" also clearly points out that *Dao* does not separate from concrete matters. That is to say, scholar-officials needed to observe and puzzle out daily life in a quiet mindset[1], switching freely between "object"

---

[1] Zhao Yuqiang. *Leisure Philosophy: The Leisure Culture of Scholar-Bureaucrats in Song Dynasty and Its Implication*. Shanghai: Shanghai Guji Press, 2017, p. 353. (赵玉强:《优游之道: 宋代士大夫休闲文化及其意蕴》,上海: 上海古籍出版社 2017 年版,第 353 页)

and "subject". Therefore, Longquan celadon naturally blended into the contented leisure space of the literati. It played the role of carrying the expectation of their moral values. This also proves that the ceramic incense burners in the Song Dynasty were mostly produced in Longquan kiln.

In a word, what the literati pursued in their leisure life essentially was the artistic conception of mellow temperament. The Longquan celadon represented by the *lilu* in this article, from its function and artistic style, presented a state of "life experiencing freedom in pleasure" because it met the real emotional needs of the literati. But such affection also linked to their moral goals. That is to say, from the perspective of the moral idea of Longquan celadon, the literati had realized the "*Dao*" and "*Li*" in a quiet state. After the oneness between object and mind, their sensation tended to be pure in nature under the guidance of the moral ideas. Then they completed the conversion from "human mind" to "*Dao* mind", and restored to the "reasonable" "temperament" before the affection was started up. In the end, it completed the meaning of the freedom of life pursued by scholar-officials.

Conclusion

The literati of the Song Dynasty in the background of Neo-Confucianism had been committed to realizing the inner "nature" of human being, highlighted the moral origin in introspection and fulfilled the meaning of individual life. Affected by this concept, the main aesthetic consciousness and standard of beauty in Song Dynasty was "valuing the truth and advocating elegance". Longquan celadon represented by the Longquan *lilu* in the Southern Song Dynasty was influenced in its craftsmanship and design. It constructed the artistic style of "elegance, simplicity and slenderness" conforming the aesthetics of the scholar-officials of the Song Dynasty, and successfully became their favour. In the process of merging into the scholars' life, its soft "green" color, jade-like glaze, and the harmonious unity of its perfect shape were transformed into the symbol of the moral ideas of "harmony and benevolence, advocating jade and virtue, and equal importance to *Dao* and instrument" in the context of Neo-Confucianism.

While arousing the "emotion" of scholar-officials, it regulated their true "nature". Then they achieved the harmony of "*Dao*", "*Li*" and "*Xin*", "*Xing*" in the process of cultivating their temperament. On the one hand, it, as the censer, participated in the leisure life of the literati with incense. It assisted the scholars to create a calm and elegant external environment in the culture of Chinese incense. On the other hand, on Longquan celadon itself, the literati completed the conversion from "human mind" to "*Dao* mind", and the unity between object and subject, body and mind, morality and leisure pursued by them in the practice part of man and thing. As a result, they realized the meaning of true life while understanding the origin of morality. So it is concluded that Longquan celadon is one of the important medium for the artistic conception of mellow temperament in the leisure life of the literati in the Song Dynasty.

(Shanghai University)

Problems and Countermeasures in the Overseas Transmission of Peking Opera

Sun Ning

On August 1, 2018, *The Revenge of the Prince*, the Peking Opera version of *Hamlet*, was staged in Kronborg Castle, Denmark (the place where the story of Shakespeare's famous work *Hamlet* took place), which acted as the prelude to the Danish Shakespeare Festival in 2018 and aroused a lot of praise from the audience. *The Revenge of the Prince* was first performed in Denmark in 2005. It infuses "fresh blood" into the classic drama of *Hamlet* with the artistic skills of speech, song, dance and combat in movement, and embodies the friendly dialogue and artistic integration between the East and the West. The artists from China reinterpreted the spirit of Shakespeare's classic play for the Danish audience with the purest traditional Chinese dramatic art form, showing the huge power drawn from the integration of Chinese and Western cultures. On August 11 of the same year, the Heilongjiang Peking Opera Theatre staged two Peking Opera plays *The Drunken Beauty* and *Flowers Scattered by the Heavenly Maids* in Denmark's Tivoli Garden. More than 2000 Danish people and tourists were immersed in the unique charm of Peking Opera. Peking Opera, as an artistic symbol condensing Chinese culture, has flowed into the hearts of the Danes through such performances, promoted Denmark's understanding of China, and deepened the friendship between China and Denmark, whose cultural value is immeasurable. As Zhang Li, director of the China Cultural Center in Copenhagen, said, "cultural exchanges play a unique and irreplaceable role in building closer people-to-people ties among different countries. Danish people have the opportunity to appreciate the quintessential charm of Chinese art, which can help them better understand Chinese culture, promote exchanges between Chinese and Danish people, and further deepen the relationship between the two countries". [1]

Peking Opera is endowed with profound Chinese cultural connotations, which is one of the oldest cultures in the world. It is the crystallization of thousands of years of human wisdom and nourishes Chinese people from generation to generation. Peking Opera represents the essence of Chinese culture, namely, the "quintessence" of Chinese culture. The reason why Peking Opera, together with "Chinese painting" and "Chinese medicine", can be called the triple "quintessence" of China is closely related to its performance techniques which combines virtuality and reality; its sophisticated system with artistic skills of speech, song, dance and combat in movement; its magnificent performance style and the national spirit contained in.

First of all, Peking Opera is an art combining virtuality and reality, which can connote the changes of time and space for the audience through the transformation of props and the performance of actors, and bring the audience a kind of "immersive" drama-appreciating experience. Secondly, Peking Opera is a stylized and sophisticated art, which involves literature, martial arts, chanting, singing, costumes, facial makeup and many other art forms. These elements work together to generate a gorgeous Peking Opera stage effect. Thirdly, the formation of Peking Opera has a history of more than 200 years. The Chinese cultural elements and national spirit contained in Peking Opera result from China's two thousand years of civilization. Each play acts as the carrier of Chinese traditional culture. Therefore, it is a window for the world to understand China and an emissary of cultural and artistic exchanges between China and the West.

In November 2010, Peking Opera was listed in the *Representative List of the Intangible Cultural Heritage of Humanity*. "Peking Opera, with its

---

[1] Xinhua News. "Chinese Peking Opera Staged in Denmark's Tivoli Garden." 2018.08.13. Online http://www.xinhuanet.com/world/2018-08/13/c_129931905.htm.(《中国京剧在丹麦古老乐园上演》,新华网,2018-08-13)

profound ideas, stylized stage performance, melodious music composition, colorful costumes and facial makeup, constitutes a unique drama culture with Chinese national characteristics."[1] Peking Opera is not only the carrier of Chinese traditional culture, but also the common cultural heritage and artistic treasure of human beings. However, the overseas spread of Peking Opera is hindered to some extent. The perception, awareness and interest of people outside China in Peking Opera do not match the cultural value of Peking Opera itself. The cultural symbols, unique rhythms, and rich performance forms of Peking Opera have not been fully and successfully displayed in front of the people across the world. Therefore, how to stimulate the horizontal vitality of this performing art is worthy of our discussion.

After Mr. Mei Lanfang's visit to the United States, Peking Opera became extremely popular there at that time and opened up a space for its overseas presence. But afterwards, the performance art of Peking Opera never reached the cultural grandeur of that time. Generally speaking, the spread of Peking Opera overseas still faces great difficulties. As an oriental theatre form which differs greatly from the western style, Peking Opera is easily misunderstood in different cultures and its acceptance is greatly hindered. In view of this, it is necessary to carry out strategic analysis of the overseas communication of Peking Opera in a scientific mode. The 5W communication mode proposed by Lasswell, the founder of American communication studies, analyzes the communication activities of human society from 5 aspects, including communication subject (Who), communication content (Says What), communication channel (In Which Channel), communication object (To Whom) and communication effect (With What Effects).[2] With the help of Lasswell's 5W mode, the author

---

[1] Liu Xizhen. "On the Aesthetic Traits of Peking Opera — Starting from Amusement and Entertainment." *Journal of Jishou University Social Sciences*, March 2006, Issue 2, pp. 45–50. (刘席珍:《论京剧的审美特质——从休闲性与娱乐性说开去》,《吉首大学学报(社会科学版)》2006 年 3 月第 2 期,第 46—50 页)

[2] Lasswell, Harold. *The Structure and Function of Communication in Society*. Beijing: Communication University of China press, 2013. (哈罗德·拉斯韦尔:《社会传播的结构与功能》,中国传媒大学出版社 2013 年版)

analyzes the problems and countermeasures of Peking Opera's overseas spread from the perspectives of communication subject, communication content, communication channel, and communication object, in order to enhance the communication effect outside China of Peking Opera.

Communication subject

The main subjects of the external communication of Peking Opera have two parts: one is relevant Chinese government agencies and official organizations, as well as other non-governmental entities related to opera.[①] The other one is the translators of Peking Opera. These two subjects are indispensable in the external communication of Peking Opera. However, the communication subject of Peking Opera now faces the problems of lack of focus, coverage, and also professional translators.

The 19th National Congress of the Communist Party of China emphasized the need to "improve our capacity for engaging in international communication so as to tell China's stories well, present a true, multi-dimensional, and panoramic view of China, and enhance China's cultural soft power".[②] The Chinese government attaches great importance to cultural exchanges between China and foreign countries, and actively promotes the spread of Chinese theatre culture to the world, which plays a dominant role in the foreign dissemination of Peking Opera. However, the non-governmental subjects such as individuals, organizations, and enterprises related to Peking Opera are still in a relatively "sporadic" state during the dissemination process. The "sporadic" here has two meanings, one is the lack of representativeness in the communication subject. Most of the overseas

---

[①] Zhang Anhua. "Strategy of Contemporary Chinese Opera's External Communication." *Drama Literature*. 2017, Issue 5, pp. 122 – 130. (张安华:《当代中国戏曲对外传播的策略探析》,《戏剧文学》2017 年第 5 期,第 122—130 页)

[②] Xi Jinping, "Secure a Decisive Victory in Building a Moderately Prosperous Society in All Respects and Strive for the Great Success of Socialism with Chinese Characteristics for a New Era — Delivered at the 19th National Congress of the Communist Party of China". October 18, 2017. Online: http://www.qstheory.cn/llqikan/2017-12/03/c_1122049424.htm. (习近平:《决胜全面建成小康社会 夺取新时代中国特色社会主义伟大胜利——在中国共产党第十九次全国代表大会上的报告》,2017 – 10 – 18)

performances of Chinese Peking Opera are in the form of "organization" and "Troupe", causing a lack of identity for the communication subject. "Compared with the conceptualized institutions or organizations, the opera actors with unique personality charm would have a more powerful impact on his audience."[4] Telling Chinese stories well needs to start from little things. To present Chinese Peking Opera well, we should also focus on the actors per se. Before Mei Lanfang visited the United States in 1930, the English-version introduction manual about Mei Lanfang had been specially printed and distributed, introducing Mr. Mei's status and influence in China to the American audience. At the same time, Mei's personal profile was also published in several American newspapers. As a result, the American people could have a specific perception of Chinese Peking Opera. Just as Denmark's national image of the "kingdom of fairy tales" is established through such concrete characters as "the little mermaid", "the ugly duckling" and "Thumbelina". The communication subject of Peking Opera must also focus on the representative characters. The second meaning of "sporadic" is that the communication subject of Peking Opera is still relatively inadequate. Wilbur Schramm, who is considered the founder of the field of Communication Studies in America, said: "Human communication is something that people do."[1] People are the carriers of Peking Opera's communication, the power source of sustainable development and uninterrupted inheritance of Peking Opera, and play a decisive role in the vitality of Peking Opera art. People are the carrier of art communication, the driving force of sustainable development and uninterrupted inheritance of Peking Opera art, and play a decisive role in the vitality of Peking Opera. China needs to further broaden Peking Opera's communication subject and absorb more social groups into the communicating process. International students in China play an important role in cultural exchanges between China and foreign countries. Since 2017, the number of international students in

---

[1] Schramm, Wilbur. *Men, Women, Message, and Media: Understanding Human Communication.* (Chen Liang, et al. Trans.) Beijing: Xinhua Publishing House, 1984. (威尔伯·施拉姆著,陈亮等译:《传播学概论》,新华出版社 1984 年版)

China has ranked third among the number of international students in the world, and ranked first in Asia.

International students have the opportunity to experience the local culture firsthand. They enjoy the most vigorous and dynamic ideas, and are the bridges between countries. In addition to overseas students in China, the Chinese residents abroad are an important social force in the communication of Peking Opera as well. "The Chinese compatriots living in foreign countries are not only recipients of information at home and abroad, but also carriers and disseminators of traditional Chinese culture. They have the ability to promote the Chinese drama art overseas through various channels." Both international students in China and the Chinese residents abroad are significant envoys of cultural exchanges between China and foreign countries. They play an important role in the spread of Peking Opera, and are potential choices to expand the communication subject of Peking Opera.

Translators are also an important subject, playing a decisive role in the external communication of Peking Opera. The translation of Peking Opera art is by no means a word-for-word translation, but the translation of cultural symbols, which makes the translation of Peking Opera extremely tricky. Professional knowledge of Peking Opera, profound foreign language literacy and cross-cultural communicative awareness are required for being a qualified Peking Opera translator. Art is interlinked among countries and has no national boundaries, but the languages expressing art spirit are various. People all over the world are deeply attracted by Peking Opera's tonality, exotic moves, colorful costumes and unique facial makeup. However, foreign audiences are confused and unable to understand the connotation of this performance art without subtitles, which leads to a gap in cross-cultural communication. However, there is a small quantity of translators specializing in Peking Opera translation and students whose major is Peking Opera translation. China should improve the training mechanism of Peking Opera translators, make full use of the talents cultivation skills of colleges and universities, further refine the division of translation majors, and guide students to learn, understand and master Peking Opera translation. It is necessary to cultivate versatile translators with extraordinary ability in

English, broad cross-cultural vision and Peking Opera knowledge. At the same time, we should strengthen the cooperation and exchange between Chinese and foreign translators, and steadily expand the professional translation team of Peking Opera through transnational research, international seminars and personnel exchange.

Communication content

The content of Peking Opera's external communication is Peking Opera itself. As a unique performance art, Peking Opera has encountered many difficulties in the process of external communication. First of all, Chinese and Western cultures are heterogeneous cultures, while Peking Opera represents the essence of Chinese traditional culture. Therefore, Peking Opera is faced with obstacles resulting from cultural differences between China and Western countries. "Chinese traditional culture is dominated by Confucian culture, advocating 'the rule of man', 'golden mean' and 'balance between the rich and the poor', emphasizing the harmonious coexistence of human beings. Chinese traditional thinking mode is the curve thinking mode of intuition and perceptual knowledge, on the contrary, Western people tend to prefer a linear logical thinking mode. What's more, China is typical of agricultural civilization while western culture is commercial and marine culture, which attaches importance to the self realization of individual rights and values and relies on rational expression."[1] Such cultural differences are also reflected in Chinese and Western dramas. Western drama focuses on "realism", emphasizing the "imitation" of real life; while Peking Opera focuses on "spiritual expression" and consequently the stage setting puts more emphasis on the artistic conception "empty", even a small table is enough for the actors to complete the whole play. Actors can travel thousands of miles with just a whip, which

---

[1] Li Xiaomin. "A Study of Chinese and Western Culture in the Perspective of Building a Harmonious Society." *Xi'an Social Science*. 2010, Volume 28, Issue 1, pp. 142-144. (李孝敏:《构建和谐社会视阈下的中西文化研究》,《西安社会科学》2010 年第 28 卷 1 期,第 142—144 页)

is a highly virtual ideographic art. This kind of "spiritual expression" makes Peking Opera highly artistic, but it may also cause foreign audiences to "misunderstand" or "misread" the play. In view of this situation, the interpretation of the play before the performance is extremely important.

Second, the plot of Peking Opera is unfolded at a slow pace, which conflicts with the fast-paced culture of Westerners. In terms of content, the plot of Peking Opera is simple and clear, focusing on describing the delicate inner world of the characters through the superb skills of the actors, stage configuration, chanting, etc. This allows the audience to enjoy it leisurely. Even if they miss one part of the whole play, they would not have to be forced to come back and watch it. For example, *The Drunken Beauty* describes that Yang Guifei (Emperor Tang Xuanzong's favorite concubine) went to the Baihua Pavilion for an appointment with Tang Xuanzong. But the Emperor did not fulfill his promise, and he went to see another beautiful concubine. Hearing the news, Yang felt very depressed and got drunk to relieve her depression. The plot of the play is simple, but with the help of actors' superb performance skills and exquisite stage costumes, the inner world of Yang is portrayed with marvellous charm. Westerners with their fast pace of life may be "impatient" in the process of watching the drama, and this affects the experience of watching.

Third, Peking Opera requires its audience to acquire certain cultural background knowledge. Peking Opera is a highly stylized art. This kind of stylization is shown as follows: "It is composed of songs and dances, with distinct rhythm, intonation, movement, gongs and drums, singing with tunes and plates, and martial arts with routines."[1] Therefore, Peking Opera has its unique content and form. The artistic skills of speech, song, dance and combat in movement are integrated in Peking Opera and these artistic forms work together to create a unique Peking Opera culture. In addition, there are four kinds of performers and roles in Peking Opera: Sheng (the main male

---

[1] Li Xiaomin. "A Study of Chinese and Western Culture in the Perspective of Building a Harmonious Society." *Xi'an Social Science*. 2010, Volume 28, Issue 1, pp. 142–144. (李孝敏:《构建和谐社会视阈下的中西文化研究》,《西安社会科学》2010 年第 28 卷第 1 期,第 142—144 页)

role), Dan (female role), Jing (a painted face male role) and Chou (a character who is witty or insidious). The pattern and color of facial makeup are symbolic, representing a certain character. Therefore, if you want to fully understand Peking Opera, a certain degree of cultural background knowledge is needed. Otherwise, it would be difficult for the audience, so that it cannot enjoy Peking Opera wholeheartedly and with ease.

In view of the cultural differences between China and the West and the stylization of Peking Opera itself, we must be fully prepared to promote the external dissemination of Peking Opera. Before Mr. Mei's visit to the United States, it took eight years to complete the preparatory work. Before departure, Mei's team made an English brochure about Peking Opera, which was published in the local newspapers in advance, and distributed to the audience for reading before each performance. Qi Rushan and other team members also meticulously drew 200 pictures about Peking Opera, which can be divided into 15 categories, including theater, costumes, headdress, beards, facial makeup, dance notation, musical instruments, bells, palace notation, and roles etc., all with bilingual introductions in Chinese and English.[1] It shows the beauty of Chinese Peking Opera more vividly and intuitively. Considering the language and cultural barriers of overseas audiences, Mei Lanfang intentionally shortened the "singing" and "chanting" parts of Peking Opera, and added the "dancing" and "combating" parts. Taking into account the fast-paced living habits of the American audience, Mei Lanfang cut the performance down to one per night, with a total of four sections of no more than two hours. Consequently, Mei Lanfang's 8-year preparatory work has also paid off. Making preparations according to the local culture can greatly reduce the cognitive load of overseas audiences in Peking Opera reception and create a relaxed and pleasant artistic experience for the audience.

Facing the audience in the heterogeneous culture, in addition to

---

[1] Shen Jing, Jing Yixin. "Crossing the Cultural Gap: An Analysis of the Reasons for Mei Lanfang's Successful Performance in the United States." *News World*, 2009, Issue 3, pp. 55 – 56. (沈静、景义新：《跨越文化鸿沟梅兰芳赴美演出成功原因探析》,《新闻世界》2009 年第 3 期,第 55—56 页)

meticulous preparatory work, we should also carry out "dialogical" innovation both on the form and content of Peking Opera, and make efforts from Peking Opera per se. The "dialogical" innovation here means focusing on the common parts between China and foreign countries with the premise of retaining the original flavor of Peking Opera to the greatest extent. The reason why Peking Opera is regarded as "the quintessence of the Chinese nation" and the representation of Chinese culture lies in the fact that Peking Opera constructs the cultural identity of the Chinese people, in its unique forms, and in its concentrated Chinese cultural symbols and values of Chinese civilization. Peking Opera should not be "banalized" in order to cater to the public's aesthetics, it should not be completely changed for innovation. Such Peking Opera is no longer Peking Opera. However, Peking Opera does follow the law of artistic development in that "continuous change and innovation is the source of youthful vitality; otherwise, it may become rigid" in the process of its external dissemination. Without innovation, Peking Opera would inevitably degenerate into songs of a highbrow type with very few people to join in the chorus. Zheng Shaohua, President of Shandong Peking Opera Theater, said that "the loyalty, filial piety, righteousness, benevolence, propriety, wisdom and faith contained in Chinese opera shows the fundamental humanity and morality, which is common to all mankind." Art is interlinked among cultures. He took the famous love drama *The Picking of Jade Bracelets* as an example. Love is the common pursuit of mankind, and what Peking Opera shows is just the love in a different culture."[1] In the process of spreading Peking Opera art, we can pay attention to and highlight the universal value and national characteristics of Peking Opera with humanity and historical connotation to reduce the artistic acceptance difficulties caused by cultural differences. Another way of "dialogical" innovation is to use the "four skills (speech, song, dance and combat in movement) and five methods (using of mouth, hand, eye, body,

---

[1] China news. "550 International Students Experience 'Beijing Opera with Explanation' and want to learn 'real Kungfu'." 2016. 11. 30. Online: http://www.chinanews.com/cul/2016/11-30/8078509. shtml.《550名留学生体验"带讲解的京剧"想拜师学"真功夫"》,中国新闻网,2016-11-30)

foot)" of Chinese Peking Opera to interpret Western classic dramas, such as a Peking Opera version of *Hamlet* and *Faust*. The great success of these adaptions is the result of "dialogical" innovation between Chinese and Western cultures. Friendly dialogue between cultures is a necessary condition for the prosperity and development of human society. As the famous philosopher Habermas said: "Different cultures should transcend the limitations of their respective cultural traditions and the basic values of life, respect each other as equal partners, eliminate misunderstandings and abandon stereotypes in a harmonious and friendly atmosphere, so as to jointly discuss the major issues related to mankind and the future of the century, and find ways to solve the problems. This should be universally observed as an ethical principle in international exchanges."[1]

Communication channel

The communication channel is an important part of the communication process, which affects the spread of the communication content. Many foreign people do not have a chance to get in touch with the art form of Peking Opera. Peking Opera must take the initiative to enter the world, and perhaps one day in the future it will take root and blossom in the hearts of a certain audience. The "going out" of Peking Opera must rely on effective channels of communication. Peking Opera, as a performance art, used to conduct physical performances through various theaters. With this form of communication, Peking Opera actors and audiences are able to have direct face-to-face contact, which greatly increases the audiences' experience. However, this kind of physical theater, on the other hand, greatly limits the spreading area of Peking Opera. Since the 1990s, with the development of the Internet, Peking Opera has been able to spread. It has been "sent" in front of the eyes of overseas people, but it failed to "walk" into people's

---

[1] Habermas, Jürgen. *From Perceptual Impression to Symbolic Expression*. (Li Li. Trans.) Beijing: China Social Sciences Press, 1999, p. 54. (《从感性印象到象征表现》,中国社会科学出版社 1999 年版,第 57 页)

hearts. With numerous cultural elements of Peking Opera compressed to a small square screen, the artistry and shock of the Peking Opera are greatly weakened.

Peking Opera should follow the footsteps of modern technology and give play to its unique charm. Virtual reality technology would be a good choice. Dr. Xiaoqing Duan from the Intangible Heritage Center of Sun Yat-sen University put forward in the *Research on the Application Mode of Virtual Reality in the Protection of Intangible Cultural Heritage of Traditional Chinese Opera*: "It is difficult for common digital protection means to comprehensively and deeply intervene in the inheritance and protection of traditional opera. As a typical representative of 'integration media', virtual reality can achieve a high degree of restoration of real space, and produce a strong sense of presence through the natural interaction of multi-channel sensory information, which provides new possibilities for the digital inheritance and protection of opera art."[1] Constructing a virtualized space of Peking Opera in a modern form, allowing the audience to interact with Peking Opera in this virtual world, is a good way of dissemination. Only by taking advantage of emerging media technologies can the dissemination of Peking Opera achieve its maximum effectiveness.

Secondly, the dissemination of Peking Opera should also take advantage of the power of the market. The relation between the government and the market is dynamic and interactive. The state must play a guiding role in adjusting the overall atmosphere in the dissemination of Peking Opera, and at the same time, we should give full play to the main role of cultural enterprises in the market. We can increase the frequency of interaction between Peking Opera and its audience by strengthening the "IP" management of Peking Opera culture. "With the deepening of people's understanding of intellectual property rights, the 'IP' management of the entertainment and cultural industry has become more

---

[1] Ni Caixia. "The Research Status, Hot Spots and Trends of Intangible Cultural Heritage: A Summary of the Symposium on Disciplinary Construction of Intangible Cultural Heritage and Ethnic Folk Art." *Cultural Heritage*, 2019, Issue 2, pp. 139-144. (倪彩霞:《非物质文化遗产学的研究现状、热点及趋势——中国非物质文化遗产与民族民间艺术学科建设研讨会综述》,《文化遗产》2019 年第 2 期,第 139—144 页)

mature, and the 'IP' management concept has become a significant reference for cross field industry management."[1] Efforts should be made to create a cultural IP of Peking Opera, and give birth to related cultural products and industries.

Last but not least, the overseas dissemination of Peking Opera can also rely on the platform of the Confucius Institute. The Confucius Institute is an important window for the world to learn about China and Chinese culture, and also an important channel for Chinese civilization to "go global".[2] Peking Opera is the business card of Chinese culture, so relying on the Confucius Institute to spread Peking Opera culture fits with the Confucius Institute's mission of "promoting Chinese and foreign cultural exchanges". As of 2018, China has established 548 Confucius Institutes and 1,193 Confucius Classrooms in primary and secondary schools in 154 countries and regions, with a total of 1.87 million students.[3] This huge group is an important force for China's friendly exchanges with the world. The Confucius Institute should give full play to the role of a cultural exchange platform and adopt various forms to stimulate students' interest in Peking Opera, such as holding Peking Opera knowledge contests, facial makeup DIY, Peking Opera seminars, Peking Opera art festivals, etc., to promote Peking Opera culture to take root in the hearts of more Chinese and foreign cultural envoys.

Communication object

"The audience is the 'destination' of information and an important link in the chain of information dissemination. The audience is also the 'monitor'

---

[1] Lu Qiang. "The History and Cultural Innovation of Shandong Rural Pottery from the Perspective of Intangible Heritage." *Journal of Nuclear Agricultural Sciences*, 2021, Issue 2, p. 516. (卢强:《非遗视角下的山东农村土陶历史与文化创新》,《核农学报》2021 年第 2 期,第 516 页)

[2] Bai Ziwei. "Research on the Transformation and Development of the Confucius Institutes." *Renmin University of China Education Journal*, 2020, Issue 4, pp. 63 - 72. (白紫薇:《孔子学院转型发展研究》,《中国人民大学教育学刊》2020 年第 4 期,第 63—72 页)

[3] Xinhuanet. "There Are 548 Confucius Institutes Around the World." 2018.12.05. Online: http://www.xinhuanet.com/world/2018-12/05/c_1210009045.htm (《世界各地已有 548 所孔子学院》,新华网,2018 - 12 - 05)

of the communication effect. Therefore, the fundamental way to improve the effect of Chinese opera in external communication is to enhance the artistic acceptance of overseas audiences." The object of the overseas communication of Peking Opera is the foreign people, who are from a heterogeneous culture and embrace different languages and cultures. The language differences between Peking Opera and its communication objects make it very difficult for Peking Opera to spread to the outside world. Therefore, how to use the language understood by people in different cultures to show the true spirit of Peking Opera is extremely important. As Sun Ping, executive director of the National Opera Research Center of Renmin University of China, said: "The key of successful communication lies in the translation of Peking Opera. From the past to the present, you will find that when domestic Peking Opera troupes go abroad to perform, there will be cases where the audience cannot understand the plot due to improper translation, and thus cannot understand Peking Opera in depth."[1] Theater translation involves not only word-to-word conversion, but the negotiation of two cultures. As David Johnston suggests, "theatre translation is a mobile practice in which nothing can be fixed, because not only are languages and cultures different, but also are theatre systems, including conventions of performance and audience expectations."[2] This greatly increases the possibility of misinterpretation of theater translations and makes artistic acceptance more difficult.

"The translation and dissemination of Chinese traditional opera cannot only protect the national character of China's intangible cultural heritage, but also promote the exchanges between various cultural groups and enhance the global character of China's intangible cultural heritage."[3] Peking Opera

---

[1] Yang Xue. "Sun Ping: The Dissemination of Peking Opera has a long way to go." *Journal of the Chinese People's Political Consultative Conference*, 2016-08-15, 009 edition. (杨雪、孙萍:《京剧的传播任重道远》,《人民政协报》2016年8月15日,第009版)

[2] Johnston, D. *Metaphor and Metonymy: the Translator-Practitioner's Visibility*. In *Staging and Performing Translation* (pp. 11-30). London: Palgrave Macmillan, 2011.

[3] Yu Qiangfu, "A Review of the Research on the Translation and Introduction of Intangible Heritage Opera 'Going Global'". *Home Drama*, 2020, Issue 35, pp. 15-16. (于强福:《非遗戏曲"走出去"译介研究述评》,《戏剧之家》2020年第35期,第15—16页)

is a unique and national art, and the huge cultural gap in it must be made up by proficient translators and mature translation methods. Peking Opera translators need to possess a certain amount of Peking Opera knowledge and advanced translation skills. Besides, Peking Opera translation can never be done by the translator alone, but must be completed by a team. As Susan Bassnett said: "When we consider translation for the theatre what becomes clear is that it is a collaborative activity, unlike other forms of translation."① In addition to translators, the team should also include native opera experts with certain English ability and foreign experts who are interested in Peking Opera. After translation, we need to take a scientific and practical way to test the translation effect. The Professor Wei Lisha of the Department of Asian Theatre and Performance at the University of Hawaii is a practitioner of cooperative translation and has achieved very good results. Her translation practice is: "Translators who speak Chinese and understand English need to cooperate with translators who speak English and understand Chinese. Both sides must be proficient in Peking Opera, and it is better to be able to perform it. Only in this way can they have an intuition about Peking opera performance and produce a good translation. Afterwards, the effect of the translation should be tested by the judgment of the Peking Opera artists and the reaction of the audience."② Objects' feedback is one of the most important ways to test the effect of communication. Before Mei's team went abroad, when they met Westerners, they would ask them which part of Mei Lanfang's performance was the best. Through such feedback, they understood the aesthetic taste of foreigners and made preparations for performing abroad. In almost six or seven years, more than 1000 foreign guests had been asked.[7] Through this kind of cooperative translation, it can be ensured that the translation of Peking opera is both readable and performable, and the artistic acceptance of the object is

---

① Bassnett, Susan. *Translation*. London/New York: Routledge, 2013.
② Huang Qinghuan, "Practice and Thoughts on the Translation of Peking Opera Scripts-An Interview with Professor Wei Lisha from the University of Hawaii." *Chinese Translators Journal*, 2019, Issue 4, pp. 99 - 103. (黄庆欢:《京剧剧本翻译实践与思考——夏威夷大学魏莉莎教授访谈录》,《中国翻译》2019 年第 4 期,第 99—103 页)

guaranteed.

Einstein once said: "Physics gives me knowledge, art gives me imagination, knowledge is limited, but the imagination opened up by art is unlimited." Excellent culture and art are worth appreciating by everyone in the world. The art of Peking Opera originates from the wisdom of generations of Chinese people, shaping the identity of the Chinese nation. China needs to face the status quo of the overseas dissemination of Peking Opera, maintain a tolerant and open mind, and take the initiative to engage in an equal dialogue with world civilization. Facing the current obstacles of the external communication of Peking Opera, China should first of all further develop and shape the representative communication subjects of Peking Opera, and optimize the translator-training mechanism of Peking Opera. Second, it is necessary to actively carry out "dialogical" innovations in Peking Opera adjusted to the audience's local culture. Third, Peking Opera should take the initiative to embrace new media and technologies to broaden the channels of communication. Last but not least, the translation of Peking Opera could take the form of cooperative translation to reveal the true nature of Peking Opera with the language understood by people in different cultures. Through all these measures, the perception and cognition of Peking Opera by audiences in heterogeneous cultures could be enhanced and the overseas communication of Peking Opera would be effectively improved and promote the prosperous development of this performance art, creating a new pattern of overseas dissemination of Peking Opera.

(Beijing International Studies University)

Jingdezhen Porcelain in China's Cultural Rejuvenation and International Communication

Guo Rongrong

Art is something universal which can cross the boundaries of time and race through the resonance of human emotions and stir people's hearts; art is fluid, and once discovered, excellent art will consciously spread out and affect other nations. Throughout history, the international communication between China and the world can be traced back to the silk trade two thousand years ago. According to the book *The Histories* by the Greek historian Herodotus (484 B. C. - 495 B. C.) in the 5th century BC, the Greeks had long referred to the great eastern country known for its silk production as the "Silk Country". Silk was seen as a rare good in the West. It was expensive and once became the largest luxury goods in the Roman Empire. Not only silk, but Chinese porcelain can also be traced to the existing early paintings and literary descriptions. At the end of the 17th century and the beginning of the 18th century, Chinese porcelain tableware became popular in Europe. Chinese utensils became a representative of the upper class, which made people full of curiosity and yearning for the mysterious oriental power. Porcelain decorated with pavilions, flowers, birds, fish and insects, famous mountains and big rivers, gods, beasts, beauties, folk religions, and drama stories became important media for the Western imagination to perceive China, allowing Westerners to see the beauty of China[1]. This means that Chinese porcelain

---

[1] Reed, Marcia. Paola, Dematte, ed. *China on Paper: European and Chinese Works from the Late Sixteen to the Early Nineteen Century*. Los Angeles: Getty Research Institute, 2011, p. 1.

plays an important role in the international communication in artistic and commercial ways.

In the thousands of years of trade and cultural exchanges, China has absorbed cultural elements from other countries to produce colored porcelain with exotic flavors, such as "enamel porcelain", "the famille rose porcelain", "Fitz Hugh porcelain" and "Jesuit porcelain" sold to Europe. At the same time, Europe also started to imitate Chinese porcelain since it was introduced to the local area. Denmark's "Royal Porcelain" is one form. The Copenhagen Kiln, established in 1775, started by imitating Chinese porcelain and later produced porcelain with its own characteristics. As the best porcelain factory in Denmark, each piece of porcelain in the Royal Copenhagen Kiln Factory is hand-painted by ceramic artists. The process is exquisite and complicated, the patterns are integrated with Danish characteristics, and the designs are ingenious. In 1790, the King of Denmark ordered a set of exquisite and representative "flowers of Denmark" porcelain to be presented to Queen Catherine II of Russia as a gift. All the porcelain patterns were based on the Danish Botanical Gardens. Porcelain as a national gift is enough to show the importance of "Danish Royal Porcelain" in Denmark and the acceptance and recognition of Chinese culture by the Danish people. The spread of the commercial trade of Chinese traditional handicrafts to Europe, and then the acceptance and internalization of Chinese goods by European countries, reflect the strong cultural soft power of ancient China. Traditional handicrafts are used as carriers to trade overseas as artworks and commodities. Therefore, porcelain is an important part of the international communication of China.

The Historical and Cultural Significance of Jingdezhen Porcelain

Jingdezhen, the city of Chinese porcelain, has a long history of producing porcelain. According to the *Nan Kiln Notes*, Jingdezhen handmade pottery industry in Jiangxi replaced agriculture thousands of years ago and is the only one city developed in a single industry in early China. Jingdezhen is located at the junction of the three provinces of Jiangxi,

Anhui, and Zhejiang. It is a transitional zone between Huangshan, Huaiyu Mountain, and Poyang Lake. The terrain is flat and the territory is dominated by low mountains and hills. The surrounding mountains contain a large number of high-quality porcelain clay resources. The superior geographical situation provided conditions for Jingdezhen porcelain manufacturing and regional trade. From the Tang Dynasty, Jingdezhen began to make porcelain. In the Song Dynasty, Jingdezhen's kiln industry suddenly emerged. In the first year of Jingde of Emperor Song Zhenzong (1004), because of the excellent quality of the blue and white porcelain produced in the town, Jingdezhen was set up under the name of the emperor's reign, and it is still in use today. The Yuan Dynasty was an important period for the development of Jingdezhen porcelain. The government set up the "Fuliang Porcelain Bureau" and turned the taxation supervisor of Jingdezhen into the leader. As a result, the national porcelain industry gradually concentrated in Jingdezhen. In the Ming and Qing dynasties, Jingdezhen, which combined the superior conditions for porcelain production, reached its heyday and formed a market-led fine porcelain production model. Different porcelain production processes are undertaken by specialized porcelain producers, which not only guarantees the quality of the porcelain but also fulfills the demand of external porcelain. In the context of traditional manual production, the advantages of the division of labor in Jingdezhen's porcelain industry ensures that it has been leading the development of the world's porcelain industry. Therefore, in the development of China's porcelain, the wisdom and labor of the porcelain workers have made Jingdezhen porcelain famous overseas and have made significant contributions to the development of China and the world's ceramic culture.

Jingdezhen porcelain has its unique aesthetic value. American scholar Abrams once proposed that the four elements that constitute the art system are the artwork, the artist, the universe, and the viewer. As a work of art, Jingdezhen porcelain satisfies people's pursuit of beauty, provides people with a visual enjoyment, interprets and externalizes people's feelings, and arouses people's spiritual resonance. Karl Marx once said, the service provided by a singer satisfies my aesthetic enjoyment. Artworks and viewers, each one of them makes the other better. Porcelains as precious works of art, spread to all parts of the world, not only as a kind of artwork for the pursuit of realizing its spiritual value, and they also satisfy the artistic aesthetic pursuits of foreign viewers.

Jingdezhen porcelain has carried the history and culture of Chinese society for thousands of years. Chinese traditional porcelain crafts are also carriers and means for the Chinese voice. Jingdezhen has embodied the core of Chinese folklore, ethics, morality, philosophy, and religion for thousands of years. Its shapes and patterns reflect the variety of Chinese society. Also, the inheritance and improvement of porcelain by Chinese porcelain workers in the era of historical change represents a turning point in Chinese social history. From the end of the Qing Dynasty to modern China, the porcelain workers in Jingdezhen struggled against foreign porcelain, so the traditional workmanship of Jingdezhen was preserved. Antique porcelains have high achievements and many sculptors, such as the "Eight Friends of Zhushan", painters and other outstanding artists stand out. Therefore, Jingdezhen ceramics carry Chinese culture and reflect the characteristics of the nation. Behind this is the guardianship and inheritance of Chinese traditional skills by Chinese ceramic workers who contributed to Chinese ceramic culture.

Jingdezhen porcelain has diverse cultural intertextuality. There are countless humanistic records about porcelain, like Chinese well-known writer Liu Zongyuan's works in the Tang Dynasty, Jiang Qi's *Tao Ji* in the Song Dynasty, and Wang Zongmu's *Jiangxi Province Dazhi • Tao Book* and Song Yingxing's *Tiangong Kaiwu • Taoman*, *Nan Kiln Notes* in the Qing Dynasty, *Jingdezhen Pottery Record* by Zheng Tinggui, *An Overview of Porcelain* by Guo Baochang, *The History of the Jingdezhen Porcelain Industry* by Jiang Siqing, *The General Situation of Jingdezhen Ceramics* compiled by Li Haoting, *Jingdezhen Ceramics Chronicle* by Xiang Zhuo, etc. Since contemporary times, there have been *Chinese Porcelain* compiled by the Jingdezhen Ceramic Research Institute of Jiangxi Light Industry Department in 1963, and *Chinese Ceramic History* by the China Silicate Association in 1982, of which Jingdezhen porcelain has a certain amount of space. Liu Xinyuan, who gained awards from Chinese government, has published articles on porcelain archaeology in foreign newspapers and has given lectures abroad many times.

The Jingdezhen porcelain industry is also a kind of science and technology. In the scientific and technological undertakings of Jingdezhen in ancient times, some people summarized the scientific achievements of porcelain making, such as *Tao Ji*. There are many professional books from the late Qing Dynasty to modern China on porcelain making. According to the *Fuliang County Chronicles* in the 48th year of Qianlong (1783), as early as the Five Dynasties, there were people who were engaged in writings on etiquette and family precepts. Later, there were a total of 172 published books divided into five categories: classics, history, anthology, and miscellaneous. Since the founding of the People's Republic of China, the number of people engaged in the research into the ceramic's development history, ancient ceramics, ancient architecture, and other social science researches has gradually increased.

Chinese Porcelain, Mainstay in the Revival and International Communication of Chinese Culture

China also means "porcelain" in the Western context. Jingdezhen porcelain is the most typical representative of Chinese traditional crafts. In recent years, social productivity has been greatly improved, science and technology have developed rapidly, international transportation has become more and more convenient, and media such as network media have spread all over the country, which has promoted more frequent cross-border cultural exchanges. Today, Chinese porcelain also has more diversified channels of dissemination, including commercial, exhibition, collection, tourism, education, and media channels.

The first is the commercial path of Jingdezhen porcelain as a commodity. Since ancient times, economic benefits have significantly and effectively promoted the commercial dissemination of Chinese traditional commodities. As the city of Chinese porcelain, Jingdezhen has produced more than 2,000 types, and more than 7,000 patterns and decorations, forming a complete range of antique porcelain, tourist porcelain, and daily-use porcelain. The ceramic product system has been exported to more than 130 countries and regions. Chinese porcelain has many sales patterns abroad. One is to retail as daily necessities in supermarkets and shopping malls, and the other is to collect as works of art in art markets. To fulfill the demand of different customers, porcelain manufacturers have developed different textures, shapes, and patterns, and modern mass production has made the Jingdezhen porcelain industry flourish again.

The second is the exhibition path of Jingdezhen porcelain as material cultural heritage. As a traditional Chinese handicraft, in recent years, Chinese porcelain has been represented in major exhibitions of Chinese traditional crafts, as an independent outreach of historical and cultural relics, in large-scale overseas art exhibitions invited by China, cooperative exhibitions between museums, and special commemorations, festive art exhibitions, international selective art exhibitions, etc. Transnational exhibitions of porcelain are mostly organized by nonprofit organizations, often accompanied by media promotion, academic seminars, special lectures, press conferences, brochures, and derivative sales to attract public attention, but not for profit. The emphasis is on cultural communication. At the same time, Jingdezhen porcelain as a traditional handicraft disseminates to the outside world, realizes the aesthetic value of porcelain as an art carrier, and promotes the exchange and development of Chinese and foreign art. Therefore, transnational exhibitions are often an important way for the international spread of Chinese culture.

The third is the collection path of Jingdezhen porcelain as artworks. Art collection combines the characteristics of the above two communication paths. First, porcelain collection is an investment method for economic accumulation, preservation, and appreciation. The non-renewability and scarcity of artworks have brought huge profits to collectors. Antique dealers and private collectors regard art collection as a kind of commercial investment; second, the art collection is also a kind of cultural communication activity. The continued collection by different collectors and the private exhibition of porcelain collections has a certain role in promoting cultural communication.

The fourth is the tourist path of Jingdezhen porcelain as local specialties. Tourism, as an effective way to show local culture to foreign tourists, is an important means of promoting cultural exchanges and international cooperation in the world today. Jingdezhen is one of the first nationally announced historical and cultural cities. Among the many ancient cultural remains, the Hutian ancient kiln site has been listed as a national key protection unit, and the northern Song Hongta in Fuliang Town and the three ancient kiln sites in Hutian, Tangxia, and Yangmei Pavilion are listed as the provincial key protection unit, 44 municipal cultural relics protection sites. Ceramic museums, ceramic history museums, ancient kiln porcelain factories, cultural relic shops, and other related cultural institutions have done a lot of work for collection, preservation, archaeology, and publicity, which attracts a large number of experts, scholars, and tourists. In terms of commercial tourism, visitors can experience the charm of oriental traditional crafts in the process of visiting museums, participating in porcelain making in ceramic workshops, and buying souvenirs. Porcelain is both artistic and practical, which is more attractive to domestic and foreign tourists and it has strong cultural attraction and artistic appeal.

The fifth is the education path of Jingdezhen porcelain and its superb skills. Jingdezhen ceramic education has initially formed a multi-level, multi-standard, multi-form education system. Jingdezhen Ceramic Institute directly under the Ministry of Light Industry, Jingdezhen Ceramic Workers College under the supervision of the Provincial Ceramic Industry Corporation, Jingdezhen Ceramic School under the Provincial Department of Light Industry, and several ceramic vocational high schools are all bases for cultivating ceramic talents. In recent years, as China's economic development is getting better and better, Chinese excellent traditional culture has received attention from home and abroad. On overseas education platforms, Chinese colleges and universities have been widely registered for education courses in Chinese studies. In recent years, foreign colleges and universities have also opened departments related to Chinese art history and sinology studies. Chinese porcelain is an important topic among them. China has opened Confucius Institutes, Chinese Cultural Centers, and other institutions all over the world to offer art courses. Porcelain, as an outstanding representative of Chinese traditional crafts, has also gained wide recognition and attention overseas.

The sixth is media path of Jingdezhen porcelain as symbols. With the development of the new media era, the development of mass media has played an important role in the overseas dissemination of porcelain. The publications issued by Jingdezhen include Jingdezhen Ceramics and Ceramic Research. The movie scripts created with ceramics as the theme include "Porcelain Doll" and "Drip Water Guanyin", which were produced by Shanghai Fine Arts Film Studio and Shanghai Film Studio, respectively, filling in the city's film creation blank. There are also several works of art, drama, music, and dance, art, calligraphy, and photography published, exhibited, or performed, reflecting the characteristics of the porcelain city and reflecting the unique cultural charm of Jingdezhen porcelain. As a cultural symbol, Jingdezhen porcelain can be seen on media platforms. Its elegant and unique cultural temperament has infected many people who are interested in Chinese culture.

To sum up, the spread of Jingdezhen porcelain overseas includes many paths. From ordinary household tableware to the characteristic national gifts presented on formal diplomatic occasions, the external promotion channels of porcelain for Chinese culture are diverse and wide. Today, with the rapid development of science and technology, there is still large room for its development.

Suggestions on Chinese Porcelain Development

Firstly, due to excessive pursuit of profit, the quality of daily-use porcelain is not guaranteed. The market competition caused by the domestic price war has seriously affected the quality of daily-use porcelain. The appearance of fake and defective products in the market has led to the phenomenon of "bad money driving out good money", which has led to daily-use porcelain manufacturers to continuously reduce the quality of porcelain.

Medium-quality porcelain has increased in price while the purchase volume has decreased. As a result, consumers' distrust of domestic products has emerged, making Japanese porcelain and Western imported porcelain more popular among consumers in China. This has further strengthened the Chinese people's "worshiping foreigners" psychology. Not only Jingdezhen porcelain, but most traditional Chinese handicrafts are faced with the contradiction of "internal price wars and external quality wars", which means some products have low prices but poor quality, and better quality but high prices. The prerequisite for cultural self-confidence is inseparable from the vigorous development of the business economy, but the bad market economy issues will indirectly affect people's psychology. This can be seen in China's current successful business cases, such as home appliances, technology products, etc. Only domestic products recognized by consumers can go abroad to impact overseas markets, spread Chinese ideas and culture, and be accepted overseas. Therefore, only by protecting traditional craftsmanship, establishing porcelain grading inspection standards, and improving market quality can it be conducive to the inheritance and development of traditional Chinese crafts and their dissemination.

Secondly, the number of porcelain artists is decreasing year by year, and so do the porcelain artworks in Jingdezhen. Although the Jingdezhen government has increased its investment in porcelain, the large-scale machine production needs more assembly line workers and the aesthetic value of porcelain is ignored by most manufacturers. It is difficult to spread China's traditional culture by these products. Therefore, it is necessary to pay attention to art education at home and the protection of artists for the inheritance of material cultural heritage, and this bring about external communication and influence.

Thirdly, Jingdezhen porcelain has the problem of low integration with modern popular culture. In recent years, Hanfu (Han Chinese Clothing) has been sought after and loved by young people. In public places such as subways, shopping malls, etc. The phenomenon of young generations wearing Hanfu robes and shawls has demonstrated cultural identity and traditional connotations. Young people are a creative and imaginative group of society. Active groups' interest in traditional culture has effectively helped the inheritance and development of Chinese culture. However, traditional Chinese crafts such as Chinese porcelain, lacquerware, and sculptures tend to be considered "outdated and old-fashioned" and "inconsistent with contemporary aesthetics". Therefore, to improve this phenomenon, it is necessary to pay attention to art and aesthetic education, strengthen the domestic and foreign promotion of Jingdezhen porcelain, enhance the interest and quality of the young generation in traditional Chinese humanistic knowledge, and inject vitality into the modern development of traditional crafts.

In short, the lack of internal force in the inheritance and development of Jingdezhen porcelain is the main problem in the international communication. In the process of foreign exchange and integration, it is necessary to expand the communication path and the scope of the audience. In external dissemination, the official and the private, the art and commerce need to be combined on diplomatic occasions or in international cooperation activities for precious heritage collections. The government should attach great importance to the study of traditional culture with folk channels, giving full play to the power of the masses, since the masses' acceptance of traditional crafts determines the depth and breadth of its external dissemination.

Conclusion

Chinese porcelain is the main carrier of Chinese culture. Trade commodities on the "Silk Road" such as porcelain, silk, and sculpture are the earliest Chinese techniques accepted overseas. Traditional Chinese aesthetics, ideology, and values are represented in the traditional crafts. Jingdezhen porcelain is one of the most typical representatives. Nowadays, the porcelain market is impacted by modern and contemporary Western-dominated pop culture. The word "tradition" seems to be incompatible with contemporary young people who pursue "fashion." The standard of fashion has been redefined by the West. With the rapid development of China's economy, the concepts of cultural self-confidence, such as "cultural soft power", "cultural competitiveness", and "cultural influence" have been continuously emphasized in recent years, and policies related to the "going out" of Chinese culture have been published. As an important part of the policy, Jingdezhen porcelain is a product with both artistic and commercial features, which would expand the international markets of Chinese goods, build the authentic image of China through artistic language, spread the excellent traditional Chinese culture.

(Beijing International Studies University)

Bibliography

1. Abrams, M. H. "The Trend of Critical Theory", translated by Luo Wuheng, *Study on Literary Theory*, 1986.
2. Chen Jinghai. *World Ceramics: The Art of Earth and Fire in the Fusion of Different Human Civilizations and Multiculturalism* (Volume 5). Shenyang: Shenyang Pictorial Publishing House, 2006.
3. Chen Jinhai. *World Ceramic Art History*, Heilongjiang Fine Arts Publishing House, 1995.
4. Guo Danying. "Research on Ancient Chinese Ceramic Tea Set for Export" [D], Zhejiang University, 2007.
5. Li Zhi. *Cultural Diplomacy: An Interpretation of Communication Studies*, Beijing: Peking University Press, 2005.
6. Li Shengli. "Thinking on Established Jingdezhen's Top Ten Porcelain Factory", *Jingdezhen Ceramics*, February 2009.
7. Wang Yichuan, *Principles of Art*, Beijing: Beijing Normal University Press, 2011.
8. Yuan Shenggen, Zhong Xuejun. "On the Relationship between Guangcai Porcelain in Qing Dynasty and Chinese and Western Cultural Exchanges" [J], *Chinese Ceramics*, June 2004.
9. Zhang Wenjing, "Inheritance and Development of Foreign Color Porcelain from the Perspective of Sino-Western Cultural Exchange" [J], *Chinese Culture Forum*, 2016.
10. Zhu Shunlong, *Ceramics and Chinese Culture*, Shanghai: Chinese Dictionary Publishing House, 2003.
11. Reed, Marcia. Paola, Dematte, ed. *China on Paper: European and Chinese Works from the Late Sixteen to the Early Nineteen Century*. Los Angeles: Getty Research institute, 2011.

The Construction of Happy Cultural Identity and Sustainable Development Countermeasures in Tianjin Cuisine

Zhang Jiachuan

Introduction: Chinese food culture is extensive and profound. The eight cuisines composed of Lu, Chuan, Yue, Su, Zhe, Min, Xiang and Hui basically emblems most of the Chinese delicacies since ancient times, and they also occupy an irreplaceable place in world cuisine. Tianjin, as a port city under the Nine River, one of the four municipalities directly under the Central Government in China, first appeared in the "Jin History" under the name "Zhigu Zhai". In the early years of the Qing Dynasty, intensive commercial areas were further developed, and a number of wealthy merchants gradually emerged during the Daoguang period. The prosperity of commerce and the activeness of businessmen naturally give rise to a huge driving force for the consumer industry. The development of the catering industry, which is the main content of people's consumption, is more obvious[1]. In 1662, the opening of "Juqingcheng", the top of the eight major "Cheng" in Tianjin ("Cheng" is a name suffix as a series) marked the official creation of the Tianjin cuisine system[2]. After years of evolution, Tianjin cuisine has become an important part of Tianjin culture and an important reference for Tianjin people to recognize their own identity. Tianjin people are cheerful, enthusiastic, optimistic and humorous. According to the

---

[1] You Guoqing. *Tianjin Wei Cuisine*. Tianjin People's Press, 2011, p. 1. (由国庆:《天津卫美食》,天津人民出版社 2011 年版,第 1 页)
[2] Lai Xin Xia. *Tianjin History and Culture*, Tianjin People's Press, 2008, pp. 218–219. (来新夏:《天津历史与文化》,天津人民出版社 2008 年版,第 218—219 页)

evaluation of the "Top Ten Happy Cities" in each year, among the big cities, Tianjin has a very high "ranking rate". Among the municipalities directly under the Central Government, it often beats Beijing and Shanghai to make the list[1]. Tianjin, as a relatively small city in China, is the same as Denmark, a European country with the same small area. It has a small scale and a big advantage in terms of the cultural soft power of "happiness".

Denmark's happiness culture is widely known. The latest "World Happiness Report 2020"[2] shows that Denmark is the second-ranked country in the world in the happiness report, only behind Finland. In fact, Denmark remains in the top two positions almost every year, and was voted the happiest country in the world in 2012, 2013 and 2016. The "Hygge" in Danish culture has spread throughout the world as a meme of happiness. In terms of food, the Danish people's dietary pursuit is to treat themselves well, to pamper themselves, to indulge themselves, and to give themselves a time to escape from the needs of a healthy life[3], which coincides with the optimistic spirit of Tianjin people. The diet of Tianjin people is mainly to please themselves. Seafood, meat, and sweets are the main ones, but salt and oil are also the characteristics of Tianjin cuisine. There are cultural codes hidden in Tianjin cuisine. Tianjin culture, as a component of Chinese culture, needs to construct its own cultural identity according to its own characteristics. Chinese culture must be critically inherited and developed, and cultural identity must be the essence, not the dross. The happiness code of the Danish diet can provide a solution for Tianjin cuisine. There is also a lot of room for improvement in Tianjin cuisine that has constructed Tianjin's cultural identity. Food, as a demonstration of cultural soft power, can also build a more distinctive Chinese cultural identity.

---

[1] Zhao Qing, Regional Analysis of Urban Residents' Happiness — Take Tianjin as an Example, *Business Culture*, 2012, Issue 11 (second half of the month). [赵青:《城市居民幸福感的地域性分析——以天津为例》,《商业文化》2012 年第 11 期(下半月)]

[2] World Happiness Report, https://happiness-report.s3.amazonaws.com/2020/WHR20.pdf, 2020 - 12 - 20.

[3] Meik Wiking, The Little Book of Hygge: The Danish Way to Live Well, *CITIC Press*, 2017, p. 71.

The history and reputation of Tianjin cuisine

There are many types of food in Tianjin cuisine, which have a long history and widely spread, enjoying a good reputation.

From the "Zhigu Zhai" in the Jin Dynasty to "Tianjin", which was officially named in the second year of Yongle in the Ming Dynasty, this place is located in the end of nine rivers and has a vast water area of "72 Gu". As the saying goes: Eat fish and shrimp, Tianjin is home. As early as Qianlong reign, there was a reputation of "Shi Li Yu Yan Xin Ze Guo, Er Fen Yan Yue Xiao Yang Zhou"[①]. In ancient Tianjin, puffer fish was abundant. At the end of Yuan Dynasty and the beginning of Ming Dynasty, when a poet Cheng shizhong passed through Tianjin, he left the verse of "Yang Liu Ren Jia Fan Hai Yan, Tao Hua Chun Shui Shang He Tun". Dong Yuandu, a Jinshi in Qianlong's seventeenth year, had been to Tianjin, and he was amazed at how Tianjin people ate puffer fish without thinking about their lives. The small yellow croaker in Tianjin has been a very precious and noble delicacy as early as the Ming and Qing Dynasties. There is a record in the "Qing Pi Cai Chao". After the emperor tasted the yellow croaker, it became a rare delicacy in the restaurant. Although the Jin Beng Li Yu was one of the delicacies that were born during the invasion of China by the Eight-Power Allied Forces, it was praised by the Tianjin celebrity Lu Xinnong in his "Food Miscellaneous Poems" as "Ming Chuan Di Yi Bai Yang Li, Peng Zuo Jin Gu Zeng Beng Yu". Tianjin loves to eat saury. There are two types: river saury and sea saury. The poet Zhou Chuliang in the Daoguang period of the Qing Dynasty recorded that "Saury is like a fiberboard on a boat. It is obtained by freshwater nets entering the river mouth … without the smell of sea, the most delicious." Except for fish. All kinds of shrimps are also delicious in Tianjin. The "Jin Men Zhu Zhi Ci" in the late Qing Dynasty said that "Zheng Si Chun Lai Xin Wei Hao, Huang Xia Shi Guo You Qing Xia." Tianjin celebrity Lu Xinnong also

---

① You Guoqing. *Tianjin Wei Cuisine*. Tianjin People's Press, 2011, pp. 4 - 180. (由国庆:《天津卫美食》,天津人民出版社 2011 年版,第 4—180 页)

said in the "Food Miscellaneous Poems":"Shu Lai Jia Jie Shuo Xin Zheng, Bai Li Yu Qun Hai Shang Zheng; Duo Ming Xiao Zhou Qing Si Ye, Qing Suo Bai Huang Gong Tiao Peng." Every spring in the April or May, Bohai Portunus crab roe is the most delicious time. Even a man is lack of money at that time, he has to eat borrowing money from others. Just like the old Tianjin saying:"Borrowing money to eat seafood is not a spendthrift." Nowadays, eating seafood is still a major feature of Tianjin.

In addition to seafood, Tianjin's old restaurants are also well-known. With the development of politics, economy and culture, Tianjin's catering industry has begun to take shape in the late Ming and early Qing dynasties, which reached its peak after the middle of the Qing Dynasty. There are hundreds of small restaurants all over the streets. To celebrate Emperor Kangxi's ascension to the throne, Juqingcheng Restaurant was born in the prosperous Baoyanlou Hutong, Guyi Street, amidst the warm sound of firecrackers in 1662. "Jin Men Zhu Zhi Ci" records:"Guyi Street Nie Zhao Hongyuan, a meal usually costs 10,000 yuan." Tianjin cuisine boomed in the 1930s, and most of the celebrity chefs in high-end restaurants mastered the skills of "five ghosts"-at the same time Control two main fires, one secondary fire and one soup fire. Vegetarian dishes are an important part of Tianjin's food culture. In the thirty-two years of Guangxu, under the initiative of the famous Tianjin cultural scholar Lin Moqing, Zhensu Building was opened in the middle of the big hutong with a west-facing facade. The word "Zhensu" quotes the sentence "(Yi Yuan Qi Xing Zhen Su) It is also due to its true nature" in "Shi Shuo Xin Yu". Gou Bu Li Bao Zi is one of the top three cuisines in Tianjin. At the end of the 1920s, Feng Wentian said in "Bingyin Tianjin Zhuzhi Ci": "Bao Zi Tiao He Xiao Yi Xiang, Gou Dou Bu Li Fan Ming Yang. Mo Kua Jin Ri Lin Feng Yue, Nan Ge Zhang Guan Jiu Shan Chang." The classic eight bowls and roasted meat, the four treasures of winter(whitebait, purple crab, iron bird, chive), and four major steaks, all represent the historical stages of Tianjin cuisine to varying degrees.

In addition to lunch and dinner, Tianjin people also attach great importance to breakfast, and even snacks and desserts after a meal have never been overlooked in Tianjin's diet, but have become a unique landscape.

Guozi was introduced to Tianjin since the Song Dynasty. People hated Qin Hui (a traitor in Chinese tales) and made him a "fried ghost". It was roughly in the Qing Dynasty and gradually changed its name to "Bangchui Guozi". Jian Bing Guo Zi is the most distinctive snack, and it is also the most popular breakfast among Tianjin people. Guoba dishes are often pronounced as "Gaba Cai" in Tianjin dialect. The image of "soup with salted black bean sauce, blue peppers at the end, water boiling in the pot, scattered golden ribbons" in Pu Songling's "Jian Bing Fu" in the Kangxi period of the Qing Dynasty is a metaphor of the situation of Guo Ba Cai. "Tianjin Ganli (chestnut)" is also a well-known brand that is well-known all over the world. It is a famous product for exporting foreign exchange and even imported food specially formulated by some countries. The "Jilue of Jinmen" in the Guangxu reign of the Qing Dynasty records that the Zheng Santang fried chestnuts under the Dongmen Archway in Tianjin are well-known, and have an excellent reputation. Other snacks such as Da Li Gao, Shu Li Gao, and Dou Gen Tang are also snacks full of Tianjin characteristics.

If one wants to learn about Tianjin cuisine, it is better to taste it. On-site inspections and tasting can better experience the delicacy described by the sages.

Cultural identity in Tianjin's happy diet

The topic of cultural identity has been controversial since the beginning of this century. After China's reform and opening up, the economy has developed rapidly, and the rapid development of society is intertwined with the influence of globalization. China's own cultural identity is no longer in a static situation, but being dynamic and developing. Globalization has stimulated national self-awareness in different countries and cultures, and strengthened the need for their own cultural identity[1]. In China, the

---

[1] Su Yong, Cultural Subjectivity in Cultural Identity and Construction, *Journal of Guizhou Normal University* (*Social Science Edition*), 2009, Issue 1. (苏勇:《文化身份认同与建构中的文化主体性》,《贵州师范大学学报(社会科学版)》2009 年第 1 期)

urbanization process of big cities is advancing rapidly, and the people's understanding of their own cultural identity is no longer limited to their own country and ethnicity, but a process of cultural integration that can be perceived. In this collision, on the one hand, we must be alert to the cultural hegemony of strong discourse, and avoid being swallowed up by the strong "Orientalist" discourse when understanding oneself and developing self-cultural identity, that is, avoiding a kind of "Orientalist" discourse. On the other hand, when constructing cultural identity, it is necessary to avoid the arrogance and intolerance of extreme nationalism[1]. If China wants to build a prosperous, strong, democratic, civilized and harmonious modernist country, cultural identity with a harmonious and high sense of happiness is worthy of respect.

Beijing is a developed capital. Shanghai, with its citizens being the most "modern", is called the modern capital, but Tianjin is called the "Gen(哏) capital". "哏" means funny and humorous in Tianjin dialect. The humor and cheerfulness of Tianjin people are mainly reflected in Tianjin's "eating culture" and "playing culture". To appreciate someone's knowledge and experience, People in Tianjin describe it as "have eaten a lot and seen a lot". This is obviously more intuitive and realistic than "reading thousands of books and traveling thousands of miles." In a deeper level of thinking, reading and traveling are suffering, but eating is blessed. Different Chinese cuisine restaurants are spread all over the city. Although Tianjin cuisine hasn't been made to the general list, the fast-food represented by "Gou Bu Li Bao Zi" and "Eighteenth Street Ma Hua" is well-known throughout the country. Eating and having fun and playing are considered to be a blessed life in Tianjin[2].

Tianjin people can feel happiness in their diet, which can be seen in the

---

[1] Su Yong, Cultural Subjectivity in Cultural Identity and Construction, *Journal of Guizhou Normal University* (*Social Science Edition*), 2009, Issue 1. (苏勇:《文化身份认同与建构中的文化主体性》,《贵州师范大学学报(社会科学版)》2009 年第 1 期)

[2] Zhao Qing, Regional Analysis of Urban Residents' Happiness — Take Tianjin as an Example, *Business Culture*, 2012, Issue 11 (second half of the month). [赵青:《城市居民幸福感的地域性分析——以天津为例》,《商业文化》2012 年第 11 期(下半月)]

production and naming of food. Gao Guiyou, the founder of "Gou Bu Li Bao Zi", was born in Xiazhu village, Wuqing County (Wuqing District Jin City in today's situation). His father got a son in his middle age. There is an old Chinese saying that a child with a crooked name is easier to be successful, so he called his child a "dog". Gao Guiyou is ingenious. After learning the craft from his master, he opened a snack shop specializing in Bao Zi- "Dejuhao". Because Gao Guiyou has exquisite craftsmanship and sufficient ingredients, the Bao Zi is soft, fresh and not greasy, and look like chrysanthemums. The business is so good that he is too busy to follow up with the shop customers to say hello. So old diners joked that noble friends "The Dog sell Bao Zi but ignore people". This way of word-of-mouth, the "Gou (means dog in Chinese) Bu Li" Bao Zi was born, and the word "Dejuhao" was dramatically forgotten by people[1]. Nowadays, Gou Bu Li Bao Zi, as the top three delicacies in Tianjin, has become a must-eat for tourists in Tianjin. Even foreign friends are deeply interested in this kind of Bao Zi with strange names. Gou Bu Li Bao Zi, as a food symbol that people will inevitably think of when they think of Tianjin, construct the culture of Tianjin people on the same side. Tianjin people are not resistant to the slightly "vulgar" name Gou Bu Li Bao Zi, and instead proudly invite friends from all over to come and taste it. The humor of Tianjin people leads to a high degree of freedom in joking in daily communication. According to Hall's theory of cultural dimensions, the power distance of Tianjin people does not seem to be large. Everyone does not particularly value their own face, but happiness is often appreciated in Tianjin culture in a larger proportion.

Sweets are also an important part of Tianjin's food culture. Eat Da Li Gao wrapped in wax paper in spring, Er Dou Bao Bing in summer, Qie Gao dipped in sugar in autumn, and Shu Li Gao selling by an old man pushing a cart in winter. Tianjin people's love of sweets will not stop throughout the year. Tianjin has a maritime climate. Winter is not very cold and summer is not unbearably hot. This makes Tianjin people like going out for walks after

---

[1] Qian Guohong, "Three Wonders in Tianjin": Tianjin's landmark cuisine, *Times Post*, 2018, Issue 7.
（钱国宏：《"津门三绝"：天津人的地标美食》,《时代邮刊》2018 年第 7 期）

dinner or in their leisure time on weekends. For families with children, it is a comfortable daily life for the children to go out to play at night and chat with their neighbors about their happiness or a rough time in daily life. Usually, there are all kinds of hawker carts on the street, and parents will often fail to withstand the request of their children to buy some sweets for the children and their friends to share. Tianjin's sweets are more present in the streets and lanes, rather than in formal gatherings and banquets. Sweets are also used as a reconciler after dinner, enhancing the relationship between neighbors. Although excessive intake of sweets is not good for health, one of the main characteristics of Tianjin people is the belief in "satisfaction and happiness." Small wealth is peace, and peace is happiness. For those who are still struggling to live a rich life, Tianjin people often show confusion: If you already have something to eat and to drink, why do you work so hard? "Unsatisfied" is a mild criticism of Tianjin people who are dissatisfied with the status quo of life. Not too wealthy or poor is the state that most Tianjin people can accept and are willing to maintain. Even if one happens to have to endure a long day of work, a few bites of Shu Li Gao that is sweet enough to alleviate most of the worries.

There are fried noodles in Beijing, braised noodles in Henan, and meat sauce noodles in Italy. The specialty of Tianjin people is "Lao Noodles". Unlike other types of noodles, Tianjin Lao Noodles does not have fixed ingredients and recipes. Generally speaking, the Lao Noodles in Tianjin is different in every family, and even each chef can make different Lao Noodles facing a different audience. Lao Noodles is naturally based on noodles, but the noodles can only be served to one-third of the bowl, and the remaining two-thirds are all filled with different dishes. There are too many dishes that can be added, with potatoes, tomatoes, fungus, eggs, shrimp as the base, bean sprouts or spinach, purple cabbage or cabbage, potato shreds fried with carrots or beans fried pork. Nothing seems to be inappropriate to be added in Lao Noodles. Traditionally, there is pepper oil made with pepper, coriander, hot oil and soy sauce. After mixing the noodles, sprinkle them on top. Finally, sprinkle with a handful of cucumber and soybeans. When eating, it is served with Baodi(a small district famous for its garlic)

garlic, which can make Tianjin people feel like a divine! Tianjin people are hospitable and accommodating. Whenever guests come to the house, Lao Noodles is an essential standard meal. Not only that, because there are too many dishes, the production process is also very cumbersome and time-consuming, so many people in Tianjin also treat the process of making Lao Noodles as a family reunion. The whole family being together, preparing family-style noodles together, is a living proof of the simple of Tianjin people's happiness.

Countermeasures for the Sustainable Development of Tianjin Cuisine and Identity

In the 21st century when the pace of life is accelerating and competition is becoming increasingly fierce, happiness has gradually become a luxury. Tianjin food culture that conforms to the country's core values should take the responsibility of promoting Chinese culture and act as a booster for the spread of Chinese culture. Food is a rigid need in people's daily life, and it is very suitable as a starting point for cultural transmission. It is especially important to make countermeasures to support its sustainable development.

First of all, Tianjin cuisine should be improved internally. Culture is developing, not static, and cannot be complacent or stagnant because of fear of losing its own characteristics. Statistics show that the obesity rate of Tianjin people is far ahead in the national rankings, which is likely to be due to the high sugar intake in Tianjin people's diet. Although with the advancement of science and technology, the popularization of medical facilities and the improvement of medical services, the cure rate of diseases has been significantly improved, but there is no scientific eating habits, heavy salt and heavy sugar can harm the body. Cardiovascular diseases can endanger life in serious cases. A happy food culture should not be at the cost of health, but should recognize the importance of healthy eating, add a layer of protection to happiness, and make happiness more long-term and lasting. Regarding Tianjin cuisine, we must take the essence and discard the dross. Tianjin people pay more attention to the sustainable development of food and reduce waste. For example, when people in Tianjin buy Jian Bing Guo Zi, they are always accustomed to bringing home eggs instead of using the eggs in the store, which is economical and affordable. Tianjin also started the implementation of a waste sorting system in 2020. The public should support waste sorting, centralized processing of kitchen waste, and attach importance to the sustainable development of the environment.

Secondly, Tianjin food culture should strengthen the awareness of cultural identity among locals, enhance their cultural self-confidence, and bring people together. Due to historical reasons, Tianjin cuisine developed earlier. Many cuisines belong to traditional cuisines and are not suitable for the fast pace of today's society. Contemporary young people are less familiar with cuisines, and the meaning of traditional cuisines is gradually forgotten. Various non-governmental organizations can organize book reading festivals, exchange reading meetings, and face-to-face with traditional chefs, leading locals to strengthen their understanding of traditional Tianjin cuisine and enhance their confidence in their cultural identity. The local government should also strengthen the support of food culture on the basis of improvement, save the endangered snacks and traditional dishes, combine material and spiritual forces, and strengthen the spread of culture on the basis of meeting social needs. For example, the Nanshi Food Street in Nankai District, which gathers various snacks in Tianjin, has not changed for many years, and the heating problem cannot be solved due to the semi-open environment. The media support is not enough at the same time. Although it is close to Nankai Joy City, the Food Street cannot attract people to go and try. The local government can strengthen corresponding safeguards to make Tianjin's food culture "be lively" and "active", which in turn strengthens the identity and cultural bound of Tianjin people, which can also promote the spread of culture.

Finally, with the wind of the development, Tianjin cuisine can combine with other Tianjin's excellent cultures, adapt to social needs, and use the rapid dissemination of new media or short videos to meet public expectations. Tianjin cuisine is not among the eight major cuisines in China, but when it comes to Xiang Sheng (a traditional Chinese talk show), Chinese people first think of Tianjin. "The name of the dish" in Tianjin classic Xiang Sheng, "steamed lamb, steamed bear paw, steamed deer tail, roasted duck, roasted chicken, roasted goose, braised salted duck, sauce chicken, bacon, Songhua eggs, small belly ..." Almost everyone in the country can remember this paragraph. This widely disseminated art method has become Tianjin's characteristic art method. It can be combined with the dissemination of Tianjin cuisine. It not only meets the audience's entertainment needs, but also spreads Tianjin culture through Tianjin cuisine and promotes the sustainability of cultural identity. development of. In recent years, short video platforms have emerged, and many traditional arts have adopted this new media method for dissemination. At present, the dissemination of Tianjin food is only through the personal account of individual Tianjin people to share the usual shop exploration and food production methods. The official media can take advantage of the development and use official short video accounts to spread Tianjin's food culture. Now that happiness is scarce, spreading the culture and values of happiness has also met the expectations of the public to a certain extent.

Tianjin cuisine, as an inseparable part of Chinese cuisine, has a new vitality in the new era due to the "happiness" element contained in it. Whether it is acclaimed seafood, traditional old shops, or snacks for breakfast, Tianjin people's happiness genes are fully displayed in Tianjin cuisine and participate in the construction of Tianjin people's cultural identity. However, culture needs progress, and cultural communication needs to be strengthened on the basis of improvement. Tianjin's culture should strengthen the cultural awareness and cultural confidence of local people on the basis of internal improvements, and use new media such as short videos to strengthen the sustainable development of cultural identity contributes to the spread of Chinese culture and strengthens China's cultural soft power.

(Beijing International Studies University)

The External Communication of Chinese Beijing Opera

Liu Qi

Brief Introduction of Beijing Opera

On November 6, 2010, the fifth session of the intergovernmental committee for the safeguarding of the intangible cultural heritage was held in Nairobi. This session is of great significance to China, 24 members jointly deliberated and adopted the declaration materials of Beijing Opera. Beijing opera successful candidate the "representative list of the intangible cultural heritage of humanity". Chinese Beijing Opera earns its place in the field of world culture and has a unique position of all the excellent traditional culture in China. It has been further recognized and accepted around the world.

Beijing Opera is the most popular, most influential and most representative type of Chinese opera. It is also known as "Chinese national essence" or "National opera". Beijing Opera got its name because it was originated in Beijing. The performing of Beijing Opera inherits and develops the tradition of singing and dancing in old Chinese opera, and gradually forms a complete system through years of practice on stage. Beijing Opera is a comprehensive performing art, integrating music, vocal performance, mime, dance and acrobatics. Beijing Opera portrays and narrates the plot and characters through stylized acting. The music, vocal performance, mime, dance and acrobatics, they all have strict procedures.[①] Different roles and professions also have different norms and styles. The characters should be closely coordinated. Actors and the band cooperate very well, they make the scene tense but orderly, and make the battle fierce but beautiful. Beijing Opera has almost all kinds of roles and they are strictly differentiated. Now the roles mainly divided into Sheng(male roles), Dan(female roles), Jing(painted roles), Chou(clowns) four categories. Each role has its own unique performance style to show the character's specialty. They may be loyal or crafty, beautiful or ugly, good or evil, each image is vivid. The costume of Beijing Opera is formed from the mainstream Chinese costume culture in China for thousands of years, which is conducive to performance skills such as mime, dance and acrobatics. Different roles have different dress code and they have a very detailed classification. Their costumes are different from the different dynasties and different status. The outlook of the costume, is an important symbol of the role in social status. Facial makeup is also an important part of dressing up. It is formed in the process of the formation of Beijing Opera by integrating the facial makeup of various types of Chinese operas and then taking advantage of them and transforming them. Facial makeup is a symbol of decorative and exaggerated character model to show the characteristic and to identify the good, evil, loyal and treacherous. It is a symbol of the character, quality and destiny of a person. It is painted with certain colors on the face. Different roles have different facial makeup. It is the key to understand the plot and is also a major feature of Beijing Opera.

The international communication of Chinese opera has a history of hundreds of years. Beijing Opera as a representation of the ancient opera culture. Its unique artistic style, oriental aesthetic and the integration of many artistic styles become the symbol of the Chinese traditional culture. It also plays an important role in introducing Chinese culture to the western world. Since the 13th century, Chinese opera has spread in Europe, America and Southeast Asia, and has been integrated with local culture and art,

---

① Zhou Yude, *Chinese Opera Culture*, China Theatre Press, 1995. (周育德:《中国戏曲文化》,中国戏剧出版社 1995 年版)

especially the local drama. Since the 15th century, cultural exchanges between China and the West became more frequent. Chinese opera and actors were introduced to Europe and appeared on the European stage. People from all over the world began to realize the unique charm of Chinese opera art. Since the 17th century, a large number of works on China have appeared in Europe, and oriental culture has provided fresh material for the creation of western drama. In the first half of the 20th century, especially in the 1920s and 1930s, a series of communication activities represented by Peking Opera is the climax of intercultural communication of Chinese opera, among which Mei Lanfang's visit to the United States is the climax. In 1915, at the request of the Ministry of Foreign Affairs, Mei Lanfang received a troupe of American priests to perform *Chang'e to the Moon*, which may be the first time that the actors of Beijing Opera officially introduced Peking Opera to foreigners on the Chinese land. Since then, his residence in Beijing has become a "diplomatic residence", hosting 6,000 to 7,000 people from various field like literature, art, politics, business and education, including Tagore, the great writer, and Bertrand Russell, the famous British philosopher.[1] Mei Lanfang changed the western prejudice against Chinese opera and even Chinese people at that time. He promoted Chinese opera, helped eastern and western cultures better understand each other, and paved a way for overseas visits. After successful visits to Japan and Hong Kong, Mei Lanfang led a delegation to the United States in 1930. The visit has been a success on the cultural communication. There were continuous coverage and commentary by the mainstream Media in the United States. And they gained the warm hospitality of people in the art world. Subsequently, Mei Lanfang visited the Soviet Union, which also set off a wave of appreciation and review of Beijing opera. In addition, from 1932 to 1933, Cheng Yanqiu, another famous opera actor, also went to the Soviet Union, France, Germany, Switzerland and Italy for culture communication, performing and

---

[1] The Cross-Cultural Barriers in the External Communication of Chinese Opera, *Journal of College Chinese Traditional Opera*, 2019(31). (刘珺:《中国戏曲对外传播的跨文化障碍》,《戏曲艺术》2010 年第 31 期)

participating in various forms of cultural activities. As a result, European countries began to gradually understand Chinese Opera and study on Beijing Opera.

Although Peking Opera has been spreading abroad for hundreds of years and has made some progress, it has never been a smooth process and always faces different difficulties in every stage in history. In the context of globalization, the cross-cultural communication of Chinese Peking Opera is once again confronted with challenges. Only by recognizing the cultural identity conflicts and difficulties that encountered in the transmission of Peking Opera, can it be carried out better under the current conditions.

The Dilemma of Beijing Opera's External Communication

Difficult to Translate, More Difficult to Understand

Language is a tool of communication. When Peking Opera troupes go abroad to perform, improper translation will make the audience unable to understand the plot and thus unable to have a deep understanding of Peking Opera. The translation of opera has always been a difficult problem. In order to translate the meaning of opera lyrics, we should neither translate literally nor completely abandon the literal meaning. We should give consideration to the understanding habits of foreign audiences, and strive to keep the rhyme of opera lyrics. Beijing Opera vocabulary translation is very hard, because a lot of words is now rarely used in vernacular Chinese expression. It is difficult to find the corresponding words in the foreign texts. In addition, many of the names of Beijing Opera are based on place names, such as *Wujiapo* and *Sanchakou*, etc., which cannot be understood by foreigners if translated in pinyin.

The performance of Peking Opera can overcome the language barrier at a certain extent, so that the audience can understand the characteristics of roles and the development of the story through the scene and performance. But this understanding is vague and does not deeply understand the plot and the emotions conveyed by the actors. When Mei Lanfang visited the United States, before each performance, he would ask the interpreter to explain the story of the play and give a general introduction of the form of Peking Opera, so that the audience could know the story when watching the play. At present, most of the plays are still in lack of suitable English translation, except for a very small number of plays performed regularly in foreign-related activities. There is a shortage of Chinese opera translators, most of whom do not know the professional knowledge of drama even cannot understand the opera lyrics. It is difficult to guarantee the accuracy of English subtitles, which often fail to convey the meaning or even lead to the opposite direction. It is more difficult to show the unique artistic conception and charm of Chinese traditional opera. The translation of opera lyrics requires the translator to have solid language skills, excellent translation skills, a thorough knowledge of Chinese and Western culture and a good knowledge of opera culture. It is an urgent problem to be solved in the in-depth cross-cultural communication of Chinese opera to improve the level of opera translation so that foreign audiences can appreciate it better.

Differences Between Chinese and Western cultures, High Threshold for Appreciation

Chinese opera has its own inherent virtuality, stylized style and unique aesthetic orientation. For those who do not know Beijing Opera, there is a relatively high threshold for appreciation, and it is difficult for the audience to understand the information conveyed by Beijing Opera.

Different from the realistic style of western drama, the movement like opening the door and sweeping, getting on the horse and traveling in Chinese drama are all expressed through certain stylized symbolic actions. Specific plots are also expressed by specific normative actions, and these symbols and norms are conventionally established. How to draw facial makeup, what color and what it represents have become regulations. Through the facial makeup, the audience can largely identify the characters and backgrounds, and further understand the plot development through the symbolism of facial makeup. These procedures are completely understandable to the audience who are familiar with Beijing Opera, but it is very difficult for the foreign audience who have known nothing about Beijing Opera before. Due to the lack of Chinese cultural background knowledge, audiences would have cognitive load in understanding the Beijing Opera, which also reduces the affinity, appeal and charm of Peking Opera.

In addition, the music of Chinese opera is very different from the western music styles. This music style has no similarity with the music of any other country, so it is difficult to gain resonate. At first, many foreign audiences could not accept the clamor of gongs and drums and the scene of the traditional Chinese instrument, like cucurbit flute and the bamboo flute, playing together. The costume of Chinese opera is also refined and created from ancient normal life, which is lack of aesthetic recognition by foreign audiences. Therefore, with only one or two opera performances, foreign audiences cannot fully enjoy the charm of Chinese opera, nor can they understand the connotation of Chinese culture.

There are many differences between Chinese culture and Western culture. We should be more brave to express and spread our own culture. Before the performance, the organizer can give background materials to the audience or hold a lecture to fill the cognitive differences and reduce the cognitive load. The workers of Beijing Opera activities should have the courage to pursue the feelings and atmosphere with Chinese characteristics, and express the vivid, freehand, introverted and lyrical genes in Chinese culture.

Lack of Interests and Market

The desire for cultural communication is mutual, not a one-side wish. Cultural communication is faced with the harsh reality that no matter how hard the communicator works, all efforts will be in vain if the target audience lacks interest in understanding. Only by truly arousing the interest of foreign audiences and attracting them to learn about Beijing Opera can it be regarded as a success of external communication. The performance of Chinese opera abroad has always focused on more about culture communication than earn the market. Even after Mei Lanfang's visit to the United States sparked the popularity of Beijing Opera, it did not succeed in establishing a fixed market. From the perspective of cross-cultural communication, Chinese opera is the representative and embodiment of the traditional culture of the Chinese nation. Through understanding the Chinese opera, people from other countries and cultures can better understand the connotation, values and aesthetics of Chinese culture. That cannot be realized if the audiences for overseas shows are concentrated among Chinese. Most foreigners who come to China will choose to watch one or two Beijing Opera performances to experience traditional Chinese culture. For these audiences, who are highly mobile and uncertain, opera performance to them is just an item on the fourist list. It is difficult for them to become regular consumers and fans of Chinese opera.

In addition to the above three aspects, in the new historical period, there are still some other difficulties in the intercultural communication of the Chinese opera, which is dominated by Peking Opera. Throughout history, these problems are fundamentally caused by culture differences. Nowadays, in the era of globalization, the distance between countries and cultures has been increasingly narrowed. The development of science and technology has provided more convenient tools for communication, which is both an opportunity and a challenge. Only by solving the difficulties in cultural communication with a positive attitude and seeking common ground while reserving differences in the process of cultural communication can we possibly solve the problems of the intercultural communication of traditional Chinese opera, so that the traditional Chinese opera culture can convey the Chinese voice and tell Chinese stories on the world stage.

the Film Communication of Peking Opera on *Farewell my Concubine*

Film, a comprehensive art, integrating music, fine arts, dance, literature and other forms, has a history of more than one hundred years at present. Compared with Beijing Opera, it is a new art form. With the development of modern society, film is more and more popular among the people. Watching movies has become an indispensable part in modern people's daily life. It is also the main form for modern people to understand different cultures.

In 1895, the first film made by the Lumiere brothers came out to the world. In 1905, China finally began to make their own film. The first film was adapted from the famous Beijing Opera *Dingjun Mountain*, which performed by the famous Beijing Opera master Tan Xinpei. In this landmark work, director Ren Jingfeng chose the theme of Peking Opera, the quintessence of Chinese culture. [1] The combination of Beijing Opera and film can not only enable Chinese people to quickly accept the fresh art form of film, but also bring Beijing Opera, the traditional Chinese art, to a bigger screen and go abroad to the world.

In 1993, the film *Farewell my Concubine* was released. The director Chen Kaige showed to the audience the love and hatred between the two actors, and describe the ups and downs of the Beijing Opera and the country. Beijing Opera runs through the film and promotes the development of the story. *Farewell My Concubine* won the "Palme D'Or" at the 46th Cannes Film Festival, the "Golden Globe Award" for "Best Foreign Language Film" and many other international awards. At the same time, it was selected into the list of "The 100 Best Films in the world history" by Time Magazine of the United States. It has exerted a profound influence on the international world. It can be seen from the success of *Farewell my Concubine* that art has no boundaries, and audiences from all over the world have a high acceptance of traditional Chinese art. Many foreign movie fans who have seen *Farewell my Concubine* show great interests in Beijing Opera art. This movie is an inheritance and transmission of traditional culture. *Farewell my Concubine* was a powerful cultural output and left a strong impression of Beijing Opera in the history of film.

Farewell my Concubine tells a moving story, with time as its thread, spanning several ages. Under the complicate historical background of extremely turbulent social political situation, the fate of the heroes and the fate of Peking Opera art experienced ups and downs together.

---

[1] Chen Xuan, On the Charm and Value of Traditional Chinese Opera in Films — Taking *Farewell my Concubine* and *To Live* as examples, The House of Drama, 2018(32). (陈旋,《论中国传统戏曲在电影中的魅力与价值——以〈霸王别姬〉和〈活着〉为例》,《戏剧之家》2018 年第 32 期)

Beijing Opera element in the film assists and promotes the narration of the story. Under the change of the period, the end of the Qing Dynasty, the Republic of China, the Anti-Japanese War, the Liberation War, the Cultural Revolution, the two heroes Cheng Dieyi and Duan Xiaolou experience the life from fame to down and out. Although foreign audiences may not know much about the history of China or the culture of Beijing Opera, they still can know about the love and hatred of the heroes. By feeling the fate of the heroes, the audience understood that they are deeply bound by Beijing Opera. The audience have gone through a life bounded with Peking Opera together with the heroes. With opera as the main narrative clue, it has strong appearance beauty and modeling beauty, which makes the film has a unique Chinese aesthetic style. The carefully designed scenes and background music in the film allow the audience to immerse themselves in an environment of promoting the art of Beijing Opera. The costumes, makeup and music in the film present a different form of beauty in the visual and auditory sense. In the film *Farewell my Concubine*, the first thing that catches people's attention is the costume art of Beijing Opera. At the beginning of the film, Cheng Dieyi and Duan Xiaolou dress up as the concubine and the King to rehearse on the stage. Cheng Dieyi wears a magnificent costume, with a phoenix crown on his head, and holds a red silk sword in his hand. Duan Xiaolou draws a black and white facial makeup, wears a warrior robe, has an imperial crown on his head, and has a long black beard. At the beginning of the film, the overall style of the opera costume is established, which makes it present a powerful visual impact, showing the delicacy of the costume and the subtlety of Beijing Opera. The background music in *Farewell my Concubine* was composed by the famous Chinese composer Zhao Jiping. It closely follows the tunes in Beijing Opera and combines a variety of traditional Chinese musical instruments. The melody blends with the sadness. The solemn and stirring band shows us the ups and downs of the characters' fate and emotional. The music conveys a strong sense of history.

Throughout the film *Farewell My Concubine*, Beijing Opera, the quintessence of traditional Chinese culture, as a national art, runs through the whole film in the vertical space and time dimension. The film art is horizontally complementary to the Beijing Opera. We can see the development history of Beijing Opera. The film vividly shows us the history, constantly leading the audience to wander in, shuttle in and immerse in it from various perspectives. The art of film gives the audience a point of view that is changing constantly from far to close, close to far. And the audiences follow the camera seems to participate in the scene. The outstanding part of *Farewell my Concubine* is not only its deep integration of Chinese traditional culture and the film art, but also its show the deep feelings towards traditional culture expressed through cross-era light. And this deep feeling shown in the film can arouse the resonance of the global audience. Through the film's aesthetic expression and emotional resonance, the charm of Beijing Opera has been amplified, and more and more audiences have developed an active interest in Beijing Opera, which is the best driving force to break the cultural differences.

The Communication of Chinese Beijinging Opera in the new era

The art of Beijing Opera is extensive and profound. From any single point of view, the opera, the performance, the music, the costumes and the stage art, they are fabulous enough to be written into a magnificent work. Face to the profound art, we need to find a balance between "specialization and refinement" and "generality and comprehensiveness", which is also a standard that Beijing Opera must to follow in its external communication.

Film and television dissemination is an effective way for China's traditional art to go abroad. We need to combine the characteristics of the era to find more scientific modes for the external communication of Beijing Opera, so as to better explore an effective way for China's excellent traditional culture to go abroad. We can make overseas audience through multiple platforms such as movies, television and Internet etc., contact and study opera knowledge, faster and better understand the classic Chinese art works. In this way they can be more familiar with the Chinese traditional culture, comprehensive grasp the emotional orientation and the values of the Chinese people, thus more interested in China's outstanding national culture.

It also increase a more effective ways to understand China.

Therefore, if we want to carry forward our traditional culture, let the Beijing Opera culture truly "go out", we should vigorously expand the market, learn to use new media platforms, and boldly innovate the forms of Peking Opera performances. We can interpret the familiar stories of western audiences in the form of Beijing Opera, embrace western civilization with an open attitude, and find a new spark in the collision between Chinese and Western civilizations. While expanding the international market, we should also understand the interests of foreign audiences, arouse more emotional resonance, attract foreign audiences to take the initiative to understand China, and let more people appreciate the infinite charm of our traditional culture.

(Beijing International Studies University)

Research on Cultural Confidence and Cultural Communication from the Perspective of the Longmen Grottoes

Shen Antong

Since the 18th National Congress of the Communist Party of China, President Xi Jinping has mentioned cultural confidence many times on different occasions. He illustrated that "Culture is a country and nation's soul. Our country will thrive only if our culture thrives, and our nation will be strong only if our culture is strong. Without full confidence in our culture, without a rich and prosperous culture, the Chinese nation will not be able to rejuvenate itself"[1]. Cultural confidence means the full affirmation of Chinese culture and represents the awakening of Chinese civilization and the direction of cultural development. It has been an important source of the confidence of the Chinese nation and the guidance for carrying forward cultural deposits, enhancing cultural soft power and realizing the Chinese dream. There are three sources of cultural confidence. The first is China's fine traditional culture, which is accumulated from the Chinese civilization of more than 5,000 years. It contains profound values, governing concepts, philosophical thoughts, literature and art, science and technology, etc., all of which are the crystallization of the wisdom of the Chinese nation and precious treasures for the sons and daughters of the Chinese nation. The

---

[1] Xi Jinping, *Secure a Decisive Victory in Building a Moderately Prosperous Society in All Respects and Strive for the Great Success of Socialism with Chinese Characteristics for a New Era — Delivered at the 19th National Congress of the Communist Party of China*, Beijing: People's Publishing House, 2017. (习近平:《决胜全面建成小康社会夺取新时代中国特色社会主义伟大胜利——在中国共产党第十九次全国代表大会上的报告》,北京:人民出版社 2017 年版)

second is the revolutionary culture formed under the leadership of the Communist Party of China. It is the result of the Chinese people's struggle for national liberation and national independence and is still the spiritual pillar of the Chinese people in times of peace such as the Jinggangshan spirit and the Long March spirit. The third is the advanced socialist culture with Chinese characteristics which is created since the reform and opening up and promotes the development of China's politics and economy.

As part of China's fine traditional culture, Chinese culture heritage is an important source of culture confidence. It witnesses the development of Chinese civilization, demonstrates the vitality of Chinese culture, and carries the soul of Chinese nation. Chinese culture has a long history, so it has a large number of cultural heritage. China has 55 sites inscribed in the World Heritage List so far, of which 37 are World Cultural Heritage and 4 are World Nature and Culture Heritage. These culture heritages enrich the connotation of Chinese culture and play an important role in demonstrating cultural confidence. The Longmen Grottoes, located in Luoyang, Henan Province of China, was listed as a World Cultural Heritage in 2000. It is one of the grottoes with the longest construction time and the most statues in the world, reflecting China's unique cultural landscape and profound historical and cultural deposits. As a cultural heritage, the Longmen Grottoes constitutes excellent national culture, stimulates national pride, and serves as a solid foundation for cultural confidence. Although Denmark's *The Little Mermaid* is not a stone carving art, it has something in common with China's Longmen Grottoes. As a Danish cultural heritage, *The Little Mermaid* contains the Danish's spiritual pursuit, creates the national image of "fairy tale kingdom", shows the excellent fairy tale literature, and becomes the national symbol of Denmark. Therefore, we should attach great importance to culture heritage and regard it as the root and soul of cultural confidence. We should carry out cultural communication through cultural heritage and realize the culture's "going out", by which we can play the role of cultural heritage and improve the soft power of national culture.

The Longmen Grottoes, as the Foundation of Cultural Confidence

The Longmen Grottoes is one of the four great grottoes in China (the other three grottoes are the Mogao Grottoes in Dunhuang, Gansu Province, the Yungang Grottoes in Datong, Shanxi Province, and the Maijishan Grottoes in Tianshui, Gansu Province.). The Longmen Grottoes is adjacent to the Yi River and close to the Xiang Hill, so it has beautiful natural scenery. In addition, the construction of it began in the Northern Wei Dynasty and lasted more than 400 years. Nowadays, there still exist more than 2,000 caves and niches, and more than 100,000 statues, so it also has rich cultural landscape. When the UNESCO World Heritage Committee enrolled the Longmen Grottoes in the World Heritage List, it complimented that "the caves and niches in the Longmen region represent the largest and the most outstanding formative art from the late Northern Wei Dynasty to the Tang Dynasty (AD 493 - 907) of China, and these artistic works depicting religious themes in Buddhism in detail represent the peak of Chinese stone carving art"[①]. Besides, the Longmen Grottoes is also one of Chinese National Key Cultural Relics Protection Units and a National AAAAA level tourist attraction. It is the epitome of ancient China and reflects the development of politics, economy, religion, culture, art, science and technology in different periods, possessing rich cultural value and cultural vitality. The Longmen Grottoes containing splendid stone carving skills, calligraphy art, Buddhist culture, historical deposits, is the strong foundation of cultural confidence.

First, the Longmen Grottoes shows excellent stone carving skills. It is known that science and technology are limited by historical conditions. Thousands of years ago, China and even the world cannot possess the advanced technologies of today, but they have left many amazing cultural heritages. For example, the Egyptian pyramids, made of stone without any

---

① The Longmen Grottoes, The Official Website of Henan Government, http://www.henan.gov.cn/ztzl/system/2009/06/12/010140064.shtml, 2009.06.12. (《龙门石窟》,河南省人民政府门户网站, http://www.henan.gov.cn/ztzl/system/2009/06/12/010140064.shtml, 2009-06-12)

glue, have been known as a wonder of the world; the Great Wall of China with thousands of miles length is a huge project and a great creation of the working people of ancient China. The Longmen Grottoes is slightly inferior compared with the former two, but its excellent stone carving skills are undeniable. Without any help of machine, people of ancient China chiseled mountains and stones, and completed the large scale project of making statues, breaking through the historical conditions at that time, which is worth marveling at. In addition, the largest statue in the Longmen Grottoes is 17 meters and the smallest is only 2 centimeters. All statues are exquisitely carved and vivid. The facial features, body proportions and clothing lines of the statues show the stone carving skills of ancient skillful craftsmen, whose carving techniques are unmatched.

Second, the Longmen Grottoes has unique calligraphy art. Chinese characters have many forms including oracle bone inscriptions, bronze inscriptions, greater seal script, small seal script, clerical script, cursive script, running script, regular script, all of which play an important role in cultural communication and cultural inheritance. The unique calligraphy art has been formed in the evolution of Chinese characters. Different forms embody different spirit of the times and value orientations, and have extremely high artistic value. The calligraphy art of the Longmen Grottoes is preserved by inscriptions on stone tablets. There are more than 2,800 inscriptions on stone tablets, reflecting calligraphy style and national character in different periods. The most famous calligraphy works are the Twelve Calligraphies and the Yique Shrine Monument. They respectively represent the steles of the Wei Dynasty and the regular script of the Tang Dynasty, with archaeological and artistic value. Taking the Twelve Calligraphies as an example, its calligraphy indicates the social characteristics of the Northern Wei Dynasty and the calligraphers' cultural quality and aesthetic concepts, and reflects the fusion of the delicacy and elegance of the Southern Dynasty and the vigor and simplicity of the Northern Dynasty.[1] Thus,

---

[1] Zhang Ting, Research on the Cultural integration of the North and South from the Longmen Grottoes calligraphy of the Northern Wei Dynasty, *Identification and Appreciation to Cultural Relics*. 2014, Issue 23, p. 50. (张婷:《从北魏龙门石窟书法看南北文化交融》,《文物鉴定与鉴赏》2019 年第 23 期, 第 50 页)

the value of calligraphy in the Longmen Grottoes is beyond its literal contents, because it bears a rich historical and cultural background and has preserved many classic literature and books.

Third, the Longmen Grottoes embodies prevailing religious culture. The Central Plains is the cradle of Chinese civilization and the ruling center of ancient China, so Buddhism was first introduced to this area. Subsequently, Buddhism took root in Luoyang, Henan Province, making this city have a strong Buddhist cultural atmosphere, with the White Horse Temple and Xuanzang's journey to the west as witnesses. Because of the worship of the rulers and the propaganda of the monks and nuns, Buddhism gradually prevailed in China. The Longmen Grottoes is produced in the development of Buddhism in China and is the artistic expression of Buddhist culture with rich Buddhist cultural connotation. The Buddha statues in the Longmen Grottoes vary in themes, including Sakyamuni, Maitreya, Amitabha, Tibetan Bodhisattva and Avalokiteshvara, etc. The Buddha statues also have many styles which can be figured out from their facial features and costumes, reflecting the evolution of Buddhist culture in China. The Longmen Grottoes has become a witness of Buddhist culture in China and a reliable source for the study of the development of Buddhism.

Fourth, the Longmen Grottoes holds profound history of ancient China. The Longmen Grottoes is not the product of a specific historical stage. Instead, it has been built over hundreds of years by several dynasties. As a result, from a diachronic perspective, it reflects the development process of ancient China, presenting the history of more than 400 years again. The ups and downs of the statue construction and the changes of the statue form reflect the change and development of the political situation, ideology, culture, art and economy, showing the magnificence and splendor of Chinese history.

The Longmen Grottoes possesses excellent stone carving skills, unique calligraphy art of ancient China, witnesses the development of religious culture in China, and reflects profound history of China, which makes it the fertile soil of Chinese culture. The fine traditional Chinese culture it contains makes it become the foundation of cultural confidence.

The Longmen Grottoes, as the Product of Cultural Communication

The Longmen Grottoes is not produced by a certain culture at a certain time. It has gone through several dynasties and is nurtured by different civilizations and cultures under the influence of many factors. The communication between the Han and minorities in China, between Buddhism and local religions, between foreign culture and Chinese culture makes contributions to the formation of the Longmen Grottoes. It can be said that without the mutual communication between different cultures, there would not be the Longmen Grottoes.

The first is the integration of the Han and minorities in China. In order to consolidate his government, Emperor Xiaowen of the Northern Wei Dynasty moved the capital to Luoyang and carried out the Chinesization policy which promotes to study the Han culture, making the Xianbei culture from the Northern China blend with the Han culture in the Central Plains. Other ethnic minority regimes in the Wei, Jin and Southern and Northern Dynasties continued to follow the Chinesization policy, learning and absorbing from the Han culture constantly, so that cultural communication and ethnic integration were realized. The Longmen Grottoes came into being under the integration of the Han and minority cultures. For instance, the statues made in the Northern Wei Dynasty retained the strong and upright physique of the Xianbei nationality, but their appearances and costumes were close to the style in the Central Plains and had the characteristics of the Han nationality. It "is the product of the great ethnic and cultural integration when the Northern Wei Dynasty moved its capital to Luoyang, and is the fusion of the Xianbei culture in the Northern China and the Han culture in the Central Plains"[1]. Since the Northern Wei Dynasty, there are more and more elements of the Han culture in the Longmen Grottoes. After the chaos of the Wei, Jin and Southern and Northern Dynasties, many national cultures

---

[1] Zhou Bin, Study on the Statue Art of the Longmen Grottoes, *World of Antiquity*. 2013, Issue 5, p. 34. (周斌:《试论龙门石窟的造像艺术》,《文物世界》2013 年第 5 期,第 34 页)

influenced each other, infiltrated into each other, and absorbed nutrients from each other. In the process of national cultural communication and integration, the Longmen Grottoes came into being.

The second is the fusion of Buddhism, Confucianism and Taoism. Since the Northern Wei Dynasty, "the fusion of Confucianism, Buddhism and Taoism has become the trend of religious development. Buddhism provides people with spiritual support and psychological comfort; Confucianism maintains the order and stability of the society; Taoism, developed on the basis of divination, is also popular among the people"[1]. As a foreign religion, Buddhism is more easily accepted by people if it integrates with the local Confucianism and Taoism. Therefore, the Longmen Grottoes retains Buddhist elements such as cassock and carcanet, while incorporating with Taoist culture like its dress and its image of flying. It also continues the essence of Confucianism "including Golden Mean and benevolence and righteousness which are reflected from its implicit and moderate aesthetic, generous and kind expression, compatible attitudes"[2].

The third is the communication between foreign culture and Chinese culture. The Silk Road, which began in the Han Dynasty, was a bridge for China to carry out cultural communication with other countries and brought China into contact with foreign culture. For example, it introduced Indian culture and Buddhism into China. After that, Indian monks came to China and preached their religion, and Chinese monks went to India for Buddhist scriptures. The frequent cultural communication between India and China began. As the cultural center at that time, the Central Plains was the main place for cultural communication so that Buddhism spread rapidly here. The Longmen grottoes was built for the Buddhist faith at that time, so it inevitably has elements of Indian culture and features of Indian Buddhist

---

[1] Xu Ting, An Analysis of the Characteristics of Female Buddhist Belief in the Northern Wei Dynasty from the Inscriptions of the Longmen Grottoes Statues, *Religious Studies*. 2020, Issue 3, p. 130. (徐婷:《从龙门石窟造像题记探析北魏女性佛教信仰特征》,《宗教学研究》2020 年第 3 期,第 130 页)

[2] Huang Zhigao, "Great change" and "invariable": The Dress of the Longmen Grottoes Statues and the Reflection of the Country, *Art Panoram*. 2020, Issue 8, p. 70. (黄智高:《"巨变"与"不变":龙门石窟造像服饰世俗载映之揆度》,《美术大观》2020 年第 8 期,第 70 页)

statues. "This kind of cultural communication between China and India made ancient China start to explore and understand the 'West' for the first time, from understanding ancient India to finally realizing the real Europe. It also made China's exploration of the Western world, not only in geography, but in cultural dissemination and communication."[1] In addition to cultural communication with India, the Longmen Grottoes also shows the trace that ancient China had cultural communication with other Asian and European countries such as Korea, Greece and Persia. The statues in the Longmen Grottoes possess exotic cultural elements such as Western instruments, European patterns and Greek stone columns, proving that the Longmen Grottoes is resulted from the integration of different civilizations and is highly internationalized. Besides, the statues have plant patterns such as lotus flower and animal shapes such as dragon, which indicates that the Longmen Grottoes is rich in traditional Chinese cultural elements. It can be seen that the Longmen Grottoes is deeply influenced by different countries, absorbing and learning from their excellent culturs. It formulated in the integration of foreign culture and Chinese culture, so the Longmen Grottoes has universal artistic value and becomes more attractive.

As fine traditional Chinese culture, the Longmen Grottoes is an important part of cultural confidence. However, cultural confidence is different from narrow ethnocentrism. While being confident in the vitality and creativity of our own culture, we should examine ourselves and accept excellent foreign culturs. The Longmen Grottoes shows the nationalization, secularism and sinicization of Buddhist culture and the long-term cultural communication and integration between different nationalities, faiths and countries. It absorbs the achievements of outstanding civilizations in the world, and demonstrates the open and inclusive cultural confidence of the Chinese nation. The cultural development of a country requires extensive

---

[1] Jin Yongqiang, Study on Transformation and Upgrading of Buddhist Culture Tourism in Henan Province from the Perspective of the Belt and Road, *Journal of Zhengzhou University of Light Industry*(*Social Science Edition*). 2017, Volume 18, Issue 5, p. 42. (金勇强:《"一带一路"视野下河南佛教文化旅游转型升级研究》,《郑州轻工业学院学报(社会科学版)》2017年第18卷第5期,第42页)

cultural communication with other countries in order to learn the excellent culture in the world, by which the circulation of excellent culture, cultural confidence, and cultural communication can be realized. Hence, we should take advantage of cultural heritage to improve cultural confidence, adhere to cultural communication with other countries on the basis of cultural confidence, and develop more excellent Chinese culture in the process of communication.

Make Use of Cultural Heritage, Adhere to Cultural Confidence, and Deepen Cultural Communication

The Longmen Grottoes is not only the representative of fine traditional Chinese culture and the source of the Chinese nation's cultural confidence, but also the result of communication between excellent cultures. The importance of cultural communication is self-evident. Therefore, while using cultural heritage to improve cultural confidence, it is necessary to deepen cultural communication, which is conductive to promote the development and spread of one's own culture. The preservation and maintenance of cultural heritage is the premise of making full use of cultural heritage, so as to continue the excellent culture and maintain the foundation of cultural confidence. In order to improve the attraction and influence of cultural heritage, it is necessary to develop cultural heritage creatively from the inside, integrating it with modern culture, and to spread cultural heritage from the outside, exporting culture by different means and making one's own culture go to the world. Finally, cultural heritage should be utilized to carry out bilateral cultural communication. Different civilizations should conduct dialogue equally to achieve mutual benefit and enrich the culture in the world.

Cultural heritage should be protected. Tangible cultural heritage is special because it is not renewable and substitutable, so we need to strengthen protection and always give top priority to its protection. As world cultural heritage, the Danxia Landform of China once experienced several devastating incidents. For example, tourists jump over the guardrail, trample on the scenic spot and carve characters in the scenic spot. These incidents cause irreparable damage to the Danxia Landform, because the damage cannot be repaired manually and it will take more than 600 years to repair naturally. Due to the inadequate supervision and protection earlier, thefts were frequent and serious in the Longmen Grottoes, which caused a huge loss of cultural relics. In addition, tourists touching the statues have also damaged existing ones. *The Little Mermaid* of Denmark has a similar experience. It was sawed, stolen and splashed with paint. As a result, cultural heritage should be protected. We should strengthen the supervision of scenic spots in order to prevent man-made damage, and should crack down on crimes of cultural relics. At the same time, we should carry out the restoration of cultural relics, so as to inherit the excellent culture of mankind and maintain the diversity of world culture.

Cultural heritage should be developed. Cultural heritage should not linger in the past, but break through the limitation of time. It should adapt to the modern society and carry out creative development, so as to stimulate cultural vitality and make great progress. Cultural heritage can give rise to many creative cultural products based on its own characteristics. Henan Museum sets a good example by creating archaeological blind boxes. Archaeological blind boxes is a kind of cultural product which uses the soil of various famous historical and cultural cities in Henan and places a duplicate of an unearthed cultural relic in the soil. Customers can utilize archaeological tools like the Luoyang shovel and small brushes in order to experience the archaeological process, feel the fun of digging treasure. This kind of product makes use of people's curiosity and combines the popular blind box culture and archaeology activities of cultural relics, attracting a lot of attention. Cultural heritage can also use modern technology and combine the Internet technology with cultural development. Many cultural heritage scenic spots adopt the mode of online ticket purchase, park visit, management and publicity, realizing the transformation and upgrading of traditional historical and cultural scenic spots. So, we should "make full use of the Internet to activate cultural heritage and enrich tourism forms, and take 'Internet+' as an effective means to activate history and culture"[1].

Cultural heritage should be spread. Video like documentary is one of the best media for cultural spread. *Masters In Forbidden City* records the story about the restoration of cultural relics of the Forbidden City, "showing the speciality of fine traditional Chinese culture, highlighting the unique style of the national culture, and demonstrating the exquisite skills and infinite wisdom of the ancients"[2]. It triggers a climax and tells the story of China's cultural heritage to the world. This year, BBC launched a documentary called *Du Fu: China's Greatest Poet*, illustrating the beauty of Chinese poetry to the world, and letting Chinese poets break cultural boundary to show their charm. This documentary proves that there is not only Dante, Shakespeare, Anderson, but also Du Fu. Therefore, cultural heritage needs to expand its path to make external communication. In addition to cultural and tourism integration, it can also make use of video and other recording forms to produce high-quality documentaries, TV dramas, variety shows and so on, promoting its own culture to the world.

Cultural heritage should initiate communication. Civilizations would make progress through mutual exchange and learning, and equal bilateral dialogue on cultural heritage is conducive to cultural development. One of the most important ways for cultural heritage communication is to hold forums for dialogue among civilizations. China and Holland once held the China and Holland Cultural Media Forum, which serves as a platform for cultural communication and allows Chinese and Dutch cultural heritage experts to exchange experiences and insights on the protection and utilization of cultural heritage and the realization of its contemporary value. The second China and Central and Eastern European Countries Cultural Heritage Forum was held in

---

[1] Man Qiwei, Tao Jianchao, Yang Hongyan, Zhang Zhenjiang, Li Songzhan, Practice and Thinking of the Longmen Mode of "Internet + Smart Scenic Spot" in Luoyang, *Henan Daily*, 2015.08.06. (满奇伟、陶建超、杨鸿雁、张振江、李松战:《洛阳"互联网+智慧景区"龙门模式的实践与思考》,《河南日报》2015年8月6日)

[2] Jing Feifei, The Value and Dissemination of Fine Traditional Chinese Culture Documentary, *Contemporary TV*. 2019, Volume 9, p.70. (敬菲菲:《中华优秀传统文化纪录片的价值与传播》,《当代电视》2019年第9期,第70页)

Luoyang. The director of the National Cultural Heritage Administration said at the forum that "cultural heritage communication and cooperation between China and CEECs have shown steady progress, and cultural relics exhibitions have become more active, personnel exchanges have become closer, and breakthroughs have been made in institutional building"[①]. Cultural heritage forums and cultural heritage exhibitions can serve as important means of cultural heritage communication, which promotes exchanges and dialogues between different cultures, and enhances cultural competitiveness and attraction through mutual learning.

Conclusion

Cultural heritage is the treasure of a nation and is an important source of national confidence. While using cultural heritage to enhance cultural confidence, it is necessary to strengthen cultural communication with other countries. As President Xi Jinping said in the Speech at the Dunhuang Research Institute, "only a civilization full of confidence can tolerate, learn and absorb different civilizations while maintaining its own national characteristics"[②]. We should draw on the splendid achievements of human civilizations through cultural communication and mutual learning, promote the establishment of a strong cultural country, enhance cultural soft power, and make world civilization more colorful.

(Beijing International Studies University)

---

① The second Cultural Heritage Forum between China and Central and Eastern European Countries opened in Luoyang, *Study on Natural and Cultural Heritage*. 2019, Volume 4, p. 12. (《第二届中国——中东欧国家文化遗产论坛在洛阳开幕》,《遗产与保护研究》2019 年第 4 期,第 12 页)
② Xi Jinping, Speech at the Dunhuang Research Institute, *Seeking Truth*. 2020, Volume 3. (习近平:《在敦煌研究院座谈时的讲话》,《求是》2020 年第 3 期)

Gone in the Soul: Study on the Directory Function for Reincarnation and Being Immortal of Mawangdui Han Tomb T Shape Silk Painting

Wang Yanhua

Studies and researches on Mawangdui Han Tomb have been on the way around 50 years since the first excavation work in 1970s. It is proved that the tomb belongs to the noble family of Licang, who is the first run of Dai prince and prime minister of Changsha kingdom in the Han dynasty. This Han tomb is a combination of 3 individual tombs of which the No.1 tomb is for Licang's wife Mrs Xinzhui, No.2 tomb for the prince of Licang, and No.3 for their son. In the first three years of the excavation work, over 3,000 historical relics were found in the Mawangdui Han Tomb. The well-preserved dead body of Mrs Xinzhui which should be rotted and eroded astonishes China and the whole world. Zhou Enlai, the prime minister of China at that time paid high attention to the related projection, and nearly 160 newspaper offices designed a special column for it[1]. Mawangdui Han Tomb's excavation leads an example of interdisciplinary studies on archaeology and extensive cooperation among different companies and institutions. It opens up a new pattern in the archaeological field of China[2].

Among the thousands of historical relics found in Mawangdui Han tomb,

---

[1] ShanxEthici Province Museum, Hunan Province Museum. *The Collection of Mawangdui Han Tomb Cultural Relics*. Shanxi Renming Publisher. 2011.4. (山西博物院、湖南省博物馆编著：《马王堆汉墓文物精华》，山西：山西人民出版社 2011 年 4 月版)

[2] Yu Yanjiao. The Historical and Cultural Values of Mawangdui Han Tomb, *The World of Cultural Relics*, 2017, Issue12, pp.23-30. (喻燕姣：《马王堆汉墓的历史文化价值》，《文物天地》2017 年第 12 期，第 23—30 页)

T shape Silk Painting, for the delicacy of aesthetic designs and the mystery of practical functions, wins the top treasure of Mawangdui Han tomb display which is held by Hunan Provincial Museum. In fact, there are two T shape silk paintings in the Han tomb, one in the No. 1 tomb for Mrs, Xinzhui and another in the No. 3 for her son, but both of them are put on the interior coffin as a covering and are made of one-layer fine silk. The silk painting is in a T shape and for the painting of Mrs Xinzhui, its top horizontal part is with the length of 92 cm and the width of 67 cm; the lower vertical part the length of 47.7 cm and width 138 cm. The total length of the silk painting in the No. 1 tomb reaches 205 cm. The horizontal part draws the patterns of sun, moon, flying dragon and the God of snake body etc.; the vertical part shows the activity of flood dragons and Mrs Xinzhui. At the top of the silk painting attaches a bamboo pole tied with a brown silk ribbon. With this, the silk can hang well and be held well. At the angles of two sides, respectively in the mid part of the silk and the end part, there are four cyan linen braids with the length of over 20 cm[1]. Based on academic studies concerning the funeral institutions, etiquettes and burial objects, it is confirmed that Taoism and Chu regional culture work together to bring the Mawangdui Han tomb into such a profound reality. Another claim is that T shape silk painting from Mawangdui should reflect the immortal thoughts of Taoism[2]. This article tries to discuss the Taoist idea of reincarnation and being immortal based on the discussion of T silk painting's function. Then, at the perspective of cross-culture studies, the view of life and death in Taoism and ancient Egypt are presented comparatively which hence echoes to a classic topic in the philosophical field, that is where are we going.

---

[1] Hunan Province Museum. *A Brief Report on Changsha City Mawangdui Han Tomb Excavation Work*. Beijing Cultural Relics Publisher, 1972, p. 39. (湖南省博物馆:《长沙马王堆一号汉墓发掘简报》,北京:文物出版社 1972 年版,第 39 页)

[2] Deng Hui, Chen Lihua. Where does the soul go: the Thoughts of Ying and Yang and Being Immortal in No. 1 Mawangdui Han Tomb T Shape Silk Painting, *Journal of Jishou University (Social Science Version)*, 2020, Issue1, pp. 94 - 101. (邓辉、陈华丽:《魂归何处:马王堆一号汉墓 T 形帛画中的阴阳、神仙思想》,《吉首大学学报(社会科学版)》2020 年第 1 期,第 94—101 页)

The Ceremony of Conjuring in Funeral Rite of the Han Dynasty

There are mainly three phases in the funeral rite of the Han dynasty according to *The Study on Han Dynasty Wedding and Funeral Custom* written by Mr Yang Shuda. The first phase calls the pre-burying ceremony which involves rituals like conjuring, bathing, putting coins or grains into the mouth, moving the body into the coffin, crying for mourning and laying down the coffin; the second phase is the burying ceremony involving sacrifice, funeral parade and placing the body in the grave; the third is a pro-burying ceremony or mourning ceremony[1]. In the view of life and death of ancient China, we find a typical idea that "the soul of the dead knows the way to home". Therefore, the Chinese folk keep the tradition from the Tomb Sweeping Day (Qingming Festival) and the Double Ninth Festival. And the ceremony of conjuring goes through the first phase and the second phase. For the unwillingness of farewell and worry of being wandering ghosts, their relatives will prepare lots of delicious foods for the conjuration. By doing this, they believe the dead person can avoid bad luck and be reincarnated in the form of the immortal.

The conjuration can be divided into two types: conjuring immediately after the death and conjuring during the burying[2]. The first type is related to the pre-burying ceremony and the second exactly to the burying ceremony. Moreover, conjuring during the burial can be subdivided into the ground ceremony and underground ceremony. As for the concrete steps (of the first type of conjuration), the conjuring master in a formal dress (named Zhao and specifically for the grand funeral) would carry one of the dead person's

---

[1] Xu Jieshun. *The History of Custom of Han Ethnic Group* (Vol. 2): *Wei-Jin and the Northern and Southern Dynasties*. Xuelin Publisher, 2004. (徐杰舜主编:《汉族风俗史·第二卷·秦汉、魏晋南北朝汉族风俗》,学林出版社 2004 年版)

[2] Wang Xiaolin. Fei Yi and Conjuring: a Comparative Study on Mawangdui, Dunhuang and Tulufanand and Other Funeral Cultures Along the Silk Road, *Journal of Nanjing Art College (Art and Design)*, 2017, Issue3, pp. 46–53. (王晓玲:《非衣与招魂——马王堆、敦煌、吐鲁番及丝路沿线墓葬文化关系研究》,《南京艺术学院学报(美术与设计)》2017 年第 3 期,第 46—53 页)

clothes (named Fu means double-layers) with the left hand. Then he goes to the roof, facing the north, and starts appealing with the words "so-and-so, come back home". After calling like this three times, the conjurer throws the cloth to another master called Si Fu (Si means managing and Fu means clothes). Si Fu at that time is standing in the ancestral hall. He catches the cloth with a basket, walks up down the stairs (called Zuo stairs which means fortune), comes to the place where the dead body settles down and finally puts the cloth on the body. Then, everyone waits for the soul back to the body[1]. But T shape silk painting from Mawangdui Han tomb is not that kind of conjuring tool applied by the master in the steps above. The ancient pays great attention to the rule of "death with life" so that people wouldn't leave a cloth used as a conjuring tool with the dead and together buried it into the underground.

With the failure of the first conjuration, the dead person unavoidably arrives at the terminal of his or her life in the human's world. He or she, turning from Yang to Ying, starts a new life in a new world[2]. People bathe and dress them, make a sacrifice, pack the body and put the body into the coffin. Until this step, people cannot see the face and the shape of the dead, so they make a Ming Jing (a long streamer inscribed with the deceased's official title and name posted in front of a coffin) as a substitute of the decease and a carrier of relatives' love and miss. Ming Jing still plays a role in the funeral procession. People hold high the streamer and walk in front of the hearse. Not only does it function for identifying the deceased and guiding the hearse, but also it guides the soul with the dead body to walk into the resting place[3]. Ming Jing finally will be put on the coffin and be buried with the coffin and the body. The soul splitting over from the body in the human world will settle down under the guidance of Ming Jing[4]. However, T shape silk painting seems not a typical Ming Jing. It is the interior coffin that the silk painting lays on and its pattern unusually faces the deceased rather than

---

[1][2][3][4] Feng Na. A Brief Discussion on the Function of No. 1 Mawangdui T Shape Silk Painting, *Technologic Information*, 2009, Issue27, pp. 491–492. (冯娜:《浅析马王堆一号汉墓 T 形帛画的功能》,《科技信息》2009 年第 27 期,第 491—492 页)

the mourners. Therefore, it is estimated that identification and condolence are not the whole functions of the silk painting. In fact, facing to the decease indicates that the targeted audience is not the mourners but the soul of the tomb master, Mrs Xinzhui[①]. Besides, the painting patterns should not be so complicated and delicate if it just functions for identification and condolence. A portrait of the tomb master is well enough. What T shape silk painting services for is nobody but the tomb master[②].

After discussing the funeral rite procedure, we can conclude that T shape silk painting is not for the conjuration in the pre-burying ceremony. While during the burying ceremony, it might play a role during the ground ceremony. Specifically, it plays a similar function as Ming Jing, identifying the deceased and guiding the soul into the coffin. However, during the underground ceremony and in the tomb chamber, T shape silk painting becomes a directory map for Mrs Xinzhui's being reincarnated in the form of the immortal[③].

Fei Yi: The Map to Be Immortal

From the funeral rite, at least two functions are found in T shape silk painting: the first, just as Ming Jing, for identifying the deceased and guiding the hearse; and the second, as a special streamer, for conjuring the soul. However, according to the funeral objects list of Mawangdui Han tomb, T shape silk painting is neither Ming Jing nor anything concerning hearse. It is named Fei Yi, which might be designed by the artist who draws the painting or Li Cang noble family who are the master of this grand Han tomb[④]. Therefore, what kind of role is played by T shape silk painting as Fei

---

[①②③] Wang Xiaolin. Fei Yi and Conjuring: a Comparative Study on Mawangdui, Dunhuang and Tulufanand and Other Funeral Cultures Along the Silk Road, *Journal of Nanjing Art College (Art and Design)*, 2017, Issue3, pp. 46 - 53. (王晓玲：《非衣与招魂——马王堆、敦煌、吐鲁番及丝路沿线墓葬文化关系研究》,《南京艺术学院学报（美术与设计）》2017 年第 3 期、第 46—53 页)

[④] Liao Jun. The Name of Changsha City Mawangdui Han Tomb T Shape Silk Painting and its Patterns, *Journal of the Western*, 2018, Issue8, pp. 67 - 69. (廖俊：《长沙马王堆汉墓 T 形帛画名称及局部内容探究》,《西部学刊》2018 年第 8 期、第 67—69 页)

Yi even beyond the function of conjuring? And where does the soul go to?

We can make a breakthrough from the shape, design and patterns of T shape silk painting. T shape in traditional Chinese culture bears the meaning of "space". Scholars of T shape silk painting studies once have put forwards that T shape highlights the superior of the celestial world. The top horizontal part draws the sun, moon, myths and legends representing the massive and admirable power of the divine of the celestial world[①]. However, besides the top part, the whole painting is a presentation of the posthumous world, illustrating Han people's faith. T shape silk painting employs the typical three-layer composition of the picture: the celestial world, the human world and the underground world. No. 4 and No. 9 Han tomb in Golden Sparrow Mount, Lin Yi city of Shandong province show a similar composition method[②]. The lower vertical part draws an ideal underground world which plays a vital role in the procedure of reincarnation and being immortal, which can be traced back to the thoughts of the Warring States period (475 - 221 B.C.), Qin dynasty (221 - 206 B.C.) and Han dynasty (202 B.C. - 220 A.D.)[③]. The middle of the silk painting draws the human world where two dragons spiral up around a conjuring jade Bi (a round flat piece of jade with a hole in the center). After the recall for the soul, it follows the hole of Bi and the body of dragons and the enters into the celestial world. The combination of Bi and dragons leads the deceased travel from the material existence into the eternity of the soul, from one world to another[④]. The top horizontal part

---

① Deng Hui, Chen Lihua. Where does the soul go: the Thoughts of Ying and Yang and Being Immortal in No. 1 Mawangdui Han Tomb T Shape Silk Painting, *Journal of Jishou University (Social Science Version)*, 2020, Issue1, pp. 94 - 101. (邓辉、陈华丽:《魂归何处：马王堆一号汉墓 T 形帛画中的阴阳、神仙思想》,《吉首大学学报（社会科学版）》2020 年第 1 期,第 94—101 页)

② Wang Xiaolin. Fei Yi and Conjuring: a Comparative Study on Mawangdui, Dunhuang and Tulufanand and Other Funeral Cultures Along the Silk Road, *Journal of Nanjing Art College (Art and Design)*, 2017, Issue3, pp. 46 - 53. (王晓玲:《非衣与招魂——马王堆、敦煌、吐鲁番及丝路沿线墓葬文化关系研究》,《南京艺术学院学报（美术与设计）》2017 年第 3 期,第 46—53 页)

③ Jiang Sheng. The Faith of Taoism in the Early Han Dynasty and Mawangdui T Shape Silk Painting, *Social Sciences in China*, 2014, Issue12, pp. 176 - 199 + 209. (姜生:《马王堆帛画与汉初"道者"的信仰》,《中国社会科学》2014 年第 12 期,第 176—199、209 页)

④ Wu Hong, Zhen Yan Trans. *Art in the Custom and Etiquette: Wu Hong the Collection of Art History of Ancient China*. Beijing SDX Publishing Company, 2016, p. 35. (巫鸿:《礼仪中的美术：巫鸿中国古代美术史文编》,郑岩等译,北京：生活·读书·新知三联书店 2016 年版,第 35 页)

is the terminal of the soul, a space for the divine. In this part, the soul reaches the Ninth Sky and transforms into the immortal[①].

As early as the first several years in Han dynasty, the faith of travelling from the underground into the celestial and being immortal has already existed[②]. Such a belief system, absorbing Chinese mythological culture and integrating Chu regional traditions, evolves into a new religious form. "Getting the essence of Taoism" before "getting into the immortal" and "earning dignity from the funeral" for "presenting the belief in Taoism". Such an elaborate ideological system leads a quest neither for the design of the tomb nor for the underground comfort, but the life transformation achieved in the tomb and through the funeral. This system encourages people to "run out of the property for scarification and funeral ceremony"[③]. Kids from poor families are even willing to be traded as slavers only for their ancestors' funeral dignity. It is rather to say the hope for being immortal after death than the responsibility of filial piety there motivates the ancient Chinese to take great efforts to build tombs and ancestral halls[④]. Mrs Xinzhui and her son are both the believer of Taoism. They firmly believe in being immortal beyond material existence. They chase for the essence of Taoism when alive, and after death, their soul drinks the jade liquid under the guidance of immortal official and then are transformed[⑤]. Their wish to be immortal merges into a technological method for transformation, which has been well-known to every household and applied in the construction of the tomb[⑥]. Therefore, the Mawangdui Han tomb equals a framework of a series of rites in terms of physical space and cultural essences. The tomb plays as the intermediate to send the discursive symbols of life transformation. Among all, T shape silk painting

---

①②③⑥ Jiang Sheng. The Faith of Taoism in the Early Han Dynasty and Mawangdui T Shape Silk Painting, *Social Sciences in China*, 2014, Issue12, pp. 176 - 199 + 209. (姜生:《马王堆帛画与汉初"道者"的信仰》,《中国社会科学》2014 年第 12 期,第 176—199、209 页)

⑤ Wang Xiaolin. Fei Yi and Conjuring: a Comparative Study on Mawangdui, Dunhuang and Tulufanand and Other Funeral Cultures Along the Silk Road, *Journal of Nanjing Art College (Art and Design)*, 2017, Issue3, pp. 46 - 53. (王晓玲:《非衣与招魂——马王堆、敦煌、吐鲁番及丝路沿线墓葬文化关系研究》,《南京艺术学院学报(美术与设计)》2017 年第 3 期,第 46—53 页)

is one of the most shinning symbols.

However, there is another voice which seems more reliable. Some scholars put forwards that what Taoism advocates in the early period of Han dynasty is not "to be immortal after death" but "during alive"①. Therefore, whether the patterns on T shape silk painting illustrate the soul's arrival in the celestial world and its transformation to be immortal demands much discussions. Instead, there is a preference to claim the conjuration help the soul rest in peace. T shape silk painting conjures the soul from the underground and directs the way to neither the heaven nor the tomb chamber, but an immortal world of eternal peace②. The deceased once has been to the immortal, can get rid of the spatio-temporal restraint like what the god can do, and can enjoy the peaceful happiness in the parallel space like what the mortal joy can be in the human world.

"Transforming to Be Immortal" Cross the Cultural Boundary

As two of the four great ancient civilizations, ancient Egypt and ancient China show their unique and outstanding funeral culture. There are typical examples like the pyramid, Sphinx, mummy, mummy case in ancient Egypt, silk painting, stone relief, and portrait brick in ancient China. Specifically, Thebes Temple mummy case with colour painting (1070 - 715 B.C.) used for the union of the well-preserved body with the soul is a mummy wooden coffin. The patterns on it illustrate how to lead the soul to be reincarnated in the immortal form③. Therefore, in terms of function, Thebes Temple mummy case and T shape silk painting reveal the same feature: directing the soul. However, what is the difference is that the former focuses on

---

①② Deng Hui, Chen Lihua. Where does the soul go: the Thoughts of Ying and Yang and Being Immortal in No. 1 Mawangdui Han Tomb T Shape Silk Painting, *Journal of Jishou University* (*Social Science Version*), 2020, Issue1, pp. 94 - 101. (邓辉、陈华丽:《魂归何处: 马王堆一号汉墓 T 形帛画中的阴阳、神仙思想》,《吉首大学学报(社会科学版)》2020 年第 1 期,第 94—101 页)

③ Deng Hongtao, Chen Xinyuan, Liu Guan. A Comparative Study on Thebes Temple Mummy Case and T Shape Silk Painting, *Art Education*, 2019, Issue12, pp. 280 - 281. (邓鸿涛、陈欣缘、刘冠:《底比斯神庙祭司人形棺彩绘与马王堆汉墓 T 形帛画形象辨析》,《艺术教育》2019 年第 12 期,第 280—281 页)

"transforming to be immortal in a well-preserved shape" while the latter "transforming to be immortal with a resting soul". These two kinds of civilization, more significantly, represent the differences in the expectation for life after death and the concept of the posthumous body.

The mummy case carries the expectation for "being an immortal god". It reproduces the figure of important god and persons like the deity, the pharaoh, and the noble with the planar sense of front. Such an Egyptian art approach (also used in carving and wall painting) presences a long-term stability because of strong religious passions[1]. On the other hand, what T shape silk painting emphasizes is "being immortal through inner cultivation and endless practice". In the Qin dynasty and Han dynasty, people preserve the body to gather refined Qi in the deceased. Then, the soul unites with the body, and the dead becomes immortal and starts a new life with the gods[2].

As for the concept of the body, the ancient Egyptian support that life comes after the combination of the visible body and invisible soul. Human as the universe is eternal, and the soul never vanishes. Therefore, as long as the material existence is well preserved, the soul can find a carrier and the deceased gains another life. Under such a concept, the Egyptian make mummy and the delicate case for keeping it[3]. However, the Chinese believe in the theory of Fangshu (an ideological mechanism involving interpromotion and interrestraint of the five elements, opposition and mutual basement of Yingyang) of which the main concept is the common eternity of both the body and the soul. And according to Taoism, the universe is made of Qi. Either the body or the soul is related to the same source Qi. The two are

---

[1] Deng Hongtao, Chen Xinyuan, Liu Guan. A Comparative Study on Thebes Temple Mummy Case and T Shape Silk Painting, *Art Education*, 2019, Issue12, pp. 280-281. (邓鸿涛、陈欣缘、刘冠:《底比斯神庙祭司人形棺彩绘与马王堆汉墓 T 形帛画形象辨析》,《艺术教育》2019 年第 12 期,第 280—281 页)

[2] Deng Hui, Chen Lihua. Where does the soul go: the Thoughts of Ying and Yang and Being Immortal in No. 1 Mawangdui Han Tomb T Shape Silk Painting, *Journal of Jishou University (Social Science Version)*, 2020, Issue1, pp. 94-101. (邓辉、陈华丽:《魂归何处:马王堆一号汉墓 T 形帛画中的阴阳、神仙思想》,《吉首大学学报(社会科学版)》2020 年第 1 期,第 94—101 页)

[3] Deng Hongtao, Chen Xinyuan, Liu Guan. A Comparative Study on Thebes Temple Mummy Case and T Shape Silk Painting, *Art Education*, 2019, Issue12, pp. 280-281. (邓鸿涛、陈欣缘、刘冠:《底比斯神庙祭司人形棺彩绘与马王堆汉墓 T 形帛画形象辨析》,《艺术教育》2019 年第 12 期,第 280—281 页)

homogenous originally. Under such a monism concept, the Chinese believe that physical immortality leads to spiritual immortality[①]. The Chinese thus pay less attention to the preservation of the body. Moreover, they wish for the immortality over the reincarnation, so they always prepare an abundant of burial objects and the grand funeral for the joy in the new life.

A falling leave tells the arrival of autumn. Thebes Temple mummy case and T shape silk painting tell the world how delicate the design mind can be and how wonderful the imagination can be as far as thousands of years ago. The uniqueness and attractiveness of the art of these two civilizations profoundly affect the development of art. Besides, the funeral ceremony is a window. From it, we can find that both ancient Egypt and ancient China, couepts of the deceased and the pondering of life which is reflected either on "transforming to be immortal in a well-preserved shape" or on "transforming to be immortal with a resting soul". And from it, we can also start philosophical thinkings though in the busy and sophistication in the real world that are: who are we? where are we from and where are we going?[②]

(Beijing International Studies University)

---

① Yu Chaowei. A Study on No. 1 Mawangdui Han Tomb Silk Painting, *Collection of Archeology in Pre Qin Dynasty to Han Dynasties*, Beijing Cultural Relics Publisher, 1985. (俞伟超:《马王堆一号汉墓帛画内容考》,载《先秦两汉考古论集》,北京:文物出版社 1985 年版)

② Wang Xiaolin. Fei Yi and Conjuring: a Comparative Study on Mawangdui, Dunhuang and Tulufanand and Other Funeral Cultures Along the Silk Road, *Journal of Nanjing Art College (Art and Design)*, 2017, Issue3, pp. 46 - 53. (王晓玲:《非衣与招魂——马王堆、敦煌、吐鲁番及丝路沿线墓葬文化关系研究》,《南京艺术学院学报(美术与设计)》2017 年第 3 期,第 46—53 页)

Research on the Dissemination of Paper-cutting in Japan and South Korea

Yu Hongjian

People all know that Hans Christian Andersen, the world-famous Danish writer, is known as the king of fairy tales. However, in his spare time, he was most interested in paper-cutting. He used symmetry and balanced techniques to make paper-cutting more fairy and romantic. In Denmark and China's northeast area, with high latitudes in the northern hemisphere, has a similar climate characteristic, but also had a similar animal and plant ecology, raccoon of rare animals of the Wusuli river in northeast China have distribution in Denmark, the Danish people Hygge life concept and the northeast people "carpe diem, humor everywhere" highly similar life attitude, culture has a lot of similarities between the two places. Denmark while never have snow all the year round in the northeast of halma scenery, but winter tourism projects are often being relish entertainment programs, in the temperate maritime climate of Danish people, although he has a unique natural resource, visitors to Denmark are always impressed by the country's cultural soft power, whether it is the high quality of life emotional appeal, or everywhere happy smiling face , can reflect the Danish culture deep strength.

The Manchu people in the Changbai Mountain area have their unique production and living customs due to their unique geographical location and characteristic life caused by the climate. Such as "A pheasant flies into the rice pot after being beaten with a stick and ladled out the fish", "The Three Great Kanto strange: window paper pastes outside, big girl in its mouth a big tobacco bag, raise a child hanging up" proverb. The living climate of the Manchu people is characterized by long and cold winters. The ancestors of the Manchu people lived in the Changbai Mountain region with four distinct seasons. It has been more than 4000 years since they lived and reproduced in the long and harsh natural environment in winter.

It is difficult to verify the historical records of the generation of the folk paper-cuts of the Manchu people in Changbai Mountain. However, it can be concluded from the development of paper-cuts that as early as the 16th century, the ancestors of the Manchu people, Nuzhen, began to cut and cut with bark, fish skin, leather, linen and so on. The patterns they cut are rough and full of national characteristics. "Original Paper-cutting" can be inferred from the Ming Dynasty, according to the "History of the Manchu" records, the Empress of Jin, Huang Taiji Nuzhen began to make paper, the emergence of paper is the "Original Paper-cutting" the emergence and development of the prerequisite. The "non-paper paper cutting" made by the early Manchu folk artists with other materials appeared before the invention of paper making. It was made of animal skin, birch bark, fish skin, corn leaf, linen and other materials to complete the paper cutting art. Changbai Mountain Manchu folk paper-cut in this unique historical environment and natural conditions formed their own appearance. In the long history of development, Changbai Mountain Manchu folk paper cutting art has become a cultural heritage retained in the folk, has been deeply loved by the folk, including living with the Manchu People of the Han people are also affected by it. Although these forms of paper-cuts did not leave more physical and written materials, they were handed down from generation to generation through oral instruction, continuous development and continuous innovation between the black waters of Baishan Mountain. After the 1920s, the Paper cuttings of the Manchus in Changbai Mountain were settled in the folk. Many of the works show the natural appearance, natural living conditions, legends and local specialties of the Changbai Mountain region where the Manchus lived. Mr. Wang Chunxin, a researcher of Manchu culture in Changbai Mountain, started fieldwork on this folk art in 1982 and conducted in-depth research and collection. It has driven the development of Manchu folk culture in northeast China. For example, Guan Yunde of Jiutai City, Jilin Province was officially recognized as the "Outstanding inheritor of Chinese folk culture" in the key project of "Rescue Project of Chinese Folk Cultural Heritage" organized and implemented by the "Chinese Folk Artists Association". In early 2000, Manchu paper cutting was listed by the Ministry of Culture as "the second batch of national intangible cultural heritage projects". Kim Ya-Zhen, a representative figure, is one of China's "top ten paper-cutting masters". Her paper cutting spread across the country and even floated to the other side of the ocean. Many paper-cut works with Manchu characteristics and natural life have been reproduced in art exhibitions and art publications around the country and even the world. Paper-cut is the treasure of Manchu ancient national culture, it is the Manchu people to life, nature and emotional art precipitation, is a reflection of Manchu custom art, extremely precious. Changbai Mountain Manchu paper-cut, a folk paper-cut art full of Manchu local flavor in northeast China, is full of strong vitality and artistic appeal. This wonderful flower of Chinese folk art will be more brilliant under our protection and inheritance.

Nowadays, under the background of the continuous integration of world cultures, international tourists are very interested in the cultural deposits of intangible cultural heritage, which is also one of the important reasons to attract tourists to travel. According to statistics. Nearly 70 percent of overseas tourists from Japan and South Korea come to Changbai Mountain, making it the top choice for tourists in Jilin Province. Changbai Mountain paper cutting art has its own characteristic pattern in the dissemination and protection of intangible cultural heritage. It takes local ethnic characteristics as the main battlefield and constantly strengthens its international influence, which is worthy of learning and reference. This paper puts forward some suggestions on the cultural communication significance of The Paper-cutting art of Changbai Mountain combined with the current situation of its communication in Japan and South Korea.

The cultural dissemination significance of The Paper-cutting art of Changbai Mountain

Manchu folk paper-cut is simple, straightforward, robust and naive, is the historical product of thousands of years of Changbai mountain culture accumulation, a comprehensive and concentrated reflection of China's folk art modeling concept, philosophical concept, to meet the aesthetic concept of the public. It not only has an extremely strong practical function, and in the development that takes root in this piece of the black land, it formed its unique artistic characteristic. The following is to discuss the practical significance of overseas dissemination of Paper-cutting art in Changbai Mountain from the perspective of artistic expression form, subject matter, and content of paper cutting, combined with cases of paper-cutting art in overseas dissemination in recent years.

First of all, in terms of the form of artistic expression, Changbai Mountain Manchu folk paper cutting has evolved into a variety of forms of expression in the long-term spread and development process, and in the continuous development and innovation process of the Manchu people. For example: " monochromatic paper-cut, color-matching paper-cut, folding paper-cut, fumigated paper-cut, hand-torn paper-cut, etc." And the most common and the most representative or monochromatic paper-cut and hand-torn paper-cut, mainly red paper. This is due to the ancient Chinese worship of red. In the color preference of the Chinese nation, red symbolizes the sun, brightness, warmth and happiness. In 2007, the second International Paper-cut Art Expo held in Wuhan attracted more than 10 countries, including China, the United States, the United Kingdom, South Korea, and more than 2,400 paper-cut works. Lady Li Xia, a folk paper-cut artist of Jilin City, won the gold medal of the Exposition for her paper-cut work *Changbai Mountain God*, which is a paper-cut work made by using Manchu techniques. It has the unique characteristics of Manchu paper-cut, such as bold and bold, simple and generous. The composition of this work is novel and orderly, mainly composed of five parts, such as "Shaman face spectrum", "three monsters of northeast China", "three treasures of Northeast China", "Four Seasons of Changbai Mountain" and "Yangko Dance of Northeast China". Although the strong national paper-cutting art is static paperwork, but because of its lifelike artistic expression form, it is a great leap forward in the overseas dissemination of paper-cut art.

Secondly, in the paper-cut on subject matter and content to the most common things in real life, things as subjects, with pure emotion and intuition to look at the image, and on this basis, gradually formed the Changbai mountain Manchu paper-cut unique pure, simple and special artistic style, concise, lively, mainly living custom, and legend story as the main content, "ginseng girl", "baishan hunting", "the sisters face," paper-cut works of each behind, will have production, seasonal, marriage funeral custom and story from folklore. In 2010, The Changbai Manchu paper cutting was officially brought to the Shanghai World Expo by Jilin Province, which made the Manchu paper cutting art with strong ethnic and regional characteristics known to more people. Tourists from all over the world stopped to watch, and paper-cut exhibits were snapped up. In 2018, at the Shenzhen Cultural expo, paper-cut artist Chen Weizhen's paper-cut works, such as "Suntan Shen Girl" and "Shaman", applied the Manchu people's hunting, marrying, fighting and other situations to the paper-cut products, which were widely welcomed and created an innovative way of combining paper-cut culture with industry.

The paper-cutting of The Manchu people of Changbai Mountain permeates almost all the folk customs of Changbai Mountain, including dress, residence, diet, etc., as an art form with national characteristics, the national traditional culture contained in it has been recognized by the general public. In particular, the folklore and stories conveyed by the shaman culture have made great contributions to the historical research of shaman culture, which can restore the original historical appearance well. In the process of overseas cultural transmission, it is full of cultural foundation. Through the small red paper-cutting, we can have a glimpse of the primitive folk customs in the northeast.

Changbai Mountain paper-cutting art in Japan and South Korea

　　Modern Japanese paper cutting takes the expression of myth, folk story, legend, natural scenery as the main theme. In the scenery paper-cutting, Mount Fuji, cherry blossoms and so on are common themes. South Korean paper cutting and Changbai Mountain paper cutting techniques are similar, are good at storytelling, constantly absorbing the way of predecessors under the study. The development of Japanese paper cutting is deeply influenced by Chinese paper cutting. The modern Japanese paper cutting mainly develops and develops gradually with Japan-China friendship activities after World War II. Shina Gilani is a Japanese female artist who lives in France and has completed much exquisite paper cutting works with scissors and dexterity. Her paper cutting art has drawn a lot of the nourishment of Changbai Mountain paper cutting art, with a typical Oriental flavor, amazing. In the cultural exchange of South Korea, Changbaishan paper cutting has also played a significant role. The art of paper-cut shines on the stage. In 2019, the Exchange group of Wendeng District performed "Building The Chinese Dream together", which combines the Chinese paper-cut culture and musical elements cleverly, fully demonstrating the excellent traditional folk art. In TV programs and variety shows, Changbai Mountain paper cutting is common. In 2019, the second China-South Korea Paper-cut Culture and Art Exchange Exhibition was held in Seoul, South Korea. A large number of paper-cut works, including the Paper-cut from Changbaishan mountain, played a great role in the China-South Korea International exchange Conference.

　　Changbai paper cutting has made great progress in the cultural communication between Japan and South Korea, but there are still great obstacles in the communication, which more or less affect overseas cultural communication. First, in terms of social environment, Japan and South Korea have paper-cut association is established in the 1980s, although the paper-cut art in Japan, South Korea's promotion and development has made great progress, at the same time, in recent years the development of Changbai mountain clipart process is relatively slow, by visiting Japan and

South Korea paper-cut association website, exist in the construction of web site update not in time, page navigation chaotic situation, by retrieving only nearly 10 or so of news reports in the Changbai mountain paper cutting, which can be seen that Changbai mountain clipart abroad attention degree of the embarrassing situation. Secondly, in terms of the commercial environment, paper-cutting has derived from various paper-cut industries, such as the application of paper-cut elements in clothing, the holding of competitions, and paper-cut products, which have achieved certain marketization results. Due to the lack of market promotion and the lack of a clear development path, the profits generated by the derivative industry cannot be fed back into the promotion of paper-cut art in the form of funds. Even some Korean and Japanese folk artisans still have the embarrassing situation of "self-financing". Finally, cultural similarities and differences often occur. All three countries adopt the method of "story telling" in the overseas transmission of paper-cut art, and export the cultural value through the stories in paper-cut, which has the advantage of cultural concept for the dissemination of Paper-cutting of Changbai Mountain containing a hundred years of cultural heritage. Especially South Korea in recent years due to the impact of the western paper-cutting culture, accept to convey aesthetic in "static", "art is used to enjoy" ideas, paper-cut art is more and more remote and Changbai mountain most paper-cut works derived from the simple country life, in contrast, Chinese paper-cutting art if not properly packaging and proper communication, I'm afraid to other countries "distraction".

Countermeasures and suggestions on the spread of Paper-cutting art in Japan and South Korea

First of all, the government should do a good job of "gatekeeper". In the context of globalization, both the person in charge of the paper-cutting the art of Changbai Mountain and the paper-cutting people should have an international perspective, abandon the single perspective and the excessive local complex, and pay attention to the international communication of the paper cutting art of Changbai Mountain from the perspective of globalization. In recent years, under the policy of Jilin Province to support the northeast Asia economic circle, the Changbai Mountain region has carried out a lot of cultural exchanges with Japan and South Korea. However, for intangible cultural heritage, compared with other cultural tourism resources, its own economic value is relatively low, the government does not pay much attention to it, and the inheritance and development efforts are relatively small. Therefore, many inheritance and protection works cannot be guaranteed. Personal level, in the case of paper-cut art, research is not deep, just stay on the level of appreciation, not continue understanding attitude, in the case of government attaches great importance to the degree is not high, Only Tonghuo Normal University carried out special protection inherits the activity center of paper-cut art, in the elective courses in paper cutting, and other colleges and universities of Jilin province attach great importance to the degree of paper-cut art, learning the lack of continuity. Due to its strong regional characteristics, this technique has been very rare in the South and can be seen in the overseas spread of resistance. At the same time, in the current situation of insufficient teaching means, many students are not interested in learning, do not see the prospect of learning such skills, and do not want to learn such skills. In addition, in the process of the protection and development of The Paper cutting art in Changbai Mountain, the government has issued corresponding policies and regulations, which are not strong in implementation, and the investment in financial expenditure is limited, so it is difficult to provide guarantee for the development of the intangible cultural heritage, and there are great obstacles in its overseas dissemination.

Given this, in the process of inheriting and developing Changbai Mountain paper-cutting art, the government must give full play to its cultural functions to provide a guarantee for its inheritance and development. First of all, local artists should be encouraged to go out and actively promote local culture through the role of "living targets" of local people, to attract more people to study paper cutting art in Changbai Mountain and provide a cultural foundation for the inheritance and development of paper cutting of the Manchu people. Secondly, the government needs to organize professional teams to protect the paper-cuts of the Manchu people in Changbai Mountain, focus on exploring the traditional art forms, and provide policy and material support and guarantee for the artists. In addition, the government has introduced corresponding policies to form a good publicity atmosphere in the whole society. For example, schools are encouraged to carry out intangible cultural heritage courses, and more young people are encouraged to enter this ancient and mysterious intangible cultural heritage and make more use of paper cuts on the street to promote their hometown culture.

Secondly, the content level should be a good "narrator" role. Changbai Mountain paper cutting is a folk art with strong cultural heritage. A good study on this aspect will help promote our folk art in the communication between Japan and South Korea and understand the historical origin behind it. Previous studies mainly focus on collection, folk customs or image analysis and other aspects. What happened in history is a long time away from me, so we do not know many cultural stories. If we do not go deep into the cultural research of "intangible cultural heritage", it will be difficult to find the root cause of the results obtained from the evolution process. Most of these studies discuss intangible cultural heritage from a macro perspective, and the scope is too wide. The current research results are not published in high quality journals. There are few national projects on the study of ginseng stories in Changbai Mountain and few high-level papers. So far, the number of relevant works and papers on the study of paper-cutting in Changbai Mountain is relatively small, and there are only about 10 papers by searching. At the same time, the depth of the research still needs to be explored. Most of the current research focuses on intangible cultural heritage ontology research, which is only superficial research. There are few studies on the specific connotation of intangible cultural heritage, cultural value, regional characteristics, and interdisciplinary and cross-disciplinary research.

Given the above situation, although the research on the paper cutting culture of Changbai Mountain has made great achievements, there are still some deficiencies in the research. The main outstanding problems are that the research content needs to be further enriched, the research quality needs to be improved and the research quantity needs to be increased. For researchers, if more stories are explored in the early stage, it will be easier for them to understand and find out the factors that suit their interests to promote the spread of paper-cut art. Should maintain and non-material cultural heritage inheritance is more closely linked, through on-the-spot visiting survey and so on, to strengthen the depth of the academic writing, should also be innovation in research methods and research perspective, to stand on the shoulders of predecessors, discovering problems, summarizing the new experiences, research of Changbai mountain ginseng story, and the intangible cultural heritage research provides new ideas.

Thirdly, at the audience level, we should lead to "guide" role, in Changbai mountain of paper-cut art, Japan and South Korea spread, sometimes in the spread of "aphasia", in face of the Japanese and South Korean tourists often can't understand our paper-cut style, a technique to convey the connotation of paper-cutting in the deep culture, also not understand in the transmission, Changbai mountain clipart to "self" as the center, did not understand the learning of the paper-cut. Among the audience, Changbaishan paper cutting art also has a lack of potential audience in its overseas communication. As the main force of propaganda, the young generation, under the influence of the growth environment, has little contact with the intangible cultural heritage, and is difficult to understand it, and is not easy to consciously form the awareness of communication. Audiences pay more attention to the programs with high adhesion to life, people's livelihood, entertainment, movies and so on. In the well-known international art exhibitions in recent years, the number of Chinese paper-cut works exhibited is less than that of other kinds of works, and the number of works favored by foreign artists is also less.

While the iron is hot still need their own hard, spread in the context of internationalization of paper-cut also should "when in Rome, do as the Romans do", to guide more people to join spread abroad, in the culture spread abroad, the main body of communication cannot be self-centered, should understand the expression of learners' demands, such as paper-cut lovers feel difficult to deal with learning difficulty of paper-cut, Changbai clipart even have the desire to Changbai mountain tourism, but the shortage or mentor abstruse difficult to understand, and many other needs, in the process of spread of Changbai mountain, to focus on the learner's own demand, adjust communication strategy, to direct, To promote a deeper understanding and learning of the art of paper-cutting. To Japan, South Korea, a potential audience of people, not on the strategy for South Korea's potential audience through the understanding of the Changbai mountain paper-cut to deeply understand the Chinese culture, and by the feedback of Chinese culture to increase their interest in learning such skills, through the living environment and cultural atmosphere of the osmosis, prompted the audience under the inertia of the national culture. Naturally accept Changbai mountain paper-cut, make personal gain recognition of Changbai mountain paper-cutting in the unconscious.

Conclusion

Changbai Mountain paper cutting art is a kind of regional original ecological culture, is the original folk culture, the accumulation of the Chinese nation's potential consciousness and social psychology. With the development and innovation of paper-cut art, this art form is more and more accepted and loved by foreign audiences. Under the cultural communication background of "going out", it is easier to have a psychological resonance with the aesthetic needs of the audience and form a dialogue and communication with the local culture with appropriate methods and strategies for external communication. Therefore, from the perspective of cultural communication, in the external communication of paper-cut art, it should not be limited to the material culture itself, but let the audience further understand the spiritual connotation of the material form in addition to understanding the aesthetic feeling of the material state presented by the modeling and skills of paper-cut. Only in this way can the audience not only recognize the works of art but also stimulate their interest in Exploring China to understand the cultural psychology of the Chinese nation and further accept and identify with Chinese culture, which is also the ultimate goal of cultural communication.

(Beijing International Studies University)

Bibliography

1. Song Chunmei. Research on the Development of Intangible Cultural Heritage Tourism in Yanbian Prefecture [D]. Jilin: Yanbian University, 2016.
2. Li Hui, Zhong Zhaoxi. Preliminary study on marketing mix strategy of manchu cultural tourism in jilin province [J]. Journal of changchun normal university (natural science edition), 2017, 36(1): 87-90.
3. Dong Renjie, Jin Shizhu, Liu Chang. Journal of Hubei university of economics (humanities and social sciences edition), 2019, 16(2): 99-102.
4. Zheng Yuanyuan. Research on the development of eco-tourism agriculture in Jilin province under the background of "One Belt and One Road" [J]. Times Agricultural Machinery, 2017, (12): 143-144.
5. Li Yang, Liu Wenchao, Liu Mingju, et al. Research on Vacation-type Complex Tourism Experience Based on Online Travel Notes Analysis — A Case study of Changbai Mountain International Resort [J]. Regional research and development, 2019, 38(1): 116-122.
6. Sun Pengcheng. Problems and Countermeasures in the development of rural ecological Tourism resources with Ethnic characteristics in Jilin Province [J]. Rural Science and Technology, 2020, (20): 26-27.
7. Ma Qianwen. Inheritance and Development of Changbai Mountain Manchu Paper cutting in preschool Art Education [J]. Art and Technology, 2017 (12): 145-146.

Hand a Name Card of China to the World: Taking Mountain Tai Porters as an Example

Zheng Tianjiao

With the rapid development of the society, people always rush forward in order to catch up with the times, but forget why they set off. People need spiritual guidance to better understand and develop themselves in this impetuous and materialistic society, in this way, the sound operation of the society can be achieved. No country can develop well without the support of the national spirits. If China have the national spirit with patriotism as its core and the spirit of the times with reform and innovation as the core, then Denmark has the well-known Danish craftsman's spirit. Although the wave of modernization after World War II was strong, the industrialization of Denmark started late. Even so, such a small Nordic country with a small population, a small land area, and a lack of resources has emerged a large number of famous companies which occupy the leading positions in the world, such as "Maersk, the world's largest container shipping company, Grundfos, the world's largest manufacturer of circulating pumps, Lego, the world's largest toy manufacturer, Topsoe, the global leader in catalysis and process technology, etc"[1]. The connotations of Danish craftsman's spirit include concentration and innovation. Danish companies have always focused on developing products and striving for perfection until they reach the highest

---

[1] Guo Fang, Why Study Denmark? — Those global leaders cast by Danish craftsman's spirit, *China Economic Weekly*, 2016, Issue 42. (郭芳:《为什么研究丹麦?——丹麦工匠精神铸造的那些全球领先者》,《中国经济周刊》2016 年第 42 期)

level in the world, they also attach importance to cultivating talents for continuous innovation. Denmark has taken its own place in the whole world with its persevering craftsmanship which has become a name card of Denmark.

The Chinese Spirit contains the essence of Chinese traditional culture. It is the ideological basis for the long-term development of Chinese traditional culture and can show the soft power of Chinese culture. President Xi has repeatedly emphasized the importance of improving the country's cultural soft power in the contemporary era, which will help strengthen national cohesion and shape the image of China. Nowadays, people are pursuing speed in all aspects of life, for example, 5G, high-speed trains, TikTok, fragmented reading, etc. However, at the same time, more and more people gradually lose their directions and motivations to move forward. In this occasion, they need to slow down, reflect on their original aspirations, so as to prepare to start again and face the future with a more positive a attitude. The spirit of Mountain Tai porters can inspire people to make continuous progress. Anyone who has climbed Mountain Tai will admire its majesty. Mountain Tai is undoubtedly a symbol of China. The spirit of Mountain Tai porters, whose cores are working hard, bearing heavy burdens, persevering in the goals, and advancing courageously, should be known and remembered by the Chinese and the world.

The Role of Mountain Tai Porters

Mountain Tai is located in Tai'an City, Shandong Province. "Tai" means greatness, smoothness and tranquility. Although Mountain Tai has the third highest altitude in the Five Sacred Mountains, it has an incomparable historical, political and cultural status. As the greatest of the Five Sacred Mountains in China, it is regarded as a symbol of social stability, political consolidation, national prosperity, and national unity since ancient times. Emperors, generals and ministers, celebrities and masters all admire Mountain Tai. A total of 72 emperors were recorded as visiting it, and six of them carried out the Fengshan(a grand ceremony of worship of heaven on the top of Mountain Tai to pray and say thanks for peace and prosperity) including Qin Shihuang (219 BC) who unified China for the first time, Wudi (110 BC) of the Han dynasty, Xuanzong (726 AD) of Tang Dynasty, etc. Royals, scholars, celebrities, writers, authorities, came to Mountain Tai to hike, acquire inspiration, compose poems, write essays, paint, carve inscriptions, and set up monuments, let alone the greatest sage of China Confucius. He reached the peak, overlooking his country Lu, and sighed with one of the most philosophical words, "the world is small". Besides the influence of Confucianism, Mountain Tai has also witnessed the development of both Buddhism and Taoism. Hence, a great many cultural relics were left on the Mountain, like grandiose temples, stone inscriptions, and tablets, etc. Many poets such as Sima Qian, Zhang Heng, Li Bai, and Du Fu have all left immortal works for Mountain Tai. Du Fu's enthusiastically praised Mountain Tai for its majestic grandeur and its beautiful scenery by using the poem "when I stand on the top of Mountain Tai, the other Mountains appear so small". Mountain Tai was announced as a World Natural and Cultural Heritage Site by UNESCO in 1987. With historical relics and masterpieces found on this magnificent Mountain, it combines the beauty of nature and culture. According to the statistics of the Management Committee of Mountain Tai Scenic Area, from 2014 to 2019, the Mountain and scenic spots receive about 5.5 million tourists from all over the world every year, which shows that Mountain Tai is attracting more and more people with its unique charm.

Mountain Tai porter is an ancient profession. The items used for the sacrifices to gods or ancestors and the materials needed for construction were all shouldered by them. They have to finish the journey of more than 7,800 steps up Mountain Tai. In 1980s, Mountain Tai began to carry out large-scale construction and the tourism industry of Mountain Tai gradually prospered, so the construction of infrastructure such as Mountain roads, temples, hotels, and cableways on the Mountain was unprecedented in scale, at that time, porters had lots of work to do, we can say the 1980s was the golden age for them. Many farmers from poor families spent their spare time working as

Mountain porters.① Gradually, there are more and more places for tourists to consume and rest along the way. Porters need to shoulder different objects, ranging from food to machines and equipment. Clearly, Mountain porters are the main force of transportation. A good Mountain climbing experience can be helpful to attract more tourists and increase the popularity of Mountain Tai at home and abroad. Therefore, porters represent the image of Mountain Tai and serve as a cornerstone in the process of promoting Mountain Tai to the world. The Jade Emperor Peak, which is approximately 1,500 meters above sea level, is the final destination of porters. They climb on the steps, sometimes even passe through some very steep sections such as the 18th Bend. They have become a beautiful and unique landscape that cannot be ignored in Mountain Tai. Feng Jicai's article *Tiaoshangong*, aka Mountain Tai Porters has been included in textbooks in China's primary schools. It is one of the famous essays about Mountain Tai. The images of Mountain Tai porters portrayed by Feng are as follows: "short and thick", "dark muscles", "a bare pole is placed on their shoulders, a few ropes hang down at both ends, and heavy objects hang on the ropes".② Porters keep climbing to the top of the Mountain step by step in a steady pace. Wang Guozhen wrote in his poem *Mountain Is High and Road Is Far* that "no Mountain is too high for a man who tries to climb and no road is too long for a man who tries to walk"③. It's a true portrayal of Mountain porters. Since the 18th National Congress of the Communist Party of China, President Xi has repeatedly quoted the story of porters who dare not stay and rest in "Kuaihuo Sanli" (flat road with 1500 meters) for a long time to inspire the majority of party members and cadres to work hard with a never-slack mental state and an indomitable attitude of struggle, and try to become Mountain Tai porters in the new era.④

---

① Xu Congfen, A Climbing Over a Thousand Years The Past and Present of Mountain Tai Porters, *Lianhe Daily*, 2019.12.31. (徐从芬:《跨越千年的攀登 泰山挑山工的前世今生》,《联合日报》2019 年 12 月 31 日)
② Feng Jicai, Tiaoshangong, 1981. (冯骥才:《挑山工》,1981 年)
③ Wang Guozhen, Wang Guozhen Classic, Writers Publishing House, 2010. (汪国真:《汪国真经典代表作》,作家出版社 2010 年版)
④ Cui Honggang, Vigorously Carrying Forward the Spirit of Mountain Tai Porters, People's Daily Online. 2019.04.03. (崔洪刚:《大力弘扬泰山"挑山工"精神》,人民网) http://theory.people.com.cn/n1/2019/0403/c40531-31010547.html, 2019 年 4 月 3 日 08:08.

Hand a Name Card of China to the World: Taking Mountain Tai Porters as an Example

Mountain Tai porters participate in and support the development of Mountain Tai. They are witnesses of history, inheritors and advocates of the Chinese Spirit. The spirit of Mountain Tai porters is a spiritual wealth accumulated over time, whose connotation should be interpreted from new perspectives due to the development of the times.

New Interpretations of the Spirit of Mountain Tai Porters

President Xi fully affirmed and praised porters' spiritual characteristics of working hard, bravely carrying heavy burdens, never slacking off, and advancing courageously. In other words, They are not afraid of difficulties in climbing, and never rest on the flat road.[1] With the accelerating pace of modern life, people are always under tremendous competitive pressure. Many people can seize the opportunity to make continuous progress. However, other people may gradually lose the motivation to work hard, reduce their requirements, and even become passive towards everything. Therefore, re-examining the spirit of Mountain Tai porters can inspire modern people who are in confusion.

The first interpretation is to work tirelessly for a clear goal. For porters, there is only one goal, in the short term, it is to shoulder things to the summit of the mountain, in the long term, it is to pursue a happy life. When the tourists enjoy the magnificent scenery of Mountain Tai or read the inscriptions of the ancients on the stone wall along the road, or wash their faces and feet by the stream, porters will pass by the tourists silently and walk quietly in front of the tourists in order to complete each task of transportation.[2] They are not confused by the scenery along the way and not frustrated by the wind and rain, but always firmly believe that they will reach the destination at last, so they never stop climbing. Modern people should also set clear and feasible goals like porters do. In the process of chasing the

---

[1] Cui Honggang, Vigorously Carrying Forward the Spirit of Mountain Tai Porters, People's Daily Online. 2019.04.03. (崔洪刚：《大力弘扬泰山"挑山工"精神》,人民网) http://theory.people.com.cn/n1/2019/0403/c40531-31010547.html, 2019 年 4 月 3 日 08：08.

[2] Feng Jicai, Tiaoshangong, 1981. (冯骥才：《挑山工》,1981 年)

goals, the pace can be steady, while laziness, hesitation and giving up should be avoided. Many well-known Danish companies are committed to reaching the highest level in the world and constantly striving for this goal. Although there will be many competitors, they still persist. It can be seen that spirit can indeed be seen as a driving force for moving forward. The second one is to challenge yourself bravely. Mountain Tai porters have to carry more than 100 pounds each time, walk more than 7 kilometers of steep mountain roads. They have the courage to pick up the heaviest load and never fear the difficulties. Nowadays, a majority of China's post-90s generation choose naked resignation which means quitting jobs without having another job lined up. One of their motives is to escape.① They decisively resign due to work pressure and interpersonal relationships. This kind of avoidance may bring relief in short time, but in the long run, it is by no means an effective way to solve the main problem. Young people should constantly try to solve existing problems when encountering difficulties, and bravely challenge themselves to adapt to the new environment. The third one is not to let pleasure take its course. Kuaihuo Sanli is located in the north of Halfway Gate to Heaven (Zhongtianmen) which has a flat terrain and pleasant scenery. Exhausted tourists can sit and relax here. However, porters never relax here because once they stop, they will become lazy and don't want to move forward, the more dangerous the 18th Bend ahead will be harder to climb.② Today, with the continuous popularization of smart phones, the number of phubbers is increasing. There is no doubt that mobile phones and other communication devices are the temptations that can make people addicted. Time is money and waits for no one, so it should be allocated to more meaningful things, instead of just indulging in the virtual world. The last one is to focus on the present, not entangling in the past, not worrying about the future. Mountain

---

① Liu Hongxia, Huang Ying, Why are the post-90s white-collar workers choose naked resignation — Based on the interview analysis of 18 post-90s white-collar workers' motivation for naked resignation, *China Youth Study*, 2014, Issue 09. (刘红霞、黄颖:《90后白领"裸辞"为哪般——基于对18位90后白领"裸辞"动机的访谈分析》,《中国青年研究》2014年第9期)

② Li Shanyu, Don't stay at Kuaihuo Sanli, *People's Liberation Army Daily*, December 16,2019. (李善禹:《"快活三里"莫流连》,《解放军报》2019年12月16日)

Tai porters are down-to-earth, walking forward step by step and focusing on each step. Danish companies apply past experiences to innovation and make continuous development in specialized fields. Being stuck in the past gains and losses is not conducive to the next move, and even causes regression. Data from the World Health Organization in 2020 shows that there are more than 350 million people suffering from depression worldwide. With more than 54 million people suffering from depression, China is one of the countries with a heavier burden of this mental disease. Pessimism and anxiety are both manifestations of depression. Mountain porters' spiritual characteristic of focusing on the current step can guide people to have a healthy mental state.

The above four points are the new interpretations of the spirit of Mountain Tai porters in combination with some problems occurred in contemporary society. Understanding and practicing this spirit will help modern people to better know and develop themselves. However, the reality is that with the building and completion of the mountain roads, vehicles can be driven from the foot of the mountain to Zhongtianmen, and there is a ropeway from Zhongtianmen to South Gate to Heaven (Nantianmen). In this way, the transportation of most groceries don't rely on porters any more. Therefore, the number of Mountain Tai porters is declining. One cannot help but worry about the future of porters and their spiritual characteristics.

Inheritance of the Spirit of Mountain Tai Porters and Telling China's Stories Well

With the innovation of science and technology, transportation methods have become diversified, and many machines that can replace humans have been created. Facing this irreversible development trend, many people will lose their jobs, especially those who rely on their strength to make a living. Of course, Mountain Tai porters also cannot change this cruel reality. At present, there are more than 50 porters in Mountain Tai and more than 30 permanent personnel because most of them choose to change their careers. Although they have played an important role in the history, the number of people who know them is decreasing, let alone the inheritance of the spirit of Mountain Tai porters. Ji Xianlin, a master of Chinese studies, once said that "Mountain Tai is one of the main symbols of Chinese culture. If you want to promote Chinese culture, you must first promote the culture of Mountain Tai." It is Mountain Tai that gives birth to the unique group of Mountain Tai porters. People should not forget the spirit of Mountain Tai porters, which can be seen as a name card of China.

At the National Conference on Propaganda and Ideological Work held on August 19, 2013, President Xi proposed that "we must do a good job in external propaganda work, innovate external propaganda methods, and strive to create new concepts, new categories and new expressions that integrate China and foreign countries, and tell China's stories well, spread the voice of China". The purposes of telling the China's stories well are to spread the voice of China, represent the Chinese Dream, elaborate the Chinese Spirit, show the Chinese features, and convey Chinese values.[①] Both internal communication in the same context and external cross-cultural communication must solve two problems: what to tell and how to tell. The former is the basis for telling a good Chinese story, while the latter determines the communication power of the story.

The first problem is the content of the story. Here, the spirit of Mountain Tai porters is the content we are going to tell. Elaborating this spirit can also be seen as telling the story of this unique group of people. The development of China relies on the hard work of all the Chinese people. Porter is also one of the ordinary professions. The stories of ordinary Chinese who have worked tirelessly to create a better life can better reflect the development of China. The history of this career, porters' main responsibilities, and the significance of their spirits to Taishan and China can all be included in the story telling.

After clarifying the content of the story, it is necessary to choose appropriate methods of communication and inheritance. In order to carry

---

[①] Su Renxian, Path Selection for Telling China's Stories Well, *China Radio & TV Academic Journal*, 2016, Issue 02. (苏仁先:《讲好中国故事的路径选择》,《中国广播电视学刊》2016 年第 2 期)

forward the spirit of Mountain Tai porters, a lot of efforts have been made. For instance, in 2016, the Management Committee of Mountain Tai Scenic Area began to compile the *Zhonghua Taishan Wenku*, which is divided into four major series of ancient books, writings, foreign and oral portraits. As one of the oral portraits, *Tiaoshangong* (*Mountain Tai Porters*) has been a complete book. Besides, Professors Zhang Runkai and Zhang Dedi of the Central Academy of Fine Arts, the first generation of sculpture artists in China, created the sculpture *Taishan Tiaoshangong* (*Porters on Mountain Tai*) in 2019. On December 19, 2020, the opening ceremony of the theater film *Tiaoshan* (*The Porters*) was held in Tai'an. Director Zheng Chunyu hopes to record the unique group of porters in the form of films and videos, so as to promote the development of his hometown. We can see that people have gradually noticed the precious spiritual qualities reflected in porters. Although the communication methods are diverse, the communication power is still not ideal. Hence, here are two suggestions for effectively elaborating the spirit of Mountain Tai porters.

First, the inheritance of spirit from generation to generation should be closely linked with schools. The future of the nation lies in the youth. The hope of the country lies in the youth. Liang Qichao said that "if young people are intelligent, China will be intelligent; if young people are wealthy, China will be wealthy; if young people are strong, China will be strong; if young people are independent, the country will be independent; if young people are free, the country will be free; if young people are progressive, the country will be progressive". Therefore, the spirit of Mountain Tai porters can be taken as an educational topic to make students of different ages aware of the significance of the spirit. It is also possible to offer relevant courses to introduce the group of porters and their spirits systematically. If conditions permit, schools can organize activities such as mountain climbing or interview with porters so that students can personally experience their spiritual qualities in the process of climbing the mountain and contacting with porters.

Second, a special promotion site can be set in Mountain Tai, aiming at introducing to the tourists the cultural and historical significance of the Mountain Tai porters. In order to speed up cross-cultural communication and let the world understand the spirit, related articles, films and other artistic creations should be translated into multiple languages to attract more foreign tourists. Besides, internet media has opened up a brand-new way of communication with advantages of diversified communicators and interactive characteristic. These advantages of internet media can expand the breadth and depth of carrying forward the spirit of Mountain Tai porters. In addition to domestic Internet media platforms such as TikTok, Weibo, we can use foreign media platforms such as Youtube, Twitter and Instagram to carry out multilingual international communication.

Porters are not only transporters of groceries but also the major construction workers of the mountain. The protection and development of Mountain Tai will never be separated from efforts made by porters. The spiritual qualities of them are also of great significance in contemporary times, and can give modern people many important inspirations. Therefore, it is necessary to carry forward the spirit of Mountain Tai porters, which can guide us on the right path and ensure the healthy operation of society. To raise people's awareness towards the spiritual inheritance from generation to generation, we need to pay attention to link the families and schools to provide spiritual guidance on the growth of children. In addition, the promotion of the spirit of Mountain Tai porters should also be carried out in accordance with the characteristics of the development of the times by applying internet media to conduct multilingual and cross-cultural communication. Mountain Tai is a symbol of China's excellent culture. The spirit of Mountain Tai porters, engraved on the name card of China, should be known to the world. The Chinese voice made by porters should be heard and transmitted to every corner of the world.

(Beijing International Studies University)